Comprehensive Literacy Instruction in Today's Classrooms

The Whole, the Parts, and the Heart

Diane Hood Nettles

California University of Pennsylvania

PEARSON

Boston • New York • San Francisco
Mexico City • Montreal • Toronto • London • Madrid • Munich • Paris
Hong Kong • Singapore • Tokyo • Cape Town • Sydney

Senior Series Editor: Aurora Martínez Ramos
Series Editorial Assistant: Kevin Shannon
Senior Development Editor: Mary K. Kriener
Senior Marketing Manager: Krista Clark
Production Editor: Janet Domingo
Editorial Production Service: Argosy
Composition Buyer: Linda Cox
Manufacturing Buyer: Andrew Turso
Electronic Composition: Argosy
Interior Design: Denise Hoffman, Glenview Studio
Photo Researcher: Sarah Evertson
Cover Administrator: Joel Gendron

For related titles and support materials, visit our online catalog at www.ablongman.com.

Between the time web site information is gathered and then published, it is not unusual for some sites to have closed. Also, the transcription of URLs can result in typographical errors. The publisher would appreciate notification where these errors occur so that they may be corrected in subsequent editions.

Photo credits appear on page 570, which constitutes a continuation of the copyright page.

Library of Congress Cataloging-in-Publication Data
Nettles, Diane Hood.
  Comprehensive literacy instruction in today's classrooms : the whole, the parts, and the heart / Diane Hood Nettles.
      p. cm.
  Includes bibliographical references and index.
  ISBN 0-205-34425-9 (pbk.)
  1. Language arts (Elementary) 2. Language arts (Middle school) I. Title.
  LB1576.N38 2006
  372.6--dc22   2005051537

Printed in the United States of America

10 9 8 7 6 5 4 3 2 1 VHP 09 08 07 06 05

Assessing Reading and Writing   92

4

Understanding the Nature of Fiction and Nonfiction   136

5

Developing Emerging Literacy   166

6

Teaching Young Children to Decode Independently   214

7

Explicit Instruction of Comprehension Strategies   332

Facilitating Your Students' Prior Knowledge 370

Facilitating Your Students' Comprehension 398

Reading, Writing, and Responding   430

13

Helping Students Become Fluent Readers   462

14

Adapting Instruction 486

Preface

When I'm asked why I wrote *Comprehensive Literacy Instruction in Today's Classrooms*, the answer is quite simple. Twenty years ago, I taught fourth grade at a school located next door to a housing project. Twice each day, I read aloud to my students. My first choice of literature for this fourth grade class was *Charlotte's Web*, by E. B. White (1952). It has always been my favorite; I felt sure that it would be a gentle, soothing story for this group of children, many of whose lives were in turmoil.

One of my students, whom I will call Shawn, was a challenge. He had a troubled home life. School was a source of continuity that he didn't have at home, yet school asked much from him that he couldn't produce. He rarely finished his schoolwork and never his homework. He tormented his peers with constant bickering, fighting, and taking things from their desks. But twice a day, Shawn was calm, content, and fascinated—with *Charlotte's Web*. I read from a copy of the book given to me by my grandfather when I was in third grade, shortly before he died. Because this was, at the time, my only copy of the book, I kept it on the classroom library shelf. During every free moment he had, Shawn grabbed it from the shelf and read the next chapter. Thus, the next day, Shawn was already familiar with the chapter I was about to read. One day, as I read aloud, I glanced at Shawn. His lips were moving in sync with mine—on each word. This happened every day until we finished the book. Shawn had every word of this book memorized.

At the beginning of the next school year, I realized that my copy of *Charlotte's Web* was missing. It broke my heart to realize that the only tangible item of my grandfather's that I owned was now gone. I don't know what happened to the book; however, I like to think that Shawn has my copy of *Charlotte's Web*. He would be about 30 years old now. I hope he has children—perhaps even students in a classroom of his own—and has read this masterpiece aloud to them, passing along one of the most wonderful tales ever written.

And that is why I wrote this book. All those years ago, when I was a relatively inexperienced teacher, Shawn showed me a few things about teaching literacy. The title of this book—*Comprehensive Literacy Instruction in Today's Classrooms: The Whole, The Parts, and the Heart* conveys the essence of what I have learned, based on my work with hundreds of students, and with many fine teachers who have inspired me and shared their classrooms with me.

First, comprehensive literacy instruction means to teach literacy with one purpose in mind: *understanding of the printed word*. Teachers must make decisions about what to teach and how to teach it, so that their students view reading and writing as meaning-making activities, rather than as a mere collection of skills.

Second, comprehensive literacy instruction means that *students need to learn to read and write whole pieces of text*, not just practice pages, computer games, or textbook materials. That's the "whole" of teaching literacy. We know a lot about how to give children the strategies and capabilities they need to read whole books, articles, web sites, letters, e-mail, poetry, newspapers, and the myriad of other texts that are part of their lives, fluently and with understanding. We also know how to teach writing, so that children can produce whole, meaningful text for real audiences. These practices need to take place in classrooms where teachers watch their students, know their needs and interests, and provide experiences and environments in which their students learn literacy with whole text that conveys meaning.

Third, comprehensive literacy instruction also means that our *students need to learn strategies and skills that enable them to make sense of text*. That's the "parts" of literacy. We also know a lot about how to give children the skills they need to decode words on their own, define vocabulary, spell, identify important ideas, and how to impart a host of other skills and strategies needed to comprehend and share the printed word. These parts are necessary, but they are just parts. Again, teachers who teach the parts of literacy in a comprehensive manner do so with one goal in mind: comprehension.

Fourth, comprehensive literacy instruction means that *teachers pass on a love of reading and writing*, and show their students its value in today's world. My fourth grade student Shawn showed me, with his unabashed excitement about *Charlotte's Web*, the last part of the title of this book—the importance of the "heart" of teaching literacy. I contend that it's the most important lesson we can learn: **Successful literacy instruction means that we produce students who *want* to read and write as much as they know *how* to read and write.**

How This Book Is Organized

When writing *Comprehensive Literacy Instruction in Today's Classrooms: The Whole, the Parts, and the Heart*, I had several goals in mind:

1. *Explain the theoretical ideas behind literacy instruction so that they make sense to you, the reader.* One of the problems that educators have is excessive use of jargon, passive writing, and discussion of theoretical ideas without relating them to the classroom. I hope to alleviate those problems with this book, using clear, concise explanations, as well as classroom scenarios and lesson examples that make theory come alive.
2. *Introduce a rich array of children's literature to you, so that you are knowledgeable about books to choose for your classroom.* Everything in this book is based upon the use of quality literature, so that your students can learn how to read and write with the best. I hope many of the titles that you read about will be old favorites, but I've also included many new ones published in the last few years. Available throughout the book as well as in various supplements are lists of children's books, from a wide array of genre. All teaching strategies that I describe use literature as a beginning point.
3. *Show you some research-based teaching strategies for five important components of literacy.* The National Reading Panel (2000a) and the No Child Left Behind Act (2001) define these five components as the most important to

teach in reading instruction: phonemic awareness, phonics, vocabulary, comprehension, and fluency. You will learn how to effectively teach them all, using strategies supported by research and based on children's literature.

4. *Show you how to move beyond No Child Left Behind.* Recently, Allington (2005) wrote of the importance of teaching components of literacy instruction that are not included in the five recommended by the National Reading Panel, but are just as important for your students. I want to show you the rationale and research-based teaching strategies for connecting writing with reading, motivating students to become readers and writers, providing access to and time for plentiful reading, teaching students from diverse backgrounds, facilitating the emerging literacy of beginning readers and writers, managing the classroom so that you scaffold your students' literacy learning, adapting instruction for all types of learners, developing students' abilities in today's "new literacies" so that they are able to successfully navigate technological resources, and making connections with caregivers and parents.

5. *Give you the confidence to make teaching decisions that belong to a knowledgeable teaching professional.* We are in an era of standards-based education, high-stakes testing, and scripted teaching. Students, especially those from diverse backgrounds, deserve teachers who are knowledgeable, observant, and articulate about why they do what they do. I'm hoping that this book will help teachers gain knowledge, skills, and confidence to teach literacy *without a script*.

6. *Share with you the excitement of teaching literacy so that you, too, will want to pass along the joys of reading and writing.* If reading is not a passion for you, I hope to at least renew your interest in it by sharing my enthusiasm for good literature with you. Teachers who read a lot tend to be interactive and strategic readers. These abilities show up in their classrooms, which benefits their students (Dreher, 2002–2003).

7. *Show you some ways to teach students from diverse backgrounds and ways to adapt instruction for all learners.* Your classroom will house a diverse group of children, either by virtue of their cultural backgrounds or their learning differences. I know the frustration of being unprepared as I tried to teach children who do not speak English, or who struggle with reading and writing, or who are bored because they're more capable than most. I hope to show you ways to capitalize on the strengths of all your learners and ensure that you are able to adapt your instruction for everyone.

Each chapter of the book is dedicated to achieving these goals:

- **Chapter 1, "Understanding the Big Picture: How Children Learn to Read and Write,"** explains the many influences on your literacy instruction: your students, the social and cultural contexts of your students, the texts they read, the politics of literacy, and the theoretical orientations to reading and writing.

- **Chapter 2, "A Model of Instruction: Making Decisions About Teaching Literacy,"** discusses how theory moves into practice in the classroom and answers two important questions as you plan instruction: "What do I teach?" and "How do I teach it?"

- Chapter 3, "Meeting the Literacy Needs of English Language Learners," introduces a myriad of specific strategies to use when teaching literacy to children who are learning English as a second language and shows you the excitement and richness that they bring to your classroom.

- Chapter 4, "Assessing Reading and Writing," offers formal, informal, and alternative assessment tools that yield the rich qualitative data that you need to make instructional decisions about your students' reading and writing.

- Chapter 5, "Understanding the Nature of Fiction and Nonfiction," introduces the elements of fiction and the structure of nonfiction, showing you how they come alive in many wonderful children's books.

- Chapter 6, "Developing Emerging Literacy," explores how to provide young children who are just beginning to grow with a learning environment that includes much exposure to quality children's literature, language activities that lead to phonemic and alphabet awareness, and literacy-based play.

- Chapter 7, "Teaching Young Children to Decode Independently," explains the true purpose of teaching phonics, which is to provide readers with the skills they need to figure out unknown words, thereby producing meaning as they decode.

- Chapter 8, "Teaching Word Study," explores types of words and introduces many strategies for teaching these words, so that students can pronounce them, use them, and remember them.

- Chapter 9, "Scaffolding Literacy Learning," shows how to support students as they learn to read and write, by providing an environment that gives them a chance to experiment, inquire, and predict without risk of failure.

- Chapter 10, "Explicit Instruction of Comprehension Strategies," demonstrates two types of explicit instruction that are especially important: explanations and mental modeling.

- Chapter 11, "Facilitating Your Students' Prior Knowledge," focuses on how to enable your students' comprehension of text by using strategies that help them connect what they already know with the author's words.

- Chapter 12, "Facilitating Your Students' Comprehension," examines at length the classic teacher behavior, questioning, so that you can see some effective ways to engage your students.

- Chapter 13, "Reading, Writing, and Responding," shows you how to offer your students aesthetic as well as efferent responses to literature. Written response activities to fiction and nonfiction are a big part of this chapter, from written retellings and summaries to journal entries.

- Chapter 14, "Helping Students Become Fluent Readers," introduces many research-based and motivating strategies that make use of the true purpose for reading aloud—to share the page with others.

- Chapter 15, "Adapting Instruction," shows you how to reach students who find reading difficult—as well as students who don't.

Special Features

Special features are included throughout the book to provide teachers of reading with an understanding of key concepts in reading instruction, as well as practical strategies for reaching the goals of this book:

- **Literature excerpts.** Each chapter begins with a relevant excerpt from a piece of children's literature, connecting the main idea of the chapter to an episode or quote from a children's book. These excerpts entice students to explore the books further; introduce good literature, as well as engage thinking about the concept of the chapter. Each is enhanced by original **reader responses** from pre-K to eighth-grade children from around the country responding to the chapter opening literature excerpt through drawings and writings. These reader responses demonstrate the purity and joy of literacy in young people. ▶

- **Personal reflections.** Boxes at the beginning of each chapter activate prior knowledge and thoughtful reflection by offering you an opportunity to ask questions and think about personal experiences with literacy. ▼

Adam, age 6

Personal Reflection

Trisha, the girl in Patricia Polacco's autobiographical story *Thank You, Mr. Falker*, grew up loving books. But when she started school, and reading instruction began, she struggled. Whenever she looked at a page in a book, all she saw were "wiggling shapes." When it was her turn to read in class, the other children laughed at her. She began to feel dumb. As the years went on, she felt dumber and dumber. Then, when Trisha was in fifth grade, a new teacher, Mr. Falker, arrived at the school. Mr. Falker was the one who made a huge difference in Trisha's life. He taught her to read.

Imagine that you have a student like Trisha. You have the opportunity to do the same thing that Mr. Falker did. What would you do? How would you begin to teach Trisha to read?

- **Diversity boxes.** Each chapter includes ▶ a brief discussion of how to work with children of diverse backgrounds, in relation to the topic of that chapter. These features engage thinking about the pressing issues of working with children who face challenges because they are from socioeconomic, cultural, and linguistic backgrounds unlike the mainstream culture of American schools. Practical teaching suggestions are offered with each.

Diversity in the Reading Classroom

Teacher–Student Interactions

The manner in which teachers communicate and interact with their students is important, especially when working with students of diverse backgrounds. Your expectations of your students' behavior and academic achievement in the classroom may be different from what is expected of them at home and in their community. For example, teachers in the United States expect their students to contribute to classroom discussions, and to be assertive about what they know. However, children of Mexican culture are taught the opposite—not to speak up or be assertive around adults (Goldenberg, 2004). This behavior gives their teachers the illusion that they are not capable of the task at hand. Likewise, Goldenberg reports that several studies indicate a mismatch between the communication styles of the teacher and that of the students. When this happens, teachers tend to lower their expectations for the students.

When teachers make the effort to make cultural accommodations, there is some evidence that students participate in class activities more and their contributions are at a higher cognitive level. Yet, to date there is little evidence that being culturally accommodating will produce higher student achievement. So why is it important to know about the communication patterns of your students? Goldenberg says, "If nothing else,

different cultural groups have different norms of behaving and interacting; teachers should understand and be sensitive to these because doing so can only help students and families feel more comfortable and welcomed in what might seem a very foreign institution" (p. 1650).

Based on reviews of the research on teaching in multicultural settings (Au, 1993, 2002; Goldenberg, 2004), here are some suggestions for adjusting your communication so that it is culturally responsive:

- A direct, explicit teaching style is more culturally familiar to some African American children. State the behavior that you want from the students, rather than indirectly implying it.

- Rather than asking questions that have known answers, teachers of African American children may get better responses if they ask questions that allow for personal interpretations or insights. Instead of asking, "What is this story about?" the teacher might ask, "Tell me why you think this story is good."

- Acknowledge and use responses of students in class discussions. Native American students tend to wait slightly longer to respond to a question than their peers. Thus, after asking a question, give everyone time to think about the answer and respond.

- With all children, keep the focus on communicating for an exchange of ideas, rather than for the purpose of correct pronunciation and grammar.

Modifying Instruction for ELL

Figurative Language and *Hey, Al*
GRADE LEVEL: 3–4

- **Objective**
  After reading or listening to *Hey, Al*, students will determine the meaning of idioms that describe the human experience.

- **Preparation**
  Type these sentences on index cards. On the back of each, glue the appropriate picture.
  - Nikko does not know what he will do after school today. He will *cross that bridge when he comes to it*. (Picture of a bridge)
  - Nadia must decide between playing on a soccer team and having more time to be with her friends. She is *at a crossroads* and does not know what to do. (Picture of an intersection)
  - Cecily's parents do not understand why she wants to stay up late and watch a movie. She thinks they are old and *over the hill*. (Picture of a hill)
  - Jaime did not listen to his grandmother's warning about staying away from kids who get in trouble all the time. He needs to *open his eyes!* (Picture of closed eyes)

- **Materials**
  - *Hey, Al* (Yorinks, 1986)
  - Brown banana or other piece of overripe fruit
  - Index cards with idioms written on them and small pictures glued to the back
  - Journals

◀ **Modified ELL lessons.** These detailed lesson plans have been modified to meet the needs of students who are learning to communicate in English. Specific adaptations are in boldface print, and the lessons relate to the topic of the chapter. Each demonstrates *how* to modify your lessons, but also *why* it is important to adapt your instruction for the students who need culturally responsive instruction.

- **Home-school connection.** Boxes at the end of each chapter provide samples of letters that can be sent to parents and caregivers, focusing on the topic of the chapter. Engaging involvement from caregivers is a critical element in developing a love for reading. Each of the letters or exercises comes directly from experienced classroom teachers who have used these letters successfully with families of students. ▶

Home–School Connection

Potluck Reading Night

One of my colleagues, Jane Bonari, who is an outstanding teacher and a wonderful cook, always says, "If you want them to come, serve food." A way to encourage your students and their caregivers to read and talk about reading is a Potluck Reading Night (Spohn, 2001). Invite everyone to your classroom on a monthly basis, in the evening. The food may be the ticket to getting the parents to attend; however, reading games and read-aloud sessions go a long way toward showing parents how to have fun with reading.

Shown below is a suggested schedule of events.

6:00—Reading game or activity
Show parents how to do activities with letter cards, word cards, or other tools such as the Story Hand. Here is a sample dialogue for showing the Story Hand to caregivers.

"One of my goals this year is to make sure your child knows the elements of a story: character, setting, plot, resolution, and theme. You can help with this by using this picture. First, read a story with your child. Then, use your hand to recall the important parts of the story. Begin with the thumb—character—and ask your child to tell about the main character as well as any other important characters. Continue with the other parts of the story. The plot may have several events, and your child should be able to recall the important ones. Let's practice!"

Plot
Setting
Resolution
Theme
Character

Caregivers, children, and the teacher enjoy learning about books together.

6:15—Group story time
Read aloud a new piece of literature. This activity gives you the opportunity to model reading aloud behaviors, as well as to introduce new books. If possible, have multiple copies of this book available for borrowing.

6:30—Family reading time
From the classroom library or from a special selection of books arranged on the table, ask caregivers and children to choose a book and read it together.

6:45—Dinner
Ask caregivers to bring a dish to share; have paper plates and utensils available.

7:15—Book swap
Ask families to bring paperback books from home and leave them on a book swap table. Invite everyone to take a gently worn book home.

Mrs. Cuervo's Lesson

Lexie is a first grader in Mrs. Cuervo's class. She is writing a story and needs to write the word "toad." She asks for help. Instead of saying, "Spell it the way you think it should be spelled," which really does not help, Mrs. Cuervo draws three boxes on her paper. She outlines the middle box in red. Then she tells Lexie that each box stands for a sound that she hears in the word "toad." She gives her three plastic chips to use as she says the word, stretching out the sounds in the word. Lexie moves a chip into a box each time she hears a different sound. She says, "t-t-t" as she pushes the chip into the first box. She says, "oh" as she pushes a chip into the second box, and she says "d-d-d" as she pushes the final chip into the third box.

Next, Mrs. Cuervo asks her to remove the chips and attempt to write the letters for the word in the boxes. She writes "t" in the first box. At the second box, which is the red one, teacher intervention is necessary. She says, "I traced this box in red because I want you to remember that this one has two letters in it. There is only one sound, but two letters are in this part of the word. The letters that go in that box are spelled the same way as the 'oh' sound in 'oak.' Can you write those letters?" Mrs. Cuervo is fairly certain that Lexie will figure this out because the word "oak" is on the word wall. She writes "oa" in that box. Last, she easily determines that the last letter is "d."

- **Lesson examples.** These appear throughout the book. Each is marked with an icon, identifying it as a place in the text where you will see theory and research being put into practice. ◀

- **Other pedagogical aids.** In every chapter are:

  Grade-level designations. Most teaching strategies in this book are marked with appropriate grade-level designations, so that you can see at a glance the intended age groups. Often there is an explanation of how to adapt the strategy for another age group. However, almost any teaching strategy can be adapted to other grade levels.

  Technology resources. A list of resources available on the Internet appears at the end of each chapter. These resources are valuable for finding out more about the topic of the chapter.

  Summary "big picture" boxes. At the end of each chapter, these provide a quick reference tool for all strategies described in the chapter. At a glance, you will see a list of all the strategies introduced in the chapter, with a description, appropriate grade levels, the type of book to use, and alignment with standards from the International Reading Association (IRA), the Interstate New Teacher Assessment and Support Consortium (INTASC), the National Association for the Education of Young Children (NAEYC), and the Association for Childhood Education International/National Council for Accreditation of Teacher Education (ACEI/NCATE).

  Comprehensive Literacy Instruction in Today's Classrooms also includes a special Internet connection that encourages you to go beyond the text to learn all that you can about literacy instruction. A **Themes of the Times** icon at the start of each chapter directs you to the companion web site **www.ablongman. com/nettles1e** and a direct link to specially selected *New York Times* articles, which present differing perspectives on contemporary literacy and education topics.

Supplements and Learning Aids

To get the most use of *Comprehensive Literacy Instruction in Today's Classrooms: The Whole, the Parts, and the Heart,* a number of useful supplements are available for students and instructors. Speak with your publisher's contact person about obtaining these supplements for your class!

For Instructors and Students

- **MyLabSchool.** Discover where the classroom comes to life! From video clips of teachers and students interacting, to sample lessons, portfolio templates, and standards integration, Allyn & Bacon brings your students the tools they'll need to succeed in the classroom—with content easily integrated into your existing courses. Delivered within Course Compass—Allyn & Bacon's course management system—this program gives your students powerful insights into how real classrooms work and a rich array of tools that will support them on their journey from their first class to their first classroom.

For the Instructor

- **Instructor's Manual with Test Items.** This supplement provides a variety of instructional tools, including chapter summaries, student objectives, activities and discussion questions, vocabulary, test questions, reflections inspired by the text, and special phonics mini-lessons you can distribute directly to your students.

- **Computerized Test Bank.** The printed Test Bank is also available electronically through our computerized testing system, TestGen EQ. Instructors can use TestGen EQ to create exams in just a few minutes by selecting from the existing database of questions, editing questions, or writing original questions.

- **VideoWorkshop.** This is a new way to bring video into your course, for maximized learning! The total teaching and learning system includes quality video footage on an easy-to-use CD-ROM, plus a *Student Learning Guide* and an *Instructor's Teaching Guide*. The result is a program that brings textbook concepts to life with ease and helps your students understand, analyze, and apply the objectives of the course. VideoWorkshop is available for your students as a value-pack option with this textbook. (A special package ISBN is required and available from your publisher's contact person.)

- **Allyn & Bacon Digital Media Archive for Literacy.** This CD-ROM offers still images, video clips, audio clips, web links, and assorted lecture resources that can be incorporated into multimedia presentations in the classroom. Please contact your Allyn & Bacon representative for details and qualifications for obtaining this supplement.

- **Professionals in Action: Literacy Video.** This 90-minute video consists of 10- to 20-minute segments on Phonemic Awareness, Teaching Phonics, Helping Students Become Strategic Readers, Organizing for Teaching with Literature, and Discussions of Literacy and Brain Research with Experts. The first four segments provide narrative, along with actual classroom teaching footage. The final segments present question-and-answer discussions by leading experts in the field of literacy. Please contact your Allyn & Bacon representative for details and qualifications for obtaining this supplement.

- **Allyn & Bacon Literacy Video Library.** Featuring renowned reading scholars Richard Allington, Dorothy Strickland, and Evelyn English, this three-video library addresses core topics covered in the literacy classroom: reading strategies, developing literacy in multiple intelligences classrooms, developing phonemic awareness, and much more. Please contact your Allyn & Bacon representative for details and qualifications for obtaining this supplement.

For Students

- **Toolkit for Teachers of Literacy.** This dynamic booklet, written by Dr. Nettles as a stand-alone aid for practicing teachers as well as a complement to the main text, contains mini-lessons; ready-to-use graphic organizers, rubrics, and assessment materials for use with students of all abilities; helpful tips and suggestions for enriching literacy instruction; and instruction on creating a literacy portfolio. Many of the materials are ready for immediate classroom use and provide literacy teachers with powerful tools for addressing all needs in the classroom.

- **Companion web site.** www.ablongman.com/nettles1e provides links to additional study items, special *New York Times* articles, annotated web links, and a complete guide to conducting research on the Internet.

- **Research Navigator™ (with ContentSelect Research Database) (access code required).** Research Navigator™ (researchnavigator.com) is the easiest way for students to start a research assignment or research paper. Complete with extensive help on the research process and three exclusive online databases of credible and reliable source material, including EBSCO's ContentSelect™ Academic Journal Database, the *New York Times* Search by Subject Archive, and a "Best of the Web" Link Library, Research Navigator™ helps students quickly and efficiently make the most of their research time. Research Navigator™ is free when packaged with the textbook, and requires an access code.

- **Research Navigator™ Guide for Education.** This free reference guide includes tips, resources, activities, and URLs to help students use the Internet for their research projects. The first part introduces students to the basics of the Internet and the World Wide Web. The second part includes many Web activities that tie into the content of the text. The third part lists hundreds of education resources on the Internet. The fourth part outlines how to use the Research Navigator™ resources. The guide also includes information on how to cite research correctly, and a guide to building an online glossary. This guide includes an access code for Research Navigator™.

Acknowledgments

Thank you from the bottom of my heart:

To my husband Tim, for his love, for his cheerful consumption of multitudes of take-out dinners, and for steadfast encouragement, even when it seemed as if this book would never end. To my son Chuck, for his winning smile, for his patience with my lack of comprehension of the game of golf, and for displaying a bumper sticker on the back of his truck that says, "I ♥ to read!" To my son Tommy, for his laughter, hugs, and his understanding as I take my work with me to all of his sporting events. To my parents Bob and Marilyn Hood, for showing me how to write and how to teach. To my sisters Tricia Harrison and Annie Eller, who have always believed in me. To Don and Helen Nettles for 26 years of encouragement.

I would also like to thank my dear colleague and friend Dotty Campbell, for listening, supporting, and keeping me out of hot water many, many times; my friend Ginny Hannan, for knowing when *not* to ask, "How's the book coming along?"; Reverend Joe Rodgers, for his daily e-mails full of wisdom, cheer, and sustaining humor; his wife Jessie Rodgers, for renewing my love for children's books; the members of my "Seekers" Sunday school class, for their unwavering faith; my college professor at the University of South Florida, Dr. Dan Purdom, who has been my role model for more than 25 years; my sixth grade teacher, Mr. Anthony Scolaro, who started it all when he said, "Don't ever stop writing"; and the many, many exemplary teachers I have known over the years, who have graciously shared their classrooms and have taught me so much—especially Cathy Hayden, Nancy Steider, Jody Grove, Vaughn Dailey, Sandy McWilliams, and Robin Teets.

A special thank you to everyone at Allyn & Bacon who believed in this book and made it happen: Senior Acquisitions Editor Aurora Martinez, for her patience, understanding, and insights; Senior Development Editor Mary Kriener, for her expertise, her uplifting way with words, and a friendship I treasure; Senior Marketing Manager Krista Clark, for her friendly encouragement; Editorial Production Administrator Janet Domingo, for working behind the scenes with a smile and keeping everyone on target; and Senior Project Manager Kevin Sullivan, at Argosy, for careful attention to detail and cheerful persistence.

Of course, there are two groups of students that need to be recognized here:

- My students at California University of Pennsylvania, who have uplifted me by laughing at all the right moments and reinforced me with their sheer joy of learning. I'm truly lucky.

- The group of young people who took time out to read the literature selections in this book and provide a "review" of each. Thank you to Matthew Ashton, Guiseppe Abbruzzo, Natalie R. Hassett, Liana Bryant, Zachary Cross, Jack Curran, Susan Curran, Ike Hanna, Lauren P. Helmrick, Marissa Johnson, Ethan Mergen, Alex Panu, Meghan Panu, Alexandra Pavinelli, Samantha Rossi, Anna Saelens, Elsa Saelens, Jacqueline Santamaria, Adam Scott, Robert C. Wiegand, and Kathryn Wittek. *(A special thank you to their parents who all said, "Sure, they'd love to do this!")*

I would also like to extend a special thank you to the reviewers who provided feedback at various stages of this project. Their insightful comments prompted valuable revisions that strengthened the text: Jean M. Casey, California State University; Laurie J. Curtis, Kansas State University; Maria Dantas-Whitney, Western-Oregon University-Long Beach; Staci Walton Duggar, Florida State University; Dennis J. Kear, Wichita State University; Maureen Kincaid, North Central College; Sara Runge-Pulte, Northern Kentucky University; Doris Walker-Dalhouse, Minnesota State University, Moorhead.

And finally, to a young boy in my fourth grade class 20 years ago, who gave me the reason to write this book.

1

Understanding the Big Picture

How Children Learn to Read and Write

And then one spring day—had it been three months or four months since they had started?—Mr. Falker put a book in front of her. She'd never seen it before. He picked a paragraph in the middle of a page and pointed at it.

Almost as if it were magic, or as if light poured into her brain, the words and sentences started to take shape on the page as they never had before. "She . . . marched . . . them . . . off . . . to . . . " Slowly, she read a sentence. Then another, and another. And finally she'd read a paragraph. And she understood the whole thing.

Thank You, Mr. Falker (Polacco, 1998)

The book that I'v read was called Thank You Mr. Falker. The book made me feel sad because she ~~trina~~ thought she was dumb and she's being bullied around ~~arr~~ alot. My mom cried

Liana, age 11

Awakening Your Ideas

If you were to start teaching reading right now, what would you do? Whether or not you have taught in the classroom, worked with children, or taken courses in education, you probably have many ideas about how children learn to read and write. Let's pretend for a moment. Look at the scenario in the Personal Reflection.

Personal Reflection

Trisha, the girl in Patricia Polacco's autobiographical story *Thank You, Mr. Falker*, grew up loving books. But when she started school, and reading instruction began, she struggled. Whenever she looked at a page in a book, all she saw were "wiggling shapes." When it was her turn to read in class, the other children laughed at her. She began to feel dumb. As the years went on, she felt dumber and dumber. Then, when Trisha was in fifth grade, a new teacher, Mr. Falker, arrived at the school. Mr. Falker was the one who made a huge difference in Trisha's life. He taught her to read.

Imagine that you have a student like Trisha. You have the opportunity to do the same thing that Mr. Falker did. What would you do? How would you begin to teach Trisha to read?

Your answer reflects a lot of things. What you already know and what you value about literacy are vitally important to your growth as a teacher. Ruddell and Unrau (2004b) state, "Everyone who teaches reading has some model of the reading process that influences, perhaps unconsciously, their instructional decision making" (p. 1116). Your past experiences at school and at home, your own reading habits, and your observations of children and classrooms shape your thoughts about teaching much more than you realize. Consciously or not, you may find that when you are faced with a problem to solve in your classroom, and you are not quite sure how to handle it, you rely on your instincts.

Some researchers have suggested that these values and past experiences are much stronger than anything a preservice teacher learns while in teacher education courses (Bunting, 1988; Lortie, 1975). Regardless, when the livelihood of children is at stake, teachers cannot rely merely on instincts. When teachers understand more about the reading process, their instruction improves and they have greater knowledge of how well their students are learning (Beck, 1989). Teachers are professionals, with the goal of shaping the literacy skills of a future generation. Thus, teaching expertise and knowledgeable decision making are essential. In *What Matters Most: Teaching for America's Future*, the National Commission on Teaching and America's Future states:

> No top-down mandate can replace the insights and skill teachers need to manage complex classrooms and address the different needs of individual students, whatever their age. No textbook, packaged curriculum, or testing system can discern what students already know or create the rich array of experiences they need to move ahead. . . . There is no silver bullet in education. When all is said and done, if students are to be well taught, it will be done by knowledgeable and well-supported teachers. (1996, p. 10)

Thus, if you are a preservice teacher learning how to teach literacy to elementary or middle school students, this book is for you. By reading, reflecting, and applying what you learn, you will be well on your way to becoming a professional who has the knowledge and confidence to make teaching decisions about reading and writing.

Factors That Affect Your Decision Making

A good teacher can effectively select appropriate materials, present lessons, and assess student learning. Other than a teacher's past experiences and value systems, what makes those things happen? What are the influences that will have an impact on your decision making? Let's look at those things now.

The Children You Teach

Good teachers know about the children they teach. Althier Lazar, in her book titled *Learning to Be Literacy Teachers in Urban Schools* (2004), says it so well:

> The question is not: How do I teach reading and writing? Rather, it is, How do I teach *my students* to read and write? (p. 132)

Certainly, it makes sense to know about the students you teach. If you are teaching second grade, you need to understand the way seven- and eight-year-olds think. Likewise, if you are a middle school teacher, some understanding of the complexities of the thirteen-year-old mind will be important to you. Moreover, knowing the personal struggles and triumphs of your students is crucial to your ability to make a difference in their learning. You must get up close and see what is going on with students like Trisha in Polacco's story (1998). You need to know who needs to be given extra support, and who needs to be given more challenges.

Knowing about the way children learn and how they respond to their environment will help you make decisions about what to teach. Terms like "developmentally appropriate practice" will make sense to you, because you will know the developmental level of the children you teach and you will be able to select appropriate learning experiences for them. Knowing their cognitive and developmental needs as well as the things that interest them will help you make decisions that will help them learn. Chapter 2, "A Model of Instruction: Making Decisions about Teaching Literacy," will show you the questions you'll need to answer as you make plans for teaching reading and writing.

Children learn by interacting with each other.

The Social and Cultural Context

You will need to know about the lives of your students outside the classroom, because this affects their classroom learning. This is a long-standing truth in education: The experiences that children have at home and in their communities shape the students that they become in the classroom. As early as 1908, Edmund Huey, in reference to children's reading abilities, said, "The secret of it all lies in parents' reading aloud to and with the child" (p. 332). Since that time, many researchers have concluded the importance of understanding how social class and culture influence literacy learning and instruction (Au, 1993; Compton-Lilly, 2003; Heath, 1983, 1994; Neuman & Celan, 2001; Purcell-Gates, 1996; Teale, 1986; Valdés, 1996). All facets of the classroom are affected by the experiences that your students bring with them to the classroom, including: communicating with your students' caregivers, providing instructional activities that meet their needs, managing the classroom in an effective yet sensitive manner, and assessing their literacy capabilities.

Chapters 3 and 4 will help you get to know your students. Chapter 3, "Meeting the Literacy Needs of English Language Learners," explains the rich variety of knowledge and experiences that students who are learning English for the first time can bring to your classroom. Chapter 4, "Assessing Reading and Writing," provides several ways to find out students' interests as well as their literacy needs.

The Text That Children Read

Your understanding of the kinds of text that your students read has an impact on the instructional decisions you make. Children's stories, poems, nonfiction trade books, textbooks, magazines, newspapers, books on CD-ROM, and web sites will all be a part of your classroom. Planning effective lessons that show students how to understand these texts requires that you know their structure and pattern (Meyer & Poon, 2004). You will need to know which books will be good ones to use when teaching an array of reading strategies, such as characterization, finding the main idea, summarizing, and interpreting the author's meaning (Duke & Pearson, 2002). You will need to know which books will motivate your reluctant readers and which ones will satisfy the readers who hunger for more. You will also need to know about the myriad of texts available to your students through the Internet, and how "new literacies" affect their reading and writing (Leu, Castek, Henry, Coiro, & McMullan, 2004, p. 497). Moreover, you will need to know the kinds of problems inherent in understanding a variety of texts, such as content area textbooks, web sites, and hyperlinked texts.

Knowing your readers' texts means that you need to be a reader as well. If you are not an avid reader, you're not alone. Applegate and Applegate surveyed the reading habits of 379 preservice teachers and found that more than 51%, of them were "unenthusiastic" about reading (2004, p. 560). With that in mind, Chapter 5, "Understanding the Nature of Fiction and Nonfiction," introduces you to the variety and richness of children's literature, both fiction and nonfiction. There, you will find out about books that contain unforgettable characters, as well as books that "hook" you into learning something new. Knowing your books will give you more confidence as you make decisions about teaching literacy.

Diversity in the Reading Classroom

Culturally Responsive Literacy Instruction for African American Children

Culturally responsive instruction is the kind of teaching that recognizes and capitalizes upon differences in culture that are apparent in today's classrooms (Au, 1993). The culturally responsive teacher recognizes an important truth: Some African American students are culturally different from the mainstream culture of American classrooms and communities (Sanacore, 2004). Culturally responsive teachers are sensitive to the challenges that some of their students face and, at the same time, see the strengths that their African American students bring to the classroom. One such strength is an understanding of Black English. This language is not an inferior dialect of Standard English; rather, it is a form of communication tied to love and acceptance from their caregivers, families, and friends (Delpit, 1995). Teachers "genuine caring" for students and recognition of their home culture and language can "go a long way in helping African American students achieve success in school" (Sanacore, 2004, p. 746).

Strategies and learning activities that respond to the cultural differences of African American students capitalize on their strengths and keep expectations high. Some of these strategies are:

- **Literature circles**—Form small groups of about four students and have them read a common book and share their responses in discussions (Daniels, 2002). Give students roles to perform in their small groups, such as questioner, recorder, or fact-finder.

- **Drama**—Give students opportunities to role-play, pantomime, sing, dance, and use puppets. Incorporate rhythm, rhyme, and music in your teaching.

- **Readers' Theatre**—Create or obtain scripts from favorite books and assign parts to the students to read. Martinez, Roser, and Strecker (1998–1999) suggest a structured format for organizing students as they prepare for Readers' Theater.

- **Daily independent reading**—Offer students opportunities to choose their own books and read independently, which is important for building confidence with the printed word. Provide a classroom library full of multicultural and traditional literature at a range of reading levels (Sanacore, 2004).

- **Talk about language**—Respect Black English for what it is—a language used in homes and communities (Teachers of English to Speakers of Other Languages, 1997). Talk about the differences between Black and Standard English and the contexts in which each is used.

The Politics of Literacy

Some of the teaching decisions you make will be based on federal and state legislation. Perhaps one of the most significant influences will be the No Child Left Behind Act (NCLB) of 2001. The NCLB statement of purpose says, "The purpose of this title is to ensure that all children have a fair, equal, and significant opportunity to obtain a high-quality education and reach, at a minimum, proficiency on challenging state academic achievement standards and state academic assessments" (No Child Left Behind, 2001, Pub. L. 107-110, Title I, Sec. 1001).

The law states that public schools must provide instruction in these five components of the reading process: phonemic awareness, phonics, vocabulary, fluency, and comprehension. Moreover, schools must ensure "the access of children to effective, scientifically based instructional strategies and challenging academic content" (No Child Left Behind, 2001, Pub. L. 107-110, Title I, Sec. 1001, #9). The term "scientifically based instructional strategies" is sometimes conveyed as "evidence-based instruction." Both terms mean "there is reliable, trustworthy, and valid evidence to suggest that when the program is used with a particular group of children, the children can be expected to make adequate gains in reading achievement" (International Reading Association, 2002).

Thus, you need to choose strategies that have been tested in educational research. You need to be familiar with a myriad of strategies that teach children how to manipulate sounds of words, decode unknown words, recognize and use vocabulary, read fluently, and demonstrate comprehension of what they read.

Your decisions will also reflect your ability to work with the standards adopted by your state. These standards, which your state legislature has written to include the five components of reading outlined by NCLB, will serve as guides for you as you plan. Appendix A lists several web sites that will be helpful to you in finding out more about standards for teachers, including the sites for ACEI, INTASC, IRA, and NCATE.

State Department Standards

The web sites of state departments of education in all 50 of the United States are included in Appendix A, because these are the ones you will most likely be using to document your abilities. Academic standards adopted by each state can be found at its web site.

National Council of Accreditation of Teacher Education Standards

Standards that are nationally accepted as guidelines for training new teachers are published by NCATE, the National Council of Accreditation of Teacher Education. This governing body regulates the accreditation of colleges of education that educate and prepare new teachers for certification. Because there are so many types of teacher certification programs, NCATE uses standards written by other organizations to evaluate university programs that prepare teachers. The Association for Childhood Education International (ACEI) authored the standards that NCATE uses to assess and accredit elementary education teacher preparation programs.

Interstate New Teacher Assessment and Support Consortium

This policymaking body (INTASC) outlines ten principles that reflect the kinds of things effective teachers do in their classrooms. I have included these principles in this book because they are nationally recognized standards that serve as guidelines for many state standards. To date, at least 37 states have indicated that the INTASC "core principles" are the model on which state departments have developed their standards. Moreover, NCATE carefully aligned its accreditation standards with the INTASC principles. Thus, the INTASC principles are frequently used by colleges of education as guidelines for assessing preservice teachers (Campbell, Cignetti, Melenyzer, Nettles, & Wyman, 2004). You might be asked to document your abilities in a professional portfolio, using any of these standards.

National Association for the Education of Young Children

This organization works on behalf of young children, ages birth to eight, and regulates accreditation in programs that offer certification for early childhood education. Its standards apply to early childhood preparation programs in universities and colleges. Additionally, the NAEYC accredits childcare and preschool programs.

The International Reading Association: Standards for Reading Professionals

This is a set of guidelines (2004) for the kinds of teaching behaviors that are associated with teaching reading. These standards specifically address all five of the NCLB components of reading, and I have aligned most of the strategies, theories, and teaching behaviors discussed in this book with the IRA standards.

In Reviewing the Big Picture boxes located at the end of each chapter in this book, I have listed standards that are reflected in the topics covered in that chapter. Standards and principles associated with the IRA, INTASC, NAEYC, and NCATE are all listed.

You will find out about the theories and research bases behind the five categories of reading instruction outlined by NCLB in this chapter. Once you understand the theoretical concepts behind the reading processes, you'll need to know how to put those into practice. Chapter 2 offers a model of instruction that can help you make teaching decisions. As you make plans, you will ask yourself, "What do I teach?" and "How do I teach it?" We will look at how you can answer those questions, which paves the way for the strategies and ideas that you will encounter in the rest of this book.

How Theory Influences Classroom Practices

A **theory** is an explanation, based on thought and observation, about how the reading process takes place. Why do you need to know theory? When you have an idea of how the reading process occurs, your teaching will be focused on ways to enable that process. In the era of No Child Left Behind and standards-based education, you will be held accountable for your teaching. Today's classrooms need teachers who are professional educators, capable of making decisions about what to teach and how to teach it. Moreover, today's classrooms need teachers who can articulate the reading process and explain their instructional decisions. Now, more than ever, today's classrooms need teachers who don't rely on mere instincts.

What ideas do you have about teaching children to read? What kinds of strategies or activities would be most important? What do your choices say about your theoretical orientation? As you think about your choices, we'll also look at some classrooms, and see how the teaching strategies of the teachers in those classrooms reflect theory. These classroom scenarios will show us the many facets of learning to read, and how theories have affected classroom-teaching practices. In reading the scenarios, you might see some of your own ideas about the teaching of literacy.

There are four major theories explained in this chapter: cueing systems, automaticity, schema theory, and the transactional theory. These theories describe the reader in four ways:

1. The reader decodes words based on the letter clues that he sees on the page and what he knows about our language.
2. The reader reads smoothly, with appropriate speed, and without the need to stop and figure out unknown words.
3. The reader comprehends print by constructing meaning based on what he already knows.
4. The reader responds to text and shares his responses with others, thus deepening his comprehension of it.

To facilitate your understanding of these theoretical orientations to literacy, I will present classroom scenarios that depict readers in each of these four ways. First, I will show you some of the teaching methods of second grade teacher Mrs. Cuesta, whose students use cueing systems to decode words and understand the story in the book *Tops and Bottoms* (Stevens, 1995). Second, we will look at Mr. Fluensee's first grade classroom. He provides his students with some fluency activities for the book *Arthur's Reading Race* (Brown, 1996). These strategies help them read smoothly, with appropriate speed, and with understanding. Third, we will visit Mrs. Skeema's fourth grade classroom, to see how readers construct meaning based on what they already know, as they read *Charlotte's Web* (White, 1952). Finally, we will observe ways that readers respond to text in Ms. Rea-Sponse's third grade classroom. They will be reading *Train to Somewhere* (Bunting, 1996).

So, let's take a look at these classrooms in the next few pages. They will help you formulate mental pictures for theories that explain the reading process.

Readers Decode Print

What happens when children approach the printed page? How do they figure out what the print says? Seeing a written word and making a mental translation is called **decoding**. Historically, theorists have had a variety of explanations for the way that readers decode. One explanation is the use of **cueing systems**, which explains what readers do as they translate print into meaning. Think about your own ideas again. Did you say that you would review or teach letters of the alphabet and their sounds? Did you want to teach an unfamiliar word to them, perhaps by showing them the word in a sentence? If your response is similar to these, you focused on helping children use available clues in text to decode words they do not know. The first teacher that we will meet does this in her lesson. Read on to find out how.

Mrs. Cuesta's Lesson

Mrs. Cuesta says to her second grade students, "I've got a great book for you to read today, called *Tops and Bottoms* (1995). Take a look at its cover. As you can see, it's a Caldecott Honor book. It's also one of my favorites and I can't wait for you to read it! But first, let's make sure that you know one of the most important words in the story." She puts a sentence strip on the board for them to see:

> This animal likes to eat carrots and lettuce. It hops around. It is a r_ _ _ _.

Mrs. Cuesta continues, "See if you can figure out what word might go in the blank, based on the clues in these sentences. Think of a word that starts with 'r' that would make sense here. Maggie?"

Maggie says, "It's gotta be 'rabbit'!"

"Yes, that makes perfect sense, doesn't it?" says Mrs. Cuesta. "You used the letter on the blank and the rest of the words in the sentences to figure that out! Good for you. Now let's imagine that the word in that blank looks different. Let's think about what might happen if the first letter was not 'r,' but something else. Take a look."

Mrs. Cuesta erases the "r" and puts an "h" in the blank, so that the sentence strip now looks like:

> This animal likes to eat carrots and lettuce. It hops around. It is a h_ _ _ _.

"And I'll give you another clue," says Mrs. Cuesta. "This missing word looks just like another word that you know. It's the word 'care.' I'll write 'care' on the board. Take a look at it. If you put the 'h' in front of the letters '-a-r-e' in this word, you'll figure out the missing word."

Several children excitedly raise their hands. Mrs. Cuesta calls on Ming Lei.

"It's 'hare'! A hare is the same thing as a rabbit!" says Ming Lei.

"That's exactly right, Ming Lei. You made an excellent prediction based on what you saw in the sentences. And a hare is one of the characters in our story. Take a look at the cover. You can see a picture of the hare standing right there, holding a piece of corn. There's also a large bear pictured on the cover, and he's sleeping in a chair. These characters have a problem to solve, and we're going to find out what it is. Remember, as you read, if you come to a word that you don't know, use your decoding bookmark that reminds you of what to do. You can make good guesses about words, if you use the clues that are on your bookmark. You may also use your sticky notes to mark words that give you difficulty."

All the students have a copy of the bookmark at their desks. The directions on this bookmark are shown below.

When you see a word you don't know:

1. Look at the letters. What word that begins with _____ would make sense there?
2. Look for a pattern that you know. Try to say the word. Does that make sense?
3. Keep your finger on the word and finish the sentence. Try a word that would make sense in this sentence.

Additionally, students have some sticky notes available on their tables. They know to use these to mark words in the story that are difficult to decode.

At this point, Mrs. Cuesta's students are ready to read. She says, "Read until you get to the page that shows Hare and his family watering and weeding the garden. Then we'll stop and talk about the story so far."

The students begin to read. While reading, Mrs. Cuesta stops them occasionally to talk about the events in the story, as well as the words that they marked with sticky notes. They write these words on cards and hang them alphabetically on the class "word wall." Later, they use these cards to create sentences and play sorting games. One of their favorites is called "Making Words," which is an activity in which Mrs. Cuesta gives them clues about words in the story and they spell the words with letter cards.

The Cueing Systems

To figure out how theory is reflected in this lesson, think about the things Mrs. Cuesta did. She began with a quality piece of literature, *Tops and Bottoms*. She provided her students with one of the tools that they will need to understand the story by teaching them an important word, "hare," using context clues and visual clues in the print. When she put the sentence strips on the board, she asked her students to figure out an unknown word, using all available clues. These clues, called the cueing systems, consist of semantic, syntactic, graphophonological, and pragmatic cues (Clay, 1991; Goodman, 1994; Halliday, 1975). Readers use cueing systems to figure out print and make sense of it. I will describe each of the cueing systems next.

Semantic cues, or meaning cues, are the ones that students get from a composite of the print, pictures, and content of the whole text. As they read a piece of text, they build an understanding of what is taking place in the words, and this understanding helps them to make predictions about words that they have yet to encounter in this text. Semantic or meaning cues help them make guesses about words that "ought to go there" because it makes sense for them to be there. For example, in the text, "This animal likes to eat carrots and lettuce. It hops around. It is a _____ " the reader makes a reasonable guess that the last word could be "rabbit" or "hare," because these words make sense, based on what she learns from the clues in the sentences prior to it.

Syntactic cues, also called structure or grammar cues, help the reader make predictions based on what makes sense in the English language. If the child is familiar with our language, he can reliably guess words based on their placement in the sentence that he is reading. Even if the child cannot name the part of speech that is in the sentence, he knows, instinctively, the types of words that are most likely to occur in different positions of a sentence. He can make a reasonable guess about the word based on its usage and placement in the sentence. Going back to our previous example, the reader of English knows that we would say, "It is a *rabbit*," but not "*It is a remove*," or "It is a *hare*," but not "It is a *how*." Even if the reader guesses, "It is a *robin*," which doesn't make sense semantically, he is making sense syntactically, because of the order of words in the sentence. This is one of the reasons that some children who are learning English as a second language have difficulty with academic tasks, because other languages do not necessarily have the same syntactical patterns as English. You'll learn more about this in Chapter 3.

Graphophonological cues, or visual and sound cues, help the reader determine the pronunciation of a word in print, based on the letters she sees. She makes guesses about words based on her knowledge of letters and sounds. This means that she is using **phonics** to figure out unknown words. If she sees a word that begins with a particular letter, she can make a prediction about the word based on a narrower selection of choices. Using the same example sentences, "This animal likes to eat carrots and lettuce. It hops around. It is a _____," the reader who uses this cueing system would not say the word "rabbit" for the last word if she sees that the word begins with the letter "h." She would put the "h" together with the rest of the word, which looks like a word she already knows,

Providing children with time to read independently allows them to become comfortable with print.

"care." Her ability to blend letters and sounds helps her figure out that this is the word "hare," which makes sense in the sentence. She knows this makes sense because she has seen pictures of hares and knows that they are related to rabbits.

Finally, your students get **pragmatic cues** from their social environment. According to Halliday (1978), children gain this information from communicating with others in their homes and communities. Dialects, which are variations in pronunciation and use of words according to geography, may affect the way they read and write. Variations of Standard English can also affect their reading and writing. Some of your students might speak African American Vernacular English, which is sometimes called Black English or Ebonics (Center for Applied Linguistics, 1997). When they see text in print and read it aloud, they may say the words differently from the way they are printed on the page. They may write using the vernacular, and while the meaning is quite clear, the words are different from Standard English. Using the example from Mrs. Cuesta's lesson, one of her students might say this when he sees the sentence strip: "Dis animal like to eat carrots an' lettuce. It hop around. It a hare." The meaning remains the same to this reader.

Sometimes, whole words are replaced when a student uses the pragmatic cueing system, because of the language patterns they use at home. They see the print, comprehend it, and translate it in their own vernacular. For example, look at this sentence from *Tops and Bottoms*:

"But all Bear wanted to do was sleep."

A child who speaks Black English in his home might read aloud:

"But Bear, all he won' do was sleep."

Figure 1.1 shows an example of what happens when the reader encounters print and uses the four cueing systems.

Using the Four Cueing Systems to Understand Print

Chad, the reader, sees:

The plumber turned off the <u>faucet</u>.

Chad moves his eyes across the words and can easily decode and understand each of the words until the last one. His eyes do not take in each single letter or word; instead, his eyes sweep across the whole sentence, taking in several letters and even several words at the same time (called *chunking*). All the time he is taking in these words, he is having no trouble, because the words are easily predictable to him. He naturally expects each of those words to be there. However, when he gets to the last word, he must fixate a bit. Chad uses clues to try to figure out the word. First, he sees the *f* and the *a,* so he uses graphophonological clues to make some guesses about that word. Is it *far, face,* or *faucet?* All of these are somewhat graphically and phonologically similar. However, the word *far* does not fit syntactically. Instinctively, he senses that this sentence calls for a noun at the end. So, he confidently eliminates that choice. *Face* does not fit because it does not make sense semantically, even though it is a noun. He eliminates that possibility. *Faucet* makes sense, but Chad is from Texas. He and his family do not call this piece of plumbing a "faucet"; instead, they call it a "spigot." Thus, when he sees the word *faucet,* because he is somewhat unfamiliar with its use, the pragmatic cueing system compels him to say *spigot.* However, the graphophonological cues tell him that *faucet* must be the word he wants, because he sees the letters and knows the sounds they represent. Thus he reads out loud, "The plumber turned off the . . . sp—sp— . . . faucet."

All of this takes about three or four seconds.

Figure 1.1 An example of a reader who uses the four cueing systems.

The teacher who encourages the use of cueing systems makes sure, just as Mrs. Cuesta did, that the classroom atmosphere is such that students are expected to make thoughtful guesses, or predictions, about words they don't know. The use of predictions is a way to facilitate their understanding; it also requires a "risk-free" environment, in which students feel comfortable about using their own judgment about the semantic, syntactic, or graphophonological clues before them. In fact, Goodman emphasizes the importance of supporting and encouraging predictions as students read, so that they use what they know about printed text to help them figure out the unknown. He calls reading a "psycholinguistic guessing game" (1967), in that readers are constantly making predictions about what is next in the print as their eyes sweep across the page. Such an environment allows them to feel comfortable about making judgments about spelling, also, so that they can concentrate on their ideas as they write first drafts, rather than on the mechanics of the appearance of words.

Of course, the teacher must also teach students the letter sounds and the meanings of words, so that they can use this knowledge as they read and write. Knowledge of letter–sound relationships is important in being able to use the cueing systems. While the reader can make educated guesses about the print she sees, she will not have much success if she does not know how to eliminate her choices based on the clues she sees on the page.

Instruction in phonics is one of the ways to ensure students' success in matching letters to sounds. Such instruction builds upon the child's **phonemic awareness,** which is the ability to manipulate sounds without any knowledge of letters (Ehri & Nunes, 2002). A **phoneme** is the smallest unit of sound in spoken language.

For example, "mud" has three phonemes, each represented by a letter, or grapheme. Say the word slowly, stretching out each of its sounds. You hear "m-m-m," "uh," and "duh." In professional literature on phonics and phonemic awareness, phonemes (or sounds) are represented by a letter or symbol within slanted lines, in this case: /m/, /u/, and /d/. Sometimes two written letters comprise a grapheme. For example, the /th/ is represented by the grapheme "th," and the /ē/ sound can be represented by the grapheme "ea," as in "teacher." (As you read this book, you'll see these symbols frequently.)

Very young children who do not yet know the letters of the alphabet are able to play with sounds in words. This is evidence of their phonemic awareness. Think about the song "Old Macdonald Had a Farm." The repetitive refrain in this song is "e-i-e-i-o." Many children play with this, singing something like this: "Old Macdonald had a farm, me-my-me-my-mo!" This ability to manipulate phonemes is an important precursor to their ability to connect letters to sounds, and then blend those sounds when they encounter unknown words in print, many years later (Yopp & Yopp, 2000).

In a meta-analysis of research since 1970 on comparisons of methods of reading instruction, the National Reading Panel (2000a) determined, after a review of 52 research studies, that "teaching phonemic awareness to children significantly improves their reading more than instruction that lacks any attention to PA [phonemic awareness]" (p. 7). Additionally, this report states that "systematic phonics instruction enhances children's success in learning to read and that systematic phonics instruction is significantly more effective than instruction that teaches little or no phonics" (p. 9). This research led to the inclusion of phonemic awareness and phonics as two of the five components of reading instruction in the No Child Left Behind law of 2001. In Chapter 6, "Developing Emerging Literacy," you will learn more about phonemic awareness and how to teach it to youngsters whose literacy skills are emerging. Chapter 7, "Teaching Young Children to Decode Independently," shows you how to teach phonics by building upon this awareness of the sounds of our language, and how to teach it for the purpose of helping your students figure out unfamiliar words.

Think again about Mrs. Cuesta's lesson. Suppose her students were able to pronounce the word "hare," but had never heard the word before. And suppose that the clues in the preceding sentences, "eating carrots and lettuce" and "hops around" were not helpful semantic clues for them. This could happen if the children do not understand the other words in the sentences, or if they do not connect the picture with the print. Their lack of vocabulary knowledge would hinder their understanding of the story. Your students' knowledge of words will certainly have an impact on their ability to read with ease and with comprehension. According to Graves and Watts-Taffe (2002), who reviewed more than 100 years of research on the subject, vocabulary knowledge is crucial for comprehending text, and children in disadvantaged situations tend to have smaller vocabularies than their peers, which is one of the reasons for their failure in school. The National Reading Panel reports, "vocabulary instruction does lead to gains in comprehension, but . . . methods must be appropriate to the age and ability of the reader" (2000a, p. 14). Thus, vocabulary is a third component of the NCLB law. In Chapter 8, "Teaching Word Study," you will learn how to teach vocabulary.

See Figure 1.2 for a summary of how teachers use the cueing systems in their classrooms.

Cueing Systems

What the Student Does

- Makes predictions about the text using clues that give her ideas about the meaning of the words in the sentences.
- Makes predictions about the text using clues that give her ideas about the correct order of words in the sentences.
- Makes predictions about the text using clues that give her ideas about the phonetic elements of the words in the sentences.
- Thinks about the text when figuring out unknown words, and thinks of words that would make sense according to what the author has written.
- Uses knowledge of letters and sounds when figuring out unknown words, and tries to make sense of the resulting pronunciation.

What the Teacher Does

- Teaches students to use context clues together with phonetic elements to figure out unknown words.
- Preteaches vocabulary before the students read only as necessary for understanding the text.
- Teaches independence in figuring out unknown words.
- Encourages predictions while reading.
- Teaches phonics for the purpose of figuring out unknown words and adding to predictions.
- Builds on students' phonemic awareness when teaching phonics.
- Gives students tools for figuring out words, such as decoding strategy bookmarks and sticky notes for marking difficult ones.
- Displays words on a "word wall" and uses them in games, sentence activities, and writing.
- Gives students letter cards and asks them to "make words" based on given clues.

Classroom Example Used in This Chapter

Before her students read the book *Tops and Bottoms*, Mrs. Cuesta taught one word, "hare," using a combination of context and phonics clues. This word was the name of one of the characters, making it a very important one to know. When encountering words while reading, Mrs. Cuesta expected her students to use clues from the print to figure them out. While reading, they referred to a decoding bookmark, which outlined a strategy for figuring out unknown words. They also used sticky notes to mark difficult words. After reading, she put words from the story on the word wall so they could make sentences and play games with them. Finally, she uses clues from the story and asks them to make words using letter cards.

Figure 1.2 Using the cueing systems.

Sources: Clay, 1991; Goodman, 1994; Goodman & Goodman, 2004; Halliday, 1978.

Readers Read Fluently

When you thought about some ways to teach a child to read, did you imagine that you might read aloud to the child first? Or did you think about asking the child to read aloud, so you could get a feel for how well she reads? Did you want to ask the child to read some words on a list, to get an idea of how many words she knows? If so, your ideas are reflective of the automaticity theory, which is a prevailing idea in Mr. Fluensee's classroom. Read on to find out how.

Mr. Fluensee's Lesson

All week, Mr. Fluensee's first grade students have been reading *Arthur's Reading Race* by Marc Brown (1994). His students are familiar with the Arthur series and enjoy listening to his adventures. Mr. Fluensee begins on Monday by reading the story aloud to them, so they could hear "how it is supposed to go." The story is about the conversation between Arthur and his sister D.W. Arthur claims that D.W. does not know how to read, but she proves to him that she does. As they walk through town, D.W. shows her brother the number of words that she knows on signs, traffic signals, and advertisements. As Mr. Fluensee reads, the students enjoy pointing to the words that D.W. knew, and they laugh at the end of the story when Arthur neglects to read a sign posted on a park bench and sits in wet paint.

After reading it aloud to them, Mr. Fluensee gives students their own copies of the story, and reads the text again. This time, he reads one sentence at a time, and asks the students to "be an echo," by repeating the sentence, using the same intonation and expression.

The next day, Mr. Fluensee puts the students in pairs and gives each pair a copy of the book. He says, "Let's read it again. This time, I'd like for you to read with your partner. One of you can be Arthur and the other one can be D.W. Take turns being the narrator." The students sit on the floor in pairs, reading their parts in the story. Mr. Fluensee circulates, sits on the floor next to the students, and listens. He makes quick notes on a chart that contains a rubric to assess their oral reading. He pays attention to the things his students do well as they read, such as using expression in characters' dialogue, phrasing, observing punctuation, and reading with appropriate speed. He also makes note of the kinds of miscues the students make, such as mispronounced words, repetitions, or slow, word-by-word reading. He is committed to listening to five students each day, and keeps these notes in a reading portfolio for each student so that he can make instructional plans.

There is a word wall in Mr. Fluensee's classroom, similar to the one found in Mrs. Cuesta's room. Mr. Fluensee writes several of the words from *Arthur's Reading Race* on cards and tapes them to the word wall. He calls out several words and asks volunteers to find them. Then they arrange these words in the appropriate sequence to create a sentence, and tape the sentence on the wall. The class reads these sentences aloud together. Additionally, each student has a "word bank." These words are added to their banks, and Mr. Fluensee often asks them to pull their word cards out to work with words. They sort the words by category, by first letter, or by rhymes.

So that his students can hear and reread the story many times, Mr. Fluensee puts a taped reading of *Arthur's Reading Race* at the listening center. During the week, they have the opportunity to visit the center and read and reread the story several times. Each time they read the book, the students become more and more familiar with the words and can read along with more appropriate speed and expression.

There is also a well-stocked classroom library in Mr. Fluensee's room, and time scheduled daily for independent reading of books of the students' choice. Mr. Fluensee has made sure that there are plenty of books that are easy to read so that his students have the chance to read and reread text without the demands of trying to figure out unknown words. Mr. Fluensee has used many of these easy books to create scripts for Readers' Theater, which is when students share a story by reading the scripts in a dramatic fashion. Stories are read in this manner very frequently in his classroom; the students love to take character parts and use their voices to "become" the character.

Finally, Mr. Fluensee's students have "home book bags" that he sends home each week. In it, each child has a copy of the book and a letter to caregivers, asking them to listen to their child read the story, and give the child opportunities to read to siblings and other family members.

Automaticity

Mr. Fluensee's teaching strategies emphasize fluid, comfortable, rapid reading. His students are learning to read with **fluency.** The National Reading Panel states that fluency is the ability to "read orally with speed, accuracy, and proper expression" (2000a, p. 11). Comprehension is also a vital component of fluency, because "fluency is the bridge or link between the ability to identify words quickly and the ability to understand text" (Johns & Bergland, 2002, p. 17). According to Samuels, "Fluency is important because it exerts an important influence on comprehension; that is, to experience good comprehension, the reader must be able to identify words quickly and easily" (2002, p. 167).

When readers read fluently, they are reading quickly and effortlessly, without conscious thought given to figuring out words or determining meaning. The reader recognizes words instantly and understands the message of the author without the need to stop and mull over the print. Moreover, when reading orally, the fluent reader sounds good. The reader gives characters expression when he reads their dialogue, and his speed is comfortable for listening.

How do all these things happen to the reader? **Automaticity** is a theory that explains fluency. Laberge and Samuels (1974) developed a model of reading that attempted to explain how readers process print. This model, which was later updated to include more findings (Samuels, 2004; Samuels & Kamil, 1984), stated that the reading process consists of two parallel functions: decoding and comprehending. Because the human brain has limited capacity to handle these two functions, a reader's attention must switch from one function to the other. The amount of attention he can give to either of these processes depends on his ability to connect letters to sounds, as well as his familiarity with the words in the text. If a reader must stop and decode too many words, he will lose the comprehension

Modifying Instruction for

ELL

The Language Experience Approach and
Arthur's Reading Race

GRADE LEVEL: K–2

● **Objective**

Students will dictate an experience chart, read the chart with help, and recognize new vocabulary.

● **Preparation**

Arrange for a walking trip around the block in the neighborhood of the school. If this is not possible, arrange to take a walk on the school grounds. As an alternative, take photographs of signs, menus, or logos from places in the community, such as fast food restaurants, gas stations, and grocery stores, or provide magazines that contain many such pictures (see "Environmental Print" section in Chapter 6).

● **Materials**

- *Arthur's Reading Race* (Brown, 1996)—This story is about a conversation between Arthur and his sister D.W., who tries to prove that she knows how to read. The siblings walk through their town and D.W. points out all the words that she knows, such as "taxi," "bank," and "ice cream."
- Pictures of these words: zoo, taxi, gas, milk, grass, bank, ice cream, wet paint.

● **Introduction**

1. Read aloud *Arthur's Reading Race*. On each of the pages that show the words that D.W. knows, point to the corresponding pictures to make sure that all students see the connection between the word and the concept. Write words on a piece of chart paper or the chalkboard. Next to each, tape a picture to illustrate the word.

2. After reading, discuss the book. Ask the following inclusive question, which allows for a variety of appropriate responses from all students: "What can you tell me about D.W.?" Then ask students to talk about the kinds of reading that they do.

● **The Language Experience Approach**

3. Provide an experience similar to the one in the story. Walk around the school or neighborhood, if possible. If not, show pictures of the surrounding neighborhood or give the students magazines with many pictures of places in a community. Say, "While we walk (or look at these pictures), find words that you know. I'll write them on a notepad so we'll remember them. I'll also draw a little picture next to each word, so we'll remember what the words mean when we get back to the classroom."

Modifications for ELL are printed in color.

(continued)

4. Back in the classroom, ask the students to gather on the rug, around a piece of chart paper. Say, "When we went for a walk, I saw a grocery store. So, on this paper, I'll write what I saw, using these words:

> Mr. Fluensee saw a grocery store.

5. Say, "Now it's your turn. What did you see? Tell me by using this sentence: <u>Student's name</u> saw a _____. If you need help, we can look at my notepad to help us remember what you saw."

6. As the students dictate sentences, write their responses on the chart paper. Then ask them to illustrate the sentence with a small picture next to or underneath the word, so that a rebus-style story is created.

7. Read each sentence to the students, moving a pointer or hand along the print. Ask students to watch.

8. Reread the text and ask them to echo it.

9. Reread the text again. Ask students to follow along.

10. The next day, duplicate the chart again, cutting the sentences apart into strips. Ask a student to look at the original chart and find the sentence that matches a sentence strip. Ask him to read the sentence and then place the strip on top of the appropriate sentence.

11. The next day, cut each strip into words. Ask students to match the words to the sentences on the chart.

12. Make a recording of this language experience chart and put it in the Listening Center for rereadings.

13. Include these words on the word wall, as well as in individual word banks at the students' desks. During the week, ask students to pull out the cards, along with other cards in their banks, and use them for sorting activities. They can sort the cards by categories, such as names of places or animal words.

14. Duplicate the chart so that each student has a copy of the text. Ask them to read the narrative to caregivers and siblings at home.

of what he is reading. Therefore, much repetition and practice with words is necessary to develop automatic recognition of vocabulary. Automaticity occurs when it no longer is necessary for the reader to figure out, or decode, words seen on the page. This situation leads to fluent reading.

An indicator of reading fluency is the student's ability to recognize words. Samuels reports that students' age and experience with reading affect the way that they recognize words (2002). Inexperienced readers tend to look at words in a letter-by-letter fashion, whereas older, more experienced readers perceive a word as an entire unit. Thus, "beginning readers cannot simultaneously decode and comprehend a text, whereas fluent readers can do both tasks at the same time" (p. 171). There are three stages in word recognition skill. At the "nonaccurate stage," the student has difficulty identifying words in very easy text. Next, the "accurate but not automatic stage" is when "the student acquires the ability to recognize some words as 'sight words' and other words by sounding them out" (p. 171). At this stage, reading is slow, because the student must stop several times and methodically sound out letters. The final stage is "accurate and automatic" (p. 172), when the student can read with accuracy and speed, as if he were talking. He can decode and comprehend simultaneously.

Mr. Fluensee worked hard to bring his first graders to the stage at which they are comfortable with the print in the texts they were reading. His strategies emphasized the development of fluency. He began by reading aloud *Arthur's Reading Race*. This step gave them the idea of how the text should sound. Then, they read the text together in a variety of ways; each time they read, the story became more familiar and more words became instantly recognized. Soon, his students did not need to laboriously sound out words; instead, they immediately said the words they saw on the page, allowing them to attend to the pleasures of understanding the story.

Much work with vocabulary is done in Mr. Fluensee's classroom, so that his students can move beyond letter-by-letter decoding and see words as whole units in text. Easy reading books that are on his students' reading levels are part of the classroom library, as is the listening center, which allows them to listen to the book being read over and over again, while they read along and pay attention to the visual features of the words. Repeated readings are an important part of his classroom instruction, because this builds comfort with print, as well as automatic recognition of words. Additionally, repeated readings are encouraged at home, where his students read books to their families—books that are by now quite familiar to them.

You may have noticed that there are some similarities between the theories that you have read about so far. These two ideas about the reading process are overlapping, because in both of them, knowledge of words is important. Think about the cueing systems for a moment. If a student is attempting to figure out a word she does not know, she will need to pick up all the clues she can from the print on the page. In order for all of the clues to work together, she needs to know most of the words on the page. For example, look at this sentence in Stevens's *Tops and Bottoms*:

"They planted, watered, and *weeded*."

If the last word in the sentence is unknown, it is most helpful for the student to know all of the other words in the sentence. But what happens if she does not know those words? She would need to stop and decode each of them, which causes her to switch her attention from a smooth and relaxed pace of reading that makes sense, to a halting and stumbling problem-solving mode in which she must attempt to decode an unfamiliar word. When this happens many times, her fluency falters,

Automaticity

What the Student Does

- Works with words so they are automatically recognized.
- Instantly recognizes most of the words in the text that he reads.
- Reads and rereads books that are easy for him to read, at school and at home.
- Listens and follows print while the teacher reads aloud.

What the Teacher Does

- Reads text aloud before asking students to read it, so that they can hear how it is supposed to sound.
- Gives students plenty of opportunities to reread text to develop fluency.
- Provides books on tape so that students can listen to a story without the demands of decoding.
- Displays words on a "word wall" and asks students to identify them and make sentences with them.
- Sends easy reading books home so students can read to family members.

Classroom Example Used in This Chapter

Mr. Fluensee reads aloud *Arthur's Reading Race* to his first graders, then asks them to read it with him. They read in echo fashion, and they read parts with partners. The book is taped and is available at the listening center for them to read. A classroom library is full of easy-to-read books so that students can experience success with reading without the heavy demands of decoding unfamiliar words. A word wall contains words from the story, and Mr. Fluensee asks the students to pick out word cards, make sentences with them, and read the sentences aloud. Book bags containing the book go home so that the students can read to their parents.

Figure 1.3 Student and teacher behaviors that reflect automaticity.

Sources: LaBerge & Samuels, 1974; Samuels, 2004; Samuels & Kamil, 1984.

and her comprehension suffers. Thus, automatic recognition of most of the words on the page is important in the efficient use of the cueing systems. Figure 1.3 shows the behaviors associated with automaticity.

Readers Comprehend Based on Prior Knowledge

Think again about the question that you answered at the beginning of this chapter: "Where would you begin to teach a child to read?" Did you say that you would provide some type of experience for the child? Or perhaps you thought about brainstorming ideas or talking about her past experiences. If so, you were thinking about teaching strategies similar to the ones we will see in this section. Here, we will focus on finding out how readers construct meaning as they read, which enables them to comprehend the page. We'll see how one teacher's classroom instruction reflects "schema theory."

Mrs. Skeema's Lesson

The lesson begins with a question about two pictures. Mrs. Skeema holds up a picture of a spider and a picture of a dog. She asks, "Which of these animals would you rather get to know?" Most students readily agree that the dog would be a preferable friend or pet. Then Mrs. Skeema leads the class outdoors, to a cluster of bushes. There is a large spider web on one of the bushes, and Mrs. Skeema asks the students to examine it, looking for the spider and noting any interesting details about the web. After taking them back into the classroom, Mrs. Skeema asks them to draw a picture of a spider, adding all the details that they can think of. Then she asks the students to share some of their ideas aloud. Mrs. Skeema writes some of these ideas on a piece of chart paper taped to the chalkboard, creating a visual web that categorizes the ideas and shows relationships between the words. Students in the class eagerly discuss their past encounters with spiders, most of which have been negative ones. Then Mrs. Skeema shows them a page from the book *Animals Nobody Loves*, by Seymour Simon (2001). In this book, Simon describes the spider, and explains why the spider is often misunderstood. The class adds new facts about the spider to the word web, and talks about how Simon's book has added some new insights about spiders to their thinking. Mrs. Skeema leaves this web hanging on the board for several days.

The next day, to introduce *Charlotte's Web* (White, 1952) to the students, Mrs. Skeema shows them a book box. In it are several items that relate to the elements of this story: a doll to represent a young girl, a picture of an ax, stuffed animals to represent barn animals (including a pig), a plastic spider, a toy replica of a barn, a spider's web decoration, a plastic rat, a package of bacon or ham, the word "terrific" torn from a magazine or newspaper, and a picture of a county fair. She says, "In this box are some objects that give you clues about the story in this book. As I pull them out, think about how they give you ideas about the story. Think about all the things we've talked about, and think about what you already know about these objects. Try to figure out the story that the author, E. B. White, wrote. Who are the characters? What is the setting? And what is the problem that needs to be solved? In your head, create a 'mind movie' that has all these things in it, and as we read, you can compare Mr. White's ideas with yours."

The students begin to read silently, stopping occasionally to talk about their predictions. As the next couple of weeks pass, they read the book, chapter by chapter. Mrs. Skeema begins each lesson by referring to the web. Reviewing what they have read so far, they add new information about spiders that E. B. White has included as part of his story. They discuss how their ideas change as they discover more about Charlotte the spider.

Mrs. Skeema precedes the reading of some of the chapters by showing the students a new word they will encounter. Words such as "metatarsus" and "coxa" and "spinneret" are discussed and pronounced before the students read. Learning about specific features of just a few important words gives the students additional knowledge about concepts in the story before they read.

At the end of the book, they draw new pictures of spiders, making sure to put in all the new details that they have learned, and write their own detailed descriptions of spiders, using the new words that they have learned. In a discussion afterwards, the students talk about how the theme of friendship throughout the book puts spiders in a new light for them. They begin to see spiders as somewhat helpful creatures in the food chain. They also recall some of the facts about spiders they learned from *Animals Nobody Loves*, and talk about how Simon's book gave them some positive ideas about spiders, too.

Schema Theory

A consistent pattern is apparent as Mrs. Skeema guides her fourth grade students through the story. Each day, she begins with discussion focused around the concept web, adding to their ideas about spiders. The fact that they begin the story by brainstorming shows that previous experiences are important to her. She adds to their background knowledge about spiders by reading *Animals Nobody Loves* to them before they encounter *Charlotte's Web*. She helps them begin thinking about the possibilities in the story by making predictions with the book box. And as each chapter is read, new ideas are discussed; in particular, Mrs. Skeema focuses on how the students' concepts are changing. Their old ideas about spiders are changed as they examine a web, then read *Charlotte's Web*. In this book, Charlotte, a spider, is a kind and selfless friend to a pig. She is personified in a very compassionate manner, but there is also a vast amount of factual information about spiders presented in the story. Mrs. Skeema's students gain new concepts as they accommodate their experiences and readings.

Mrs. Skeema was very carefully activating background knowledge. This means that she was making sure that they knew some concepts that were related to what they were reading. It was important to her that the students remember some things that they already knew about spiders, because she felt that this would facilitate their understanding of the story. It was also important to her that her students had some firsthand experiences with observing a spider, and recalling information that they already knew about them. The discussions about some of the words, such as "spinnerets" and "metatarsus" were also important, because these discussions added to their understanding of specific vocabulary that would be crucial to their story comprehension. All of this background knowledge about spiders helps to put them in a more positive light, which will help her students empathize more deeply with the main character, Charlotte the spider, as they read this classic piece of fiction.

Students in Mrs. Skeema's class are constructing meaning as they read. **Constructivism** has been defined in many ways (Cambourne, 2002). Simply put, it is the idea that learners create new knowledge by connecting what they already know to their experiences in an environment that is thought-provoking and engaging. This theory is largely based on the work of Jean Piaget, a child psychologist who developed some of the most influential ideas about learning and teaching ever written. He said that children learn new ideas by interacting with things and people in their environment. As a child experiences something, he modifies previously held ideas about the things in that environment. This means that the child is constantly adapting his old ideas to create new ones (Piaget, 1969; Pulaski, 1971). Remember when the students began to form new ideas about spiders based on their readings, experiences, and discussions? Concepts were being changed in this stimulating environment.

Piaget's work and the work of other constructivists inspired researchers interested in the way children comprehend text. Thus, **schema theory** evolved. This theory states that what the reader brings to the page is just as important as what is printed on the page (Anderson, 2004; Anderson & Pearson, 1984; Rumelhart, 1980). A reader's background knowledge is what enables her to understand what she reads. Schema theory applies constructivist ideas to the act of reading. **Schemata** are the concepts that the reader brings to the page, and they help the reader understand what is written. In Mrs. Skeema's lesson, the ideas that her students already had about spiders were their schemata.

One way to understand schema theory is to envision two kinds of schemata that are important in understanding text: (1) knowledge of world topics, and (2) knowledge of print. Knowledge of world topics is a huge category; this is everything the child knows about life in general. All of his understandings about people, animals, things, places, ideas, and feelings make up this type of knowledge. In addition to things he has learned through firsthand experiences at home and in his community, this category includes subject matter content learned in school (Adams & Bruce, 1982).

Knowledge of print is more specific; this is his understanding of how text works. This includes all of his knowledge of the alphabet, the sounds of the letters in our alphabet, understanding and use of words, how words are put together, the makeup of stories, the fact that we read English print from top to bottom and from left to right, the fact that we use commas and periods in sentences to add meaning, understanding of the language and structure of stories, and many other characteristics of the written word. Both kinds of knowledge must be present in order for reading to be truly meaningful.

As you recall, when Mrs. Skeema activated the background knowledge of her students, both kinds of knowledge were part of her lesson. Discussion about spiders helped them recall their general knowledge about things in this world; this would enhance their understanding of a story about barn animals. Discussion about the words "spinnerets" and "metatarsus" added to their knowledge of print, which would facilitate their understanding of this story because of the importance of viewing Charlotte in a sympathetic light. Mrs. Skeema clearly believes in the schema theory, and helps her students use their prior knowledge to facilitate their understandings of what they read and write.

Just as the cueing systems and automaticity were related, schema theory is also connected to the cueing systems. The background knowledge of your students is vitally important to all aspects of their reading. Remember the scenario from Mrs. Cuesta's classroom? Her students were decoding the word "hare" in this passage:

> This animal likes to eat carrots and lettuce.
> It hops around. It is a h_____.

In order for the word "hare" to be one of the possibilities that the student might guess when he approaches the final word in the sentence, it has to be part of his schema. If he has never heard of a hare, seen a picture of one, or realized that it is an animal related to the rabbit, his limited knowledge of world topics prevents him from using the semantic cueing system to make that prediction.

Figure 1.4 summarizes the main ideas behind schema theory.

Sources: Anderson, 2004; Anderson & Pearson, 1984; Rumelhart, 1980.

Readers Respond to What They Read

When I ask undergraduate students in my classes to share ideas about how to teach reading, I often get responses such as, "I would ask them to choose a book and read it, then draw a picture of their favorite part of the book," or, "I would have them read and tell how the story is like something that has happened to them," or, "I think they should talk to their classmates about how they feel about books they have read." Does your answer to this question sound similar to this? If so, you are enabling your students' comprehension of the text based on their personal reaction to it, and their interactions with others about it. Take a look at Ms. Rea-Sponse's classroom to see how readers are encouraged to respond to literature.

Ms. Rea-Sponse's Lesson

Ms. Rea-Sponse is preparing her third grade students to read *Train to Somewhere* (Bunting, 1996), a piece of historical fiction about an orphan girl who was on an orphan train in the late 1800s. The book describes the trip this train made from New York City to several points west, stopping to let the dozens of orphans on board file off and stand before their potential adoptive parents. As the train moves further west, there are fewer orphans on board, as people who want to adopt children take the most attractive and personable children immediately. The main character, Marianne, is heartbroken, because she hopes to find her biological mother at each train stop, but does not. Finally, Marianne is the only one left on the train. At the last stop, a town called Somewhere, Iowa, a childless elderly couple adopts her, and she begins to understand acceptance.

To begin, Ms. Rea-Sponse tells her students: "Close your eyes, and put a mind movie in your head as I talk." The children readily do this; they have participated in visual imagery before.

Ms. Rea-Sponse continues, "Think about being on the playground with your classmates, getting ready to play a game of kickball. There are two team captains, Jeff and Courtney. They begin to choose their team members, one at a time. Of course, they want to pick the strongest players first. So they each choose a really good athlete. Continuing, they pick the four best kickball players in the class. Then, they begin to pick the smart ones, and the funny ones, and the ones with the coolest sneakers. After both sides choose ten players, there are two children left, waiting to be selected. Finally, Courtney picks one of these last two. That leaves the final person waiting to be picked. That person is you. Reluctantly, Jeff gets you for his team. He scowls. All the kids snicker. Think about that for a moment. Now, open your eyes."

Ms. Rea-Sponse asks the students to share with each other their thoughts about not being chosen for the team. After the students have talked for a few moments, Ms. Rea-Sponse shows them a nonfiction book, *Orphan Train Rider: One Boy's True Story* (Warren, 1996). She explains the history behind the orphan train of the years from 1854 to 1930 and shows them the pictures in this book. She reads aloud portions of the first four chapters, which explain what happened to a young boy's family and how he and his brothers came to be a part of an orphan train. Then she reads part of Chapter 8, "When the Orphan Trains Came to Town," which uses newspaper accounts to explain how children were often chosen for adoption from the trains.

Finally, Ms. Rea-Sponse says, "Think about how you felt when you imagined no one picking you for the kickball game. How is that similar to the information that we are finding out from this book?"

The children discuss this for a few minutes. Ms. Rea-Sponse then says, "Today we are going to read a story about a girl who was on the orphan train. This is a story written by Eve Bunting, called *Train to Somewhere*. It is based on a true event, which we found out about in this other book, *Orphan Train Rider*. *Train to Somewhere* is historical fiction, while *Orphan Train Rider* is nonfiction. What is the difference between these two books?"

Several students contribute a response to the question, explaining that one book tells facts, while the other is a story created by the author, even though it may be based on facts. Ms. Rea-Sponse continues, "Now that we know something about this book, we can read it and think about it without having to worry about finding out any information. We already know the background information about the orphan train. When we read *Train to Somewhere*, let's think about the main character. Her name is Marianne, and this is her picture." Ms. Rea-Sponse shows the page from the story depicting Marianne. "Let's remember how we felt when we pretended we were the last to be picked for the kickball team. How might Marianne be like each one of us?"

The students make predictions about this, and make further predictions when Ms. Rea-Sponse shows them some more pictures from the story that hint at the sequence of events. She relates all of her questions back to the prereading kickball team scenario.

They begin to read silently. Ms. Rea-Sponse stops them periodically and asks them to think about how the main character reacts to the most recent turn of events, and to record ideas in their reading logs. After reading, the children discuss the events in the story and compare them to those in the nonfiction account, *Orphan Train Rider*.

Now that her students have read this book by Eve Bunting, Ms. Rea-Sponse invites them to join a **literature circle** (Short & Klassen, 1993) and read additional books by Bunting. In a literature circle, they choose a book they wish to read, and join their peers who have chosen the same book in small group discussions about their responses. On a sheet of chart paper, Ms. Rea-Sponse makes a list of six other books by Eve Bunting: *How Many Days to America?* (1988), *Gleam and Glow* (2001), *Dandelions* (1995b), *I Am the Mummy Heb-Nefert* (1997), *So Far from the Sea* (1998), and *Cheyenne Again* (1995a). She shows the students each of the books and tells them a little bit about each one in a short "book talk." All of the books are thought-provoking historical fiction accounts. Then she asks them to write their names and a "1" or a "2" on the chart under the titles to indicate their first two choices. During her planning time, Ms. Rea-Sponse creates groups based on this chart and gives students either their first or second choice. She plans meeting times, number of pages per day to read, how the students will record responses, and when she or a parent volunteer will meet with the group to facilitate discussion. The students meet in these groups for the next several days. Each student in the literature circle has a role, such as "fact finder" or "personal connector." When all groups have finished reading, the whole class gathers to talk about their experiences and reactions to the literature.

Transactional Theory

Students in this classroom have become so involved in what they have read that they respond to it in a very active way. This is an important feature of the **transactional theory** (Rosenblatt, 1938, 1978, 2004), which states that learners transact with the text. In other words, they think about what they are reading in rather complex ways. They think about their personal reactions to the text and how it makes them feel. They also think about what the author is trying to tell them, whether it is explicitly stated or merely implied. They think about how they should approach a piece of text, because they know that different texts are read for different purposes, such as reading for enjoyment or reading for information (Many, 2004; Squire, 1994). All of these transactions with the text add to their comprehension of it, because, "We learn from experience. . . . It is the thinking during and after reading that translates the activity of reading to experience" (Squire, 1994, p. 644).

Additionally, the transactional theory, also called the **reader response theory,** explains how text is understood (Rosenblatt, 1978, 2004; Squire, 1994). This theory says that a single piece of text can be understood in many ways, depending upon who is reading it. Each reader brings a unique set of experiences, interests, abilities, and understandings to a piece of text. His personal background affects how he reacts to what he reads. He can respond *aesthetically,* with emotion. He can also read a piece *efferently,* for the purpose of gaining information.

Sometimes, the line between these two purposes is not so clearly drawn. For example, suppose a world-renowned chemist picks up a scientific journal that contains an article about the chemical properties of everyday materials. This information is not new to her, but she is interested in the article because this subject is her life's work and it brings her enjoyment. Thus, she reads the article aesthetically. She responds to it on a level that is quite different from the way those of us who have no interest in chemistry would respond to it.

Responding to literature is personal as well as social. Ms. Rea-Sponse recognized the importance of allowing her students the chance to share with others their understandings of the book. She used literature circles in her classroom to give her students the opportunity to talk to each other in small group settings, sharing their views and insights. The social nature of literacy is an important part of the transactional theory, because "the value of the reading experience comes from thinking about, talking about, or writing about the work. . . . Response must be active. Individuals must talk about their reactions with others" (Squire, 1994, p. 644).

Transactional (Reader Response) Theory

What the Reader Does

- Approaches the text in a personal way, searching either for information (efferent reading), or for emotional satisfaction (aesthetic reading).
- Reacts to the text in a personal way by relating it to his own life experiences.
- Brings a unique set of experiences to the text that allow him or her to understand it in a way that is unlike anyone else's understanding; there are as many meanings of the text as there are readers.
- Responds to the text covertly by thinking about what the author has written and relating it to his experiences.
- Responds to the text overtly by talking, writing, drawing, creating, role-playing, acting, or reading aloud expressively.

What the Teacher Does

- Talks with the students about their purposes for reading a particular piece of text.
- Provides opportunities for students to respond to the text in efferent and in aesthetic ways.
- Helps students see parallels between the text and their own lives.
- Asks questions and leads discussions about the text, expecting a variety of possible answers and responses.
- Uses literature circles.

Classroom Example Used in This Chapter

Ms. Rea-Sponse uses the nonfiction book *Orphan Train Rider* to help her third graders understand the historical background for *Train to Somewhere*. As they read, she asks her students to put themselves in the place of the main character and think about how it feels to be left out and unwanted. Later, she helps them form literature circles to read other books by Eve Bunting and discuss their responses.

Figure 1.5 The premise and instructional implications of the transactional, or reader response, theory.

Source: Rosenblatt, 1938, 1978, 2004.

Back to Ms. Rea-Sponse. She has helped her students use their reading and writing skills to respond to a story that has implications for their own lives. She also organized her classroom so that they met with each other in small groups to talk about their responses to books of their own choosing. She immersed the students into the whole text, without much emphasis on mechanical skills such as phonics or vocabulary. While she may teach these objectives in other lessons, she is more concerned with their understanding of and reaction to the meaning of the book in this lesson. This is the transactional theory—or reader response theory—at work.

As with all the theories explained in this chapter, there is an overlapping nature to the transactional theory. Students' responses to the printed page depend upon their prior experiences (Duke & Pearson, 2002; Rosenblatt, 1938). Squire tells us, "How important for comprehension it is, then, to select literature related to young readers' personal experiences" (1994, p. 641). Thus, the transactional theory, which says that each reader responds to text in his own unique way, is related to the schema theory, which says that prior knowledge about the topics in the author's work aids the reader in his comprehension of it.

Figure 1.5 summarizes the ideas in the transactional theory.

Putting It All Together

We visited four classrooms headed by fictional teachers who are based on teachers at work in real life. You saw some very strong ideas that are reflected in the work of these teachers. You learned about cueing systems, which are clues that the reader picks up from the page, enabling him to decode the print and translate text into meaning. You read about fluency, in which the reader reads effortlessly and smoothly. When he reads without any need to decode unknown words, because they are all part of his sight vocabulary, this is automaticity. You learned about how the reader's ideas and past experiences, or his schemata, help him construct an understanding of text. Schema theory explains the fact that knowledge of world topics and knowledge of print work together to enable the reader's comprehension. Finally, we looked at the ways that readers respond to text, as explained by the transactional theory, and the resulting implications for personal understanding and social interaction around literature. These theories have been posited by researchers and teachers who have observed children at work and have noticed what happens to their learning when teachers set up their classroom environments in certain ways. Because these theories make sense to them, the teachers we have visited utilize teaching behaviors, strategies, and materials that influence the learning of their students.

What makes sense to you? Throughout this chapter, I have asked you to think about the strategies or activities that you chose in response to this question: "What would you do to teach a child to read?" In comparing your response to the classroom teaching strategies that you have seen in the scenarios presented in this chapter, you can see the theoretical orientations of your ideas. Figure 1.6 shows some of the teaching strategies and activities that my students have commonly listed as their response to this question.

You may be able to determine the theoretical orientation of the strategy or activity that you chose. If so, this orientation simply reflects your current value system, and it may change. As you continue to study literacy and its instruction, you may revise your ideas quite a bit. It is important to remain open to the possibility

"Where Would You Begin to Teach a Child to Read?"
Classroom Activities or Strategies

Strategies or activities that focus on decoding print by using all available clues in the print:	Strategies or activities that focus on automatic recognition of words and fluent reading:	Strategies or activities that focus on comprehending text based on prior experiences:	Strategies or activities that allow readers to respond to the text and share responses with others:
• Show pictures in a book, look at the title, and ask for predictions based on clues from the book. • Show vocabulary from the book and ask for predictions. • Teach or review important vocabulary using context clues. • Teach or review letters of the alphabet. • Teach or review phonics generalizations and patterns. • Create a word wall.	• Review vocabulary. • Read aloud a book and then read it again together. • Reread a favorite, familiar story. • Play word card games. • Create a word wall. • Listen to a book on tape.	• Provide an experience related to the book. • Prior to reading, talk about past experiences and how they relate to the book. • Prior to reading, brainstorm ideas related to the book. • Ask for predictions about the book based on past experiences with the topic.	• Read a book together, ask students to draw a picture about the story or the information in the book. • Talk about the reason for reading a book. • Talk about what the reader needs to get out of the book. • Read a book together, ask students to relate the events to events in their own lives. • Ask students to read a book and write about their favorite part of the story. • Read a book of interest with other people and talk to them about it.
Reflective of using the cueing systems	Reflective of automaticity theory	Reflective of schema theory	Reflective of transactional theory

Figure 1.6 Categorizing the responses to the question: "If you were to start teaching reading right now, what would you do?"

of changing your ideas, because there are so many choices available to the teacher. Moreover, you may find that as you write lesson plans and make teaching decisions, all four of these theories will become part of your literacy instruction. Routman (2000, p. 15) advises us to ask ourselves, "What needs to be done to ensure that children become literate?" To accomplish this, we ought to be "thoughtfully applying beliefs and practices that are supported by research as well as by our own teaching practices and life experiences" (p. 14).

Home–School Connection

Explaining the Reading Process to Caregivers

It is important to know how to communicate your teaching decisions to the caregivers of your students. Your rapport with them and their trust in you will increase based on your ability to explain why you do the things you do in the classroom. Literacy is one of the most difficult topics to teach because of its political nature. Moreover, just as you had ideas about how you might begin teaching reading when you started reading this chapter, the caregivers of your students might also have opinions and value judgments about teaching literacy. Shown in the rest of this section is an example of an informational flyer that you can send home to help explain reading processes.

What Happens When Children Read

There are four major ways that we can look at what happens when children read. These theoretical ideas influence the way that I teach and the things that your child will be doing in my classroom. Let's look at these ideas now.

First, the reader tries to decode words. This means that he or she is trying to translate the words on the page into some meaning. This translation process is called using the *cueing systems.* He or she uses clues on the page to do that—clues about the letters and their sounds, clues from the sentences, and clues from pictures. In order to be successful, your child needs to know the alphabet and the sounds that each of the letters make. Your child needs to make logical predictions about words on the page, based on what he or she sees in the print. The student also needs to read repeatedly, so that he or she does not always need to rely on decoding letter-by-letter. Your child needs a strategy for figuring out words that he or she doesn't already know. Thus, I will be asking students to keep a decoding strategy card at their desks, which should help with unknown words and with making logical predictions about words. The card looks like this:

> ### When you see a word you don't know:
>
> 1. Look at the letters. What word that begins with _____ would make sense there?
> 2. Look for a pattern that you know. Try to say the word. Does that make sense?
> 3. Keep your finger on the word and finish the sentence. Try a word that would make sense in this sentence.

Summary:
Look Again at the Big Picture

In determining what to do when faced with a classroom of students who need to learn to read, you will rely on many things. In this chapter, you read about how your values system as a teacher affects decisions that you make, and how your past experiences influence your ideas about teaching. However, teachers are professionals, so expertise and knowledgeable decision making are essential. Indeed, many factors will have an impact on your teaching decisions.

First, you need to know your students—their abilities, their needs, and their interests. Second, you need to know about their lives outside the classroom, because of the huge effect that their homes and communities have on their learning at school. Third, knowledge of children's literature is essential, so that you can

Second, readers build confidence in reading by knowing many, many words instantly. This helps them read quickly and with expression, because they do not need to stop and sound out many words. This is called *automaticity*. I will be sending home paperback books that are not too difficult, and not too easy for your child to read. Please listen to your child read and reread these stories, because this will help him or her gain confidence with the print.

Third, it is important to think about your child's understanding of what is on the page based on what he or she already knows. Your child's past experiences with letters and sounds, as well as experiences with people and things at home, at school, and places traveled, are very important to his or her understanding of what he or she reads. For example, when we read stories about animals, your child's past experiences with animals will help him or her better understand those stories. I will brainstorm ideas with them and talk about prior experiences with them before they read, so that this knowledge is fresh in their minds when they pick up the book.

Fourth, the reader reacts to what he or she reads. This is something that we all do as adults. When we read novels, we think about how this story relates to our own lives. The stories that we like best are the ones that make us laugh or cry, or that touch a nerve in us somehow. When we read for information, we search for things that we need to know. Often, we think deeply about a book we've enjoyed or something that we found out on the Internet. And sometimes, as we read, we think things like, "Gee, I wonder why that author said *that*." Responding to the written word is an important part of the reader's life. In

Communicating instructional decisions with families is important.

my classroom, your child will have many opportunities to talk about and write about books, newspapers, magazines, web sites, and other printed material. Another thing we do as adults is talk about things we've read with other people. We write notes and letters for the purpose of communicating with others. Children do the same thing. In order to grow as readers, they need to talk to each other, share ideas with each other, and write for each other. In this classroom, many reading and writing activities will take place in groups and with partners.

These four ways of looking at the reading process will be evident in the activities, materials, lesson plans, and homework assignments that I will use with your child this year. •

choose texts that are well suited for the lessons you have planned, as well as for the students who read them. Last, you need to understand the impact of federal and state legislation on your classroom. The No Child Left Behind Act of 2001 will most likely place some demands on your teaching; namely, you will need to be able to ensure that your students learn strategies and skills in five areas: phonemic awareness, phonics, vocabulary, fluency, and comprehension. The methods that you use when teaching these strategies and skills must be research-based, backed by experimental research that shows the strength of the methods. The law also stipulates that your students demonstrate proficiency in standards specified by your state, which should reflect these five components of reading as well.

So that you are able to articulate the research upon which your teaching strategies are built, I introduced four prevailing theories of reading in this chapter: cueing systems, automaticity, schema theory, and transactionalism. To do that, I introduced four teachers, and showed you the type of reading instruction that goes on in their classrooms. All four of the teachers in this chapter have one goal—their students' understanding of what they read.

The way in which readers figure out print is explained by the cueing systems. Four cueing systems are available to help the reader decode words she doesn't know: semantic cues, syntactic cues, graphophonological cues, and pragmatic cues. The reader continually makes educated guesses about the print as she sees it, based on the myriad of clues available on the page.

Automaticity is the idea that readers must see print and automatically recognize what it means; thus, they must learn to decode words and then commit them to long-term memory in order to read fluently with comprehension.

As they read print, readers construct meaning based on things that they already know. This manner of reading is explained by the schema theory. Based on Piagetian ideas of concept development, the schema theory tells us that readers form ideas about print by building upon their past experiences and by relating new concepts to those that they already know.

Readers respond to what they read in personal ways. Transactionalism is the theory that explains this process. Readers do not passively decode print; rather, they interact with it, think about how it relates to them, and wonder about the author's intentions. Readers respond to print either aesthetically (emotionally) or efferently (cognitively). Moreover, every reader's response to a single piece of literature or text is unique. Sharing these responses with others adds to the reader's understanding of it.

Putting it all together means that your literacy instruction includes strategies connected to each of these theories. Indeed, the interrelatedness of the theories dictates that you do so. Moreover, you will achieve a balance of instruction if you use strategies that support all four theories. In Chapter 2, I will explain more about how to balance your instruction so that it encompasses all of the knowledge and skills your students need to read and write. The Reviewing the Big Picture box lists the theories discussed in Chapter 1, as well as their alignment with standards and principles from IRA, INTASC, NAEYC, and ACEI/NCATE.

Technology Resources

The web sites listed here are helpful for finding out about the reading process.

- **www.reading.org**   This is the homepage of the International Reading Association. An archive of articles from the journal publications of the IRA is available. You can access abstracts for free; a fee is charged for article reprints.
- **www.ed.gov/pubs/StateArt/Read/index.html**   The site of the United States Department of Education is a valuable source of government articles and information on reading. There is a very helpful archive of government-sponsored articles, as well as a link for searching government articles stored in the ERIC database.
- **www.readingrockets.org**   The public television station in Washington, D.C., WETA, produces this web site. Articles on a variety of topics related to teaching reading are available, as well as a very helpful Frequently Asked Questions link.
- **www.nichd.nih.gov/publications/nrp/findings.htm**   The Report of the National Reading Panel is published at this site, including reports organized by topic areas on several reading processes and components such as phonemic

awareness, comprehension, and many more. The U.S. Congress commissioned the report in 1997; it examined empirical research to assess the effectiveness of several approaches to teaching reading.

Reviewing the Big Picture
Theories Introduced in Chapter 1

Theory	Description	IRA Standards	INTASC Principles	NAEYC Standards	ACEI/NCATE Standards
Cueing systems (Clay, 1991; Goodman, 1994; Halliday, 1978)	As the reader perceives chunks of print, he anticipates words; thus, he makes predictions based on semantic, syntactic, and graphophonological clues.	1.1, 1.2, 1.4, 4.1, 4.2	1, 2, 3, 4, 7	1, 4b, 4d	1, 2.1, 3.1
Automaticity theory (Samuels, 2002, 2004; LaBerge & Samuels, 1974; Samuels & Kamil, 1984)	In order to understand print, decoding effort must be minimal. When a reader perceives print, either he recognizes the words instantly or he must decode them. Repeated meaningful exposure aids automatic recognition and fluency.	1.1, 1.2, 1.4, 4.1, 4.2	1, 2, 3, 4, 7	1, 4b, 4d	1, 2.1, 3.1
Schema theory (Anderson, 2004; Anderson & Pearson, 1984; Rumelhart, 1980)	Reading comprehension is based on the reader's knowledge of print and of the world.	1.1, 1.2, 1.4, 4.1, 4.2, 4.4	1, 2, 3, 4, 7	1, 4a, 4b, 4d	1, 2.1, 3.1, 3.2, 3.4
Transactional theory (Rosenblatt, 1938, 1978, 2004)	The reader transacts, or becomes involved with the text, constantly thinking about how the author's words relate to him personally. Readers read aesthetically as well as efferently.	1.1, 1.2, 1.4, 4.1, 4.2, 4.4	1, 2, 3, 4, 7	1, 4a, 4b, 4d	1, 2.1, 3.1, 3.2, 3.4

2

A Model of Instruction

Making Decisions About Teaching Literacy

But things can come together in strange ways. The wood was at the center, the hub of the wheel. All wheels must have a hub. A Ferris wheel has one, as the sun is the hub of the wheeling calendar. Fixed points they are, and best left undisturbed, for without them, nothing holds together.

Tuck Everlasting (Babbitt, 1975)

Tuck Everlasting was an amazing book. This book is about a family, the Tucks, and there life that would never end. This family drank from a magica spring, which gave them eternal life. Because of this curse, the Tuck family was constanly on the move. They had finally settled down in a small house in the woods, which was owned by a wealthy family, the Fosters. This very wealthy family, had one daughter named Winnie. Winnie Foster was sick of her life, and ran away. She then met the Tuck family. She also figured out about there secret. She wanted to drink from the spring herself. The Tucks then had to explain to her, the circle of life, because of this went they could not be part of this circle, they where rocks on the side of the rode. The Tucks could never find true happiness because they could not complete the circle of life. Later in the story when all seems in place, they find out that a stranger followed Winnie to the magica spring. He is planning to market this water. The Tucks with the help of winnie have to stop this man. This book was very interesting and had great detail. I highly recomend this book.

Susan, grade 7

Reflecting on a Commonly Taught Lesson

To grasp the importance of decision making while teaching, let's visit another classroom. Ms. Menshin is a student teacher assigned to third grade. Her objective in the lesson we are about to witness is for her students to determine the problem in a story. Her students have not yet been taught this strategy. She begins by telling the class, "Today, class, we are going to learn a very important reading strategy. We will learn how to determine the problem in a story. This is important, because it will help you better understand the story that you are reading. If you can do this, you will be able to enjoy stories more, too."

She passes out copies of the book *Hey, Al*, by Arthur Yorinks (1986). She gives them these directions: "Read this story silently. When you think you have found the problem in the story, raise your hand."

The students comply, and several students raise their hands after the first few pages.

Ms. Menshin asks, "What is the problem?"

Michael volunteers the answer: "Al and Eddie live in a really small apartment and they don't like it there."

Ms. Menshin says, "Excellent, Michael! You've found the problem. See, that wasn't so hard at all, was it?"

After her lesson, Ms. Menshin gives the students a practice page, which shows some short stories with problems. They are to read the stories and choose the problem from among multiple-choice answers. After the students hand in their work, Ms. Menshin examines these practice pages, and she is disappointed to discover that more than half of her students were unable to accomplish the objective.

What went wrong? Think about this in the Personal Reflection.

Personal Reflection

Why do you suppose that half of Ms. Menshin's students could not determine the problem in the story? Given the same objective, what would you do?

Let's reexamine the methods that Ms. Menshin used. She provided the students with appropriate reading materials, assuming that they could read at the third grade level. She carefully explained the purpose for the lesson. She gave very clear directions on what the students were to do. These are effective teaching behaviors.

Now think about what Ms. Menshin did *not* do. She never showed them how to find the problem in a story, nor did she provide them with any experiences, tools, or strategies for accomplishing this strategy. She simply asked them to do it. Her entire lesson focused on the product of the act of reading, placing her students in the position of having to produce something that they had not been taught.

Durkin terms this type of practice "mentioning," which is "saying just enough about a topic to allow for an assignment related to it" (1978–1979, p. 505). In her now-famous study of comprehension instruction, Durkin found that instead of planning lessons that teach children how to comprehend, teachers spent a great deal of time simply manipulating materials that accompanied the published reading program or **basal** textbook adopted by their school.

Good teachers do more than merely mention things. They make decisions about what to teach, and they make decisions about how to teach it. They use instructional techniques that show students how to accomplish reading strategies, rather than simply expecting students to perform a task. They teach the processes of reading in addition to asking students to produce something from reading. They show students how to accomplish reading tasks, and set up situations and environments that make it more likely for these strategies to be employed successfully. In short, they liken their teaching to a wheel, like the one that Natalie Babbitt (1975) spoke of in the prologue to her book, as quoted in the opening of this chapter. At the hub of the wheel, good teachers have established their goal: their students' success in reading. This desired outcome supports all the spokes of the wheel—their classroom environment, the materials they use, and their teaching methods.

Instructional planning involves decisions about what and how to teach.

A Model of Comprehensive Instruction

Perhaps the most important part of your job is the instructional planning that you do. You need to make decisions about what is best for your students. What conditions will be optimal for their learning?

Vygotsky introduced the idea of a **zone of proximal development** (Dixon-Krauss, 1996; Vygotsky, 1978), which is the level at which children learn the most. He said that children learn best when the task that they are attempting is not too hard, or too easy for them to tackle. It is challenging enough to be interesting, without being overwhelming. In addition, they have a more knowledgeable person to show them how to accomplish the task. Showing them how to do something can take many forms. Vygotsky said that when people who know more provide verbal directions and models, their interaction with children serves as stepping stones, or **scaffolds,** toward the intended goal. Scaffolds are the instructional supports that help students accomplish a learning task; **scaffolded instruction** enables students to succeed in a sufficiently challenging environment. Chapter 9 reviews specific ways to scaffold your students' literacy.

To provide such an environment for your students, the two most essential questions you can ask yourself as you plan instruction are: "What is important to teach?" and "Which teaching method do I use?" Knowing the answers to these questions on a daily basis makes you a professional, rather than a manipulator of materials and young people. As Durkin states, "superior teachers do not rely on recipes—not even on good recipes. Rather, they have cookbooks in their heads from which they make selections based on what needs to be taught to whom" (1993, p. 21).

Comprehensive instruction relies on a sense of balance. **Balance** usually refers to an "eclectic or multifaceted approach to teaching" (Robinson, McKenna & Wedman, 2000, p. 8). I contend that a model of instructional balance is necessary to ensure that reading is taught rather than merely "mentioned." Achieving balance means that you will plan two different dimensions to your curriculum and its lessons. First, you need to balance the content of your instruction. Second, you need to balance your method of teaching the content. Such a model is shown in Figure 2.1.

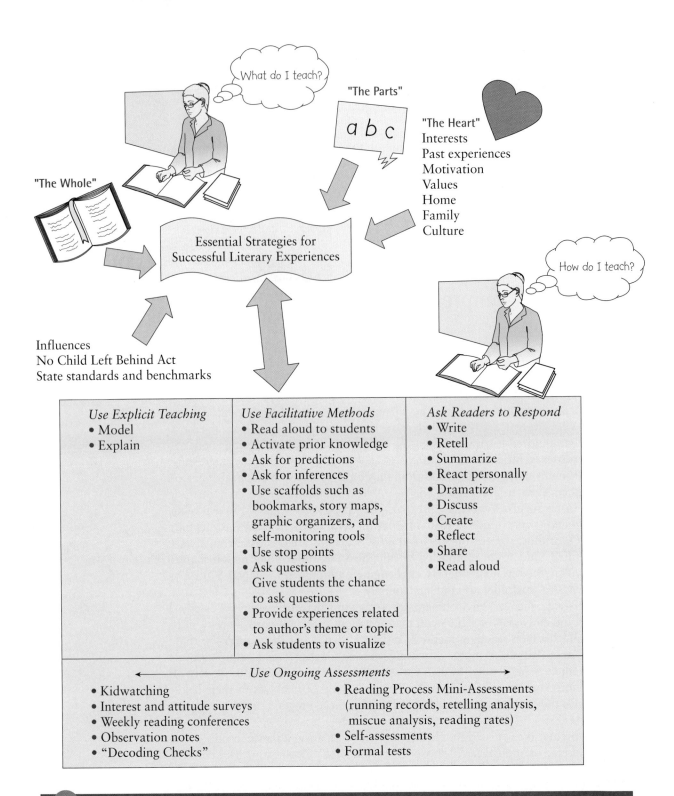

Figure 2.1 A decision-making model of Comprehensive instruction.

What Is Important to Teach?

As you can see in Figure 2.1, the teacher first reflects upon the balance of content—or, very simply, what to teach. Yet literacy is a multifaceted, very complex activity. Knowing what to teach children as they learn to read is not easy. What knowledge is needed for literacy?

It goes without saying that any teacher who teaches reading does so with one goal in mind—to develop good, enthusiastic readers. Thus, it is important for teachers to know what good readers do, and always ask themselves as they teach: "Why am I teaching this? Is this important for learners to know in order to become good readers?"

The balance of content included in the model of comprehensive instruction presented here is designed for the purpose of developing skilled, motivated readers. I contend that, in order to do that, classroom instruction must include the three encompassing facets of literacy: the whole, the parts, and the heart.

Teach the Whole

It makes sense that the teaching of literacy needs to include lots of reading. Books, newspapers, magazines, and web sites have an important place in your classroom. Balanced instruction includes teaching activities that focus on understanding at the whole-text level and that allow children to spend much time reading selections of fiction and nonfiction literature. According to Weaver, "Learning to read is a process that develops over time, but in complex ways—not a skill or strategy at a time" (2000, p. 163). Be reflective about the amount of time spent in your classroom on reading whole texts. "There is ample evidence that independent reading does considerably more to develop reading ability than all the workbooks and practice sheets children typically complete" (Weaver, 2000, p. 163).

Additionally, "teaching the whole" refers to the understanding of reading as a social endeavor. As you may recall from Chapter 1, the transactional theory (Rosenblatt, 1938, 1978, 2004) tells us that each reader derives a different meaning from the text. Thus, teaching reading involves helping children glean the author's message from the printed page, and relate this to their own experiences, values, beliefs, emotions, experiences at home, and repertoire of past reading. It also involves sharing these experiences and understandings of the text with each other, reflecting the idea that reading is best learned when it is talked about, lingered over, enjoyed together, and compared.

Finally, "teaching the whole" also refers to an understanding of the reciprocal processes of reading and writing. Good readers also write. They use writing to help them understand a text, and they use it to respond to a text. They think about the texts they read in terms of authorship—reacting to and wondering about the author's word choices, style, and main ideas. Indeed, when readers write for authentic purposes and audiences, they are more sensitive to the "ways that words and genres express meaning" (Polette, 2005, p. 53).

In summary, "teaching the whole" of reading means to teach children by allowing them to read the way reading is meant to be done—from whole stories, articles, books, and texts. Allow them to read and write for personal pleasure, for specific information, and for sharing with others.

Teach the Parts

Reading is indeed a complex human behavior. It consists of a myriad of abilities that work together to produce one effect—understanding. But it will be necessary for you to isolate portions of the text—letters, words, and sentences—to focus on the skills needed to manage the mechanics of processing the print. Paying attention to letters, words, and sentences is unavoidable in learning to read the English language, which depends upon letter–sound relationships for its substance. Some research studies tell us that an early and systematic emphasis on teaching children to decode words leads to better achievement than a later or more haphazard approach (Adams, 1990; Chall, 1989, 1996; National Reading Panel, 2000a).

Students who can process print easily can also manage larger portions of text.

Young children need to understand that meaning is derived from print, and that there is a relationship between the sounds of our language and the letters that represent them.

Thus, "teaching the parts" of reading includes instruction in decoding. According to Beck and Juel, "early learning of the code leads to wider reading habits both in and out of school" (1992, p. 102). This approach allows readers to use the cueing systems in a balanced manner; if they are comfortable with the "parts" of our language, they can use semantic, syntactic, graphophonological, and pragmatic cues seamlessly. This learning also leads to automaticity, which, as you learned in Chapter 1, is the idea that readers need to be able to instantly recognize many, many words, so that they do not need to painstakingly decode each letter and sound they encounter (LaBerge & Samuels, 1974; Samuels, 2004; Samuels & Kamil, 1984). Adams (2004) reports on the importance of teaching students words, and that research on direct vocabulary instruction shows an increase in word knowledge as well as comprehension.

Readers also need to go beyond the word level and learn how to manage larger portions of text. The strategies used by good readers to comprehend text are dependent upon a combination of their knowledge of the world around them, as well as their familiarity with the printed page. Pearson, Roehler, Dole, and Duffy (1992) advocate a curriculum that ensures that readers are able to accomplish things such as self-monitoring, synthesizing information, and making inferences. Duke and Pearson (2002) add to this list several other strategies: integrating prior knowledge with the text, thinking about the authors, thinking about the characters and setting of narrative text, constructing and revising summaries of expository text, and reading different kinds of text differently. Thus, "teaching the parts" of reading also refers to presenting children with the strategies involved in processing print beyond the single word.

Teach the Heart

Children think with their brains, but they remember with their hearts. The things and people that they love and hold dear, the things that they like to do, and the things that make them care are your tools for helping them learn. To remember something, a child must "own" it. He will do that if you can connect new understandings with what he cares about. You learned in Chapter 1 that readers learn about text by connecting what they already know to new information—this is schema theory at work (Anderson, 2004; Anderson & Pearson, 1984; Rumelhart, 1980). Thus, when you include your students' interests in a lesson, you are incorporating what is familiar to them, and what they are able to accomplish successfully. This technique gives them a base on which to rest the new and unfamiliar.

The power in your teaching lies in your ability to make your learners care. In other words, when choosing literature and other materials to teach, you will need to consider the interests, needs, cultural background, family experiences, and prior knowledge of your students. There are many decisions that you will make that reflect your inclination to teach to the heart. For example, when you choose a particular book to read aloud to your class, or when you purchase certain books to put in your classroom library, you are making decisions that affect the aesthetic—or emotional—side of learning.

You will make instructional decisions pertaining to your students' attitudes. Mathewson (2004) reports that persuading students that certain books are worth reading is an important part of your daily instruction. You can do this by generating excitement and interest with strategies such as talking about books, using concrete objects, telling personal stories, and including your students' families in your classroom instruction.

Minimizing **extrinsic rewards** for reading is also important, so that your students develop a desire to read for the sake of reading, not to win a prize. **Intrinsic motivation** to read is when readers want to read because they are interested in it and feel successful at doing it. Guthrie, Wigfield, Metsala, and Cox (2004) report that students who feel competent, know how to cope with failure, and can comprehend well also seem to be the most intrinsically motivated readers. Thus, you will need to make plans for developing confidence, for showing students strategies for when comprehension breaks down, and for providing interesting, engaging reading.

These decisions are vitally important, because when you help children connect to reading through their hearts, they remember what they have learned. Recall from Chapter 1 the transactional theory, in which Rosenblatt (2004) describes the importance of encouraging an aesthetic transaction between the reader and the text.

The goal of this model of balanced content is to develop a reader who can—and does—read. This means building enthusiasm for reading and helping children have successful experiences with literacy. According to Pearson, Roehler, Dole, and Duffy, "motivated students are those whose encounters with reading are reasonably successful" (1992, p. 181).

Decide on the Essentials

Determining what to teach will sometimes be a difficult decision. You will have many demands on your time and resources. There will be occasions when you must decide between objectives, because there simply isn't enough time to teach them all. When determining what is important to teach, keep in mind the real goal—that of developing readers who choose to read and who can do so independently and with confidence. Figure 2.2 lists sixteen essential reading strategies, supported by research findings.

As you study this list of strategies, keep in mind your responsibilities. According to the No Child Left Behind Act of 2001, your students need to be at a proficient level on state standards and assessments (Pub. L. 107–110, Title I, Sec. 1001,

What Is Important for Readers to Know How to Do?

Before Reading

1. Establish a purpose for reading and make decisions about choosing text to read, for pleasure as well as for information (Brown, Palincsar & Armbruster, 2004; Rosenblatt, 1978; Tierney & Cunningham, 1984).

2. Make logical predictions about text, based on clues on the page, as well as on knowledge of story structure, text structure of nonfiction, theme, and the topic chosen by the author (Duke & Pearson, 2002; Goodman, 1967).

3. Think about what the reader already knows and relate prior knowledge to the text (Anderson, 2004; Dewitz, Carr & Patberg, 1987).

During Reading

4. Use knowledge of letters and sounds to decode unknown words (Adams, 1990; Berent & Perfetti, 1995; Cunningham & Cunningham, 2002; National Reading Panel, 2000a).

5. Use knowledge of word structure to decode unknown words (Graves & Watts-Taffe, 2002; National Reading Panel, 2000a).

6. Use context clues to determine meanings of words (Goodman, 1973; Johnson, 2001; Moustafa, 1997; National Reading Panel, 2000a)

7. Read with accuracy, appropriate speed, expression, and comprehension (Adams, 2004; Johns & Berglund, 2002; National Reading Panel, 2000a; Samuels, 2002).

8. Make inferences, using clues from the author together with things the reader already knows, to guess the author's hidden meanings and implications (Anderson & Pearson, 1984; Anderson, 2004; Hansen, 1981; Kintsch, 2004).

9. Self-monitor and generate questions while reading for pleasure, as well as for information (Lysynchuk, Pressley & Vye, 1990; National Reading Panel, 2000a; Rosenshine & Meister, 1994; Wagoner, 1983).

10. Visualize fiction or nonfiction text with mental pictures (Gambrell & Bales, 1986; Gambrell & Koskinen, 2002; Harvey & Goudvis, 2000; Pressley, 2000).

11. Transact with the text efferently by thinking about the author's word choices and purposes (Beck, McKeown, Hamilton & Kucan, 1997; Rosenblatt, 1978, 2004).

12. Transact with the text aesthetically by relating the author's words to real-life experiences and feelings (Many, 2004; Rosenblatt, 1978, 2004).

After Reading

13. Identify all the story elements in a retelling, verbally and in writing (Gambrell, Koskinen & Kapinus, 1991; Ruddell & Unrau, 2004a).

14. Summarize stories verbally and in writing (Glazer, 1998; National Reading Panel, 2000a; Winograd & Bridge, 1986).

15. Identify and summarize the main ideas of nonfiction text, verbally and in writing (Baumann, 1986; Duke & Pearson, 2002; Meyer & Poon, 2004; National Reading Panel, 2000a).

16. Relate the text to personal experiences and share those ideas in a variety of ways, including writing (Galda & Beach, 2004).

Figure 2.2 Sixteen essential strategies for successful literacy experiences.

2001). Naturally, standards will drive many of your decisions about what to teach. A list of web sites that will connect you to standards for each of the 50 states is in Appendix A. Let's look at three of these standards, shown in Figure 2.3. Each of the examples, taken from the state education departments for California, Florida, and Pennsylvania, are standards for third grade students.

Do you notice the similarities? All three of these standards reflect the same reading behavior, summarizing after reading, which is also one of the sixteen essential strategies shown in Figure 2.2. Moreover, the National Reading Panel report includes summarization as one of the categories of text comprehension instruction for which there is a "solid scientific basis" (National Reading Panel, 2000a, p. 15). While each state standards framework is different, and there is some argument about what constitutes a "research base" (Shanahan, 2002, p. 8), in general, state departments of education recognize many of the important behaviors that readers ought to be able to do. "Teaching Children to Read," the report of the National Reading Panel (2000a) that is the foundation of the No Child Left Behind Act, is the result of an extensive review of research; it outlines five components that represent a broad view of the process of learning to read: phonemic awareness, phonics, fluency, vocabulary, and comprehension. This report, along with the standards outlined by your state department of education, is one of the resources that can help you decide what is important to teach. Use these as guides; however, remember that to develop readers who can and will read willingly, you will need to consider motivation, amount of reading, and time to read as well.

English Language Arts Content Standards for California Public Schools—Kindergarten Through Grade 12
Distinguish the main idea and supporting details in expository text.
  (California Department of Education, 1998, p. 17)

Grade Level Expectations for the Sunshine State Standards Language Arts—Grades 3–5
The student understands explicit and implicit ideas and information in third grade or higher texts (for example, main idea, implied message, relevant supporting details and facts, chronological order of events).
  (Florida Department of Education, 1999, p. 4)

Pennsylvania Academic Standards for Reading, Writing, Speaking, and Listening
Retell or summarize the major ideas, themes, or procedures of the text.
  (Pennsylvania Department of Education, 1999, p. 3)

Figure 2.3 Examples of grade level standards from three states.

Diversity in the Reading Classroom

Making Decisions About What to Teach

In *Teaching Children to Read* (2000a), the National Reading Panel made several recommendations to federal lawmakers, and concluded that teachers need to devote their instructional time to five components of reading: phonemic awareness, phonics, vocabulary, comprehension, and fluency. This recommendation is based on findings from an extensive review of experimental research, which is when the researcher attempts to determine the effects of a particular treatment on groups of people. The panel did not review correlational studies, which attempt to determine whether two variables are related. However, several recent, large-scale correlational studies have identified important relationships for the teacher to consider. One such relationship is that between highly achieving readers and the amount of time they spend reading. As Allington reports, these studies have found that "more reading generally accompanies improved reading" (2001, p. 28). He concludes: "The consistency of the evidence concerning the relationship of volume of reading and reading achievement is surely strong enough to support recommending attention to reading volume" (p. 32). Thus, the NRP leaves out something vitally important: Motivating children to read—and read a lot.

To date, only a few state departments have included volume of reading as part of their curriculum. For example, standards for New York and Pennsylvania suggest that children read 25 books per year. (See Appendix A for standard web sites.) When the No Child Left Behind Act became law in 2001, it stipulated that schools receiving federal monies must ensure that all of their students are proficient in the standards of their state, as determined by statewide achievement tests (No Child Left Behind, 2001, Pub. L. 107–110, Title I, Sec. 1001). There are serious implications for teachers of students of diverse backgrounds. Schools in low-income areas with large diverse populations typically have lower achievement scores (Au, 2002). The standards-based emphasis has led to pressure on teachers to raise their students' test scores. As a result, the curriculum narrows and more instructional time is devoted to lower-level skills. "An emphasis on test scores leaves teachers with less time for . . . involving the students in the full process of reading. . . . In this sense, an emphasis on standardized testing can have a detrimental effect on the learning to read of students of diverse backgrounds" (Au, 2002, pp. 407–408).

So, when you make teaching decisions based solely on state standards, you might be leaving out something that your readers of diverse backgrounds need most—the time to read books. While it is important to teach reading skills, it is equally important to give your students time to read. When deciding what to teach, consider these things:

- Give students uninterrupted time to read every day.

- Teach reading strategies all day—in science, social studies, and math lessons.

- Provide plenty of books that they can read independently.

- Teach skills only in the context of meaningful reading experiences.

Ultimately, the greatest factor in making an instructional decision is the student. Thus, when faced with choices of objectives or demands on your instructional time, you should ask yourself, "If I teach this, will it help my students become independent, confident readers?" Make sure that you include in your curriculum all aspects of literacy—thoughtful reading of whole text; meaningful strategies for tackling letters, words, and whole pieces of text; and inclusion of student interests and motivations.

Which Teaching Methods Are Important?

In this book, comprehensive instruction refers to how you teach, as well as what you teach. The No Child Left Behind Act, state assessments, and state standards may influence your decision making about what to teach, but how to teach should be your decision. It is important that you are able to make informed decisions about the manner in which you will accomplish goals in your classroom. "Children deserve teachers who understand them, know the content of the subjects they teach, and are able to effectively engage students in learning content" (Stewart, 2004, p. 732).

The teacher balances instruction when he does all of these teaching behaviors:

1. Shows students how to accomplish reading behaviors with explicit instruction—carefully explaining and modeling the processes of reading.
2. Facilitates students' reading by providing tools, materials, environments, and strategies that make it highly likely for them to independently construct meaning from print.
3. Gives students opportunities to respond to and share what they have read in efferent and aesthetic ways.
4. Checks continually for understanding by assessing student needs during all lessons.

I contend that balance does not happen unless all four of these teaching behaviors take place consistently. Let's look at them more closely.

Explicit Teaching

Explicit teaching techniques are teacher-directed, and when done "within the context of a specific text," they help prepare students to construct meaning from what they read (Cooper, 2003, p. 295). As you learned earlier, according to Vygotsky, this interaction between the adult and the child creates a "zone of proximal development," and is known as "the distance between the actual developmental level as determined by independent problem solving and the level of potential development as determined through problem solving under adult guidance or in collaboration with more capable peers" (1978, p. 86).

When you teach explicitly, you put students in this range of learning, and provide clear, direct, and explanatory interaction between you and your students. This does not mean that packages of scripted lessons are necessary, nor does it mean that a particular program or set of commercial materials needs to be purchased. Instead, explicit teaching means using your communication skills well to explain, model, demonstrate, and make the skills of literacy clear. In a study of effective literacy teachers' practices, Pressley, Rankin, and Yokoi (1996) surveyed primary grade teachers who had been nominated as effective instructors of literacy. These primary grade teachers reported that "overt modeling" was an important teaching strategy in their classrooms, "making clear to [their students] what is meant by reading" (p. 371). According to the Center for the Improvement of Early Reading Instruction (CIERA), explicit teaching is a scaffold for students' learning, which means that it provides students with the support they need to be successful at literacy skills. Such teaching "includes explicit explanation and modeling of a strategy, discussion of why and when it is useful, and coaching in how to apply it to novel texts" (2004, p. 128).

There are two kinds of explicit teaching strategies discussed in this chapter: (1) explanations and (2) mental modeling. Usually, in a planned lesson, you will use both of them before your students begin reading a selection, or while they are reading selected pages. Teaching in this manner helps you to focus on the process of reading. On the next few pages, I'll explain these two types of teaching strategies in detail.

Explaining

An **explanation** outlines the desired behavior in a set of steps or procedures. As Duffy (2003) says, "Specifically, explanations contain 'how-to' information, presented in forthright and unambiguous ways early in lessons, and sometimes, repeatedly across several lessons" (p. 9). Readers can use specific strategies for deriving meaning from text. Making these strategies clear to them so they can use them independently is the key to good explanations when teaching reading. Your students need "cognitive clarity" about literacy, which is a clear understanding about what they need to do when they read and write, and how they need to go about these tasks (Cunningham & Cunningham, 2002, p. 88). A good explanation can get them there.

Take a look at Figure 2.4, which is a page from *The Little Old Lady Who Was Not Afraid of Anything* by Linda Williams (1986). In Figure 2.5, you can read an example of an explanation that Mrs. Raymond, a second grade teacher, used to teach the strategy of making inferences, using this page from Williams's book.

Many times, your verbal explanations need to be written, so that they can serve as reminders and scaffolds for your students as they work and read. To create written explanations, I suggest the use of strategy charts, bookmarks, or desk cards. A strategy chart outlines the steps needed for the strategy in a format that the whole class can see. Hang it prominently and refer to it when modeling or using shared reading. Bookmarks or desk cards contain the same information, in a reduced size. Children can keep the bookmarks handy for use while reading, or tape the desk cards on the corner of their desks for quick referral. Throughout this book, you will see many strategy charts to use in explaining reading processes.

Rationale for Explanations

Why are explanations important for teaching the reading process? First, explanations allow you to put into words a process that is often taken for granted. The reading processes are hidden. Students often assume they know "how to read," when in reality, they know very little about how to comprehend. Likewise, teachers often assume that children know what to do to help themselves understand, when they do not. This may be especially true of students from diverse backgrounds, who have not had the advantage of a lifetime of immersion in the semantics and syntax of Standard English. Au (1993) explains that explicit instruction in the form of mini-lessons would be helpful. Second, explanations help turn an ambiguous process into a procedure or set of steps that make sense. That helps to make the reading process concrete and workable.

The next morning she woke up early.

She went to her window and looked out into her garden.

And what do you think she saw?

Two shoes go CLOMP, CLOMP,

One pair of pants go WIGGLE, WIGGLE,

One shirt go SHAKE, SHAKE,

Two gloves go CLAP, CLAP,

One hat go NOD, NOD,

One scary pumpkin head go BOO, BOO…

Figure 2.4 From *The Little Old Lady Who Was Not Afraid of Anything.*

Source: Text copyright © 1986 by Linda D. Williams. Illustrations copyright © 1986 by Megan Lloyd.

Characteristics of a Good Explanation

Explanations that make sense and help produce desired results have the following characteristics:

1. The language of an explanation is clear and direct.
2. The vocabulary used in the explanation is age-appropriate.

An Example of an Explanation

"Sometimes, the author of a book does not tell you everything you need to know in order to understand the book. You must figure out some ideas for yourself. Authors do this so that they don't have to repeat the same words over and over, which makes their writing more interesting. But there are usually some very good clues that you can use to figure out what the author means. For example, look at this page in *The Little Old Lady Who Was Not Afraid of Anything*. The lady is looking out the window, and obviously is looking outside at something. But the author doesn't tell us what that 'something' is. So, we have to figure that out, or make a good guess. There are three types of clues in the story that will help us do that. Here they are:

1. Read the author's words. What do they tell you?
2. Look at the pictures. What do you find out?
3. Use ideas you already know. What can you guess?

If you think about all of these things, you can make guesses about how these items of clothing might go together to scare something in the lady's garden."

Figure 2.5 Mrs. Raymond's explanation of the process of making an inference.

3. The teacher does not assume that the students already know how to accomplish the objective.
4. Terms that refer to parts of words, parts of sentences, or specifics about syntax are made clear.
5. Whenever possible, the teacher gives options for students to develop independence.
6. Illustrations and demonstrations are used often.

When to Use Explanations

Explanations are not always necessary—or even a good idea. Sometimes, it is best to allow children to figure things out for themselves. But there are times when a more direct approach, or an explanation, is needed. These times are as follows:

1. When you present examples of a new topic, and your students determine a generalization for these examples, you have now reached the point at which an explanation is needed. The topic needs to be named and explained so that it is clear. Thus, the students construct their own ideas, and you add structure and depth to those ideas.
2. When students are unsure about a strategy, topic, or process, you need to make an intentional plan to explain it so that it is demystified.
3. When you want students to apply a strategy to their reading, it is necessary to explain the importance of the strategy.

The Value of Explanations

Making reading processes and strategies visible and distinctive to children is vital to their ability to construct meaning, especially if they are at risk for failure. In spite of differences and limitations in the designs of research studies, Wilkinson and Silliman (2000) report that there is still "compelling evidence" that "instructional conversations" such as direct explanations will scaffold, or support, the learning of African American, bilingual, and learning disabled students (pp. 345–346). In fact, lack of explicit instruction in a meaningful context is actually detrimental to students of diverse backgrounds (Au, 1993).

In your instructional conversations, combine explaining with mental modeling, which is the second type of explicit instruction I'll discuss, and you'll have shown your students how to comprehend.

Mental Modeling

Mental modeling is the teaching behavior that teachers use when they model their own cognitive activity by making "their reasoning visible to the novice" (Duffy, Roehler & Herrmann, 1998, p. 163). Also called "think-alouds" (Wilhelm, 2001, p. 8) or "cognitive modeling" (Graves, Juel & Graves, 2001, p. 62), this technique "describe(s) mental maneuvers illustrative of what one does when doing the reasoning so students have enough information to assume metacognitive control of the mental processing" (Duffy et al, 1998, p. 167).

Rationale for Mental Modeling

Think about learning how to read. Learning this skill is different from learning to swing a bat or make a cake. The unique problem with reading is that its process is covert, or hidden from view. In order to accomplish reading, a process must go on inside the reader's head. Other people cannot see the things that are taking place in the human brain to accomplish the act of reading; they can only see—or hear—its result. Thus, in order to show a young reader how to accomplish a reading capability, you must make those reading processes that are going on in your head visible, making the process of reading overt. You must think out loud.

Look at the page from *The Little Old Lady Who Was Not Afraid of Anything* (Williams, 1986) once again. Shown in Figure 2.6 is a mental model that Mrs. Bell used to show her second graders how to make inferences. You will see that mental modeling is different from providing an explanation. In the next few paragraphs, I will tell you what mental modeling looks like, as well as what it does not look like.

Uncovering Reading Processes

In this example, Mrs. Bell points to her forehead and tells her students what is going on inside her head. She talks about the three clues that she uses to put together the meaning that the author conveys. She points out the pages and the pictures that contain these clues. Notice also that she talks about the author, stating explicitly that the author made decisions to use certain words or place certain pictures on the page. It is important, especially with young children, to convey the message that books are products of the author's imagination, and that authors

An Example of a Mental Model

Mrs. Bell asked the students to sit on the floor and look at the last two pages of the book, as she put her index finger to her forehead and said: "Now, let's look at these last two pages of this story. The author, Linda Williams, tells me with her words that the old lady is looking at her garden through the window. But I see on this page that Ms. Williams does not show us the picture of these things—not yet! As I read, I'm going to need to make a guess about what the lady is looking at out the window, because the author isn't telling me exactly what it is. H-m-m; I'm asking myself, 'Why would something in the garden say BOO?' Well, I can make a guess. I've seen my neighbor put out pieces of clothing to scare the birds away from the plants growing in her garden. She makes a scarecrow out of those clothes. So, I think to myself, 'Could this be a scarecrow?' This is my guess. I turn the page, and I see the scarecrow! Yes, that's it! I read, 'And scare all the crows away!' Now, she didn't actually say that there is a scarecrow there, but she hinted at it. So, the author gives me clues in the pictures, and in the words. Then I put that together with what I already know about gardens. That is called *making an inference*."

Figure 2.6 Mrs. Bell's mental model for making inferences.

make decisions about text and pictures in order to add interest and meaning to the piece of literature. This technique helps to alleviate some of the mystery behind reading, because it reveals the things that happen in an experienced reader's head as she completes the act of reading.

Mental modeling, or the teacher think-aloud strategy, has been tested in several research studies, during which the strategy was "part of a package of reading comprehension strategies" (Duke & Pearson, 2002, p. 214). These studies tell us that "teacher modeling is most effective when it is explicit, leaving the student to intuit or infer little about the strategy and its application, and flexible, adjusting strategy use to the text rather than presenting it as governed by rigid rules. Teacher think-aloud with these attributes is most likely to improve students' comprehension of text" (p. 215).

In Chapter 10, you will learn about comprehension strategies that your students can use to grasp the meaning of text. For each of those strategies, you will see examples of mental modeling.

Some things do not need to be taught with mental modeling. Concepts that need to be explained, demonstrated, or described are not served well with this strategy. For example, suppose I want to teach my second graders about mammals. I want them to know what mammals look like, their characteristics, and their habitats, so I need to present examples, describe them, and perhaps show them nonexamples. No thinking aloud is needed here. Teaching students about concepts that can be seen does not require mental modeling. Teaching about reading does.

Sharing Personal Accounts

Children listen with fascination when the teacher says, "Let me tell you what I'm thinking about this. . . ." When the teacher talks about what he is thinking while he reads, children see reading as an activity that not only interests their teacher, but also engages their teacher in some thoughtful activity. Because children feel connected to their teacher, they begin to see the reading process as something important for themselves, too.

Not Asking Many Questions

Many times, preservice teachers attempt a mental model in a lesson plan; however, they do not do enough modeling. Instead, they ask multiple questions. Look at this nonexample:

> Ok, now, we're on the last two pages. The little old lady is looking at something outside her window. What words tell us that? (Student response.) Ok, now, we know she's looking, but at what? What's there? What could be in the garden that says 'BOO'? What do you think it is?

While it is a good thing to get children involved through the use of questioning (and you'll learn how to do that in Chapters 11 and 12), this is not modeling. To model, you must show them how. When you model by thinking out loud, you are assuming that this idea or skill is new to the students, so questioning them would be expecting them to do the very same skill that you are trying to teach them, but without the benefit of having been taught how to do it! With a mental model, show them now, and ask questions later, once you believe they have learned the strategy.

Mental Modeling versus "Teacher Telling"

Mental modeling makes cognitive processes come alive. Thus, you verbalize the thoughts going on in your mind as you read. This is not the same thing as telling your students how to accomplish the skill. It is not a simple list of steps in a procedure or a "how-to" lecture. Take a look at another nonexample of a mental model:

> Making an inference is when you try to figure out what the author means, even though the author is not coming right out and telling you everything. There are three clues in stories that will help you make guesses about what the author means. They are: words, pictures, and your own ideas. So, all you have to do is read the words, look at the pictures, then think about what you already know. After that, see if you can make a guess about what is outside the lady's window.

In this nonexample, the clues are listed and the teacher gives directions for making an inference, but she does not show the students how this is done, nor does she reveal how she would accomplish this herself. In the example that you read in Figure 2.6, the nature of the reading strategy—inferencing—is such that a reader's prior knowledge about the topic in the text is important. It helps to know something about what gardeners do to scare unwanted creatures out of their gardens. To make an inference on this page of text, the reader needs to use that prior knowledge. An immature reader needs the explicit revelation of this thought process. However, the nonexample that you just read does not reveal this at all.

Student Benefits

Mental modeling makes the reading process visible; thus, this demystifies reading for all students. Good readers will probably enjoy mental modeling, because it tends to personalize the reading act; the teacher is "chatting" about the things he does while reading, and many students find this reinforcing.

Struggling readers benefit as well. According to Duffy, Roeher, and Herrmann (1988), "Decreasing uncertainty is particularly important for poor readers because their background knowledge about what reading is and how it works is sparse. . . . In short, [mental] modeling minimizes the guesswork in learning how reading works" (p. 162).

One caveat of mental modeling is its length. Sometimes, modeling a complex reading process can be difficult to do with brevity. It is important to plan what to say so that the talk does not become too long-winded and students become bored. In addition, you will need to "intersperse modeling with student opportunities for expression so that the students' reasoning when reading can be observed" (Duffy, Roehler & Herrmann, 1998, p. 167). Students who have difficulty focusing or paying attention will be lost if modeling is not done clearly and succinctly, and if they do not have the chance to talk, too.

To help students become actively engaged in their learning of the reading processes, you'll need to combine these explicit instruction techniques with facilitative instruction. I'll describe that next.

Facilitative Teaching

In contrast to explicit teaching strategies, **facilitative teaching** is the type of instruction that is less direct, yet enables students to comprehend what they read. It consists of activities and strategies that help learners figure things out for themselves. Facilitative methods discussed in this book are:

1. Reading aloud to students
2. Activating background knowledge
3. Asking for predictions
4. Asking students to make inferences
5. Asking questions before and during reading
6. Using reading scaffolds (such as graphic organizers, story maps, bookmarks, and self-monitoring tools)
7. Providing stop points
8. Giving students a chance to ask questions
9. Providing experiences around a theme related to the text
10. Asking students to visualize

You will use these strategies to help make it possible for your students to comprehend what they read; they are the scaffolds, or instructional supports, that you will provide for students. Some scaffolds are tangible, such as story maps or graphic organizers. Others are verbalized, such as discussions, predictions, or questions. Many of these strategies prepare the students to read, so you will use them before students begin reading. Facilitative methods also help students maintain comprehension, so your students also use them while they are reading. There is a myriad of ways to use these supports, and all of these teaching strategies will be described at length in Chapters 9, 11, and 12.

Recall the theories that you learned in Chapter 1. Schema theory is reflected in the strategies that teachers use before their students read to help them build background and common experiences (Anderson, 2004; Anderson & Pearson, 1984; Rumelhart, 1980). These are the types of activities that you will need to plan for the purpose of enabling your students' understanding of words as well as whole pieces of text.

Once you've shown students the processes of reading and given them a chance to participate in the construction of meaning as they read, you will need to find out how they respond to what they've read. Let's look at ways to do that.

Providing for Reader Responses

Reader responses are ways that you ask the students to think about and show their reactions to what they have read. Providing opportunity for response often occurs after reading, once comprehension has already taken place. Providing response opportunities can also take place during reading, if the teacher and students pause and reflect upon the text as they move through it. Response is simply a time for the students to think about how the text relates to what they have experienced; to think about what they have learned; or to show how the text affects them personally, to react to it with joy, anger, sorrow, or worry.

Responses can be overt or covert. **Overt responses** are most commonly used because they show evidence of the reader's thoughts. They can be written, verbal, artistic, dramatic, or graphic. However, **covert responses,** those that are going on in the student's head as he reads, can be facilitated through skillful questioning and setting up environments conducive to reflective thought.

As you learned in Chapter 1, responses are also either efferent or aesthetic (Rosenblatt, 1978, 2004; Squire, 1994). Efferent responses are those that require the students to think about what they learned from the text. When they can retell it, summarize it, identify its main idea, compare it to other texts, or critically analyze it, they are responding in an efferent manner. Aesthetic responses, on the other hand, are emotional. When students place value judgments on the text, claim their favorite parts of the story, relate to it personally, or seek out similar texts to enjoy, they are responding aesthetically.

Allowing children to respond to the texts that they read adds value to their reading experience. When they think, talk, or write about the work, they are deeply involved as readers. Rather than focusing on mere explicit understanding of text, this type of teaching gives students the opportunities and the instruction they need to evaluate the author's point of view, fuse emotional and intellectual responses, and talk about their reactions to the text with others. This is what Rosenblatt (1978) meant when she wrote about the transactional theory of reading, and warned us that we need to cultivate more aesthetic responses to literature. Chapter

13 shows you many response activities to do with your students, using fiction as well as nonfiction, and aesthetic as well as efferent responses.

Response takes place after reading the entire selection, or after reading portions of the selection. Interpreting literature is a personal thing, but it is also a social endeavor. Students respond to literature by thinking about how it relates to them personally, but they also think about the social and cultural ramifications of the written word. Many times, readers begin to understand the world they live in as they read about social issues in literature (Galda & Beach, 2004).

Galda and Beach (2004) also tell us that students can respond to literature by using a variety of methods of presentation, such as drama, discourse, technology, journal writing, drawings, and questions for the author. Students can rewrite their own versions of literature by using multimedia computer productions. They compose responses in writing, but they also use images, songs, photos, and video clips.

Students can respond at a more specific level, too. One of the more conventional teaching behaviors associated with effective literacy teaching in the study done by Pressley and others (1996) is that of providing practice. Teachers can give students opportunities to practice their newfound literacy skills in meaningful, high interest contexts, such as independent reading of books, word games, writing, and carefully planned activities that allow them to apply newly learned strategies.

You will want your students to become good at responding to the text personally as they read, and then sharing their responses with others. One way of doing this is through quality oral reading. This is another way that your students can respond to the literature that they read—presenting it aloud to others, using appropriate speed and expression, so that the beauty of the author's words are preserved and passed on. Chapter 14 will show you many ways to encourage your students' responses to literature by reading aloud to others.

Ongoing Assessments

"**Kidwatching**" is an approach to assessment that is part of this model; this is a type of teaching behavior in which teachers watch their students carefully, making notes and conducting quick, informal assessments to determine their abilities and needs (Goodman, 1985). The teacher makes plans and decisions based on what she sees. Kidwatching is part of a philosophical orientation to the assessment of children that is quite different from the typical model of teaching followed by testing. A teacher who engages in this type of assessment believes that it is important to choose materials, make lesson plans, and form groups based on the interests and needs of her students. While she uses as her guide specific objectives and standards-based benchmarks that are necessary for all of her students to accomplish, she knows how to reach those goals by involving the students in activities that are meaningful and interesting to them. She also informs her students of the observations she has made of their reading, and asks for their help in forming goals for meeting their own needs and overcoming their weaknesses.

Chapter 4 will show you a myriad of ways to assess your students before they begin reading in your classroom, as well as on a daily basis. Ways to assess "the whole, the parts, and the heart" of reading are included in that chapter. While formal tests such as standardized tests will be a part of your classroom, such tests provide only one small picture of your students' capabilities. Observational methods will be important, "so that a full picture of students' developmental strengths and educational needs may emerge. Teachers are faced with the challenge of variability among students in their language and literacy skills and how best to assess and promote the development of these skills" (Wilkinson & Silliman, 2000, p. 353).

Thus, I advocate a collection of informal assessments to use on a daily basis. Alternatives to standardized tests, such as observations, reading conferences, running records of oral readings, and retellings are some of the assessment tools you will explore in Chapter 4. Additionally, a sample of an assessment that you can complete in five minutes or less, and that is taken from the running records of your students' readings, is included in Appendix B. If you observe five students per day, you can collect a wealth of information about how they process print, understand the author's message, and respond to the text.

Balancing Content and Instruction

Remember Ms. Menshin? At the beginning of this chapter, I told you that this fictional student teacher asked her students to identify the problem in a story, without first showing them this process. Thus, her "lesson" was lopsided, and many of her students didn't "get it." She needed balance in her teaching. She had chosen a good thing to teach, and a very necessary strategy for her students to learn, but she had not organized her teaching so that she made this process of reading visible first.

In order to have a balanced approach to teaching literacy, a teacher needs to use all four of the types of teaching behaviors that I have discussed in this chapter: (1) explicit, (2) facilitative, (3) providing for reader responses, and (4) ongoing assessments. I contend that this balanced approach to teaching reading actively engages the thinking of students as they learn more about literacy. It involves them on two levels. First, they interact with their teacher and with each other as they learn about print. Second, they interact with the text, construct their own understanding of it, and respond to it. All the while, the teacher who balances instruction in this manner constantly watches the students to determine their level of involvement—in other words, this teacher would always be asking, "Are these children learning?"

Ms. Menshin's Lesson Revisited

Let's visit Ms. Menshin, our third grade student teacher, again. She wants her students to learn how to determine the problem in a story. She has chosen to use *Hey, Al*, by Arthur Yorinks (1986). This book is about Al, a janitor, who lives in a small apartment in the city with his dog, Eddie. They are not happy with their home, because it's so small and they keep working hard and getting nowhere. Good news arrives one day, though, from a bird who appears in the bathroom window. He offers to fly them away to a paradise, where there will be no worries or cares. Al and Eddie, after much discussion, decide to go. When they get to an island in the sky, life is wonderful, until one day, when they discover that they're turning into birds.

To begin her lesson, she says, "I'd like to show you a book in which the main characters have a real problem. In fact, you may have had a similar problem. Let's take a look at *Hey, Al,* by Arthur Yorinks." Ms. Menshin asks her students to look at the cover and the title, and make some predictions about the story based on these clues. Then, from a book box, she shows a few objects that relate to the story: a picture of a janitor or custodian; a plush dog; a picture of a messy, cramped apartment; a mop; a plush exotic bird; and travel brochures of tropical islands. She says, "Class, what do you think these objects and pictures tell us about this story?" She asks the students to talk to each other and offer ideas to the class.

To accomplish reading the story together, Ms. Menshin asks her students to read along while she reads aloud for the first page. This method enables her to stop at the end of the first page and talk with them about the action in the story so far.

She reads to the bottom of the first page, where the text finishes on the words, "What could be bad?" At this point, Ms. Menshin says, "I'd like to share my ideas about what I have read so far. I'll think out loud so that you know what I'm thinking." Ms. Menshin points her forefinger to her forehead and says, "Well, this is interesting. The author is asking, 'What could be bad?' And it's only the first page! Mr. Yorinks, the author, has already introduced me to the two main characters, Al and his dog, Eddie. And he tells me about the setting—a small apartment on the West Side of what might be New York City. So, when I read this sentence, I'm wondering, 'Well, what *could* be bad?' I know that most good stories have problems, and it seems as if the author is trying to tell me the problem at this point in the story. Those are the last words on this page, so I think that if I turn the page, I'll see the answer to the question, and I think that Mr. Yorinks is going to tell us that Al and Eddie have a problem. Perhaps there's something wrong with Al's job. Or perhaps he doesn't like his tiny little apartment. I'll turn the page to find out."

Ms. Menshin turns to the next page, and reads it aloud. She asks the students to join in with her as she reads. Then she says, "Well, my prediction is confirmed. Al and Eddie do have a problem. And the author described it on this page with the dialogue. Eddie the dog thinks their apartment is a dump. He wants a house and a yard to run around in. That, I think, is a big problem, because the pictures show me that Al is looking a little bit glum. And the words tell me that Al doesn't really want to move. I'm using the word clues and the picture clues to figure out the problem in this story." She continues the story, reading aloud while the students join her. At some points in the story, she stops and asks her students to talk to each other. At the end, she asks a volunteer to reread the final sentence in the story: "Paradise lost is sometimes heaven found." She asks, "Why did Mr. Yorinks write this sentence?" She asks the students to share ideas with their partners.

The next day, students write in their journals. She asks them to explain the problem in the story, and then describe a similar problem in their own lives.

Throughout the week, Ms. Menshin asks the students to think about problems in stories as they read independently. While the class is reading books independently, she meets with five students each day and talks with each of them privately about their reading. Prior to each conference, she gives them small sticky notes to mark the places in the book that give them clues about the problem in the story that they are reading. During individual conferences, she looks for their understanding of this story element and makes notes for her records. She realizes that she will need to model this reading process again for some of her students and makes plans to do so.

How can you achieve instructional balance? You must first decide what you want to teach, and then determine which instructional stance you need to take. Sometimes, a lesson can include both explicit and facilitative strategies. Other times, a lesson can include opportunities for response. At all times, assessment is ongoing. Figure 2.7 shows the kinds of teaching behaviors that can take place when you balance your instruction in this model of comprehensive instruction.

Balanced Literacy Instruction: Teacher Behaviors

Explicit Teaching	Facilitative Teaching	Teaching with Reader Responses
• Giving examples and non-examples to apply to definitions • Explaining rules, procedures, and strategies before reading • Modeling reading strategies by thinking aloud before and during reading • Modeling appropriate reading aloud behaviors • Explaining and demonstrating letter–sound relationships	• Reading aloud to students before they read • Providing concrete experiences before reading • Activating and using background knowledge before reading • Asking for predictions before and during reading • Providing story maps and graphic organizers to use before and during reading • Asking questions that lead to construction of thought and meaning before and during reading • Setting purposes before reading	• Giving opportunities for social interaction around books during and after reading • Asking students to relate texts to personal lives during and after reading • Giving meaningful practice opportunities so that students can apply what they learned after reading • Asking students to write, draw, talk about, or dramatize their understandings of text • Asking students to read aloud favorite characters' dialogue, important quotes, and dramatic parts

Teacher Behaviors Related to Ongoing Assessment

• Kidwatching
• Observing and taking notes on five students per day
• Using informal assessments such as observations, conferences, running records, and retellings, along with formal assessments such as standardized tests for a complete picture of the literacy abilities of students
• Adjusting instructional plans based on observations of students

Figure 2.7 Balanced instruction.

Ms. Menshin's Instructional Decisions

How did Ms. Menshin balance her lesson? First, Ms. Menshin determined what is important to teach, to achieve her balance of content. She knew that reading comprehension involves the understanding that stories contain characters that go through a series of events in order to solve a problem. One of the academic standards for third graders in her state says, "Students will determine the problem in a story." Ms. Menshin valued this one as a high priority. She contended that understanding the story is much easier if her students realize the problem that the main character is having, and begin to search for solutions in their minds, just as the main character is doing. Thus, she made the decision to teach the strategy of determining the problem in a piece of fiction.

She also made the decision, as she has always done with all of her lessons, to teach this strategy by relating it to something that interested her students. She decided to "teach the heart," by selecting a piece of literature that she knew they would relate to very easily. Her students love picture books, even though many of them are already reading chapter books. *Hey Al,* a Caldecott Award winner, is a particularly good one to use because of intriguing use of figurative language, making it an interesting story to talk about. Its pictures are fascinating, and add much to the story. She knew her students would find many clues about the outcome of the story in its illustrations. Her book box objects, which she used to introduce the book, would start the conversation and social interaction around the message of this book. When planning, she always tries to find some way of motivating them or to relate their learning to something personal.

The second instructional decision Ms. Menshin needed to make was how to teach the lesson. She decided to teach this lesson using a combination of explicit and facilitative methods. The book box was a facilitative strategy. These objects gave the children ideas for predictions about the story, enabling them to think about the story before they read it, and then confirm their predictions as they read. This teaching reflects schema theory, because her students were using prior knowledge to build their comprehension of the text (Anderson, 2004; Anderson & Pearson, 1984; Rumelhart, 1980).

Shared reading was the method that Ms. Menshin used for this story. This means that she read parts of the story aloud while her students read silently. She made the decision to use this strategy because she felt that the decoding demands of the text were high for some of her students. This story was being used as a vehicle for teaching a reading strategy; thus, it was important that all of her students understand the story line. She felt that this would best be accomplished by providing a "scaffold." Reading the story aloud while her students silently followed along enabled her to keep the entire group together as they read the book, and enabled her to lead a discussion about the elements of story. This strategy put her students in the zone of proximal development (Dixon-Krauss, 1996; Vygotsky, 1978).

She decided to use mental modeling to show how to find the problem of a story, because this method shows students how to accomplish a reading task in the same way that mature readers do. This was the explicit portion of her lesson, in which she made specific plans to teach her students in a rather direct manner, telling them her thoughts as she read.

Modifying Instruction for

ELL

Figurative Language and *Hey, Al*

GRADE LEVEL: 3–4

● **Objective**

After reading or listening to *Hey, Al*, students will determine the meaning of idioms that describe the human experience.

● **Preparation**

Type these sentences on index cards. On the back of each, glue the appropriate picture.
- Nikko does not know what he will do after school today. He will *cross that bridge when he comes to it.* (Picture of a bridge)
- Nadia must decide between playing on a soccer team and having more time to be with her friends. She is *at a crossroads* and does not know what to do. (Picture of an intersection)
- Cecily's parents do not understand why she wants to stay up late and watch a movie. She thinks they are old and *over the hill.* (Picture of a hill)
- Jaime did not listen to his grandmother's warning about staying away from kids who get in trouble all the time. He needs to *open his eyes!* (Picture of closed eyes)

● **Materials**
- *Hey, Al* (Yorinks, 1986)
- Brown banana or other piece of overripe fruit
- Index cards with idioms written on them and small pictures glued to the back
- Journals

● **Introduction**

1. Talk about the pictures on the cover and title page of *Hey, Al*. Make predictions.

● **Shared Reading**

2. Begin reading. Stop on the page where a large bird appears and offers to take Al and Eddie away. Talk about the problem in the story and make predictions.

3. At the page that says, "Ripe fruit soon spoils," stop and write these words on the board. Then show them a brown banana or other piece of overripe fruit.

4. Use a mental model: When I read this, I needed to stop and think, "This story is not about fruit. I wonder why the author says, 'Ripe fruit soon spoils.' Then, I think about buying bananas. I buy them when they are yellow, and I like to eat them very quickly after I buy them. Why? Because in just two or three days, the

Modifications for ELL are printed in color.

(continued)

banana looks like this! It's too brown to eat! It's spoiled! So, the author, Mr. Yorinks might be telling me that when Al and Eddie were on the island, they had a good life. But, just like this banana that spoiled, things can quickly go wrong. I think Al and Eddie will have another problem now. I think they will be unhappy with the island. What do you think?

5. Elicit responses, continue reading, and verify the prediction about the problem.

6. At the end of the book, write the author's last sentence on the board: "Paradise lost is sometimes heaven found." Talk with students about the meaning of this figurative language, relating it to the lesson that Al and Eddie learned about being satisfied with life.

● Response

7. Explain: Mr. Yorinks used figurative language to describe the life of Al and Eddie. There are lots of types of figurative language. One type is called an idiom. This means that the words say one thing, but mean something else. Show students one index card. Model your thoughts about the idiom: "I see this sentence: 'Tomas got in a fight with his friend. He was mad for a week, but now he needs to forget about it. He needs to *move on*.' OK, so Tomas was mad at his friend, but he needs to stop being mad. The next words say that he needs to 'move on.' The picture of the moving van on the back of my card makes me think that when you move, you start again in a new place. Maybe that's what Tomas can do. He can start all over again with his friend, just as if he had moved."

8. Ask the students to read their sentence together, talk to their teammates about what the words mean, and illustrate the idiom that is on the card.

9. Ask students to choose and address one of these questions in their journals:

Is it better to plan ahead or to cross the bridge when you come to it?

What age is over the hill to you?

Have you ever been at a crossroads? Tell about it.

Tell about a time when you had your eyes closed about something.

Think of an idiom in your language. What does it mean?

The last part of the lesson gave her students an opportunity to respond. They responded aesthetically by writing in their journals and describing a similar situation in their own lives. Her students were transacting with the text, reflecting upon the reader response theory (Rosenblatt, 1978).

She also used kidwatching by asking her students to think about finding story problems when they read during the week, and to use sticky notes to mark the clues that they use. As she observed each student, she was able to make plans for further instruction.

In this lesson, the teacher chose an important objective, provided interest and motivation, used explicit as well as facilitative instructional techniques to reach this goal, and assessed her students' abilities to apply the strategy right away. That is balance.

Home–School Connection

Sharing the Modeling Strategy with Caregivers

Mental modeling, one of the teaching strategies described in Chapter 2, is one of the most powerful techniques you will use. Caregivers of your students can use it too, as they read to and interact with their children at home. Shown here is a letter that you can send to caregivers explaining the importance of modeling and talking about books. ●

Modeling and talking about books can take place at home, too.

Dear Families,

When your child brings home books to read, one way you can help him or her is to talk about the book while he or she shares it with you. Stop on some of the pages and talk about what you are thinking as you read these words. You can say things like:

> "I'm thinking about how the main character feels right now. It reminds me of when I was little, and. . . ."

> "I think there's going to be a big problem on the next page, because the author keeps leaving me little hints on this page."

> "Look at this picture of the boy's bedroom. It reminds me of your bedroom!"

> "I wonder why the author put this photograph of a leaf on this page. I'm thinking maybe we'll find out about photosynthesis on this page."

When you say these things, you are letting your child know about some of the reading strategies that you use, like predicting, relating the story to your own experiences, and self-questioning. These are important reading behaviors, and you can make them seem very easy and natural if you simply talk about them as you read. Give it a try!

Sincerely,

Your child's teacher

Summary:
The Importance of Balance

Planning two different dimensions to your curriculum and to the lessons you teach is the essence of comprehensive instruction. In this model, you achieve balance in two ways. First, you need to balance the content of your instruction. Second, you need to balance your method of teaching the content.

What is important to teach? Curriculum must include content that includes whole text and the understanding of it. After all, that is what reading is all about—the ability to pick up a book and read it with understanding. It must also include the nuts and bolts of reading—strategies for decoding and automatically recognizing letters and sounds, so that words, sentences, and paragraphs can be understood. Thus, the "whole" and the "parts" of reading are equally important for inclusion in your lessons. A third facet to include is the "heart" of reading. Knowing your students' interests, attitudes, concerns, joys, and pastimes helps you in the classroom. Choosing materials and methods that reflect your knowledge of who your students are as people is crucial to your success in developing lifetime readers.

How do you teach all of this? First, you show your students how reading is done. You explain reading processes to them by clearly defining the steps and procedures they need in order to make sense out of print. You also model by thinking out loud. Called the mental model, this technique tells them the kinds of decisions that go on in your mind as you encounter print and uncovers the mysteries of the thought processes behind reading. This is explicit instruction, which puts students in an environment of comfortable learning called the *zone of proximal development.*

The other way to teach strategies is to enable your readers to experience the reading process themselves. To do this, you provide reading materials that are appropriate and interesting. You also provide tools and strategies that will make it more likely that comprehension will occur. As they grow with these enabling tools and strategies, they become more independent readers. Including strategies such as making predictions, brainstorming, self-monitoring, and questioning while reading enables your students' comprehension. In addition, scaffolds such as reading guides, stop points, bookmarks, story maps, and advance organizers are all ways to focus on and enable the process of reading. This is called *facilitative instruction;* it reflects schema theory in that such teaching helps students rely on their prior knowledge to construct meaning.

To continue with balanced instruction, you also give your students an opportunity to use what they know about reading to gain from it. You ask students to respond and react to what they have read, by writing, dramatizing, reading aloud to others, reflecting, summarizing, retelling, discussing, and creating multimedia productions. *Transactionalism* tells us that responses are important to the growth of the student as a reflective reader and writer.

Additionally, while all this is going on, you are watching your students—watching, waiting, encouraging, listening, and taking notes. Called kidwatching, this manner of assessing enables you to evaluate your own teaching and make adjustments as necessary. It also enables you to do more planning, by capitalizing on what your students are capable of doing, and building upon that experience to help them grow even more as readers.

Balanced instruction is multifaceted. It includes a myriad of decisions. It involves the whole, the parts, and the heart of reading. But then, so does literacy.

To review these teaching behaviors, look at the Reviewing the Big Picture box. In it, I have aligned the behaviors with IRA, INTASC, NAEYC, and ACEI/NCATE standards and principles.

Technology Resources

- www.readingonline.org   This web site, sponsored by the International Reading Association, lists many links to articles, all of which are available for free online.
- www.stenhouse.com/pdfs/0307fm.pdf   *Reading with Meaning: Teaching Comprehension in Primary Grades,* by Debbie Miller (2002), is reproduced in its entirety and offers some good explanations of strategies I discuss in this chapter.

- www.schoolchangeinreading.org/CI/EEI_RDGS.html#IB   This web site contains many articles on balance, modeling, and offering response opportunities.

- www.balancedreading.com   This web site contains an alphabetical set of 26 links to sources that offer information about balanced reading programs. The organization was designed to provide research-based information about reading programs to educators.

Reviewing the Big Picture

Teacher Behaviors Described in the Decision-Making Model of Comprehensive Instruction

Type of Teacher Behavior	Description	IRA Standards	INTASC Principles	NAEYC Standards	ACEI/NCATE Standards
Explicit teaching	The teacher shows students how reading is done.	2.1, 2.2, 4.3	3, 4, 6, 7	4b	1, 2.1, 3.1, 3.2, 3.4, 3.5
Explanations	This explicit teacher behavior is a way of verbally and visually making reading strategies clear. Steps to the procedures and helpful hints are parts of explanations.	2.2, 5.1	3, 4, 6, 7	4b	1, 2.1, 3.1, 3.2, 3.4, 3.5
Mental modeling	This explicit teacher behavior is "thinking out loud," in which the teacher verbalizes his thought processes as he reads.	4.3, 5.1	3, 4, 6, 7	4b	1, 2.1, 3.1, 3.2, 3.4, 3.5
Facilitative teaching	The teacher enables understanding by providing materials, tools, and teaching strategies that make it more likely that children will be successful at reading on their own.	2.1, 2.2, 2.3	3, 4, 6, 7	4b	1, 2.1, 3.1, 3.2, 3.4, 3.5
Reader responses	The teacher gives students an opportunity to react to and use information from reading.	2.1, 2.2, 2.3, 4.4	3, 4, 6, 7	4b	1, 2.1, 3.1, 3.2, 3.4
Ongoing assessments	The teacher watches students so that he is aware of needs and strengths	3.1, 3.2, 3.3.	8	3	4

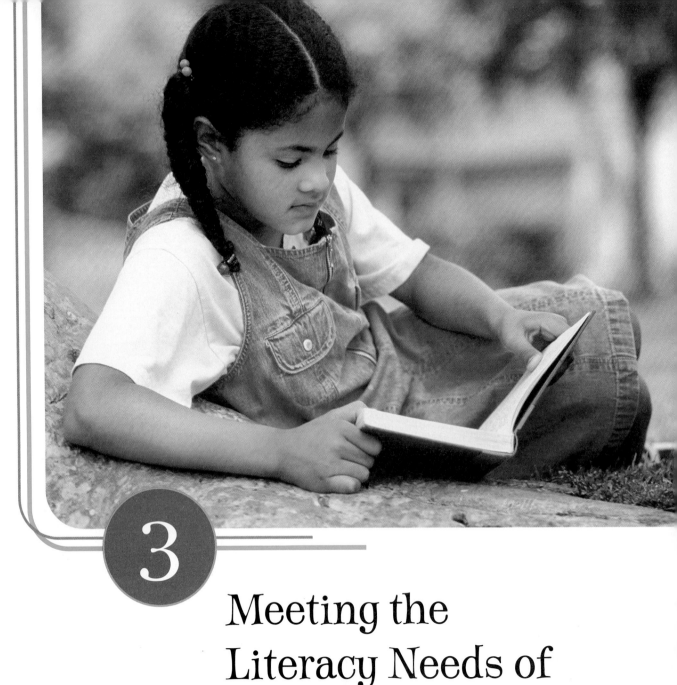

3

Meeting the Literacy Needs of English Language Learners

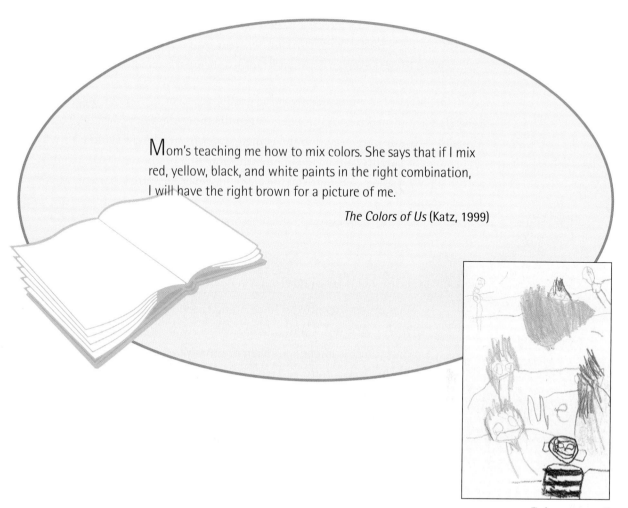

Mom's teaching me how to mix colors. She says that if I mix red, yellow, black, and white paints in the right combination, I will have the right brown for a picture of me.

The Colors of Us (Katz, 1999)

Guiseppe, age 5

What do you need to know to understand the things you read? Imagine the following scenario.

Miss Osburn says to her second grade group, "Students, this morning I'd like for you to read a book with me. I've chosen *Arthur's Thanksgiving*, by Marc Brown (1983). Since Thanksgiving is just around the corner, it will be a great one for us to share."

The children settle at their desks and begin to read. On the fourth and fifth pages of the book, the words are:

Arthur's first job as director was to assign parts. The narrator would have the most to say, but the turkey, the symbol of Thanksgiving, had the most important role of all. Secretly, Arthur was glad he wouldn't have to be the turkey. But who would play that part?

At lunch, Francine gave Arthur two chocolate cupcakes. She wanted to be the narrator. Buster even let Arthur borrow his Captain Zoom spaceman. He wanted to be Governor William Bradford. Being the director seemed like fun.

Chu-Mei, one of the students in the group, fixes her eyes on the page. When the group is finished reading and begins to talk about the story, she keeps quiet. Chu-Mei's family immigrated to the United States from China's Canton province last year. Her parents cannot speak English. Chu-Mei has begun to speak conversationally with some of the girls in the class; however, she rarely participates in book discussions.

Now, answer the questions in the Personal Reflection.

Personal Reflection

- What must you know to understand the words on the two pages of *Arthur's Thanksgiving*?
- What troubles might Chu-Mei, or any child not familiar with American culture, have with this book? Why?

This scenario shows us how texts that seem simple and straightforward to us might be confusing and difficult for students who do not speak English, and who are not familiar with American culture. To understand and enjoy *Arthur's Thanksgiving*, the reader must know something about Thanksgiving, directing theatrical plays, American history, popular toys, and bribery in the school cafeteria!

While reading the first two chapters of this textbook, you have no doubt seen the importance of the reader's background knowledge while reading. Schema theory, as you learned in Chapter 1, tells us that what the reader brings to the page is just as important as the print on the page (Anderson, 2004; Anderson & Pearson, 1984; Rumelhart, 1980). A reader has two kinds of knowledge that contribute to his understanding of the printed page: knowledge of print and knowledge of world topics. Recall that knowledge of print refers to the reader's grasp of the alphabet, letter–sound correspondences, and the mechanics of the English language in print. Knowledge of the world is the reader's understanding of people, relationships, things in nature, and a vast store of knowledge gained from being a living, breathing human being. But suppose that the reader that you're teaching has knowledge of print in a language other than English, and knowledge of a world quite different from yours. How will you teach him to read?

This chapter focuses on some answers to that question. First, I will describe English language learners. Second, we will examine the strengths and knowledge that these learners bring to the classroom, enabling skilled teachers to capitalize on those strengths and maximize their learning. Third, we will take a look at how the needs of English learners are different from the needs of other learners in the classroom. In the fourth section of the chapter, I will explain how you can make your classroom a welcoming place for children whose native language is not English. Finally, in the last section, I will list specific strategies that you can use with English language learners to teach them the whole, the parts, and the heart of reading, so that you have the "right combination," as Katz says in *The Colors of Us* (1999), for all of the students in your classroom.

Who Are English Language Learners?

Children whose home language is not English are, first of all, people. When a child enters your classroom, it is possible that you will know very little about each other's language, culture, and traditions. But what you both share is the human condition. Miller (2004) tells of empathy, "the extraordinary capacity for one human being to see things through the eyes of the 'other,' the source of compassion, tolerance, and understanding that leads us away from egocentrism to a world view that lies at the heart of multicultural education" (p. 92).

Such a view is not optional in today's classrooms. According to the International Reading Association's *Reading Today* ("Meeting Spotlights ELL Issues," 2004), 41% of nearly 3 million teachers surveyed by the U.S. Center for Educational Statistics reported teaching students whose home language is not English. The same report shows that 20% of U.S. students currently live in homes where English is not the primary language. However, "by 2015, up to 55% of the K–12 population will not have English as a first language" (p. 34). It makes sense to get to know these young people, the strengths that they bring to the classroom, and their special needs.

There are a variety of acronyms used in professional literature to name the group of students who enter American classrooms with little or no knowledge of the English language. Figure 3.1 shows a list of these acronyms and their meanings. The purpose of listing them here is to familiarize you with the many

Terms and Acronyms

These terms and acronyms are associated with students who speak languages other than English.

ELL—English Language Learners

ESL—English as a Second Language

EFL—English as a Foreign Language

LEP—Limited English Proficient

ESOL—English for Speakers of Other Languages

Bilingual—Knowledge and use of two languages

Figure 3.1 Terms and acronyms.

terms that you will see in the literature on this subject. Throughout this book, when an acronym is necessary, I will use "ELL."

English learning students in the United States are a magnificently diverse group. While the majority of English learners in this country speak Spanish (Helman, 2004), there are many other languages spoken by children in American classrooms, including Vietnamese, Korean, Cambodian, Cantonese, a variety of Native American languages, and many more (Elmore & Rothman, 1999). Often, the teacher does not speak the language of the ELL students in her classroom. Such diversity requires that teachers become knowledgeable about their students' interests, abilities, and family backgrounds, as well as their native culture and traditions. According to Peregoy and Boyle (2004), "This kind of information makes it possible to validate students for what they *do know* and build from there" (p. 113).

What Do English Language Learners Already Know?

What can your English learners do when they arrive in your classroom? What are their strengths? Knowing this will help you provide what Peregoy and Boyle call "positive transfer" (2004, p. 111) from what they already know about language in general to an understanding of the English language in particular. In the next few sections, I will discuss some of the things that these students bring with them when they enter your classroom.

Literacy in the Primary Language

English language learners who are literate in their home language have a basic understanding of many of the concepts of print that are necessary for understanding English learning. Many languages, such as Spanish and French, are read in the left-to-right and top-to-bottom manner, so the student who can already read in such a language is likely to be comfortable and familiar with the organization of English print. Even learners who are literate in languages that are very different from English, such as Thai and Arabic, bring to the classroom much familiarity with concepts that they will need. For example, they realize that print is speech written down, and that symbols on the page have meaning. These learners know what reading is about.

More than 13% of minority students in this country are Latino/Hispanic students, making them our largest group of minority students (Jiménez, 2004), so it is helpful to know that English and Spanish share phonemic qualities. Alphabet letters are shared in these two languages, and several consonant sounds are the same or similar. Similarities exist at the word level as well. Spanish and English are called "cognate languages," because many of the words in these languages look similar and can even be found within each other. For example, English "flower" is Spanish "flor," "insect" is "insecto," "paper" is "papel," and "number" is "numero."

This similarity gives English language learners who already know Spanish a "base for working with an unfamiliar oral language" (Helman, 2004, p. 453).

Such understanding of the purpose of literacy, as well as some familiarity with sounds and vocabulary of our language, gives these learners an edge in learning English. In fact, "to the extent that the writing systems are similar, positive transfer can occur in decoding" (Peregoy & Boyle, 2004, p. 110).

Understanding of Verbal Speech

Many English language learners begin to understand verbal speech fairly quickly, and "develop peer-appropriate conversational skills in about two years" (Drucker, 2003, p. 23). Even though many of these students do not hear English at home, they adapt quite quickly to social situations in the classroom, and can converse with friends, participate in playground games and organized sports, and speak with the teacher on a one-to-one basis. Often, they can accomplish day-to-day tasks and classroom routines; these environmental and social skills are the first ones that they acquire. These skills enable them to "fit in" with their peers and give them a basis for building new understandings of English.

Past Experiences

Your students who are learning English will bring to the classroom a variety of experiences and cultural influences. This background knowledge is a rich source of schema for reading and writing. Additionally, such variety will enhance your classroom and provide opportunities for your students to learn from each other. Your English language learners may know about different holidays, traditions, geography, storytelling, and a myriad of other experiences that can add much richness to your teaching (Kamil & Bernhart, 2001). Often, their family units are strong and their parents place great importance on learning. These influences can strengthen your curriculum.

What Are the Needs of English Language Learners?

Along with their strengths, English language learners bring some challenges to the classroom teacher. Your recognition of these challenges is important to their success in the classroom, because many times these students are unable to express their needs to you. Moreover, some of the behaviors that they exhibit may appear to be symptomatic of something other than their true needs. For example, if a student doesn't immediately answer a question, he or she may appear to be disrespectful of authority or incapable of grasping the content. In actuality, cultural differences may be influencing this behavior. Thus, teaching students who are learning English requires that you look beneath the surface and be reflective about making instructional decisions to meet their needs. The next few sections describe those needs.

Proficiency in Academic Language

The classroom is full of all kinds of language: books, printed material on the wall, web sites, teacher verbal directions, children's conversations, directions written on the chalkboard, group discussions, teacher explanations, teacher modeling, printed directions on worksheets, and a myriad of other ways to communicate. Each of these forms of communication serves a different purpose and requires varying degrees of cognitive attention. In particular, using reading and writing for information as well as for enjoyment requires greater cognitive demand than does conversational language or reading environmental print. The English language learner, while competent at chatting with a buddy, may not yet have a proficient level of English mastery needed to meet the demands of the more academic types of communication. Cummins terms this "cognitive academic language proficiency (CALP)" (1994, p. 40). English language learners typically are behind their peers in this type of language proficiency—often by six to eight years (Collier, 1987). These students need to gain more proficiency with reading and writing each year than do their native English-speaking peers.

Period of Silence

Because English language learners have not yet mastered verbal abilities in English, they sometimes give the impression that they do not understand concepts or are not paying attention. Take a look at this classroom interaction:

> Mrs. Reed, a first grade teacher, asks Min-Ling, a Vietnamese-speaking girl in her class, "What was your favorite part of *Tacky the Penguin*?"
>
> Min-Ling, who really enjoyed the book, thinks to herself, in Vietnamese, "I thought Tacky was really funny when he sang a funny song and scared the hunters away." However, she can't verbalize this in English, so she says nothing.
>
> Mrs. Reed, not wanting to embarrass her, says, "That's okay, Min-Ling. Billy, will you tell us your favorite part?"

There is a gap between Min-Ling's conceptual understandings and her ability to articulate this in English. Often, English language learners can understand much more speech than they can generate. Unfortunately, teachers might mistake this silence for lack of understanding or lack of cognitive ability. Even worse, educators sometimes assume English learners are learning disabled because of this gap (Flores, Cousin & Díaz, 1998).

Cultural Differences

Here is another classroom scenario to imagine:

> Miss Gold reads *Cook-a-doodle-do* (Stevens & Crummel, 1999) to her kindergarten students. Afterwards, she helps the students make straw-berry shortcake, using the recipe in the book. She asks Miguel, one of

her students, to help her with stirring the ingredients in the bowl.
He stares at the floor and shakes his head.

Unfortunately, Miss Gold didn't realize that, in Miguel's family, men and boys do not cook, and consider such an expectation an insult.

The same thing that makes a classroom so rich in learning resources for all of your students—their cultural diversity—can also make learning more difficult for some of them. Facial expressions, body movements, and gestures are affected by cultural influences. Some of these behaviors may make a difference in classroom interaction.

In many Asian cultures, a smile sometimes means embarrassment, confusion, or anger. A giggle can be a sign of embarrassment, especially if the child has been reprimanded or caught doing something wrong (Pennycook, 1985). Another commonly misunderstood gesture is that of eye contact. Many Haitian and Puerto Rican children look at the floor to show respect to an adult. Looking at an adult in the eye shows defiance (Ariza, 2002a).

These types of reactions can lead to misunderstanding if the teacher is not aware of such differences. Likewise, your students who are learning English in your classroom and are not native to this country may have difficulty understanding your verbal and nonverbal communication. Moreover, their cultural differences can affect their comprehension of printed material. On top of that, some students may come from cultures that value schooling and literacy in ways different from yours. These differences can present enormous challenges, but awareness of them helps.

Phonemic Differences

Phonemes are the smallest units of sound in a language. There are vast differences between English and other languages, and these differences may make learning to read difficult. While Spanish and English share many consonant sounds, the vowel phonemes are very different. Other languages, such as Vietnamese and Chinese, are tone languages, meaning that the speaker uses voice pitch to differentiate between words and syllables. Given the fact that phonemic awareness is vitally important for learning to read English, such differences make literacy instruction a huge task for these learners and their teachers.

Ways of Communicating

Teachers who teach children of diverse backgrounds are sometimes puzzled because their students seem to misunderstand them, even when language differences are not a factor. Instead, cultural differences in communication styles contribute to misunderstanding or to making erroneous teaching decisions. For example, some Asian American children are not assertive about what they know. They have been taught not to draw attention to themselves or to offer information (Ariza, 2002b; Willis, 2000). Thus, the teacher who is not aware of this tradition may misconstrue the child's silence or reluctance to mean that she does not know the information asked for.

Establishing a risk-free atmosphere, using humor, and providing culturally responsive instruction are ways to engage all students in learning.

Likewise, children from many Native American groups are not accustomed to being called upon in front of a large group. Called "teacher spotlight effect," the teacher, in a typical question–answer recitation lesson, calls on the child to answer a question. Without the benefit of volunteering or preparing for the question, the Native American child is embarrassed or offended (Au, 1993, p. 111).

The culture of American classrooms is such that children are expected to assert themselves and respond when called upon; however, this type of interaction can create discord for some students.

How Can You Make Your Classroom a Welcoming Place?

Your classroom can be one in which all of your students feel accepted, welcomed, and successful. Such an atmosphere of learning and an acknowledgement of your students' strengths and needs is part of **culturally responsive instruction,** which Au defines as "instruction consistent with the values of students' own cultures and aimed at improving academic learning" (1993, p. 13). There are many ways to respond to the needs of your English language learners, as discussed in this section.

Maintain a Risk-Free Atmosphere

Your English language learners will be trying out many things—reading, writing, speaking, answering questions, and working in groups, among others. In order for them to feel comfortable using English, they need to be able to take risks without fear of failure or ridicule. Establishing this from the first day of school is important. Write classroom rules that emphasize cohesiveness as a class community. Allow them to work with buddies who can assist them with tasks such as revising and editing, or decoding unfamiliar words. Additionally, model risk-taking behaviors for your students, such as making predictions, trying to decode unknown words, brainstorming, and writing. Show them how you accomplish these things, and that you are willing to make mistakes.

For example, take a look at one simple way that Mrs. Brown, a fourth grade teacher, encouraged risk taking as she read *The Sweetest Fig* (Van Allsburg, 1993) to her students.

Mrs. Brown's Lesson

Mrs. Brown showed the students some of the pictures at the beginning of the book, and then she said, "After the dentist pulled the woman's teeth, I see her giving figs to Monsieur Bibot. He looks angry. He wanted her to pay him with money, not figs. I think he will throw them away because he's angry. I don't think he would believe what the old lady said about the figs being magical. Let's read and find out."

Mrs. Brown read aloud while the students read silently. They discovered that Monsieur Bibot did not throw the figs away; in fact, he ate one of them. So Mrs. Brown said, "Well, my prediction did not happen. I thought he would throw them away. But instead, he ate one! I'm surprised that my prediction was wrong, but it's okay. I made a prediction that made sense."

Mrs. Brown let her students know that reading is a risk-taking activity, and that sometimes, good readers don't get it "right." But sensible guesses are necessary in making sense of print, and the opportunity to take risks without fear is essential to the classroom atmosphere.

Make Time for Laughter

Humor can go a long way in the classroom. Laughter eases anxiety and gives children a sense of comfort. It brings people together and encourages a positive, trusting atmosphere. Allowing your students to work and chat with each other leads to an atmosphere that is receptive to humor. Reading to your students daily gives you a chance to bring humor into the classroom, because you can read aloud funny books. Many teachers use a "morning meeting" time to gather and begin the day in a positive and socially accepting manner. The first few minutes of every day can be a time to share jokes or funny stories. This activity sets the tone for the entire day.

Encourage the Use of the Primary Language

Many immigrant families are anxious for their children to "fit in," and to become part of the mainstream American society. While this is important for their children's well-being, it is often at the expense of their native language fluency. As immigrant children begin to learn conversational English, they lose touch with

Modifying Instruction for

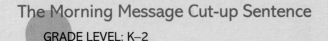

ELL

The Morning Message Cut-up Sentence

GRADE LEVEL: K–2

● **Objective**

After listening to the teacher's morning message, students will reread it for fluency, cut one of the sentences into word cards, and then reassemble the words into a sentence.

● **Preparation**

Begin each day with a "morning message," which is a written statement that awaits the students as they arrive to school. It should contain the date and a simple statement of information that tells students what to expect during the day. Some teachers include the weather, birthdays, holidays, and any other pertinent information about the day in the message.

● **Materials**

- Chart paper for the morning message
- Scissors
- Plastic bag for taking word cards home
- Instructions on how to use the cut-up message at home

● **Procedure**

1. Invite students to sit on the rug and look at the morning message printed on chart paper and displayed on an easel. Tell the students that today's morning message gives them some information about the day. A typical message would say something like this: "Today is Tuesday, December 14, 2004. It is Miata's birthday! We will eat cupcakes and sing a song."

2. Read the message to them, then repeat, asking them to read it aloud, too. Discuss the message. Talk about its meaning. Keep the message displayed throughout the day, giving students a chance to reread it.

3. At the end of the day, take the message from the easel and cut it into word cards. (Early in the year, cut apart only the most predictable part of the message, such as the date. Later, cut apart a sentence that is less predictable.)

4. Show the cut-up words and ask students to read them. Model the decoding process as needed.

5. Put the word cards on the floor in random order and ask students to reconstruct the cut-up message, putting it in any order that makes sense.

Modifications for ELL are printed in color.

6. Reread the morning message together before leaving for the day. Give the cut-up word cards to a student in a plastic baggie to take home, with instructions to reconstruct the message for his or her family.

7. As students become more capable of this, duplicate a smaller copy of the morning message for each. Ask them to cut it apart themselves, and reconstruct it. Once they have determined the correct sequence of words, they can glue it on a blank sheet of paper.

● **Adaptation of the Strategy**

Language experience charts can be used in the same manner. Also, have students create their own predictable sentences after reading predictable books such as Bill Martin Jr.'s (1983) *Brown Bear, Brown Bear, What Do You See?* Cut up their sentences and ask them to reconstruct and glue them on a blank sheet of paper.

their own language. Their parents might not have the time to learn English because of long hours on the job, as they make their way in their new home. All of this leads to the loss of the child's primary language, and a deterioration of communication in the home. This is unfortunate, because, as Fillmore says, "For immigrant children, learning English as a second language and dealing with school successfully are just one set of problems to be faced. Hanging on to their first language as they learn English is an equally great problem. Hanging on to their sense of worth, their cultural identities, and their family connections as they become assimilated into the school and society is a tremendous problem for all immigrant children. What is at stake in becoming assimilated into the society is not only their educational development but their psychological and emotional well-being as individuals as well" (2004, p. 78).

Thus, you need to encourage parents to find time to talk with their children. The children need to know their family stories, backgrounds, and traditions. Many families have rich oral traditions and histories that should be passed on. Convincing parents of the need for this might not be easy, especially if they are working long hours and find it difficult to get to school. Moreover, sometimes these parents are not comfortable talking with teachers, and often will not attend parent meetings because they believe the school alone has authority over their children's learning.

You may need to enlist the help of interpreters if you do not know their language. But it is crucial that your students and their caregivers see that you value their native language and the gifts that they bring to the classroom. In fact, "primary language development, including literacy, is a valuable educational goal for English learners themselves and for U.S. society as a whole" (Peregoy & Boyle, 2004, p. 114).

One way that you can help caregivers is to send home books on a weekly basis. Cooter, Mills-House, Marrin, Mathews, Campbell, and Baker (1999) describe the use of "reading backpacks," which are bags that contain trade books written in English and Spanish, activities for caregivers to do with their children printed on cards, a video, and some writing supplies. These bags go home for a

Building on students' background knowledge helps them better understand the books they read.

couple of days and then the children bring them back with feedback notes from their families. Web sites that aid in finding bilingual trade books are listed in the "Technological Resources" section at the end of this chapter.

Family message journals will also help bridge the gap in communication, as well as provide authentic opportunities for your students to write (Ganske, Monroe & Strickland, 2003). Have your students write a message in a journal about something learned that day or some special event in school. They take it home, and read it to a family member, who writes back. If necessary, these exchanges can take place in the native language.

As you send notes, bulletins, and parent/caregiver information home, remember that it is important to be cautious in the manner in which you communicate to the caregivers of your English language learners. Many times, parents assume that anything written and sent home is bad news, and this is conveyed to their children. Thus, notes sent home might not make it home! Explain to your students the purpose of all home communications; in fact, read them aloud together and talk about them. Avoid sealing notes in their envelopes, which could connote a negative message. Another thing to keep in mind is that parents may be more apt to read "official" publications than handwritten notes. So, attach your notes to informational brochures, flyers, and typewritten letters, and send them home in the book bag or backpack. One good resource to use, a U.S. Department of Education booklet series for parents, called "Helping Your Child," is available at **www.ed.gov** (n.d.). Several of these booklets are printed in Spanish, such as "Cómo Ayudar a Su Hijo a Ser Un Buen Lector (Helping Your Child Become a Reader)" available online at **www.ed.gov/espanol/parents/academic/lector/index. html** (2002).

Bring Cultural Experiences to the Classroom

Think about the following scenario:

> Mrs. Smith teaches fifth grade. In December, she teaches a unit called "Holidays Around the World," during which she reads books aloud, shows pictures, cooks food, and plays music from several winter celebrations, including Christmas, Hanukkah, and Kwanzaa. In February, she teaches a unit called "Black History," in which the students read biographies of Martin Luther King Jr.. Additionally, they learn about slavery in the United States. Because her curriculum is crowded, this is the only way she can "fit" any objectives for multiculturalism.

The problem with such an approach is that the experiences are not real. Students are left with the impression that these cultural experiences are "add-ons." Moreover, stereotypes, misconceptions, and over generalizations are likely when students are given only limited exposure to other cultures, taught during one month out of the year.

Make multiculturalism real. Make it a part of your everyday experiences for all of your students. One of the easiest and most effective ways to do this is with children's literature. Using these books throughout the year, you can share with all of your students stories, biographies, poetry, and nonfiction that give them exposure to worlds outside their own. Additionally, matching the background knowledge and cultural schemata of your English language learners with the literature that you read in the classroom gives them the advantage of building upon what they already know as they learn literacy skills.

These books need to respectfully and positively depict the experiences of people and their heritage, so careful selection is necessary. Figure 3.2 shows some criteria for selecting multicultural literature. Figure 3.3 lists some excellent titles.

Read Aloud Daily

Reading aloud to all of your students is crucial to their literacy growth; it is particularly important for your English language learners. By reading aloud, you are modeling appropriate reading behaviors, sharing your enthusiasm for the printed word, building background knowledge, and developing vocabulary. Reading aloud gives you the opportunity to immerse these students in the sounds and structure of our language in a low-key, relaxed manner.

Hickman, Pollard-Durodola, and Vaughn (2004) recommend a read-aloud strategy that uses the literature to teach vocabulary and concepts. First, the teacher breaks a story or piece of nonfiction into several segments of about 200 to

1. Choose books that are accurate and current.
2. Look for hidden agendas. Choose books that do not show the same people in the same roles all the time.
3. Watch for stereotypes, such as all Native Americans living in teepees or all Chinese looking alike.
4. Choose books that emphasize the commonalities in the human condition.
5. Choose books that have interesting stories that all children would like, regardless of their ethnicity.
6. Avoid books that have neat, unrealistic answers to complex problems; instead, choose books that depict problems honestly and offer resolutions that are realistic.
7. Avoid books that are condescending,
8. Avoid books that portray a whole group of people with one personality trait.

Figure 3.2 Criteria for selecting multicultural children's books.

Children's Books That Celebrate Many Cultures

Picture Books

Brother Eagle, Sister Sky: The Words of Chief Seattle (Jeffers, 1991). A speech given by Chief Seattle, a chief of Suquamish and Duwamish Native Americans, conveying the central belief of Native Americans to white settlers of the Pacific Northwest in the 1850s. (Grades 3–4, 26 pages)

The Butterfly (Polacco, 2000). A story of two friends during the Nazi occupation of France. (Grades 3–4, 48 pages)

The Colors of Us (Katz, 1999). A seven-year-old girl wants to paint a picture of herself, and thinks that "brown is brown." But her artist mother takes her for a walk and shows her that there are many shades of brown on many different people. (Grades K–1, 28 pages)

Chato's Kitchen (Soto, 1995). Chato and his friend Novio Boy, two cool cats, invite some mice to dinner, expecting some *chiles rellenos, enchiladas,* and *chorizo con mice.* But they get a real surprise. (Grades 2–3, 32 pages)

Cheyenne Again (Bunting, 1995a). Young Bull, a Cheyenne, is forced to go to an off-reservation boarding school in the late 1880s. (Grades 2–3, 32 pages)

Gleam and Glow (Bunting, 2001). Based on a true story, about a villager who gave his sons two goldfish, in 1990, before the Bosnian War. (Grades 3–4, 32 pages)

How Many Days to America? (Bunting, 1988). A family flees its country and lands in America on Thanksgiving Day. (Grades 2–3, 32 pages)

How the Stars Fell Into the Sky (Oughton, 1992). A retelling of a Navajo folktale, in which First Woman tries to write the laws in the sky. (Grades 1–2, 32 pages)

In My Family/En Mi Familia (Garza, 1996). Carmen Garza, a Mexican American artist, portrayed several family events in paintings and wrote descriptions of each. (Grades 3–4, 32 pages)

Is My Friend at Home? Pueblo Fireside Tales (Bierhorst, 2001). Seven friendship-themed Hopi stories. (Grades K–1, 32 pages)

Joseph Had a Little Overcoat (Taback, 1999). The author's favorite song as a child was a Yiddish folk song, on which he based this book. (Grades 1–2, 32 pages)

The Leaving Morning (Johnson, 1992). An African American family moves from their apartment in the city. (Grades 1–2, 28 pages)

The Legend of the Bluebonnet (DePaola, 1983). A retelling of a Comanche legend that explains how the Texas state flower, the bluebonnet, covers the land every spring. (Grades 2–3, 30 pages)

Life Doesn't Frighten Me (Angelou, 1993). Jean-Michel Basquiat illustrated Maya Angelou's poem, which speaks of confidence against the odds. (Grades 2–3, 32 pages)

Listen to the Desert/Oye al Desierto (Mora, 1994a). The animals of the desert are shown on each page, and each line is repeated twice in English and twice in Spanish. (Grades 1–2, 32 pages)

Lon Po Po: A Red-Riding Hood Story from China (Young, 1989). A Chinese version of Red Riding Hood. (Grades 3–4, 32 pages)

Moon rope/Un Lazo a la Luna (Ehlert, 1992). An ancient Peruvian tale told in Spanish and English. (Grades K–1, 32 pages)

My Name Is Yoon (Recorvits, 2003). A young Korean girl, adjusting to life in America, does not like her name written in English. (Grades 1–2, 32 pages)

The Old Man and His Door (Soto, 1996). The old man gets in trouble when he doesn't listen to his wife, who tells him to bring *el puerco,* a pig, to a barbeque. Instead, he brings *la puerta,* the door. (Grades 1–2, 32 pages)

The Piñata Maker/El Peñatero (Ancona, 1994). Don Ricardo is a piñata maker in a village in Mexico. This book, written in Spanish and English, shows how he makes them. (Grades 2–3, 40 pages)

Figure 3.3 Multicultural books.

Pink and Say (Polacco, 1994). Pink, a slave boy fighting for the Union, finds Say, a wounded Union soldier, in a battlefield in Georgia. Pink takes Say home for his mother to care for him, but they must return to battle soon. (Grades 3–4, 44 pages)

The Rebellious Alphabet (Diaz, 1993). Written by a Chilean who is now in exile, the story is about an illiterate dictator who bans all reading and writing in the land. An old man trains birds to print and deliver messages. (Grades 3–4, 30 pages)

The Rough-Face Girl (Martin, 1992). An Algonquin version of the Cinderella story. (Grades 3–4, 32 pages)

So Far from the Sea (Bunting, 1998). Laura Iwasaki and her family, who are Japanese American, visit her grandfather's grave at the site of the Manzanar War Relocation Camp. (Grades 2–3, 30 pages)

Suki's Kimono (Uegaki, 2003). On her first day of first grade, Suki chooses to wear her kimono. (Grades 1–2, 32 pages)

Tikki Tikki Tembo (Mosel, 1968). An old Chinese folktale about the giving of long names to the firstborn son in the family. (Grades 1–3, 40 pages)

Too Many Tamales (Soto, 1993). As Maria helps her mother make tamales for Christmas, the phone rings. When her mother answers it and leaves her ring on the table, trouble begins. (Grades 1–2, 30 pages)

Chapter Books

Before We Were Free (Alvarez, 2002). Anita tells of life in the Dominican Republic in the last years of the Trujillo dictatorship, 1960–1961. (Grades 4–6, 166 pages)

Fires of Jubilee (Hart, 2003). Abby is a 13-year-old who still lives on the plantation where she was raised as a slave. But it is 1865 and the South is conquered and slaves are now free. Abby's mother is gone and no one will tell her why. (Grades 4–5, 85 pages)

Homesick: My Own Story (Fritz, 1982). An autobiography of Jean Fritz, who lived in China as a 10-year-old. (Grades 5–6, 173 pages)

A House of Tailors (Giff, 2004). A story of life in Brooklyn in the 1870s, through the eyes of Dina, a 13-year-old German girl. (Grades 5–7, 176 pages)

A Jar of Dreams (Uchida, 1981). Rinko is a Japanese American growing up in California in the 1930s. A visit from her aunt helps her learn to be proud of her heritage. (Grades 4–6, 144 pages)

Li Lun: Lad of Courage (Treffinger, 1947). A classic tale of a boy who lives in a fishing village on the coast of China, but is afraid of the ocean. He refuses to fish and is banished to live alone on the mountaintop. (Grades 4–5, 96 pages)

Little Firefly: An Algonquian Legend (Cohlene, 2003). An Algonquian legend similar to the Cinderella story. (Grades 2–3, 48 pages)

Morning Girl (Dorris, 1992). Morning Girl and her brother Star Boy are two Taino children whose family lives in harmony with nature. At the end of the book, the reader discovers the year is 1492. (Grades 4–5, 80 pages)

Parvana's Journey (Ellis, 2002). In the Taliban-controlled Afghanistan, Parvana's father has just died. She leaves Kabul, disguised as a boy, to find her mother, sister, and brother. (Grades 5–6, 176 pages)

Sees Behind Trees (Dorris, 1996). Walnut, a Native American boy who is near-sighted, uses his other senses keenly and earns the respect of his tribe by guiding an old man on a dangerous journey. (Grades 4–5, 128 pages)

The Skin I'm In (Flake, 1998). Maleek is a dark-skinned African American teenager who hates her color. A new teacher at school who has a rare skin condition helps her gain confidence. (Grades 5–7, 171 pages)

The Skirt (Soto, 1992). Miata lost the skirt that belonged to her mother as a child in Mexico. It's Friday afternoon and she needs to find it before Sunday, without telling her parents. (Grades 2–3, 74 pages)

(continued)

The Star of Kazan (Ibbotson, 2004). Annika is raised in early twentieth-century Vienna by a cook and maid. One day, an aristocratic woman who claims to be her mother appears and takes her to a castle in northern Germany. (Grades 5–7, 405 pages)

Why Do They Hate Me? Young Lives Caught in War and Conflict (Holliday, 1999). Twenty-five excerpts from real diaries of young people whose lives are interrupted by hate, war, and imprisonment. (Grades 6–7, 293 pages)

Year of Impossible Goodbyes (Choi, 1991). Sookan and her family are Koreans in 1945. This is the story of how her family endures the Japanese occupation of Korea, as well as the takeover of North Korea by Communist Russian troops. (Grades 6–7, 169 pages)

Figure 3.3 Continued.

250 words. The teacher chooses three new words from the book, and teaches them to the students. Then, he reads. After the first reading, he talks with the students about the selection, and then rereads it aloud, stopping at each vocabulary word to review and clarify. He repeats this procedure for several days, until the segment is read. This chunking procedure makes the literature manageable and teaches vocabulary in meaningful context.

Make Every Lesson a Language Learning Experience

Every lesson that you teach will be a more intense learning experience for your English language learners than anyone else. Why? Because they are listening to and conversing in a language that is unfamiliar to them. Thus, when you explain things to your students or give them verbal directions, make sure that you are clear and direct. Use all modalities: write important terms on the board, point to them, and say them clearly. Remember that you may need to use gestures, and that these need to be very clear. If you point to a word on the board and say, "Write this word," some of your students may not realize that you want them to write it. You may need to gesture the act of writing the word. Use as many ways of communicating as you can.

Teach from Whole to Part

Reading strategies, by themselves, do not mean much. Strategies such as recognizing letters and sounds, decoding unknown words, making predictions, making inferences, and finding important ideas cannot be done meaningfully in isolation. It is crucial for English language learners to remain grounded in purposeful learning; thus, always begin your lessons with whole text. For example, when teaching a phonics element such as short vowels to your students, read aloud to them a story such as *The Cut-Ups* (Marshall, 1985) first, and then list and work with vocabulary from the story. This gives your students an understanding that the letters and sounds come from text that has meaning.

Offer Scaffolds

Au describes how "rearranging reading instruction" helped two researchers (Moll & Diaz, cited in Au, 1993, p. 143) create a positive learning experience for children who spoke Spanish and limited English. First, they read a story aloud to the students, then reviewed the plot and discussed the story in English. Next, they asked simple questions, and elaborated on their responses as much as possible, so that the students and the teacher interpreted the story together. Then, they discussed unfamiliar vocabulary. Finally, the next day, the teacher asked challenging questions from the teacher's manual, and allowed the students to use Spanish for answers, if needed. When they used their native language, the students could answer questions as well as their English-speaking peers. Yet, at the same time, they were able to tackle a grade-level piece of text.

Reading aloud first, so that students can hear how the story goes, allowing the native language for answering some questions, and talking about difficult vocabulary after reading are examples of scaffolds that can support your students' learning.

Begin with Common Letter–Sound Correspondences

One of the strengths that some of your students will bring to the classroom is their knowledge of phonemes in their own language. In order to build upon what your English language learners already know, when teaching phonics, start with letters and sounds that are similar in their home language. In particular, Spanish and

---

Cognates in English and Spanish:
Words Associated with the Zoo (El Zoologico)

Cognates—Words That Are Similar in Both Languages	Words That Are Not Similar
animals—los animales	bear—el oso
camel—el camello	deer—el venado
coyote—el coyote	fish—el pez
crocodile—el cocodrilo	fox—el zorro
elephant—el elefante	parrot—el loro
flamingo—el flamenco	walrus—la morsa
giraffe—la jirafa	wolf—el lobo
hippopotamus—el hipopótamo	
jaguar—el jaguar	
kangaroo—el canguro	
koala—el koala	
lion—el león	
monkey—el mono	
tiger—el tigre	
toucan—el toucán	
zebra—la cebra	

Figure 3.4 Cognate words related to the zoo.

English share these consonants: b, d, f, k, g, l, m, n, p, s, w, y, and ch. These letters provide a good place to start when teaching phonics to your students, because they will quickly recognize these phonemes and may also recognize the letters as well (Helman, 2004). Vowel phonemes are somewhat similar; however, they are spelled differently in Spanish. For example, the /ā/ phoneme, as in "lake," is similar to the "e" in the Spanish word for three, "tres." Thus, your Spanish-speaking students will recognize English vowel phonemes, but may make spelling errors based on the spellings they are familiar with in Spanish (Helman, 2004).

Use Cognate Vocabulary

Starting with what your students know makes everyone's job so much easier. There is a great deal of overlap in many languages, and this is good news, because vocabulary knowledge is an important predictor of success for English language learners (Hickman et al, 2004). Look for opportunities to teach vocabulary that looks similar in English and in your students' languages. These words are called cognates.

English and Spanish cognates are especially helpful, because the majority of English language learners in American schools are Latino/Hispanic. Figure 3.4 shows the close similarity between these languages in words that would interest children—animal words. Note that out of 23 animal words, 16 are cognates, which means that they are spelled similarly or the same.

Allow for Time to Learn

Students who are still trying to master English are going to need time to process literacy tasks, especially reading. Because they are not yet proficient at using language for academic tasks, they will take longer than the rest of your students when attempting to read English. According to Kamil and Bernhardt (2001), you have several options for providing them with this time:

1. Give them a chance to finish during free-choice activities.
2. Allow them to take their reading home to finish.
3. Give them the questions before they read, so they know what to look for as they read.
4. Summarize parts of the selection for them.

Another way to allow for time is to use the strategy of wait-time (Rowe, 1974). To do this, ask a question, and then pause for about three seconds before asking for a response. Pausing after asking questions is especially helpful to learners who are assimilating English. This pause gives them time to think of a response, and slows down the pace of the lesson.

Above All, Expect Excellence

Throughout all of your instruction, planning, and interactions with your English language learners, remember that there is only one true difference between them and the rest of your students—the lack of proficiency in English. Avoid the trap of

Diversity in the Reading Classroom

Teacher–Student Interactions

The manner in which teachers communicate and interact with their students is important, especially when working with students of diverse backgrounds. Your expectations of your students' behavior and academic achievement in the classroom may be different from what is expected of them at home and in their community. For example, teachers in the United States expect their students to contribute to classroom discussions, and to be assertive about what they know. However, children of Mexican culture are taught the opposite—not to speak up or be assertive around adults (Goldenberg, 2004). This behavior gives their teachers the illusion that they are not capable of the task at hand. Likewise, Goldenberg reports that several studies indicate a mismatch between the communication styles of the teacher and that of the students. When this happens, teachers tend to lower their expectations for the students.

When teachers make the effort to make cultural accommodations, there is some evidence that students participate in class activities more and their contributions are at a higher cognitive level. Yet, to date there is little evidence that being culturally accommodating will produce higher student achievement. So why is it important to know about the communication patterns of your students? Goldenberg says, "If nothing else, different cultural groups have different norms of behaving and interacting; teachers should understand and be sensitive to these because doing so can only help students and families feel more comfortable and welcomed in what might seem a very foreign institution" (p. 1650).

Based on reviews of the research on teaching in multicultural settings (Au, 1993, 2002; Goldenberg, 2004), here are some suggestions for adjusting your communication so that it is culturally responsive:

- A direct, explicit teaching style is more culturally familiar to some African American children. State the behavior that you want from the students, rather than indirectly implying it.

- Rather than asking questions that have known answers, teachers of African American children may get better responses if they ask questions that allow for personal interpretations or insights. Instead of asking, "What is this story about?" the teacher might ask, "Tell me why you think this story is good."

- Acknowledge and use responses of students in class discussions. Native American students tend to wait slightly longer to respond to a question than their peers. Thus, after asking a question, give everyone time to think about the answer and respond.

- With all children, keep the focus on communicating for an exchange of ideas, rather than for the purpose of correct pronunciation and grammar.

thinking that your students who do not speak English are not as intelligent or capable of higher-order thinking as the rest of your students. Expect them to think critically, and give them opportunities to do so. At the same time, be sure to provide them with practice in basic skills such as grammar, spelling, and phonics. Teaching these skills within authentic contexts such as writing for purposes and teaching skills from whole texts will help. Convey your expectations while you provide scaffolds, materials that build on their background experiences, and positive emotional support.

What Strategies Can You Use to Meet ELL Needs?

There are a myriad of solid, research-based strategies that are helpful for teaching your students who are learning English as a second language. The good news is that these strategies are excellent for all learners; thus, using them will help you to meet the needs of everyone in your classroom. The other good news is that you will learn all of these strategies in this book. The sections that follow show you strategies for the whole, the parts, and the heart of teaching literacy. I've listed the strategies as well as the chapters in which you can find them.

Strategies to Teach the Whole

Strategy	Description	Location in This Book
Daily read-aloud sessions	Read aloud whole texts (fiction and nonfiction) every day. See Hickman, Pollard-Durodola & Vaughn (2004) for a read-aloud strategy that helps students learn new vocabulary.	Chapter 9
Shared reading	Read aloud from predictable text while the students read along with you.	Chapters 6 and 9
Choral reading	Have the whole group read aloud together. Usually short, rhyming pieces such as poems are used.	Chapter 14
Paired reading	Put students together with partners for reading.	Chapters 9 and 14
Before-reading strategies that allow for previewing and predicting	Look at pictures and words before reading. Talk about past experiences before reading.	Chapter 11
Taped books	Let students listen to a tape recording of the selection, and then they can read it alone.	Chapter 14
Language experience approach	Provide an experience, then ask the students to dictate a narrative about it. Use the resulting text for reading and writing activities.	Chapters 6 and 8
Interactive writing	Provide an experience, then "share the pen," as you and the students negotiate sentences to write about it. Allow the students to write, scaffolding as they do.	Chapters 6 and 8
Dialogue journals	Share journals by asking partners to respond to each others' journal entries about topics of interest or books they have read.	Chapter 13

Figure 3.5 Strategies for teaching the "whole" of reading to ELL students.

Teaching the Whole of Reading and Writing

One of the ways to make your classroom a welcoming and meaningful place for English language learners is to teach from the "whole." This means grounding all of your activities and strategies in meaningful text. Otherwise, skills, activities, and practice exercises make no sense. Figure 3.5 lists strategies that are related to whole text, and where you can find them in this book.

Teaching the Parts of Reading and Writing

The same principles for teaching the "parts" of reading, shown in Chapter 2, apply to teaching English language learners. As mentioned before, individual letters, words, and skills need to make sense. Thus, you will need to teach them in context. But it is important to provide your students with plenty of opportunities to practice basic skills such as recognizing vocabulary, sounding out unfamiliar words, and spelling words phonetically. Students who are unfamiliar with the English alphabet will need to learn letter recognition as well. As always, it helps to begin with what they know. Specific strategies are shown in Figure 3.6.

Strategies for Teaching the Parts

Strategy	Description	Location in This Book
Alphabet books	Fill your classroom with many alphabet books that can be used to enhance alphabet recognition.	Chapter 6
Children's literature characters associated with consonant and vowel phonemes	Have students make consonant and vowel charts "starring" characters whose names represent the phonemes. A variation of this is to have students bring in samples of logos, menus, and advertisements to represent each letter, such as "Wendy's" for "w."	Chapter 7
Making words	Give students letter cards or tiles and say words for them to spell. Vary this by using words in the students' native language, enabling everyone to achieve success and learn new words.	Chapter 7
Phonics word sorts	After reading a book, have students sort words from the book into common phonetic patterns.	Chapter 7
Using words you know	From familiar words in everyday life, such as names of cereals, candies, or fast food restaurants, have students find phonetic patterns to make new words. Vary this by using color words, number words, and bilingual words.	Chapter 8

Figure 3.6 Strategies to use when teaching the "parts" of reading.

Home–School Connection

Survey

The letter shown below can be sent to parents before school starts. You may need to translate it into the child's native language. ●

Your child is an important part of our class this school year. I would like to know more about him or her. Please answer the following questions and return this letter by Friday. Your answers will help me see your child through your eyes!

Thank you,

Teacher's name

- List five words that describe your child.
  _____
  _____

- What does your child like most?
  _____
  _____

- What upsets your child? Any suggestions for calming your child?
  _____
  _____

- What can your child do well?
  _____
  _____

- What does your child need help with?
  _____
  _____

- What else do I need to know about your child?
  _____
  _____

Helpful Web Sites for Parents and Children

Web Sites for Elementary Children
- www.ajkids.com Ask Jeeves Kids
- www.ala.org/parentspage/greatsites American Library Association Great Web Sites for Kids
- www.enchantedlearning.com Enchanted Learning
- www.pbs.org/wgbh/pages/arthur Arthur, PBS Kids
- www.pilkey.com Dav Pilkey's Extra-Crunchy Web Sites o' Fun

- www.timeforkids.com Time for Kids
- www.4kids.com 4Kids TV
- www.whitehouse.gov/kids White House Kids
- www.yahooligans.com Yahooligans Web Guide for Kids

Web Sites for Middle School-Age Children
- www.afterschool.gov/kidsnteens.html Web Sites for Kids and Teens
- www.howstuffworks.com How Stuff Works
- www.carnegielibrary.org/teens/index.html Carnegie Library of Pittsburgh Teens "Real Life"
- www.rif.org/parents/tips/tip.mspx?View=19 Reading is Fundamental "Choosing Books for Preteens and Teens"
- jfg.girlscouts.org Girl Scouts
- quizhub.com/quiz/quizhub.cfm Quiz Hub

Web Sites for Parents and Caregivers
- www.cbcbooks.org Children's Book Council
- www.ala.org/alsc American Library Association, Association for Library Services to Children
- www.eduhound.com EduHound
- www.funbrain.com Fun Brain
- www.kidsdomain.com Kids Domain
- www.scholastic.com Scholastic
- www.pta.org/parentinvolvement/index.asp National PTA, Parent Involvement

The National PTA offers this brochure, also available in Spanish at:
- www.pta.org/parentinvolvement/standards/pdf/app_e1spanish.pdf The brochure shows 100 ways for parents to be involved in their children's education.

Caregivers and their children can enjoy many types of prints together.

Strategies for Teaching the Heart

Strategy	Description	Location in This Book
Interest and attitude surveys	Find out from your students and their parents what they like to do at home. Use their responses as you plan classroom activities.	Chapter 4
Partner reading	Assign a buddy to your ELL students so that they can share books with each other.	Chapters 9 and 14
Poetry parties	Have students share their favorite poetry with each other.	Chapter 14
Series books	Provide and/or suggest series books titles for your students to read for enjoyment.	Chapter 15
Large classroom library	Make sure that your classroom library is sufficiently large for the range of abilities in your class. Include many multicultural titles.	Chapters 5 and 15

Figure 3.7 Strategies for "heart" teaching.

Teaching the Heart of Reading and Writing

Many of the suggestions that I made earlier are associated with "heart-minded" teaching. These are the kinds of strategies that make children feel welcome in your classroom, regardless of their language or home background. Shown in Figure 3.7 are some additional strategies, described throughout this book, for making sure that your students feel valued, welcomed, and wanted in your classroom.

Summary: Reaching Across the Divide

In this chapter, you learned who your English language learners are. They are a tremendously diverse group, speaking any language, with any number of past experiences. Their experiences are important, because these are the strengths that they bring to your classroom, enabling you to build upon what they already know. Schema theory, as you learned in Chapter 1, tells us that the reader's background knowledge is of utmost importance, and that a reader has knowledge of print as well as knowledge of the world. Many English language learners have much experience in knowledge of print. They may be fluent in their native language, and they may have some experiences with reading and writing in that language, which gives them concepts that are important, such as the understanding that print carries meaning. Moreover, some languages, such as Spanish, share many phonemes and even words, making the transition to English much easier. As for knowledge of the world, English language learners have a variety of experiences with their families that can be used to support their learning.

You also learned the needs of English language learners. The task before them is huge. Their conversational skills and abilities to "fit in" the school environment often lull us into thinking that they understand more than they actually do. Their cognitive academic language proficiency (CALP), or the language abilities they need to process print for academic purposes, usually lags behind their social and conversational skills. Research has shown that it takes five to seven years for English language learners to reach the same reading proficiency level as their English-speaking peers.

Cultural differences present challenges as well. Verbal and nonverbal ways of communicating vary in all cultures, which teachers must be aware of so that they can work around them and reach students as well as parents. Bridging the gap between the school and the home of the English language learner is especially important, so that parents feel comfortable contributing to the formal education of their children.

You learned ways to make your classroom a welcoming place for children whose native language is not English by maintaining a risk-free atmosphere filled with humor and cooperative learning. Starting with what your students already know about phonemes as well as vocabulary is essential. Additionally, filling the classroom with quality multicultural literature helps to broaden the perspective of everyone in the classroom.

And finally, I listed specific strategies that you can use with English language learners. These strategies are explained throughout the book, and are helpful for all of your students in learning the whole, the parts, and the heart of reading. Your understanding of the concepts presented in this chapter reflects your abilities relative to the standards and principles shown in Figure 3.8.

IRA Standards	INTASC Principles	NAEYC Standards	ACEI/NCATE Standards
1.3, 1.4, 2.2, 2.3, 4.1, 4.2, 4.3, 4.4	3, 4, 5, 6, 7	2, 4a	2.1, 3.2, 3.4, 3.5

Figure 3.8 Standards and principles addressed in Chapter 3.

- **www.ala.org/ala/alsc/alscresources/booklists/bilingualbooks.htm**   The Association for Library Service to Children offers this extensive annotated bibliography of children's books that are written in two or more languages, published from 1995 to 1999. The books appeal to ages up to 14 and "were determined to be of high literary quality in each language." Twelve languages are represented.

- **www.education.wisc.edu/ccbc/books/detailListBooks.asp?idBookLists=42**   The Co-operative Children's Book Center at the School of Education of the University of Wisconsin-Madison offers this link, called "50 Multicultural Books Every Child Should Know," compiled by Ginny Moore Kruse and Kathleen Horning in 2001.

- **www.archive.ala.org/alsc/American_Experiencebib.html**   The American Library Association web site contains this annotated list of books that celebrate the diversity found in communities in the United States.

- **www.tsl.state.tx.us/ld/projects/childcare/bibliography.html**   This Texas State Library Archives and Commission web site provides a list of books suitable for preschoolers, many of which are Spanish/English.

- **childrensbooks.about.com/od/bilingualforeign/**   This about.com web site offers several resources for bilingual children's books.

- **www.co.fairfax.va.us/library/Reading/Elem/bilingualbooks.htm**   Lists of bilingual books are offered on this web site, including books of different genre and readability levels.

- **www.pvsd.k12.ca.us/library/Alphabet.htm**   Bilingual alphabet books are featured at this web site.

- **www.eslkidstuff.com/Classroomgamesframe.htm**   Classroom games are offered at this web site.

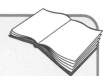

expect the world
The New York Times
nytimes.com

Themes of the Times

Expand your knowledge of the concepts discussed in this chapter by reading current and historical articles from the *New York Times* by visiting the "Themes of the Times" section of the Companion Web Site.

4

Assessing Reading
and Writing

"But we have received a sign, Edith—a mysterious sign. A miracle has happened on this farm. There is a large spider's web in the doorway of the barn cellar, right over the pigpen, and when Lurvy went to feed the pig this morning, he noticed the web because it was foggy, and you know how a spider's web looks very distinct in a fog. And right spang in the middle of the web there were the words 'Some Pig.' The words were woven right into the web. They were actually part of the web, Edith. I know, because I have been down there and seen them. It says, 'Some Pig,' just as clear as clear can be. There can be no mistake about it. A miracle has happened and a sign has occurred here on earth, right on our farm, and we have no ordinary pig."

"Well," said Mrs. Zuckerman, "it seems to me you're a little off. It seems to me we have no ordinary *spider*."

Charlotte's Web (White, 1952)

> My favorite part of the story was when Fern got to keep the baby pig because her father did not have to kill him. My favorite character is Wilber because he is cute. The lesson he learned from Charlotte was don't worry and don't hurry.

Marissa, grade 2

Mrs. Zuckerman was right. Paying attention to what is going on in the barnyard is sensible advice for a farmer. The same holds true for the classroom. When teaching, you need to know your readers. Think about that as you answer the questions in the Personal Reflection.

Personal Reflection

What do you need to know about your students before you begin to teach them about literacy? How can you find out?

To help you think about how you view learners, let me tell you a story about a first grade teacher, Mrs. Edwards, and one of her students, Christopher.

Mrs. Edwards' Lesson

Early in the school year, Mrs. Edwards was conducting an individual reading conference with Christopher. She told him that she wanted him to read aloud to her from the book *Monkey See, Monkey Do*, by Marc Gave (1993), but that he could read it silently first. The book is a very simple rhyming picture book, leveled for beginning readers. After a few pages, he was visibly upset, and he tossed the book aside.

"I'm not reading that book anymore. It's stupid," he muttered.

"But, Christopher, you seemed to be enjoying the book. What's wrong?" Mrs. Edwards asked.

"The book is stupid. I hate it. I won't read it."

"Why?" she asked.

"It doesn't make sense."

"Show me what doesn't make sense."

So Christopher reluctantly picked up the book and turned to the page that read: "Monkey in the middle. Monkey out of sight."

"What's wrong with this page?" Mrs. Edwards asked.

"It says, 'Monkey out of sig-ut.' That doesn't make sense. That's stupid."

Smiling, his teacher said, "Chris, you're absolutely right. The word that you are saying does not make sense. In fact, it's not really a word. I'm so glad you figured that out! Now, let's see if we can figure it out so that it does make sense. Look back at this page, at this word."

She pointed to the word "right" on a previous page, knowing that he had recognized the word earlier. She then asked, "Do you see how similar they are? They're the same except for the first letter. Do you remember how to say this word?"

Christopher said, "Right."

"That's correct," Mrs. Edwards said. "Now, figure out the one that didn't make sense to you."

"S-s-s-ight. Sight!" said Christopher. "Monkey out of sight!"

"Hooray for you!" she said, as Christopher continued reading the book.

Mrs. Edwards' first reaction was mild concern. Tossing books aside in frustration is not the kind of behavior that teachers like to witness in their students. But she knew that it was important to get up close and pay attention to Christopher's error.

And once she did that, she discovered that his decoding skills were well developed, and that he was using many clues to figure out what he did not know. More importantly, Mrs. Edwards discovered that he viewed reading as a meaning-making process, and expected nothing less from books than a good read; hence his frustration when the page did not make sense to him. Based on this observation, Mrs. Edwards knew that Christopher was good at monitoring his own comprehension, and decoding letter by letter. She also determined that he would benefit from more work in viewing words as members of word families.

As you can see, the careful observations made by the teacher are very important. Even more important is the attitude of the teacher as she observes. You've heard the cliché, "The glass is half full, not half empty." These truly are words to live by in the classroom. When children make mistakes or refuse to complete tasks, we need to gather information from this behavior. We are much better off trying to figure out what children *do* know, rather than what they *do not* know, because what they know gives them a place from which to grow.

When Christopher threw the book aside in frustration, his teacher could have assumed that the book was too difficult and told him to choose another one. She could also have assumed that he was having difficulty with decoding because he couldn't figure out the word "sight" on his first try. But in getting up close and asking questions, she discovered that he knows a lot about decoding and making meaning as he reads, because he figured out a pronunciation for the word and tried it out in the sentence. This produced nonsense for him, and that, he knows, is not supposed to happen when one reads. Thus, she could guide him back to comprehension by helping him connect the unknown word, "sight," to a known word, "right." Once that happened, he was on his way to finishing and enjoying the book.

What should you know about your students? Your answer to the Personal Reflection question depends on what you think is important for learners to be able to do as they read and write. In a model of the reading process, Ruddell and Unrau state, "Readers—even beginning readers—are active theory builders and hypothesis testers" (2004a, p. 1,463). This is the view of literacy taken in this book; learners are involved actively, not passively, in their quest to make sense of the printed word. This is the **engagement perspective,** which is described by Wilkinson and Silliman as a view of teaching and assessing that "emphasizes students' active learning" and "focuses on motivation for reading." When teachers instruct and assess in such a way that oral and written language learning are integrated, and students are guided to become "motivated, strategic, and competent readers," the use of "alternative assessments is a necessity, because the mastery of certain aspects of reading can be revealed only by rich qualitative data" (2000, p. 352).

Viewing the student as an active learner affects the way you teach, as well as the way you assess. If you assume that students are trying to make sense of the printed page based on what they know, you can guide them in that direction when they falter. Moreover, if you assume that the learner is actively pursuing comprehension while reading and writing, you will realize that one standardized, multiple-choice test per year will not yield the information that you need to make teaching decisions for each student in your classroom.

Diextrsity in the Reading Classroom

High-Stakes Testing

High-stakes testing is when the results of standardized tests—usually based on state standards—are used to punish or reward schools. Federal and state monies are awarded based on results of these tests; additionally, results are publicized so that parents—and perhaps even teachers—can make decisions about leaving a school that performs poorly. The premise behind standards-based education is a commendable one; it is hard to argue that any child should be "left behind." However, this type of testing and use of the data often results in merely rewarding or punishing educators, without providing support for serving the students who need the most help. In fact, Au says, "Placing a premium on achievement results alone may discourage schools from making a commitment to serve struggling learners of diverse backgrounds or to keep these students from leaving school" (2000, p. 845). Testing programs often "drive out thoughtful classroom practices" (Shepard, 2004, p. 1,622), especially for students of diverse backgrounds.

There are several ways that teachers can meet the needs of these students, at the same time honoring the premise that high standards are desirable for all learners. Some suggestions include:

● Review state standards and the tests that assess them so that you are familiar with the things that are asked of your students (Temple, Ogle, Crawford & Freppon, 2005).

● Have older students keep two sets of notes. One set would be for real knowledge needed for a task, and the other set would be for skills and knowledge needed for the test (McNeil, cited in Shepard, 2004).

● Make assessment part of your instruction on an ongoing basis. Do not wait until the spring of the year to find out about your students, based on the results of their standardized tests. Keep records of their reading and writing abilities in the classroom all year long (Glazer, 1998).

● Increase your students' self-efficacy, which is their belief that they can handle the tasks of literacy. Teach strategies such as using prior knowledge and self-monitoring to build students' self-confidence in tackling literacy tasks (Guthrie & Wigfield, 2000).

● Have high expectations and teach toward those expectations (Au, 2000).

● Give students practice for a skill, task, or strategy in a variety of situations (Shepard, 2004).

Formal assessments of your students' achievement, such as standardized tests, will give you one snapshot of their learning, and will undoubtedly be an important part of your classroom life. Standardized tests are those that are created by commercial testing companies or state educational agencies to compare a student's performance on a variety of literacy skills to the performance of students in the same grade level across the country. Usually, results from these tests determine students' eligibility for special services in school. They are also particularly important in today's classrooms because of the No Child Left Behind Act of 2001. This federal law states that all public school students must be tested in grades three through eight, beginning in the 2005–2006 school year. Schools will be compared with the data from these tests. Parents of children who attend schools that do not perform at the "proficient" level for their state standards may receive vouchers to send their children to other schools. Thus, parents and caregivers, administrators, and politicians will be extremely interested in the results of these tests. It is your responsibility to make sure that your students are comfortable with these types of tests and do well on them.

At the same time, it is your responsibility to make sure that such tests do not take over your curriculum. Standardized tests are not designed to help you plan individual instruction. Shepard states, "Yes, end-of-year tests can be used to evaluate instruction and even tell us something about individual students, but such exams are like shopping mall medical screenings compared to the in-depth and ongoing assessments needed to genuinely increase learning" (2004, p. 1,633). **Alternative assessments** are those that go beyond formal standardized tests. These assessments include those in which the "actual language and literacy behaviors of students are described over time, and the progress of individual students is documented" (Wilkinson & Silliman, 2000, p. 353). This type of assessment is done frequently; usually, at least weekly. It includes a collection of the student's writing as well as records of reading abilities in a variety of situations. These are **informal measures,** which include data gathered from anecdotal notes from observations, reading and writing strategies checklists, samples of student writing for portfolios, interest inventories, running records of oral reading, decoding checks, concept of print observations, and many others. Assessments such as these are not standardized, and are generally created by the teacher to give an in-depth look at specific objectives that the teacher has taught on an ongoing basis. These types of informal measures of your students' abilities give you the complete picture of their literate lives.

In this book, assessments are viewed from the engagement perspective. This approach means that a variety of assessments are necessary. This chapter will show you what to look for as you get to know your students. It will introduce to you the factors that affect the development of someone who can read and write and chooses to do so. It will also help you make decisions that will enable you to teach in such a way that all of your students care about their learning. Most importantly, it will show you how to get up close as you observe children, and really look at what they are accomplishing as they learn. There are many assessment tools introduced in this chapter; however, as you read this book, you will discover additional ways to assess your students while they read and write in each chapter. Throughout this chapter and the rest, you will learn how to look beyond a single test score on a standardized test, and watch what happens when your students read and write.

What factors influence your students? What is important to know about them as you teach literacy? In the next several sections, I will introduce factors that influence your students' performance in literacy tasks—affective as well as cognitive factors. We'll look at these separately, and examine how they influence reading as well as writing behaviors.

Affective Factors

When you wrote your ideas in the Personal Reflection, did you include interest-related things? Did you want to know your readers' hobbies, likes, and dislikes? If so, you were interested in the **affective** knowledge of your students. The affective domain of human thinking is concerned with feelings and emotions. The power in your teaching lies in your ability to make your learners care. When you know what your readers do in their spare time, what motivates them, and the kinds of books that they would enjoy, you can reach them in ways that you otherwise would not. More important, as Calkins observes, "Children should immediately and always sense our interest in the wholeness of each of them as a reader" (2001, p. 141).

Knowing your students' affective concerns will help you to teach to children's hearts. If you can connect new understandings with the things they care about, your job becomes much easier. Thus, you need to know your students. You need to find out their interests and attitudes towards reading and writing.

How can you do this? There are several ways to assess your students' affective lives: conversations, interviews, observations, interest inventories, and attitude surveys. Let's look at those now.

Conversations and Interviews

One of the most exciting things about teaching is getting to know your students as people. A fine teacher I know, Mr. Vaughn Dailey, once told the parents of his students at an open house night at the Pennsylvania middle school in which he taught, "One thing I never forget is how important these children are to you. I hope to get to know your child and see him or her in the same way you do—as a very precious human being."

It is important to start at the beginning of the school year. In personal interviews, you can ask your students questions that help you to get to know them, especially the kind of reader that exists within themselves. Calkins advocates asking questions about how they view reading and how reading fits into their everyday lives (2001, p. 142). Likewise, you can ask questions of your students about how they view writing and how they view themselves as writers. Examples of such questions are shown in Figure 4.1.

Taking notes during a brief interview is helpful; asking older children to respond in writing to one or two of these questions will give you many insights into their literate lives. In addition, this sets the stage for promoting literacy in your classroom. When you begin the year with the conversation focused on reading, children see right away that reading and writing are valuable to you, and will be a part of the everyday life of your classroom.

Observations

Make a regular habit of watching children as they learn. Appropriately, Yetta Goodman calls this *kidwatching* (1978, p. 37). While it may seem obvious that a teacher needs to watch the kids, this type of assessment is easily swept aside in the everyday bustle of the classroom. Make anecdotal notes, which are useful for gaining and storing information about how a child approaches reading (Au, Carroll & Scheu, 1997). One way to manage this technique is to set up an observation plan. Set a goal to talk with at least five students per day, and write notes on their strengths and needs. Resolve to maintain a system of note taking; make these observations a part of your daily plan. As you observe your students, make notes

Questions to Ask about Reading Relationships

- What do you do when you read?
- With whom do you share books?
- What is the best part about reading?
- What is the worst part about reading?
- When you're at home, when do you read?
- Tell me about how you read.
- What kinds of reading material do you have at home?
- Who reads a lot at your home?
- What do you like about reading at school?
- What do you dislike about reading at school?

Questions to Ask about Writing Relationships

- What kinds of writing do you do?
- When do you write?
- Why do you write?
- What is the best part about writing?
- What is the worst part about writing?
- Who writes a lot at your home?
- What do you like about writing at school?
- What do you dislike about writing at school?

Figure 4.1 Finding out about your students' relationships with reading and writing.

accordingly, and concentrate on finding what the child knows about reading, you will experience the joy and excitement in children's learning. Below are a couple of ways to keep track of these observations.

- **Five-a-Day Folder System.** Obtain five different-colored file folders, one for each day of the week. On the outside, label each folder with a day of the week. Inside each folder, attach five 5″ × 7″ index cards, accordion-style. On each index card, write a child's name and the date. These cards are the place for writing notes about each student in the classroom. This system can accommodate 25 students. You can adjust the number by adding or reducing the number of index cards in each folder. Daily, you carry the folder for that day with you as you move about the classroom, put the date on each card, and make notes on the children whose names are in the folder. Once the cards are filled with notes, transfer them to a portfolio for each child or file box.
- **Stick-to-It Notes.** Keep a pad of notes on a clipboard as you circulate the room. Make notes on the sticky notes, including the child's name and date. Stick them to your clipboard, to be transferred later to the child's folder. (This can also be done with blank address labels.) Set up a plan to observe five students each day. Keep a class list on the clipboard and make a checkmark next to each child that you observe that day.

Stop and watch your students as readers. Calkins advises us to observe with specificity, and to watch for the kinds of reading behaviors and attitudes that they exhibit. When you "pull alongside" a child, and watch very closely, you will discover some fascinating things about how children construct meaning, process print, and make choices (2001, p. 101). See Figure 4.2 for a list of behaviors to observe.

Interest Inventories

Mathewson says that reading interest is "favorable attitude with high action readiness" (2004, p. 1,444). For example, a child who regularly and voluntarily reads many biographies about sports personalities could be said to have "high action readiness," because he acts upon that interest in sports by reading. However, this does not mean that all children who are interested in sports will be readers of sports biographies, due to their possible lack of reading ability or maturity. It also does not mean that the child who spends a week or two reading such biographies is doing this because of interest; instead, the student might be preparing for a required school research report.

Researchers tell us that interest can have an affect on children's reading. Shirey and Reynolds (1988) found that children spent more time on reading interesting sentences and learned them better. Mathewson determined that "interesting reading done on an ongoing basis breaks down barriers to initiating reading activity and forms desirable habits" (2004, p. 1,456).

To capitalize on interests, find out first what your students like. Use an **interest inventory** to determine what interests them, and stock your classroom library with titles that reflect these interests. Interest inventories can help you select books for your students, plan themes, and form literature circles. Knowing your students' interests can help you encourage voluntary reading, and guide them in experiencing the joy of reading. When this happens, as Rosenblatt explains, they have an aesthetic **stance** (1978). A stance is the manner in which a reader approaches a piece of text, or the way in which the reader mentally prepares to read. Readers who look at reading with an aesthetic stance are expecting enjoyment, personal connections, and meaningful encounters. Rosenblatt suggests that our aim when teaching our students to read should be the development of an aesthetic stance.

Many (2004) reports that readers' stance can affect their understanding of text. If they are encouraged to look at literature from personal perspectives, or affective views, they will have greater comprehension. Conversely, teaching practices that focus on answering efferent-type questions narrow the experience that children have with literature. "When teachers use Ping-Pong questioning techniques, where students parrot back responses to questions listed in the teacher's manual, students may assume the only appropriate focus when reading literature is to analyze the selection and retain important information." Instead, "inviting students to fully relive the literary experience could lead them to greater heights of understanding" (p. 926).

It is helpful to fill your classroom library with books and other printed material that match the interests of your students. For example, suppose you find out that several members of your class play on sports teams. Sports fiction books (such as those written by Matt Christopher), biographies about sports heroes, sports

Reading Behaviors to Observe

Look at the reader's eyes:

- How does the reader move his or her eyes around the page?
- Does the reader search for clues in the pictures, charts, maps, or figures?
- Does the reader glance from one page to the next, searching for clues in the print and the pictures?
- Does the reader look around the room, searching for clues in the classroom environment?
- What signs of interest do you see?
- Does the reader point to words on the page?
- Does the student slide his or her finger across the line of print?
- Does the reader attempt to cover up portions of a word to figure out its parts?
- Does the reader mark pages, write down notes, mark difficult words?
- When the reader comes to a difficult or unknown word, what does he or she do?
- Resist the temptation to offer immediate assistance. What is the reader's choice of strategies for decoding? For determining meaning?
- Does the reader stop when something does not make sense?
- Does the reader reread?
- Does the reader read ahead to figure out the unknown?

Writing Behaviors to Observe

- Does the writer use brainstorming tools or lists of ideas to generate writing?
- Does the writer prefer to generate his or her own ideas for writing?
- Does the writer need help selecting topics?
- How does the writer approach a writing assignment?
- Does the writer persist with revising and editing?
- Does the writer give up and "publish" work that is not yet finished?
- Does the writer collaborate with others about the writing?
- Is the writer open to suggestions and comments about the writing?
- Does the blank page inhibit the writer?
- Do the mechanics of writing and handwriting overwhelm the writer?

Figure 4.2 Observation notes.

magazines, and newspapers would likely be popular reading material in your classroom library.

Knowledge gained from interest inventories can also help you interact with your students in meaningful and personal ways. For example, suppose your middle school students are reading *The Skin I'm In* (Flake, 1998). This book is not considered a sports story; the main character, Maleeka, does not play a sport.

However, she must make many important decisions about the friends she hangs around with, her relationship with her mother, and her behavior at school. When talking to your students about the book, you can ask them to relate the problems she has to the ones they might have. You can ask them to think about how the author might change the story. Because your students are interested in sports, talk about how playing on a sports team might have given Maleeka a different perspective on things. Thus, knowing your students' interests enables you to choose materials for them, but it also helps you think about ways to make personal connections to the printed page.

Generally, the purpose of any interest inventory is to determine what students enjoy, what they care about, and what motivates them. Topics and questions in an interest inventory might include:

- What do you like to do in your spare time?
- What sports do you like?
- What kinds of books do you like?
- What television shows do you like?
- How much time do you spend reading at home?
- What do you like/dislike about reading?
- What do you like to do when you are with friends?
- What is your favorite time of year?
- What is your favorite school subject?
- Who do you most admire?
- Who is your favorite famous person?

Choose the ones that will be of most help to you. Then determine the manner in which you want to survey your students' interests. Figures 4.3 and 4.4 show some formats. The format you choose depends on the age level of your students and manner in which you want to record and store their responses. Some formats are questionnaires or surveys; others are artistic creations done by the students. Create your own interest inventory using the topics that you want to know about, combined with the format that will work best for you and your students.

Attitude Surveys

Why do some of your students love reading and others hate it? Knowing the answer to that question can make a real difference in your instruction and your impact on the children with whom you work. It is important to find out what motivates your readers, as well as the attitudes they have about the act of reading, because "the environment for reading instruction is optimum when students are enthusiastic about reading and have an I-can-do-it attitude" (Pearson, Roehler, Dole & Duffy, 1992, p. 181). Many times, you will find that some of your students do not like to read and avoid it as much as possible. This information is helpful, too, because you can include materials in your classroom that are of high interest, such as Dav Pilkey's *Captain Underpants* series or *Ricky Ricotta's Mighty Robot* series. Books such as these, while they are not necessarily high-quality literature, can give your reluctant readers some much needed practice with the printed word in easy-to-read and motivating formats. Young reluctant writers often enjoy writing silly stories of this nature, too.

Ways to Survey Interests

Sentence Completions

Using this method, you will create "sentence starters," and ask the students to complete the sentence by filling in the blanks. This format works best for children who are comfortable composing and spelling on their own. Examples of sentence completions are:

I enjoy _____.

My favorite subject in school is _____.

What I like to read most is _____.

My favorite thing in the whole world is _____.

When I have free time, I like to _____.

The very best present anyone could give me is _____.

Teacher-Read Survey

This type of survey provides more support for children who are not proficient or confident writers, or for younger children. You will read the question, and then the child marks the appropriate face symbol, indicating his or her level of interest. Some prior discussion of the symbols will help. Shown below are some sample items.

1. How much do you like books about animals? ☺☹
2. How much do you like math? ☺☹

Open-Ended Questions or Prompts

When you choose some questions or writing prompts that have a wide possibility of answers, you may get rich and interesting responses, which provide you with a wealth of information for planning. This type of inventory works well for children who are comfortable with writing and are given sufficient time and space to write lengthy answers. Some examples of these questions are:

- Imagine you have three hours of free time after school. What would be the best way to spend this time?
- Tell about the best family vacation you ever had.
- Who is your favorite famous person? Why?
- What is your favorite section of the library?
- If you had $100 to spend on anything you wanted, what would you buy? Why?

Figure 4.3 Ways to survey student interests.

(continued)

Glyphs

A glyph is a chart that shows any type of information, using a picture legend (Bamberger & Hughes, 1995). Shown below are directions for a bookworm glyph, in which your students can portray their reading interests. The completed glyph (Figure 4.4) was designed and created by one of my students, Jodi Murray.

Bookworm Legend—My Reading Interests

Before you begin your glyph, read all directions first.

1. How much do you like to read?
   Not very much—Color your bookworm's body one color.
   A little bit—Color your bookworm's body two colors.
   Very much—Color your bookworm's body two colors and add some polka dots.

2. What is your favorite type of book?
   Mystery—Draw glasses on your bookworm.
   Adventure—Add a cowboy hat to your bookworm.
   Science fiction—Draw antennae on your bookworm.
   Other—Add a top hat to your bookworm, then write your favorite type of book on the back.

3. Do you have a favorite author? Who is it? Write the author's name along the tail of your bookwork.

4. What is the title of one of your favorite books? Write the title on the cover of your bookworm's book.

5. What is one of your favorite things to do?
   Play sports—Color the shoes purple.
   Watch TV—Color the shoes orange.
   Artwork—Color the shoes red.
   Listen to music—Color the shoes green.
   Other—Color the shoes blue, and write your favorite thing to do on the back of the bookworm.

6. How do you feel when your teacher asks you to read?
   Good—Draw ⌣ on the bookworm.
   Uncomfortable—Draw ⌣ on the bookworm.
   Awful—Draw ⌢ on the bookworm.

7. If you could have three wishes, what would they be? Write your three wishes on the thought cloud. Please put your name on the back of the bookworm when you are finished.

Figure 4.3 Continued.

Figure 4.4 Example of a bookworm glyph that depicts a student's interests.

In order to foster an environment that generates enthusiasm, Mathewson discusses the need for linking "students' previously held values, goals, and self-concepts to reading" (2004, p. 1,455). In other words, you'll want to know your students' responses to two questions as they relate to the act of reading: "Can I do this?" and "Is it worth my efforts?"

There are several ways to determine your students' attitudes toward reading and writing. Let's take a look at some **attitude surveys** that can help you do this.

Elementary Reading Attitude Survey

McKenna and Kear (1990) created a survey that uses the popular Garfield cartoon character. The questions ask the students to tell how they react to a number of reading activities, in and out of school. When you give this survey to your students, you can obtain estimates of your students' attitudes toward two types of reading—recreational and academic. Individual scores will enable you to complete a picture of each of your students, and class averages will provide you with a profile of the entire group. Both kinds of information will help you plan instruction as well as provide classroom materials that are most conducive to keeping your students motivated to read.

Using the survey, you can ask your students to read a question that relates to how they feel about reading. (You can read the survey to younger students.) For example, one question reads: "How do you feel when you read a book on a rainy Saturday?" Another one asks, "How do you feel about getting a book for a present?" (McKenna & Kear, 1990, p. 630). Four pictures of the cartoon character Garfield are shown next to each question. These cartoons represent moods ranging from elation to anger, and students choose the picture that best represents how they would respond to the question. A copy of the complete survey of reading attitudes, available for use by teachers, is in the May 1990 edition of *The Reading Teacher*.

Writing Attitude Survey

More recently, a similar survey was created for the measurement of writing attitudes (Kear, Coffman, McKenna & Ambrosio, 2000). Garfield once again provides the stimulus for students to respond to questions, on a Likert scale, that ask them about how they feel about writing. Some questions ask students about types of writing, such as, "How would you feel writing to someone to change their opinion?" (p. 17). Other questions pertain to the writing process, such as "How would you feel if your teacher asked you to go back and change some of your writing?" (p. 20). The instrument can be used with any grade level; the teacher can read the items to the students in primary grades. A complete copy of the survey and its estimates of reliability and validity are in the September 2000 edition of *The Reading Teacher*.

Reader Self-Perception Scale

Building upon the same idea with older readers, Henk and Melnick created the Reader Self-Perception Scale (RSPS) to "measure how intermediate-level children feel about themselves as readers" (1995, p. 471). The scale is based on the "self-efficacy" idea, which is a "person's judgments of her or his ability to perform an activity, and the effect this perception has on the ongoing and future conduct of the activity" (p. 471). Designed for children above fourth grade, the scale measures four different factors related to reading self-perception: progress, observational comparison, social feedback, and physiological states. Students are asked to read each of the 33 items and rate their agreement with statements such as "I think I am a good reader" and "I understand what I read as well as other kids do." The teacher can compare the students' scores in each area with the norms established by the researchers, and determine if their self-perceptions are in the normal range. Performance of whole groups can also be examined, so that the teacher can modify classroom practices and materials as needed. The scale in its entirety, along with directions for administration and scoring, is available in the March 1995 edition of *The Reading Teacher.*

Writer Self-Perception Scale

The idea of self-efficacy is also the basis of the Writer Self-Perception Scale, or WSPS (Bottomley, Henk & Melnick, 1997–1998), which is designed in the same manner as the Reader Self-Perception Scale. The authors contend that "individuals who hold positive writer self-perceptions will probably pursue opportunities to write, expend more effort during writing engagements, and demonstrate greater persistence in seeking writing competence" (p. 287), and this assessment tool makes it simple for you to determine your students' perceptions of themselves as writers. This scale consists of 38 items and is appropriate for upper elementary or middle school grades. It is available in the December 1997/January 1998 edition of *The Reading Teacher.*

Motivation to Read Profile

Students' self-concepts as readers, along with their perceptions of the value of reading, are measured in the Motivation to Read Profile, or the MRP (Gambrell, Palmer, Codling & Mazzoni, 1996). This team of researchers recognized the need for teachers to assess both of these factors as they get to know their students' reading lives.

There are two parts to the profile: the reading survey and the conversational interview. The survey, which consists of 20 items that are read aloud to the group by the teacher, is designed to assess readers' self-concept, measuring how well they perceive their own competence as well as how they compare it to that of their peers. Additionally, the survey elicits information about the value students place on reading, usually in terms of how often they engage in reading behaviors and activities. The conversational interview consists of three sections, gathering information about the student's reading of fiction and nonfiction as well as information about general reading behaviors. The interview is unique in that it is given individually and can "glean information that might otherwise be missed or omitted in a more formal, standardized interview approach" (Gambrell et al, 1996, p. 525). Individual information can lead to instructional plans such as suggesting certain books to children or providing additional support in small groups. Class averages can help the teacher to determine overall motivation of her students at different points in the school year, which may lead to modified plans, changes in materials, or implementation of home programs.

Some of the questions asked in this profile are shown in Figure 4.5.

Reading Survey

My friends think I am _____.

_____ a very good reader

_____ a good reader

_____ an OK reader

_____ a poor reader

When my teacher asks me a question about what I have read, I _____.

_____ can never think of an answer

_____ have trouble thinking of an answer

_____ sometimes think of an answer

_____ always think of an answer

Conversational Interview

Tell me about the most interesting story or book you have read this week.

Think about something important that you learned recently . . . from a book. What did you read about?

Figure 4.5 Example items from the Motivation to Read Profile.

Source: Gambrell, Palmer, Codling & Mazzoni, 1996, pp. 520–523.

Cognitive Factors

What was your answer to the question in the Personal Reflection, "What do you need to know about your students before you begin to teach them about literacy?" Did you think about gathering information about your students' abilities to recognize letters and sounds, read aloud, pronounce words, retell what they've read, spell correctly, or write clearly? These are abilities that are reflective of cognitive factors related to literacy.

As Calkins said so eloquently, "Respect the intelligence in your students' efforts" (2001, p. 9). Remember the story about Christopher, who threw his book in frustration because the word he was trying to pronounce did not make sense? That incident is an example of a child's attempt to construct meaning as he reads. Although the effort failed momentarily, Christopher was clearly able to do the things that readers are supposed to do. Many mental abilities are involved in the act of reading, and the child's capacity for mustering up all of them simultaneously and smoothly results in his reading strength.

I mentioned before the importance of considering the glass as half full when assessing your students' reading abilities. This is sometimes hard to do, especially when needs are so great that they seem to overwhelm the child's strengths. A few years ago, in my graduate-level reading course, most of my students were practicing teachers. One, in particular, was a highly respected teacher who had been teaching in the primary grades at a local elementary school for several years. She was returning to the university to earn her master's degree in reading. A requirement of the course was to work in our reading clinic with a child whose parents brought him to the clinic because he was having difficulty learning to read. I assigned a second grade boy to this teacher to work with in the clinic, because of her work with children in primary grades. After about a week, she came to see me, and said with frustration that she really did not think she would be able to work with the boy, and wondered if I would consider assigning another student to her. I was quite surprised, and wondered if she was having difficulty managing his behavior or if he was not able to stay focused.

"No, it's not that," she said. "It's just that . . . well . . . he's just too low! He can't read!"

I assured her that this was the very reason the child was in a university reading clinic, and that, no matter how "low" he was, she would be able to teach him how to read. And she did!

Sometimes, we have expectations of the way our students should be when they walk into our classrooms. An engagement perspective of assessments helps us to see students in terms of the things they can do over a period of time, which in turn helps us make plans, determine starting points, and specify needs.

Cognitive factors are the mental skills needed to complete the acts of literacy. In order for literacy to be complete, with understanding of print or an articulate written message as the end result, all of these abilities need to be present and working together. What kinds of cognitive abilities are involved in literacy? There are several abilities needed to read and write print. The questions to ask about your students are:

1. How well can the beginning reader manipulate sounds of the language?
2. How well does the beginning reader know the mechanics of print?
3. How well can the student decode unknown words?
4. How well can the student comprehend?
5. How well does the student monitor his own understanding as he reads?
6. How well does the student express his thoughts in writing?

The answers to these questions will help you get a clear picture of your readers, no matter which grade you teach. We'll look at each of these areas of assessment separately.

Assessing Phonemic Awareness

Young children need some understandings about how our language works. Phonemic awareness, which you will learn more about in Chapter 6, is the awareness that young children have about the sounds of language. They instinctively know that spoken words signify meaning, but they also know that words can be manipulated so that additional words result. Phonemic awareness is "an insight about speech itself" (Graves, Juel & Graves, 2001, p. 99). For example, a child who is phonemically aware knows that the word "hat" can be changed to become the word "cat" or even the word "has." This child may also know that "hat" sounds very much like "fat" and "sat" and "bat" and "flat." All of these understandings are important prerequisites to the understanding of letter–sound relationships, which is one of the essential skills used when figuring out unknown words. Listening to and repeating nursery rhymes, nonsense verse, and silly songs delight many children. They often like to play with the language and create rhymes or songs of their own. This is evidence that they are beginning to develop phonemic awareness.

You can cultivate additional evidence of phonemic awareness with the use of a simple informal assessment, called the Yopp-Singer Test of Phoneme Segmentation (Yopp, 1995). This assessment consists of a list of 22 words. The teacher says each word, and asks the child to repeat the word in segments, so that it is broken into each of its phonemes. For example, if the teacher says, "dog," the child must say, "duh," "ah," "guh," indicating the three sounds in the word "dog," which are /d/, /o/, /g/. The teacher uses his own judgment about the need for instruction in this area, based on the number of correct responses given by the child. Figure 4.6 shows the Yopp-Singer Test of Phoneme Segmentation.

Assessing Concepts of Print

Marie Clay, in *Becoming Literate: The Construction of Inner Control* (1991), describes what happens when the teacher of very young children does not make clear what she means when she uses words that are associated with print:

> Suppose a teacher has placed an attractive picture on the wall and has asked her children for a story which she will record under it. They offer the text "Mother is cooking" which the teacher alters slightly to introduce some features she wishes to teach. She writes,
> Mother said,
> "I am baking."
> If the teacher then says, "Now look at our story," 30 percent of her new entrant class will attend to the picture. (p. 141)

When learning to read, the very young need to learn some concepts of things that experienced readers take for granted. Print concepts, such as "letter," "word," "sound," "sentence," "writing," and "picture" need to be pointed out and defined. **Concepts of print** include all of the terms and entities of print that a reader needs to successfully sort out the connections between speech and written language. Additionally, these terms need to be familiar and recognizable so that the child can talk to others about the acts of reading and writing. Harris and Hodges define "print concept development" as "in emergent literacy, the growing recognition that print needs to be arranged in an orderly way to communicate information in reading and writing" (1995, p. 194).

There are several ways to measure your young students' concepts of print. I'll describe them in the next few sections.

Yopp–Singer Test of Phoneme Segmentation

Student's name _____ Date _____

Score (number correct) _____

Directions: Today we're going to play a word game. I'm going to say a word and I want you to break the word apart. You are going to tell me each sound in the word in order. For example, if I say "old," you should say /o/-/l/-/d/." *(Administrator: Be sure to say the sounds, not the letters, in the word.)* Let's try a few together

Practice items: *(Assist the child in segmenting these items as necessary.)*
   ride, go, man

Test items: *(Circle those items that the student correctly segments; incorrect responses may be recorded on the blank line following the item.)*

1. dog _____	12. lay _____
2. keep _____	13. race _____
3. fine _____	14. zoo _____
4. no _____	15. three _____
5. she _____	16. job _____
6. wave _____	17. in _____
7. grew _____	18. ice _____
8. that _____	19. at _____
9. red _____	20. top _____
10. me _____	21. by _____
11. sat _____	22. do _____

Figure 4.6 The Yopp–Singer Test of Phoneme Segmentation.

Source: Yopp, Hallie Kay. (1995, September). A test for assessing phonemic awareness in young children. *The Reading Teacher,* 49(1), 20–29. Reprinted with permission of Hallie Kay Yopp and the International Reading Association. All rights reserved.

Graves, Juel, and Burns Emergent Literacy Assessment

A young reader, in order to be successful at reading, needs to have alphabet knowledge, as well as an understanding of what happens when letters come together. Graves, Juel, and Burns (2001) developed an emergent literacy assessment that can help you determine the youngster's ability to differentiate words. In this assessment tool, the teacher shows the child a picture and its accompanying sentence: "He can run." The teacher reads the sentence aloud while pointing to the picture. Then, the teacher says one of the words in the sentence, and asks the child to repeat it verbally. After that, the student must write the word on a space provided in the test, writing as many letters as he or she can figure out, based on knowledge of letter–sound correspondences. Points are given for each part of the word that the child can reproduce verbally and in writing. Another feature of the test asks the student to point to each word in the sentence as he reads. This helps the teacher determine the student's ability to match spoken words to their printed equivalents—an indication of the concept of word. The test in its entirety, in addition to other useful classroom assessment tools, is available in *Rubrics and Other Tools for Classroom Assessment for Teaching Reading in the 21st Century* (Graves, Juel & Burns, 2001). Morris (cited in Tyner, 2004) offers a similar assessment tool, in which students finger-point as they recite the words on the page of a four-page book.

Clay's Concepts About Print Test

Marie Clay's Concepts About Print test (1993) can help you determine what the child knows about the mechanics of reading, such as moving the eyes from left to right, and differentiating between words. The child is given one of two available books, each of which has errors intentionally placed throughout. These books, titled *Stones* (Clay, 1979) and *Sand* (Clay, 1972), contain pictures and words that are upside down, letters in words that are backwards, and words in a sentence that are in the wrong order. The teacher asks the child to help her read the book. While the child interacts with the book, the teacher checks to see whether he or she notices any of the errors. Questions to ask and record sheets for recording information are in Clay's *An Observation Survey of Early Literacy Achievement* (1993). The two children's books needed for completing the assessment must be obtained separately.

Checklist for Observing Young Children

Figure 4.7 shows a checklist that can be used when observing a young child as she "reads" a book. The checklist is a simple way to determine what a child knows about books. It can be used as soon as you notice that a youngster shows interest in reading, such as when she picks up a book and pretends to read, or listens attentively as you read to her. The age at which this begins varies according to the child, but generally, the checklist can be used with children as young as three years old. Note that the directions indicate that you are to ask the child to choose a book and "share it" with you. The reason for this wording is that some children are acutely aware of the fact that they cannot yet decode individual words phonetically. When asked to read a book, they will point out that they cannot, and may refuse to try. Thus, if you ask the child to simply share the book with you, you may get a more enthusiastic response. This checklist can be used over a period of time to chart growth in reading awareness.

Checklist for Observing Young Children

Directions: Ask the child to choose a book and say, "Please share this book with me." Record his or her behaviors as well.

Reading Awareness Description	
1. The child demonstrates understanding that a book holds meaning.	11. The child matches individually spoken words with the individual written words in the text.
2. The child treats a book differently from the way he treats another object, such as a toy.	12. The child's verbal story or retelling matches the written text.
3. The child holds the book right side up.	13. The child uses "book language" to tell or read the text.
4. The child turns to the beginning of the book.	14. The child phonetically decodes words: most some none
5. The child begins sharing a book on the first page.	15. The child can, when asked, point to individual words.
6. The child moves from left to right through the book.	16. The child can, when asked, point to the beginning of a word on the page.
7. The child moves from left to right on the page.	17. The child can, when asked, point to the end of a word on the page.
8. The child moves across the page and down to the left, moving down the page.	18. The child can, when asked, point to the middle of a word on the page.
9. The child "keeps place" with his finger or some other method of marking.	19. The child can, when asked, point to the beginning of a sentence on the page.
10. The child uses pictures to read or tell the text.	20. The child can, when asked, point to the end of a sentence on the page.

Figure 4.7 A reading awareness checklist to use with beginning readers.

Alphabet Recognition Checklists

Of course, beginning readers must also recognize the letters of the alphabet. The interesting thing about alphabet knowledge is that a youngster does not actually need to know the names of the letters in our English alphabet in order to read. Conceivably, a child could see the written word "hat," and say its verbal equivalent. To accomplish this task, whether by phonetically decoding or through instant recognition, the child would not need to be able to tell you that the first written symbol in this word is the letter "h." As long as he or she can make the sound represented by this little scribble on the page, it would seem that it doesn't matter whether the child can say "aitch" when you point to the "h" and ask him or her to identify it. However, in order for children to be able to converse with others—namely, their teachers, their parents, and their peers—about the mechanics of reading, they must know what names to call all of these written symbols on the page. It is most helpful for a five-year-old to know which one of the symbols in the word "hat" is the "h."

Thus, an alphabet recognition checklist is helpful. Several are available (Clay, 1993; Graves, Juel & Burns, 2001; Morris, cited in Tyner, 2004; Shanker & Ekwall, 2000), and they all ask children to name the letter that is written and shown to them. Figure 4.8 shows directions for an alphabet checklist checklist. Figure 4.9 shows part of a record sheet, as well as two different sets of student pages, printed in different fonts. Some teachers find it useful to assess a child's ability to recognize the alphabet as it is printed in different type faces, because certain letters, such as the "a" and the "g," are reproduced differently, depending on the font. Sometimes children become confused with the differences in appearance of these letters.

Also notice that the assessment contains two components: naming and writing. You can use this checklist to record how well the child can verbally name letters of the alphabet, as well as how well he can reproduce the letters in writing.

Alphabet Recognition Checklist

Directions:

1. Have available the uppercase alphabet recognition sheet and some lined writing paper. Ask the child to write his or her name on the lined paper.
2. Show the uppercase alphabet recognition sheet in the font of your choice. Point to the first letter and ask the student to name it.
3. Ask the child to write the letter.
4. Repeat the procedure for each of the letters on the recognition sheet. Be sure to stay in the same order as shown on the sheet; do not present the alphabet in its usual sequence.
5. Repeat the assessment using the lowercase alphabet recognition sheet in the font of your choice.

Figure 4.8 Alphabet recognition checklist and assessment sheets.

Record Sheet

Child's Name:	Names the Letter		Writes the Letter	
	Uppercase	Lowercase	Uppercase	Lowercase
Aa				
Bb				
Cc				
Dd				
Ee				

Student Uppercase Alphabet Recognition Sheet

W	F	R	T	S	A	M
Q	Y	O	Z	B	C	X
N	L	I	J	E	V	H
D	G	P	U	K		

W	F	R	T	S	A	M
Q	Y	O	Z	B	C	X
N	L	I	J	E	V	H
D	G	P	U	K		

Student Lowercase Alphabet Recognition Sheet

w	f	r	t	s	a	m
q	y	o	z	b	c	x
n	l	i	j	e	v	h
d	g	p	u	k		

w	f	r	t	s	a	m
q	y	o	z	b	c	x
n	l	i	j	e	v	h
d	g	p	u	k		

Figure 4.9 Student recognition sheet.

Assessing Decoding Abilities

Decoding means to "use symbols to interpret a unit that bears meaning" (Beck & Juel, 1992, p. 104). Knowing how to decode unfamiliar words is a vitally important skill for the reader, because this allows children the independence and opportunity to read more widely than children who cannot decode well. Decoding skills lead to automaticity, which, as you learned in Chapter 1, is when the reader knows a word instantly and does not need to think about its construction. Children need to know that letters correspond to sounds in spoken words (Beck & Juel, 1992), and that letters have a relationship with the sounds in printed words (Adams, 1990). There are many formal tests available for determining decoding ability; however, many of them test simple letter–sound correspondence, using pictures. It is important to keep in mind the reason for assessing decoding skills, which is to determine how well children can decode words that are not known. Pictures do not allow for this; nor do familiar words. If a test asks students to decode the word "house," which is already in their reading vocabularies, the test is not assessing their abilities to figure out a word by using what they know about letters and sounds (Shanker & Ekwall, 2000).

Thus, assessments that are most useful for determining your students' true decoding abilities fit the following criteria:

1. Unfamiliar or nonsense words are used; students are asked to read them aloud.
2. Assessment is done individually and privately.
3. Students are asked to show their ability to blend and segment phonemes in a written word or nonsense word.

Names Test

The Names Test (Cunningham, 2005, p. 176) is one such assessment that fits these criteria. Students are shown a list of first and last names that include common phonetic elements. They are asked to read the list of names as if they were taking roll in a classroom. The teacher writes the phonetic spelling for each name that is mispronounced, which offers some idea of the types of phonetic elements that give the student trouble. For example, if a child cannot pronounce the name "Grace," the teacher can conclude that the child might not be familiar with the "gr" blend, or with the "CVCe" phonics generalization. Common patterns can be determined, and instruction planned accordingly.

One disadvantage of using this test is that some names might be familiar to the students, which defeats its purpose. Additionally, the authors could not find names for some common syllables such as "-ion," which limits its usefulness. Another disadvantage, acknowledged by the authors, is the fact that children of diverse backgrounds may find the test difficult because of its lack of ethnic names. The list of names used in this test, available in Cunningham's *Phonics They Use: Words for Reading and Writing* (2005), is shown in Figure 4.10.

El Paso Phonics Survey

The El Paso Phonics Survey (Shanker & Ekwall, 2000) is another assessment that requires students to read unfamiliar words; however, this test uses nonsense words. It is based on the assumption that words consist of two parts—onsets and

Jay Conway	Wendy Swain	Floyd Sheldon
Kimberly Blake	Dee Skidmore	Neal Wade
Cindy Sampson	Troy Whitlock	Thelma Rinehart
Stanley Shaw	Shane Fletcher	Yolanda Clark
Flo Thornton	Bertha Dale	Gus Quincy
Ron Smitherman	Gene Loomis	Patrick Tweed
Bernard Pendergraph	Chuck Hoke	Fred Sherwood
Austin Sheperd	Homer Preston	Ned Westmoreland
Joan Brooks	Ginger Yale	Zane Anderson
Tim Cornell	Glen Spencer	Dean Bateman
Roberta Slade	Grace Brewster	Jake Murphy
Chester Wright	Vance Middleton	

Figure 4.10 The names test.

Source: From Patricia M. Cunningham, *Phonics They Use: Words for Reading and Writing*, 4th ed. Published by Allyn and Bacon, Boston, MA. Copyright © 2005 by Pearson Education. Reprinted by permission of the publisher.

rimes. An **onset** is the first phoneme of a word, such as the "b" in "bat," or the "ch" in "chill. A **rime** is the remainder of the word, or the part that makes it a member of a word family. In my examples, the rime in "bat" is "-at," and the rime in "chill" is "-ill." In the El Paso Phonics Survey, there are 58 nonsense words that begin with consonant units, and all are comprised of the rimes "in," "up," and "am." The student is shown the word that is broken into two parts, and asked to say the first letter, then pronounce the rime, and finally, say the resulting nonsense word that is made when the letters are blended together. For example, one item appears as this:

n   up   nup

The child is expected to say, "n," "up," "nup."

Knowledge of vowel phonemes is also assessed, and the items are used in a similar fashion. The child is asked to say the vowel letter or letters first, then the nonsense word in which the vowel phoneme is heard. For example, one of these items looks like this:

ŏ   sot

The child is expected to say, "short o," "sot."

Extensive directions and a recording sheet are included in the *Ekwall/Shanker Reading Inventory* (2000).

Classroom Decoding Checks

You can create your own simple classroom assessments. One excellent teacher, Nancy Steider, who teaches first grade in Pennsylvania, creates a ten-item assessment every nine weeks (N. Steider, personal communication, March 12, 2002). She makes a list of nonsense words, using onsets that she knows her students have learned, and rimes that she knows are part of their sight vocabulary. She asks them

Teachers can use running records to discover much about the reading processes of their students.

to pronounce the onset first, then the rime, then the entire word. This is a true decoding assessment, because the nonsense words are unfamiliar, yet they contain phonemes that she knows her students have been taught. The assessment for each child takes about a minute. Figure 4.11 shows an example of one of Steider's decoding checks.

Assessing Comprehension

A reader's ability to say the words on the page is just one part of reading. The ability to translate those words to meaning is the remainder of the act of reading, and is the key to success as a reader. Decoding assessments show only half of the picture; in addition, you'll need to assess how well the reader can recognize and understand vocabulary, as well as understand the explicit and implicit messages of the text. I will introduce and discuss three useful assessment tools that can help you do this: running records, miscue analysis, and retelling analysis.

Running Records

It makes sense that the best way to determine how well a student can read is to ask him or her to read. A very powerful assessment tool called the **running record** accomplishes this. Marie Clay designed this assessment tool to be used by the classroom teacher. "The prime purpose of a Running Record is to understand more about how children are using what they know to get to the messages of the text, or in other words, what reading processes they are using" (2000, p. 8). It is designed to assess text difficulty for the student, as well as to give the teacher information about oral reading behaviors, which aids in making instructional decisions. You can determine how well the student recognizes words instantly, as

Classroom Decoding Check

Directions: Ask the child to say the first sound in each of these nonsense words, then the second sound, then the entire blended word. For example, for the nonsense word "drass," the child would say, "druh . . . ah . . . s—s—s— . . . drass." On the spaces provided, write the pronunciation that the child makes.

Phonetic elements:

Digraphs: qu, ch, tch, th

Final consonants: ss, s, b, ff, f, m, p, ck, ll

Short vowels: a, e, i, o, u

r-blends: br, cr, dr, fr, gr, pr, tr

mog _____   druck _____

bram _____   cress _____

chib _____   prell _____

thuss _____   quiff _____

fatch _____   groth _____

quoll _____   shep _____

Figure 4.11 A classroom decoding assessment that matches classroom instruction.

Source: N. Steider, personal communication, 2002.

well as how the student figures out words he or she does not know. Ideally, the running record can be done with any text selection, at any time, with any student who can attempt to read out loud. It is administered on a one-to-one basis with the student, and once you are comfortable with the notations of the record, you can complete it in five to ten minutes. A sample assessment is shown in Appendix B. Directions and scoring sheets are provided in the *Toolkit* booklet.

Miscue Analysis

Based on the oral reading that you record, you can determine trends and consistencies in the student's reading behavior by analyzing her miscues in an assessment called the **miscue analysis**. A **miscue** is anything the student says that is different from what is printed on the page. When you analyze what a student says when reading out loud, comparing it to what is written on the page, you obtain a qualitative analysis, which often reveals that the student is extracting meaning from the page, despite word recognition errors. This analysis helps you become aware of the language functioning of a student who speaks a variation of English or is learning to speak and read English at the same time. You also find out the strength of the student's reading strategies. The idea of miscue analysis came to us from Yetta and Kenneth Goodman more than 25 years ago. Recently, they said that readers' mistakes reveal much more about readers' capabilities than their incapabilities, and that "miscues are the windows on language processes at work" (2004, p. 638).

Modifying Instruction for

ELL

Self-Assessment of Retelling

GRADE LEVEL: 3–5

- **Objective**

  After reading *The Skirt* (Soto, 1992), the student will retell its story elements and assess his or her own ability to describe each element.

- **Preparation**

  On index cards, write each of the story elements, one per card: setting, characters, problem, events, and resolution. Prepare a story-retelling checklist like the one shown below.

- **Materials**

  - *The Skirt,* by Gary Soto (1992)
  - Items related to Mexican dancing: musical instruments, articles of clothing, photographs
  - Retell checklist for each student
  - Drawing supplies

- **Introduction**

  1. Meet with the student individually.
  2. Prepare to read *The Skirt* by talking about the title and cover picture. Activate prior knowledge about Mexican dances and the colorful skirts women dancers wear. If possible, encourage the student to talk about any personal experiences. Show and talk about some of the items related to Mexican dances, such as articles of clothing, musical instruments, or photographs.
  3. Ask the student to make predictions about the story and write them down on a chart.
  4. Show the student a retelling checklist, similar to the one shown below. Remind the student to look for the elements as he or she reads.

Story Retelling Checklist

Setting	I know the setting of the story.	During Reading _____	After Reading _____
Characters	I know the most important character in the story.	During Reading _____	After Reading _____
	I know the other characters in the story.	During Reading _____	After Reading _____
Problem	I know the problem in the story.	During Reading _____	After Reading _____
Events	I know how the character tries to solve the problem.	During Reading _____	After Reading _____
Resolution	I know how the problem was solved.	During Reading _____	After Reading _____
What I Think	I can think about this story and tell others what I think.	During Reading _____	After Reading _____

Modifications for ELL are printed in color.

● Guided Reading

5. Read the story, stopping at appropriate places to talk about the elements. Refer to the retelling checklist and check off the elements in the "During Reading" box, as she finds them and verbalizes them.

6. As each element is found, give the student an index card. Write the name of the element on the front of the card. On the back, ask the student to draw the element. For example, the character card will look like this:

Front	Back
Characters	Picture of Miata and Ana

● After Reading

7. Putting the retelling checklist out as a reminder, ask the student to retell the story, using the sequence of elements on the checklist. If necessary, pull out the pictured story structure cards that the student created, to help him or her recall important parts of the story. Check off the "After Reading" portions of the checklist.

8. Talk with the student about the retelling, and put the retelling checklist and cards in the student's portfolio. If the student had difficulty remembering the elements, use sticky notes the next time he or she reads a book. Mark the pages with each of these elements and ask the student to refer back to the book as necessary while retelling.

The analysis is based on the student's use of cueing systems. As you learned in Chapter 1, readers use the four cueing systems to figure out meaning from the print on the page. The reader determines meaning based on graphophonological, syntactical, semantic, and pragmatic cues. By completing the miscue analysis, you can determine which of these cues is most supporting the reader.

To see what miscue analysis can do for you, look at this sentence, taken from Marc Brown's *Arthur's Family Vacation* (1993). Let's imagine that you ask a student, Tanya, to read a portion of this book for a running record. One sentence in the book reads:

For the next few days, it rained and rained, but Arthur didn't mind.

Tanya reads the sentence aloud, and says this:

"For the next four days, it rained and rained, but Arthur didn't mind."

Miscue analysis tells you that Tanya is getting some clues from all of the cueing systems. Her miscue is the word "four," which she says instead of the word "few." Semantic cues indicate to her that the word must be one that connotes a number and describes the word "days," and she uses a word that does just that. Graphophonological cues tell her that the word she must say begins with the letter "f," and she obviously knows the sound represented by that letter. The remaining letters in the word, however, she ignores. Thus, Tanya's miscue indicates to us that she is deriving meaning from the page, and has used a miscue that probably will not inhibit her understanding of the print. The word "four" makes sense in this sentence, and will most likely not have a negative affect on her comprehension of the whole story.

Let's look at another student's miscue. Mitchell reads the sentence this way:

"For the new days, it ran and ran, but Arthur didn't mind."

Mitchell's miscues reveal much about his use of clues from the page as he reads. The words "next" and "few" seem to run together for him; thus producing the word "new." He pronounced the word "rained" as "ran," which is visually similar to the word "rained." Thus, Mitchell seems to be relying on graphophonological cues. These miscues will probably affect his comprehension, because while they are visually similar, they are not semantically similar to the words that the author uses.

Other types of miscues reveal important information about the reader. For example, when a reader makes a miscue, pauses, and then corrects him- or herself, this is called a self-correction. Use of a self-correction indicates something you hope all students are doing—deriving meaning from the page. Suppose Mitchell had stopped himself after saying the word "ran," and corrected himself, saying, "rained." This step would indicate that he was asking himself as he read, "Does this make sense?" His self-monitoring ability would be evident, which is an important strategy for readers to cultivate.

Retelling Analysis

Apart from assessing the child's accuracy with words, you need to know how well he understands what he reads. A **retelling analysis** is a "viable alternative to teacher follow-up questions" (Routman, 1991, p. 323) that allows the student to tell what he remembers from his reading. I prefer retellings to teacher questioning as an informal assessment, because the child guides this assessment. You can truly determine what the child remembers from the reading, as well as the ability to sequence the details, and the ability to include all the story elements or main ideas of the text. After the child reads aloud, ask him or her to retell the story or the text, as if telling it to someone who has never before read the book. As he or she retells, record all of the remembered details and then prompt for more, if necessary.

Some children are uncomfortable with retelling because they are accustomed to answering teacher-directed questions, and are unsure of what to do when they must generate thoughts about the text on their own. That makes retelling even more important for them, because they are "in charge of telling in their own words what they have understood" (Routman, 1991, p. 323). This technique helps them develop confidence and autonomy as readers who think about their own reading. Retelling is proactive, not reactive, in that children are told before reading that they will be asked to retell the story. Thus, they can begin thinking about the text before they read, rather than waiting until after reading and reacting to the teacher's questions. Hoyt (1999) offers some excellent suggestions for using retelling analysis. Additionally, the *Toolkit* provides two checklists for retelling analysis.

Matching Readers to Texts

One of the most important things you will do is help your students find books that fit their abilities and interests. A running record will reveal the student's word recognition ability, which is the number of words pronounced just as they are printed on the page. This number, called the *word recognition rate,* is helpful in determining a comfortable reading level for the child. To help you understand the concept of reading levels, let's look at three kinds of reading materials: independent, instructional, and frustrational. Each of these levels is summarized in Figure 4.12.

When your student can pick up a book, read it fluently, understand it, and personally react to it, without help, the book is at the "independent level" for that student. Generally, this means that he or she can recognize about 95% or more of the words in the text; however, an important consideration is the student's interest. In order for the text to be one that the child can truly read independently, the child needs to be engaged as he or she reads it. The child needs to be interested enough in the book to react personally to it. Most of the time, students choose this book on their own. He can say of this book, "I can—and I want to—read this text by myself."

Books that are just a little bit too hard to tackle alone fall in the instructional level. These are books in which your students can read about 90% to 94% of the words with no help. These books would not be ideal for reading independently. Instead, they would be the ones that you use in teaching lessons about

Text Difficulty Level

Independent Level ("I can read this text by myself.") This is the type of text desired for sustained silent reading in the classroom, or reading for pleasure at home.	95% or higher word recognition accuracy, and the retelling: • was full and detailed. • was mostly unassisted. • was correct. • included personal connections or reflections.
Instructional Level ("I can read this text with help.") This text is used in guided reading lessons.	90%–94% word recognition accuracy, and the retelling: • was partial, but satisfactory. • needed to be prompted for about half of the details. • was accurate after questioning or prompting. • was not independently done; the child needed guidance.
Frustrational Level ("This book is not for me right now.") This text would be more appropriate, depending on interest, for read-alouds by the teacher.	Below 90% word recognition accuracy, and the retelling: • was fragmented. • was confusing. • was incomplete; important details were missing. • was indicative of misunderstanding or difficulty with the selection.

Figure 4.12 Text difficulty levels based on word accuracy and retelling ability.

reading. Typically, you choose these books for your students. Often, they are valuable for meeting certain objectives that you have. Or, they are simply good books that offer a good read, but with which your students will need some support. Your students can say of these books, "I can read this text with help."

Books at the frustrational level are too hard for your students to decode. Attempting to read them alone would be a frustrating task—thus their label. Word recognition is below 90%. However, many times, these books are highly interesting to your students. Keep in mind that children need to listen to good books and to see a model of reading. So these are the books that you will need to read to your students. They can say of these books, "This book is one I can listen to right now. I can read it later."

Sometimes it is quite easy to determine the difficulty level of a book. Many publishers tell you; all you have to do is look on the front or back cover and find a grade level. For example, HarperTrophy, a division of HarperCollins Publishers, publishes books under the label "An I Can Read Book," and the grade level for which the book is most appropriate is printed on a top corner of the cover of the book. Bantam Doubleday Dell Publishers publishes the Bank Street Ready-to-Read series of books, which are categorized according to grade levels. Scholastic Books offers the "Hello Reader!" set of books, which show the age and grade that would most likely use them. Some Scholastic Book company books are printed with a label on the back cover of the book, on one of the bottom corners. The label "RL," followed by a number, represents the "reading level" of the book, which is its approximate grade level. Random House also has sets of leveled books, and has had the label "I Can Read It All By Myself—Beginner Books" on its Dr. Seuss books (as well as others) for more than 40 years.

Grade levels of books are most often determined by the difficulty of the vocabulary in the book, as well as the difficulty of the sentence structure. Generally, shorter words and fewer sentences are easier to read. This is the premise of a formula for determining the **readability** of a book. There have been several readability formulas available over the years; one is the Fry Readability formula (Fry, 1977, 2002). It is a graph that determines the approximate grade level that matches the difficulty of the book, based on word length and number of sentences. The Fry Readability formula yields a grade level number based on the number of syllables and the number of sentences in passages of the text. When you compute the readability of a book, and derive a grade level, you can assume that it is approximately appropriate for an average reader who is in that grade in school. This formula and others like it are objective measures of readability, and do not account for more subjective measures such as the interests of your students or their motivation to read. Proper nouns, such as Anastasia, Encyclopedia Brown, or Benjamin Franklin, can increase the grade level score of your text, even though the content of the book might be of lower readability. Moreover, the Fry Readability formula does not work well for books for younger children, because it is based on an average of three 100-word counts. Most books for beginning readers do not have that many words. Thus, the formula is most useful for chapter books. See Figure 4.13 for the Fry Readability graph.

Crawford created a readability formula for Spanish text (Temple, Ogle, Crawford & Freppon, 2005, p. 530). This formula works on the same premise as the Fry Readability graph. The teacher counts the number of syllables and sentences in the first hundred words of the Spanish text, and determines the approximate grade level of the text.

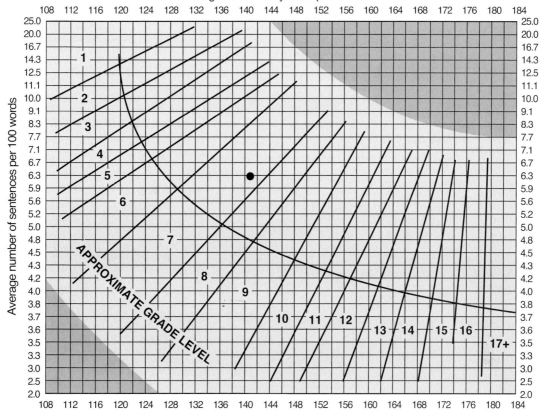

Average number of syllables per 100 words

DIRECTIONS: Randomly select 3 one hundred word passages from a book or an article. Plot average number of syllables and average number of sentences per 100 words on graph to determine the grade level of the material. Choose more passages per book if great variability is observed and conclude that the book has uneven readability. Few books will fall in gray area but when they do grade level scores are invalid.

Count proper nouns, numerals and initializations as words. Count a syllable for each symbol. For example, "1945" is 1 word and 4 syllables and "IRA" is 1 word and 3 syllables.

EXAMPLE:

	SYLLABLES	SENTENCES
1st Hundred Words	124	6.6
2nd Hundred Words	141	5.5
3rd Hundred Words	158	6.8
AVERAGE	141	6.3

READABILITY 7th GRADE (see dot plotted on graph)

Figure 4.13 The Fry Readability graph.

Source: Fry, E. (2002). Readability versus leveling. *The Reading Teacher,* 56(3), 286–291.

Other ways of determining the suitability for books have been developed more recently. Published lists of **leveled books** are available, including two by Fountas and Pinnell: *Matching Books to Readers: Using Leveled Books in Guided Reading K–3* (1999), and *Guiding Readers and Writers Grades 3–6* (2001). Fountas and Pinnell describe "hard texts," "easy texts," and "'just right' texts"; the latter is the type of text teachers need to use with students when instructing them (1999, pp. 2–3). These books are just a little too difficult to use independently, but can be read easily with support from the teacher. Fountas and Pinnell also describe five categories of readers: emergent, early, transitional, self-extending, and advanced. They explain how books are leveled according to their characteristics, so that each group of readers would be matched with books that are suitable for their needs and developmental stages. For example, books for early readers would have larger font size, a greater number of pictures, a simpler theme, and a simple narrative point of view. Characteristics that are considered are:

1. Length
2. Print
3. Page layout
4. Punctuation
5. Illustrations
6. Content
7. Themes
8. Ideas
9. Organization of narrative texts (fiction)
10. Organization of expository texts (nonfiction)
11. Perspective
12. Language structure
13. Literary language or devices
14. Sophistication of vocabulary
15. Number and range of words

In both of the books mentioned earlier, Fountas and Pinnell list hundreds of books and their levels, and all of these characteristics are considered when leveling the books.

An excellent source that gives an honest appraisal and a practical explanation of leveling books is Calkins's *The Art of Teaching Reading*, Chapter 7, "Teaching Readers Within a Leveled Classroom Library" (2001, pp. 119–135). Additionally, several web sites can help:

> studentview.org/instruct-svcs/booklist/home.htm
> registration.beavton.k12.or.us/lbdb/
> www.pps.k12.or.us/curriculum/literacy/leveled_books/
> www.geocities.com/teachingwithheart/levelbooks.html
> www.pps.k12.or.us/instruction-c/literacy/leveled_books/
> users.oasisol.com/daireme/book.htm
> www.expage.com/page/kikiteachersleveledbooklinks
> www.leveledbooks.com/booksearch.html

When you use the running record, you'll select a book that, based on your best guess, is not too easy or too hard for this child, choose a passage of about 150 words, and complete the assessment. Once the student has finished reading, you can determine how well that piece of text "fits" him or her, as well as some valuable information about what he or she does to decode unknown words and monitor understanding. At that point, you can make instructional decisions. For example, let's say that the child reads a selection that has a readability of about second grade level. If the child can accurately read 95% of the words in that passage, clearly retell the passage in detail with personal meaning attached, and self-correct most of the word recognition errors, then the child is able to read second grade materials independently.

Another good way to match readers to texts is with an **informal reading inventory**. This assessment tool is commercially available. Some excellent ones are listed in Figure 4.14, including one that is a bilingual reading inventory for grades K–12. An inventory consists of a set of graded passages. The teacher determines the grade level that would be a comfortable place to begin, and asks the student to read the passage aloud. While the student reads, the teacher records errors. Afterwards, the teacher asks a few comprehension questions (usually four of them) about the passage. Based on the number of words recognized, as well as the number of correctly answered questions, the teacher determines the level at which the student would be most comfortable for instruction as well as for independent reading.

You can also make your own informal reading inventory (IRI) by selecting passages from graded basal reading anthologies and writing four comprehension questions for each. If you have Spanish-speaking students, you may want to create an IRI in Spanish. Crawford's Readability formula for Spanish texts will be helpful for this (Temple, Ogle, Crawford & Freppon, 2005, p. 530).

One effective way to use the informal reading inventory is to determine the student's listening capacity. In this assessment, the teacher selects the graded passage that corresponds to the student's current grade level, reads it aloud to the student, and then asks the comprehension questions. Because children can comprehend what they listen to better than what they read, the listening capacity level gives you an idea of their capacity for comprehending text in English. Typically, students can comprehend a passage that is at their grade level or higher, even if they cannot read it.

Crawford (2004) suggests using the listening capacity level as a measure of "readiness" for English language learners. For example, suppose you have a third grade student who is learning English and can read in his native language. Read a third grade IRI passage to him, and ask four comprehension questions. If the student answers three of the four questions correctly, then he is ready to begin instruction in third grade reading materials in English.

English-Espanol Reading Inventory for the Classroom (Flynt & Cooter, 1999)
Informal Reading Inventory, Sixth Edition (Burns & Roe, 2002)
Qualitative Reading Inventory—3 Third Edition (Leslie & Caldwell, 2000)
The Stieglitz Informal Reading Inventory: Assessing Reading Behaviors from Emergent to Advanced Levels, Third Edition (Stieglitz, 2001)

Figure 4.14 Informal reading inventories.

Assessing Metacognition

Have you ever been reading a book—perhaps a textbook like this one—and suddenly stopped reading because you realized that you did not understand the words anymore? Perhaps you were doing what I call "reading without really reading," or calling out the words to yourself, without fully understanding what the author was trying to say. If you caught yourself doing this and stopped in your tracks, then your metacognition was at work. **Metacognition** is the ability of students to monitor their own thinking while they read. It is important for you to know how well your students can monitor their own reading, because good readers are able to do this, and poor readers are not.

Observing your younger readers as they read is also important for determining metacognition abilities. You can make anecdotal notes about your students' behaviors when they come to words they do not know, when they mispronounce words, or when they make several repetitions as they read. The running record is an excellent way to record students' reading behaviors. The "self-correction rate" is indicative of the student's ability to recognize his or her oral reading errors and correct them without help. Young children who are skilled at reading are far better at doing this than those who are struggling with reading (Paris, Lipson & Wixson, 1994). (See the *Toolkit* for further information.)

Think-Alouds

A strategy that is useful for determining metacognitive abilities is the student think-aloud. This strategy asks students to stop at certain places in the text and think out loud, saying what makes sense and what does not, as well as explaining the strategies that they use as they try to make sense of the text. According to Oster, "readers' thoughts might include commenting on or questioning the text, bringing their prior knowledge to bear, or making inferences and predictions. These comments reveal readers' weaknesses as well as their strengths as comprehenders and allow the teacher to assess their needs in order to plan more effective instruction" (2001, p. 64). To use this strategy as an assessment, first list the kinds of things that readers "should be thinking about all the time while reading" (p. 65), such as:

1. Information about characters or story that they think is important
2. Predictions about the characters' actions or the story
3. Questions they have about the characters or story
4. Personal reactions about the characters or story

Then, model the think-aloud, using a selection from a piece of literature in which you show the students how you grasp understanding of the passage. You will find numerous examples of mental modeling, which is when the teacher thinks aloud, in Chapter 10 of this book. After modeling, have the students talk about the kinds of comments that you made in your mental model. One way to reinforce this strategy is to write down your thoughts and give them a copy of your notes. Then, help them categorize the sentences according to the type of information you are using in the mental model. Next, do a think-aloud together as a group. Read one sentence aloud at a time, and ask students for comments about the text, identifying them according to the categories that you listed, and writing them on the board or overhead. Finally, have pairs of students practice think-alouds together with the next two paragraphs in the passage you have chosen, and write down their comments to share.

Once your students have learned the think-aloud procedure, you can use it as an assessment of their metacognitive abilities. Think-aloud comments can be written down so that you can save them and read them later; this step eliminates the need to be everywhere at once in your classroom as the children read. They reveal information about the strength of your readers' prior knowledge, vocabulary understanding, ability to interpret, and ability to gather important information.

Metacomprehension Strategy Index

If you desire a more formal assessment tool for determining metacognition, try the Metacomprehension Strategy Index, or the MSI, created by Schmitt (1990). Designed for use with middle and upper elementary children, this questionnaire measures readers' awareness of strategies to use when their comprehension breaks down. It is a 25-item multiple-choice survey, which asks questions about what readers do before, during, and after they read stories. For example, one item asks, "Before I begin reading, it's a good idea to . . ." (Schmitt, 1990, p. 459), and a choice of four answers are given. The correct answer, "Read the title to see what the story is about," is indicative of a previewing strategy that aids in comprehension. Directions for scoring, as well as reliability information, are given in the March 1990 edition of *The Reading Teacher.*

Assessing Writing

Reading and writing processes are reciprocal. According to Rosenblatt, "the parallels in the reading and writing processes . . . and the nature of the transaction between author and reader make it reasonable to expect that the teaching of one can affect the student's operations in the other" (2004, p. 1,388). Chapters 9 and 13 will show you many ways to connect reading with writing instruction, and involve your students in authentic purposes for writing. I will show you the **process approach,** which is a method of teaching writing that mirrors the way true authors write. When writing for authentic purposes and genuine audiences, your students will need to articulate themselves clearly, using appropriate voice, acknowledging an audience, developing a pleasing writing style, and being courteous to readers by using conventional punctuation and spelling. Spandel (2001) outlines the Six Traits model of assessing writing, in which the teacher evaluates students' writing in these areas: (1) ideas and content, (2) organization, (3) voice, (4) word choice, (5) sentence fluency, and (6) conventions. Spandel's *Creating Writers Through 6-Trait Writing Assessment and Instruction* (2001) is an excellent source for direction on how to assess writing. Additionally, Spandel offers a thorough explanation of how to help your students assess themselves as they revise their work. Appendix B shows a partial sample rubric adapted from the Six Traits model to be used in first grade. The *Toolkit for Teachers* (Nettles, 2006) includes more rubrics.

Home–
School Connection

A Parent Letter

This letter is used by Cathy Hayden, a third grade teacher in Pennsylvania. ●

Children can participate in family conferences with the teacher.

Dear Family,

Our conference is scheduled for
_____. Could you please respond to this brief list of questions and return this note to school with your child on _____ to help me better prepare for our conference?

Additionally, I would like to have something to share about your child with his or her classmates, following our conference. Although I can certainly discuss some of the positive views of your child that you and I have in common, I would like to have learned "something special" about your child at our conference. So, could you share something special with me about your child that I don't already know? For example, perhaps you could tell me about an athletic accomplishment, a hobby, participation in Scouts or a club, a special story about a relative or pet. I welcome any picture, trophy, or other memorabilia that you may have to accompany this information.

Your child is welcome to attend our conference. In fact, you and your child might enjoy sharing the "something special" together! I look forward to meeting with you. Thank you!

Sincerely,

Mrs. Cathy Hayden

Please complete, clip, and return by _____.

1. How does your child feel about school?

2. What concerns do we need to be certain to address in our conference?

3. What can I do to make your child feel more comfortable or be more successful in school?

Summary: Assessing Your Students

The reflective teacher thinks about students constantly while teaching. This habit makes sense, because if the teacher loses sight of his students, there is no point in teaching. Getting wrapped up in the mechanics, strategies, theories, and materials of teaching can cause us to forget why we're here.

As you plan, think about how you will assess. When you teach a lesson, determine how well the students learned what you wanted them to learn. When you make decisions about materials to use, strategies to teach, and instructional methods to use, consider what you already know about your students, based on what you've learned through observations and the simple assessment methods that you learned in this chapter. The Reviewing the Big Picture box lists the assessment tools that were shown or described in this chapter, along with their alignment with standards.

Remember, teaching is not about the teacher. It's about the students. That's why getting to know the nature of the children with whom you work is so important.

Technology Resources

- **www.fdlrssprings.org/instructreslinks.htm#topinstructreslinks** This web site for Florida Diagnostic and Learning Resources Systems offers several links to sites that provide information about readability.

- **www.plainlanguagenetwork.org/stephens/readability.html** This web page explains readability formulas from the writer's perspective.

- **school.discovery.com/schrockguide/fry/fry.html** Sponsored by Discovery School. com, Kathy Schrock's Guide for Educators gives a nice explanation of the Fry Readability graph.

- **pathways.thinkport.org/resources/reading.cfm** Maryland Public Television sponsors this web site, called "Pathways to Freedom: Maryland and the Underground Railroad." Click on "Reading Tips" for information on matching books to readers as well as the use of readability formulas.

- **www.man.canterbury.ac.nz/courseinfo/AcademicWriting/Flesch.htm** Rudolf Flesch, in this article called "How to Write in Plain English," describes his Flesch Readability formula.

expect the world

The New York Times
nytimes.com

Themes of the Times

Expand your knowledge of the concepts discussed in this chapter by reading current and historical articles from the *New York Times* by visiting the "Themes of the Times" section of the Companion Web Site.

Reviewing the Big Picture

Assessment Tools

Assessment Tool	Source	Grade Level	Type of Information Assessed	IRA Standards	INTASC Principles	NAEYC Standards	ACEI/NCATE Standards
Questions to ask about reading relationships	Calkins, *The Art of Teaching Reading*, 2001	K–2, 3–5, 6–8	Records students' perceptions of reading with interview questions.	3.1, 4.1, 4.4	8	3	4
Reading and writing behaviors to observe	Calkins, *The Art of Teaching Reading*, 2001	K–2, 3–5, 6–8	Records the manner in which the reader approaches reading, including physical factors and apparent comfort with reading.	3.1, 4.1, 4.4	8	3	4
Interest inventories questions	Nettles, this text	K–2, 3–5, 6–8	Determines interests, hobbies, likes, dislikes, leisure-time activities of students.	3.1, 4.1, 4.4	8	3	4
Ways to survey interests	Nettles, this text	K–2, 3–5, 6–8	Shows several formats for use with interest inventories, including the glyph (Bamberger & Hughes, adapted by Murray).	3.1, 4.1, 4.4	8	3	4
Elementary reading attitude survey	McKenna & Kear, *The Reading Teacher*, 1990	K–2, 3–5, 6–8	Measures attitudes toward reading by using a survey that primary grade students fill out independently by circling pictures of the cartoon character Garfield.	3.1, 4.1, 4.4	8	3	4
Writing attitude survey	Kear, Coffman, McKenna & Ambrioso, *The Reading Teacher*, 2000	K–2, 3–5, 6–8	Measures attitudes toward writing by using a survey that all ages of elementary students can complete by circling pictures of the cartoon character Garfield.	3.1, 4.1, 4.4	8	3	4
Reader self-perception scale	Henk & Melnick, *The Reading Teacher*, 1995	3–5, 6–8	Measures how older readers perceive themselves as readers by using a survey in which students rate their agreement with statements about reading.	3.1, 4.1, 4.4	8	NA	4

Assessment	Source	Grade	Description				
Writer Self-Perception Scale	Bottomley, Henk & Melnick, *The Reading Teacher*, 1997–1998	3–5, 6–8	Measures how older students perceive themselves as writers by using a survey in wh ch students rate their agreement with statements about different aspects of writing.	3.1, 4.1, 4.4	NA	3	4
Motivation to Read Profile	Gambrell, Palmer, Codling & Mazzoni, *The Reading Teacher*, 1996	3–5, 6–8	Measures students' self-concepts as readers and their perception of the value of reading using a survey and a conversational interview.	3.1, 4.1, 4.4	NA	3	4
Yopp-Singer Segmentation Test	Yopp, *The Reading Teacher*, 1995	K–2, 3–5	Measures phonemic awareness by reading words to the child, who must repeat it by "stretching it out" and saying each of its phonemes.	3.1, 3.2, 3.3, 3.4	8	3	4
Emergent literacy assessment	Graves, Juel & Burns, *Rubrics and Other Tools for Classroom Assessment for Teaching Reading in the 21st Century*, 2001	K–2	Measures ability to differentiate words by asking students to reproduce them and by asking students to point to words as they are read.	3.1, 3.2, 3.3, 3.4	8	3	4
Concepts about Print Test	Clay, *An Observation Survey of Early Literacy Achievement*, 1993	K–2	Measures awareness of the conventions of print by asking the child to "read" a specially prepared book; the child's ability to point out errors and nonconventional items in the text are recorded.	3.1, 3.2, 3.3, 3.4	8	3	4
Checklist for observing young children	Nettles, this text	K–2	Measures awareness of print conventions by asking the student to "share" a book with the teacher.	3.1, 3.2, 3.3, 3.4	8	3	4

Reviewing the Big Picture (continued)

Assessment Tool	Source	Grade Level	Type of Information Assessed	IRA Standards	INTASC Principles	NAEYC Standards	ACEI/NCATE Standards
Alphabet recognition checklist	Nettles, this text	K–2	Measures ability to recognize upper- and lowercase letters in two different fonts.	3.1, 3.2, 3.3, 3.4	8	3	4
The Names Test	Cunningham, *Phonics They Use*, 2005	K–2, 3–5	Measures decoding ability by asking students to read a list of first and last names.	3.1, 3.2, 3.3, 3.4	8	3	4
El Paso Phonics Survey	Shanker & Ekwall, *Ekwall/Shanker Reading Inventory*, 2000	K–2, 3–5	Measures decoding ability by asking students to read a list of nonsense words.	3.1, 3.2, 3.3, 3.4	8	3	4
Classroom decoding checks	Steider, this text	K–2, 3–5	Measures student's ability to blend and segment, using nonsense words that reflect word families.	3.1, 3.2, 3.3, 3.4	8	3	4
Running records	Clay, 2000	K–2, 3–5	Measures word recognition in context and ways that the reader processes print. Determines independent, instructional, and frustrational reading levels.	3.1, 3.2, 3.3, 3.4	8	3	4
Miscue analysis	Goodman & Goodman, 2004	K–2, 3–5	Measures use of cueing systems; shows ability to self-correct miscues.	3.1, 3.2, 3.3, 3.4	8	3	4
Retelling analysis	Hoyt, 1999; Routman, 1991	K–2, 3–5, 6–8	Measures ability to recall important ideas in text and retell them.	3.1, 3.2, 3.3, 3.4	8	3	4

Fry Readability formula	Fry, *The Reading Teacher*, 2002	K–2, 3–5, 6–8	Uses a graph to plot the approximate grade level of reading materials based on number of sentences and number of syllables in 100 words.	3.1, 3.2, 3.3, 3.4	8	3	4
Spanish Readability formula	Temple, Ogle, Crawford & Freppon, 2005	K–2, 3–5, 6–8	Uses a graph to plot the approximate grade level of reading materials written in Spanish based on number of sentences and number of syllables in 100 words.	3.1, 3.2, 3.3, 3.4	8	3	4
Informal reading inventories	Flynt & Cooter, 1999; Burns & Roe, 2002; Leslie & Caldwell, 2000; Stieglitz, 2001	K–2, 3–5, 6–8	Students read increasingly difficult graded passages and answer comprehension questions until they are at the frustrational level. This determines the match of text with reader.	3.1, 3.2, 3.3, 3.4	8	3	4
Think-alouds	Oster, 2001	3–5, 6–8	Students voice their thoughts as they read, and the teacher records notes about their metacognitive abilities.	3.1, 3.2, 3.3, 3.4	NA	3	4
Metacomprehension Strategy Index	Schmitt, *The Reading Teacher*, 1990	3–5, 6–8	A multiple-choice survey of students' reading habits and behaviors.	3.1, 3.2, 3.3, 3.4	NA	3	4
Writing Assessments	Spandel (2001)	K–2, 3–5, 6–8	Rubrics are used for analyzing students' writing with six traits.	3.1, 3.2, 3.3, 3.4	8	3	4

5

Understanding the Nature of Fiction and Nonfiction

*E*verybody knows the story of the Three Little Pigs. Or at least they think they do. But I'll let you in on a little secret. Nobody knows the real story, because nobody has ever heard *my* side of the story. I'm the wolf. Alexander T. Wolf. You can call me Al. I don't know how this whole Big Bad Wolf thing got started, but it's all wrong.

The True Story of the Three Little Pigs! (Scieszka, 1989)

Robert, age 9

If you are going to teach children how to read books, it makes sense to know your books—to know, as Alexander T. Wolf said, the "real story." This chapter will help you understand the unique features of **fiction** and **nonfiction,** and how these understandings can inform your teaching. Getting your students "hooked" on books requires knowledge of the types of books that are available to them. To facilitate their understanding of books, it is necessary to teach them about some ways in which authors typically organize both fiction and nonfiction writing. This knowledge makes books more user-friendly; it also allows your readers to develop expectations for books, which enables them to make logical predictions before they read and to monitor themselves as they read. Because of the unique nature of two different broad categories of text, fiction and nonfiction, I will discuss each separately in this chapter.

The Nature of Stories

Knowing the unique features of stories helps you to teach reading more effectively. It's like teaching someone how to bake an apple pie. Of course, it's helpful to know the ingredients necessary for making a pie, such as flour, shortening, and salt for the crust, and apples, cinnamon, sugar, and nutmeg for the filling. But a more proficient pie baker also knows that certain kinds of shortening make flakier crusts, and certain types of apples make tastier fillings. So let's look at the nature of stories.

Think about what makes stories interesting to you by answering the Personal Reflection questions.

Personal Reflection

- What is your favorite piece of fiction? What do you like most about it?
- What was your favorite children's storybook? Why was it your favorite?

What makes a good story? The answer to that question is as varied as the number of people who would attempt to answer it, because everyone has his or her own idea of what makes stories interesting. However, stories generally fit a pattern. This pattern can help you teach your students how to read fiction, because when you show them what stories are and how they look and sound and feel, they know what to expect when they read them. These are the elements that most stories share: characters, settings, problems, events, resolutions, and themes.

Characters

Characters make us love stories. They are why we keep returning to certain books, and why we seek out more books about them. We can identify with certain characters, because we see ourselves in their thoughts and actions. Some characters make us laugh; others make us cry. Characters are the reason we become "hooked" on some books. They give meaning to the term "aesthetic response," because we become emotionally involved in reading stories through characters.

Characters carry the action in a story. They are the personalities that cause—or react to—the action in the story. Stuff happens to characters. Their reactions and decisions make the story go in one direction or another. Without characters, stories would be mere descriptions or narratives of events.

One of the most popular stories in children's literature is *Tales of a Fourth Grade Nothing* by Judy Blume (1972). Peter is the main character, and the title of the book is a humorous play on how he is portrayed. Fudge is Peter's younger brother, whose pesky antics cause many confrontations between the two brothers. Children enjoy Blume's writing style, because she uses much dialogue, making the characters seem all the more real. Moreover, in this book, Peter is the first-person narrator. It seems as if Peter is talking to the reader, because Blume wrote the narration in the manner of a fourth grader describing his little brother. In this excerpt, Fudge has lost his two front teeth in a playground accident. Notice how Peter's thoughts and dialogue make him seem real.

> I started calling him Fang because when he smiles all you can see are the top two side teeth next to the big space. So, it looks like he has fangs.
>
> My mother didn't like that. "I want you to stop calling him Fang," she told me.
>
> "What should I call him?" I asked. "Farley Drexel?"
>
> "Just plain Fudge will be fine," my mother said.
>
> "What's wrong with Farley Drexel?" I asked. "How come you named him that if you don't like it?"
>
> "I like it fine," my mother said. "But right now we call him Fudge. Not Farley . . . not Drexel . . . and *not* Fang!"
>
> "What's wrong with Fang?" I asked. "I think it sounds neat."
>
> "Fang is an insult!"
>
> "Oh . . . come on, Mom! He doesn't even know what a fang is!"
>
> "But *I* know, Peter. And *I* don't like it."
>
> "Okay . . . okay . . ." I promised never to call my brother Fang again.
>
> But secretly, whenever I look at him, I think it. *My brother, Fang Hatcher!* Nobody can stop me from thinking. My mind is my own. (Blume, 1972, pp. 40–41)

Peter is a strong character whom eight-to-ten-year-olds readily enjoy meeting. Peter is just like most children; he has conflicts with siblings, friends, parents, and school. Blume makes Peter come alive through his actions and reactions; she includes very few descriptions of him. That is what makes characters strong—their dialogue, their narration, and their actions.

One rule of thumb for determining whether the characters in the story are strong: If you took out that character and his traits, would the story be the same? Would it be as interesting? If the story would not be the same without the main character, then the character is strong enough to carry the story.

There are a few teaching strategies that are helpful for showing your students the importance of characters. Jim McIntyre, a middle school teacher in New York, uses a teaching strategy called the Body Map. This teaching tool is a way of recording personal responses to the story using pictures of the main character in the story and the student as prompts. See Figure 5.1 for a description of this motivating strategy.

Body Map

1. After students have read a book that has a strong main character, give them each a large piece of paper. Ask them to fold their papers in half and have them draw a full-body picture of the main character on the left side of the fold.

2. To respond to the book, show them the body map key shown below, and have students write or draw symbols to represent the character's thoughts, actions, personality traits, and events.

3. Next, tell students to draw a full-body picture of themselves on the right side of the fold.

4. Using the same key, have them draw or write symbols to represent the categories for their own lives, which allows them to make a personal connection to the main character.

5. Students can explain verbally or in writing how they are similar to and different from the main character.

6. You can adapt this activity to include fewer categories. Use only the categories that correspond with the book that the students read.

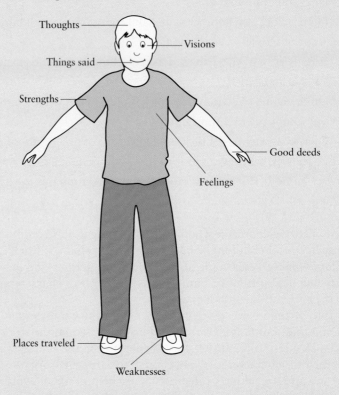

Figure 5.1 Body Map procedure and example.

The Character Evidence Map is a table that students can use to record character traits and provide evidence from the page in the book. See Figure 5.2 for a copy of the map and directions for its use. Books with strong characters include *My Name is Yoon* (Recorvits, 2003) and *Joey Pigza Loses Control* (Gantos, 2000).

Settings

Stories have places and times. These are **settings.** They are often overlooked as an element of any particular importance, yet settings help the reader create a visual image of the story. The time and place of a story add to the richness of the tale. Try to imagine *Charlotte's Web* (White, 1952) without the barnyard. Can't do it? Of course not! It is integral to the story. Without the setting, it just would not be the same.

Sometimes, the setting of the story is so vital that it affects the plot and resolution. For example, in *Hatchet* (Paulsen, 1987), the main character, a 12-year-old, makes a crash landing of a small airplane in a Canadian forest. The rest of the book chronicles his quest for survival. Clearly, without such a setting, there would be no story.

One of the best examples of a story with an important setting is *Cloudy with a Chance of Meatballs* by Judi Barrett (1978). In this story, the setting actually causes the plot; the entire story is about how the setting affects the characters. At the beginning of the book, Barrett tells us about the tiny town of Chewandswallow:

> In most ways, it was very much like any other tiny town. It had a Main Street lined with stores, houses with trees and gardens around them, a schoolhouse, about three hundred people, and some assorted cats and dogs. But there

Title of Book: _____ Title of Chapter: _____

For each, answer the question and write the page number that gives you the evidence.

What is the character's name?	What does the character look like?	How does the character act?	What does the character say?	What word describes the character's actions?
Page:	Page:	Page:	Page:	Page:
Page:	Page:	Page:	Page:	Page:
Page:	Page:	Page:	Page:	Page:

Figure 5.2 **Character Evidence Map.**

were no food stores in the town of Chewandswallow. They didn't need any. The sky supplied all the food they could possibly want. The only thing that was really different about Chewandswallow was its weather. It came three times a day, at breakfast, lunch, and dinner. Everything that everyone ate came from the sky.

In a book that fascinates children with its imaginative plays on words and hilarious events such as "storms of hamburgers" and "a brief shower of orange juice," the setting is the most important element of the story. Utilizing visual imagery is a reading strategy that can be used quite well with this and other books that have strong settings. Chapter 10 will demonstrate this strategy, using *Cloudy with a Chance of Meatballs*. Books with settings that make a real difference in the story include:

Picture Books:
Arrowville (Boedoe, 2004)
The Butterfly (Polacco, 2000)
The Color of Home (Hoffman, 2002)
Gleam and Glow (Bunting, 2001)
A Quiet Place (Wood, 2002)

Chapter Books:
Among the Betrayed (Haddix, 2002)
Fat Camp Commandos (Pinkwater, 2001)
A House of Tailors (Giff, 2004)
Parvana's Journey (Ellis, 2002)
Roll of Thunder, Hear My Cry
    (Taylor, 1976)

Many older readers enjoy historical fiction, in which the setting—time and place—is critical. Such books show your students worlds they do not know, and introduce them to historical events they might not otherwise investigate. One book of interest is *Parvana's Journey* (Ellis, 2002). Amid the backdrop of war, the main character, Parvana, whose father has just died, searches for her mother and siblings in Taliban-controlled Afghanistan. As she travels, she picks up refugees who are also lost in the war.

Often, stories have more than one setting; sometimes, several. To help students keep track of all the places in a story, as well as to use literature to teach important geography and social studies objectives, I suggest a strategy called *literary mapping* (Pritchard, 1989). Using this excellent strategy, your students will create "page-by-page depictions of the setting and then compare them to authentic maps or drawings from the illustrators" (D. Farrer, personal communication, June 8, 2004). See Figure 5.3 for a description of this strategy, as well as some books that have multiple settings, making them conducive to mapping.

Children need time to read books of their choice independently.

Problems and Events: The Plot

The **plot** of a story is its action, its conflict, and its excitement. You've heard people comment on a movie or a book, saying, "Well, I didn't like it, because it didn't have much of a plot." Such people

Literary Mapping

1. Introduce the book to the students, explaining that the setting is very important to the story. Tell them to pay attention to the details of where and when the story takes place.
2. Read the book together. Stop at descriptions of the settings. Discuss the details. Make note of how the setting changes from page to page.
3. Once the book is finished, go back to the beginning, and page by page, draw small pictures or symbols to represent the setting, based on the author's descriptions. Cut these pictures out and place them aside.
4. After drawing all the necessary pictures or symbols, place them in the proper positions on a large sheet of chart or bulletin-board paper. This creates a map. Include compass directions and a map key for the symbols.
5. Reread the story to check for accuracy of the settings as depicted on the literary map.

Books to Use with Literary Mapping

Arthur Meets the President (Brown, 1991)
Dandelions (Bunting, 1995b)
Henry Explores the Jungle (Taylor, 1968)
Horton Hatches the Egg (Seuss, 1940)
Katy and the Big Snow (Burton, 1943)
Little Black Bear Goes for a Walk (Freschet, 1977)

Make Way for Ducklings (McCloskey, 1941)
Peter Rabbit (Potter, 1987 [reissue edition])
Rosie's Walk (Hutchins, 1968)
This Is the Place for Me (Cole, 1986b)
The True Story of the Three Little Pigs (Scieszka, 1989)
Where the Wild Things Are (Sendak, 1963)

Figure 5.3 Literary mapping directions and book list.

prefer to read about events, rather than descriptions of characters or settings. Undoubtedly, most good stories are considered so because of their well-developed, interesting plots.

A plot is what happens to the characters. Usually, a plot involves a problem that must be solved, and the characters go through a series of events to solve the problem. Roadblocks along the way prevent the problem from being solved right away, but this gives the story depth and strength.

Sometimes, authors make the problem of the story obvious. Some authors even open the story by stating immediately that the characters have a problem. Arthur Yorinks (1986) does this with *Hey, Al*. He describes Al, a janitor who lives in a one-room apartment with his dog, Eddie. Then he says:

> They worked together. They ate together. They played together. What could be bad? Plenty.

Yorinks goes on to describe the dog Eddie's discomfort in the cramped apartment in which they live, and his desire to seek a better life. Al, however, is somewhat re-sistant to change. Thus, the problem begins, and a chain of interesting and thought-provoking events follows.

Conflicts can take place in many ways. Sometimes, the character has a conflict with another character. For example, in Gary Soto's *The Old Man and His Door* (1996), the problem is introduced on the first page:

> This is the story of an old man in a little village who was good at working in the garden, but terrible at listening to his wife.

The story continues in a series of hilarious events, all stemming from the fact that the old man didn't listen to his wife's instructions as she left the house. She was off to a *comadre*'s barbeque, and she wanted him to join her there, as soon as he finished giving the dog a bath. As she left, she yelled, "Did you hear me? *El puerco*. Don't forget to bring the pig!"

The conflict continues, because when the old man left, he took with him not *el puerco,* the pig, but *la puerta,* the door! He couldn't imagine why she wanted him to take the door off the hinges and take it to a barbeque, but he did what she told him to do. Or so he thought! The rest of the story tells of the adventures he has as he attempts to take the door to a party.

Young adolescent readers particularly enjoy books that have conflicts in which the main character, usually an adolescent, has a problem with another adolescent character. This is the kind of turmoil that teens know so well. Often novels for adolescents are narrated in first person, which makes it easier for the reader to relate to the character's problems. Sharon Flake's *The Skin I'm In* (1998) illustrates this beautifully:

> Up till now, I just took it. The name calling. The pushing and shoving and cheating off me. Then last week something happened. I was walking down the hall in one of Char's dresses, strutting my stuff, looking good. Then Char walked up to me and told me to take off her clothes. There was maybe eight or nine kids around when she said it, too. Including Caleb. I thought she was kidding. She wasn't. So I went to the girls' room and put my own stuff back on. That's when I made up my mind. Enough is enough. I deserve better than for people to treat me any old way they want. But saying that is one thing, making it happen is something else.
>
> So you see, I got my own troubles. (p. 5)

Other conflicts can be between the character and nature, such as that between the teenager Sam Gribley and the harsh environment of a forest in the dead of winter. In *My Side of the Mountain,* by Jean Craighead George (1959), Sam runs away from his home, an apartment in New York City, and finds the location, in a thick, uninhabited forest, of what was once his great-grandfather's farm. He carves a home for himself in the hollow of a tree and lives there for a year. This classic book is his chronicle of the adventure, and contains many of Sam's journal entries that explain how he finds food and maintains his shelter in the winter, such as this one:

> This night I am making salt. I know that people in the early days got along without it, but I think some of these wild foods would taste better with some flavoring. I understand that hickory sticks, boiled dry, leave a salty residue. I am trying it. (p. 53)

Sometimes, conflict can take place within the confines of the character's own mind, such as when Ira cannot decide whether he wants to spend the night at his best friend's house in *Ira Sleeps Over,* by Bernard Waber (1972). Children everywhere can relate to the difficulty of making a decision while being torn between the familiarity and comfort of home, and the excitement and promise of doing a "grown-up" thing such as sleeping over at a friend's house.

Story maps help children see plots. Because they are ways to graphically represent the elements of a story, they can aid children in seeing the nature of the plot of a story. If a story is episodic, in that the main character attempts to solve a problem three times before its resolution, the story map can depict this. Figure 5.4 shows a rather generic story map that can help students record story elements and enables them to remember important events.

Story maps can take many forms, and they should reflect the unique features of the story that you are using. They also need to be developmentally appropriate, in that the age of your students will affect the number of details that you expect. Figure 5.5 shows a B-M-E Map, which gives younger students room to draw pictures for the beginning, middle, and end of the book.

One way that you can aid students to recall the elements of a story is to use the "Storytelling Glove" (Hoyt, 1999). On a plain white garden glove, write the elements, one per finger, starting with "characters" on the thumb. Draw a heart in the center for the author's theme or purpose of the story. Students wear the glove and start at the thumb to retell the elements of the story. Hoyt suggests that you

---

Title and Author of This Book

_____

Characters

Main character—_____

_____

Setting

Time—_____

Place—_____

Problem

_____

Events (Things the characters do to solve the problem)

_____

_____

Resolution

_____

Figure 5.4 A story map.

Directions: In this map, ask the students to write or draw the characters, setting, and problem in the "beginning" section. Events go in the "middle," and the resolution goes in the "end" section.

Beginning

Middle

End

Figure 5.5 B-M-E Map for younger students.

purchase a box of food handler's gloves, write the elements on these, and send them home with students to use in practicing with parents. A variation of this is to ask students to trace their hand on a piece of paper and write the elements on the fingers. Use this tracing to help them retell the story.

Additionally, story frames can help. These are written equivalents of story maps, in that they help students verbalize the elements of the story in writing. Samples are included in the *Toolkit*.

Resolution

Ah, the satisfaction of a tale well told! The **resolution** of a story is the place where all readers want to be eventually when they delve into a good book. This is how the problem is solved, what happens when the character is no longer struggling, and ultimately, how the reader is satisfied.

Surprise endings are fun for readers, too. These books lend themselves very well to discussions and responses. Chris Van Allsburg is a master at this, as evidenced in many of his works. In particular, *The Sweetest Fig* (1993) chronicles the events that happen to a mean-spirited dentist who is given two magic figs. These figs will make dreams come true, but the dentist discovers that he cannot escape his bad behavior. The clever plot twists in this book never fail to fascinate; the conclusion of *The Sweetest Fig* is one of the most startling, yet satisfying story resolutions you will find. In fact, you may find yourself sitting for a moment and staring at the page, marveling at what has just happened to the two main characters.

Another book that ends with a surprise is Audrey Wood's *Little Penguin's Tale* (1989). Wood begins with the Grand Nanny Penguin telling the little penguins a tale of long, long ago but the problem was Little Penguin, because he "didn't listen to his Grand Nanny's tales."

Throughout the book, Little Penguin wanders into one adventure after another, not paying attention to the sensible advice of his Grand Nanny. By the end of the book, he is so tired that he lies down to take a nap, and "everyone knows that a little penguin can get eaten by a whale if he falls asleep by the deep, dark sea." Fortunately for her readers, and for Little Penguin, Audrey Wood gave this book two conclusions, and readers may choose the one they like.

Generally, in children's literature, closure occurs in the resolution, leaving the reader with a feeling that the characters are either satisfied with or resigned to the solution to their problem. However, sometimes problems are not fully solved. Mercer Mayer addresses childhood fears in his book *There's Something in My Attic* (1988). A young girl hears noises in the attic of her new home on the farm and investigates. She finds a creature that has just stolen her teddy bear, and lassoes it downstairs to her parents' bedroom, to show them what she had captured. However, as Mayer writes, "But nightmares are very tricky, and sometimes they just slip away." The little girl does not get rid of the creature but resolves to face up to it again, the very next day.

Responses to books help readers express their reaction to the resolution. Calkins (2001, p. 484) also suggests the use of "ways to linger," which are ways in which the students can reflect upon the book as a whole. In light of its resolution, your students can think about why authors chose endings that they did, and what they are trying to tell readers. Chapter 13 will tell you more about ways to linger. Books with resolutions that will make your students want to linger include:

Picture Books:
Boxes for Katje (Fleming, 2003)
If You Take a Mouse to School (Numeroff, 2002)
A Plump and Perky Turkey (Bateman, 2001)

Chapter Books:
Gathering Blue (Lowry, 2000)
Hoot (Hiaasen, 2002)
The Same Stuff as Stars (Paterson, 2002)

Theme

The **theme** is the author's purpose for writing the story. Often, the author has a message that he or she wants to get across to readers—a message that makes a point about life. Remember *Hey, Al?* In it, Arthur Yorinks (1986), the author, tells of a janitor and his pet dog who are dissatisfied with their small apartment in New York City. They are swept away, literally and figuratively, by a large bird, which promises them a blissful life in paradise. When things on the paradise island start to go awry, Al and his dog Eddie decide that life at home is not so bad after all. Yorinks resolved his story very eloquently with figurative language in the last sentence, "Paradise lost is sometimes Heaven found." (In Chapter 2, you saw how *Hey, Al* could be used in a lesson for students learning English as a second language.)

Such eloquence is in books and stories that gently nudge the reader toward a basic truth about life, such as Arnold Lobel's *Fables* (1980). Based on Aesop's fables, Lobel's adaptation is a delightful collection of stories that teach us lessons. Each ends with a moral, such as "The Bad Kangaroo," which is a story about a kangaroo who was misbehaving at school. He threw spitballs, put thumbtacks in chairs, and put glue on the doorknobs, so the principal paid a visit to the home. There, when invited to sit, he discovered a thumbtack in the chair. As he sat talking to Mr. and Mrs. Kangaroo, a spitball landed on his nose. As Mrs. Kangaroo said, "Forgive me, but I can never resist throwing those things." The moral? "A child's conduct will reflect the ways of his parents" (Lobel, 1980, p. 28).

Many times, children of elementary age (especially in the primary grades) will not comprehend the author's theme, because it is only implied and depends upon the child's ability to infer information that is not explicitly stated. An example of a book that does not state its theme explicitly is *Swimmy*, by Leo Lionni (1963). This is the story of a tiny black fish, Swimmy, whose family and friends were all red fish. One awful day, the entire school of fish, except Swimmy, was devoured by a tuna fish, leaving him alone in the sea. After exploring for a while, Swimmy sees a school of little red fish, like his. He begged them to swim with him and see and do things, but they were afraid of being eaten by the big fish. So, after much thought, Swimmy solved the problem by telling them to gather together as they swam, so that they would make themselves look like a large red fish. And Swimmy, the black fish, placed himself in the position to be the eye.

Why did Lionni write this book? Besides being a delightful tale with beautiful illustrations, it seems that this book is telling us the value of thinking of a plan and working together to solve problems. Yet, Lionni never tells us that this is his intention. He allows us to draw that conclusion as we enjoy the story. And sometimes, as Rosenblatt tells us in her description of the transactional theory, each of us can draw a different conclusion from the same story, based on our unique experiences (1978).

Themes cannot be forced on children. It does no good to ask rhetorical questions such as, "Wasn't Swimmy trying to teach the red fish a lesson?" They might figure out the answer to your question, but they probably won't get the point. Instead, ask questions that allow for multiple levels of understanding, such as these:

1. "Why did the author write this book?"
2. "What is the author trying to tell us?"
3. "What does the author want us to figure out?"
4. "What life lesson can we learn from this book?"
5. "How can this book help us understand things that happen to us in our lives?"

Reread stories with strong themes a few times, because often the subtle messages become clear after the second or third time students are exposed to the story. Books with strong themes include:

Picture Books:
Pink and Say (Polacco, 1994)
Suki's Kimono (Uegaki, 2003)
Thank You, Mr. Falker (Polacco, 1998)

Chapter Books:
Before We Were Free (Alvarez, 2002)
Because of Winn-Dixie (DiCamillo, 2000)
Is My Friend at Home? Pueblo Fireside Tales (Bierhorst, 2001)

The Importance of Knowing the Nature of Stories

It is important to know the look, feel, and sound of the text that your students will be reading. Sharing your love of good literature with children will be one of the most exciting parts of your job. Helping them to know it, to own it, and to turn to it again and again, will be more important than all the skills lessons you could muster. Don't like to read yourself? Don't enjoy stories and poetry? As I mentioned in Chapter 1, Applegate and Applegate (2004) found that more than half of the preservice teachers they surveyed did not like to read. It will be difficult to convey enthusiasm about reading when you do not feel it. Yet your students deserve a chance to love reading. To be the most effective at teaching reading, a teacher must "transform one's own comprehension of the subject matter, one's own skills of performance or desired attitude values, into pedagogical representations and actions" (Pearson, Roehler, Dole & Duffy, 1992, p. 178).

A large classroom library and time to read together help children's literacy abilities grow.

This point was once made clearly by a young friend of mine, Alex. It was his first day of seventh grade, and when he got home, his mother asked him about his teachers. She was particularly interested in his language arts class, because reading was not his favored choice of activities.

"Oh, yeah," he said. "He's a really good teacher. I can tell."

"How can you tell?" his mother asked.

"He likes it."

"He likes—what?"

"He likes reading—a lot. You can't be good at it if you don't like it."

"How do you know he likes reading? Did he tell you?"

"No, but I can just tell. He's excited about teaching us and reading with us. I can just tell he likes it."

I urge you, right now, to pick up some children's books and become familiar with the richness that is available to you. Start collecting books for your classroom library, and as you do, read them yourself. Get books from garage sales, flea markets, library book sales, children's book clubs, and bookstore sales. Read them! As you delve into the array of children's literature available to you, you'll feel more comfortable sharing it with children, and helping them learn to love it, too.

The Nature of Nonfiction

Begin examining the nature of nonfiction by taking a look at the report card for a fourth grader, shown in Figure 5.6. Why does Jake do well in reading, but not in the subject areas? Wouldn't it make sense for him to achieve good grades in social studies and science, also? Wouldn't his good reading abilities help him succeed in the subject areas?

Not always. Reading for information, which is what we can assume Jake needs to do in his social studies and science schoolwork, is not the same kind of reading that he does otherwise. While his reading performance may be satisfactory, his grade may also reflect a use of text that contains fiction—in particular, stories. He may have not yet developed the specialized skills necessary to read nonfiction. Also, informational, or expository, text is different. It is not the same kind of text that Jake may be accustomed to.

Figure 5.6 A report card for a fourth grader.

Inside the figure:

Report Card

Name: Jake
Grade: Fourth
  Reading—B
  Science—D
  Social Studies—D

What can you surmise about Jake's academic abilities?

There are several ways in which nonfiction text is different from fiction. First, nonfiction text contains difficult vocabulary. These words are more difficult to decode than the kinds of words that are found in children's stories. Second, once they are decoded, children have not yet developed schemata for them, which is essential for their comprehension of the whole text (Anderson, 2004; Anderson & Pearson, 1984; Rumelhart, 1980). For example, even if a child is able to decode a word such as "photosynthesis," and say the word, he or she may not be able to conjure a picture or concept of the word. Third, most nonfiction works look different from their fiction counterparts. Pages are busier, containing graphs, charts, tables, and photographs with captions; children sometimes find this type of presentation difficult to navigate. Readers who are searching for information must also deal with features that are different from the content of fiction, such as the index, the table of contents, and the headings (Dreher, 2002). Fourth, much of the nonfiction that your students will read is electronic. Many web sites are difficult to read because of the amount of distracting material on the page—additional links, animated graphics, and colorful fonts. Reading and comprehending these visuals requires a bit of skill (Leu, 2002; Moss, 2004). Fifth, some nonfiction texts are not user-friendly. Sometimes they are not written in terms that children can understand, are watered-down so much that they lose their significance in helping children understand the concept, are not visually appealing, or have pictures that do not match the text (Donovan & Smolkin, 2002; Kletzien & Dreher, 2004). And finally, reading for information in elementary classrooms is awash with weak teaching practices. In many classrooms, children are asked to read nonfiction texts in round-robin fashion, because the teacher knows of no other way to cover the text material. Moreover, many primary grade teachers tend to use fiction rather than nonfiction in their classrooms, so children in the lower grades are not exposed to texts that convey information (Moss, 2004; Palmer & Stewart, 2003; Richgels, 2002).

In spite of all these difficulties with the nature of nonfiction, it is an extremely useful genre, not only because of the wealth of information that these books and other types of text provide, but also because children love to read about things that interest them (Palmer & Stewart, 2003). Many times, reluctant readers attempt

Diversity in the Reading Classroom

The Importance of Multicultural Literature

Multicultural literature can be a catalyst for helping your students understand the world they live in. What is multicultural literature? Bishop states that it includes "books that reflect the racial, ethnic, and social diversity that is characteristic of our pluralistic society and of the world" (1997, p. 3). Au (2000), in a review of the research on the literacy learning of students of diverse backgrounds, reports several recommendations, one of which is to increase the amount of and use of multicultural literature in the classroom. Knowledge and use of such literature can help teachers who are outsiders to a culture learn to teach in a "culturally responsive manner" (p. 838). Although the study of the impact of such literature is new and more studies need to be done, Marshall (2000) reports that students can gain positive attitudes toward diversity through the use of literature. Yet Marshall also reports that sometimes students resist these books. Likewise, Lazar (2004) describes preservice teachers who were reluctant to use multicultural literature in their internship classrooms. Sometimes, teachers have a "tourist view" of multiculturalism, which does little more than "create access to certain stories" (Hade, 1997, p. 237). Instead, a deeper empathy for social injustices is necessary, in which teachers help students think about the issues of race, class, and gender.

Becoming acquainted with multicultural literature is the first step to understanding how it can enhance your students' learning. Bishop (1997) makes suggestions for choosing books for your classroom library and for instruction. She recommends that teachers include the following when choosing multicultural literature:

- Books about people from many diverse groups

- Books written and illustrated by people from many diverse groups

- Books that reflect the many experiences of people within any group, such as varying occupations and differing socio-economic backgrounds

- A variety of genre, such as realistic fiction, poetry, historical fiction, folklore, biographies, and nonfiction

- Books that contain themes that can be compared with other books

- Books in which the discussions of race, class, and gender do not appear to be forced

- Books that portray differing perspectives on issues and events

- Books that will encourage readers to reflect upon the human condition

Such a balanced collection will "make it more likely that no one book will bear the burden of being the only experience a child has with literature about a so-called minority group" (Bishop, 1997, p. 18). A bibliography of some multicultural titles is included in Chapter 3.

nonfiction because the topic is motivating to them. Additionally, reading for information is something that your students need to know how to do. Most of the reading passages on standardized tests are nonfiction passages (Calkins, Montgomery, Santman & Falk, 1998), and most state standards reflect the need to read nonfiction (Kletzien & Dreher, 2004). Thus, nonfiction will be very helpful in your classroom.

In order to enable your students' understanding of nonfiction, it is necessary to know the nature of this type of text. We will examine that now.

Organizational Patterns of Informational Text

Good nonfiction writers organize their text in ways that help the reader understand the topic. There are five types of organizational patterns that are prevalent in children's literature: descriptive, sequential, comparison, cause-effect, and problem-solution (Meyer & Freedle, 1984; Meyer & Poon, 2004). While many books will reflect a combination of these patterns, most are predominantly one or the other.

Descriptive Informational Texts

Some authors explicitly describe the topic, telling the reader what it is like, where to find it, and so on. This is **descriptive text structure.** An example of a good descriptive book is *Whales*, by Seymour Simon (1989). Using photographs as well as clear, clean prose, the author gives the reader a sense of what these creatures are like. Words that help signal the reader to a description are the ones that signify color, size, shape, habitat, and location, such as in this passage from Simon's book:

> Perhaps the best known of the toothed whales is the killer whale, or orca. That's because there are killer whales that perform in marine parks around the country. A killer whale is actually the largest member of the dolphin family. A male can grow to over thirty feet and weigh nine tons.
>
> Orcas are found in all of the world's oceans, from the poles to the tropics. They hunt for food in herds called pods. Orcas eat fish, squid, and penguins, as well as seals, sea lions, and other sea mammals, including even the largest whales. Yet they are usually gentle in captivity, and there is no record that an orca has ever caused a human death.

 To help students gather important information from descriptive text, show them a graphic organizer first. Such an organizer should reflect the number of important ideas described in the text. For example, an organizer for the excerpt from *Whales* might look like the one shown in Figure 5.7. Books with descriptive patterns include:

Primary:
Beaks! (Collard, 2002)
Spiders (Otto, 2002)
You Can't See Your Bones with Binoculars: A Guide to Your 206 Bones (Ziefert, 2003)

Intermediate:
Baseball in the Barrios (Horenstein, 1997)
Going to School in Colonial America (Sateren, 2002)
Palindromania! (Agee, 2002)

Sequential Informational Texts

Events in time or the order of events in a procedure must be explained using **sequential text structure.** Authors who are interested in describing how things happened over a period of time use a chronological order of events. Most biographies and autobiographies fit this pattern, as do books about history. Sequentially

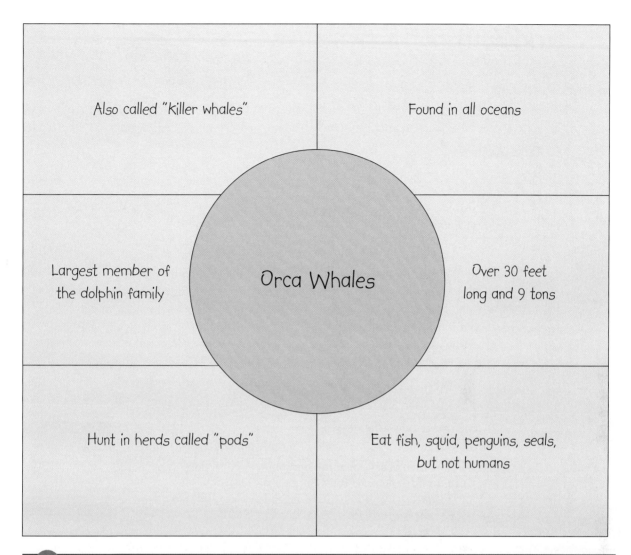

Figure 5.7 Graphic organizer for a selection from the descriptive text *Whales*.

Source: Simon, 1989.

organized text often contains signal words such as "first," "next," "then," "last," "after," "when," "years," "months," "days," and "finally."

David Adler wrote a series of biographies that present factual information about famous people in concise, easy-to-read narratives. This excerpt, from *A Picture Book of Helen Keller* (Adler, 1990), shows the sequential nature of his text:

Helen Keller was born in Tuscumbia, Alabama on June 27, 1880. She was a pretty baby. She was happy and smart.

When Helen was just six months old, she began talking. But a year later, in February 1882, she became sick. . . . After a few days the illness was gone.

Modifying Instruction for

ELL

Shared Reading and Writing with
In My Family/En Mi Familia

GRADE LEVEL: 3–4

- **Objective**

  After reading a selection from *In My Family/En Mi Familia* (Garza, 1996), students will retell the selected story and write an autobiographical account of a family tradition.

- **Preparation**

  - Assign reading buddies, which are partners who work together during the lesson.
  - Collect pictures or items that can help students recall events from *In My Family/En Mi Familia:* Picture of a lizard, cactus, squash or sweet potato, barbeque tool, Easter egg, piece of newspaper, piece of incense, picture of *La Llorona* (the weeping woman), a rose, picture of a water tank, crochet needle, wedding veil, guitar.

- **Materials**

  - Items for recalling the story
  - Multiple copies of *In My Family/En Mi Familia* (Garza, 1996)
  - One copy each of several autobiographies or collections of memoirs:
    Catch and Connect—Tony Gonzalez (2004)
    I Dreamed I Was a Ballerina—Anna Pavlova (2001)
    Kids Like Me in China—Ying Ying Fry (2001)
    La Mariposa—Francisco Jiménez (2000)
    My Diary from Here to There/Mi Diario De Aqui Hasta Alla—Amada Irma Pérez (2002)
    Sue Bird: Be Yourself—Sue Bird (2004)
    Thank You, Mr. Falker—Patricia Polacco (1998)
    Through My Eyes—Ruby Bridges (1999)
    Upside Down Boy/El Niño de Cabeza—Juan Felipe Herrera (2000)

- **Introduction**

  1. Tell the students a story about your childhood. Share a family tradition, a humorous story about a relative, a favorite pastime, or a hardship overcome.

  2. Show them the book *In My Family/En Mi Familia* (Garza, 1996). Tell them its title in English as well as in Spanish. Invite the students to look at the cover picture and make predictions about the book.

  Modifications for ELL are printed in color.

3. Explain: "An autobiography is a book that a person has written about his or her own life. Many famous people write them to tell us about their lives. Other people who are not famous write about their lives because they want to share with us some of their stories. Here are some examples of books that are autobiographies." Show the students the autobiographies and point out their authors. Briefly describe some of them, and explain that these books will be available for reading independently during the week.

● Before Reading: Predicting with Objects

4. Each page of this book contains one story about Garza's family during her childhood. Give each reading buddy pair one page to read, and the story object that corresponds to their story. For example, Garza's story "Earache Treatment" tells of a time when her mother rolled newspaper into a cone, lit the top of the cone with a match, and put the bottom end of the cone in her father's ear. This was a way to evaporate the trapped water in his ears, which was a result of a war injury. Use a piece of rolled newspaper as the object for this story. Have students look at the picture for their story and make predictions with their partners about how their story object goes with the story. Talk to each other about predictions.

● Silent Reading

5. Students should read silently with help from their buddies, if needed.

● After Reading Response: Retelling

6. After reading, ask students to talk to each other in their pairs about the story, and decide how to share it with the class.

7. Ask each pair to retell the story they read, using the story objects as prompts.

8. After retelling in the large group, ask students to share with their partners a family story.

● After Reading Response: Writing

9. After talking with their partners, students can write their autobiographies.

To reinforce the idea that this book follows a sequence, you can create a time line from a roll of butcher paper or craft paper and hang it on your board. As you read the book aloud, or as children read and stop at certain points, record important events in Helen Keller's life on a time line. When older students are reading biographies about people in the same time period, you can ask each of them to create a time line for the biography that they are reading. Hang them in the room, and have the students compare the lives of the people in their time frame.

K–8

Another way that authors sequentially represent the content of a book is to provide a set of steps in a procedure. This technique is typical of instructional books, which show readers how to do things, such as Louise Colligan's *Help!*

I Have to Write a Paper! Scholastic's A+ Junior Guide to Good Writing (1988).
Here is how this author begins to list ideas sequentially:

> Now to answer the question every student writer worries about—What do I do first? Let's break down the big job of writing a paper into ten smaller jobs that even the most nervous writer can manage one by one. (Colligan, 1988, p. 3)

Colligan then lists "Ten Steps to A+ Writing," and describes each of those steps in detail. From there, each chapter follows the same sequence. Writing a description, a how-to paper, and a persuasive paper, among others, are addressed in subsequent chapters. For each, the author follows the same ten-step guidelines for writing a paper. Colligan makes frequent use of words to signify sequence, such as: "first," "next," "then," and many ordinal numbers.

To organize this information, tell the students before reading that there are some important steps to follow in writing a paper. They can number a piece of paper from one to ten, and list these steps.

Other authors have written books that explain how things are produced, such as *How a Book Is Made* (Aliki, 1986). While this book is clearly sequential, in that it chronicles the making of a book from start to finish, it makes minimal use of signal words. Even so, you can tell students that there are five basic steps to making a book, and ask them to find action words that indicate these steps and list them. Notice that in the following example only two sequential signal terms, "starts" and "at last," are used:

> A book starts with an idea. The author thinks of a story. She writes it down. It is harder than she expected. Sometimes she can't find the right words. She has to look things up. At last she is satisfied. She sends off her manuscript to her editor at Goodbooks Publishing Company. (Aliki, 1986, pp. 6–7)

A fascinating example of a sequentially ordered book is *The Ever-Living Tree: The Life and Times of a Coast Redwood* (Vieira, 1994). The author chronicles the life of a redwood tree, and to illustrate how old it is, she simultaneously chronicles world events that are taking place as the tree grows. Across the top of each page, she includes a timeline of dates. As students read or listen to this book, you can have them compare the two timelines. Read a sample of Vieira's work:

> Time went on and on. The ever-living redwood tree kept growing bigger and bigger. It stood tall and silent in the middle of its fair circle of younger trees.
>
> The United States of America declared itself an independent nation in the New World with thirteen colonies along the eastern coast of North America. General George Washington led the colonists through the bitter Revolutionary War with Great Britain to establish that independence. After the war, General Washington became the first president of the United States.
>
> The giant redwood tree was now more than 300 feet tall—one of the tallest living things on the face of the earth.

Books that fit the sequential text structure pattern include:

Primary:
One Day at Wood Green Animal Shelter (Casey, 2001)
A Voice of Her Own: The Story of Phillis Wheatley, Slave Poet (Laskey, 2003)
What You Never Knew About Fingers, Forks, and Chopsticks (Lauber, 1999)

Intermediate:
First to Fly (Busby, 2003)
Lives of Extraordinary Women: Rulers, Rebels (and What the Neighbors Thought) (Krull, 2000)
September 11, 2001: The Day That Changed America (Wheeler, 2001)

Comparison Informational Texts

In order to clarify a concept, authors like to help the reader compare two ideas, which gives a **comparison text structure.** Sometimes this approach helps define the concept. For example, an author might describe frogs. Since many people confuse frogs with toads, the author compares these two animals so that their differences are distinct. Comparison writing patterns are common in nonfiction books about animals, and the words often used by these authors include: "different," "alike," "same," "compare," "share," and "common." As students read comparison texts, have them draw the two things being compared, such as a frog and a toad, or a crocodile and an alligator. As they draw, they should also illustrate and label the details that make them different, based on what they have learned from the book.

One interesting comparison account is of earth formations in *The Sun, the Wind, and the Rain,* by Lisa Westberg Peters (1988). In this book, Peters compares the evolution of Earth's mountains to a young girl's building of sand mountains on the beach:

> The earth cracked and shifted again. Bending and breaking the sandstone layers slowly rose to become a new mountain.
>
> Elizabeth finished her new sand mountain. She brushed sand off her hands, picked up her bucket, and walked back up the beach.

Books that contain comparison texts include:

Are Trees Alive? (Miller, 2002)
Giving Thanks: The 1621 Harvest Feast (Waters, 2001)
No One Saw: Ordinary Things Through the Eyes of an Artist (Raczka, 2002)

Cause/Effect Informational Texts

Most events in history or natural phenomena happen as a result of other events. Authors who tell about these events must organize their writing in the **cause/effect text structure.** These relationships can be complex; usually, one event does not simply lead to another event. Multiple effects can occur from a single cause. Authors who use cause/effect writing patterns are seeking to answer the questions "What happened? And why?" Words to describe these relationships include: "if," "then," "why," "purpose," "what happens," "cause," "because," "effect," and "as a result."

Lindsay Barrett George illustrates cause and effect relationships in nature quite beautifully in her book *In the Woods: Who's Been Here?* (1995). In this book, which describes a walk in the woods by two children, George tells of clues that have been left behind in places throughout the forest, and the children guess which animals have been in those places:

> Cammy and William climb over a smooth gray tree that has fallen across the trail. The bark has been gnawed off the branches close to the ground. Who's been here?

The reader turns the page to find that it was a snowshoe hare. Before explaining the cause/effect relationships in this book, you can prepare students by explaining that the entire book is about the things that animals do in the forest. Therefore, the animals cause all of the things that are found in the book, such as a flower blossom missing from the stalk or bleached bones on the ledge of a cave. Use a simple graphic organizer like the one in Figure 5.8 to help the students see the nature of this relationship.

Another example of cause/effect relationships comes from Seymour Simon. In *Animals Nobody Loves* (2001), Simon tells us about animals that are feared and despised, and explains why:

> If a person bothers a Gila, it turns and snaps with lightning speed. It sinks its teeth deep into the person and holds on like a bulldog. Poison slowly flows through its mouth and into the victim. Few people are bitten by Gila monsters—only those foolish enough to try to handle one. (p. 26)

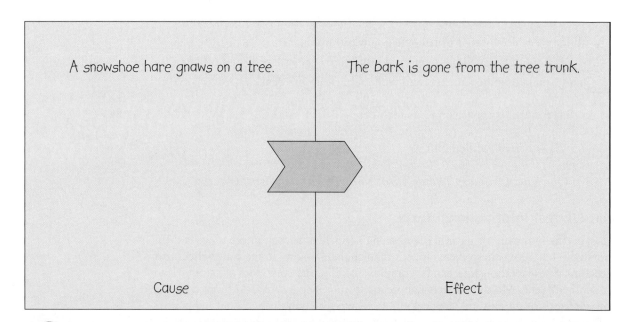

A snowshoe hare gnaws on a tree.

The bark is gone from the tree trunk.

Cause

Effect

Figure 5.8 A cause/effect relationship in *Who's Been Here?*

Source: George, 1995.

To help students see the cause/effect relationship in this passage, tell them to look for the signal word "if," and the action that follows it. The author wrote, "If a person bothers a Gila . . . ." Explain that this is the action that caused something else to happen. Then ask, "What two things happen as a result of bothering the Gila?" This effect is a chain reaction that can be depicted in a graphic organizer like the one shown in Figure 5.9. Books that contain cause and effect text structure include:

Primary:

If the World Were a Village: A Book About the World's People (Smith, 2002)

They Call Me Wooly: What Animal Names Can Tell Us (DuQuette, 2002)

What Makes an Ocean Wave? (Berger & Berger, 2001)

Intermediate:

Food Rules! The Stuff You Munch, Its Crunch, Its Punch, and Why You Sometimes Lose Your Lunch (Haduch, 2001)

Weather! (Rupp, 2003)

Toys! Amazing Stories Behind Some Great Inventions (Wulffson, 2000)

Problem/Solution Informational Texts

A special type of cause/effect relationship is the **problem/solution text structure.** In this pattern, the author is explaining an event that is a problem for the people involved. This type of event causes people to search for solutions and act upon them. These two questions are answered: "What was the problem?" "And what did people do to solve it?" Signal words include "if," "then," "effect," "resulting in," "because," "problem," "solve," "solution," "possibilities," "think," "plans," "idea," and "determined."

Cause	Effect #1	Effect #2
If a human bothers a gila monster, then . . .	it snaps and bites, holding on with its teeth, and then . . .	the poison flows into the human.

Figure 5.9 Graphic organizer for a cause/effect relationship in *Animals Nobody Loves.*

Source: Simon, 2001.

Cause/effect and problem/solution texts are very similar. You may have noticed that they share many of the same signal words. Additionally, both types of texts often describe chain reaction events. The main difference between them is the fact that cause/effect relationships occur in nature, as well as with inanimate objects such as machinery. Problem/solution relationships occur only when people are involved.

An example of a problem/solution writing pattern is found in *Garbage! Where It Comes From, Where It Goes,* by Evan and Janet Hadingham (1990):

> And because we're running out of landfills, Americans now face a big garbage problem. While the total amount of trash we all throw out grows steadily each year, landfills are shutting down everywhere. In fact, during the next twenty years, over three-quarters of all the landfills in the United States will shut down. (Some will close simply because they're full, others because they're breaking health and safety regulations.) So by the year 2010, there won't be many places left for our trash to go. This book is about our garbage problem, and explores what we can do to help solve it. (p. 7)

After reading this text, ask the students to think about possible ways to solve the garbage problem. Put their predictions in a graphic organizer like the one shown in Figure 5.10. As they read, list the solutions explained by the authors in another organizer.

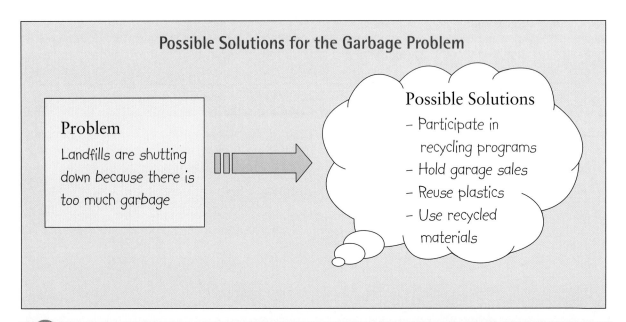

Figure 5.10 Graphic organizer for predictions for *Garbage! Where It Comes From, Where It Goes.*

Source: Hadingham & Hadingham, 1990.

Home–School Connection

Potluck Reading Night

One of my colleagues, Jane Bonari, who is an outstanding teacher and a wonderful cook, always says, "If you want them to come, serve food." A way to encourage your students and their caregivers to read and talk about reading is a Potluck Reading Night (Spohn, 2001). Invite everyone to your classroom on a monthly basis, in the evening. The food may be the ticket to getting the parents to attend; however, reading games and read-aloud sessions go a long way toward showing parents how to have fun with reading.

Shown below is a suggested schedule of events.

6:00—Reading game or activity

Show parents how to do activities with letter cards, word cards, or other tools such as the Story Hand. Here is a sample dialogue for showing the Story Hand to caregivers.

"One of my goals this year is to make sure your child knows the elements of a story: character, setting, plot, resolution, and theme. You can help with this by using this picture. First, read a story with your child. Then, use your hand to recall the important parts of the story. Begin with the thumb—character—and ask your child to tell about the main character as well as any other important characters. Continue with the other parts of the story. The plot may have several events, and your child should be able to recall the important ones. Let's practice!"

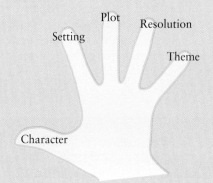

Plot
Resolution
Setting
Theme
Character

Caregivers, children, and the teacher enjoy learning about books together.

6:15—Group story time

Read aloud a new piece of literature. This activity gives you the opportunity to model reading aloud behaviors, as well as to introduce new books. If possible, have multiple copies of this book available for borrowing.

6:30—Family reading time

From the classroom library or from a special selection of books arranged on the table, ask caregivers and children to choose a book and read it together.

6:45—Dinner

Ask caregivers to bring a dish to share; have paper plates and utensils available.

7:15—Book swap

Ask families to bring paperback books from home and leave them on a book swap table. Invite everyone to take a gently worn book home. ●

Take a look at the example of problem/solution text written by Jean Fritz, in *Shh! We're Writing the Constitution* (1987):

> Once during the war Washington had decided it would be a good idea if his troops swore allegiance to the United States. As a start, he lined up some troops from New Jersey and asked them to take such an oath. They looked at Washington as if he'd taken leave of his senses. How could they do that? they cried. New Jersey was their country!
>
> So Washington dropped the idea. In time, he hoped, the states would see that they needed to become one nation, united under a strong central government. (p. 8)

 To help students see that the author is presenting a situation that posed a problem, you can use the mental modeling strategy. This strategy, described in detail in Chapter 2, shows your students how to arrive at the conclusion that there is a problem presented in the text. See Figure 5.11 for a mental model used by a third grade teacher. Books in all age ranges that have problem/solution text structure include:

Fight On! Mary Church Terrell's Battle for Integration (Fradin & Fradin, 2003)
Left for Dead: A Young Man's Search for Justice for the USS Indianapolis (Nelson, 2002)
Shutting Out the Sky: Life in the Tenements of New York, 1880–1924 (Hopkinson, 2003)
When My Name Was Keoko (Park, 2002)

> As I read this, I realize that George Washington had a real problem! The author, Jean Fritz, tells me he wanted his soldiers to pledge allegiance to the country, just like we do every morning with our flag. No one had ever done this before! I know that the country was very new at the time and it was made up of 13 states. I remember reading earlier, on page 7, that Jean Fritz told me that people weren't really ready to call themselves Americans. They were just happy to be free from England, and didn't care much about making a whole new country. So, when George Washington wanted them to say a pledge, they simply said no! This was a problem to Washington, who was trying to get them to see how important it was to be united for their country. As I read, I am going to look for ways that he attempts to solve this problem.

Figure 5.11 Mental model for showing students the problem/solution structure in the text *Shh! We're Writing the Constitution.*

Source: Fritz, 1987.

What Teachers Need to Know About Nonfiction

The nature of nonfiction is truly different from fiction. It is important to know the differences and to use this knowledge in your teaching of content area reading. How can this knowledge inform your teaching?

First, good teachers teach their students the difference between reading fiction and reading nonfiction. Every time a new piece of text is introduced, you can talk about its genre or type. Even the youngest children can begin to differentiate between stories and information. Use the terminology associated with the text. Good teachers avoid using the term "stories" for all texts, because they know that nonfiction books are not stories.

Second, good teachers teach strategies for reading nonfiction, so that children approach this kind of text in the manner in which it was written. For example, if children know that an author is attempting to compare one animal with another in the text, they can look for such comparisons as they read, and organize this information in their notes accordingly. Signal words help readers look for this type of pattern, and graphic organizers help children organize their thoughts and notes about the information in a logical manner.

Finally, good teachers use nonfiction—a lot! Often, read-aloud times in the classroom consist of reading favorite stories to children; however, the teacher who includes quality nonfiction during these times is doing his or her students a huge favor.

The *Toolkit* includes a sample of a report frame. This strategy gives students a framework for writing about what they have found out from reading nonfiction. Prior to reading, show them the frame, so they know what type of text structure to expect and what to look for as they read. After reading, have them write a brief summary of their findings, using the frame as a guide for composing sentences.

Summary: Knowing the Nature of Text

You've just read about the importance of knowing your students' books. I described the two main types of literature—fiction and nonfiction. Fiction contains story elements: characters, settings, problems, events, resolutions, and themes. These are the nuts and bolts of stories; they constitute the essence of stories. Without them, stories are not complete. Nonfiction contains writing patterns, or text structure: description, sequence, comparison, cause and effect, problem and solution. With these writing patterns, authors make their main ideas clear. Some books contain several types of text structure; however, most are indicative of just one or two of these types. These text structures are shown in the Reviewing the Big Picture box, with the corresponding grade levels, teaching standards, and principles.

Become familiar with the ways in which the authors of your students' books have chosen to present stories and information. This knowledge helps you facilitate your students' understandings of what they read, because you can prepare them to read with appropriate leading discussions, predictions, and purpose-setting activities. As they read, your knowledge of the uniqueness of the piece of literature will help you provide scaffolds such as mental models, graphic organizers, and story maps. These strategies are described in later chapters.

Most importantly, get to know your students' books, so that when you introduce yourself on the first day of school, your students will be able to tell right away that you too are genuinely excited about reading.

Technology Resources

- wiredforbooks.org/kids.htm   This is the Kids Corner web site, sponsored by Ohio University. Audio and written stories are available.

- storybookonline.net/Default.aspx   Children's original stories are featured on this web site, and children are invited to participate in writing stories online.

- www.readingonline.org/editorial/december2001/index.html   "Teaching Students to Evaluate Internet Information Critically," by Bridget Dalton and Dana Grisham, provides insight into reading nonfiction electronically.

- yahooligans.yahoo.com/tg/evaluatingwebsites.html   The issue of critically reading web sites is addressed in this article. The authors suggest the "Four A's" as a way of evaluating sites: accessibility, accuracy, appropriateness, and appeal.

- www.geocities.com/abcsoftheinternet/, www.siec.k12.in.us/~west/slides/abc/   Students can learn the basics of using the Internet with these simple web sites.

---

expect the world

The New York Times
nytimes.com

Themes of the Times

Expand your knowledge of the concepts discussed in this chapter by reading current and historical articles from the *New York Times* by visiting the "Themes of the Times" section of the Companion Web Site.

Reviewing the Big Picture

Text Structure Strategies

Story Element	Strategy	Grade Level	IRA Standards	INTASC Principles	NAEYC Standards	ACEI/NCATE Standards
For Fiction Text						
Characters	Body map	K–2, 3–5, 6–8	1.4, 2.2, 2.3, 4.1, 4.2, 4.3, 4.4	4, 5, 7	4b (Use with read-alouds or shared reading)	2.1, 3.1, 3.2, 3.3, 3.4
Characters	Character Evidence Map	3–5, 6–8	1.4, 2.2, 2.3, 4.1, 4.2, 4.3, 4.4	4, 5, 7	NA	2.1, 3.1, 3.2, 3.3, 3.4
Setting	Literary mapping	3–5	1.4, 2.2, 2.3, 4.1, 4.2, 4.3, 4.4	4, 5, 7	NA	2.1, 3.1, 3.2, 3.3, 3.4
Plot	Story map	3–5, 6–8	1.4, 2.2, 2.3, 4.1, 4.2, 4.3, 4.4	4, 7	NA	2.1, 3.1, 3.3, 3.4
Plot	B-M-E Map	K–2	1.4, 2.2, 2.3, 4.1, 4.2, 4.3, 4.4	3, 4, 7	4b (Use with read-alouds or shared reading)	2.1, 3.1, 3.2, 3.3, 3.4
Plot	Storytelling glove	K–2, 3–5	1.4, 2.2, 2.3, 4.1, 4.2, 4.3, 4.4	3, 4, 5, 7	4b (Use with read-alouds or shared reading)	2.1, 3.1, 3.2, 3.3, 3.4
Plot	Story frames	3–5	1.4, 2.2, 2.3, 4.1, 4.2, 4.3, 4.4	3, 4, 7	NA	2.1, 3.1, 3.2, 3.3, 3.4
Resolution	Ways to linger	3–5, 6–8	1.4, 2.2, 2.3, 4.1, 4.2, 4.3, 4.4	3, 4, 5, 7	NA	2.1, 3.1, 3.2, 3.3, 3.4
Theme	Questions to ask	3–5, 6–8	1.4, 2.2, 2.3, 4.1, 4.2, 4.3, 4.4	4, 6, 7	NA	2.1, 3.1, 3.2, 3.3, 3.4, 3.5
For Nonfiction Text						
Descriptive	Descriptive text graphic organizer	K–2, 3–5, 6–8	1.4, 2.2, 2.3, 4.1, 4.2, 4.3, 4.4	1, 4, 7	4b, 4c (Use with read-alouds or shared reading)	2.1, 2.8, 3.1, 3.3, 3.4
Sequential	Time line	K–2, 3–5	1.4, 2.2, 2.3, 4.1, 4.2, 4.3, 4.4	1, 4, 7	4b, 4c (Use with read-alouds or shared reading)	2.1, 2.8, 3.1, 3.3, 3.4
Sequential	Sequential graphic organizers	K–2, 3–5, 6–8	1.4, 2.2, 2.3, 4.1, 4.2, 4.3, 4.4	1, 4, 7	4b, 4c (Use with read-alouds or shared reading)	2.1, 2.8, 3.1, 3.3, 3.4
Comparison	Comparison drawings	K–2, 3–5, 6–8	1.4, 2.2, 2.3, 4.1, 4.2, 4.3, 4.4	1, 4, 7	4b, 4c (Use with read-alouds or shared reading)	2.1, 2.8, 3.1, 3.3, 3.4
Cause/effect	Cause/effect graphic organizers	3–5, 6–8	1.4, 2.2, 2.3, 4.1, 4.2, 4.3, 4.4	1, 4, 7	NA	2.1, 2.8, 3.1, 3.3, 3.4
Problem/solution	Problem/solution graphic organizers	3–5, 6–8	1.4, 2.2, 2.3, 4.1, 4.2, 4.3, 4.4	1, 4, 7	NA	2.1, 2.8, 3.1, 3.3, 3.4
Problem/solution	Mental modeling	3–5, 6–8	1.4, 2.2, 2.3, 4.1, 4.2, 4.3, 4.4	1, 4, 7	NA	2.1, 2.8, 3.1, 3.3, 3.4
All text structures	Report frames	3–5	1.4, 2.2, 2.3, 4.1, 4.2, 4.3, 4.4	1, 4, 7	NA	2.1, 2.8, 3.1, 3.3, 3.4

6

Developing
Emerging
Literacy

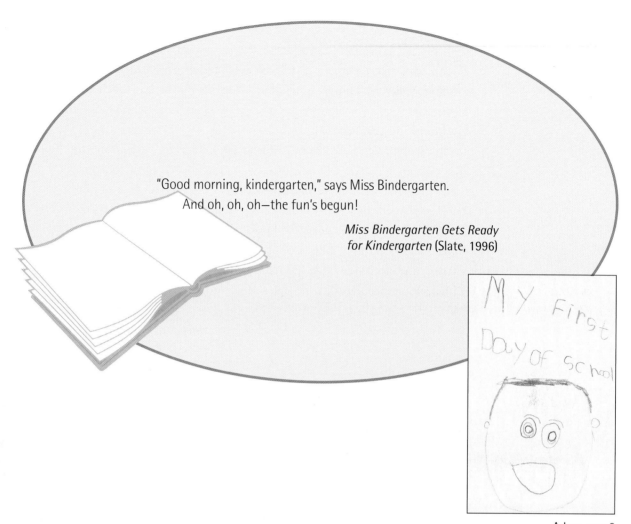

"Good morning, kindergarten," says Miss Bindergarten.
And oh, oh, oh—the fun's begun!

*Miss Bindergarten Gets Ready
for Kindergarten* (Slate, 1996)

Adam, age 6

Take a look at the Personal Reflection and think
about what is going on.

Personal Reflection

Sammy is two years old. He is in his family's apartment, while his grandmother cooks supper. On a low bookshelf that he can reach are several children's books. Sammy starts looking through all the books, searching for one in particular. After he has piled a stack of books next to him on the floor, he finally finds the one he is looking for: *The Three Bears* by Byron Barton (1991). When he picks it up, the book is upside-down. He turns it around and begins on the first page. He turns each page of the book, saying all the words on each page. When he gets to the last page, he says, "The End!" In a box on the bookshelf is a stack of scrap paper and some markers. Sammy takes a piece of paper and a marker, runs to the kitchen, and sits at the table. He makes several scribbles on the page, along with a simple circular drawing. He shows it to his grandmother, and says, "My bear! My bear is eating!"

Is Sammy reading? Is he writing? Why or why not?

Well, what do you think about Sammy's literacy abilities? Years ago, many educators would say, "Sammy is absolutely not reading or writing. He's too young. He'll be ready to read in about four years, when he is able to understand enough about the alphabet and its corresponding sounds to decode print that he sees on the page. Even though he is saying the words on the page, he has simply memorized those words because his mother has read that book to him several times. And he's not writing. He's drawing and scribbling on the paper."

Many people would still make these assertions about Sammy's behavior, based on their contention that reading is an act of decoding and writing can be done only by writers who make correctly spelled, neatly formed letters on the page. The idea that Sammy cannot yet read because he is not ready is based on the concept of "reading readiness," which prevailed in literacy education for years. Chall (1983) describes reading development in stages; the point at which the child knows letter–sound correspondences and can decode print is when he is ready to begin reading. In fact, many times, teachers who held this idea simply waited for the children to reach the "right" age before they taught them to read and write.

This concept is challenged by other educators, who would say, "Sammy is certainly beginning to read. He understands many things about books. He knows which book to look for. He sees an association between the words and pictures in the book with real-life things. He knows the entire story from beginning to end, and coordinates the words of the story to the pages on which those words appear. He knows how to hold the book, and where the story begins and ends. These are all important reading behaviors, connected to the idea that readers read for meaning. He also knows that writing is done to convey a message. His message about

Very young children who interact with books have sophisticated knowledge about print.

the bear may not be spelled in conventional English, but he clearly has attached meaning to his scribbles. This is an important concept in writing." Today, this second idea about Sammy's literacy abilities is more prevalent, and reflects the concept of "emergent literacy" (Teale & Sulzby, 1986; Strickland & Morrow, 1989).

Emergent literacy is the idea that young children acquire reading and writing abilities as they grow. There is no beginning point at which children are "ready" to read; their literacy emerges as they grow. In fact, all the experiences that children have as infants, continuing as they go to school, collectively add to their abilities to read and write.

It is the premise of this book that children's understandings of literacy grow just as the children themselves grow, and that reading emerges based on their experiences with the world in general, as well as on their experiences with print. The emergent literacy of some children at early ages is closer to mature reading than that of other young children; however, there is no magical age at which all—or even most—children are "ready" to decode printed words on the page.

Durkin (1966) studied children who had learned to read at an early age and found that many young children developed concepts about literacy long before they reached the maturational age at which they were "ready" to read. These behaviors showed sophisticated knowledge about books, print, and meaning that is derived from print. Teachers who accept the idea that children's development of literacy is a gradual process over a period of years also accept the fact that "when children enter school they will be at different points in the emerging literacy process" (Clay, 1991, p. 19). So, when they come to school for the first time, and the "fun's begun," as Slate declares in his book, *Miss Bindergarten Gets Ready for Kindergarten* (1996), what do very young children already know about reading? Let's examine some of these behaviors now.

Children Derive Meaning from Print

Sammy, the child in the Personal Reflection scenario, has a great deal of knowledge about print, even at his very young age. Evidence of this knowledge includes turning the book so that it was in the correct position to read. He knows that books have a top, bottom, front, and back. He also knows that books carry meaning, as evidenced by the fact that he drew a picture of a bear, similar to the one in the story. His storytelling ability indicates that he knows that there are words and pictures in the book that convey this story. All of these concepts are essential to being able to read. Several concepts of print, as well as ways to teach them, are described in the sections that follow.

Books Have Meaning

If you observe a baby with a picture book over a period of time, you might notice a pattern. At first, the book is simply a plaything, or something to chew. Eventually, as the baby grows older and is read to more often, he or she begins to see the book differently. The baby looks at the pictures and searches for familiar ones, and may even begin paying attention to the print. The book is no longer treated as a toy; the baby realizes that it is a thing he or she can turn to for a story or a familiar picture. There are many ways to enable this growth of understanding about books. Let's look at some of them now.

Daily Read-Alouds

The best way to teach children this concept is the simplest—read to them often. Making books a part of children's lives is the way to show them that books are important, that they are enjoyable, and that they are sources of information. When children ask questions, you can answer them with statements such as, "Let's look it up in a book to find out more," or "Here's a picture of one in this book." Read and reread favorite story books and big print books, because this is a way for children to become familiar with the structure of a story at a very young age.

When you read aloud to children, remember that oral language is the bridge to literacy with print. Clay says that "the preschool child's language development is vital to his progress in reading. . . . After all, reading is a language activity" (1991, pp. 37–38). Reading aloud to children is a skill that takes practice, yet it is one of the most enjoyable experiences you'll have as a teacher. There are ways to make the read-aloud experience one that your students will eagerly anticipate. See Figure 6.1 for some tips on how to read aloud to children, as well as ways to

Book Interactions

1. Always introduce the book as a product of an author.
2. Talk about the author as a person who wrote some words for others to enjoy and learn from. Point out the dedication page, which helps children see authors as real people. Talk about other books by the same author, and similarities you can see.
3. Talk about the decisions that the author made in the book, such as the setting, names for the characters, and problems in the story.
4. Think aloud, telling the children how you are reacting to the book as you read. Examples of ways to begin are:

   "Hm-m-m. This is a surprise. I wonder why the author said this."
   "Wow. I wonder what will happen next?"
   "Ok, so wait a minute. I want to be sure that I have things straight in this story. So, this book is about. . . ."
   "Oh, I think this sentence might be a clue. Listen!"
   "I really love the way the author used that word. Listen to it again. . . ."
   "This reminds me of the time. . . ."
   "I did not know that. I'm going to keep reading to find out more. I'll turn the page."
   "Oh, I see a picture on this page. It's giving me a clue."

5. Encourage predictions based on pictures, words, the title, and the author.
6. Point to pictures and name them. Ask questions like, "What do you notice about this picture?" or "What does this picture show you?"
7. Encourage children to talk with each other about the book. After reading the book once, reread it and ask them to "say something" to a partner at stop points throughout:
   - Turn to your partner and tell him or her the funniest thing on this page.
   - Turn to your partner and talk about the character.
   - Turn to your partner and make a face that shows what the character is feeling right now.

Figure 6.1 Ways to interact with books.

[handwritten note: Is it ok to break up the story, or should you read it a 2nd time + then "think aloud"]

interact with children as you read to them, so that their understanding of books grows as they listen and enjoy.

Any teacher or parent of young children knows that a single reading of a good book is never enough. It's easy to tell which books in the home or classroom library are the children's favorites! They are the ones with the worn and wrinkled pages, smudged fingerprints, and curled covers. These are the books that children love and return to again and again. Don't hesitate to reread books to children; in fact, make it part of your plan to read a good book several times. This repeated exposure gives them the schema that they need to begin reading it on their own, as well as the understanding of what stories and informational books are like.

Frequent rereading of a familiar book gives students background knowledge of the story so that they can "integrate with the graphic clues they see" (Schickedanz, 1989, p. 104). **Rereadings** of books should be encouraged, even though decoding is not yet taking place. These rereadings help your young students to internalize the print. Sulzby found that many children will read with help from the pictures, but rereadings help them become more familiar with the appearance and sound of the print. This information from previous rereadings can "be integrated with the children's budding graphic phonemic knowledge" (1989, p. 105).

Pretend Readings

The toddler introduced at the beginning of this chapter, Sammy, was doing what we call **pretend reading** (Cox, Fang & Otto, 2004). Also called **emergent story-book reading** (Teale & Sulzby, 1989), a pretend reading consists of a verbal page-by-page retelling of the text. Children who have been exposed to a book several times often know the text word for word on each page of the book. This behavior shows that the child is remembering the words, rather than decoding them, and sometimes parents and teachers overlook the importance of this remarkable achievement of the young child. The child is doing more than merely memorizing the text. He is beginning to understand print. He is beginning to know these things about the meanings that are conveyed in books:

1. Many books have stories in them.
2. Stories have characters, with problems.
3. Every story has a beginning, middle, and end.
4. Sometimes books have words that rhyme, and these words often look and sound alike.
5. Many books contain information about the world around them.
6. Books contain pictures of familiar things.
7. The words in books help explain the world around them.

Pretend reading is a natural result of reading aloud to children. After hearing a book read aloud to them several times, children are familiar with its contents and are usually eager to experience the book on their own. It is exciting to a young child to realize that he does, indeed, know what is contained within the covers of a book. Thus, he "pretends" to read, by retelling the words verbally as he turns the page. Dr. Seuss so aptly described this behavior in his book of this same title, "I can read with my eyes shut!" (1978).

Encourage this important indicator of growth in your classroom by providing plenty of books in your classroom library. Do not worry about making sure that these are all "easy-to-read" books that can be decoded by your children. If you did, you would severely limit the books that your preschoolers or kindergarteners would know. Have available books that might be familiar to them, such as fairy tales, Dr. Seuss selections, and nursery rhyme books. These books are true candidates for pretend reading, because they might already know the story and narration behind them from listening to their parents or preschool teachers read to them. Make sure that your own curriculum consists of many, many read-alouds, because listening to a book gives them the schema that they need to attempt to "read" a book on their own (Gadsden, 2000; Martinez & Roser, 1985; Paratore,

2002; Strickland & Taylor, 1989; Tierney & Readence, 2005). If you are teaching English language learners, encourage their attempts at pretend readings, using partners and providing plenty of bilingual books, because these readings promote emergent reading for them (Goldenberg, 2004).

Shared Book Experiences

The **shared book experience** is a strategy that gives children support as they learn to read text (Harste, Short & Burke, 1988; Holdaway, 1979; Tierney & Readence, 2005). The term **shared reading** is often used to describe this strategy as well. "Shared reading" means to support students' reading by decoding the words for them while they listen and read along where possible. "Shared book experience" refers to the experience that teachers provide for a group of students. Usually, the shared book experience is done with an enlarged edition of the book, called a "big book." The book should be a quality piece of children's literature with predictable, repetitive text; perhaps some rhyme; intriguing pictures; and a plot that captivates the students.

To use this strategy, have the children sit on the floor in front of you, and put the big book on an easel in front of them. It is important that everyone can see the pictures as well as the print, which is the advantage of the enlarged size. Using this type of text makes it more likely that your students will be able to follow the text and read aloud with you. Read aloud and move your finger across the print as you read the page; invite them to join you when they can. Some teachers specify when the children may want to join in (usually at a rhyming word or predictable phrase), with a prearranged signal. After the initial reading, engage your students in a variety of activities in which they interact with and respond to the book, such as rereading, talking about specific words in the text, art, drama, puppetry, and writing responses. Have small copies of the book available for the students to read on their own, and audio copies of the story at a listening center. Give them the opportunity to reread the book throughout the week.

The shared book experience can also be done with poems, chants, or songs that you have duplicated for the overhead projector. These types of texts and the shared reading strategy are particularly valuable for students who are learning to speak English (Peregoy & Boyle, 2004).

I describe shared reading in greater detail in Chapter 9, along with some advice for purchasing big books and a list of appropriate ones to use in the shared book experience. As you will see in Chapter 9, scaffolded reading is a way to give students a chance to read on their own, with your help. Shared reading is just one way that you can scaffold your students as they learn to read.

Predictable Books

As explained in the previous section, **predictable books** are an important part of the early childhood classroom. Young children love books that are predictable, because they can read them! These books give nonreaders the confidence they need to see themselves as readers, because the text is so easy to predict. As you'll recall from Chapter 1, readers are constantly using cueing systems to make good guesses about what comes next on the printed page (Goodman, 1967, 1973; Smith, 1997). Predictable books allow them to do this with ease. The text uses some phrases

Modifying Instruction for

ELL

Shared Reading with *Silly Sally* (Wood, 1992)

GRADE LEVEL: K–1

● **Objective**

Students will recognize new vocabulary, read with fluency, and retell the events of the story in the book *Silly Sally*.

● **Preparation**

Choose "rug buddies," which are partners assigned to sit with each other every time the class gathers for literacy lessons on the rug. This practice ensures the participation of all students, so that they can talk to one another without the anxiety of speaking to the whole group.

● **Materials**

Silly Sally by Audrey Wood (1992), in big book and small book forms.

● **Introduction**

1. Invite the students to sit on the floor with their rug buddies and show them the big book.

2. Say, "The title of the book is *Silly Sally*. Look at this picture on the cover."

3. Point to the picture of Sally and ask an "inclusive" question, which allows for a variety of appropriate responses from all the students: "What can you tell us about Sally?"

4. When students respond, point to the features of the picture that correspond to the child's statement. For example, if the child says, "She has a purple dress," point to the picture of the dress. This practice helps reinforce the visual cue from the picture for all students; in particular, it is vital for English language learners to see the connection between the picture and the word.

5. Write the responses on chart paper.

6. Invite the students to read and find out the silly things that Sally does.

● **Shared Reading**

1. Read the first page aloud to the students, which shows Silly Sally walking to town backwards and upside down.

2. Ask for predictions: "What will happen to Sally when she walks to town upside down? Turn to your rug buddy and whisper your idea."

Modifications for ELL are printed in color.

3. Continue in this manner throughout the book, stopping every time Sally meets a new animal. Ask students to join in the reading of the repetitive rhyme, and be sure to point to words as they are read.

4. Use the stop points to talk about words and phrases in the book that require schema that some of the students might not have. Write these words on the board, then explain them, using concrete examples and role-play, so that students can see connections between the words and their experiences.

   a. *Leap-frog*—Show the students how two people can play this game by jumping over each other, much like frogs.

   b. *Loon*—Write the word on the board and show students a picture of a loon. (You can find good photographs and much information by typing "loon" into Google or your favorite search engine.)

   c. *Jig*—Explain that a "jig" is a dance. Have students role-play a "jig."

   d. *Right-side-up*—Show students the difference between "right-side-up" and "upside-down" with a chair or other large object.

5. Ask another inclusive question: "What do you know about Silly Sally now? Turn to your buddy and share your answer."

6. Ask students to share their answers with the whole group. As they respond, turn to the appropriate page and point to the corresponding picture.

7. Ask, "How did Neddy Buttercup help Silly Sally get to town?" Discuss responses.

● Response Activities

   1. Put a tape of this story in the Listening Center for rereadings.

   2. Send a copy of the book home in a family reading bag.

   3. Put a picture of Sally on the table, along with a toy pig, a plush dog, the picture of the loon, a plush sheep, and a picture of Neddy Buttercup. Ask students to retell the story, using the objects and pictures to help them recall the sequence of events. Use a retelling checklist to record and assess their retellings.

repeatedly, and often contains rhyming words within these phrases. This makes the words easy for the youngest reader to figure out without the demands of decoding every word. Many predictable books do not have a story plot, with a character, problem, and resolution, as typical children's story books do. Rather, the narrative is often sillier, more playful, and simply describes an event or a character's condition. Some excellent predictable books include:

Slowly, Slowly, Said the Sloth (Carle, 2002)
The Surprise Garden (Hall, 1998)
Polar Bear, Polar Bear, What Do You Hear? (Martin, 1991)
If You Give a Mouse a Cookie (Numeroff, 1985)
Mouse Mess (Riley, 1997)
There Was an Old Lady Who Swallowed a Fly (Taback, 1997)
Silly Sally (Wood, 1992)

Playing with Literacy

To help children appreciate and internalize the language of stories, make story books an everyday part of the classroom. One easy and effective way to do this is with **prop stories** (Glazer, 1989). This strategy capitalizes on children's natural tendencies to play, and on their ability to dramatize as they play. After reading a good story to your students, tell them that it will be available to them for play. Put the book in a sturdy plastic box, a cloth bag with a drawstring, or even a cardboard box. Label this receptacle with the title of the book. Also place in the box or bag several items that could help the students reenact the story. Items can be costumes, toys, or props that pertain to the story. Once these are available, your students can retell these favorite stories, using the props that are provided in the kits. Figure 6.2 shows some examples of kits that you can make.

In addition, you can invite your kindergarten students to play with reading and writing by making play areas in your classroom full of the stuff of literacy (Neuman & Roskos, 1989). Play areas are places set aside in the classroom for specific types of play, such as a housekeeping center that contains a child-sized refrigerator, stove, table and chairs, and doll beds. In this play area, include a telephone with a pencil and pad sitting next to it. Also include a cookbook, telephone book, and shopping lists to hang on the refrigerator. This area gives students an opportunity to think about how writing and reading fit in the household, and

The Very Hungry Caterpillar (Carle, 1969). A homemade fuzzy pompom caterpillar (or stuffed animal), wax or plastic fruits, pictures of foods, silk or plastic leaves, homemade butterfly.

The Three Billy Goats Gruff (Galdone, 1981). Three stuffed animals of graduated sizes (they do not have to be goats—children will pretend or create another story!), a troll or monster, a box to serve as a bridge.

The Little Old Lady Who Was Not Afraid of Anything (Williams, 1986). A small female doll (or a shawl that a child can wear to represent the lady), a man's shirt, an old pair of shoes, a hat, a pair of white gloves, a pair of pants, a plastic jack-o-lantern.

Caps for Sale (Slobodkina, 1947). At least one each of the following colors of caps: red, brown, grey, blue; at least two stuffed animals that can serve as monkeys; one checked cap; man's jacket for the peddler.

The Three Bears (Barton, 1991). Three teddy bears of graduating sizes, one blonde doll, three bowls of graduating sizes, three chairs of graduating sizes, three small bed pillows of graduating sizes.

The Old Man and His Door (Soto, 1996). A plush pig, hat for the old man, a large piece of sturdy cardboard for the door, washcloth or scrub brush, a baby doll, a small plastic bee, a plush goose or duck, a plastic egg, dollhouse furniture, two balls to represent watermelons.

Figure 6.2 Story book kits for playing with stories.

include these ideas in their play. Other types of play areas can include literacy props, such as a grocery store play area (cash register receipts, grocery lists, newspaper advertisements, and coupons), or a restaurant play area (menus, waiter's memo pad, cookbook, and bill for the meal). If your classroom space is limited, you can make play boxes filled with appropriate props for playing in these venues, and store them on low shelves. Children can select the box they want for playing.

Books Have Boundaries

We read English from left to right, and from top to bottom. This is a concept that very young children begin to internalize. If they pick up a book and see the picture upside-down, they know to turn it around. They also know that there is a beginning and will turn to the first page in the book. Later, they begin to consistently move from left to right through the book, and from left to right on the page. As sophistication with books grows, the child knows that he must make his eyes move to the right across the page, then drop down to the left, and continue in this manner as he covers the entire page.

These important understandings can be modeled and explained to students as you read and write with them (Clay, 1991; Schickedanz, 1989). Encourage the development of the idea that books and pages have boundaries with activities such as these:

1. When you read aloud from a book, tell them that you are starting from the beginning of the book.
2. When you finish reading, tell them that the last page is the end of the book.
3. Point to text on the big books that you read. Move your finger or a pointer across the page as you read aloud, pointing to each word.
4. When you turn the page, say, "I'm going to turn the page, and then start reading right here." Point to the words.
5. Put a green dot beside the first word on lists and charts that hang in the classroom.
6. When you write on charts, point to the left side of the page and explain that your writing must start there, so that it makes sense to people who read English.

Pictures Add to Meaning

Pictures in the book help to tell the story or explain the topic. When Sammy, the little boy described in the Personal Reflection at the beginning of this chapter, picked up *The Three Bears* and began "reading" or telling the story, he used pictures as an aid. Pictures are more than just decorative; as children grow older and more savvy about books, they realize that the pictures are essential elements of the story, and that they can retell the entire story, often by simply looking at the pictures.

To capitalize on the use of pictures, you can use **wordless picture books.** Invite children to tell the story from the pictures alone. Examples of such include:

The Red Book (Lehman, 2004)
Clown (Blake, 1996)
Sidewalk Circus (Fleischman, 2003)

Diversity in the Reading Classroom

Creating Learning Climates for All Young Children

Allington and Cunningham (2002), in their book *Schools That Work: Where All Children Read and Write,* state, "It is the children who arrive at kindergarten with a history of few home experiences with print, book, story, and pencil activities who are most likely to occupy the desks in the basic skills and special education class-rooms in high school 10 years later. . . . The schools we have are better at sorting and labeling children than at accelerating their academic development" (2002, p. 1).

Programs designed to help our youngest students, such as the Head Start program, have been around for years. Yet evaluations of Head Start have also shown disappointing results for years (Austin, Rogers & Walbesser, 1972; Zigler & Muenchow, 1992). Wide-scale reforms and mandates from the government may call attention to the need for solutions; however, sometimes the things that matter most are simply a matter of common sense. What makes sense?

First, children who are at risk for learning literacy need more books. Schools in which poor children are enrolled have fewer books in their libraries than do wealthier schools (Guice, Allington, Johnston, Baker & Michelson, 1996). Krashen (1996) tells us that many studies relate school library quality to reading achievement. Allington and Cunningham (2002) suggest that school libraries are one of the most important places in a school that enrolls at-risk young children, and that they should be well stocked, serviced by a knowledge-able librarian who works on flex-time, and available year-round for community use.

Second, children deserve good teachers. The quality of classroom instruction is more important than the curriculum materials being used. For too long, educa-tors—and, more recently, national and state govern-ments—have been concerned about the "best" way to teach literacy. Access to high-quality teaching is what matters for children, especially those who are at risk (Allington & McGill-Franzen, 2004). Teachers who know how to choose from the variety of materials available to them, who know their students well, and who know a myriad of strategies that will meet their students' needs are what all children deserve. Classroom practices that these teachers rely upon for their students having diffi-culty learning to read and write include:

● Reading to children daily from several different types of texts, including plenty of predictable books

● Use of shared book and interactive writing experi-ences

● Explicit instruction and mental modeling of strategies

● Frequent rereadings of favorite books

● Authentic assessments, rather than reliance solely on standardized tests

● Large classroom libraries containing literature by and about people of diverse backgrounds

● Large blocks of time to read books that are easy enough to read independently

● Programs that involve families

(Allington & Cunningham, 2002; Strickland, 2002b)

Oh! (Goffin, 2000)
Clementine's Cactus (Keats, 1999)
Man's Work! (Kubler, 1999)
The Ring (Maizlish, 1996)
Dinosaur! (Sis, 2000)

Using picture books that have words in them, pictures can be connected to the text by using them to make predictions. In the popular **picture walk** strategy, the

Using the Picture Walk Strategy

First Day

Look at the cover and the author's name, and then make predictions about the book based on these. Introduce the theme or main idea of the book, and make additional predictions. Write students' predictions on a chart. Next to each child's prediction, write his or her name or initial.

Second Day

Look at each page without reading the words. Talk about the pictures and how they add to the story. Talk about what the pictures tell you about the story or the main idea of the author. On each page, make some predictions based on the pictures. Write them on charts that you have numbered or otherwise identified so that you know to which page in the book they refer.

Third Day

Read the book aloud, with expression and drama. Do not comment or check on predictions yet. Simply read the book for the pleasure of hearing the author's words.

After enjoying the book, reread it. Page by page, check the predictions that you and the students made from the picture walk. Make sure your comments affirm rather than praise predictions that are "correct." Remember that predictions are merely a good guess, and sometimes they do not match the print. Make comments like these:

"You got lots of clues from the pictures!"
"Your prediction made a lot of sense."
"Your prediction matched the author's words."

Figure 6.3 The picture walk procedure.

teacher shows pictures from the story to the children before they read or listen to the story (DeFord, Lyons & Pinnell, 1991; Goldenberg, 1991). The teacher asks the students for predictions about the story based on these pictures. The procedure is shown in Figure 6.3. A similar strategy is **storyboards,** which also capitalizes on the use of pictures to make predictions, and reinforces the process of putting events in sequential order. See its procedure in Figure 6.4.

Printed Words Match Spoken Words

Without actually decoding letters and sounds, children know that words on the page represent words that are spoken. Young children are often able to retell familiar stories, repeating word for word the text that is on a particular page. This

Storyboards

To prepare:

1. Choose a book that has clear illustrations that depict the story well, with a storyline that has a definitive beginning, middle, and end. Find three paperback copies of the book, two of which will be cut apart. Search flea markets, library sales, garage sales, and old school storage closets for multiple copies of old books.
2. Tear out each page. Remember to include the pictures on the back of each page, so that every page in the book is represented. You may leave the words intact, or, if you prefer, cut the words off.
3. Glue each page to squares of tagboard, posterboard, or stiff construction paper.

Procedure:

1. Show the students the intact copy of the book and tell them that they will be trying to put a mixed-up version of this story in order. Prepare to read it by making predictions from the front cover. For example, when reading *Hey, Al* (Yorinks, 1986), model by saying, "This picture on the cover makes me think that the book will be about a man who cleans places—a custodian or a janitor. What does the cover picture tell you?"
2. Show the students the picture cards, in the correct sequence. Ask them to make predictions based on these pictures. For each prediction, write the name of the student making it on a sentence strip or sheet of paper. Tape the prediction above the storyboard picture, displayed along the chalk ledge.
3. Read the book in its entirety, without stopping, and with appropriate expression.
4. Return to the predictions and verify them. Talk about the clues that the pictures give the students, enabling them to make good predictions.
5. Remove the storyboards and the predictions from the board and chalk ledge. Shuffle the storyboards and display them in mixed-up order. Ask the students to retell the story in sequence, using the pictures as clues. Have them put the storyboards back in the proper sequence.
6. For students who need a challenge, do not read the book first. Instead, show them the shuffled storyboards out of sequence. Ask them to make predictions from these pictures, then read the story to confirm. After reading, put the storyboards in the proper sequence.

Figure 6.4 The storyboards procedure.

ability does not mean that the child is able to decode, or recognize the word out of context; however, it means more than simple memorization of words in a story. An essential element of reading is the knowledge that the squiggly little lines on the bottom of a page hold meaning. Connecting those flat, two-dimensional symbols with words and ideas is a giant leap forward in the journey of reading.

Language Experience Approach

To help your students see that print represents words that can be spoken, use the **language experience approach** with them. This technique has been around for more than 30 years, and it is still a sound one for helping students see the connection between language and print. Its premise is that every child eventually conceptualizes these ideas:

- What I can think about, I can talk about.
- What I can talk about, I can write.
- What I can write, I can read.
- I can read what others write for me to read. (Allen & Allen, 1967, p. 1)

The language experience approach is based on the idea that students can talk and write about their experiences, then read and learn from their own text (Stauffer, 1970; Allen & Allen, 1967). To use this strategy, provide your students with an experience, and talk about it with them. This experience gives them a shared schema for a topic of interest. When they dictate a narrative that describes their experience, and you record it, they are seeing the results of authorship—language that is written down for everyone to see and share. This student-generated piece of text can be used in many ways, from learning new words to sequencing story events. It is especially helpful for English language learners, as their command of English grows (Lenters, 2004 & 2005). Figure 6.5 shows the procedure for this strategy.

Environmental Print

Yetta Goodman (1986) wrote of the importance of **environmental print** for emerging readers. This is the kind of print that surrounds us every day: "McDonald's," "Wal-Mart," and "Nike" are a few words that your students may see in their homes and neighborhoods. Other environmental words are "stop," "women," "men," and "exit." Many teachers capitalize on their students' interest in words around them by labeling objects and furniture in the classroom, as well as labeling students' desks, mailboxes, and cubbyholes with their names. However, Yaden, Rowe, and MacGillivray (2000) report that experimental studies do not show strong support for depending upon environmental print to help children develop reading abilities. Instead, "conventional reading" experiences from books are better for word recognition and development of writing (p. 439).

Yet environmental print can be motivating for young children, because it is highly recognizable and often associated with things that are important and familiar to them. Later, when they begin to see the connections between letters and sounds, you can use words from their environment as a stimulus for learning new words. Cunningham (2005) suggests a strategy called "Using Words You Know," which is a decoding activity in which students learn how to make new words from words they already know, such as the word "hut" in "Pizza Hut," or the word "it" in "Kit Kat" candy bars. Chapter 7 shows you that strategy in use with words from children's books, and Chapter 8 shows you how to use it with words taken from surveys of your students' interests. Additionally, children's names and objects in the classroom provide great stimulus for kindergarten and first grade journal writing.

> ## Creating Language Experience Texts with the Language Experience Approach
>
> 1. Provide students with a concrete experience, such as walking through a park, visiting the school cafeteria, or planting seeds. The experience can also be a vicarious one, such as listening to a favorite story.
> 2. Talk about this experience together. Recall sights, sounds, smells, and feelings.
> 3. Ask students to dictate sentences that describe their experience.
> 4. As students talk, record these sentences on chart paper. Try to incorporate students' names in the narrative as much as possible. Some teachers write each contributor's name next to his or her sentence, or use the name in the sentence.
> 5. Upon completion, read the chart aloud to the students.
> 6. Reread it, asking the students to read it with you. Tell them to read any of the words that they know.
> 7. Keep the chart hanging in a highly visible spot. Reread the chart several times over the next few days.
> 8. Duplicate the chart and cut it into sentence strips. Have the students put the strips back in sequence.
> 9. Type the narrative so that each student has his own copy. Send it home for the students to read to their families.

Figure 6.5 Creating language experience texts.

Thus, environmental print can be used in strategies in which students need to use words they already know to create new words or provide text that they can read. Suggestions for doing this are listed in Figure 6.6.

Words Have Boundaries

As the young child grows in his understandings of the printed page, he realizes that words are separate entities, and that they have several qualities. First, they are different from pictures, and represent language. Second, a word is made up of a unique set of sounds. Third, each word has a beginning and end, and there are labels for different parts of a word. A child whose literacy is emerging can, when asked, point to individual words, and eventually, point to the beginning, end, and then the middle, of a printed word (Clay, 1991; Nagy & Scott, 2004). Children have these understandings in various degrees, regardless of whether they can verbalize them (Clay, 1989). Moreover, research indicates that concepts of word develop quite slowly (Gombert, 1992; Nagy & Scott, 2004). Piaget determined as far back as 1926 that these concepts of words are not fully present even in children as old as 9 or 10.

The language experience approach can be used to show this concept to your students. Be sure to display the student-generated text for all to see. As you write their dictations, tell them that you are leaving spaces between words. Make comments about the boundaries of words, such as, "Look at this. The word 'Tuesday'

Using Environmental Print

Logo Scrapbooks

Cut out logos from familiar items such as cereal boxes, toy labels, can labels, old paper menus, boxes such as those containing' McDonald's French fries, and so on. Put these in a scrapbook or magnetic page photo album. Children like to find words and logos that they recognize. Have them dictate sentences about the places where they have been.

Photograph Albums

After taking pictures of classroom activities, put them in a photo album. Label them with captions that the children dictate. You can also ask the children to bring in baby pictures and other photographs from home, and create individual albums with captioned pictures or a class album called "When We Were Very Young."

Classroom Labels in Sentences

Many early childhood teachers label objects in the classroom, so that students can see words like "desk," "chair," "chalkboard," and "clock." Go one step further, and use labels that show a complete sentence, such as, "This is a chair," or "This is the clock." Underline or put a box around the target word.

Charts and Classroom Directions

Wherever possible, put your organizational techniques in writing. Create charts that help students know their classroom jobs, or where items belong. Create lists such as the daily schedule, attendance records, and group arrangements. Give the students opportunities to read and find out these housekeeping types of things for themselves.

Figure 6.6 Creating text that comes from the children's environment.

ends with a 'y,' just as the word 'Monday' does!" Or, "Here's the end of that word, so now I need to leave a space, then write the next word." When you read the chart aloud with the students, point to words with your hand or pointer. Allow students to do the same with a pointer.

Another good way to show students about word boundaries is with big books. Pointing to words as you read is easy because the print is large enough for all to see it. In addition, you can talk about how the author and publishing company made decisions about where to place words and pictures on the page.

"Book Language" Is Unique

Even though the young child can understand that printed words mean spoken words, the child who is familiar with books knows something more about text. Stories in books are spoken in a special style, which differs from the way we talk

(Hayes, 1988; Nagy & Scott, 2004). For example, authors usually use the word "said" to convey dialogue. They must also do lots of describing, which is unnecessary in normal speech. Additionally, stories have flavor, in that they consist of words and phrases that we do not often use in speech, such as "Once upon a time," or "And they lived happily ever after," or even "The end."

To reinforce this, when reading aloud, talk about book language. Make remarks such as, "That's such an interesting way for the author to describe this. I never would have thought of that." Or, "Gee, a lot of stories begin with 'Once upon a time,' don't they?"

Words Consist of Letters

A young child's understanding of words develops over time (Ehri, 1994), and one of the most important concepts children grasp is the idea that words are made of letters (Goswami, 2000). Usually, the alphabet is introduced, sung, or taught as a separate entity from words on a page; however, it needs to be made clear to children that the alphabet is a set of letters, and that these letters serve a purpose in words. When writing words on a chart, or pointing out words in a big book, it is helpful to be specific about naming a letter. For example, if you encounter the word "today" in a language experience chart, you can point to it and say, "This word begins with the letter 't.' I know I need to get my mouth ready to make the /t/ sound because I see the letter 't.'"

Word Size Does Not Matter

A child who is beginning to understand concepts of print knows that there is no relationship between the length of words and the size of the concept they represent. For example, the name "Tim," even though it is a short, three-letter word, does not necessarily connote a smaller person than the name "Samantha," which is a much longer word. This helps them to understand the idea that words have their own qualities, unrelated to the concepts they represent.

Environmental print is helpful in reinforcing this concept (Schickedanz, 1989). When your students see names of classmates on charts and on desks, they begin to realize that the size of the name does not indicate the size of its person. Similarly, labeling objects in the classroom accomplishes this same objective. Talking about this helps, too.

Charting the size of words is another way to teach this idea. Have students count the number of letters in words that have been written on cards. Then place the word cards on a chart to graph the size of the words. An example is shown in Figure 6.7.

Sentences Have Boundaries

As the child's familiarity with print grows, he knows that sentences are collections of words. When asked, he is able to point to the beginning of a sentence on the page, as well as the end of a sentence on the page. This distinction is important,

The Size of Words

1-letter words	2-letter words	3-letter words	4-letter words	5-letter words
I	in	the	fish	Chris
A	to	cat	Mike	chair
	we	Kim	door	board
	on	all	desk	lunch

Figure 6.7 Charting the size of words.

because it shows the child's ability to recognize conventions of print. **Metalinguistic awareness** is the understanding of the ways that we talk about our language, and is evident when the child is able to identify components of print (Nagy & Scott, 2004). In school, we often address concepts of print by including things such as these in our talk: "the first word in that sentence" or "the period at the end of the sentence" or "the capital letter." Many times, we simply assume that our students know what we are talking about. When a child begins to see sentences as entities, his or her awareness of how our language looks on paper is growing and he or she is better able to manipulate it and talk about it.

To foster this understanding, the language experience approach is helpful once again. After you read the chart with your students, point out the sentences. Say, "Let's read the first word of this sentence," and "Now, this period tells us that this is the end of the sentence." Another way to increase sentence awareness is to duplicate the chart, then cut it into sentence strips. It will look similar to a puzzle, because sentences do not all stop at the end of the line or the edge of the page. Ask your students to read the original chart in its entirety, and then put the sentence strips in order. It may be necessary for them to leave the original chart handy so that they can refer to it as they read the strips.

Big books are helpful for this type of print awareness, too. As you read to students or have them participate in shared reading, move your hand along the print. When you get to the end of a sentence, tap the page with your finger or with the pointer, to indicate a punctuation mark such as a period, which signifies the end of the sentence.

Be sure to talk with your students about books in which sentences have been printed on multiple pages. An example of this is the classic *Where the Wild Things Are* by Maurice Sendak (1963). This book is a delightful story book with pictures, but it is difficult for some children to read, because they must turn the page several times in order to read just one sentence. There are a few books like this, and you can increase children's awareness of sentence boundaries with them. First, read the book aloud for them to enjoy. Then, read the book again, and as you read, say, "I'll turn the page for the rest of the sentence." Examples of books with sentences that go beyond the page boundaries include: *Angus and the Ducks* (Flack, 1997) and *If You Take a Mouse to School* (Numeroff, 2002).

Children Become Phonologically Aware

One of the most significant milestones in a youngster's development is the ability to think about and verbalize sensitivity to the sounds of our language. Children have **phonological awareness** when they can talk about words that rhyme, count syllables in a word, or separate the beginning of a word from its ending (Yopp & Yopp, 2000). One part of phonological awareness is phonemic awareness, which is the child's "awareness that the speech stream is made up of a sequence of small units of sounds" (p. 130). These units of sounds, the smallest units in our language, are called *phonemes*. They make a difference in our communication and our understandings of what is spoken. For example, the difference between the words "cat" and "hat" is one phoneme. The word "cat" begins with the /k/ phoneme, and the word "hat" begins with the /h/ phoneme. Otherwise, the words sound the same; yet that one small sound amounts to a big difference in meaning. Thus, a child's ability to pay attention to, manipulate, and talk about the differences between the sounds of these two words is phonemic awareness. This type of awareness is crucial to the child's future ability to associate sounds with letters; thus, phonemic awareness is critical for success in phonetic decoding, and eventually reading with understanding the words they encounter in print (Ehri & Nunes, 2002; National Reading Panel, 2000a; Yopp & Yopp, 2000). The importance of phonemic awareness is underscored by the No Child Left Behind Act, which stipulates that it is one of the five areas in reading in which students in U.S. schools must be proficient.

Phonemic awareness is not the same thing as phonics. It is an awareness of the smallest sounds of our language and how they can be manipulated; it requires no knowledge of the alphabet. Children who are phonologically aware do not necessarily know alphabet letters and their corresponding sounds at all! Phonics knowledge is different. It requires recognition of the alphabet, and an understanding of the correspondence between those letters and the sounds that they represent. But phonemic awareness is very helpful for knowing how to take apart and blend sounds together—something that is needed later, when trying to decode unknown words.

Suppose you give Joey, a student in your kindergarten class, this task: "Tell me the first sound you hear in the word 'house.'" Joey should be able to make the /h/ sound by opening his mouth and blowing out air. That would indicate that he has some phonemic awareness. He knows the sound, or the phoneme that he hears at the beginning of the word. If you tell him, "Tell me the sound that is the same in 'house,' 'hat,' and 'here,'" he should still be able to say that the /h/ sound is in each word, indicating that he has phonemic awareness. Or, suppose you ask, "What is 'house' with the /m/ sound at the beginning of the word?" His phonemic awareness abilities kick in when he answers, "Mouse!"

Notice that there is no discussion of the written letter "h." Joey's phonemic awareness indicates that he knows the sounds that are in these words, but he does not necessarily identify that sound with its corresponding letter. Suppose, however, you ask Joey, "Which letter in the word 'house' makes the /h/ sound?" If he can answer, "h," then he has knowledge of the correspondence between that letter and the sound it represents. If you tell him, "Change the word 'house' by taking away

Type of Phonological Awareness	Example of Activity
Rhyming words	"Tell me a word that rhymes with *cat*."
Syllables	"Clap three times—one clap for each part of Jennifer's name."
Onsets and rimes	"Change the word *hat* to another word, just by changing the first sound."
Phonemes	"Stretch out the sounds in the word *dog*. How many sounds are there?"

Figure 6.8 Sequence of instruction for phonological awareness activities, as suggested by Yopp and Yopp (2000).

the 'h' and putting an 'm' at the beginning of the word. Now tell me the new word," he should be able to produce the word "mouse," and pronounce it. Successful completion of these tasks indicates that he has some understanding of phonics because he knows which letters represent the sounds he hears in a word.

Yopp and Yopp (2000) offer a sequence for instruction, which begins with the largest (and easiest to grasp) sound units—the whole word—and ends with the smallest (and most difficult to grasp) sound units—individual phonemes. This sequence is helpful in planning classroom activities for the emergent reader and is shown in Figure 6.8. Each component of the sequence is discussed next.

Rhyming Activities

Larger units of sound are easier to manipulate than smaller units of sound. Thus, it is helpful to begin with rhyming activities using whole words. The best place to start is in children's books. Books for the very young abound with playful language and rhyming words. Read these books daily, and join the children as they play with rhymes. Figure 6.9 shows some of my favorite rhyming books and some rhyming activities to do with them. Figure 6.10 shows an example of one of these activities.

Activities with Syllables

In order to understand that word parts can be manipulated, which is important in decoding, children need to begin thinking about separating words into some components. Syllables are the word parts with which most children are able to begin. Cunningham, Moore, Cunningham, and Moore suggest that clapping is the "easiest way to get every child involved, and the children's names are naturally appealing words to clap" (2000, p. 40). You can model this by calling a child's name, then repeating it and clapping the number of syllables at the same time. The name

Title of Rhyming Book	Activity That Focuses on Rhymes
Alligator Pie: Special Edition (Dennis Lee, 2001)	Have children make up their own "if I don't get some" rhymes. Nonsense words may also be used. For example: "Alligator cake, alligator cake. If I don't get some, I think I'm gonna shake." "Alligator pasta, alligator pasta. If I don't get some, I think I'm gonna shasta."
Play Day: A Book of Terse Verse (McMillan, 1991)	Terse verse is a type of poetry, with each poem consisting of two rhyming words. One such verse is in the title of this book: "play day." Ask children to create and illustrate other verses, such as "cool school," or silly ones such as "jet pet."
Does a Mouse Have a House? (Miranda, 1994)	Told in rhyme, this book is about animals and his or her habitats. Give each student a frame for filling in his or her own animal names and rhyming habitats. For example: "Does a *snake* have a *lake?*"
There's a Bug in My Mug (Salisbury, 1997a)	This book contains silly rhymes similar to its title. Ask students to make up rhymes about animals that could be found in unusual places; for example: "There's a *rat* in my *hat.*"
My Nose Is a Hose (Salisbury, 1997b)	This is another book with silly rhymes that mimic metaphors. Ask students to make up similar rhymes, and illustrate them: "My *leg* is an *egg.*"
Green Eggs and Ham (Seuss, 1960)	Ask the children to think of two words: an animal word and a place. These two words must rhyme. Then, have them create another page for this book, indicating places where they would not eat green eggs and ham. For example: "I would not eat them with a dog. I would not eat them on a log."
A Giraffe and a Half (Silverstein, 1964)	This cumulative, rhyming tale tells of a giraffe that has a bee on his knee and many other silly things. Ask the children to draw pictures of silly things that they could have on themselves, such as "jelly on his belly," or "pies on her eyes."
The Hungry Thing (Slepian and Seidler, 1967)	Ask the children to guess the food that the Hungry Thing wants to eat, based on the nonsense rhyme used in the book. Then, create a meal of their own, using any words, nonsense or real, that rhyme with the food words, such as "quananas" for "bananas" or "nice dream" for "ice cream."
Silly Sally (Wood, 1992)	This book uses rhyme to describe Silly Sally's travels. Her antics rhyme with the names of animals she meets along the way. Ask students to create their own rhymes, such as this: "Silly Tommy went to town, walking backwards, upside down. On the way he met a rat, a silly rat, they wore a hat!" See the example of a "Silly Sally" rhyme produced by a first grader, shown in Figure 6.13.

Figure 6.9 Rhyming activities that use children's books.

Figure 6.10 A "Silly Sally" rhyme.

"Angelo" is represented with three claps, and just one clap represents the name "Mike." Children do not need to learn the term "syllable," and many teachers find it more age-appropriate to use the word "beat." Practice clapping beats during routine activities such as morning roll call, circle time, or lining up. You can give directions such as "Anyone who has a two-beat name may line up!"

Yopp and Yopp (2000) suggest visually representing the number of syllables in the children's names. Have each child draw a self-portrait and write his or her name. Then, ask them to glue the appropriate number of colored paper squares on the paper to represent the number of beats in their name. Finally, ask the students to move around the room with their portraits in hand, to physically group themselves according to the number of syllables in their name.

This idea can be applied to other words; for example, interesting words from a children's book can be categorized according to their number of beats. Children will begin to see that longer words usually signify more syllables; however, some words have many letters in them but only one or two beats. Thus, as they gain experience with listening to the beats in words, it is helpful to also show them the words. (See Figure 6.11, on p. 190). In this activity, Mrs. Dickenson, a kindergarten teacher, read aloud *Armadillo Rodeo* (Brett, 1995). She printed interesting words and names from the book on a chart, then pronounced them for the

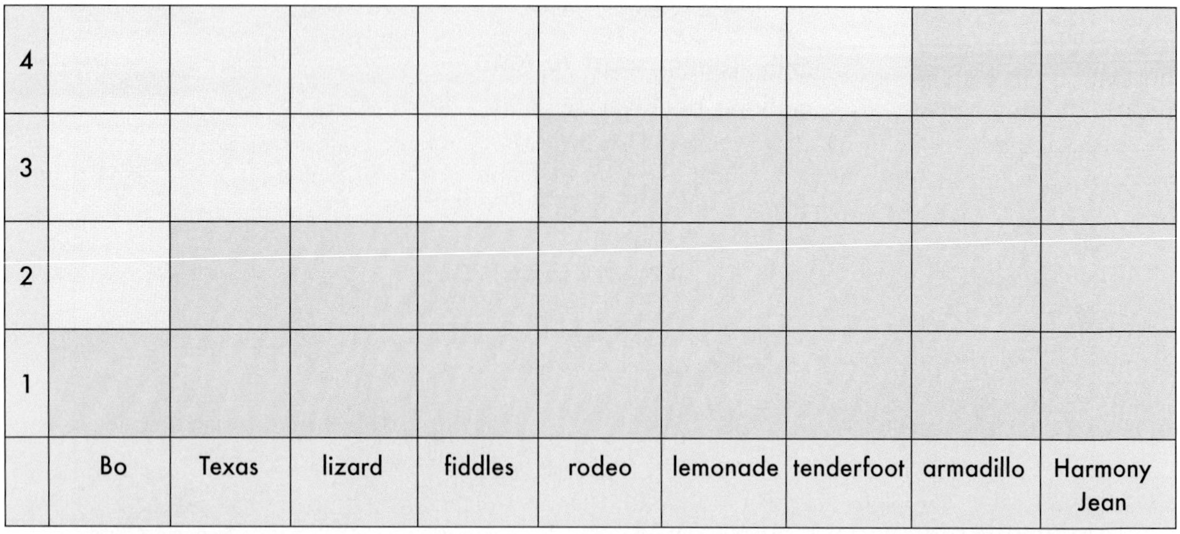

	Bo	Texas	lizard	fiddles	rodeo	lemonade	tenderfoot	armadillo	Harmony Jean
4								▓	▓
3					▓	▓	▓	▓	▓
2		▓	▓	▓	▓	▓	▓	▓	▓
1	▓	▓	▓	▓	▓	▓	▓	▓	▓

Figure 6.11 Words and names from *Armadillo Rodeo* (Brett, 1995) and their syllable counts.

students and asked them to clap the beats in each word. Once the number of beats was determined, students pasted colored squares above the word to signify the number of syllables in the word. Notice that some words have longer spellings but fewer syllables.

Another fun and challenging way to examine the "beats in a name" is to use two children's books: *Tikki Tikki Tembo* (Mosel, 1968) and *Tingo Tango Mango Tree* (Vaughan, 1995). Both of these books introduce characters with very long names that will entice children to clap the many beats in the name.

Finally, Yopp and Yopp show us that a traditional children's song can be helpful in blending syllables. The song begins:

> Clap, clap, clap your hands,
> Clap your hands together.
> Clap, clap, clap your hands,
> Clap your hands together.

After singing this, introduce a new verse:

> Say, say, say these parts,
> Say these parts together.
> Say, say, say these parts,
> Say these parts together.
> Teacher: "Pen" (pause) "cil!"
> Children: "Pencil!"
> Teacher: "Ta" (pause) "ble!"
> Children: "Table!"
> Teacher: "Com" (pause) "pu" (pause) "ter!"
> Children: "Computer!"

(2000, p. 138)

Activities with Onsets and Rimes

Imagine a young reader who is trying to decode the unknown word "mouse." If the student is already able to recognize the word "house," then decoding this new word can be quite simple. He or she simply substitutes the /h/ phoneme for the /m/ phoneme. This act of substitution is a skill that is used readily by good decoders. Good decoders can also segment phonemes in words, such as the child who says that "mouse" consists of two parts: "m-m-m" and "ouse."

These two skills—substituting one onset for another, and segmenting words into onsets and rimes—are important capabilities for success in decoding unknown words. An onset is the part of the syllable that precedes the vowel, such as the "b" in "ball" and the "sp" in "spill." The rime of a word is the vowel and any consonants that follow it. (Some rimes are words too, such as "all," "oat," and "eel.") Words that share the same rime are in the same word family, such as "bar," "car," "far," "star," and "tar." Word families sound alike, except for the first consonant phoneme. Thus, the word "war" would not be a part of the example word family; it does not sound like the other examples.

It is not necessary to teach children the terms for these word parts; instead, give them lots of opportunities to play with words, substitute sounds, and create new words in the same family (Ehri & McCormick, 2004). One way to do this is with children's literature that lends itself to word play. Dr. Seuss was the master of this genre! In *There's a Wocket in My Pocket* (1974b), he began:

> Did you ever have the feeling there's a WASKET in your BASKET?

The entire book tells of nonsense creatures found in the narrator's house, most of which are named with words in the same word family as the places they inhabit, such as the "nupboards in the cupboards" and the "vug under the rug." After hearing this book, encourage your students to make up their own nonsense creatures, such as the "zalkboard on the chalkboard" or the "hountain by the fountain." Have them write and illustrate these rhymes, then hang them in the appropriate places around the classroom.

Yopp and Yopp (2000) describe an activity that can be used many times in the classroom, using different words. Get the children started by reading aloud *We're Going on a Bear Hunt* (Rosen, 1989). Then, ask them to sit on the floor with their knees bent up, so that they can easily touch their toes as well as their knees. As the teacher chants, the students echo, tapping their toes and slapping their knees, using the chant that is shown in Figure 6.12. The easiest words to use are those that begin with sounds that are produced with a continuous flow of air and can be elongated, such as the /m/ phoneme: "m-m-m-m-m-m." These are easier to say and also easier for children to hear. Easier continuant sounds are also shown in Figure 6.12. As children develop, you can use words that begin with consonants that are "stopped"; in other words, they must have the "uh" sound added to them when pronouncing them in isolation, such as the /d/ phoneme: "duh." As you say this phoneme and slide your hands up to your knees, as shown in the chant, repeat it several times: "duh, duh, duh, duh, -ig—dig!"

Working with Spoken Phonemes

Before children know how to decode, they are users of our language. Prior to becoming aware of the relationship between letters and sounds, they are aware

Word Hunt

Example One: Using Continuant Sounds

Teacher: Going   on a   word   hunt!
(tap toes)   (slap knees)   (tap toes)   (slap knees)
Children repeat the words and motions.
Teacher: What's   this   word?
(tap toes)   (slap knees)   (tap toes)
Children repeat the words and motions.
Teacher: /r/   /at/
(tap toes)   (slap knees)
Children repeat the words and motions.
Teacher and children together: r-r-r-r-r-r-r-r-r-rat   Rat!
(slide hands from toes to knees)   (slap knees)

These are the consonant phonemes to use with beginners: /m/, /s/, /h/, /r/, /n/, /y/, /z/. They are continuant consonants and are easier to pronounce than others.

Example Two: Using Stop Consonant Sounds

Teacher: Going   on a   word   hunt!
(tap toes)   (slap knees)   (tap toes)   (slap knees)
Children repeat the words and motions.
Teacher: What's   this   word?
(tap toes)   (slap knees)   (tap toes)
Children repeat the words and motions.
Teacher: /b/   /ug/
(tap toes)   (slap knees)
Children repeat the words and motions.
Teacher and children together: "buh, buh, buh, buh, -ug bug!
(bump hands from toes to knees)   (slap knees)

These are the consonant phonemes to use as the students become more sophisticated: /b/, /w/, /d/, /v/, /l/, /g/, /t/, /f/, /p/, /k/. They are the stop consonant sounds and are more difficult to pronounce in segments.

Figure 6.12 Onset–rime chant suggested by Yopp and Yopp (2000).

that the language consists of sounds. When they begin to decode, they will need to understand that a written word represents a certain set of sounds, and moreover, that some words look very similar to other words that sound almost the same way; they will also need to be able to manipulate sounds in our language. Thus, they will need to work with spoken phonemes.

Because children naturally love to play with language, working with phonemes is not as difficult or as dull as it may seem. "Ghost talk" is one way to capitalize on children's interest in and propensity for rolling words around on the tongue. To get them interested in ghost talk, read aloud a children's ghost story, such as "In a Dark, Dark Room" or "The Ghost of John," two particularly good ones. Both are retold by Alvin Schwartz in his collection *In a Dark, Dark Room and Other Scary Stories* (1984). Have some pictures from the book ready to show them and tell them that you will "stretch out" the sounds of the words in the pictures as if talking like a ghost. For example, show a picture of a dog, and say, "This is a d-d-d-d-d-o-o-o-o-o-g-g-g-g." Be sure to pronounce each phoneme clearly and separately as much as possible.

To help children visually represent phonemes, you can use **Elkonin boxes.** Clay (1985) describes this strategy, which is based on an idea from the Russian psychologist D. B. Elkonin. The teacher and students "stretch out" the phonemes of a word, then use a concrete object to represent each one. The procedure is shown in Figure 6.13, and two examples are shown in Figure 6.14, on p. 194.

Children Become Aware of the Alphabet

One of the rites of passage in early childhood is learning the alphabet. Letters in the alphabet are the building blocks of our language; as adults, we have known and understood them for so long that we now take them for granted. Yet, looking at these

1. Choose words from literature with which your students are very familiar. These words should consist of only three or four phonemes.
2. Draw or affix a picture for each word on a card.
3. Underneath each picture, draw a matrix of three or four boxes.
4. Provide each child with a set of chips, counters, or other small objects.
5. Say the word, slowly and distinctly. Stretch out the sounds of the word without exaggerating them.
6. As you say each phoneme, slide a counter or chip into the box on the matrix, representing the number of phonemes in the word. Encourage the child to join the process with you, eventually sliding the chips into the boxes himself.
7. Remember that the number of phoneme spaces will not necessarily match the number of letters in a word; for example, the word "sick" has four letters and three phonemes. Additionally, consonant clusters consist of two phonemes; thus, the word "clip" has a total of four phonemes. Consonant digraphs represent only one phoneme; therefore, a word such as "that" has a total of three phonemes.
8. Make the task more difficult by removing the matrix and having the child represent the phonemes with chips only.
9. As the child gains experience, remove the picture and just say the word. The child represents the phonemes with chips, deciding how many sounds there are in the word.

Figure 6.13 Procedure for Elkonin (sound) boxes.

Elkonin box for a three-phoneme word: "dog"

Elkonin box for a four-phoneme word: "frog"

Figure 6.14 Two examples of Elkonin boxes.

letters through the eyes of a young child can give us a renewed respect for the complexity of the task that lies before the nonreader. Look at the letter shown below.

> **B**
>
> **What is this?**
>
> **What does it mean?**

How do you answer the question, "What does 'B' mean?" When you attach meaning to this flat, one-dimensional figure printed on the page, you're doing so by associating it with something else—something that is real, personalized, and bigger than it actually looks. The only way that the symbol printed on the page has any meaning is to attach it to something else—by itself, it means nothing. One might say that it says "buh," which is true, but by itself, what does "buh" mean?

Young, emerging readers must see each letter symbol as a unique, separate entity; be able to name it with a nonsense sound (such as the word "aitch" for "h" or "double-you" for "w"), recognize its upper- and lowercase forms; distinguish it from other letters (even the ones that look very similar to it); and finally, connect it to sounds and concepts that have meaning. This requires a number of abstractions and complex learning for a young mind that usually operates on concrete things.

"A teacher can provide the child with many opportunities to learn how to recognize the distinguishing features of a letter and use this information to form the letter, but the child must develop a personal basis to visually discriminate one letter from another" (Lyons, 1999, p. 60). This personal basis is how a concrete operational mind can handle such abstractions. Through multiple experiences and exposure, young children begin to associate letters with things that they know, or they begin to remember the visual idiosyncrasies of the letter. Children know letters in personal ways that may be different from the ways their classmates know letters. Additionally, they may have different ways of knowing different letters. For example, a kindergartener, Joey, knows the name of the letter "K" because of the sign he sees in front of the K-Mart store. However, he has not yet associated the sound of "K" with a noise like "kuh." He knows the letter "J" by its name as well as by its sound, and associates this letter with his own name. In fact, he says that "J" is "my J," and can reproduce the letter quite well. He also knows the "m-m-m-m" sound, but sometimes calls the "M" either "em" or an "en," and has trouble writing this letter. Joey is just beginning to know letters as separate entities, and has his own ways of remembering them.

While it is desirable for most kindergarteners to learn most of their letters before entering first grade, it is not necessary for them to know all of the letters of the alphabet before learning to read. In fact, some children learn to read before they know the entire alphabet. But, "learning a few letters is the first necessary step in gaining control of this complex process" of attending to and sorting out the visual information presented to them when reading (Lyons, 1999, p. 64). Identification of letters is important, because it helps children know what readers refer to when talking about printed forms of text. They also need to know letters so that they "use this visual information to monitor and check on themselves while reading and writing" (p. 64).

What kinds of experiences can you provide that will facilitate your young students' personal knowledge of letters? Let's look at some of those strategies now.

Using the Alphabet Song

One of the milestones in the growth of toddlers is their ability to sing this old, familiar song. It is part of growing up! Yet knowing a letter means "knowing it as a distinct entity, not just being able to name or sing the letters of the alphabet" (Lyons, 1999, p. 57). Sometimes, parents and even teachers are surprised when a child can recite the alphabet or sing the song, yet cannot identify single letters. Moreover, one of the difficulties with relying on the song is the "l-m-n-o-p" problem; sometimes children think that "elemenopee" is one letter.

The alphabet song is part of so many childhoods. It is hard to ignore it, so why not capitalize on it? Having the alphabet sequence intact gives the child a scaffold to hang onto when learning individual letters. Sometimes, when introducing a new letter, you will see your students singing the song and pointing to letters to figure out which letter you are talking about.

Create an alphabet chart that is synchronized with the song, like the one shown in Figure 6.15. As children sing, point to the individual letters, placed on the lines of the chart according to the pauses in the song. This helps them match the spoken letter with its written equivalent.

You can also create a big book using the same idea. Give each line a separate page. This way, children see the letters separately. You can make individual booklets, have the students illustrate them, and send them home for the children to share with their parents.

Using Children's Names

When teaching individual letters, it is not necessary to teach them in the same order as their appearance in the alphabet; instead, teaching letters in personally meaningful ways is most important. Cunningham, Moore, Cunningham, and

A	B	C	D	E	F	G
H	I	J	K			
L	M	N	O	P		
Q	R	S				
T	U	V				
W	X					
Y	Z					

Figure 6.15 The alphabet song chart.

Moore (2000) advocate using children's names as a guide for teaching the alphabet. To do this, make a list of your students' first names, and take note of the first letter of each name. Now determine which alphabet letters are represented by the names in your class. For example, Michelle, Santiago, Garret, Emily, and Latisha are in Mr. Campbell's kindergarten class. Thus, he begins teaching the letters "m," "s," "g," "e," and "l." He makes sure to spread out the easily confused letters over a period of time. Letters children often visually confuse are:

d b
m n
r h
w v
p q

They should not be taught in consecutive weeks.

Using Three Parts of the Brain

Luria (1980) tells us that people remember more when they learn something new by using the three parts of the brain simultaneously: the occipital lobe (accessed through the eyes), the temporal lobe (accessed through the ears), and the parietal lobe (accessed through the hand). Thus, when teaching a child a letter, show the letter, tell the child how to make it, and have the child make the movements needed to produce it. This procedure also reflects the need for explicit instruction with some students, particularly those who have had little exposure to alphabetic concepts (Duffy, 2003). Figure 6.16 shows steps adapted from Luria's work in this simple but powerful procedure.

Three-Parts Letter Learning

1. Tell the student that you will show him or her how to make the letter, then take the child's hand and trace the letter shape in the air, very slowly.
2. While tracing the letter, verbalize the movements needed to make the letter. For example, for lowercase "a," say, "Go around and close. Now go back to the top, and go down."
3. Now show the child a large card with the letter printed on the card. The letter should be about 12″ high. Take the child's hand and trace the written letter, verbalizing the movements again.

Figure 6.16 Learning letter formation using three parts of the brain.

Reading Alphabet Books

There are many beautifully illustrated and written alphabet books available. Make these books part of your classroom library and read-aloud times. When choosing alphabet books, look for clear depictions of the letters themselves, without embellishments or pictures that are integrated into the physical shape of the letters. Your young students need to see the letter itself without distractions.

Also, look carefully at the words that the author associated with each letter. Make sure that these words represent the most commonly used phoneme represented by the letters. When you begin to introduce phonemes to your students, they need to see and hear the "pure" phoneme represented by the letter first. Sounds associated with consonant combinations such as blends and digraphs are more difficult for children to hear. For example, the letter "t" should be represented with words like "turtle," "Tom," and "tickle," not words like "Thanksgiving," "tree," or "twister."

Below is a sampling of alphabet books that depict the letters clearly and plainly, and for the most part, associate the letters with the most common pronunciation of the phoneme.

A Is for Annabelle (Tudor, 2001)
The Alphabet Room (Pinto, 2003)
Alphabet Under Construction (Fleming, 2002)
Dog's A-B-C (Dodd, 2000)
Girls A–Z (Bunting & Bloom, 2002)
Miss Spider's ABC (Kirk, 2000)
Museum ABC (Metropolitan Museum of Art, 2002)
Quilt Alphabet (Cline-Ransome, 2001)
Z Is for Zamboni (Napier, 2002)

Using a Word Wall

A **word wall** is a large space on the wall in the classroom, on which the teacher hangs word cards. It is used as a source of information throughout the year in primary grade classrooms, especially if you are teaching struggling readers, English language learners, or students who need help with writing. Teachers of older students can use word walls, too, as resources for writing.

Students and their teacher create the wall together, using words from children's books and other texts that they are reading. Throughout the year, students will refer to it for spelling words as they write, playing word games, collecting words that interest them, learning phonics patterns, and more. You will need at least one empty wall in your room for this strategy; as the year goes on, you will expand the wall, requiring plenty of space.

To get started, display each letter of the alphabet horizontally across the wall. If you have primary students or English language learners, write the first names of each of your students on cards. Tape these cards to the wall below the first letter of each name. That starts the wall with the words your students know best—their names. Now you are ready to add important words to the wall. Using children's books as a stimulus, you can add favorite words, words that interest your students, theme-based words, colors, days of the week, or numbers. Write the words on construction paper with a bold black marker. Cut around the words so that their configuration is apparent. (This technique makes words like "where" and

Word wall activities give students valuable word recognition practice.

"were" more visibly different.) Put these words up gradually and do not inundate the wall—or your students—with too many new words at once. Cunningham (2005) suggests no more than five words per week.

There is no point to having a word wall unless your students use it. It is extremely helpful for building a variety of skills your students will need in reading and writing, and particularly useful for English language learners. Following are some suggestions for ways to use the wall. Additionally, Cunningham's *Phonics They Use* (2005) is an excellent source for word wall ideas for teachers of primary grades.

- Use pictures. After reading a book, put pictures of important words in the book on the wall, labeled with the appropriate word. For example, after reading *Silly Sally* (Wood, 1992), you can put up the main character's picture and her name, "Sally," as well as pictures labeled with the words "pig," "dog," "loon," and "sheep." The pictures will be a helpful aid for your youngest readers or your English language learners.
- Use different colors for words that are easily confused, such as "their" and "there." You can also highlight the difference between confusing words with clues. For example, next to the word "four," write the numeral "4." Next to the word "for," draw a gift tag that says, "For you."
- Make the word wall a spelling resource. Tell students that all words that are on the wall must be spelled correctly in their writing. Older students can create their own mini–word walls, using a file folder—have them copy words from the wall onto an alphabetical list in the folder. This project gives them a handy resource for words they need while writing.
- Use the wall for phonics and word study. Point to a word, and then ask students to say it and spell it. On their paper, ask them to write another word that looks and sounds just like it. For example, if you have the words from

Silly Sally on the wall, you can point to the word "pig" and ask them to write a word that rhymes with it and looks just like it. Possible words include "big," "dig," "fig," "jig," or "wig." (Notice that each of the words used with *Silly Sally* can be used to spell new words. When choosing words to go on the wall, pay attention to how useful they are for making new words, and display the words with the greatest number of possibilities.)

- Use the wall for word-building activities. For example, ask students to find a word on the wall and make it plural ("house"/"houses"), or write it in past tense ("walk"/"walked" or "run"/"ran").
- Play games with the words on the wall. Students can have word races, play bingo games, or search for words based on riddle clues.
- Use the word wall to cross-reference words in other languages. Multicultural literature will give you plenty of ideas and words for doing this. For example, *The Old Man and His Door* (Soto, 1996) is a delightful story of how an old man in Mexico mixed up the words "puerta," which means "door," and "puerco," which means "pig." You can put the word "door" under the letter "d," and next to it display its Spanish equivalent. Likewise, under the letter "p," put the words "la puerta," and display its English equivalent. You may want to include pictures. See the example figure.

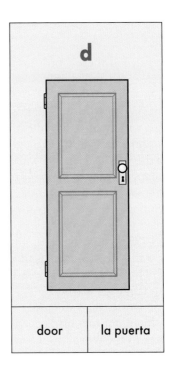

Children Become Writers

Two-year-old Sammy, our little friend in the Personal Reflection box at the beginning of this chapter, drew a picture of a bear accompanied by some scribbles after reading *The Three Bears* (Barton, 1991). He showed the paper to his grandmother, telling her the message that he had written about the bear. In the emergent literacy view of writing development, Sammy is most definitely well on his way to becoming a writer. He is using his own production of symbols and drawings to convey meaning, and share that meaning with others. Isn't that what writers do?

Chomsky (1971) tells us that writing development may be easier than reading development for children. Readers must decipher unknown messages. When they tackle the print, they are attempting to decode a message written by someone else. They must connect sounds to the letters on the page, and these letter–sound correspondences may be unfamiliar to them. Thus, they are moving from the unknown to the known. In contrast, a writer already knows the message, because it is in the writer's head. All he or she needs to do is to put this down on paper so that someone else can read it. This is the unknown part, where the writer must figure out which letters will convey the appropriate sounds. In this way, writers move from the known to the unknown, which makes writing easier than reading for many children.

When you give young children a chance to write, you discover amazing things. First, you discover that they can, indeed, write. Secondly, you find out that they search for ways to express what they want to say, and use their prior knowledge to do that. Children's written compositions at two, three, and four years old show lots of things about what they already know about literacy. Let's look at some of the ways that your young students develop writing abilities, as well as ways to facilitate their growth.

Early Writing Development

Given the expectation that they can write, your youngest students will develop writing literacy in a somewhat predictable pattern, with some recognizable forms of writing that usually appear, as shown in Figure 6.17, on pp. 202–205.

Generally, when very young children are encouraged to write and are surrounded by an environment that invites writing, they will begin experimenting with paper and pencil and produce scribbles and drawings. As Sammy did, they will connect meaning and messages to these markings. As they get older and have been exposed to more print, children will begin writing symbols that look like letters, and will use these symbols in addition their scribbles and drawings. Strings of letters and letter-like symbols are often written all over the page, and many times are repeated in lines across the page. Single letters are also common, sometimes representing whole words, such as "K" for "Kaitlin," or "GM" for "grandma." As children begin to understand more about the alphabet, you will see phonetic representations of some words, such as "KT" for "cat," or "LOT" for "looked." Later, they usually begin to use **invented** or **temporary spellings** on a regular basis, producing writing that can usually be deciphered by someone else. These are spellings that closely approximate the real word, using some of the correct letters, but not all of them and not in the correct sequence. As children begin kindergarten and first grade, around six years old, many commonly used words are spelled conventionally (such as "I love you"). Invented spellings usually are written the way they sound to the writer. Children older than six use many conventionally spelled words on a regular basis, falling back on invented spellings for unknown words (Bissex, 1980; Clark, 1988; Clay, 1991; DeFord, 1980; Sulzby, Teale & Kamberelis, 1989; Temple, Nathan & Burris, 1982).

Forms of Emerging Writing

In the earliest stages, scribbling and drawing are predominant, often with meanings attached. Scribbles often stretch across the page in horizontal lines. Children in preschool produced these writings.

Later, conventional letters appear. Use of single letters for whole words is common. In this writing, the "T" represents "Tommy," who wrote this as a four-year-old.

Figure 6.17 Forms of emerging writing.

Sometimes young children use letter-like symbols, along with alphabet letters. This was written by four-year-old Tianna.

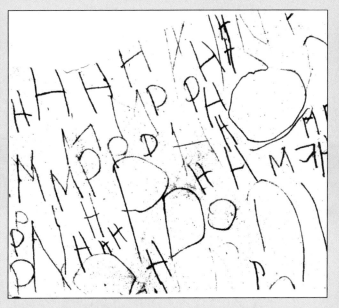

Letters or symbols often are repeated in strings across the page. Kindergarteners wrote these.

Figure 6.17 Continued.

(continued)

Written by a kindergartener, Maria, this writing says, "Once upon a time there was an elephant playing with another elephant." Many kindergarten writers begin to use phonetic spellings. Notice that Maria wrote "eleft" to spell the word "elephant."

With more experience, more phonetic representation of words takes place, alongside conventional spellings. This was written by Edward at the beginning of first grade. He wrote, "I went to the batting cage with my dad."

Figure 6.17 Continued.

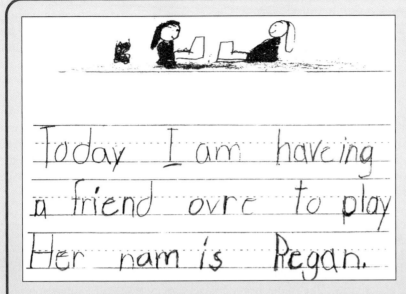

By the time they are in first grade and have had experiences with writing, first graders spell most commonly used words conventionally, and use invented spellings for unknown words. Vowel combinations, word endings, and silent letters are yet to be developed; however, most messages can easily be read by others.

Figure 6.17 Continued.

These stages of development are not fixed. But they are the most general and common types of writing that emerge when you ask youngsters to write on a regular basis.

Ways to Encourage Writing

Daily Opportunities to Write

In my undergraduate classes, I assign my students projects in elementary classrooms. I ask them to teach lessons in which reading and writing activities are merged. Many, many times, students have come to me, worried that they could not complete the assignment. When I ask them why, they tell me it's because they teach kindergarten or first grade, and they know that these children most certainly cannot write!

If young children cannot write, it is most likely because they have not been expected to write. When teachers give their kindergarten and first grade students time and opportunity to write daily, they can, and do, write (Epstein, 2002; Sulzby, 1992; Sulzby, Teale & Kamberelis, 1989; Temple, Nathan & Burris, 1982). Make room for this time in your daily schedule. Many teachers provide their students with blank journals and use the first 10 or 15 minutes of the day for journal writing. Some teachers use prompts to get students started, but other teachers expect the students to generate their own ideas. There are many ways to accomplish journal writing, as discussed in Chapter 13.

Another way to provide writing opportunities is to provide a writing center where your students can go to write for a variety of purposes. In this center, provide the materials needed for writing, such as different types of paper, writing utensils, and supplies for illustrating. You may want to specify a type of writing for the students to accomplish, such as a thank-you letter for a classroom volunteer or an invitation to an Open House for their families. This center should be located near the word wall so that students can take advantage of the wall for spelling assistance.

Connections with Literature

When your students listen to and read literature that "grabs" them, they have experienced the power of written words. There is no better way to motivate them to write than to introduce them to children's writers who are masters of the craft. You can connect literature to writing in many, many ways, some of which I have already discussed in this chapter. Other ways are listed here:

- The very youngest students can write in patterns. Read a book that repeats a pattern to your students, and then ask them to write their own words in the same pattern. For example, read aloud *The Very Busy Spider* by Eric Carle (1984), which is a story in which barn animals ask the spider to join them in a variety of activities. The spider never answers because she is too busy spinning her web. Students can then write their own sentences, using different animals, such as: "'Grr-grr!' said the bear. 'Want to eat in a cave?'"
- Kindergarten and first grade students can write riddles. Read a book such as *What Am I?* (Charles, 1994). Its riddles follow a pattern like this one, describing an apple: "I'm red, I'm round, I fall to the ground. What am I?" Ask your students to create their own riddles, filling in the blanks: "I'm _____, I'm _____, I _____. What am I?"
- As students get older and more sophisticated with writing, ask them to write parallel stories. Read aloud books with clear, interesting plots, and ask the students to use the same problem in the story, using different characters. For example, *Tacky the Penguin* (Lester, 1988) is the story of a penguin who saves his friends from hunters because of his wacky personality and goofy songs. Ask students to write what would happen if Tacky were an alligator or a horse. Or, ask students to use the same characters from the story, but give them different problems.

Some good resources for more ideas for writing with literature are:

- *Using Literature to Enhance Writing Instruction* (Olness, 2005)
- *Getting the Most from Predictable Books* (Opitz, 1995)
- *Read and Write It Out Loud!* (Polette, 2005)

Teacher Interventions

Sipe (2001) warns that while teachers should encourage the use of invented spellings when their youngest students write, they cannot merely stand by and watch. Children will do what is expected of them, and if a first grader figures out that all you want from him is to "come close" in spelling a word, that is what you will get from him, even if he should know the word or has previously spelled it correctly. Sipe says that there is concern that "the constructive theory of literacy learning has been translated into laissez-faire classrooms" (p. 267). Instead, an active role is required of the teacher, so young writers will use what they know as they write, rather than slide by with minimum growth. Sipe adds, "It may be that some children (particularly children whose culture does not match the school's 'culture of power') will fare best when teachers are explicit in their directions and in their teaching, without harming children's independence and sense of self-worth" (p. 267). There are several ways to help students as they attempt invented spellings, two of which are Elkonin boxes and interactive writing.

A variation of Elkonin boxes, described earlier in this chapter, helps students visually represent the spoken sounds in a word. In this variation, students use the boxes to figure out the sounds in the words first, and then use them to determine the spellings of words. Let's look at an example of how this works.

Mrs. Cuervo's Lesson

Lexie is a first grader in Mrs. Cuervo's class. She is writing a story and needs to write the word "toad." She asks for help. Instead of saying, "Spell it the way you think it should be spelled," which really does not help, Mrs. Cuervo draws three boxes on her paper. She outlines the middle box in red. Then she tells Lexie that each box stands for a sound that she hears in the word "toad." She gives her three plastic chips to use as she says the word, stretching out the sounds in the word. Lexie moves a chip into a box each time she hears a different sound. She says, "t-t-t" as she pushes the chip into the first box. She says, "oh" as she pushes a chip into the second box, and she says "d-d-d" as she pushes the final chip into the third box.

Next, Mrs. Cuervo asks her to remove the chips and attempt to write the letters for the word in the boxes. She writes "t" in the first box. At the second box, which is the red one, teacher intervention is necessary. She says, "I traced this box in red because I want you to remember that this one has two letters in it. There is only one sound, but two letters are in this part of the word. The letters that go in that box are spelled the same way as the 'oh' sound in 'oak.' Can you write those letters?" Mrs. Cuervo is fairly certain that Lexie will figure this out because the word "oak" is on the word wall. She writes "oa" in that box. Last, she easily determines that the last letter is "d."

The intent of Elkonin boxes, which is to visually represent phonemes, carries over into spelling phonetically, offering teachers a more concrete and supportive way to help children spell while they are writing (Sipe, 2001).

Interactive writing is another way to support young writers. Using the same principle as shared reading, interactive writing allows students to create messages with support from the teacher. It is a strategy designed for beginning writers who have some knowledge of letters and sounds but are not yet spelling conventionally (Button, Johnson & Furgerson, 1996; Henry & Wiley, 1999). It is based on the language experience approach, described earlier; however, this strategy gives the students more control over the mechanics of writing than does the language experience approach. With interactive writing, the teacher and students share the pen

Interactive Writing

Before Writing

The teacher gathers materials needed: chart paper on an easel, thick black markers, and correction tape or small squares of white paper and scotch tape (for covering errors).

The teacher and students talk about what they'd like to write. This needs to be purposeful as well as short. Begin with one sentence, gradually building up to three or four lines of text. If a longer message or class story is being written, the lesson will take several days. Some possibilities for text are:

- Morning messages
- Lists of words
- Brief descriptions of a story book character
- Brief descriptions of the events of a story
- Recipes
- Directions
- Statements of facts learned from informational books

Decide together what the sentence will say.

During Writing

- The teacher says the sentence out loud and the students count its words.
- The teacher chooses students to write letters or words that they know, such as words on the word wall and frequently used words.
- The teacher writes words that are unfamiliar or irregularly spelled.
- If a word is unfamiliar, but the students can make reasonable predictions about its spelling by saying the sounds they hear, the teacher guides them in figuring out its spelling.
- Mistakes are covered with correction tape or small pieces of white paper and scotch tape. Students then make revisions.
- The teacher can use a different color marker for the words he or she writes, to keep track of the amount of writing students are actually doing.
- Students and teacher talk about where to start writing on the page, putting spaces between words, which words should be capitalized, and other mechanical details.
- Students can write the messages individually on whiteboards with dry-erase pens, while following along with the group's writing of the chart.

After Reading

- The teacher and students reread the message.
- The teacher leaves the chart hanging for a few days so that students can reread it.
- The teacher can make word cards using the same words on the chart, mix up the cards, and ask students to reproduce the sentence with them.
- Students can illustrate the chart.

Figure 6.18 Procedure for interactive writing and an example.

Home–School Connection

Early Childhood Resources on the Web

There are many great resources that you can access on the Internet. A few are listed below.

- **www.naeyc.org/resources/eyly** This is one of the web pages included in the National Association for the Education of Young Children web site. It is called "Early Years Are Learning Years," and contains a series of short articles designed for parents.
- **www.brighthorizons.com** Bright Horizons is a provider of child care and early childhood information. The pages "Child Care Checklist" and "Resource Room" are valuable sources of information.
- **www.pocketparent.com** Pocket Parent is a source for parents, offering frequently asked questions, stories, recipes, book lists, articles about education, and much more.
- **www.ProfTim.com** This web site authored by Tim Graves, a popular early childhood advocate, offers a myriad of articles on many topics in prekindergarten and kindergarten education.

Very young children learn by playing and interacting with others.

to write a brief message—usually just a sentence. The teacher writes words that the students do not know and guides them while they attempt to write words that the teacher believes they can handle. Its procedure is listed in Figure 6.18. Notice the sample of interactive writing, by four-year-old Tommy, who describes his craft project. In the title of the piece, the teacher wrote the first portion of the word "sailboat," as well as the "a" in "boat." She supported him in these spellings because he was unaware of silent vowels. However, the second time the word "sailboat" was needed, Tommy wrote it himself.

Summary: Emerging Readers and Writers

Facilitating the growth of very young readers is one of the most important jobs you will have as a teacher. The whole, the parts, and the heart of reading must all be part of the early childhood classroom. This chapter focused on ways to facilitate your youngest students' encounters with print so that they become familiar with the nature of the "whole"—books and the understandings that can be gleaned from them. One of the things that young children who have been exposed to literature know is that print in books has meaning. Several strategies for encouraging growth in this understanding were introduced, such as reading aloud to them, pretend readings, shared book experiences, and using predictable books.

Emerging readers have understandings of the "parts" of literacy as well, such as letter knowledge, concepts of words, and phonemes. I have shown you some strategies that help your students begin to understand concepts of words and letters, as well as learning how to manipulate the sounds of our language. All of these types of strategies include elements of interest to young children, such as using their names, doing rhyming activities with quality literature, and making sure that all activities are appropriate for the young mind, which thinks in terms of things that are personal and concrete. Alphabet knowledge and phonemic awareness activities lead to an understanding of the relationship between letters and the sounds that they represent—which is what phonics is all about. The next chapter shows you how to teach phonics in a manner that leads to independent reading.

See the Reviewing the Big Picture box for summaries of these strategies, including their alignment with standards and principles.

Technology Resources

- **www.naeyc.org**   The National Association for the Education of Young Children is a well-known and respected academic society for early childhood education. Click on "Information for Families" at this site, and you will find several helpful resources, such as brochures and lists of children's books. You can also click on "Early Childhood Issues" to find a link to "NAEYC Position Statements." This page offers links to documents that explain the philosophical stand taken by the NAEYC on a variety of issues. In particular, the concept of school readiness is explored in this document: *www.naeyc.org/about/positions/pdf/readiness.pdf*.

- **www.songsforteaching.com**   This web site lists sites that show songs to teach concepts to your students. There is an extensive list of preschool and kindergarten songs, many of which include sound clips.

- **www.educationworld.com/a_issues/chat/chat036.shtml**   The Education World web site contains many articles on topics of interest in early childhood education. This web page is a discussion on phonics and phonemic awareness.

- **ceep.crc.uiuc.edu/poptopics.html**   The Clearinghouse on Early Education and Parenting sponsors this web site, featuring many articles on popular topics.

---

expect the world

The New York Times
nytimes.com

Themes of the Times

Expand your knowledge of the concepts discussed in this chapter by reading current and historical articles from the *New York Times* by visiting the "Themes of the Times" section of the Companion Web Site.

Reviewing the Big Picture

Emerging Literacy Strategies

Strategy	Description	Emerging Literacy Concept	Most Appropriate Genre/Grade Level	IRA Standards	INTASC Principles	NAEYC Standards	ACEI/NCATE Standards
Daily read-alouds	Talk with your students about books as you read them together.	Books have meaning	Fiction and nonfiction/K–2	4.3	2, 4	1, 4b, 4d	1, 2.1, 2.8, 3.1, 3.2, 3.4
Rereadings	Give students the opportunity to reread favorite books many times.	Books have meaning	Fiction and nonfiction/K–2	1.4, 4.1, 4.3	2, 4	1, 4b, 4d	1, 2.1, 3.2, 3.4
Pretend readings or emergent storybook readings	Do not discourage students from pretending to read a familiar story. They may retell the story from memory, or look at clues in the book to help them say the printed words.	Books have meaning	Fiction/K	1.4, 4.1, 4.3	2, 4	1, 4b, 4d	1, 2.1, 3.2, 3.3, 3.4
Shared reading	Read a book together as a group. Share the page by reading predictable phrases and words aloud in unison. Usually an enlargened version of a predictable book is used.	Books have meaning	Fiction and nonfiction/K–2	2.1, 2.2	2, 4	1, 4b, 4d	1, 2.1, 3.1, 3.2, 3.4
Predictable books	These books can be easily read by beginning readers, because they can easily figure out what is next on the page without heavy decoding demands.	Books have meaning	Fiction/K–2	2.3	2, 4	1, 4b, 4d	1, 2.1, 3.1, 3.2, 3.3, 3.4
Prop stories	Give students props that help them "play-act" stories.	Books have meaning	Fiction/K–1	2.3, 4.1	2, 4	1, 4b, 4d	1, 2.1, 2.8
Play areas	Fill play areas with props that are related to literacy.	Books have meaning	Fiction/K	2.3, 4.1	2, 4	1, 4b, 4d	1, 2.1, 2.8

Reviewing the Big Picture (continued)

Strategy	Description	Emerging Literacy Concept	Appropriate Genre/Grade Level	IRA Standards	INTASC Principles	NAEYC Standards	ACEI/NCATE Standards
Wordless picture books	These books help beginning readers form story schema without decoding demands.	Pictures add to meaning of books	Fiction/K–2	2.3, 4.2	2, 4	1, 4b, 4d	1, 2.1, 3.1, 3.2, 3.3, 3.4, 3.5
Picture walk	Before reading, show students pictures in the book to make predictions about the upcoming story.	Pictures add to meaning of books	Fiction and nonfiction/K–2	2.2	2, 4	1, 4b, 4d	1, 2.1, 3.1, 3.2, 3.3, 3.4, 3.5
Storyboards	Cut apart a book and ask students to put it in sequence before reading it to them.	Pictures add to meaning of books	Fiction/K–2	2.2	2, 4	1, 4b, 4d	1, 2.1, 3.1, 3.3, 3.4
Language experience approach	Provide an experience, have children talk about it, and dictate a narrative about it. Transcribe their narrative to produce a student-generated piece of text.	Printed words match spoken words	Fiction and nonfiction/K–2	2.2, 4.1	2, 4	1, 4b, 4d	1, 2.1, 2.8, 3.1, 3.2, 3.3, 3.4, 3.5
Charting word sizes	Show words on cards, have children count and graph the number of letters in the words.	Word size does not matter	Fiction and nonfiction/K	1.4, 2.2	2, 4	1, 4b, 4d	1, 2.1, 3.1, 3.3, 3.4
Rhyming activities	Use children's literature as a springboard for creating rhymes with students.	Language consists of sequences of sound	Fiction and nonfiction/K–1	1.4, 2.2	2, 4	1, 4b, 4d	1, 2.1, 3.1, 3.2, 3.4
Charting syllables	Say some interesting words from a children's book, ask students to clap the syllables, then chart them according to their number.	Language consists of sequences of sound	Fiction and nonfiction/K	1.4, 2.2	2, 4	1, 4b, 4d	1, 2.1, 3.1, 3.3, 3.4

Strategy	Description	Concept	Genre/Grade				
Word hunt	Use the chant "I'm Going on a Bear Hunt" to clap syllables in words.	Language consists of sequences of sound	Fiction/K	1.4, 2.2	2, 4	1, 4b, 4d	1, 2.1, 3.1, 3.3, 3.4
Ghost talk	"Stretch out" sounds in words when studying them, making your voice sound like a ghost.	Language consists of sequences of sound	Fiction/K–1	1.4, 2.2	2, 4	1, 4b, 4d	1, 2.1, 3.1, 3.3, 3.4, 3.5
Elkonin boxes	Have students represent phonemes in a word using chips.	Language consists of sequences of sound	Fiction and nonfiction/K–2	1.4, 2.2	2, 4	1, 4b, 4d	1, 2.1, 3.1, 3.3, 3.4, 3.5
Using the alphabet song	Synchronize a chart with the song, and point to the letters as you sing or say the alphabet.	Alphabet is basis of print	Fiction/K	1.4, 2.2	2, 4	1, 4b, 4d	1, 2.1, 3.1, 3.2, 3.4, 3.5
Using names	Use the names of your students to help them learn the alphabet.	Alphabet is basis of print	Nonfiction/K	1.4, 2.2	2, 4	1, 4b, 4d	1, 2.1, 3.1, 3.2, 3.4
Three-parts letter learning	Trace a letter while verbalizing how it is made.	Alphabet is basis of print	Fiction and nonfiction/K	1.4, 2.2	2, 4	1, 4b, 4d	1, 2.1, 3.1, 3.2, 3.3, 3.4
Alphabet books	These books aid letter recognition because they depict the alphabet for beginning readers.	Alphabet is basis of print	Fiction and nonfiction/K–1	1.4, 2.2	2.4	1, 4b, 4d	1, 2.1, 2.8, 3.1, 3.2
Word wall	As students find out about new words, display them under the appropriate letter on the wall.	Alphabet is basis of print	Fiction and nonfiction/K–2	1.4, 2.2	2, 4	1, 4b, 4d	1, 2.1, 2.8, 3.1, 3.2, 3.4
Connecting writing to literature	Read quality literature aloud; have students respond in writing.	Writing emerges as reading does	Fiction and nonfiction/K–2	1.1, 4.3	2, 4	1, 4b, 4d	1, 2.1, 2.8, 3.1, 3.2, 3.3, 3.4, 3.5
Interactive writing	Share the pen with students as they write messages.	Writing emerges as reading does	Nonfiction/K–1	1.1, 4.3	2, 4	1, 4b, 4d	1, 2.1, 3.1, 3.2, 3.3, 3.4, 3.5

7

Teaching Young
Children to Decode
Independently

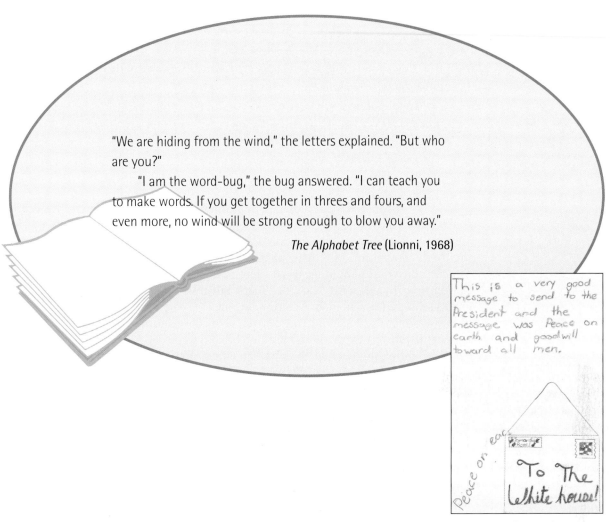

"We are hiding from the wind," the letters explained. "But who are you?"

"I am the word-bug," the bug answered. "I can teach you to make words. If you get together in threes and fours, and even more, no wind will be strong enough to blow you away."

The Alphabet Tree (Lionni, 1968)

This is a very good message to send to the President and the message was Peace on earth and goodwill toward all men.

Peace on earth

To The White house!

Samantha, age 10

When letters "get together in threes and fours," sometimes they sound as we expect them to, and sometimes they don't. See an example of this in the Personal Reflection.

Julius, a first grader, is reading *I Went Walking* (Williams, 1989). He encounters this sentence: "What did you see?"

He does not recognize the first word in the sentence, and looks up at his teacher, Mrs. Martinez, for help. She says, "Sound it out, Julius."

Imagine being Julius, attempting to sound out the word "what." If Julius knows anything about the phoneme represented by the letters "wh," he knows to pronounce the beginning consonant by blowing air out while making the "wuh" sound for "w." After that, he must tackle the vowel sound. He might associate the word with other words that look like "what," and attempt a pronunciation that rhymes with "cat" or "hat," but this would not yield anything that makes sense in the sentence. Additionally, once he's figured out the word "what," he moves on to "did," and then "you," which is another tricky word to pronounce! If Julius is expected to continue breaking the code in this laborious manner, a delightful, predictable book will quickly become a source of frustration.

Indeed, often words like "what" are frustrating to young or immature readers. "What" is a phonetically irregular word, in that it is not pronounced in the expected manner based on its spelling pattern. Its pronunciation is a puzzle to inexperienced readers because of its irregularity. Thus, it is counterproductive merely to tell the child to "sound it out" every time he struggles with a word. Students must know a variety of ways to figure out unknown words.

Phonics is the understanding of the relationships between letters and the sounds that they represent. When you use phonics to determine an unknown word, you attempt to pronounce the word, either out loud or silently, based on what you know about the combination of letters that you see in that word. Sometimes it is the most useful way to determine an unknown word; sometimes it is not.

Many people consider phonics to be the only way to determine an unknown word. Think about times when, as a child, you did not know a word you came across as you were reading. When you asked a parent or teacher, what did he or she say? Most of us got this response: "Sound it out." And many times, "sounding it out" alone did not work, just as it did not work for Julius. As this example illustrates, it is not possible to "sound out" many of our English words, because they do not sound the way we expect them to sound.

Why Teach Phonics?

Phonics is one method of translating written English spellings into meaningful ideas. When reading aloud, readers can use phonics to approximate the correct sounds represented by the letters in the words. When reading silently, pronunciation is not important, but instant recognition of written words is very important. Phonics is helpful with word recognition in two ways.

First, if instant recognition breaks down, the use of phonics is helpful. If a word is troublesome or unknown, the reader can use knowledge of letters and sounds to make reasonable guesses about word choices.

Second, when you teach letter–sound correspondences along with predictable word patterns, you have equipped your students with the ability to remember the spelling sequences of words. The spelling sequence of a word makes it entirely unique; even though words look and sound similar, most words are distinguishable because of the way they are spelled. Once readers have been taught to pay attention to letter sequences, "(k)nowledge of letter–sound relations provides a powerful mnemonic system that bonds the written forms of specific words to their pronunciations in memory" (Ehri & McCormick, 2004, p. 369). Thus, readers store this sequence of letters in their memory banks, which allows them to recognize the word when they encounter it again. Eldredge says that sight word learning is "a process involving the establishment of systematic connections between spellings and pronunciations of words. Phonics knowledge facilitates these connections" (1999, p. 130). This leads to automaticity, or instant word recognition without the process of decoding letter by letter (LaBerge & Samuels, 1974; Samuels, 2004; Samuels & Kamil, 1984).

There is much support for the teaching of phonics. According to Groff, "the great majority of experimental findings on reading development make clear that explicit, direct, systematic, intensive, comprehensive, and early teaching of phonics information is the most productive way to develop children's automatic word skills" (1998, p. 140).

The National Reading Panel, in a report to the U.S. Congress, describes phonics in this way: "Phonics instruction is a way of teaching reading that stresses the acquisition of letter–sound correspondences and their use in reading and spelling. The primary focus of phonics instruction is to help beginning readers understand how letters are linked to sounds (phonemes) to form letter–sound correspondences and spelling patterns and to help them learn how to apply this knowledge in their reading" (2000a, p. 8). The importance of teaching phonics is emphasized by the No Child Left Behind Act (2001), which includes decoding unfamiliar words as one of the five most important reading strategies for which teachers in public schools will be accountable.

Keep in mind that true reading requires the reader to understand the message. A reader who decodes words and pronounces them correctly must also derive meaning from those words. There are several ways to gain meaning from words. A reader can figure out an unknown word by looking at all the other words in the sentence and thinking about what makes sense. The reader can also think about what he or she already knows to make predictions about words that might make sense. A reader can look at pictures if there are any available. And, a reader can analyze a word to determine how its parts, such as prefixes and suffixes, add to its meaning. A good reader has all of these skills, plus knowledge of letters and sounds, at his or her disposal. Thus, phonics is just one of the necessary tools needed for reading. Using all of these available tools is a **balanced approach** to teaching reading, and avoids the issue of which method is the "best" way to teach children how to read.

Thus, teaching phonics to young readers has only one purpose, and that is to add to their repertoire of strategies for figuring out unknown words and remembering known ones. The National Reading Panel adds:

> Teachers must understand that systematic phonics instruction is only one component—albeit a necessary component—of a total reading program; systematic phonics instruction should be integrated with other reading instruction in phonemic awareness, fluency, and comprehension strategies to create a complete reading program. While most teachers and educational decision makers recognize this, there may be a tendency in some classrooms, particularly in 1st grade, to allow phonics to become the dominant component, not only in the time devoted to it, but also in the significance attached. It is important not to judge children's reading competence solely on the basis of their phonics skills and not to devalue their interest in books because they cannot decode with complete accuracy. It is also critical for teachers to understand that systematic phonics instruction can be provided in an entertaining, vibrant, and creative manner. (2000a, p. 11)

Let's look at some ways to follow the NRP recommendations.

Phonics Instruction

What is the best way to teach phonics? Ask any reading educator that question, and you are likely to start a very lively conversation! How to teach phonics is part of one of the most persistent and, I contend, unnecessary debates in our profession. If we focus on the purpose for reading, which is to understand the message on the printed page, the answer to the question of how to teach phonics becomes clear. All phonics instruction is done for the purpose of arriving at understanding whole text. The next few pages will show you some useful, research-based strategies and ways to accomplish this.

Phonemic Awareness

In Chapter 6, you read about phonemic awareness. I mention it again here because it is important to build upon your students' phonemic awareness, and to reinforce the point that phonemic awareness and phonics are two separate ideas. "Phonemic awareness is awareness of sounds of spoken words; phonics is the relationship between letters and sounds in written words" (Stahl, 1992, p. 621). Before your students are able to break apart words and try to figure out their sounds as well as their meanings, they need to know that the sounds in words *can* be manipulated. In fact, many children have difficulty with separating sounds in words. They need explicit instruction and practice so that they recognize that a word such as "dog" has three phonemes, but a word like "frog" has four. Manipulation of phonemes is difficult for some children, because they attach meaning to the word, and they don't think of words as composites of the phonemes that are joined together to make them. Stahl (1992) describes asking a child, Heather, to remove a phoneme from a spoken word:

> I had Heather say "meat" and then repeat it without saying the /m/ sound (*eat*). When Heather said *chicken* after some hesitation, I was taken aback. (p. 621)

Heather was not aware of the fact that she could separate the phonemes in the word "meat." Thus, "for her, a little less than *meat* was *chicken*" (p. 621). Yet, when she begins to decode unknown words, she will need to be able to take off the /m/ phoneme and put others there, so that she can recognize quickly words like "beat," "heat," "neatly," "bleat," and "repeat."

Early phonemic awareness is associated with reading achievement in the later elementary school years. If your students can identify and manipulate sounds as youngsters, they will be able to build upon this ability once they gain alphabet knowledge. This skill equips them for tasks that will enable them to figure out unknown words when they read (Ehri & Nunes, 2002; National Reading Panel, 2000a; Yopp & Yopp, 2000).

It is important for you to know some phonemic awareness strategies if you are teaching young or immature readers. The National Reading Panel (2000a) also identified phonemic awareness as one of the five most important components of successful reading, and it is expected of teachers, according to the No Child Left Behind Act (2001). In Chapter 6, I introduced some strategies that can help you develop the phonemic awareness of your students. Now, in this chapter, you will see some strategies to build upon this awareness.

Sequence of Instruction

Once again, the purpose of teaching phonics is to provide your students with a useful tool for figuring out words. Thus, the sequence of phonics instruction needs to be determined by what would be most useful for your students. While published materials and basal programs usually offer a sequence of instruction, organizing the order in which you "should" teach letters, much of this sequence is arbitrary. Spiegel tells us, "Systematic instruction does have scope, but it does not necessarily have a prescribed *sequence*" (1992, p. 40). What matters is that you give your students what they need—knowledge of letters and their corresponding sounds in the literature selections that they are currently reading. State standards often stipulate benchmarks for when students must have been taught elements of phonics, but again, there is no "correct" sequence, and benchmarks vary from state to state.

Usually, children are somewhat familiar with much of the alphabet by the time they reach kindergarten, but knowing the sounds associated with letters is a concept that takes time to sink in. In many schools, teachers teach letter recognition in meaningful contexts at the beginning of the kindergarten year. Then, at about halfway through the kindergarten year, teachers begin to systematically teach letter sounds.

Consonant phonemes are generally easier than vowel phonemes to say, hear, and see. Additionally, consonants are more consistent in the sounds that they represent. Many preschool and kindergarten teachers start with the consonants that

Students can learn new words by comparing them to words they already know.

are easiest to pronounce and are the most useful. Vowel phonemes are much more complicated; each vowel represents at least two sounds. Thus, teachers often teach vowel phonemes later, usually in first grade.

Ruddell (2006, p. 211) suggests that "consonant continuants" be the first letters introduced in early childhood classrooms, because of their relative ease in pronunciation and blending with other sounds. Durkin (1993) warns that similar sounds should not be introduced consecutively. For example, /b/ and /p/ are phonemes made by placing the mouth in the same position. The only difference between the two sounds is that one is voiced (/b/) and the other is not (/p/). Thus, you should not introduce /p/ soon after introducing /b/. In addition, Durkin advocates usefulness as a guideline for teaching letters; thus, the most commonly used initial consonants in words that occur in children's books ought to be taught first.

Eldredge (1999) explains that children have developmental stages in their ability to decode, and that these stages are also evident in their invented spellings. The easiest type of word for beginning readers is a one-syllable word that begins and ends with a consonant, and has one vowel in the middle position. The most difficult words are those that contain silent letters, such as "knight," "gnaw," and "write."

Based on all of this, a suggestion for the sequence of letters and sound instruction is shown in Figure 7.1. You may find the sequence helpful in making instructional plans or developing your curriculum. However, keep in mind the purpose of phonics, which is to provide your students with tools for figuring out unfamiliar words. Strictly adhering to a sequence of objectives and skills is not as important in achieving this goal as emphasizing the use of phonics as a problem-solving tool.

Vowels, which represent a much greater variety of sounds, can be introduced later. Sometimes teachers like to introduce one vowel at a time, between consonants.

Which should come first, long vowel sounds or short vowel sounds? Educators and researchers differ on this, and actually, it is simply a matter of choice. Some say that long vowels are easier to learn because the letters simply represent the sound of their own names. However, long vowel sounds are represented by a variety of spellings that often include vowel teams rather than single vowels, such as in the words "bake" and "team." Short vowels, on the other hand, are more often represented by themselves, in simple words that are common in children's literature, such as in the words "cat" and "dog." Thus, many teachers turn to short vowels first, and I recommend this approach.

Suggested Sequence for Introducing Consonant Phonemes to Young Children

Teach first ◄─────────────────────────────────────► Teach last

Sounds that are produced with a continuous flow of air:	Voiced consonant sounds that are "stopped" and must have the "uh" sound added to them:	Voiceless consonant sounds that are "stopped," and a faint "uh" sound is heard:	Consonant letter that has no phonemes of its own:	Infrequently used consonant sounds:
/m/, /s/, /h/, /r/, /n/	/b/, /w/, /d/, /v/, /l/, /g/, /y/	/t/, /f/, /p/, /k/	/c/	/j/, /z/, /qu/, /x/

Easier and more useful ◄──────────────────────────► Harder and less useful

Suggested Sequence for Learning Words

This sequence is based on decoding and spelling development in children. Types of words that young readers recognize are listed from easiest (#1) to hardest (#6).

1. CVC words containing:
   n, b, t, z, l, p, m, f, k, x (as in fox), c (as in cat), d, r, s, h, j, g, y, w, v, qu, c (as in city)

   Easiest ─────────────────────────────► Hardest

2. Words containing digraphs:
   sh (as in ship), ch (as in chip), ng (as in "sing"), th (as in "them" or "thin")

   Easiest ─────────────────────────────► Hardest

3. Words containing blends at the beginning:

   Words that start with "sl" (as in sleep) and "fl" (as in flag)
   Words containing blends at the end:
   Words that end with "-ft" (as in "soft"), and "-st" (as in "last")

4. Words that contain simple vowel teams, such as "beep," "beat," and "main"
5. Words that fit the CVCe pattern, such as "ride"
6. Words with complex consonant clusters, such as "ranch," "stitch," "graph," "shrimp," and "scream"

Figure 7.1 Suggested sequence for teaching initial consonants and word patterns.

Sound Charts

Once you have determined the sequence in which you plan to introduce letters and sounds, you can help your kindergarten or first grade students remember them with **sound charts.** These are charts that teachers hang in their classrooms to show the phonics elements that they want their students to remember. For example, one of the most familiar is a chart that shows each of the vowels, with pictures to represent their short and long phonemes, such as "apple" and "acorn" for "a." Any teacher supply store offers a variety of these charts. Generally, after a brief, initial inspection, children ignore these posters. You can make these much more interesting—and useful.

Read a story about a character whose name begins with the consonant sound you want to teach. Show them the character's name and identify its first letter and sound. Have your students draw pictures of the character, and attach them to the chart, along with words found in the book that have the represented sound. For example, your sound chart for the short "a" sound would feature the Cat from Dr. Seuss's *The Cat in the Hat* (1957). Have your students put pictures of the Cat in the Hat around the border of the chart. Then fill the chart with words that contain the short "a" sound, such as "hat," "bat," "apple," "man," "fan," and "Sally." Students can help you find these words as you reread the book together.

Figure 7.2 shows a list of books containing characters or themes whose names contain clear examples of a phoneme, such as "Hester the Jester" for the /e/ phoneme. The list includes several multicultural books.

Explicit Instruction

Many children need explicit instructions on the sounds that letters make and cannot determine the sounds of letters unless they are separated from other sounds in the word; this is particularly true of students who are English language learners or struggling readers (Durkin, 1993; Duffy, 2003). Look at this example:

Mrs. Kline's Lesson

Shana, a first grader, sees the word "cheat" and cannot decode it. Her teacher, Mrs. Kline, says, "Shana, it begins the same way that your friend Charlie's name begins, and then sounds like 'eat.' What is the word?"

Shana still struggles with this, because she is not able to draw the same conclusions that Mrs. Kline can. Instead, she needs an explicit explanation, and then Mrs. Kline can connect the information with what Shana already knows. Look at this example, which includes explicit instruction:

When Shana cannot pronounce "cheat," her teacher says, "Shana, this word begins with the letters 'c' and 'h.' Both of those letters together make this sound: /ch/. Get your mouth ready and make that sound with me."

Shana does this, and then Mrs. Kline says, "That's right. Let's say it together again. '/ch/.' Good! Now, the /ch/ sound is the one that you hear at the beginning of Charlie's name. Do you hear it? I'll say it: '/ch/,' like in '/ch/—arlie.' Say that with me. Ok! So, start with /ch/. Now, the rest of the word looks like a word you know, 'eat.'" She writes the word "eat" on a whiteboard, and continues, "Do you see how they look alike? So, say, '/ch/,' and then say 'eat,' and then put them together, like this: '/ch/—eat.' Try that. What word do you have?"

Single Consonant Phonemes Represented in Children's Literature Characters

Bb
My Brown Bear Barney (Butler, 1988)
Tough Boris (Fox, 1994)

Cc
Corduroy (Freeman, 1968)
Carlos and the Squash Plant/Carlos y la Planta de Calanza (Stevens, 1995)*

Dd
D.W. the Picky Eater (Brown, 1995)
David Gets in Trouble (Shannon, 2002)
Go, Dog, Go! (Eastman, 1961)

Ff
Feathers and Fools (Fox, 1989)
Fox in Socks (Seuss, 1965)

Gg
Curious George (Rey, 1941)
Mr. Gumpy's Outing (Burningham, 1970)

Hh
Clean Your Room, Harvey Moon! (Cummings, 1994)
Harold and the Purple Crayon (Johnson, 1955)

Jj
Jamaica's Find (Havill, 1986)*
Jesse Bear, What Will You Wear? (Carlstrom, 1986)

Kk
Mr. Katapat's Incredible Adventures (Barroux, 2004)

Ll
Leo the Late Bloomer (Kraus, 1971)
Leo Cockroach, Toy Tester (O'Malley, 1999)

Mm
Madeline (Bemelmans, 1958)
Magda's Tortillas/Las Tortillas de Magda (Chavarria-Chairez, 2000)*
You're a Good Sport, Miss Malarkey (Finchler, 2002)

Nn
Nate the Great (Sharmat, 1972)
Nicholas Cricket (Maxner, 1990)
Uncle Nacho's Hat (Rohmer, 1989)*

Pp
Pablo's Tree (Mora, 1994b)*
The Paper Bag Princess (Munsch, 1980)
Pickle Things (Brown, 1980)

Qq
Little Granny Quarterback (Martin & Sampson, 2001)
Recess Queen (O'Neill, 2002)

Rr
Rip Roaring Russell (Hurwitz, 1983)
Watch Out, Ronald Morgan! (Giff, 1985b)

Ss
Sagwa, the Chinese Siamese Cat (Tan, 2001)*
Silly Sally (Wood, 1992)
Suki's Kimono (Uegaki, 2003)*

Tt
Tacky the Penguin (Lester, 1988)
A Birthday Basket for Tia (Mora, 1992)*

Vv
Vera Rides a Bike (Rosenberry, 2004)
"Viola Swamp," from *Miss Nelson Is Missing!* (Allard, 1985)

Ww
Whistle for Willie (Keats, 1964)*

Yy
My Name Is Yoon (Recorvits, 2003)*
Yertle the Turtle and Other Stories (Seuss, 1958)

Zz
Zachary's Ball (Tavares, 2000)

Consonant Phonemes Represented in Children's Literature Characters

Ch
Chato's Kitchen (Soto, 1995)*
Chicken Little (Kellogg, 1987)
This Little Chick (Lawrence, 2002)

Figure 7.2 Phonemes represented in children's literature characters, for use in sound charts.

(continued)

Th
Hans Christian Andersen's Thumbelina
(Mills, 2005)
Theodore All Grown Up (Walsh, 1981)

Sh
Sheep in a Jeep (Shaw, 1986)
Sheila Rae, the Brave (Henkes, 1987)

Wh
Whales Passing (Bunting, 2003)
Whizz! (Lear, 1973)

Short Vowel Phonemes
/a/ as in "cat"
      The Cat in the Hat (Seuss, 1957)
/e/ as in "Hester"
      Hester the Jester (Shecter, 1977)
/i/ as in "Jillian Jiggs"
      Wonderful Pigs of Jillian Jiggs (Gilman, 1988)

/o/ as in "Moppy"
      Mop Top (Freeman, 1955)
/u/ as in "Cut-ups"
      The Cut-Ups (Marshall, 1985)

Long Vowel Phonemes
/ā/ as in "Jake"
      Jake Baked the Cake (Hennessey, 1990)
/ē/ as in "teeny"
      The Teeny Tiny Woman (Galdone, 1984)
/ī/ as in "Ira"
      Ira Sleeps Over (Waber, 1972)
/ō/ as in "Oma"
      Oma's Quilt (Bourgeois, 2001)*
/ū/ as in "Trudy"
      Tell Me a Trudy (Segal, 1977)

*Multicutural titles.

Figure 7.2 Continued.

Such directness is necessary for many students to hear the sounds they need and to make the connections with the letters they see. You need to write the word, show them its letters, and pronounce its sounds for them. Thus, explicit instruction tells students exactly what needs to be produced when they blend sounds. For some students, this is the only kind of phonics instruction that makes sense. Studies of reading-disabled students support the use of explicit instruction (Allington, 2002; Ehri & McCormick, 2004). Moreover, some students from diverse backgrounds need teachers to make statements in a direct manner, rather than making implications or expecting the students to draw conclusions (Au, 1993), and many older students or English language learners may need explicit instruction so that they can hear differences in sounds (Duffy, 2003).

Connections to Meaningful Text

Because phonics is a tool for determining unknown words in text, it is important to make sure that phonics instruction is connected to text that your students will read (Stahl, 1992). Sometimes a textbook's teacher's edition lists a phonic element to be taught alongside the reading of a selection that has no examples of that element in its vocabulary. It's a waste of time to teach phonics lessons that have little to do with reading words. Asking students to spend time cutting and pasting, making crafts, and looking at or drawing pictures is valuable time that could be better spent reading texts that are matched to their abilities and allowing them to apply what they have learned.

Diversity in the Reading Classroom

Teaching Phonics to Students with Diverse Dialects and Languages

Children of diverse backgrounds need to be able to hear and manipulate speech sounds and learn the graphemes that correspond to those sounds (Au, 1993), as do all learners of English. The ability of students to do this depends on their proficiency in their native language (Peregoy & Boyle, 2004). Explicit, direct instruction may be best for learners from diverse backgrounds, because they typically have not been immersed in the language and print-rich environments that their mainstream peers have been (Delpit, 1988; Cambourne, 2002).

On the other hand, students whose language is not English may have difficulty with phonics-based reading instruction. Focusing on letters and sounds in isolation can be confusing, because English words are not always phonetically regular, and emphasis is on pronunciation rather than on comprehension. Phonics drills, practice pages, computer software, and coloring sheets are not authentic reading experiences. "When English learners are beginning to read English, attention to meaning is paramount at every step in instruction" (Peregoy & Boyle, 2004, p. 114).

Thus explicit instruction of letters and sounds, grounded in practice with authentic reading for understanding, is important (Stahl, 1992). Using a whole-part-whole approach to teaching phonics helps to accomplish this (Trachtenburg, 1990). This approach means to read a book to students first, and then isolate a letter–sound correspondence that occurs frequently in the book and teach a mini-lesson about that phonic element. Afterwards, reread the book and others that contain the same element.

"Sheltering strategies" (Peregoy & Boyle, 2004, p. 114) are those that support English language learners as they grapple with a new set of understandings. Some supportive strategies for learning phonics elements are:

- Use poems, recipes, songs, pattern books, and other short pieces of text, especially with older students.

- Use trade books that contain many examples of a letter–sound correspondence in a meaningful context.

- Use student-generated text, based on an experience, especially with older students. Take sentences from this text and create cloze exercises for students to complete. For example: Maria can make tortillas. _____ can _____ tortillas with _____ and _____.

- Use high-interest/low-vocabulary books. You can find many titles searching for the phrase "high interest low vocabulary" with an Internet search engine such as Google. Moreover, there are some publishers that specialize in these books, such as High Interest Publishing, available online at **www.hip-books.com/**, or Patnor Publishing, at **www.patnorpublishing.com/ field_trial.htm**.

- When you want students to read a selection on their own, read it aloud to them first, so that you model pronunciations. Be explicit about how to make the sounds.

- Always point to letters and words as you teach their corresponding sounds.

Some educators have concluded that in order for beginning readers to be successful at applying phonics knowledge, they must be given texts that are called **decodable text.** These books contain only the few words and sentences that the beginning reader can decode by putting letters together with sounds. Sentences would look something like this:

Mag had a rag. Mag wags.

Dan can fan. Van can tan.

The problem with such text is that it sometimes makes little sense, and the content is highly limited. Many children, especially struggling readers, have no patience for working hard at decoding words that produce little meaning. Likewise, good readers, who do not struggle with decoding anyway, are disappointed when they search for meaning as they read. Boredom quickly sets in. Cunningham and Cunningham conclude, "Although there is general agreement that children need text in which they have to apply their decoding to some words, there does not seem to be any support in the research for recommending highly decodable text as the exclusive beginning reading material for all children" (2002, p. 94).

Mental Modeling

The units of written English that are most easily processed by the human eye are words (Ehri, 1994). Words that are instantly recognized are words that the reader does not need to figure out. However, if a reader does not know a word by sight, he or she must use other ways to figure it out, depending on the text and the circumstantial context of the reading. Decoding, or "phonological recoding," as some researchers call it (Ehri, 1994, p. 349), is when the reader translates the spelling of a word into its pronunciations by matching the written letters with their corresponding sounds, then searches his or her lexicon for a word that matches this pronunciation and makes sense in the context. This is what people commonly call the act of "sounding out" the word, and is a much slower process than reading a word by sight. In fact, the automaticity theory of reading suggests that this process hampers the reader's comprehension; thus, it is desirable for all words to be recognized instantly (LaBerge & Samuels, 1974; Samuels, 2004; Samuels & Kamil, 1984).

These word-processing abilities are thought processes; therefore, they are covert and cannot be seen by others. In order to show students the process of figuring out unknown words, you must model it. Automatic word recognition grows as time goes on, but young readers need to know what to do when they encounter unfamiliar print. To help them develop independence in processing print, you must make this reading process visible.

Mental modeling, as you learned in Chapter 2, is the term given to the teaching behavior that teachers use when they model their own cognitive activity by making "their reasoning visible to the novice" (Duffy, Roehler & Herrmann, 1998, p. 163). Such modeling helps to ensure that "students have enough information to assume metacognitive control of the mental processing" (p. 167). Mental modeling is a teaching tool that is helpful for showing students how to accomplish any reading strategy. It is also sometimes called "think-aloud modeling," and is frequently done with comprehension strategies such as making inferences or summarizing (Wilhelm, 2001). You will

Explicit instruction of phonetic elements, along with mental modeling, helps students understand the process of decoding unknown words.

see many examples of mental modeling in Chapter 10, when you learn about how to show children how to construct meaning from whole text.

But decoding unknown words is also somewhat mystifying to readers. Often they are unsure of how other readers translate all those symbols on the page into something that is recognizable. Thus, modeling the act of decoding by letting them hear your thoughts is very useful. To model the process of determining an unknown word, use a difficult word in the text and show what you do to tackle it.

Read the example below of a mental model from a lesson that Mrs. Williams taught to her second graders with *Hey, Al,* by Arthur Yorinks (1986). Notice that her instruction is explicit and direct while she focuses on the process of figuring out print. She shows her students the decoding process.

Mrs. Williams' Lesson

First, Mrs. Williams put this sentence with the unknown word on the board: "The days passed <u>blissfully</u>." She covered up the word "blissfully" with an index card taped to the board. Then, she modeled:

"As I'm reading this story, I see this sentence. I get to the last word and I don't know what it is. So, I begin to make guesses. I think about all the possible words that could go there: 'slowly,' 'quickly,' 'happily.' There are probably lots of words that could go there. But it doesn't help me to just put any old word there. I need to think of what makes sense in this story. So, I look for clues. I look at the pictures, and see Al sitting in a pool, sunning himself and having some punch. He's smiling. So, I think that 'happily' is a good choice. I'll write that down.

But, if I look further, I see another clue—the word itself. (She uncovers the 'bl' portion of the word.) I see that it begins with the 'bl' blend. That means that 'happily' can't go there. (She erases the word 'happily.') As I look at the word again, I see that the 'bl' is followed by this word part: '-iss.' (She uncovers this portion of the word.) I've seen this in words that I already know: 'kiss' and 'miss.' Now all I have to do is blend these together: 'bl' and 'iss,' which makes 'bliss.' Oh, I've heard of this word before, but I'm not sure of the meaning, so I look at the pictures on the page again. Al looks happy. This is a beautiful place. I'm guessing that the word 'bliss' means something like being happy. And I look at the rest of the word, and see 'fully' in it, which makes the word mean 'in a way full of bliss.' Ok, I'm going to guess that 'blissfully' is a lot like the word 'happily.' Let's double-check my guess by looking up the word in our dictionaries.

Inductive Word Solving

One of the fallacies about phonics instruction is that it must be didactic, full of drill and skill worksheets, and boring. But if you set up your lessons so that students are constructing knowledge about letters and sounds with your guidance, you can challenge their thinking, allow them to use their problem-solving skills, and keep them interested. For example, suppose you read to your kindergarten or first grade students the book *Too Many Tamales,* by Gary Soto (1993). This is a delightful story about Maria, who helped her mother and father make 24 tamales on Christmas Eve. She was playing with her mother's ring while cooking, and later thought it was cooked into one of the tamales. So, she convinced her cousins to help her eat all of the tamales to find the ring! In this book, you will find the following words. Print them on a chart in a column.

too
tamales
telephone
toys
tears
tired
taste
took
tugged
tell

To teach your students the sound represented by the letter "t," ask them to look at the list and tell how all of the words are alike. To do this, ask, "How do these words look alike?" and "How do they sound alike?" If necessary, ask them to pay attention to the first letter in each word. Model for them the stretching out of each phoneme so that they can hear the likenesses in the first consonant sound of each of these words. Based on their conclusions, ask the students to generalize. Ask them, "What sound goes with the letter 't'? Get your mouth ready and show me how to make the sound."

This method can also be used with vowel phonemes, although it's a bit harder to do, so it would be best for first or second graders. For example, you can read aloud *Seven Blind Mice,* by Ed Young (1992). Show the students these words:

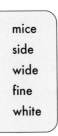

mice
side
wide
fine
white

Now, read the words aloud and have the students say them aloud, too. Ask:

"What letter do you see in the middle of all of them?" (i)
"What letter do you see at the end?" (e)

"Do you hear the 'e'?" (no)

"What vowel sound do you hear in the middle of the word?" (/ī/)

"How do they all sound alike?" (They all have the /ī/ sound in the middle of the word.)

Explain, "In lots of words, you will see a pattern like this. There will be a vowel in the middle of the word and an 'e' at the end. What can we say about words like this?"

Students can help you write a statement to help them remember this letter pattern. Keep in mind, however, that the amount of guidance that you will need to provide varies with your students. You may need to combine this use of examples and drawing conclusions with explicit instruction. Figure 7.3 summarizes this procedure.

Generalizations

In the English language, there are some consistent spelling patterns that are useful to know. Understanding some of these patterns can give your students an edge when figuring out words they do not know. Some of the patterns are very consistent; others are not. These generalizations are noted with acronyms, with "C" representing "consonant" and "V" representing "vowel." For example, one common

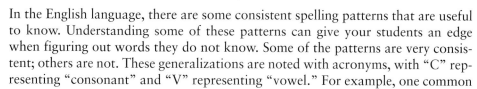

Teaching Phonics Generalizations and Elements with Inductive Learning

1. Decide which phonetic element or generalization needs to be taught.
2. In a piece of children's literature, find several words that clearly serve as examples of the element or generalization. In order for this step to be most helpful, many of the words in this list should be known to your students.
3. List the words, and show the list to your students. Read the list to them while they read along silently. Then read it again and ask them to read aloud with you.
4. Ask them to talk to each other about these words. They need to determine how all the words are alike.
5. Use questioning to lead your students to a conclusion about the words. Ask, "What looks the same in each word? What sounds the same in each word?" Then name the element or pronounce the sound.
6. Based on their conclusions, ask the students to dictate a generalization that would be helpful to remember the next time they see such words.

Figure 7.3 How to use inductive teaching with phonics elements or generalizations.

generalization is the CVC pattern. The words "dog" and "wet" fit this pattern. The CVC pattern refers to a word or syllable that begins with a consonant, has a vowel in the middle, and a consonant at the end. The generalization associated with this type of word is that the vowel in the middle will most likely represent a short vowel sound, just like the "e" in "wet" and the "o" in "dog."

Theodore Clymer, in a classic research study that was reproduced in 1996, studied the usefulness of the generalizations that are usually taught in elementary classrooms. He examined 45 phonics "rules," or generalizations, that at the time of his study (1963) were commonly taught in reading basal materials. His procedure was this: If a generalization was listed in the basal materials as one that needed to be taught, he looked for words that appeared to fit the generalization. Of those words, he counted the number that actually fit the pattern. For example, the CVVC generalization states that the first vowel in the middle of the word will be long, and the second one will be silent, such as in the word "boat." He looked for words like "boat" in the stories that children were expected to read. He might have found "goat," "mail," "beat," and "rain." These words fit the CVVC generalization, because the first vowel in each of them is long. However, he might also have found words like "belief," "couch," and "head." These words do not fit the generalization, even though they contain two adjacent vowels. The long sound of the first vowel is not pronounced in any of them. This sort of finding lowered the generalizability of that generalization! In fact, he found that the CVVC pattern actually works in only 45 percent of the studied words that contained adjacent vowels in the same syllable (1996, p. 184). Clymer determined that a utility rate of 75 percent was necessary in order for the generalization to be considered useful in the classroom (p. 186).

Clymer's results have been interpreted in a myriad of ways over the years. Perhaps the most important conclusion that can be drawn is that so-called phonics rules are rarely actually rules. There are too many exceptions to call them such. "Effective decoders see words not in terms of phonics rules, but in terms of patterns of letters that are used to aid in identification" (Stahl, 1992, p. 622). Teaching phonics rules is counterproductive, because there are too many exceptions to them.

Knowledge of some generalizations can be useful for students in grades higher than first grade, as long as they realize that these are patterns of letters and not rules. Even a generalization such as the CVVC, with its low utility rate, can be a useful one, because it gives readers a place to start if they have no other way to determine the word. It is reasonable to say that if a reader encounters a word that contains adjacent vowels, is unfamiliar with the word, and cannot recall a word that looks similar to it, the reader could predict the word by trying to pronounce the long sound of the first vowel. If that does not produce a recognizable word that makes sense in the context (which it won't, about half the time), then the student could try another vowel sound or another method of determining the word. Shown in Figure 7.4 is a list of generalizations suggested by Clymer that may be useful for your students to know.

Helping your students see generalizations and patterns can be accomplished with a **word sort.** In this strategy, you ask students to find words in a story or basal selection. Once they find the words and write them on cards, they then sort them according to the way they sound. When they put words in categories of this nature, they can see patterns emerge. See Figure 7.5 for the procedure, and Figure 7.6 for an example.

Useful Phonics Generalizations for Teachers to Know

CVC—In this pattern, the vowel is short. Also, consonants can be in blends or digraphs, representing a consonant unit, such as in the word "sick" or "blot." The same pattern holds true for words or syllables without the first consonant, such as in the words "an" and "at."

Words that fit the generalization:

fat, him, leg, sod, cut, duck, crab, it

Words that appear to fit the generalization, but do not:

play, drew, for

Generalizability: 62%

CVCe—This generalization says that when an "e" is added to the end of a CVC combination, the vowel in the middle represents a long vowel sound. The final "e" is silent.

Words that fit the generalization:

lake, bike, hole, mane, fume

Words that appear to fit the generalization, but do not:

give, have

Generalizability: 60% (Clymer applied this generalization only to words that contain "a" or "i" as the middle vowel.)

CVVC—This generalization says that when two vowels are adjacent in the middle of the word or syllable, the first vowel is long and the second vowel is silent. The same pattern holds true for words or syllables without the first consonant, such as in the word "aim" and "oak." All CVVC words contain vowel digraphs; however, not all vowel digraphs fit the CVVC pattern. For example, the word "boat" contains two adjacent vowels and its first one is long; therefore, it fits the CVVC pattern. However, the word "coin" contains two adjacent vowels, but it does not fit the CVVC pattern because the first vowel, "o," is not long.

Words that fit the generalization:

team, reach, coat, main

Words that appear to fit the generalization, but do not:

boil, head

Generalizability: 45% for all studied words that contain any adjacent vowels; more for combinations "ai" (64%), "ea" (66%), "oa" (97%)

CV—This generalization says that when there is a single vowel at the end of a word or syllable, the vowel is long. This pattern applies also to words that have no consonant at the beginning, such as in the word "able," or single vowel words such as "I."

Words that fit the generalization:

he, she, acorn, music, icicle

Words that appear to fit the generalization, but do not:

do, ability

Generalizability: 74%

Figure 7.4 Helpful phonics generalizations.

1. Read a book or story aloud to students. Be sure that the book contains words with the spelling patterns that you want students to learn.
2. Pair up the students and assign each pair a page from the story.
3. Ask students to look for words that contain a letter or combination of letters that you want to target. When they find them, they are to write each word on a card. Do not write duplicates.
4. Make a chart that helps students sort the words. It can consist of two to four columns, depending on the words that are in the book. At the top of each column, write a word from the story to serve as a target word. This word should be highly recognizable, such as the main character's name or a word from the title.
5. Have students look at each word card and pronounce the word, then determine the column that it best fits in. They can tape the cards to the chart, or rewrite them on the chart. Duplicates should not be added to the chart.

Once columns are complete, students can see the number of ways that a phoneme can be spelled. The teacher chooses a word from one of the columns and asks the students to make a list of all words they can think of that are in the same word family.

Figure 7.5 Word sort procedure.

Decoding by Analogy

As you may recall from Chapter 6, an onset is the consonant that precedes the first vowel in a word or syllable and a rime is the part of the syllable that contains the vowel and any letters after it. For example, in the word "tap," "t-" is the onset and "-ap" is the rime. Words that contain the same rime are part of a word family. Words that contain the "-ap" rime include: "cap," "lap," "map," "strap," and "wrap." These are said to be in the "-ap" word family. Longer words also contain the "-ap" rime, such as "happening," "laptop," "capital," and "tapestry." Knowing about rimes is a powerful tool for the young reader. Once a child realizes that many words look alike, figuring out unknown words—even longer words—becomes much simpler. He can process spelling patterns by searching his memory bank for the pattern and producing a pronunciation based on a word he knows. Decoding letter by letter is not necessary, and the speed of the entire process is much quicker. This strategy is called **decoding by analogy,** and is the way that many researchers believe we decode most of the unknown words we encounter (Adams, 1990; Cunningham & Cunningham, 2002; Trieman, 1985).

Remember all of those generalizations that Clymer researched? He found that many of them are not very stable. But the use of rimes and decoding by analogy helps them to make more sense. For example, the CVVC generalization holds true in about 45 percent of words in which there are two adjacent vowels in the same

Phonics Word Sort Using Words from *The Cut-Ups*
by James Marshall (1984)

1. Have your students look through the book *The Cut-Ups* and find all the words in it that contain a "u." They should then write these words on cards. (Or, you can have these words printed on cards already, and give them to the students.) They should each have the following words:

   Spud—Turner—cut—up—full—murder—guys—built—Spurgle—just—used—binoculars—much—stuff—hurried—bushes—run—rushed—education

2. Have the students remove the words "used," "binoculars," "bushes," "full," "built," "guys," and "education" from the list and place them aside. Now they are to place only the words shown below on the desk in front of them.

   Spud—Turner—cut—up—murder—Spurgle—just—much—stuff—hurried—run—rushed

3. Ask the students to sort this list of words according to the way they look by presenting these criteria:
   • Find words that have the "u" followed by an "r."
   • Find words that have the "u" between two consonants. The second consonant should not be an "r."
   At this point, the following categories should be made:

   Turner, murder, Spurgle, hurried
   Spud, cut, just, much, stuff, run, rushed

   They will need to put aside the word "up."

4. Now ask the students to pronounce the words in each of these groups. What sound do you hear in each word of the two groups?

   Turner, murder, Spurgle, hurried: The /ėr/ sound
   Spud, cut, just, much, stuff, run, rushed: The /u/ sound

5. You can now divide the groups further by creating word families. Have the students make them into column headings and find or think of additional words that would fit in these families. See the following word family groupings, produced from the second group of words from Step #4.

spud	cut	just	much	stuff	run	rush
bud	but	bust	such	buff	bun	gush
dud	gut	dust		cuff	fun	lush
mud	hut	must		huff	gun	
stud	nut	rust		muff	nun	
muddle	rut				sun	

6. Create a generalization from these groups. For the families shown in Step #5, the students can generalize the following: Words that begin with a consonant unit, have the "u" in the middle, and end with a consonant unit are called **CVC words.** They contain the short "u" phoneme in the middle position.

7. You can also create word families from the other groupings and generalize. For example, the grouping that contains the name "Spurgle" leads to a generalization about the r-controlled vowel phoneme.

8. Now ask about the word "up." Have the students think of words in its family, such as "cup" and "pup." Show them how the word "up" also fits the CVC generalization, even though there is no consonant at its beginning.

9. Talk about the words that they put aside in Step #2: "used," "binoculars," "bushes," "full," "built," "guys," and "education." How are they different from the words discussed so far?

Figure 7.6 Phonics word sort example.

syllable. This generalization says that the first vowel represents the long sound and the second one is silent. Words with the "-eat" rime almost always have the long /e/ sound, just as words with the "-ain" rime almost always have the long /a/ sound. So, to help students realize that the CVVC does work, it is often helpful to teach them how to recognize and spell words with rimes.

Stahl (1992) reports that there are 37 rimes that can be used to derive almost 500 words. They are listed in Figure 7.7, in order by the first vowel.

Your students can do all sorts of activities using onsets and rimes to learn new words. Eldredge (1999) suggests the use of **hink pinks** to give your students practice in combining onsets and rimes. Show them several onsets, and one rime. Show them how to find two words that sound alike and create a mental picture when used together, such as "fat cat." Students can create hink pinks and publish a class collection of them. Also called **terse verse,** this is actually a form of poetry; you can introduce the idea with a book by Bruce McMillan, *Play Day* (1991), which contains several such verses, illustrated beautifully with photographs. Be careful to use only words that contain the same rime for this exercise. Some terse verse rhymes, but the rimes are not the same, such as the words in the title of another McMillan book, *One Sun* (1990).

A strategy that gives students the chance to manipulate rimes and onsets is called **Making Words.** Devised by Cunningham and Cunningham, it is "an activity in which children are individually given some letters that they use to make words" (1992, p. 107). Making Words is a fast-paced, concrete, and mentally challenging way to build upon what your students already know about some words, and learn new words in the process. It's quite simple to do, and can be done with all elementary age children. Look at Figure 7.8 for directions on how to use "Making Words with Books," an adaptation of the strategy using children's books. Figure 7.9 shows an example of a Making Words with Books lesson.

Cunningham (2005) offers another strategy that is useful for teaching patterns in words. Called **"Using Words You Know,"** it helps them spell and read new words, based on known words. Figure 7.10 shows an adaptation, along with an example, using this strategy with words from children's literature. This activity is good for any elementary grade, because you use the selections they are reading and you can tailor it to their needs. It helps your students see the similarities and differences in spelling patterns.

Rimes That Will Create Many Words

-ack , -ain, -ake, -ale, -all, -ame, -an, -ank, -ap, -ask, -at, -ate, -aw, -ay
-eat, -ell, -est
-ice, -ick, -ide, -ight, -ill, -in, -ine, -ing, -ink, -ip, -ir
-ock, -oke, -op, -or, -ore
-uck, -ug, -ump, -unk

Figure 7.7 A list of rimes that will make almost 500 words.

Source: Stahl, 1992.

Making Words with Books

1. From a book that your students are reading, choose a target word. This word should be long enough to make some smaller words out of it.
2. Make a list for yourself of all of the words that can be made from the target word, using these criteria:
   a. Words that contain the same rime
   b. Little words as well as big words (to help the struggling readers and challenge the better readers)
   c. Words that can be made by placing one letter in a different position
   d. A proper name (so that capital letters can be used)
   e. Words that are in the listening or speaking vocabularies of your students
3. Choose about six or eight of these words, ordering them from shortest to longest. These will be your "mystery words." Make up clues about each of them, beginning with the shortest word. Ideally, your clues would connect to ideas or characters in the children's book.
4. Write all of these mystery words on index cards and order them from shortest to longest.
5. Make all the letter cards that you will need to complete your words. On the back of each, write its capital letter.
6. Store the word cards, letter cards, and list of clues in an envelope. On the outside of the envelope, write the target word, the six to eight mystery words, and the rime patterns that you are using.

Figure 7.8 Directions for the Making Words with Books activity.

Invented Spelling

As you will recall from Chapter 6, invented spelling is the natural, unsolicited spelling that occurs when young children are asked to write unassisted. It reveals much about a student's understandings of letter–sound relationships, and research indicates that the process of figuring out letters to represent sounds while writing gives students some valuable skills for decoding unknown words (Clark, 1988; Ehri & McCormick, 2004). Research also tells us that spelling patterns that are evident in children's writing closely parallel their decoding development (Eldredge, 1999); therefore, observing your students' invented spellings will give you a window into their decoding abilities.

Make the time for your students to write informally, and use this time to observe the strategies your students use as they write. However, as Sipe (2001) suggested, do more than merely observe. Their spelling mistakes are opportunities for

Making Words with *Little Penguin's Tale* by Audrey Wood (1989)

1. Read aloud the story.
2. Give each student a set of letter cards: o, p, s, t, and u, w.
3. Give the students the following clues to make words. After making each word, show the index card on which you have written the word, and hang it on the chalkboard or word chart.
   a. You will need three letters. This is the word that tells the part of the bottle that the gooney birds were blowing. (top)
   b. You will need the same three letters. Rearrange them to make a word that means something you can beat on to make loud noises. (pot)
   c. Add another letter, to make four letters. If there are lots of gooney birds, there is more than one pot. So, make the plural of the word "pot." (pots)
   d. Rearrange the letters to make a word that finishes the following sentence: "The Walrus Polar Club was a great gathering _____ for meeting other animals who did whatever they wanted to do." (spot)
   e. Take away a letter, then add another letter and rearrange them to make a word that contains a vowel diphthong. It means something that Little Penguin might do if he did not get his own way about everything. (pout)
   f. We will use up all the letters now. What word do you think we will make? Add a letter to make a word that means something you see on the whale's back. (spout)
4. Show the students the words that were made: top, pot, pots, spot, pout, spout. Ask them to put the words in groups according to word families:

   top

   pot, pots

   pout, spout

   Now have them think of additional words that can be made to put in these categories.

Figure 7.9 Example of a Making Words activity.

you to teach new letter–sound correspondences or word patterns. When they ask for help or appear to be "stuck," help them to stretch out the sounds of words they do not know and identify letters that represent these phonemes (Dahl, Scharer, Lawson & Grogan, 1999).

Using Words You Know
from Books

1. Read aloud a book. Make sure that it contains examples of words that contain phonics elements you want to teach.
2. On a chart, make two to four columns, depending on the ability of your students. Head each column with a word from the book. Each word should be a distinctly different phonics element, and a highly recognizable word, such as the main character's name, a word in the title, or a frequently repeated word. These are your target words.
3. Make a master list of easy words and hard words that can be categorized in one of the columns. From this list, make large word cards for half of the words. Each word should be a member of the word family of one of the target words.
4. Show students the word cards one at a time. Have students pronounce them, and then write them in the column that best fits them.
5. Now say the remainder of the words on your list aloud for the students, but do not show them the word. Ask them to find the column that best fits these words and write them there.

See the following example from *Joseph Had a Little Overcoat* (Taback, 1999).

Words from that story to head the columns:

coat   worn   got

Easy words: boat, born, hot, float, pot, torn, goat, horn, tot, spot

Harder words: overcoat, forlorn, bloated, pottery, trotting, morning, popcorn

coat	worn	got
boat	born	hot
float	torn	pot
goat	horn	tot
overcoat	forlorn	spot
	morning	pottery
		trotting

Figure 7.10 Using words you know from books.

Modifying Instruction for ELL

Using LEA as a Stepping Stone to Phonics

GRADE LEVEL: 3–5

- **Objective**

  Students will use LEA stories or narrations to find words that are members of word families and make new words with them.

- **Preparation**

  Provide interesting and relevant experiences for your third to fifth grade students. Write language experience stories or narratives together, based on these experiences. However, because these are older students who may feel that wall charts are "babyish," after writing the stories on chart paper, type them, and then duplicate them for each student. Keep them in a booklet for each student, which gives them access to their own written words. Be sure to give students the opportunity to read and reread these stories and narratives. (Following is a list of suggested experiences and types of writing.) Assign students to partners for paired reading. Examine the selections in your students' booklets. Make a "master" list of words from the selections that contain common rimes. Use the list of 37 rimes in this chapter.
  - Cooking—Recipes
  - Collecting—Descriptions of collectibles
  - Classroom visits from family members of students, community members, or authors—Interviews
  - Art or craft projects—How-to articles
  - Science experiments—How-to articles and description of results

- **Materials**
  - Language experience booklets
  - Blank word cards

- **Introduction**
  1. Ask students to sit with their reading partners and bring their language experience booklets with them.
  2. Have each pair of students choose a selection from the language experience booklet to read together.

Modifications for ELL are printed in color.

3. After reading, ask students to find words that fit a particular pattern. For example, if you know that the language experience story contains the word "nice," write the word "rice" on the board and ask them to find a word in their stories that looks like it. Partners work together to find "nice."

4. When they find the word, students should write it on a list that looks like this:

rice	same	tore
nice	game	wore
twice	name	bore
slice	blame	sore
		more

5. Students then work together to write new words from the same family, in the appropriate column, even if they are not sure of what the word means. Because these words are members of word families, students should be able to pronounce them.

6. Use this list as a starting place for learning new vocabulary. Over the next few days, teach students the new words that they created on their lists. Use pictures or props to show the meanings. Encourage students to put the words on the classroom word wall and to use them in their writing.

Home–School Connection

Parent Bulletin: Making Words at Home

Shown below is a letter to send home. ●

Dear Families,

One of the activities that your child will be doing in my classroom is called "Making Words." This simple activity helps your child practice what he or she knows about letters and sounds. It also helps your child become aware of spelling.

Each week, I will send home a list of words, a set of letter cards, and some clues. Your job will be to read the clues aloud and ask your child to make the word for the

Reading with caregivers and parents gives children the chance to learn new words and practice familiar ones.

clue. Shown below are the letters and clues for the book *Maybe You Should Fly a Jet! Maybe You Should Be a Vet!* (LeSieg, 1980).

First, read the book with your child. We have read it together at school, so your child is familiar with many of the words. Then, get ready to make words! You will need these letter cards: t, v, j, s, r, and two e's.

Directions to give to your child:

1. You will need two letters. This is something that shows cartoons and other programs. (TV)

2. You will need to add a letter, so now you will have three. This is a person who takes care of animals. (vet)

3. Add another letter, to make four. This is something that you can wear, and it has no sleeves. (vest)

4. Add two letters, to make six. The author of this book shows a picture of this person who makes vests. (vester)

5. Change one letter. You will still have six letters. This is a person from days long ago who made the king laugh. The author of this book shows a picture of him. (jester)

Enjoy!

Your Child's Teacher

Summary: Phonics Instruction That Makes Sense

Many times, phonics instruction is thought of as drudgery. Because it is one of the tools your students will need to read our language, it makes sense for you to teach phonetic elements and generalizations in ways that are meaningful and interesting. This chapter showed you some strategies that capitalize on children's curiosity about language, their interests, and the things that they already know. The Reviewing the Big Picture box summarizes these strategies and their corresponding standards and principles.

Few people who teach reading have a neutral stance on the teaching of phonics—it is seen as a "cure-all" for whatever ails reading education by some, and as a needless, workbook-oriented skill by others. Regardless, phonics instruction is one of the five components of reading stipulated by the No Child Left Behind Act, making it an area for which you will be held accountable. In actuality, the teaching of phonics can invoke much inquiry and discovery. Think about the reason for teaching phonics—to provide a tool for determining an unknown word. Thus, the use of phonics involves an attempt to make sense of an unknown entity (a new word) by making discoveries about it, and comparing this to what is already known (a familiar, similar-looking word). Constructing knowledge about words is truly what phonics instruction is all about.

Technology Resources

- www.readingcenter.buffalo.edu/center/research/word.html   This web page is an article edited by Debra Carlin, which explains the Making Words strategy.

- www.wordles.com/default.asp   This web site, called "Wordles," is a "place to have fun with words." On one of its pages, "Words in Words," you can type any phrase or word into its search box, and the program produces a list of all the "little words" within your phrase or word. Such a list is helpful for planning Making Words or word sort activities.

- www.kidsource.com/kidsource/content2/phonics.html   This is an article by Constance Weaver titled "Phonics in Whole Language Classrooms," which explains how teachers can use whole text to teach phonics skills.

- www.teacher.scholastic.com/reading/bestpractices/phonics.htm   The Scholastic. com web site contains several web pages on understanding and teaching phonics.

expect the world
The New York Times
nytimes.com

Themes of the Times

Expand your knowledge of the concepts discussed in this chapter by reading current and historical articles from the *New York Times* by visiting the "Themes of the Times" section of the Companion Web Site.

Reviewing the Big Picture
Strategies Described in Chapter 7

Strategy	Description	Appropriate Text/Grade Level	IRA Standards	INTASC Principles	NAEYC Standards	ACEI/NCATE Standards
Phonemic awareness	Build upon what your students know about sounds heard in words. (See Chapter 6 for phonemic awareness strategies.)	Fiction and nonfiction/K–2	1.4, 2.2	4	4b	1, 2.1, 3.1, 3.4
Sequence of instruction for phonics	Teach the easiest and most useful phonemes first.	Fiction and nonfiction/K–2, 3–5	1.4, 4.1	4	1, 4b, 4d	1, 2.1, 3.1, 3.3, 3.4
Student-generated sound charts	Associate a sound with a well-known character from children's literature. Ask students to draw a picture of him and attach the pictures on the chart. List words that contain that sound on the chart.	Fiction/K–2	1.4, 2.2, 2.3, 4.1, 4.3, 4.4	4	1, 4b	1, 2.1, 3.1, 3.4
Explicit instruction	Teach phonetic elements directly. Let students hear and see how letters represent sounds.	Fiction and nonfiction/K–2, 3–5	1.4, 2.2, 2.3, 4.3	4, 6	1, 4b	1, 2.1, 3.1, 3.4, 3.5
Connections to meaningful text	Use texts that make sense and enable students to immediately apply what they've learned about phonics.	Fiction and nonfiction/K–2	1.4, 2.2, 2.3, 4.1, 4.4	4, 5,	1, 4b	1, 2.1, 3.1, 3.4
Mental modeling	Show students how you use letter clues to sound out words. Think out loud as you model this process for them.	Fiction and nonfiction/K–2, 3–5	1.4, 2.2, 2.3, 4.3	4, 6	4b	1, 2.1, 3.1, 3.2, 3.4, 3.5

Strategy	Description	Genre/Grade				
Inductive word solving	Give examples of a phonics pattern found in a piece of literature. Ask students to determine how the examples are alike. Write a generalization to go with the examples.	Fiction and nonfiction/K–2	1.4, 2.2, 2.3, 4.1, 4.3	4	4b	1, 2.1, 3.1, 3.3, 3.4
Generalizations	Teach the most useful generalizations.	Fiction and nonfiction/K–2, 3–5	1.4, 2.2, 2.3, 4.1	4	1, 4b	1, 2.1, 3.1, 3.3, 3.4
Word sort	Have students find words of a certain phonic element in a story. Sort by categories.	Fiction/K–2	1.4, 2.2, 2.3, 4.1	4	4b	1, 2.1, 3.1, 3.3, 3.4
Decode by analogy	Once students learn a rime, have them figure out many new words by substituting the onset.	Fiction/K–2	1.4, 2.2, 2.3, 4.1	4	4b	1, 2.1, 3.1, 3.3, 3.4
Hink pinks or terse verse	Students create a two-word verse, in which the words rhyme.	Fiction/K–2, 3–5	1.4, 2.2, 2.3, 4.1, 4.4	4	4b	1, 2.1, 3.1, 3.3, 3.4
Making words	Give students letter cards and clues for making words that come from books you have read in class.	Fiction and nonfiction/K–2, 3–5	1.4, 2.2, 2.3, 4.1, 4.4	4	4b	1, 2.1, 3.1, 3.3, 3.4
Using words you know	Ask students to compare new words to words they know. This aids in decoding and in spelling.	Fiction and nonfiction/K–2, 3–5	1.4, 2.2, 2.3, 4.1, 4.4	4	1, 4a, 4b	1, 2.1, 3.1, 3.2, 3.3, 3.4
Invented spelling	Give time for writing daily, especially in response to literature. Allow your students to spell unknown words according to their sounds and familiar patterns.	Fiction and nonfiction/K–2	1.4, 2.2, 2.3, 4.1, 4.4	4	1, 4b	1, 2.1, 3.1, 3.2, 3.3, 3.4

8

Teaching Word Study

Nick raised his hand first thing after the bell rang and said, "Mrs. Granger, I forgot my frindle."

Sitting three rows away, John blurted out, "I have an extra one you can borrow, Nick."

Then John made a big show of looking for something in his backpack. "I think I have an extra frindle, I mean, I told my mom to get three or four. I'm sure I had an extra frindle in here yesterday, but I must have taken it . . . wait . . . oh yeah, here it is."

And then John made a big show of throwing it over to Nick, and Nick missed it on purpose. Then he made a big show of finding it.

Mrs. Granger and every kid in the class got the message loud and clear. That black plastic thing that Nick borrowed from John had a funny name . . . a different name . . . a new name—frindle.

Frindle (Clements, 1996)

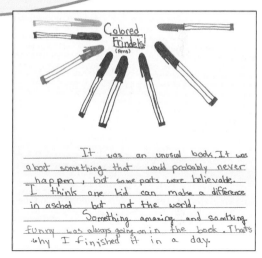

It was an unusual book. It was about something that would probably never happen, but some parts were believable. I think one kid can make a difference in aschol but not the world.

Something amazing and somthing funny was always going on in the book. That's why I finished it in a day.

Elsa, grade 4

Begin by reflecting on your own ideas about teaching words. Look at the three words shown in the Personal Reflection, and answer the questions.

The Personal Reflection illustrates that sometimes the smallest word can create the biggest questions. Did you find the word "of" to be a problem? If you did, that is because "of" has no real, tangible meaning of its own. Trying to describe "of" is nearly impossible if you are talking to children.

And yet you are responsible for making sure that your students know words well enough to recognize them and use them. The National Reading Panel (2000a) specifies vocabulary as one of the five most important components in reading. Without knowledge of words, your students' reading will not be smooth and fluent, and they will need to stop and sound out letters painstakingly, or depend upon pictures. How can you help children feel comfortable with reading so that they do not need to rely upon decoding? How can you help children's vocabularies grow, so that they immediately recognize many, many words, and know what they mean in context? How can you make words as important to your students as they were for Clements' character Nick, who created his own word for a pen? We will explore these questions in this chapter.

The premise of this book is that there is one goal of all word instruction: independence. For your students to achieve this goal, you will need to do three things. First, you will need to teach strategies that enable children to confidently decode unfamiliar words, using all the clues that are available to them. Second, you will need to provide much practice with words that your students have already encountered, so that these words become automatic and are part of your students' everyday reading vocabulary. Finally, you will need to make teaching decisions that lead to independence. When your students read, there will be words that are unfamiliar to them. You will need to decide whether it is necessary for you to show them these words prior to reading and make them familiar. This is called preteaching vocabulary, and it is quite a common practice, especially in instruction recommended by basal programs. It is the premise of this book that preteaching too many words fosters dependence, rather than independence. So, in this chapter, you will learn how to choose such words for instruction.

Fostering Independence with Words

Say this word: "sarcosporidiosis." Do you know this word? If not, how did you figure out the pronunciation of the word? Do you know its meaning? Without looking up the word in the dictionary or asking for help, can you use the word in a sentence? If not, what would be the most helpful thing for you to do?

It probably is obvious to you that to know this word, you need more information. In order to be able to understand it and use it on your own, you probably feel the need to see it in a sentence or read its definition.

One of the fascinating things about words is that correct pronunciation of them does not necessarily lead to understanding and correct usage of them. Thus, not only do we need to teach children how to figure out a word so that they can say it and recognize it when they see it again, we also need to teach them how to figure out its meaning so that they can generate, on their own, the appropriate mental image or concept represented by the word. When making decisions about what to teach about words so that our students become independent readers, we need to teach two things:

1. How to say the words that they see in print
2. What these words mean in the context in which they are being used

When teaching children how to figure out unknown words, you need to give them all the tools they need to become familiar with them, on their own. You need to consider the whole context in which a word is used, as well as the parts that make up the word, in order to decode. As you learned in Chapters 1 and 7, *decoding* is when the reader sees a written word on the page and makes a mental translation. In his or her mind, the reader translates the clustered set of letters that he or she sees into a possible known word. The reader uses any clues that are available in the word or in the context to determine a correspondence between letters and the sounds they represent. At the same time, the reader conjures up a mental picture or understanding about the concept that the word represents.

Look at this sentence: "The horse was not doing well because its muscles were weakened from the disease sarcosporidiosis." Do you have a better idea of the meaning of the word now? This disease, found in animals, is caused by a fungus parasite that attacks the muscles of animals. All of the available clues in the sentence can help you translate the letters of the word "sarcosporidiosis" into meaning.

Early in the school year, begin modeling for children how to figure out an unknown word, using a set of decoding strategies. Thus, when you say to them later, "Try out a sound," or "Use the clues to help you," your students will know what to do. Moreover, it is important to send a message to your students: a message that says that figuring out words is a multifaceted—and independent—endeavor.

See Figures 8.1 to 8.3 for some examples of bookmarks made by teachers who taught their students to be independent word users. These bookmarks show students a series of behaviors to try when solving an unknown word puzzle.

Figures 8.1 and 8.2 show some bookmarks for children who are just beginning to decode. These bookmarks are based on the work of Brown (2003), who suggests that teachers take their students' age and development as readers into consideration when providing prompts for them as they read. The first one is for readers who are just beginning to decode and have little sight vocabulary. These readers depend on word beginnings and pictures to give them clues. The second one is for readers who can decode simple words and have a greater sight vocabulary, and most importantly, have begun to recognize onsets or patterns in words. Figure 8.3 is a bookmark for older readers. It directs the students to skip the unknown word and attempt to use clues from the rest of the sentence, which is what more mature readers often do when they encounter difficult words (Goodman & Goodman, 2004; Smith, 1997).

What to Do with Hard Words

1. Look at the first letter.
2. Get your mouth ready.
3. What is the first sound?
4. Look for clues on the page.
5. Say the word. Does it make sense in this sentence?

Figure 8.1 Decoding bookmark for earliest readers.

What to Do with Hard Words

1. Look at the word. Do you see a pattern you know?
2. Use the pattern to say the word fast.
3. Does it make sense in this sentence?
4. If not, try another vowel sound. Does it make sense?

Figure 8.2 Bookmark for beginning readers who recognize onsets and patterns.

In Figure 8.4, you'll see a mini-poster created by Cathy Hayden, who teaches third grade in Pennsylvania. Her decoding reminder is very simple; she calls it "Be So Careful." She asks students to "bleep" the unknown word, then search for phonic elements, and last, check with a dictionary, partner, or teacher. Her goal is to remind her students of the most essential self-help decoding strategies.

How to Figure Out an Unknown Word

NOW

1. When you see a word you don't know, read the sentence for clues.

2. Still don't know? Mark it and come back to it later.

LATER

3. Think about the author's clues.

4. Look for word parts you know and sound them out.

5. Try the word again. Does it make sense here?

6. If you still don't know, write it down so you can look it up or ask for help.

Figure 8.3 Decoding bookmark for older readers.

When you come to a new word,
Be So Careful!

Bleep the word and finish the sentence!

Search for the word parts and letter sounds!

Check with a dictionary, and then find help from a partner or the teacher.

Figure 8.4 Decoding strategy mini-poster used by Cathy Hayden's third graders.

In order for your students to be able to use decoding strategies such as these, you need to show them how to do things such as locating familiar word parts, blending, trying out possible vowel sounds, determining the meanings of prefixes and suffixes, reading the context for clues, and making predictions about the meaning of the word. This book focuses on both facets of teaching words—constructing meaning from all available clues, as well as decoding phonetically for accurate pronunciation—so that your students instantly recognize and can use the words they encounter in print. In Chapter 7, you learned how to teach phonics meaningfully, so that your students gain independence as they encounter unfamiliar print. In this chapter, you will learn how to teach words so that your students recognize, remember, and use them. Now, let's return to those words shown in the Personal Reflection. We'll look at the three types of words and how to focus on the process of constructing meaning as you teach them to your students.

A Function Word: "Of"

The word "of" is similar to these words: "the," "to," "some," "were," "have," "was." How are these words alike?

You probably noticed their relative size. These are small words, often consisting of only four letters or fewer. You may have also noticed that these words do not mean much on their own. They need other words surrounding them in order to make sense. They cannot be easily described. Try defining one! In fact, they are not easily defined in a dictionary. In the *World Book Dictionary,* two of the eight definitions for the word "the" contain the word "the"! If you were unfamiliar with the word, would this definition help? Probably not. Finally, you may have noticed that these words are phonetically irregular—that is, they are not pronounced the way we would expect based on the way they are spelled.

These words are **function words.** They are also high-frequency words. They serve a function in a sentence, such as to indicate a certain subject or number, a state of being, or the position of a thing. They are prepositions, articles, and connectives. But they have little meaning without other words.

Function words are the most frequently used words in our language (Hiebert & Martin, 2002). It is therefore very important for children to know them, because they will encounter these words most often. They are often phonetically irregular and do not generate mental pictures; therefore, they are difficult for many students to master. You will spend much time with these words if you teach primary grades, especially first grade. How can you teach such words?

Using Context

If a function word has no meaning by itself, it makes no sense to teach it out of context. When teaching these words, always put them in meaningful, clear sentences, then read them and show them to your students. Highlighting these words, underlining them, or typing them in a bold font helps to make them stand out. You can also use a window card, which is a blank index card or square of construction paper in which a word-size window has been cut out. This cutout frames the word that you want to target in a sentence.

Using Repetition

Repetition is the key. If a word is not easily decodable, it needs to be repeated more often in the texts that children read (Hiebert & Martin, 2002). First grade readers of average ability need to see a word at least four times before they instantly recognize it (Reitsma, 1983). Thus, you need to provide your students with reading materials that repeat many of these high-frequency functional words. Some basal publishers, in attempts to make texts easier, have created stories that omit many function words; however, this technique may confuse young readers (Hiebert & Martin, 2002). One good way to make sure that your students are exposed to function words repeatedly is to provide easy-to-read books that are interesting and have many function words. Another way is to have many predictable books available. Reading and rereading predictable pattern books, along with sentence and word activities, tends to help children remember these function words (Bridge, Winograd & Haley, 1983). A list of some favorite easy-to-read books is shown in Figure 8.5. Refer to the Companion Web Site for a list of predictable books.

Using the Language Experience Approach

One way to use repetition is by using the language experience approach (LEA). As you may recall from Chapter 6, this method gives students the opportunity to dictate or help write a story or narrative about a common experience. The stories or narratives can be used for reading instruction with primary grade students. It is also an extremely valuable strategy for use with students in any grade whose native language is not English (Cunningham & Allington, 2002).

Concrete experiences such as going on trips, making things, conducting experiments, interacting with classroom visitors, playing games, going on outdoor walks, and participating in holiday activities provide topics for student-generated texts. Vicarious experiences, especially those with books, are also valuable. Additionally, many experiences with technology will provide students with ideas for writing, such as CD-ROM stories, informational texts, and software games.

Once you read a book to your students, the entire class has a shared experience to which they can respond. After the experience or after listening to the book, have the students dictate a few sentences that describe it, resulting in a brief narrative that clearly shows the relationship between spoken words and print. Now the students can read aloud the text together, then independently from individual copies made by the teacher (Durkin, 1993; Allen & Allen, 1967; Stauffer, 19).

To make the most of this **language experience text** when teaching function words, set up the experience and the chart dictation so that you know it will lead to the use of the words you wish to target. For example, suppose the word "was"—a difficult function word to master—is the word that you want your students to practice. You can have the students play a "hide and seek" game, and tell

Providing Repetition of Function Words with Easy-to-Read Books

Berenstain, M. (1991). *Nose, toes, antlers, tail.* Racine, WI: Western Publishing.

Brown, M. (1980). *Pickle things.* New York: Trumpet.

Brown, M. (1996). *Arthur's reading race.* New York: Random House.

Brown, M. (1999). *Arthur in a pickle.* New York: Random House.

Browne, A. (1988). *I like books.* New York: Scholastic.

Canizares, S. (1998). *Storms.* New York: Scholastic.

Canizares, S. & Moreton, D. (1998). *Sun.* New York: Scholastic.

Canizares, S. & Reid, M. (1998). *Coral reef.* New York: Scholastic.

Carle, E. (1969). *The very hungry caterpillar.* New York: Philomel.

Coxe, M. (1996). *Cat traps.* New York: Random House.

Eastman, P. D. (1961). *Go, dog, go!* New York: Random House.

Galdone, P. (1986). *Over in the meadow.* New York: Simon & Schuster.

Herman, G. (1996). *There is a town.* New York: Random House.

LeSieg, T. (1972). *In a people house.* New York: Random House.

Lewison, W. (1992). *Buzz said the bee.* New York: Scholastic Cartwheel.

Lobel, A. (1971). *Frog and Toad together.* New York: Scholastic.

Lobel, A. (1976). *Frog and Toad all year.* New York: HarperCollins.

Maccarone, G. (1996). *Recess mess.* New York: HarperCollins.

Marshall, J. (1984). *George and Martha back in town.* Boston: Houghton Mifflin.

Oppenheim, J. (1989). *"Not now!" said the cow.* New York: Bantam Doubleday Dell.

Oppenheim, J. (1993). *"Uh-oh!" said the crow.* New York: Bantam Doubleday Dell.

Packard, M. (1993). *My messy room.* New York: Scholastic.

Schulman, J. (1993). *The Random House Book of Easy to Read Stories.* New York: Random House.

Seuss, Dr. (1960a). *Green eggs and ham.* New York: Random House.

Seuss, Dr. (1960b). *One fish, two fish, red fish, blue fish.* New York: Random House.

Seuss, Dr. (1963b). *Hop on pop.* New York: Random House.

Seuss, Dr. (1974a). *Great day for up.* New York: Random House.

Vinje, M. (1996). *The new bike.* Grand Haven, MI: School Zone.

Wilhelm, H. (2002). *I love my shadow.* New York: Scholastic.

Williams, R. L. (1994a). *All through the day with cat and dog.* Cypress, CA: Creative Teaching Press.

Williams, R. L. (1994b). *Cat and dog.* Cypress, CA: Creative Teaching Press.

Williams, R. L. (1994c). *Where do monsters live?* Cypress, CA: Creative Teaching Press.

Wiseman, B. (1959). *Morris the moose.* New York: HarperCollins.

Ziefert, H. (1984). *Sleepy dog.* New York: Random House.

Figure 8.5 Easy-to-read books.

them to remember where everyone hid. Afterwards, they dictate a narrative. Begin the narrative by asking them, "What did we play? Where was everyone? Let's write the questions, then the answers." Your resulting chart would be similar to the one shown in Figure 8.6. You can see how the word "was" is repeated

Where Were We?

We played hide and seek.
Where was Miguel? Miguel was under his desk.
Where was Tiffany? Tiffany was by the sink.
Where was Jeffrey? Jeffrey was behind the door.
Where was Patrick? Patrick was under the bean bag chair.
That game was fun!

Figure 8.6 Language experience text resulting from a classroom game.

throughout the narration. Notice also that other function words, such as "where," "the," and several prepositions are repeated.

The language experience approach is very adaptable to all learners. Middle school students can use it with photography and computer technology (Stratton, Grindler & Postell, 1992), and English language learners benefit from seeing their spoken words written (Dixon & Nessel, 1983).

Another way to make sure that function words are practiced is to choose predictable books that contain at least one target word. After the students have enjoyed listening to the book and reading it together, ask them to write their own version of a predictable story, using the same pattern used by the author in the shared book. One popular example is Martin's (1993) *Brown Bear, Brown Bear, What Do You See?* Years ago, my first graders wrote a Halloween story version of this book, called, "Black Cat, Black Cat, What do You See?" Since then, I have seen many variations of Martin's patterned story written by kindergarten and first grade students, using all kinds of themes and characters. Once this chart or book is written, it is important to give your students many opportunities to read it. Use the procedures shown in Figure 8.7 on page 254.

Over the years, in working with young readers and their teachers, I have used and observed several experiences that lead to language experience narrations that reinforce targeted function words. Figure 8.8 on page 255 lists some of these ideas.

Interactive Writing

As you may recall from Chapter 6, a strategy that is very similar to the language experience approach is called interactive writing (Button, Johnson & Furgerson, 1996). Interactive writing is different from LEA in that the teacher shares the pen with the students, allowing them to write as much as they can, using what they already know about letters and sounds. It is a way to support emerging writers as they move from invented spellings to conventional spellings. Using interactive writing, you and your students collaborate on the text that they want to write. As the group watches, give the pen to a student and ask the student to write the agreed-upon sentence on a chart for all to see. Students can then take turns sharing the pen, writing a sentence that the group dictates. As the students write, you might ask questions like these:

- Where should we start?
- How many words are in this sentence?
- Say the word slowly. What sounds do you hear?
- What letter stands for that sound?
- Read what we have so far. What should come next?
- Look at our alphabet chart. Which letter do we need to write next?
- Would that word make sense here?

As you ask questions, guide the scribe while he or she writes. When the students need to write words that they do not know how to spell, provide a scaffold by helping them determine sounds and syllables. If students misspell words or make other types of word errors, ask them to reread what they have written and ask, "Does that make sense?" You can use correction tape over the mistakes and help them write the word conventionally.

Button, Johnson, and Furgerson explain, "Interactive writing provides an authentic means for instruction in phonics and other linguistic patterns within the context of meaningful text. Children learn the conventions of spelling, syntax, and

Experiences that Become "Talk Written Down"

Target Words	Experience	Sample Sentences from Chart
and	Find things that go together, such as "salt and pepper," or "paper and pencil." Show them to students and ask them to think of more pairs of things.	**What Goes Together?** Salt and pepper go together. Paper and pencil go together. Catsup and French fries go together.
want	Read the book *Maybe You Should Fly a Jet! Maybe You Should Be a Vet!* (LeSieg, 1980). Ask students what they want to be when they become adults.	**What We Want to Be** Mark said, "I want to be a fireman." Maria said, "I want to be a fashion model." Cassie said, "I want to be a doctor." Lin said, "I want to be a pilot."
if, but, give	Read "Alligator Pie" by Dennis Lee (2001). Think of favorite things that the children cannot part with, and words that rhyme with them.	**Alligator Cake** Alligator cake, alligator cake, if I don't get some, I think I'm gonna shake. Give away my gingerbread, give away my snake, But don't give away my alligator cake.
what, do	Read *Brown Bear, Brown Bear, What Do You See?* by Bill Martin Jr. (1983). Ask the students to create additional animals or characters (related to a theme, if you wish), that can fit into this pattern. Begin by writing the first line to serve as a model.	**Green Cat, Green Cat, What Do You See?** Green cat, green cat, what do you see? I see an orange snake looking at me. Orange snake, orange snake, what do you see? I see a purple dog looking at me.
to	Have students look through magazines to find pictures of favorite foods. Ask them to pick one that they like best, and dictate a sentence that tells this. Write the dictation, then ask them to glue the picture next to the sentence.	**We Like to Eat** Tammy likes to eat pizza. Angelo likes to eat hot dogs. Marcus likes to eat cheeseburgers. Ella likes to eat candy.

Figure 8.8 Providing experiences that lead to useful language experience text.

Children benefit from reading and rereading their own writing.

semantics as they engage in the construction of letters, lists, and stories" (1996, p. 453). With interactive writing, your students begin to gain control over their use of words.

Using Word Banks

One way to give young readers lots of exposure to words is to provide them with word cards. Personal word collections can be used in a myriad of ways with primary grade students. Give them a box or envelope—a **word bank**—to hold small word cards. You can make these cards yourself to start, but as their vocabularies grow, children can write their own word cards. Keep stacks of small cards or squares of construction paper in the classroom for this purpose. Make sure that your students' word banks contain words of all kinds, so that they can make sentences. Function words alone do not make sentences! Figure 8.9 shows some word bank activities.

Using Word Walls

Word walls give your students a place in the classroom to collect words they encounter in their literacy experiences. Word walls are used in primary grade classrooms; there are several types of word walls. The first is the kind introduced in Chapter 6, the alphabetic word wall, where you put words on the wall alphabetically. The second kind of word wall is a word family wall, in which words are listed by their rime pattern. Finally, words can be categorized by content areas, themes, or concepts, such as Thanksgiving words, ocean words, or words that

Word Bank Activities

Grade Level: K–2

The following suggestions are things that your students can do with their word cards. These activities are arranged from easiest to hardest.

1. Find words that the teacher calls out.
2. Find words that rhyme with words called out by the teacher.
3. Organize word cards into categories such as colors, numbers, action words, or prepositions. For example, if "words that tell where" is the category, possible words are "on," "over," "up," and "in." The categories can also reflect the story that the students are reading. For example, you can say, "Find the words that tell all the things that the third little pig did." Words could be: build, make, slam, cook, shout, dance.
4. Find the word that fits in an incomplete sentence.
5. Find the word that describes a character in a book, a family member, or a friend. Or, add such a word to your bank.
6. Arrange word cards to match dictated sentences.
7. Use sports cards together with word cards in sentences. For example: If the child has a Mario Lemieux card, he or she could make up a sentence using the hockey card as a word and the rest of the word cards. The sentence could be:

   Mario Lemieux can skate very fast.

8. Make up a sentence with the word cards.

Figure 8.9 Word bank activities.

describe. Most likely, the alphabetical word wall will remain active all year in your classroom. The others may be removed after their use with the thematic unit or lesson.

You can add words to the word wall by isolating sentences in a book and asking students to look for words with certain qualities. For example, Fuhler (2000) suggests the use of *Buffalo Dreams* (Donner, 1999) for a lesson on homonyms. Show the students some sentences from the book. Then ask them to find words that sound like a word in the sentence, but are spelled differently. For example, look at this sentence: "The next day, when the tribe awoke, their village was surrounded by a herd of buffalo." The homonyms in the sentence are "their," "by," and "herd." Students can locate them, write each pair of homonyms on a card, and display them on the word wall.

Displaying the words on the wall helps your students spell as they write. Some teachers tell students that any word on the wall should be spelled correctly in their writing. This means, of course, that students need frequent activities with the wall to keep them familiar with the words. There are many ways to do word wall games and activities. For example, give the students a sheet of paper and ask them to find, in two minutes, all the words on the wall that look like and sound like a familiar word, such as "see." You can also ask them to find words related to a children's book. For example, after reading *Tio Armando* (Heide & Pierce, 1998), ask them to find a word on the wall that describes Tio, or have them find a word that tells how Suki feels in *Suki's Kimono* (Uegaki, 2003).

A Content Word: "Lake"

The word "lake" is similar to these words: "car," "girl," "seven," "run," "drive," "sleepy," "red," "quickly," and "happy." What do you notice about these words?

If you compare the meanings of these words at face value, they seem to be quite dissimilar. But closer inspection can tell much about them. First, each of these words can be named or described, and once doing so, they can be visualized. They are nouns, verbs, adjectives, and adverbs, and they have meaning by themselves. These words are called **content words**.

The content words listed are phonetically regular, in that their spelling patterns conform to what you would expect, based on familiar phonics generalizations; however, not all content words are phonetically regular. For example, the word "love" is a content word, but it does not fit the CVCe pattern.

As you might recall, function words must have context surrounding them in order for them to make sense. They are not usually associated with mental pictures. However, when reading a content word, a child either recognizes it instantly or figures out how to say it. At this point, if the word connotes an idea or concept with which the child is familiar, he or she conjures a mental image of the meaning of the word.

For example, suppose that David, a second grader, is reading this sentence: "Josie works at the hospital as a nurse." He needs to think about the word "hospital" for a second or two; it does not look familiar to him. But when he sees the word "nurse," his brain puts all the letter, sound, and meaning clues together in this sentence. That momentary hesitation when he saw the word that begins with "h" gives way to understanding, because it makes sense to him that the word "nurse" might be connected to the word "hospital." Thus, in his mind, he pictures a large building filled with people taking care of the health needs of other people, and a woman named Josie in a uniform. Of course, he needs to have had prior experience with or exposure to the concept of hospitals in order to do this. He also needs to have enough phonological knowledge to be able to connect the letters in the word "nurse" with their pronunciations. Therefore, the following facts are important for teaching content words:

1. *Children need large speaking vocabularies.* In order to connect words in print with their meanings, children need to have had prior experience with the concepts behind the words. For example, if a child sees the word "grits," he may be able to pronounce it; however, it is possible that the child will not know

what grits are. If a child has never heard of grits or has never eaten a bowl of them, he or she will not be able to conjure a mental image of this delicious hot breakfast cereal. Thus, if the word "grits" is not part of a student's speaking vocabulary, connecting those five letters to meaning is difficult. Making words part of children's speaking vocabularies means that they need experiences, both concrete and vicarious. They also need opportunities to talk about experiences, and opportunities to listen to the language of books (Nagy & Scott, 2004).

2. *Children need large sight vocabularies.* When a word is instantly recognized, it is said to be recognized on sight. No hesitation, no thinking about the word, no figuring out of letters need to take place. When a reader sees such a **sight word,** he or she accesses information stored in his or her "mental dictionary" (or lexicon), based on previous experiences with the word (Ehri, 1994, p. 323). Automatically reading words by sight is the goal of all vocabulary instruction, because once we teach a word, we want it to stay in the child's memory bank (LaBerge & Samuels, 1974; Perfetti, 1985; Samuels, 2004). Ideally, all words would be sight words. If this were the case, a child would never stumble, never need to stop and think about a word, never mispronounce a word, never misunderstand. Thus, it is important that as many words as possible are instantly recognized. This requires lots and lots of experience with words. In short, this means that children need to read books—lots of them.

3. *Children need to see words in context.* Content words produce mental images, to be sure. However, the surrounding context of a word can help children figure it out. They need to know that it is acceptable—and often necessary—to make predictions and educated guesses about words based on the sentences that house them. Sometimes, these words cannot be decoded without surrounding context. Consider this word: "read." Its pronunciation is quite different in these two sentences:

> I am anxious to read that book.
>
> I read the book yesterday.

Without context, homonyms remain a mystery.

4. *Children need strategies for independently figuring out unknown words.* Of course, even mature readers do not instantly recognize all words. So children need to know what to do when they encounter an unfamiliar one. They need knowledge of phonetic patterns, as you learned in Chapter 7.

Given these considerations, the way to teach a content word depends upon the word. If it is phonetically regular, then it is important that children know to use phonics generalizations and word families. If it is not, or if it is dependent upon context for its meaning, then it is important that children know how to use context to infer its meaning. Using the phonetic elements of the word and the generalizations of our language were discussed in Chapter 7. Using other available clues is discussed in the following sections of this chapter.

Diversity in the Reading Classroom

The Power of Words

Students of diverse backgrounds need solid instruction in the teaching of vocabulary. Language barriers as well as cultural barriers add to the challenge of helping them gain the vocabulary knowledge they need to understand unfamiliar text. And yet, some of the same efforts to help struggling readers may hinder them. For example, because of the No Child Left Behind Act, school administrators might increase the amount of reading instruction time in school. While more time for reading may appear to be beneficial at first glance, the number of hours in school is fixed; therefore, increasing reading instruction time may mean cutting back on subject area instruction, such as science or social studies. According to Crawford, this is not in the best interest of English language learners (1993). Content area studies involve rich learning experiences and vocabulary growth, which students of diverse backgrounds need but would not get if such programs are discontinued.

Additionally, "schools tend to provide students of diverse backgrounds with rote instruction in isolated skills and little opportunity to develop higher-level thinking about text. Constructivist approaches to literacy instruction offer the possibility of reversing this pattern" (Au, 2000, p. 846). Vocabulary instruction that engages the students' thinking needs to be part of the curriculum for these students.

Specific suggestions for accomplishing this are:

- Do not limit instruction to a single textbook. Use multiple resources, including web-based and software resources.

- Integrate curricular subject areas throughout the day. Teach the vocabulary of specialized subjects.

- Make sure all students have access to plenty of reading material appropriate for their abilities, and allow them to take these materials home to share with their families.

- Pair English language learners with buddies for vocabulary learning activities. Allington and Cunningham (2002) describe a project in which "language buddies" created bilingual dictionaries together, and the school kept these on file year after year.

- Allow English language learners to help teach words from their native language to English-only students.

Content Word Meaning Strategies

Content word meaning strategies help your students know the word, understand it, and use it appropriately. These strategies are dependent on the use of **context clues;** therefore, when you use these strategies, you will need to introduce new words to your students in meaningful context. Showing them the word in isolation on the chalkboard or on a word card will not be sufficient. In order to do this, you need to know a few things about context clues.

Not all context clues are created equal! Look at this nonsense word: "dremock." Even though you are likely to pronounce it correctly, its meaning is a mystery. It would be helpful to read the word in context to determine what it means. Let's look at some sentences that could help us decode the meaning of the word.

Suppose the sentence in which you encounter the word reads: "I love dremock!" This tells you almost nothing, other than the fact that the word is most likely a noun. Thus, asking a student to depend upon such a sentence for clues about the meaning of an unknown word would be fruitless.

Try this sentence: "Dremock plays all day from my radio." This sentence tells a bit more, indicating that it is something that comes from the radio and that it "plays." Notice what you must do to use the sentence clues. In order to know that "dremock" is something that plays from the radio, the reader must skip the unknown word and go all the way to the end of the sentence to figure this out. This is an appropriate strategy for using context to determine an unknown word; however, it requires an effort to hold the thought of the unknown word in place, while searching the remainder of the sentence for clues about its meaning.

Here's a sentence that is a bit more helpful: "I enjoy listening to the dremock as it plays from the radio." Now, the unknown word is in the middle of the sentence. Prior to this word, we read that the narrator in the sentence enjoys listening to this unknown thing called "dremock." More clues are evident here. Plus, the reader picks up an idea at the beginning of the sentence, before he or she encounters the unknown word.

Finally, read this sentence: "One of my favorite things to do is to turn on the radio and sing along with the dremock." This is the most helpful of the sentences for determining the unknown word. Why? Notice that the nonsense word "dremock" is at the end of the sentence. This placement allows the reader to gain all the necessary information needed about the unknown word prior to encountering it! Thus, even before the reader says "dremock," he knows that it is something that comes from the radio and that the narrator can sing with it. These clues would lead to the conclusion that "dremock" most likely means "music."

The point is that context clues are most helpful if they occur at the beginning of a sentence. If the unknown word is at the beginning of the sentence, the clues are helpful, but more difficult to access, because the reader must skip the word and "hold that thought." Then, the reader must read to the end of the sentence, glean the information, and mentally return to the unknown word. Figure 8.10 shows this sequence of difficulty levels, adapted from Durkin's work in this area (1993). Keep this sequence in mind as you make decisions about teaching words. When you ask students to use context clues to make logical guesses at the meanings of words, make sure that the clues available to them are helpful enough to warrant this. When you develop exercises and use strategies for teaching new words in context, write sentences that enable their understanding of the words with strong, useful context clues. Strategies that capitalize on the use of text to teach new words will be described in the next few pages.

Usefulness of Context Clues

Unknown word at the beginning of the sentence	Unknown word in the middle of the sentence	Unknown word at the end of the sentence

Hardest ◄——————————————————————► Easiest

Figure 8.10 The usefulness of context clues.

Predict-o-gram

The Predict-o-gram strategy (Blachowicz, 1986) relies on predictions to categorize words according to their usefulness in a story. The students' understanding of story structure is important to the use of this strategy; thus, it can be used with any students who are familiar with the story elements: character, setting, problem,

---

How to Prepare a Predict-o-gram

Grade Level: 3–5

1. Make a list of vocabulary words that are very important to the story. If you need to provide more support for your students, put the words in sentences.
2. Have the students discuss the words with their teammates.
3. Now have them put the words into categories according to how the words might be related to the story.
4. After reading, verify these category choices.

An example for use with *Hey, Al*, by Arthur Yorinks (1986) is shown here.

Predict-o-gram with Hey, Al
Look at the words from *Hey, Al*. Write them in the spaces to show where you think you will find them in the story.

janitor	pigeons	ferried	blissfully
faithful	struggling	thousands	ecstasy
Al	West Side	island	plumed
Eddie	conversation	cascaded	paradise
lost	heaven	found	bird

Characters		
Setting	Where	When
Problem		
How the problem was solved		

Figure 8.11 The predict-o-gram strategy.

events, and resolution. Students read the word list prepared by the teacher, and then determine which story element it most closely reflects. This procedure is shown in Figure 8.11.

Cloze Passage Definitions

The cloze procedure has long been used as a reading assessment (Bormuth, 1968; Harp, 1996; McCormick, 1987; Shearer & Homan, 1994). In the cloze test, the teacher prepares a passage in which he or she omits every fifth word, leaving a blank for the word. The child reads, attempting to insert the correct word in the blank. This activity gives the teacher a measure of the child's reading abilities.

The strategy shown here is different from the typical cloze activity in that it is designed as an instructional technique rather than as an assessment. It relies on the reader's cueing systems, because the reader uses clues in the passage to determine the missing words. It can be adapted for any grade level, depending upon the passage you use. Take a look at the example in Figure 8.12. Now, try filling in the blanks. The same word goes in both blanks.

What word did you put in the blanks? Most people put "book bag," "backpack," or "schoolbag." These words make sense in this context. However, the author, Johanna Hurwitz (1987), used the less common word "knapsack." Even if you'd never heard of this word before, you have thought of at least one synonym that could help you define the word "knapsack." This same procedure for figuring out an unknown word can be done with children, and it reinforces the idea that we can decode words in lots of ways. The procedure for preparing the cloze passage definition is shown in Figure 8.13 on page 264.

Word and Sentence Prediction Charts

Adapted from one described by Yopp and Yopp (2001, p. 45), this strategy is designed for use with expository text in upper elementary grades. It could also be

---

Now that Russell Michaels was six years old, he was in the first grade. His mother had bought him a lunchbox last year when he was in kindergarten. This year he had a _____, too. In it he carried his notebook and his reader. Often, when he returned from school, his _____ was filled with worksheets that he had completed in the classroom. At home the refrigerator was covered with the pages that Russell had done.

Figure 8.12 Example of a cloze passage for *Russell Sprouts* (1987, pp. 17–18).

Cloze Passage Definition

Grade Level: 3–5

To prepare:
From a story that the students are going to read (but haven't read yet), select a passage of about 100 words. (This length can vary.) The passage should contain at least one, and preferably more, of the targeted word or words that you want the students to learn. Reproduce the passage, keeping the first and last sentence intact. After the first sentence, delete the targeted word and put a blank instead. Remember that deletions at the beginning of the sentence are hardest to figure out, and deletions at the end of the sentence are the easiest.

Procedure for the students:
1. Have the students read the entire passage.
2. Ask them to fill in the blanks with words that would make sense.
3. Poll the class and list all the words that they used.
4. Reveal the "answer," or the word that the author used in the text.
5. Determine, from the students' list, which words can be used as synonyms for the targeted word.
6. Together, write a definition of the targeted word.
7. Confirm this definition with the dictionary.
8. Repeat this procedure with any other words that you wish to target in the cloze passage.

Figure 8.13 Cloze passage definition instructional strategy.

adapted for use in middle school. It relies on predictions to construct understandings of vocabulary. Its procedure is described here, and an example is shown in Figure 8.14 on page 265.

1. Give the students a copy of the selection and have them spend a few moments looking at pictures, charts, subtitles, and graphs.
2. Ask them to close their books.
3. Have the students generate as teammates a list of words that they anticipate will appear in the text. They must offer an explanation for their predictions and write their reasons on the chart.
4. Have the students create a sentence that contains at least two of the words that they anticipate being in the text. This should be a sentence that they believe would appear in the selection, based on their predictions, and must make sense in the context. They write this sentence on the chart.
5. Now ask students to read and confirm their predictions. As they read (or afterwards), the students check off the words that were actually in the selection and write their own definition of the word. Then they check the sentence for its validity and make changes to it as necessary.

Word and Sentence Prediction Chart

Grade Level: 3–5

Book: _____

Before Reading Write words that you think will be in this passage.	Before Reading Why did you make this prediction?	After Reading Did the author use this word?	After Reading What does this word mean? Write or draw.

Before Reading
Write a sentence that you think the author will use in this passage. Use two words that would make sense together.

After Reading
Did the author use a sentence like yours? Write the author's sentence here:

Figure 8.14 Word and sentence prediction strategy.

Semantic Feature Analysis

In the semantic feature analysis (SFA) strategy, students develop an understanding of vocabulary by seeing how a group of words are different and how they are alike (Johnson & Pearson, 1984). It can be used before, during, or after reading, with grade levels above second grade. Typically, this strategy is used after reading to reinforce understanding of pertinent words in the selection; however, here it is described as a prereading exercise, where the students make predictions about the words and the text. It helps students think about the specificity of word meanings and how the author uses them in his writing.

Using the strategy before the students read, you must assume that your students are not yet familiar with the vocabulary in the selection; you will therefore need to provide them with the targeted words in some interesting and meaningful context, so that they can make logical predictions about attributes. Directions for preparing the SFA are shown in Figure 8.15. An example of a "before reading" SFA is in Figure 8.16.

Using Semantic Feature Analysis Before Reading

Grade Level: 3–8

1. Select a category or class of words.
2. List items that fall into this category down the left side of the grid.
3. List attributes or features that some of the items have in common across the top of the grid. Make sure to include attributes that all of the items will have in common, as well as some attributes that are specific to only a few of the items.
4. Write some sentences for target words that contain clear, descriptive context clues.
5. After reading the sentences, have the students put pluses, minuses, or question marks in squares of the grid to indicate whether the items in the category have or lack the feature under consideration. Discuss words that can be characterized by multiple features.
6. If there are words that have the attributes at different times, put a slanted line through the grid cell and mark it with a plus and a minus. (For example, apples can be green or red; a character can be happy or sad in different parts of the book.)
7. Examine the patterns of pluses and minuses to determine the likenesses and differences of words. Discuss these, and save the grids. They can become part of the students' own dictionaries.
8. Question marks in the grids are a basis for additional research. Students need to read further for more context clues, or consult other sources.
9. Character traits, names of people and places, parts of speech, and figurative language are some examples of other types of items that can be used.

Figure 8.15 How to prepare semantic feature analysis.

Mnemonic Strategies

Remembering the meanings of words, particularly in content area subjects, can be a daunting task. So many times, children in the upper elementary grades attempt to learn new words by looking them up in a glossary and copying a definition. I'm sure you remember the success of that practice!

Instead, mnemonics help students learn—and *remember*—words. In the **keyword method** (Levin, Levin, Glasman & Nordwall, 1992), students remember the meaning of a new word because they have associated it with a familiar word, and can picture it in their minds. Several studies support the use of the keyword method (Konopak, Williams & Jampole, 1991; National Reading Panel, 2000b; Pressley, Levin & Delaney, 1982) for vocabulary learning.

It is an effective learning strategy for all readers, including struggling readers and ELL students (Avila & Sardarki, 1996; Tierney & Readance, 2005).

Before Reading Vocabulary Predictions:
Using Semantic Feature Analysis

First, read the following sentences. Next, think about what the underlined words mean. Then, fill in the grid.

1. Some people grow crops, or plants used by people for food or other needs.
2. A natural resource is something found in nature that people can use.
3. A mineral such as silver, gold, or iron is a resource found in the earth.
4. Some fuels, such as coal and oil, are found in the earth and can be burned to make machines work.

	Found inside the earth	People grow them	Used to make things	Used for food	Help provide power	Towns built near them	Part of nature	Help give people jobs
Crops	−	+	+	+	−	+	+	+
Natural resources	−	−	+	−	+	+	+	+
Minerals	+	−	+	−	−	+	+	+
Fuels	+	−	+	−	+	+	+	+

Figure 8.16 A semantic feature analysis grid completed before reading a selection from a third grade social studies text.

Source: "Communities Are Built Near Resources," from Living in Our World, Boehm, Hoone, McGowan, McKinney-Browning & Miramontes, 1997, pp. 106–109.

Here is an example of the keyword method, using the new word "shun":

"Shun" rhymes with "sun." The word "sun" becomes your keyword. Now picture someone sitting under a beach umbrella, shaded from the sun. This person "shuns the sun." This mental picture of someone avoiding the sun at the beach can help you remember the meaning of the word "shun."

Students enjoy creating their own dictionaries of words and keywords, with illustrations that help them remember the meaning of the word.

Modifying Instruction for

ELL

Taking Home Key Words

GRADE LEVEL: 1–6

● **Objective**

After reading a story or nonfiction selection at school, students will recognize and use important vocabulary.

● **Preparation**

Assign reading buddies, which are partners who work together during the lesson.

● **Materials**

- Index cards
- Basal selection or trade book
- Concrete items to go with word definitions

● **Procedure**

1. Introduce the reading selection or book. Tell the students that they will need to look for important words in the text as they read.

2. Read the selection, keeping a stack of index cards nearby.

3. When students approach a word they are unsure of, tell them to write it on a card.

4. After reading, discuss the words together, putting them in sentences, role playing meanings of words, and associating them with concrete objects.

5. Students may illustrate their word cards once they know its meaning.

6. Punch a single hole in the cards, and take them home. Ask caregivers or older siblings to write the word in the home language on the back of the card.

7. Students should bring these cards back to school and choose one word to share with their teammates.

Modifications for ELL are printed in color.

Word Part Strategies

As students get older, the number of words to which they are exposed grows. **Affixed words**, which are words containing a prefix, suffix, or both, are prevalent in the reading materials of students in grades three and higher. In these grades it becomes very important to teach students how to use their knowledge of root words and affixes to decode unknown words.

A **root word** is the word to which one or more affixes has been added. **Affixes** is the term given to any type of word part that is "affixed" to the word. A **prefix** is the word part attached to the beginning of a word, while a **suffix** is attached to the end. All affixes alter the meaning of the root word in some way. Sometimes, the meaning is changed entirely, as with the word "unhappy." The root word "happy" becomes its opposite when the prefix "un-" is added. Other times, the affixed word does not change in meaning, but only in number, tense, or degree. We call this an inflected word. When the word "flag" is inflected and becomes "flags," its meaning is still the same, except for its plurality. The word "hot" can be changed to the word "hotter"; the "-er" inflectional suffix indicates only that the heat is turned up.

All of this complicated information is made simpler by the fact that just a few affixes account for a great number of the affixed words in the English language. Thus, once you introduce the concept of root words to students and show them just four or five common affixes, they will know how to tackle more than half of the affixed words they will encounter. According to White, Sowell and Yanagihara (1989), the top six prefixes in written English are:

Prefixes	Examples
un-	unwrap, unhappy
re-	rewrite, replace
in-, im-, ir-, il- (all of these mean "not")	inability, impossible, irresponsible, illegal
dis-	disable
en-, em-	enable, empower
non-	nonfiction

The top six suffixes are:

Suffixes	Examples
-s or -es	chairs, buses
-ed	worked
-ing	playing
-ly	slowly
-er, -or (agentive, indicating a person or thing performing an action)	teacher, actor
-tion, -sion, -ation, -ition	action, invasion, medication, demolition

Cunningham (2005) suggests that teaching affixes should follow these guidelines:

1. Begin with affixed words that your students can already read and spell.
2. Show students several examples of words so that they can find the commonalities.
3. Show students how to "peel off" the affix, revealing the root word.
4. Have students draw conclusions about the affixes based on examples that they already know.

Take a look at how Mrs. Kline teaches her fourth grade students the meaning of the prefix "un-."

Mrs. Kline's Lesson

First, Mrs. Kline shows students the sentences shown below. Each contains an affixed word. She chose these words because she knows her students use these words in their speaking vocabularies; thus, the students are familiar with the words.

Mike said, "The snowstorm we had last week was **unbelievable!**"

Simona figured out the **unknown** word in the sentence.

The weather made Alexa very **unhappy.**

She asks the students, "Read these sentences and think about what they mean. Try to picture in your head the action in each sentence. Talk to your partner about the picture in your head."

Students discuss the sentences for a minute or two, and then Mrs. Kline says, "Suppose I changed these sentences a little bit. Watch what I do."

Mike said, "The snowstorm we had last week was **believable!**"

Simona figured out the **known** word in the sentence.

The weather made Alexa very **happy.**

After she erases the "un-" prefix from each word, Mrs. Kline asks, "How does the sentence change when I erase that word part?"

"The second sentence about me says that I'm happy about the weather. But in the first one, I'm unhappy about it."

"That's right," said Mrs. Kline. "So, tell us about your mental pictures. How did that change the picture in your head?"

"Well, in the first sentence, I was picturing a rainy day that would ruin my soccer game. But in the second one, I was thinking about a nice sunny day that wasn't too hot, just right for a soccer game."

"Yes! We can see that the whole meaning of the sentence changed. Many times, those two little letters, 'u' and 'n,' when added to the beginning of a word, make the whole word different. 'Unknown' is different from 'known.' In fact, these words are opposites! When you see a word that begins with 'un-,' you can think about how that little word part changes the whole meaning of the word. Now, take a look at this list." Mrs. Kline writes these words on the board:

under

uniform

uncle

She continues, "These words are different from the words 'unhappy' and 'unknown.' Try taking off the 'un' in the first word. What happens?"

Bridget says, "You get 'der.' That doesn't make sense."

"You're right, Bridget. These words stand alone. They are not words that have the 'un' prefix added to them. Now, I want you to make two columns on your paper, head the first column with the word 'unhappy,' because we know this word. Then, head the second column with the word 'uncle.' That's another one I think you're all familiar with. I'll call out some words and you decide which column to put them in."

Mrs. Kline calls out the words "unlike," "unicycle," "unappealing," "unusual," "united," "unit," "unmarked," and "undercover." Students work to put the words in the appropriate columns, like this:

Unhappy	Uncle
unmarked	united
unlike	undercover
unappealing	unit

As her students read during the week, they look for other words that contain the prefix "un-" and add them to the list. Explicit instruction, combined with a facilitative strategy such as word sorting, helps students use what they already know about familiar words to figure out unknown words.

An Interest Word: "Dinosaur"

The great thing about a word like "dinosaur" is that it requires little, if any, teaching. Even children as young as first grade almost always know it. They also know words like: "McDonald's," "ninja," "soccer," "pizza," "Wendy's," "Barbie," "Pokemon," "hockey," and "football." Obviously, not all of these words are easy to figure out phonetically. Yet many children know them. Why?

These are **interest words**. Words such as these interest children, and are part of children's environment, play, and everyday lives. Many children recognize these words long before they can identify letters or decode even the simplest of content words. For example, when my son, Charlie, was three, he instantly recognized the words "Pizza Hut" in a flyer that came in the mail. These were the first words that he ever read! Of course, the familiar red roof symbol helped this identification; however, the words were eventually internalized and became part of his reading vocabulary.

All children have words that are special to them. "Dinosaur" and all of the names of each species of dinosaurs, such as "Tyranosaurus Rex" and "Brontosaurus" are instantly recognized by many children who cannot decode, or distinguish between words such as "was," "saw," "were," and "where." That is because these words interest them. Many interest words are also environmental, and are part of the things that surround children daily. Proper nouns, such as names of sports figures and names of popular restaurants, are common interest words. These words differ according to age, gender, and the current "in" toys or movies on the market.

It makes sense to capitalize on interest words. Use them to help you teach other, perhaps more useful, words. Here's how.

Strategies for Interest Words

Using Interest Words You Know

Recall from Chapter 7 the strategy offered by Cunningham, Moore, Cunningham, and Moore, called Using Words You Know (2005). The strategy is based on the premise that readers can decode unknown words based on what they already know about words that are familiar to them. Using interest words from the children's environment for this purpose is especially helpful, because these words add an element of motivation. Lower elementary grades would benefit from this strategy; however, you can also use this with older English language learners. This practice is demonstrated in Figure 8.17.

Interest Word Banks and Word Walls

Be sure to include interest words in your students' word banks. These words are readily recognizable, and make it possible for them to create many sentences. This approach gives them the opportunity to link function words and content words, and gives them practice in using words that are not as familiar to them. Some teachers have their students make their own interest word cards by asking them to bring one favorite word per week to the classroom as part of a homework assignment. Others will feature "the word of the week," offered perhaps by the students themselves, based on current interests or local events. These words should be added to word banks or word walls so that they can be used in making sentences, sorting, and categorizing.

Making Decisions About Teaching Words

The classroom is a busy place, and like any other busy place, it is run by the clock. You will always be making decisions about time, because there is never enough of it. You will need to weigh the myriad of possible objectives that you want your students to meet against the amount of time you have to teach them and their relative importance. This axiom holds true of anything you teach; in particular, you will be making such decisions daily about reading.

Most school districts use basal programs. Basals are programs developed by publishing companies for the purpose of teaching children to read. Because they do seem to take on a life of their own in our schools, you might consider them to have split personalities. One side of basal programs is that they offer a complete set of materials, including anthologies of children's literature. In one place, you have all the copies of stories and nonfiction selections that you need for your class to read, all at appropriate reading levels for your grade level. This convenience is extremely helpful, especially to beginning teachers whose classroom libraries have not yet

Using Interest Words You Know

Grade Levels: K–2

1. Prior to the activity, survey the children to find out their favorite restaurants, candy bars, and cereals. Other interest words, such as toys and sports, could be surveyed as well. These would also be good questions to ask in an interest inventory the first day of school:
   a. What is your favorite restaurant?
   b. What is your favorite candy bar?
   c. What is your favorite breakfast cereal?
2. Once you have gathered these words, choose those that would help create word families, write them on a list, and set them aside for future planning.
3. On the day of your lesson, show your students three to five of these words taken from the same categories of interest, and have them write the words in columns. Highlight or bold the parts of the name that you want to use and have the children do the same. For example:

Sk*itt*les	St*ar*burst	Sw*eet* Tarts	Milky W*ay*

4. Explain that parts of words that we already know can often help us figure out how to spell and how to read words that we don't know.
5. Show some word cards and ask them to write them under the word that has the same pattern. For example, you could show the following for the words used here: "car," "day," "feet," "hit," "far," "bar," "play," "spit."
6. Explain that thinking of rhyming words can help students read as well as spell. For this step, read the words to them, but do not show them. After you say the word, the students need to decide which of the known words on their list it rhymes with. Then, they try to spell it and put it in its correct column. Some words you can use for this example are: "meet," "street," "may," "sway," "fit," "split." When doing this, begin with easier words and then add words that contain consonant blends and digraphs.
7. On another day, if your students are ready for more advanced words, continue the lesson in the same manner. Show them the first set of harder words, and have them place them in the correct columns. Then, say the second set of words, and have them place them in the columns. Words you can use for this example are: "today," "Friday," "cockpit," "admit," "fleeting," "wayside," "visit," "carton," "streetwalk."
8. End these lessons by stating, "Thinking of a rhyming word or looking for a word pattern helps us in spelling and reading."

Figure 8.17 A lesson that "uses interest words you know."

Source: Cunningham, 2005.

Word bank activities help students become familiar with vocabulary in interesting and meaningful ways.

fully developed. The other side of the basal personality is a distrust of teachers. They are designed to be "teacher-proof," meaning that if you simply follow the directions given, you cannot mess up your children's learning. Thus, an enormous amount of directions are given to teachers. If you adhere strictly to a basal program, much of your decision making is done for you. This prescription is unrealistic. A basal program does not know your students. Nor does it watch the clock.

This discussion is relevant because of the treatment of vocabulary in a typical basal lesson. Usually, a list of words is chosen for the teacher, to be taught before the students read a particular selection. Suggestions are given for teaching each word. Often, sentence charts accompany the basal materials, so that the teacher can simply show the students the chart so that they learn the words in context before they read. Usually, the number of words on this list is more than five; often it includes ten or more words. There is not enough time to teach these words well before the students read, nor is it necessary. To develop independence, students need to use their decoding skills to figure out unknown words on their own.

Thus, it is important to make a decision about which words will be pretaught from the list suggested by the basal. I suggest that no more than two or three words be pretaught prior to any scaffolded reading lesson. Base your decision on the following criteria:

1. Do your students already know the word? Many times, you will need to answer this question based on what you know about your students and what you know about their past classroom experiences. But if they already know a word, why teach it?
2. Is the word vitally important to the understanding of all or part of this selection? If so, it is a candidate for preteaching.
3. Is the word surrounded by helpful context? If so, do not preteach it. Allow the students to use their knowledge of reading for context clues to figure out this word.

4. Is the word easily decoded, based on the phonics elements that the students have already been taught? If so, do not preteach it. Allow the students to use their knowledge of decoding to figure out this word.

This list of guidelines assumes that your students have been taught decoding strategies and are given many opportunities to practice them. It also assumes that you teach the unknown words so that your students will remember them, making sure they see the words in the same contexts as they do in the literature selection.

A strategy that is helpful for determining whether your students already know vocabulary that they will encounter in a literature selection is one that I call Vocabulary Cover-up. It allows you to use your students' prior knowledge about words to make quick, on-the-spot decisions about vocabulary to teach. The procedure is described in Figure 8.18.

Vocabulary Cover-up

1. To prepare, type a list of vocabulary that your students will encounter in the selection that you want them to read. Use large font and spread the words across the page so that they can easily be seen.
2. Cut several pieces of construction paper or tagboard in word-card sized rectangles, making sure that these pieces will cover the words that are on your list.
3. Make a list of sentences that contain the words on your vocabulary list. You can lift them as quotes from the book or write your own. Make sure that these sentences offer clear context clues for defining and understanding the words.

To use the strategy:

1. Put the students in pairs. Give each pair a copy of the vocabulary list and ask them to determine which words they know "for sure." Give them the rectangle pieces. Ask them to cover up all the words that both members of the pair know. Both members of the pair must agree that the words they cover up are words that they already know.
2. Once all the known words are covered, the students need to look carefully at the uncovered words, because these are the ones that they don't know. At this point, give them the copy of sentences. Ask them to read the sentences that contain the words they don't know, and see if the context clues help. After talking about these words, have the students agree on which words they feel comfortable with at this point. Have them cover up additional words that they now know.
3. Circulate the classroom and watch. Take note of the words that are uncovered. These are the words that your students still need to learn. Make plans to teach them.

Figure 8.18 The Vocabulary Cover-up strategy for determining words to preteach.

Home–School Connection

Word Card Games

Shown here is a letter that you can send to caregivers of your primary grade students, showing them how to play word card games with their children. ●

Dear Families,

Your child will be bringing home some word cards for practice. You can help him or her by spending about five minutes each day with these words. There are several ways you can have fun with words. See my suggestions below.

1. Make two of each card, then play Concentration.
2. Put three or four cards out on the table. Make up a sentence for your child, leaving one word out. Ask your child to find the word that completes the sentence.

Reading books together is another way to have fun with words.

3. Put three or four cards out on the table. Ask your child to find the word that best describes a character in a book, a favorite sports figure, or a member of the family.
4. Ask your child a question. Have him or her answer it by stringing cards together to make a sentence. For example: The parent says, "Billy, do you like cookies?" Billy finds these cards and strings them together: I do like cookies.
5. Put all the words out on the table and ask your child to group them into categories. The child may choose any logical categories, or you can specify them. Here are some examples: Words that start with a particular letter, words that sound alike, happy words, food words, people words, words that show movement.
6. Make note of the words that "bug" your child. Include these in repetitive sentences. For example, if the troublesome word is "where," make five cards that say "where." Then have your child make up five sentences, using the word cards, that include the word "where." He or she could create sentences like these:

   Where is my cat? Where is my dog?

   Where is my mother? Where is the book?

7. Use your child's favorite trading cards or sports cards to string together words into sentences. Make a sentence with word cards, and place the trading card in the sentence where it makes sense; for example: Tiger Woods hits the ball.

Please let me know if you have questions.

Sincerely,

Your Child's Teacher

Summary: Teaching Words Wisely

You are the teacher, trusted with the education of many youngsters every year. Use that trust to make solid, sensible professional decisions based on your students' needs. Don't let a teacher's manual make those decisions for you. Use strategies that capitalize on your students' prior knowledge and interests, and focus on the meaning of the text in which they will encounter the words. This chapter has shown you some of those strategies—techniques that can help your students learn and use function words, content words, and interest words. Strategies that focus on the use of context were introduced in this chapter, and are summarized in the following Reviewing the Big Picture box, along with the corresponding standards and principles from IRA, INTASC, NAEYC, and NCATE.

Technology Resources

- **teacher.scholastic.com/reading/bestpractices/vocabulary.htm** From the Scholastic web site, this page shows best practices in teaching vocabulary. The author, Francie Alexander, answers questions, provides lists, and shows several activities and strategies.
- **school.discovery.com/brainboosters/** The link called "Word and Letter Play" offers several interactive activities with vocabulary.
- **www.readingonline.org/articles/art_index.asp?HREF=/articles/curtis/index.html** This web page includes an article by authors Curtis and Longo titled, "Teaching Vocabulary to Adolescents to Improve Comprehension."

expect the world
The New York Times
nytimes.com

Themes of the Times

Expand your knowledge of the concepts discussed in this chapter by reading current and historical articles from the *New York Times* by visiting the "Themes of the Times" section of the Companion Web Site.

Reviewing the Big Picture

Vocabulary Strategies

Strategy	Description	Appropriate Type of Text/Grade Level	IRA Standards	INTASC Principles	NAEYC Standards	ACEI/NCATE Standards
Decoding bookmarks	List a decoding strategy on a bookmark for students to use as they read.	Fiction and nonfiction, all words/K–2, 3–5	1.4, 2.2	4, 7	4b	1, 2.1, 3.1, 3.4
Using context	Introduce function words in context, and highlight or frame the words to make them stand out.	Fiction and nonfiction, function words/K–2	1.4, 2.2	4, 7	4b	1, 2.1, 3.1, 3.4
Easy-to-read books	Books that repeatedly use function words are helpful for providing meaningful repetition of vocabulary.	Fiction and nonfiction, function words/K–2	1.4, 2.3, 4.1, 4.2	4, 7	1, 4b	1, 2.1, 3.1, 3.4
Language experience materials	Provide an experience for the students and ask them to dictate to you an account of the experience. Read the resulting narrative together.	Fiction and nonfiction, function words/K–2, 3–5	1.4, 2.2, 2.3, 4.1	4, 7	1, 4b	1, 2.1, 3.1, 3.4, 3.5
Interactive writing	Decide with your students on a topic for writing, and then share the pen. Negotiate the words and sentences, then choose students to write the words on a chart.	Fiction and nonfiction, function words/K–2	1.4, 2.2, 2.3, 4.1	4, 7	1, 4b	1, 2.1, 3.1, 3.4, 3.5
Word bank activities	Put function, content, and interest words on cards. String them into sentences, play games, and categorize these words.	Fiction and nonfiction, function words/K–2	1.4, 2.2, 2.3, 4.1	4, 7	4b	1, 2.1, 3.1, 3.2, 3.4
Word walls	Display words on the wall in a variety of ways. Use the words in many categorizing, spelling, and writing activities.	Fiction, nonfiction, all types of words/K–2	1.4, 2.2, 2.3	4, 7	1, 4b	1, 2.1, 3.1, 3.2, 3.4

Strategy	Description	Genre/Level				
Predict-o-gram	List words from the story and have students determine how they reflect the story elements.	Fiction, content words/3–5	1.4, 2.2, 2.3	4, 7	NA	1, 2.1, 3.1, 3.2, 3.3, 3.4
Cloze passage definition	Choose a target word. Type a short passage from a book, deleting words that are synonyms of the target word. Ask students to fill in the blanks and determine the meaning of the target word.	Fiction and nonfiction, content words/3–5	1.4, 2.2, 2.3	4, 7	NA	1, 2.1, 3.1, 3.2, 3.4
Word and sentence prediction charts	After previewing pictures, charts, and maps, ask the students to generate a list of words they anticipate will appear in the text. Then write sentences that they believe might be in the book.	Nonfiction, content words/3–5	1.4, 2.2, 2.3	4, 7	NA	1, 2.1, 3.1, 3.2, 3.4
Semantic feature analysis	Give students a grid on which they compare vocabulary to a set of attributes.	Fiction and nonfiction, content words/3–5, 6–8	1.4, 2.2, 2.3	4, 7	NA	1, 2.1, 3.1, 3.2, 3.3, 3.4
Mnemonic strategies	Give students a key word and picture to associate with the target word.	Fiction and nonfiction, content words/3–5, 6–8	1.4, 2.2, 2.3	4, 7	NA	1, 2.1, 3.1, 3.2, 3.3, 3.4
Word parts strategies	Give students examples of affixed words that they know, draw conclusions about them, and sort words into categories.	Fiction and nonfiction, content words/3–5, 6–8	1.4, 2.2, 2.3	4, 7	NA	1, 2.1, 3.1, 3.2, 3.3, 3.4
Using interest words you know	Survey students to find out some favorite environmental words. Have them use these familiar words to determine unknown words.	Fiction and nonfiction, interest words/K–2	1.4, 2.2, 2.3, 4.1	4, 7	4b	1, 2.1, 3.1, 3.2, 3.3, 3.4
Interest word banks and walls	Give students word banks for stringing sentences, categorizing, and playing word games. Be sure to include interest words in the bank.	Fiction and nonfiction, interest words/K–2	1.4, 2.2, 2.3	4, 7	4b	1, 2.1, 3.1, 3.2, 3.3, 3.4
Vocabulary Cover-up	Give students a list of words. After reading the words in meaningful context, have them cover up words they already know.	Fiction and nonfiction, all types of words/3–8	1.4, 2.2, 2.3, 4.1	4, 7	NA	1, 2.1, 3.1, 3.2, 3.3, 3.4

9

Scaffolding Literacy Learning

That night after we ate, Moe Moe Bay came back to the table with a worn old Bible. She was so happy. My heart ached at the thought of tellin' her we'd be leavin' soon.

"Master Aylee showed him how paper talks. Show him, Pink," she said.

He took out a pair of spectacles from his pocket and opened the Bible to the Psalms of David and started to read. His voice was steady and had such wonder. Just hearin' them words made pictures come into my head.

"I surely do wish I could read," I announced to them without thinkin'.

When Pink saw I was ashamed, he took my hand.

"I'll teach you, Say, some one day. I'll teach you."

Pink and Say (Polacco, 1994)

I like the part when Pink finds Say, in the beginning of the book. It was really nice of Pink to provide hospitality to the injured boy. The book showed Pinks character as a young kid. But, in my eyes, I picture him as a hero because he reached out to a person of a different color in their time of need.

Zachary, age 12

Pink and Say never got a chance to finish that reading lesson. You can read to find out what happens in Patricia Polacco's moving story of two young Union soldiers, a black slave from Georgia and a white farm boy from Ohio who deserts the Army and is deeply ashamed of it. But "some one day," in your classroom, you'll be teaching children to read and write. Supporting them as they read and write will be one of the most important things you do, because it enables them to find a comfortable spot with print, figure out how it "is supposed to go" (Calkins, 2001, p. 164), and gain the confidence that breeds success as readers and writers.

What is reading like for you? Think about that in the Personal Reflection.

Do you like to read? Do you like to write? Why or why not?

What do you like about teaching children to read and write?

What is your greatest challenge in teaching children to read and write?

Are your answers to the first two questions negative? If so, look around you. If you are sitting in a room of teachers, inservice or preservice, about half of the people sitting around you will feel the same way (Applegate & Applegate, 2004; Gray & Troy, 1986). Many teachers do not value reading (Searls, 1985). There are many reasons, but your experiences as a child in school probably have much to do with this. Applegate and Applegate tell us that, based on a survey of preservice teachers, "It was clear that significant numbers of respondents were affected, either positively or negatively, by the instruction they received during their early school years" (2004, p. 560). Yet your feelings about literacy spill over in the classroom; Morrison, Jacobs, and Swinyard (1999) found that there is a positive relationship between teachers who read a lot and their use of effective literacy practices. Dreher says, "In short, teachers who are engaged readers are motivated to read, are both strategic and knowledgeable readers, and are socially interactive about what they read. These qualities show up in their classroom interactions and help create students who are, in turn, engaged readers" (2002–2003, p. 338).

Your experiences with reading might not have always been positive ones, even if you enjoy reading as an adult. The classroom is where young readers learn the technicalities of literacy. But sometimes, these technicalities seem to take over, and everyone involved—teachers as well as students—lose sight of what literacy is all about. You might have experienced this yourself. But literacy is about a connection to others, an awakening of a world that would never otherwise be known. Reading and writing in the classroom do not have to be joyless. Regardless of what you have experienced in the past, you can support your readers without suffocating them. You can provide an environment that invites experimentation, trial and error, inquiry, and prediction, without risk or fear of failure. You can provide the right amount of instructional support and expectations for independence, without killing your students' enthusiasm for the written word.

It is necessarily true that reading and writing in the classroom are different from reading and writing anywhere else. When your students read a book before going to bed or when they plop down on the couch with a magazine on a Saturday afternoon, they are reading casually. When they write a note to a friend or send instant messages on the computer, they are writing casually. These are very different experiences from the kinds of literacy tasks they do in the classroom. There, they interact with others while they read, talk to the teacher about what they've understood, and respond to the author's words in a variety of ways. The books they read at school may be slightly more difficult than the ones they would choose to read on their own. Likewise, they talk with each other about ideas for writing and ways to revise their work, as well as experiment with many forms of writing. The most important difference between casual literacy experiences and the ones they have in the classroom is *you*. You are the one who supports them as they learn new strategies and skills, guide them as their literacy abilities grow, and provide them with a classroom environment for optimal learning without fear of failure.

How can you do this?

Think about Vygotsky's zone of proximal development (1978), which you learned about in Chapter 2. You may recall that this is an educational environment that provides optimal learning, and is the kind of learning environment in which the teacher gives his students just the right amount of challenge. Tasks are not too hard, nor are they too easy. The teacher supports learning by offering scaffolds (Graves & Graves, 2003; Wood, Bruner & Ross, 1976). Scaffolded instruction helps students accomplish more than they would be able to do on their own. Scaffolds can be any instructional tool or technique that you use to enable your students' literacy efforts. Your interventions provide students with the amount of support they need to comprehend text or to create text for others to read. Figure 9.1 on page 284 shows the kinds of activities that you can use to scaffold your students before, during, and after their reading and writing. *[handwritten margin note: give them a purpose]*

Prereading and prewriting activities prepare students for the literacy tasks that they have to do. Brainstorming ideas and activating background knowledge are important strategies, as are motivating students to read or write. When reading, you may find it necessary to help students make predictions or build anticipation. Sometimes, you need to provide experiences for your students so that they will have the necessary prior knowledge to read a selection or to write about a topic. You may need to teach mini-lessons that show students how to accomplish a reading task such as selecting an appropriate book to read or a writing task such as determining an audience. Other strategies for activating background knowledge and preparing to read and write are described in Chapter 11.

During reading and writing, you can offer support in a myriad of ways. Readers may need you to stop and discuss parts of the story or selection with them, clarify misconceptions, check comprehension, confirm predictions, or help with decoding difficult words. You may need to read all or part of the text to them, and ask them to follow along whenever possible. During writing, you can scaffold your students' efforts by teaching mini-lessons on the mechanics of writing; talking to students as they write and refine their writing; providing spelling help such as word walls or personal word banks; and allowing students to work collaboratively with others to create books, reports, or messages. Chapter 12 shows many strategies that support students as they read and write.

After reading is finished, your students can respond to the text with retellings, discussions, or artistic expressions, among many other response activities (shown in Chapter 13). They can respond by writing in journals, letters to the author, or stories written in the same pattern. Students also like the opportunity to share with each other either books they've read or pieces that they've written.

This is the kind of environment you need for your students. You want them to be able to read and write on their own, but in order for them to do this, you need to support them. When the book is too difficult for them to read alone, you can read it with them, talking about it with them as you read. This type of support will enable their understanding of the book, and provide them with skills they will need for the next book they attempt. When they are unsure of what to write or how to write it, you can share the pen with them, helping them formulate ideas and spelling words that others can read. These supports will enable them to write a message and lay a foundation for the next message they attempt to write. All of this, and more, is part of providing the zone of proximal development for literacy learning.

Ways to Scaffold Your Students' Reading and Writing

Before Reading

- Activate background knowledge.
- Talk with students about predictions and inferences.
- Set purposes for reading.
- Talk about the author's purpose for writing.
- Preview the text together.
- Provide real-life experiences.
- Read aloud to students so they know how it is supposed to sound.

During Reading

- Use stop points throughout the book, which are places to stop, discuss predictions, and monitor comprehension.
- Give students printed reading guides, which have questions to answer or reminders of things to look for as they read.
- Decode hard words for them by reading the book aloud as the students follow along.

After Reading

- Talk with students about the book, reflecting upon it and reacting to it.
- Invite students to share responses with others.
- Ask students to retell all the elements and events of the story or all the important ideas of nonfiction.
- Ask students to summarize only the most essential story elements or main ideas.

Before Writing

- Activate background knowledge.
- Help students determine audience and purpose.
- Help students list ideas for writing.
- Talk about authors' styles and use of words.
- Make lists of words and phrases that students can use in writing.
- Keep a word wall in the classroom.
- Provide real-life experiences.

During Writing

- Read and reread drafts with the students.
- Allow students to discuss drafts with their peers.
- Hold conferences with students as they write drafts, to determine areas of need.
- Provide help with spelling and grammar as needed.
- Share the pen and write as students dictate.
- Provide models, patterns, and frames for writing, based on quality children's literature.

After Writing

- Talk with students about what they've written, reflecting upon it and reacting to it.
- Give students authentic opportunities to publish writing for others.

Figure 9.1 Ways to scaffold before, during, and after literacy.

Supporting students as they read and write is important. However, letting go is even more important. Scaffolding supports, but it also enables independence. "Scaffolding," as defined in *The Literacy Dictionary* (Harris & Hodges, 1995), is "the gradual withdrawal of adult (e.g., teacher) support, as through instruction, modeling, questioning, feedback, etc., for a child's performance across successive engagements, thus transferring more and more autonomy to the child" (p. 226). This "gradual release of responsibility," originally explained by Campione, is "a progression in which students gradually assume increased responsibility for their learning from the teacher" (cited in Graves & Graves, 2003 p. 45).

Thus, as your students get older, more mature, and more capable of reading and writing, you can allow them to do more on their own. However, the difficulty of the text they need to read plays a role in this progression, too. For example, if you are teaching first graders, they may start the school year dependent upon you for decoding words, even in the very simplest and most predictable text, such as *I Went Walking* by Sue Williams (1989). This book contains just one sentence per page with pictures that give the reader clues about what happens on the next page. But as the weeks go on, they will be able to read this book on their own, as well as many similar books. Thus, you can decrease your support with books like these, but offer support with slightly more difficult ones such as *Arthur's Reading Race* (Brown, 1996), which has limited vocabulary but is not as predictable. This type of recursive support continues throughout the elementary grades and middle school. The amount of support you give them depends on the texts your students need to read, the amount of background knowledge they have about the topics they are reading and writing, their reading and writing abilities, and their motivation to tackle the literacy tasks before them. As any of these variables change, your level of support may need to change, as well (Fountas & Pinnell, 1996; Graves & Graves, 2003).

Take a look at Figure 9.2. Literacy instruction is represented as a triangle. The triangle itself represents the amount of teacher intervention needed for teaching reading. As you can see, the base of the triangle is its widest part, which represents the greatest amount of support offered to the students as they read and write. These methods of instruction are the ones in which you do most of the decoding or writing for your students. The amount of support decreases at each higher level of

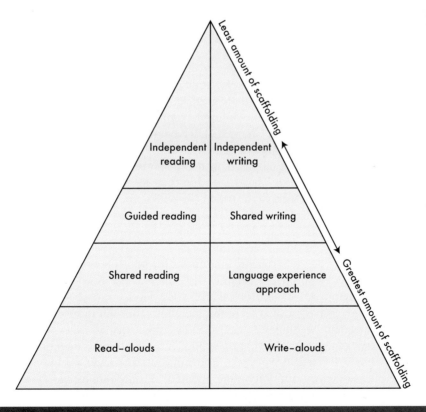

Figure 9.2 Scaffolding literacy instruction.

the triangle, showing strategies that allow for more student-initiated efforts. The top, which is the smallest portion of the triangle, represents the least amount of support by the teacher. In these methods, the students read or write on their own.

Now let's look closer at supporting your students' literacy efforts, including discussion of reading and writing frameworks.

Ways to Scaffold Reading

To provide scaffolds for your students as they learn to read, you will need to do two important things: (1) Find reading materials that are appropriate for your students, and (2) determine the amount of scaffolding they need. Read on to find out ways to do both of these things.

Matching Readers to Text

In order to choose reading materials that would be best for your readers, you'll need to know your readers as well as the text you want them to read. Assessing your readers' abilities can take place in a variety of ways; you learned about running records and miscue analysis in Chapter 4. These valuable tools give you an idea of how well your students can process print, and help you determine how easy or hard their texts ought to be.

You may also remember from Chapter 4 that there are a variety of ways to determine the reading level of a book. Many children's books have been labeled by the publisher with approximate grade levels. If the reading level of a book is not identified, you can determine an approximate grade level using the Fry Readability formula (mentioned in Chapter 4), which mathematically determines the grade level of text based on number of sentences and number of syllables in one hundred words of text (Fry, 1977, 2002). This formula is easy to use for a rough estimate of the difficulty of the text. There are additional formulas that objectively and consistently assign grade levels to thousands of books, such as the New Dale-Chall Readability Formula (Chall & Dale, 1995), and the Lexile Framework (Stenner, 1996). However, as with anything that is easy to do, these formulae may be too simplistic, because they do not account for student interests or background experiences, and because they lack specific gradations for books for the very youngest readers.

As mentioned in Chapter 4, Fountas and Pinnell (1999, 2001) provide lists of thousands of books, along with reading levels for each. They determined levels with an extensive list of criteria that take into consideration many aspects of books that readability formulas do not, such as complexity of ideas, perspective, and organization of the text. Moreover, leveling "usually provides finer gradations at the primary levels" (Fry, 2002, p. 291). You can look for books on these lists, as well as other lists that you can find online. Related web sites are listed in Chapter 4, but you can find additional ones by typing "leveled books" in your favorite search engine.

Moreover, you might want to determine the readability of your readers' text on your own, and try leveling them. Whether you are trying to select books, or you are evaluating the ones provided for you in the basal series, it's a good idea to know how to determine text difficulty. Graves and Graves (2003) suggest several considerations, including your students' background knowledge and interests, as well as the author's quality of writing and ability to hold interest. Allington (2001) explains how to level books on your own, by first choosing some benchmark books. These are books that have already been established as representing grade levels. You can use the leveled booklists in the work of Fountas and Pinnell (1999, 2001) to help establish benchmark books, or use selections in the basal textbook adopted by your school district. Compare the books that you want to level with the benchmark books by considering vocabulary, pictures, size of print, predictability, and familiarity of topic. It is best to do this leveling process in a group, involving all teachers in the school. This approach allows for continuity across grade levels, and capitalizes on the collective wisdom of the faculty.

You may also recall that there are three levels of reading—independent, instructional, and frustrational—introduced in Chapter 4. Review them and see how they can help you scaffold your students' reading.

Instructional Supports for Reading

Depending upon the amount of scaffolding that you need to provide, the text can be read in one of the following ways:

1. The students read silently and independently, from text of their own choosing. The teacher assesses and monitors their progress or participates in discussions after they read. This method offers the least amount of support (Anderson, 2000; Atwell, 1998; Daniels, 2002; Harste, Short & Burke, 1995; McCracken & McCracken, 1972; Cunningham, Hall & Defee, 1991, 1998).
2. The students read the text silently, in a small group setting called guided reading. Texts are matched to the readers' abilities, and the students and teacher interact with each other while reading (Fountas & Pinnell, 1996; Cunningham, Hall & Defee, 1991, 1998). This offers scaffolding in that the text is chosen and the teacher supports students while they read silently.
3. The teacher uses shared reading, in which the teacher reads the text aloud while students follow along, looking at the print and decoding as much as possible (Harste, Short & Burke, 1988; Holdaway, 1979; Tierney & Readence, 2005). This method scaffolds the reading of students who cannot decode many of the words in the text, but are beginning to read simple or predictable texts.
4. The teacher reads the text orally to the students while they listen, called a read-aloud (Smith, 2000; Trelease, 2001). This provides complete support in that it eliminates the demands of decoding.

Scaffolding your students' reading requires that you match your teaching strategies to your students' needs as well as to the reading materials that they use. If your students read, understand, and enjoy a book that is relatively easy for them, there is little need for your intervention. On the other hand, suppose that your students are immature readers and are not yet capable of decoding most words on their own. You need to help by decoding for them and allowing them to

This teacher offers instructional support to a group of students as they read and interact with each other.

join in where possible. Your support is crucial to their success and confidence in their ability to read. So, deciding on the amount of support you will provide, along with choosing the appropriate level of text, is the essence of scaffolding your students' reading experiences.

Choosing the method that you use to scaffold a reading lesson depends on the difficulty of the book, the objective you want to meet, and the abilities of your students. The triangle of scaffolds shown in Figure 9.2 provides a guideline for making these decisions. This framework of reading scaffolds includes ways to provide support based on the work of several researchers, who have introduced us to frameworks such as Four Blocks (Cunningham, Hall & Defee, 1991, 1998); Guided Reading (Fountas & Pinnell, 1996); Reading Recovery (Clay, 1979); the Reading Workshop (Atwell, 1998); Scaffolded Reading Experiences (Graves & Graves, 2003); Students Achieving Independent Learning, or SAIL (Bergman, 1992); and Success for All (Slavin, Madden, Dolan, Wasik, Ross & Smith, 1994). Starting at the top of the triangular model shown in Figure 9.2, we'll look at each of the ways that you can scaffold reading.

Independent Reading

Children need to be able to read alone. They need time to enjoy, reflect, learn, ponder, and relax with a book. If we are to help our students "author richly literate lives for themselves" (Calkins, 2001, p. 8), it makes sense to give them daily opportunities to read. This simple direction is a fundamental need in the teaching of reading; if we want children to appreciate the value of reading, we must give them time to experience this activity in the classroom (Atwell, 1998; Calkins, 2001; Krashen, 1993).

Many teachers over the years have done just that, implementing programs with names such as DEAR, for Drop Everything and Read, or SSR, for Sustained

Silent Reading. Essentially, the students are asked to read silently and independently in books that they choose, for a few minutes every day (Anderson, 2000). The idea is for the teacher to read silently during this time as well, for the purpose of modeling good reading behavior (McCracken & McCracken, 1972).

However, the National Reading Panel (2000a) has cast some doubt on this practice. This group of reading researchers was asked by the U.S. Congress to conduct an extensive review of educational research, in the interest of finding evidence of best practices that lead to reading achievement. The NRP, in examining the topic of independent reading, reported that many correlational studies do show that children who read a lot also have better reading scores on tests. Yet, the NRP also warns that correlational research does not necessarily indicate a cause or reason, for students' improvement. Thus, readers who do lots of independent silent reading may indeed be better readers, but the amount of time spent reading may not be the cause of their higher achievement. Thus, only experimental research was included in the report of the National Reading Panel.

In its report, the NRP reviewed 14 experimental studies in which researchers tried to determine the effects of "independent silent reading with minimal guidance or feedback" (2000a, p. 12). They concluded that this type of treatment did not produce improvements in reading comprehension, vocabulary, or fluency. While educators disagree with the amount of emphasis that the National Reading Panel placed on experimental research (Allington, 2001), the fact remains that its report has been influential in changing educational policy throughout the country. This conclusion has led others to debate the value of such practices, and even to state, "we can no longer recommend such a procedure until research has revealed the conditions under which encouraging more reading in the classroom might produce gains in reading achievement" (Armbruster & Osborn, 2002, p. 5).

Part of the problem with the programs studied in this report may be the lack of teacher participation in them. "Minimal guidance or feedback" implies a hands-off approach, in which students are to read on their own, with little intervention from the teacher. Perhaps these programs were not structured enough to realize their full potential.

In this book, independent silent reading means a period of time in your school day when your students are reading books that they have selected, while you are intensely involved. Remember that your classroom may be the only place your students get a chance to read by themselves. Waiting for researchers to draw conclusions from experimental research may be depriving these students of the thing they need most—time to read books. Routman says:

> The growth of the Internet, cable television, entertaining computer programs, and increasingly adultlike movies for children all contribute to the acceleration of childhood and the demand for ultra-sophisticated stories. If books are to continue as the lifeline for future generations, we teachers must provide the uninterrupted time and quality resources that foster the motivation to read. . . . As school may well be the last place where books are valued and promoted, we teachers must do everything we can to keep the magic and beauty of books alive for our students. (2000, p. 62)

Children need to time to read real books; they need to develop their confidence as readers who can select their books on their own; and they need to learn how to maintain their own pace with silent reading. Researchers have found that the amount of time reading literature contributes to reading achievement

(Morrow, 1992); and they have found that students, especially struggling readers or children from diverse backgrounds, need access to books and time to read them (Allington, 2001; Krashen, 1993). Moreover, children who read voluntarily have teachers who give their students opportunities to choose their own books and spend class time reading them (Morrow, 1991).

Thus, it is important to set aside time each day for independent reading, when all children in the classroom are expected to read independently. It needs to be part of the daily routine, not an add-on or something for the children to do when they are finished with their "real" work. Allowing children to select their reading material is important, because this is one of the reading abilities that you want to cultivate. Independent reading requires several conditions:

- Your students need access to plenty of books. Allow the students to select their own books, but make sure you have plenty to choose from. In your classroom, you will need books at all readability levels, easily accessible to your students. Increase your classroom library by visiting yard sales, flea markets, and book warehouses. When resources come your way, use them to buy books. Set up programs where families can donate and swap used books. Ask your school librarian to loan you sets of books that can be part of your classroom library for a while. See Figure 9.3 for a list of criteria for building a quality classroom library.
- Students must have books with them at all times. Some teachers keep boxes near each table of students to house books they will need throughout the day.

Creating a Quality Classroom Library

Classroom libraries that are used by students and contribute to the quality of reading instruction have the following qualities:

- Boundaries or partitions set the library apart from the rest of the classroom.
- Comfortable seating is available, including chairs, pillows, and carpet.
- The library area is big enough for about five children to sit.
- Open shelves are available for books to be displayed with the front cover showing.
- There are at least eight books per child. (The minimum number of books should be one per child.)
- Books are organized by categories for ease of access.
- Posters, puppets, flannel boards, taped readings, and student-written reviews are part of the library displays.
- The library area is labeled and has a name. For example, in one teacher's classroom in an inner-city area in which more than 98% of the students were Latino/Hispanic, the library was labeled "Teirra de Fantasía/Fantasy Land."

Figure 9.3 Quality classroom libraries.

Sources: Fractor, Woodruff, Martinez & Teale, 1993; Morrow, 1991.

Others give students special boxes or bags in which to keep books that are "just right" for them to read independently (Routman, 2000).

- Your students need to know how to select books. One simple and popular way is to use their fingers, with the "Five Finger Rule." Students read any page in the book, and count the number of words they do not know, starting with their pinky finger. At each unknown word, they put one finger down. If, at the end of the page, the thumb is still up, the words in the book are not too hard. Allington (2001) suggests that this strategy be modified to the "Three Finger Rule," so that your students are reading the books that are most comfortable for them. You also need to model, by thinking out loud, the process of choosing a book. Students, especially those who are reluctant to read on their own, need to know how to find the right book for the right occasion (Duffy, 2003).
- Your classroom needs to provide an atmosphere conducive to quiet, private reading. Independent readers need quiet spots in the room to relax with a book, and they need an atmosphere that is free of discord. While it is not necessary to make your classroom as quiet as a tomb, it is counterproductive to expect children to read silently when the room is full of distractions and extraneous noise. Thus, establish rules for this period of time so that your students know what is expected of them and so that they respect this time as an important part of the day (Calkins, 2001; Routman, 2000).
- You need to be involved. As your students read, move around and read with them. Ask students to sit with you as you read, or ask students to share their book with you. You can use this time for kidwatching; for modeling; or for private, quiet reading conferences (Cunningham, Hall & Defee, 1991, 1998).
- Students' independent readings need to be recognized as important. You can group students who have read similar books and have them share their responses with others in a workshop-type format (Atwell, 1998). The Reading Workshop method is discussed later in this chapter.

Guided Reading

As you look at the next step down the triangle in the literacy instruction framework shown in Figure 9.2, you'll see guided reading. This method provides many more scaffolds than independent reading. **Guided reading** is a method of teaching reading to small groups of children who read from text that is chosen by the teacher and is at their instructional level. In the framework of guided reading as defined by Fountas and Pinnell, students are placed in homogeneous small groups, so that the teacher can provide scaffolds for students "who use similar reading processes and are able to read similar levels of text with support" (1996, p. 1). On the other hand, Cunningham, Hall, and Defee (1991, 1998) included a component of guided reading in their popular Four Blocks reading program, in which students work in mixed-ability small groups. By working with students in small groups, providing appropriate reading material, and staying close by as they read, you provide a scaffold for your students who are capable of decoding.

In guided reading, your job is to choose a selection that all students in the group will read, and that is on their instructional reading level, which means that they can recognize at least 90% of the words in the book. You also need to select the students who will be in each group, and be flexible enough to regroup whenever necessary. After introducing the selection to the students and setting purposes

Modifying Instruction for

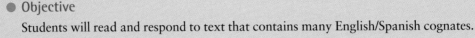

Using Cognates in Guided Reading with Middle School English Language Learners

GRADE LEVEL: 5 AND HIGHER

- **Objective**

  Students will read and respond to text that contains many English/Spanish cognates.

- **Preparation**

  - Write a paragraph or dialogue that includes several English/Spanish cognates, which are words that look similar in both of these languages and have the same meaning. For example, "comenzar" and "commence" are cognates. Write a second narrative, using English words that are synonyms for the cognates, but are not visibly similar in Spanish, such as "begin" for "commence." You can find several web sites for English/Spanish cognates through your favorite search engine.

  - Find short book passages that contain cognates. Type them, along with a corresponding passage that contains an English synonym for the cognate. For example, if the sentence reads, "That night, the ocean was tranquil," rewrite it like this: "That night, the ocean was calm."

  - Divide students into mixed-ability small groups.

- **Materials**

  - Copies of the teacher-created cognate narratives printed on paper, one copy on overhead transparency, or MS PowerPoint presentation

  - Highlighting markers

- **Introduction: Before Guided Reading**

  1. To the whole class, explain the term "cognate," which is a word that looks like and means the same thing in two languages. Show students a list of these in English and Spanish, such as "elect-elegir," "signify-significar," and "occupied-ocupado." Discuss the meanings of these words.

- **During Guided Reading**

  2. Put students in small groups or with partners. Distribute copies of the sample narrative provided at the end of this section, and highlighters. Explain that this is a paragraph about Mara, who is having a party. Ask students to read the narrative silently, highlight any words that look similar to Spanish words, and use context to think about what they mean.

- **After Guided Reading**

  3. After reading, write the cognates on the board and talk about their meanings. Show pictures and objects or use body movements to explain as needed.

  4. Show the text on the screen and reread, while students follow along. Point to the words as you read, so students can see and hear the words.

Modifications for ELL are printed in color.

5. Distribute the second narrative, with synonyms for the cognates. Have students read it silently.
6. After reading, compare the two texts. Point out the non-cognates in the second text, and show how they have similar meanings to cognates. For example, point out the word "begin," which was used instead of "commence." Write these words on the board. You can also make word cards to add to the word wall, or ask students to write words in their reading logs or personal dictionaries.

● After Reading
7. Ask students to retell the story or write a summary of the narrative.
8. In another lesson, show students a book passage that contains cognates. Repeat the procedure with this passage.

Getting Ready for the Party (with English cognates)

Mara opened the door and pulled her best friend, Tiana, into the apartment.

"Come on in! My party will commence at 6:00 tonight," said Mara. "But we will need the entire morning to get ready."

"I'll help you," said Tiana, who was an amicable girl. "Let's decorate the patio first!"

The girls decorated with giant balloons, flowers, and candles. The effect was very elegant. They even put a palm tree on the patio.

"Fabulous!" Mara said later. "Now I'm ready for the party. I hope everyone will dance!"

Getting Ready for the Party (with English synonyms for cognates)

Mara opened the door and pulled her best friend, Tiana, into the apartment.

"Come on in! My party will begin at 6:00 tonight," said Mara. "But we will need the whole morning to get ready."

"I'll help you," said Tiana, who was a friendly girl. "Let's decorate the patio first!"

The girls decorated with very big balloons, flowers, and candles. The way it looked was very pretty. They even put a palm tree on the patio.

"Great!" Mara said later. "Now I'm ready for the party. I hope everyone will dance!"

The cognates and synonyms in this passage are:

English Cognate	Spanish Cognate	English Synonym Replacing Cognate in Second Story
apartment	el apartamento	(no replacement needed)
commence	comenzar	begin
entire	entero	whole
amicable	amigable	friendly
decorate	decorar	(no replacement needed)
patio	el patio	(no replacement needed)
giant	gigante	very big
effect	el efecto	way it looked
elegant	elegante	pretty
palm	la palma	palm tree
fabulous	fabuloso	great
dance	danzar	(no replacement needed)

for reading, invite the students to read silently and independently. Fountas and Pinnell explain, "The reading is usually soft or silent, but all members of the group are operating independently as readers at the same time. This is not 'round robin' reading, in which children take turns reading aloud. In guided reading each child has the opportunity to solve problems while reading extended text and attending to meaning" (1996, pp. 8–9).

While students read, you may need to assist them, or listen in as they read. You can watch what the students are doing as they read, and make notes. Depending on the length of the selection, you can either finish reading it together with the group or send the students back to their desks to finish. After reading, talk with students about what they've read, or assign a response activity. Sometimes you might want to have them reread the book to practice fluency strategies. Guided reading instruction should be short; Routman (2000) describes reading group instruction that lasts no more than 12 minutes. Typically, you might have three groups to meet on a daily basis. The procedure for guided reading is shown in Figure 9.4.

Shared Reading

You can offer even more scaffolding with shared reading. **Shared reading** is a method of supporting students' reading by decoding the words for them while they look at the print and read along (Harste, Short & Burke, 1988; Holdaway, 1979; Tierney & Readence, 2005). Holdaway introduced this strategy more than 25 years ago, modeling it after the kinds of things that parents do and say while reading aloud to their children at home. Teachers still find it a useful way to support children who are just beginning to decode.

The **big book,** which is an enlarged version of a piece of children's literature, is an important part of this strategy when teaching very young children. It enables everyone to see the words as the teacher reads the book aloud and the children follow along. Books with predictable text or lots of rhyming words are most helpful, because the teacher can invite the students to read these portions of the text aloud. Sometimes, the teacher specifies the words that she wants them to read aloud; other times, she lets them chime in whenever they can. Most of the time, the predictable refrains are the ones that the children can quickly remember and read. Eventually, after several rereadings of the text, the students know the entire text and can read it, either with the teacher's help or without.

Once the text is read, the teacher uses it to teach new words, language skills, and reading strategies. If there are little book versions of the text, students can read the story independently after the shared reading has provided enough support for doing so. The procedure for shared reading is summarized in Figure 9.5.

When should you use shared reading? When you want to offer lots of scaffolding along with expectations for independence, shared reading is appropriate. The shared reading strategy is designed to give support to beginning or immature readers. Decoding demands are minimal, because you are reading aloud most of the text, and because the book used is predictable or has repetitive text. Students will probably begin to chime in quite easily on the predictable parts of the text, and continuing to offer repeated readings will eventually lead to recognition of words and help young readers to gain confidence. Shared reading allows inexperienced readers to begin to feel as if they are "really reading."

Guided Reading

1. Form groups of 3 to 6 children. If you are working with first graders or struggling readers, Fountas and Pinnell (1996) recommend grouping them homogeneously, with students of like abilities working together. Older and more experienced readers can work in mixed-ability groups. Cunningham, Hall, and Defee (1991, 1998) recommend using guided reading with mixed-ability groups; however, they do say that first grade readers may need to be more homogeneously grouped.

2. Select a book or other text that is at an appropriate instructional level for all students in the group. They should be able to recognize at least 90% of the words in the text.

3. Prepare the students to read by building background knowledge related to the theme of the book. Look at selected pictures or concrete objects and invite predictions. Keep a list of predictions for checking later. Direct students to a purpose for reading, such as, "Read to find out why. . . ." or "Read to see whether your predictions come true." Strategies you can use before reading are described in Chapter 11.

4. Direct students to read the text silently. If you are working with very young readers who are just beginning to decode, they might need to hear themselves as they read, so "silent reading" may be "soft reading" or "whisper reading." Decide what you will do as students read. Depending on the text, there are several options, listed as follows. Chapter 12 will give you additional ideas for strategies to use while students are reading.

   a. *Stop points*—Choose one or two stop points in the selection. Make sure these stop points are at important episodes in the story or, if it is nonfiction, after an important idea. As the students read silently, ask them to give you an agreed-upon "silent signal" for letting you know when they have reached the stop point. When everyone reaches this cut-off point, discuss what was read so far in relation to the predictions made.

   b. *Kidwatching*—As the students read, make note of their behaviors. Watch carefully for the ways that they monitor themselves, or the words that give them difficulty. Look for

behavior that indicates that they do not understand, or that they are not really paying attention to the page. Look for potential problems such as these:
   - Text is too difficult.
   - Pictures or graphics are too distracting.
   - Students are not attempting to figure out unknown words.
   - Students are reading too quickly.
   - Students are not really reading; they glide their fingers along the print without decoding the words.
   - Students are not interested in the text.

   c. *Self-monitoring*—Ask students to keep a spiral-bound notebook handy, to use as a reading journal. They should date each page of the journal and write the title of the book before reading. As they read, they should copy down words that give them trouble. They should mark page numbers, too. They should cross out words that they want to figure out later on. Another way to do this is to use sticky notes to mark the words. Be sure that students know that if they are not marking many difficult words, they can serve as "expert word readers" to help out other students.

   d. *Responses*—When you set a purpose for reading, ask a question that students need to answer after they read. They can write the answer in a sentence or phrase in their reading journals. Other response opportunities are described in Chapter 13.

   e. *Questions*—Check for meaning with one or two questions that require students to think about the author's implications.

   f. *Discussion*—Talk about the story and how it relates to their own experiences.

5. At the end of the small-group time, give an assignment for students to read at their seats. Depending on the group and the length of the text, you can ask students to finish reading the selection, or ask them to choose another book to read.

6. You might want students to reread the story orally; choose an appropriate strategy from Chapter 14. Choose oral reading activities carefully; not all selections need to be read orally.

Figure 9.4 Guided reading procedures for small groups.

Shared Reading with Big Books

1. Select a big book that is appropriate for the theme or topic that you wish to emphasize. It should be predictable, or the vocabulary should be simple enough to present few decoding problems for your group.

2. Prepare the students to read by building background knowledge related to the theme of the book. Encourage predictions and write them down for all to see. Explain how the reading will be done together, by pointing out predictable words or phrases that the children will read along with you.

3. Read the book aloud, using your finger or a pointer to point to the words. The first time you read the book, read it aloud, in its entirety, by yourself. During subsequent readings, pause when you come to the words or phrases that you want the children to read aloud. Some teachers use a hand movement or other signal that invites the children to chime in.

4. Once the book has been read, use the text to teach skills and strategies. Suggestions are:
   - On each page, cover up an important word with a sticky note. When rereading, ask students to guess the covered word. Write the students' predictions on the sticky note. Then reveal the first letter and ask them to adjust the prediction.
   - Make word cards for each of the words in a predictable sentence. Give each student a set of the cards and ask students to construct the sentence as it was written in the book.
   - Talk about punctuation on the page. Read the story as if there were no punctuation marks and ask students to tell what is wrong.
   - As you read aloud, intentionally make errors. For example, say "pow" instead of "cow." Ask students to catch your errors and point to the letters that give them the clues.

5. Make the little book versions of the text available for independent reading.

6. Make taped readings of the book and put the tape in the library or listening center.

Figure 9.5 The shared reading procedure.

Shared reading should be attempted only if everyone can see the print. The purpose of the big book is to allow all the students to see the words and hear the correspondence between the spoken word and its printed equivalent. It is helpful to have young children sit near you on the floor, not at their desks. This setup enables everyone to see the print of the big book, which is so important. Moreover, it is important to make sure your students see the words as they are spoken; use your hand or pointer to point to the words.

If you are teaching very young children, you will need to add big books to your classroom library. A word of caution is necessary. Not all big books are of high quality, nor are they all appropriate for shared reading! Remember that the purpose of shared reading is for everyone to be able to see the text and begin to feel successful at reading the text. Your big books must have highly visible words and should also consist of text that is predictable or rhyming. Figure 9.6 shows a list of criteria for purchasing big books. Some favorite big books for shared reading include:

The Three Billy Goats Gruff (Appleby, 1984)
The Very Hungry Caterpillar (Carle, 1981)
The Surprise Garden (Hall, 2000)
"Not Now!" Said the Cow (Oppenheim, 1994)
Mouse Mess (Riley, 1999)
Horse and Toad: A Folktale from Haiti (Wolkstein, 1993)

Once you have read and reread the text several times, and its content and words are quite familiar to your students, you can use it to present mini-lessons. You can teach new words by making word cards, and then asking your students to put words together into sentences, categorize the words, and put words on the word wall. You can teach language skills, such as punctuation marks and sentence order. You can teach reading strategies by using mental models to show how you would find main ideas, identify story elements, or make inferences. Shared reading gives you the opportunity to teach the same kinds of lessons to non-decoders that you would to accomplished decoders.

If you have older readers who struggle with the demands of decoding, and you want all of your students to experience the same book, you can use shared reading to scaffold their needs (Routman, 2000). Give everyone a copy of the book, and read aloud as they read silently with you, pausing occasionally and asking them to supply a word or phrase you know they can handle.

Criteria for Selecting Big Books That You Can Use in Shared Reading

1. Print in the book should be clear and large enough to be visible to the entire group when they are sitting around you on the floor. Ideally, the print should be large enough to place a small sticky note or window marker over a word.
2. The pictures and text should be true to the original version of the book.
3. Text should be predictable or rhyming, so that the advantages of shared reading can be realized. Children should be able to begin "reading" the book quickly.
4. Print and pictures should match; the action taking place according to the print should be the same as the action depicted by the illustrations.
5. Busy-ness should be minimal. Print and illustrations should be clear, free of extraneous details, and designed so that position of text on the page is in a predictable place at each turn of the page.
6. The amount of printed text on each page should be no more than a sentence or two.
7. Little book versions are usually offered by publishers; these should be made available after reading the big book.

Figure 9.6 Criteria for selecting high-quality big books.

Shared reading can also be done with a single child and the teacher or other adult. This type of reading looks much like the type of interaction that takes place when a parent reads aloud to a child before bed at night. Read aloud, pointing to print as you read, while the child follows along. Invite the child to join in, reading orally, in as many places as possible in the text. A parent volunteer or a student helper from an older grade can help out in this capacity, too.

Reading Aloud to Students

Almost all of the most pleasurable classroom experiences that I have had involve reading aloud to my students. Choosing a good book—one that is too difficult for most of them to tackle on their own—and sharing it in the way that books are meant to be enjoyed is the greatest gift you can give your students. One of the most important things you can do in your classroom is to read aloud to your students daily (Adams, 1990; Anderson, Hiebert, Scott & Wilkinson, 1985), and talk to them about what you've read (Beck & McKeown, 2001). By reading aloud to them and interacting with them about the book, you teach them so many important things, including these:

1. When you are engaged in reading, the words come alive. You give words expression and ignite their power to create mental images and thoughts.
2. The language of books is different from the language that we speak. The vocabulary is more elaborate, the structure of sentences is more sophisticated. Descriptions are more detailed and dialogue is more exact.
3. Authors write for the purpose of conveying meaning.

When your students are involved in the tasks of decoding, especially if they are inexperienced or struggling readers, or if they are also learning to speak English while they are learning to read, they cannot fully appreciate these facets of books. Thus, reading to all of your students is important, so that they are exposed to these important understandings and use of language (Bus, 2002).

What kind of reader are you? Being a teacher of reading means that you will need to read—a lot. You will need to be familiar with children's books; if you are not already, begin adding them to your list of readings. Vow to read at least one or two picture books or chapters, silently, daily. If reading aloud to others is bothersome to you, begin practicing now. Read aloud to yourself, and then read aloud to someone close to you—preferably a child. Then practice reading aloud to groups. You can also listen to audiotapes of books, so that you hear a model of expressive reading.

A rule of thumb to remember is this: Always read silently first what you have chosen to read aloud. This step allows you to practice the pronunciation of unusual proper nouns; additionally, it allows you to discover the content of the book. Some books are best suited for silent, private reading, due to the sensitivity of their topic. Moreover, you may not be comfortable reading some books aloud. You'll need to decide for yourself before you have an audience.

A good resource for reading aloud is Trelease's *The Read Aloud Handbook* (2001). It offers suggestions for improving your own oral reading ability, boosting your confidence, and choosing good books. Additionally, several guidelines for reading aloud are listed in Figure 9.7.

1. Select books that are of a difficulty above the reading level of your audience. At the same time, remember that children must be developmentally ready to listen to the content in the book. Do not choose a book that has a theme that is too mature for the audience.

2. Select books that will be of interest to the students. If necessary, provide background information. This step is especially necessary for biographies and historical fiction.

3. Communicate the mood of the book. Use facial expressions, adjust your timing, change your voice pitch, and move your body the way the book feels. Be dramatic.

4. If you are reading a longer book, select the parts of the book that you will be reading in one sitting. Make sure you select a place in the story that fosters excitement and makes the students want to hear more the next time you read. (Most picture books can be read in one sitting.)

5. When reading picture books, hold the book to your side with one hand. Make sure everyone can see the pictures. Do not read the book upside-down in your lap. If you can, move your finger or hand along the print. (Don't do this if it causes you to obstruct the view of the pictures.)

6. Prepare for all of your read-alouds. Never read a book to children that you have not already read yourself. This is necessary for your own practice, but also because you may find that the book is inappropriate for your audience. While you are reading to them, it is too late to find out.

7. Allow time for discussion about the book, but don't force questions upon the students. Often they need time to reflect upon what they have experienced with the book. Do not follow every read-aloud with a lot of comprehension questions. Instead, if they are responsive, begin a discussion about the motives of the character, similar experiences the students may have had, or the interesting setting that was introduced. Remember that discussions are not always necessary to appreciate a book.

8. Always make the book available to the students to read on their own.

Figure 9.7 Read-aloud guidelines.

Sources: Trelease, 2001; Smith, 2000.

When should you read aloud to your students? Daily, of course; however, there are specific situations for when reading aloud enhances reading instruction. Hoffman, Roser, and Battle (1993) contend that merely reading aloud for a few minutes a day is not enough; teachers need to read at least 20 minutes per day; interact with students in lively, thought-provoking discussions; and offer a variety of experiences connected to the reading.

You might want to select a book that introduces your students to an author, a theme, an idea, or a particular writing style. If they do not recognize 90% of its vocabulary, eliminate the demands of decoding from them and read it to them. Reading aloud to them alleviates the need to match their decoding ability with the difficulty level of the book. Therefore, you can select books that are above their reading level, so that you are immersing them in new vocabulary and language structure within a meaningful context (Horowitz & Freeman, 1995). All students benefit from read-alouds. Strickland explains the importance of reading aloud to African American, at-risk children, to "help strengthen their vocabulary and concept development and broaden their background knowledge" (2002a, p. 329).

Sometimes, it is necessary to scaffold your students' understanding by completely removing the demands of decoding, even though you hadn't planned it that way. For example, on occasion, I have watched my undergraduate students prepare lessons in which they chose the book, wrote a plan for guided reading, and carefully facilitated the understanding of their students, only to have the lesson teeter on the brink of disaster because they overestimated the reading ability of the children. It happens, even to experienced teachers! In situations like this, when teachers quickly decide to read the selection to the students rather than insist on independent decoding, many of the objectives of the lesson can be met. Graves and Graves (2003) emphasize the importance of reflective teaching, in which you make decisions like this on the spot, so that the needs of your students are met.

Reading aloud reinforces the social aspects of literacy. If you read a book to your students, everyone in the room now has a common bond with the book, its author, and its ideas. This experience can be very useful for writing language experience materials and holding discussions. There are times when a book is simply too good to pass up and you have only one copy. Reading aloud to your students allows you to share it with them quickly. Even if you do not read the entire book to them, you can introduce the book with a few passages that are laden with expression, whetting their appetite for reading the book on their own. Routman (2000) recommends doing this for older readers, especially reluctant readers, who might need to be convinced of the value of spending their time reading. An excellent source for read-aloud selections for your older students is Trelease's *Read All about It! Great Read-Aloud Stories, Poems, and Newspaper Pieces for Preteens and Teens* (1993).

Ways to Scaffold Writing

As an undergraduate in college, I took an English course in creative writing, and during a conference with my professor, he asked me to tell him how many books I read in a year. I stumbled a bit at the answer, but I thought maybe 25 or 30 books would be about right. My professor, who was also a published author, then informed me that he read more than 500 books a year. I have always loved to read, but was, and still am, amazed at his tenacity with the printed word. His point? If you want to be a writer, you need to be a reader.

Likewise, teachers of reading are also teachers of writing. Tracey and Morrow, in a discussion of their observations of two exemplary classrooms, state: "The most striking feature of these teachers' instruction was the degree to which they integrated their language arts literacy program. . . . An area in which this integration was very apparent was in linking reading and writing. . . . Teachers' writing assignments were based on what the students had read and were designed to create thoughtful, high-level processing of texts. Thus much reading comprehension was fostered through the relating of reading and writing assignments" (2002, p. 228).

Writers and readers have a common bond—the printed page. Writers want to be heard; that is the purpose of their writing. Readers seek information or enjoyment; that is the purpose of their reading. Thus, neither process is solitary. Literacy is a social endeavor, and teachers who recognize this teach reading and writing processes simultaneously (Atwell, 1998; Graves, 2003).

Because writing skills are so crucial in today's world, it needs to be a vital part of your literacy instruction and curriculum. When children view themselves as writers, they have greater appreciation for the written word. They begin to truly transact with the text, because they begin to think like authors as they read, and to think like readers as they write (Graves, 2003; Lancia, 1997).

Just as you scaffold your students' reading, you can support their writing efforts with scaffolds as well. This is quite different from merely making writing assignments and grading them. Instead, you can do these things:

1. Give students time to write independently, for authentic purposes and audiences (Calkins, 1994). While you provide the environment for ease of writing, you offer the least amount of instructional support in this method.
2. Expose students to excellent literature so they see what good writing looks like. Invite students to use writers' patterns, styles, and devices in their own writings (Lancia, 1997). This technique provides a scaffold, because students are not entirely independent as they compose.
3. Support emerging writers' efforts by taking dictations in the language experience approach (Allen & Allen, 1967) or "sharing the pen" in interactive writing (Button, Johnson & Furgerson, 1996; Wiley, 1999). These methods offer much scaffolding, because you transcribe their words into print and guide them to the realization that print consists of thoughts and spoken words written down.
4. Show students how writing is done by demonstrating it and thinking aloud as you write, called "writing aloud" (Routman, 2000). This offers the most amount of scaffolding, as you model the writing yourself.

Looking back at Figure 9.2 on page 285, you can see that these types of teaching methods support students as they write, and offer increasing amounts of scaffolding, with the most support being offered with writing aloud, and the least offered with students' independent writing. Let's start at the top again, and examine each method of scaffolding writing separately.

Independent Writing

At the top of the scaffold triangle is independent writing. Using the **writing process approach,** students write formally and informally, for authentic purposes and real audiences. Your support consists of strategies and activities that will enable your students to write on their own, without sharing the pen or using frames. You will need to hold individual conferences, during which the student shares his writing with you, and you give feedback, suggestions for revisions and editing, and materials for publishing.

When writing for the purpose of sharing with others, there are five stages that writers usually use: (1) rehearsal, (2) drafting, (3) revising, (4) editing, and (5) publishing (Calkins, 1994; Graves, 2003). It is important to note the recursive nature of these stages. They are listed here in sequential order because it makes sense to explain them in that manner. However, most writers do not write in a linear fashion, starting with an idea and moving it toward publication in a step-by-step manner. Most writers are far messier than that! Drafting, revising, and editing can occur simultaneously as the author uses print on the page to think about ideas, try them out in a variety of ways, and rethink them again.

On the next few pages are some ways to facilitate the writing process. The strategies and activities are suggestions for helping your students stick with a piece of writing from beginning to end, and for providing the type of environment needed to cultivate writers. You will see additional strategies in Chapter 13, including how to use written literature responses in the classroom.

Rehearsal

In the **rehearsal** phase, students prepare to write and think of topics for their writing. It is often the most difficult stage of writing, because many times children do not know what to write about. Choosing topics is an argumentative issue; many researchers in writing advocate allowing children to choose their own topics (Calkins, 1994; Clark, 1987; Graves, 1994; Spandel, 2001), while teachers know how difficult and time-consuming this can be. Cramer (2001) advocates an approach in which teachers make some topic suggestions, while giving students the option to choose their own topics if they prefer to do so. Another approach is to give students a broad topic, such as the Revolutionary War. Within such a topic, students can choose to write about causes of the war, influential people during the war, life in colonial times, and so on.

Give your students folders in which they can keep lists of possible topics, composition drafts, spelling lists, and other useful documents needed as they write. The folders should be easily accessible to the students and used on a daily basis. Students will need a huge bank of ideas for writing. You can ask them to brainstorm for just a few minutes daily, giving them ideas such as: "Write your favorite names to use as characters," "Write some mood words," "Write some favorite quotes from books," or "Observe things in nature and describe them." One good way to present the ideas is to have one per day displayed. As students enter the classroom, or at the start of their writing session time, they can jot down the idea in their folders. Once students have written these, they can keep them and use them in stories and expository pieces.

A good writer keenly observes the world around him. But young writers lack the experiences and observations that adult writers have. Help sharpen your students' powers of observation by giving them activities that require them to pay attention to detail. Some suggestions, which can be used in mini-lessons, include the following:

- Introduce lots of nonfiction books to students as springboards for ideas. Many students will never become fiction writers, but they will use nonfiction writing throughout their lives. Provide plenty of good nonfiction models for them to know (Spandel, 2001).

- Give each student a piece of fruit or vegetable, such as a potato, an orange, or a carrot. Ask them to look at it carefully, smell it, touch it, and get to know it well. Then, ask them to write about their fruit or vegetable, describing it in detail. After they finish writing, collect the pieces of produce, making sure to mix them up well. Spread them on a table, and ask students to find their own again (Solley, 2000).

- Ask students to watch a hamster or turtle for several minutes, and then write down what they see. Pay attention to details that are not obvious (Spandel, 2001).

- Divide the class into small groups. Ask each group to create a character. Describe the character in a paragraph, making sure to include all the details that make this character "visible." Give the paragraph to another group and have them draw a picture of the character (Solley, 2000). The same idea can be used for settings.

- Ask students to write "how-to" instructions on something they know and love. This gives them a starting place and adds confidence. They can begin with a simple list, then add to this to create a draft. Jean Roach, a middle school teacher in Pennsylvania encountered a seventh grader who refused to write (J. Roach, personal communication, 2005). The boy crossed his hands on his chest and steadfastly refused to pick up a pencil, saying, "I can't write. I don't have anything to write about." Roach sat next to him and suggested that they put that pencil away for a while. She asked, "What do you know how to do real well?" He insisted he knew nothing that was worth writing about. Roach continued to chat with him, forgetting about the impending need to put something on paper. She asked him if there was something he thought he might be able to do that she couldn't do. Suddenly, he brightened and said, "I know how to change a tire. I learned how last week." Roach told him that was a skill she had never learned, and asked him to write its procedure for her so that she would be able to follow his directions. During the next several days he produced a manual of step-by-step directions on changing a tire!

Drafting

Getting the words on paper—or **drafting**—can be the hardest part of writing. Facing a blank page, as any writer knows, is a daunting, humbling task. Your students need to know that this is hard for everyone. Sugarcoating it and telling them otherwise is simply not fair. Writing is hard work, and students deserve to know it.

Additionally, children often have difficulty with the idea that a draft is a temporary thing. Many times, young writers think that once they put words on paper, they are finished. They are unwilling to revisit their work and change it. Often, they write in a strict linear fashion, starting at the beginning and plodding through to the end. But mature writers know that drafting requires writing bits and pieces here and there in the manuscript, and revisiting sections of the work over and over again. Many children do not have the patience or the endurance to do this without help.

You can provide them with drafting support. First, you might need to make drafting visible for them by thinking out aloud. Use the overhead projector or computer screen to show them, using a mental model, the thought processes that you use as you put words to paper. It is important that your students see your attempts at authorship, because it will show your students that you care about their efforts, and also because it will establish your credibility as a writer and a teacher of writing.

Second, give them some drafting strategies that might help them get their words on paper. Not all strategies will work for everyone, because all writers are different. Thus, you'll want to expose your students to as many strategies as possible. Some ideas are listed here:

- Encourage your students to write several possibilities for the beginning of their draft. Using their topic idea, students write three or four possible sentences for the opening of their paper. This helps to get them over the "blank page" hurdle, because now they have several possibilities from which to begin (Spandel, 2001).

- Encourage your students to experiment with different types of leads, such as quotes from literature, flashbacks, questions, and biographical accounts. Model this experimentation by showing them on the overhead projector how you think of several ways to begin a draft that you are writing.

- Tell students to write words, phrases, or complete sentences down the left side of the page. Using a word processor makes this easy, but it can be done manually. Once the student has listed everything possible, he or she should go back to the top of the list and begin putting ideas together. Sometimes, phrases become whole sentences, and sentences can join together to become paragraphs. Anything can be arranged as needed.

- Cramer suggests that writers can "start in the middle and work inside-out" (2001, p. 90). This strategy allows the writer to start with what he or she knows best. This type of drafting works best if your students are composing at the keyboard, rather than writing longhand on paper. However, if your students don't have access to the computer, you can encourage inside-out writing by giving students small index cards or strips of paper on which to write their sentences. These can be manipulated and rearranged in any order, then taped to a larger piece of paper.

Revising

While researchers define the term **revision** in many ways, I like the one offered by Cramer, who says, "Any change in a written text constitutes revision, whether it be large or small, form or substance, minor or major. Hence, editing and proofreading are revision of a specific sort, occurring and reoccurring at unpredictable times during writing, according to the habits of a given writer" (2001, p. 104).

Thus, when writers make changes in their drafts, they are revising. It is sometimes difficult for students to understand this phase without putting the revision process in a step-by-step list of procedures. Some teachers teach their students to follow the stages of writing in a strict sequential manner, such as drafting first, then revising for content, then editing for vocabulary choices, and finally proofreading. While this approach puts the writing process into what appears to be a manageable framework, it is not the way most writers write. Many writers revise and edit simultaneously. Others continually proofread, taking care of mistakes as they go along, so they can avoid a big clean-up when they finish. Revision, editing, and proofreading can happen in any order, in a circular fashion. Cramer (2001) offers further definition with an outline of the "Three Faces of Revision":

- **Revising**—The goal of revising is to improve content. The writer asks, "What do I have to say?"
- **Editing**—The goal of editing is to refine language. The writer asks, "What is the best way for me to say it?"
- **Proofreading**—The goal of proofreading is to make final corrections. The writer asks, "What needs to be corrected?"

Another problem with revising is that teachers are often unrealistic about expectations for revising. Routman (2000) describes revising as having two extremes. Sometimes, teachers expect students to revise everything they write, which is not the way of real writers. She suggests that students and teachers need to talk more about purposes for writing. Authentic purposes lead to a concern for the finished product. Many times, students just don't care whether their paper hangs on the bulletin board. Thus, there is no incentive to put effort into the real work of revising.

The other problem with revising is that teachers sometimes accept poor work. It is important to encourage young writers, but at the same time, make sure to keep your expectations appropriately high. Students need to know that, while writing is hard work, you will not accept half-hearted attempts at shoddy work. Drafts need to be "friendly," in that they must be legible. Perfect handwriting and spelling are not necessary, but it is necessary to be able to read and understand your students' drafts. Avoid calling a draft the "sloppy copy," which is a commonly used term in classrooms, because such a title may mislead them. Wherever developmentally appropriate, insist on conventional spelling in drafts that are ready to be read by others, using a "No Excuses" list of words (Routman, 2000, p. 185b). This is a list of words that you can distribute early in the school year, and it contains all the words that your students should know how to spell at this point in their academic career. All of those words should be spelled correctly, even on rough drafts. Many teachers apply this rule to the word wall; any word on the wall should be spelled conventionally. These expectations will help you avoid the problem of trying to decipher what your students' drafts say; additionally, it will help students as they help each other with revising. Thus, while your first priority should always be the content of the children's written work, it is important that students know that you and their peers need to be able to read their papers. Meet with your students individually on a regular basis and talk about their drafts. Use this time to teach mini-lessons and discuss problems with their work.

Publishing

When students publish their work, they accomplish the goal to which authors aspire, which is to share their words with other people. Not all pieces of writing should be published. There are many reasons to write that do not require publishing, such as journal writing, retelling, summarizing, and writing notes for learning. However, when your students write for genuine audiences for real reasons, they have reason to publish their work. This is much more purposeful than writing for the teacher alone.

Knowing the audience affects the quality of their work. Young authors, especially emerging writers, often have difficulty writing for an audience. Their concern for getting words down on paper precludes any thought of the people who may be reading their words. Often, they write only for themselves, forgetting that others will need to understand their message. An authentic audience helps your students to focus their writing. Ask them to mentally picture the people who will read their paper and imagine talking to them. This practice often helps them develop a sense of audience as they write.

Some of the types of pieces that your students can publish include a big book created on their own or a bilingual book worked on with a classmate. These writings give meaning to the writing that your students do, because they are designed to be read by other people, for authentic reasons. Appendix B includes a list of student publishing projects.

Shared Writing

The next level of scaffolded writing is shared writing. There are various forms of shared writing, each of which give the students more control over writing. Shared writing includes lessons in which the teacher offers support, shares the pen, models writing, and provides patterns and frames from which to write. Read on to find out about these methods.

Interactive Writing

Chapter 6 introduced interactive writing. It is an excellent way to support students as they move from invented to conventional spellings. To use the strategy, you and your students negotiate a message to write. Give volunteers the pen to write one word at a time, stretching out their sounds and spelling them conventionally. When there are words that are too difficult for the students, you can write them for the students, showing them how you figure out the spelling of these words. Button, Johnson, and Furgerson describe this approach, and explain, "Through questioning and direct instruction, the teacher focuses the children's attention on the conventions of print such as spaces between words, left-to-right and top-to-bottom directionality, capital letters, and punctuation" (1996, p. 447).

Robin Teets, who teaches in Virginia, uses interactive writing with students who are learning to speak English. She gives the students as much chance as possible to use the pen to write morning messages, simple responses to stories from children's literature, or facts learned from information books. Because many words need to be stretched out so the child who has the pen could figure out which letters

This teacher scaffolds her students' reading by meeting with a small group of readers who read the same book together.

to write, one sentence written interactively could take several minutes. This produced problems with getting the rest of the children in the group to pay attention, which she solved with whiteboards and socks. Each student got a whiteboard and a sock to put on the non-writing hand. As the interactive message was being composed, all the students in the group copied the message on the whiteboard, using the sock to erase mistakes as needed.

Literary Borrowing

Lancia describes an approach that provides a model for writing using quality children's literature. He writes, "As any novice learns by imitating a role model, children learn about writing by interacting with professional writers. . . . Additionally, children rely upon their past experiences with literature as springboards for ideas" (1997, p. 471). As a second grade teacher, Lancia collected his students' writings during the school year and categorized them according to the ways in which they borrowed ideas from children's literature. He found that his students borrowed:

- Entire plots for retellings
- Characters for use in new situations or continuations of the original story
- Stylistic devices such as descriptive language, patterns, and humor
- Genre elements in which several books of the same type were used as models
- Information from nonfiction

Lancia's students seemed to find literature a natural starting point for writing their own pieces, and many times did not realize that they had borrowed ideas from another author. Lancia hypothesized that they had internalized their reading so deeply that writing like their favorite author was unavoidable. He suggests that literary borrowing should be encouraged, because of the model it provides for good writing.

Borrowing can begin as early as kindergarten, when the teacher reads aloud predictable books, and then asks students to write a sentence that fits the same pattern. For example, *I Went Walking* by Sue Williams (1989) can be used, like this:

The teacher writes: I went walking. What did I see?

The student writes: I saw a rooster looking at me.

Each child in the class can write a page to be added to a class book.

Later, as children grow more sophisticated in their writing and become more familiar with authors' styles, characters, and plots, they begin to borrow on their own. Lancia does not consider this to be plagiarism, as it suggests a mentor-type relationship between the author of a book and the child reader/writer. In fact, it is a way to help students develop their own writing styles as they become more confident writers.

Frames and Reminders Checklists

Another way to scaffold writing is to provide students with frames and reminders checklists. This technique scaffolds their writing so that they see the way words need to be structured in a report, retelling, summary, or other efferent type of writing. You'll find several frames in *Toolkit for Teachers of Literacy* (Nettles, 2006) and one sample in Appendix B. To use frames, model the writing first by writing aloud. Then show students a frame that matches the writing you did and ask students to follow it when they write the first report. You may find that students need this scaffold for another report or two. Some teachers prefer for the students to use the frame, and then recopy or type the report on plain paper so that the frame no longer is visible. When they are ready to compose a report without a frame, give them a list of reminders that will help them remember all of the parts of the paper to include. See an example in Figure 9.8 of a Writer's Reminders Checklist created from a report frame. Notice that it also reminds the writer to indent. You can scaffold your writers as much or as little as you want, using the reminders checklist.

Language Experience Approach

The language experience approach (Stauffer, 1975; Allen & Allen, 1967), described in Chapters 6 and 8, is accomplished by providing an experience for your students, and then asking them to talk about it. They dictate a narrative, which you record for them. This activity gives them the chance to compose without the demands of physically writing the words on the page.

Over the years, there has been some debate over whether teachers should change students' dictations if the words and syntax do not reflect Standard English. If a student says, "I ain't seen nobody in the room," should the teacher write that on a chart? If dictation is done privately, and its purpose is for the student to see the connection between spoken and written words, you will need to record what he has said. To do otherwise means that he will not be able to read back what he has written.

However, if the dictation is being done in a group, and the purpose is to write a narrative about a group experience, you can negotiate the written words with the students. Using the example, you can say, "I'll write, 'I haven't seen anyone in the room.' How's that?" This change does not compromise the meaning of your students' words; it merely provides a model for writing in Standard English. The resulting narratives are wonderful sources of reading material for students who are learning English as a second language (Temple, Ogle, Crawford & Freppon, 2005).

The language experience approach is an excellent way to use technology as model writing. Nancy Steider, who teaches first grade in Pennsylvania, asks her students to gather around her as she sits at the computer. While they dictate and negotiate sentences, she types. When revisions are suggested or words need to be changed, she verbalizes how she does that, by saying things like, "Ok, let's change the word 'said,' to 'asked.' I'll just use the backspace key to go back over those letters and change them. Watch what I do." Using the word processor allows you to quickly make copies for everyone in the group, and to share their writing via e-mail and web sites.

Writing Aloud

The most support you can offer to your writers is to model it for them. **Writing aloud** is a strategy in which you show the students how you write (Routman, 2000; Calkins, 2001). Recall the strategy of mental modeling from Chapter 2, which is a powerful

Changing Scaffolds: Moving from a Frame to a Checklist

The following frame can be used with a book that compares one topic or concept to another. After students use it to write a report, let them be more independent by using a Writer's Reminders Checklist.

Title: _____

The author of this book compares _____ to _____ .

They are alike in two ways. First, _____
_____ .

Second, _____
_____ .

They are different in two ways. First, _____
_____ .

Second, _____ .

In conclusion, _____ .

Writer's Reminders: A Report that Tells about Comparisons

If the author of your book compared two things, you can write a report that tells about it. Use this checklist:

_____ I told my reader the two things that are being compared.

_____ I told my reader the number of ways they are alike.

_____ I wrote a sentence that tells the first way they are alike.

_____ I wrote a sentence that tells the second way they are alike.

_____ I told my reader the number of ways they are different.

_____ I wrote a sentence that tells the first way they are different.

_____ I wrote a sentence that tells the second way they are different.

_____ I wrote a sentence that wraps up my report.

Read your paper and see how you like it. Make any needed changes.

Figure 9.8 Writer's Reminders Checklist, based on a report frame.

strategy involving explicit instruction (Duffy, Roehler & Herrmann, 1998). The teacher thinks out loud, verbalizing her mental processes as she completes a task. In writing aloud, the teacher tells the students her thoughts about composing a message, explicitly showing them the phases of writing. You can use the computer screen, an overhead projector, a piece of chart paper, or the chalkboard to write down your thoughts as you compose out loud. It is important not to overplan this; you want students to see how you get ideas and put them together to create a message.

Before the students write, you can write aloud to show them the recursive nature of the writing process. Use the computer screen and think out loud as you show them how you add, delete, substitute, and rearrange your words when you write. If they are working without a computer, show them editorial symbols such as the caret to show where they wish to insert new words in their drafts. Model for them how to cross out words rather than erase when deleting or substituting. Finally, show them how to cut and paste and draw arrows as they revise.

You can also show students how to stop and read what they've already written. Model this by writing two or three sentences on the overhead projector or on the computer screen, thinking aloud as you write. Then stop and reread what you've written so far. Sometimes, rereading makes errors and misconceptions very clear. Other times, rereading helps the writer feel better about what she's written so far.

You can make all of these strategies apparent by writing aloud, and your students can benefit from these lessons without the demands of generating ideas on their own . . . yet. Writing aloud can take place with any age group; middle school students who are seasoned writers can learn from these mini-lessons, as can first graders who are just beginning to find their writing voices.

Workshop Approaches

So far in this chapter, I've shown some teaching methods that teachers use to provide instructional scaffolds for students as they learn to read and write. Here, I want to discuss ways to use some of those methods in organizational structures called *workshops*. Recall from Chapter 1 the transactional theory (Rosenblatt, 1938, 1978), which states that readers respond to what they have read. Responding can take many forms, from the personal and covert act of thoughtful reflection about an author's words, to the public and overt acts of writing, dramatizing, or talking about the book to others. **Workshop approaches** are literature-based methods of helping students read and write in social settings about works of fiction and nonfiction. Workshops are based on the idea that readers get the most out of what they read when they respond to, transact with, and write about literature with and for other people. The next section of this chapter describes literature circles, reading workshop, and writing workshop.

Literature Circles

When you read a great book, what do you do? Most adult readers who are excited about a book want to share it with others. They make recommendations, talk about how the book relates to their lives, exchange paperback copies of books, and compare books to movies. Enthusiastic readers who have read the same book share a common bond and excitedly talk about how this book affected them. Compare that kind of response to the way many children are required to respond to books in the classroom. Book reports, practice pages, and coloring sheets quickly take away the enthusiasm young readers feel when they read a good book. Soon, desire to read shuts down and getting students excited about reading is a problem for their teachers.

One way to encourage your students to read more and to become more involved as readers is to implement **literature circles** (Daniels, 2002; Harste, Short & Burke, 1995), a method of teaching literature that puts the teacher in the back seat as the students assume more responsibility for their reading. They choose the book they want to read, read it independently, and afterwards meet with other students who have chosen the same book. During these meetings, students respond to their reading through discussion. The teacher participates, not in the traditional sense of evaluating the students, but as a facilitator and a reader who is interested in responding as well (Eeds & Peterson, 1991).

To implement literature circles, planning and preparation are very important. You will need several sets of books with multiple copies. These book sets need to be at appropriate reading levels for your students, and need to be of high interest to them. Books can be fiction or nonfiction, and they can reflect a theme, an author, or a genre. Create five or six sets of texts, and then introduce each of them to the whole class. To do this, talk about the book set, telling just enough about it to pique curiosity.

Once you've introduced the book set, give students the opportunity to choose the book they want to read. Many teachers ask students to pick their top two choices, so that numbers in groups are manageable. Some teachers ask students to sign up for a particular interest, topic, or genre, such as mysteries, books about sports, or funny stories. Students who choose the same book form a circle; depending on the number of titles available, they form three or four literature circles.

Students in the groups read their books and then meet to discuss their responses. You can provide a list of questions to help generate discussion. Students ask questions of each other and participate in response activities. Questions that reflect story elements and that can start discussion include asking about the character *(Why did the main character act in this manner?)*, the setting *(Tell how the setting in this story reminds you of a place or time in real life.)*, events *(Tell what you were thinking when _____ happened.)*, or the resolution *(How would you have solved the problem differently?)*. Nonfiction questions might explore the author's point or might ask what readers have learned that they did not know before. You can guide, observe, and encourage active engagement through discussion. After reading, the students choose a new book and join another group. See Figure 9.9 on page 312 for the procedure for literature circles.

When the students meet, there are a variety of ways that they can conduct their groups. Daniels (2002) suggests the use of roles, in which everyone in the group has a job to do, such as to summarize the selection read so far, illustrate the character or events, or investigate some outside information about the book. When students join the literature circle, the teacher gives them roles and assignment sheets that reflect those roles. Role assignments work best with students higher than second grade. See Figure 9.10 on page 313 for a list of possible roles, adapted from Daniels's work.

Another way to conduct the group is for everyone to generate questions. This procedure might be difficult for your students, if they are not accustomed to asking the questions, and they might feel awkward at first. A good way to help is to model the act of question generating for them by thinking out loud. Question

1. Collect multiple copies of interesting, high-quality books (fiction or nonfiction) that are written for the reading level of your students.

2. You might want to create sets of books that relate to themes you are teaching in social studies or science. Or you can highlight a genre, such as historical fiction or animal fantasies.

3. Introduce each book with a book talk, a brief talk that tells the students a summary of the book, giving them just enough information to entice them to read it.

4. Ask students to sign up for the book that they want to read. Some teachers ask students to sign up for a topic, such as historical fiction, and the book title changes weekly.

5. After receiving his or her book, each student reads it, either during independent reading time or at home.

6. Once everyone in the group is finished reading, the group meets to discuss it.

7. You can give students assigned roles, like the ones shown in Figure 9.10, or you can ask them to generate questions for each other. Some teachers like to make suggestions for questions that reflect story elements.

8. If you have parents or paraprofessionals who can help guide your literature circles, enlist their help. One first grade teacher, Nancy Steider, asks four parents to commit to meeting twice a month with a literature circle. She provides a brief training session, a packet of response questions and ideas, and a copy of the book. She meets with a group, too, which keeps the groups small and provides plenty of models for first graders.

9. As you meet with literature circles, encourage student participation and keep teacher intervention to a minimum. Make sure students know the following guidelines:
   • You must read the whole book before meeting with the group.
   • You do not need to raise your hand to speak.
   • Always look at the members of the group when talking.
   • Always listen when someone is speaking.
   • Make sure to do your assigned role before you come to the group.
   • Show respect for what other people have to say.

10. Encourage groups to share with each other.

Figure 9.9 Procedure for literature circles.

Role	What the Student Does
Summarizer	Writes a summary of the selection and begins the discussion by reading it to the group.
Quotes Finder	Finds favorite quotes or passages and reads them to the group, explaining why he or she chose them.
Word Wizard	Looks for important or difficult words in the selection, and looks them up. During the discussion, he or she shares the words with the group. (The teacher can make suggestions for one or two words and ask the Word Wizard to find two or three more.)
Investigator	Searches for information about the author, book, theme, or topic. An Internet search or reference books can be used. The investigator makes copies of the information and shares it with the group.
Connector	Helps the literature circle members tie this book to their lives. The Connector looks for events in the school or the surrounding community that connect with events in the book.
Illustrator	Illustrates a character, an event, a prediction, or theme, and shares the picture with the group for discussion.

Figure 9.10 Literature circle roles.

Source: Daniels, 2002.

generating is difficult for many children; you may need to model this a few times. The following lesson is one example of question generating.

Mrs. Worthy's Lesson

In the following example, read the words of Mrs. Worthy, who is showing her third graders how to generate their own questions after reading *So Far from the Sea* (Bunting, 1998). This book is about Laura Iwasaki, a young Japanese American girl, whose family visits the Manzanar Relocation Camp in California for the last time before they move to Massachusetts. They go there to remember Laura's grandfather, who died after he was held prisoner there during World War II. He was one of thousands of Japanese Americans held in concentration camps after Japan bombed the United States at Pearl Harbor. Mrs. Worthy models:

"Ok, I've read *So Far from the Sea,* and all of the students in my group have read it, too, and now I need to ask my group a question. Now, I could ask a question like this: 'What are some of the things that people left at the Manzanar Relocation Camp?' And probably, someone will be able to give me the right answer, because they can see the picture of the origami birds and some coins. But I want to ask a question that makes everyone think a little bit more than that. I want the kids in my group to think about how this book makes them feel. I know that when I read it, I couldn't believe that we actually had concentration camps in this country. It made me sad to think that Americans were put in prison just because they were from Japanese families, but it also made me think about the way many American people felt back then. They were angry that Japan had attacked Pearl Harbor. I know how I felt on September 11. I was angry and confused, too. OK, so, let me ask a question that will make my group talk about that. Here is my question: 'What makes you mad when you read this story?' I think that would be a good one because it'll get my group talking."

Literature circles work for beginning readers, too. First and second grade students benefit from the relaxed, informal exchanges that take place when they meet with their groups. Nancy Steider, who teaches in Pennsylvania, organizes her literature circles a bit differently for her first graders. She selects the group members based on abilities, and recruits parent volunteers to manage each group. Steider gives the volunteers several choices of book titles that she has judged to be appropriate for their group. When the parent volunteers meet with their students, they decide on the books they want to read, and hold lively discussions during and after reading.

Carmen Martinez-Roldán and Julia López-Roberston describe their work with first grade bilingual children in literature circles:

Our purpose in the circles was not to teach the students how to read the book, but to facilitate meaningful discussions about books. We held a transactional perspective of the reading process, but did not follow a specific model or guide for leading the discussions. Instead, we encouraged the children to listen to one another, not to raise their hands but to talk when they were prepared, and to respond to or ask questions of the other members of the group. Our questions invited the children to share what they thought of the book. We also shared what we thought of the stories, prompted sometimes by the students' questions or invitations, as when one of them said to Julia [one of the authors] during the fourth discussion, "It's your time to talk." (1999/2000, p. 273)

Reading Workshop

One of the greatest paradoxes in reading education is that teachers spend lots of time teaching reading in school, yet school is one of the places where kids never have a chance to read. Reading instruction often consists of lots of activity and talk about reading, and very little actual reading. Nancie Atwell recognized this problem in her book about teaching reading to middle school students, *In the Middle: Writing, Reading, and Learning with Adolescents* (1998). Her work is considered the primary source for information on the **reading workshop.** The reading workshop is a method of teaching reading with literature; using this approach, the teacher sets aside time for independent reading of quality children's books, along with opportunities for students to respond to their reading through journals and conferences with the teacher. Additionally, the teacher teaches brief mini-lessons on reading strategies based on students' needs as evidenced in their reading

The following activities take place in reading workshop; you may organize the schedule as it suits you and your students:

- Provide a large classroom library, filled with books on every readability level. You will need a wide variety of genres from fiction and nonfiction. Also have multiple copies available.
- Read aloud a book or selection, and discuss it with students.
- Invite students to choose their own reading material and read uninterrupted for a period of time. They may sit wherever they want.
- After reading, students record responses in a reading journal. They need to date the entry, and record the title and author of the book they read.
- Teach a mini-lesson on a reading strategy, based on students' needs.
- Hold an individual conference with each student in the class at least weekly. In the conference, discuss reading strategies, responses to books, and suggestions for the next reading selection.
- Set aside a share time for students to share responses to their books with others.

Figure 9.11 Reading workshop elements.

journals and conferences. Students read independently and choose their own books from an extensive classroom library. A list of the elements of reading workshop is shown in Figure 9.11.

Bryan (1999) explains how he developed a reading workshop for his kindergarten classroom by gradually implementing procedures and mini-lessons during DEAR (Drop Everything and Read) time. He provided gallon-sized plastic "shopping bags" and showed students how to "shop" for two books—one that was familiar and that he had already read to the class, and another that was a new book of their choice. Additionally, Bryan gradually added the mini-lessons to the DEAR time, during which he taught alphabet skills as well as strategies such as predicting.

A key component of the reading workshop at any grade level is the mini-lesson, which is a teacher-directed lesson, about 10 minutes long, in which the teacher uses explicit instruction to teach strategies, skills, or concepts that readers need for successful reading. This mini-lesson makes reading workshop different from a period of sustained silent reading, because of the element of teacher involvement. You may recall that the National Reading Panel (2000a) did not recommend independent reading programs like SSR or DEAR, because of the lack of teacher guidance. The reading workshop, with its teacher read-aloud and mini-lesson, alleviates that concern. Explicit instruction is described in detail in Chapter 10, where you will see explanations and models of essential reading strategies.

Writing Workshop

Based on the relationship between reading and writing, Atwell also introduced the idea of the writing workshop (1998). The concept of the writing workshop approach is much the same as the reading workshop. You would provide uninterrupted, quiet time for the students to write, and have individual writing conferences with each student every two or three days. Students keep ongoing writing projects in a folder and follow the writing process as they complete them. Just as in reading workshop, the mini-lesson is a key element in writing workshop; it is a brief lesson on one of the strategies that students need while they are writing. You can plan mini-lessons to follow the writing process. Figure 9.12 shows several essential strategies that you might want to teach in mini-lessons. In addition to Atwell's *In the Middle* book (1998) on writing workshop, these three resources offer excellent ideas for teaching writing:

> *The Art of Teaching Writing* (Calkins, 1994)
> *Creative Power: The Nature and Nurture of Children's Writing* (Cramer, 2001)
> *Creating Writers Through 6-Trait Writing Assessment and Instruction* (Spandel, 2001)

At the end of writing workshop, students share their written pieces with each other. Some teachers call this the **author's chair.** Whoever sits in the author's chair has the opportunity to read his or her writing to the rest of the class. This is a celebratory time, in which students applaud each other's efforts at the difficult task of writing. Additionally, you may want to have your students try sharing their work electronically. They can write book reviews for Amazon.com, and publish stories and other pieces in a variety of places. Figure 9.13 lists some web sites that are useful for young authors; in addition, you can find many by typing "publishing children's writing" in your favorite search engine.

Strategies for Writing Mini-Lessons

Model and explain these strategies:

Rehearsal
- How to select a topic for writing
- How to use past experiences as a framework for writing
- How to find an audience for the written piece

Drafting
- How to keep writing when the page is blank
- How to write, revise, and edit recursively
- How to string phrases or sentences
- How to select colorful and meaningful vocabulary

Revision
- How to help classmates revise their work
- How to move blocks of writing around

Editing
- How to use the word wall for spelling help
- How to determine if a sentence is complete
- How to use editing marks such as carets and word substitutions

Figure 9.12 Mini-lesson topics for writing workshop.

Places for Children to Publish on the World Wide Web

Stone Soup

www.stonesoup.com/main2/writing.html   *Stone Soup* is a magazine for young writers. This web site allows children to publish their stories online.

Scriptito's Place

members.aol.com/vangarnews/scriptito.html   This is a writing resource center hosted by Vangar Publishers. Students from ages 7 to 15 can publish here.

Kid Pub

www.kidpub.org/kidpub/   One of the oldest web sites for children's writing; this one has been around since 1995. A large database of children's stories written by children. Teachers can set up a separate page to post the work of their class. The address for more information on this is *schools@kidpub.com*. There is a small fee for membership, which allows for unlimited story posting. As of 2005, there are more than 42,000 stories in the database.

Aaron Shephard's Young Author's Page

www.aaronshep.com/youngauthor/index.html   Children's author Aaron Shephard has set up this web site, which offers information for children who want to publish their writing.

MidLink Magazine

longwood.cs.ucf.edu/~MidLink/   This is an online magazine for children ages 8 to 18, which offers links to schools who want to participate in collaborative web projects, as well as web quests on a variety of subjects.

Figure 9.13   Internet sources for publishing children's writings.

Managing the Scaffolds: A Daily Plan

One of the hardest things to do when running a classroom is to get everything done! There is never enough time to teach all the things you want to teach, to let the children say all that they want to say, and to read as much as you'll want them to read. Managing time is also one of the skills that new teachers find the most frustrating, because this is not something you can easily learn in a university classroom. Experienced teachers who have been juggling their classrooms along with the clock have devised some ways to maximize efficiency and learning, and we'll look at some of those methods.

Additionally, several reading researchers have developed and tested programs for organizing and teaching literacy, especially for struggling readers. These programs are well organized and well structured, and are supported by experimental research or scientifically based ideas (Tierney & Readence, 2005). Four Blocks (Cunningham, Hall & Defee, 1991, 1998); Guided Reading (Fountas & Pinnell, 1996); Reading Recovery (Clay, 1979); Reading Workshop (Atwell, 1998); Scaffolded Reading Experiences (Graves & Graves, 2003); Students Achieving Independent Learning, or SAIL (Bergman, 1992); and Success for All (Slavin, Madden, Dolan, Waski, Ross & Smith, 1994) are programs that offer teachers and students ways to include all of the components of scaffolded reading and writing described in this chapter. Suggestions for managing your literacy instruction include ideas or elements from the research that backs these programs.

A daily routine for teaching reading and writing can be helpful. There are many ways to approach it; the main goal is to focus on putting books and writing utensils in your students' hands as much as possible, in as many ways as possible. In Figure 9.14, you will see elements of a daily routine. There are many ways to accomplish some of the components; for example, there are many ways to offer independent reading. Thus, options are listed where appropriate.

The following sections cover these elements of a daily plan: (1) class meeting and read-alouds, (2) journal writing, (3) independent reading, (4) group reading, and (5) independent writing. Notice that there are several options for management of independent reading, group reading, and independent writing.

You can arrange these elements in any fashion that suits your needs. Other than the class meeting, which should occur first, the sequence of these elements is not important—do whatever works for you. The important thing to remember is that your students need each of these elements in order for reading and writing to come together, and they need them in large blocks of time and on a daily basis. As you read about each of these parts of a plan, notice that if you include all of the elements in your day, you've included "the whole, the parts, and the heart" of teaching literacy.

Managing the Class Meeting

Begin the day together. No matter what grade level you teach, gathering the students together at the beginning of the day helps to instill a sense of community, togetherness, and social connectivity that is so important in teaching reading. Many teachers use this time to talk with the class about plans for the day, and to help students organize their daily goals. They talk about the things they will do and read, and put these plans in writing, in a space on the board for all to see. Other teachers use this time to read aloud to their students, tying the book into a theme or important idea they want to convey. If you teach in a middle school or an elementary school with several classes per day, hold a brief meeting at the beginning of each of your sessions.

Calkins tells of teachers and students using this time to talk about reading—and to really listen to each other. She describes how one teacher, named Kathy, makes this a daily habit that starts the first day of school. Kathy has asked her students to bring in favorite books to share during the morning minutes:

> These books may not have been Kathy's idea of great children's literature, but they did come into the room layered with life stories. Josh, holding up his cross-section book of

Elements of a Daily Plan for Literacy Instruction

Class Meeting and Read–Aloud

Reserve about 20 minutes of the day for this step, and include all of your students. This is a good time to talk about books and reading. Also spend some time reading aloud to them, which is one of the ways to scaffold their reading and provide a common bond for all students in the class (Calkins, 2001).

Journal Writing

Give your students 15 to 20 minutes to write in journals privately. Use the journals as a way to respond personally to text and to practice writing skills. This requires little scaffolding, but is valuable for developing confidence in writing. Invented spellings give you a window to their knowledge about letters and sounds (Clark, 1988; Ehri & McCormick, 2004; Eldredge, 1999).

Independent Reading

Students of all ages and all backgrounds need time to read independently (Allington, 2001). This activity requires the least amount of scaffold, but provides the most meaningful practice. Use this 20 to 30 minute block of time to allow students to read books of their own choosing.

Ways to organize independent reading:

- *Uninterrupted Sustained Silent Reading (USSR) or Drop Everything and Read (DEAR)*—Children silently read books of their own choice, uninterrupted. The teacher reads as well, to provide a model (Anderson, 2000; McCracken & McCracken, 1972). No other teacher intervention is required; however, the National Reading Panel (2000a) did not support the use of sustained silent reading without teacher intervention or involvement other than just reading.
- *Self-selected reading and conferencing*—Students read books of their own choosing while the teacher moves around the room and holds conferences with five students per day (Cunningham, Hall & Defee, 1991, 1998).
- *Reading workshop*—Students read books of their own choosing and hold a conference with the teacher about their reading. The teacher begins each session with a mini-lesson on reading strategies (Atwell, 1998).
- *Literature circles*—Students read books that they have chosen from a selection of books gathered by the teacher. They form small, flexible groups to discuss their responses after reading. Each student can take a role, such as Summarizer or Illustrator, shown in Figure 9.10. The teacher guides without leading the discussion (Daniels, 2002; Harste, Short & Burke, 1995).

Group Reading

Reserve about 30 to 45 minutes for this time block. Students read text that you have selected at their instructional level. Scaffold their reading by using any variation of shared reading or guided reading that suits the needs of your students.

Ways that you can organize group reading:

- *Shared reading*—Read the text aloud while your students follow along. You can do this with the whole class, a small group, or with individual students (Harste, Short & Burke, 1988; Holdaway, 1979; Tierney & Readence, 2005).
- *Guided reading using the Fountas and Pinnell (1996) model*—This framework uses flexible groups of children grouped by ability. Each group reads its own leveled book chosen by the teacher. The teacher meets with each group daily.

Figure 9.14 Daily plan elements.

(continued)

- *Guided reading in the Four Blocks model* (Cunningham Hall, & Defee, 1991, 1998)—This framework is used with mixed-ability groups. The students can meet with the teacher, meet with a self-guided group, read in pairs, or read alone.

Writing

Students can work independently on response projects that involve writing, researching, or creating multimedia pieces. Usually, you will need about 30 to 45 minutes for this type of work. Use the writing process and publish for authentic purposes and audiences. You may need to add 10 to 15 minutes to this time for word study. Work with decoding rimes, word wall activities, making words, and other word-related activities (Cunningham, Hall & Defee, 1991, 1998).

Ways that you can organize writing:

- *Writing workshop*—Begin with a mini-lesson on some aspect of the writing process that students need, such as writing for an audience, word choice, or clarity. Use writing aloud to model strategies by thinking aloud (Calkins, 2001; Routman, 2000). Give students 30 minutes to write independently. Revising and editing comes from peers in groups, as well as during individual conferences with the teacher (Atwell, 1998).
- *Shared writing*—Meet with the whole class or in small groups to write, using language experience charts (Stauffer, 1975; Allen & Allen, 1967), interactive writing messages (Button, Johnson & Furgerson, 1996), literary borrowing (Lancia, 1997), and story or report frames and checklists.

Figure 9.14 Continued.

automobiles and trains announced, "My dad reads it to me." That was all Josh planned to say. He was done. A flurry of hands popped up as the circle of children clamored onto knees and waved frantically, speaking, "Call-on-me, call-on-me!"

But Kathy's attention remained steadfastly fastened on Josh. With one hand, she quelled the appeals as if to say, "Wait, I'm listening to Josh. Listen with me." Looking into Josh's face, Kathy said, "You read with your dad? That is *so cool*." (2001, p. 19)

Thus, the morning class meeting can be a time for setting the tone for the whole school day—indeed, the whole school year. Talk about reading during this time together. Ask your students to bring a favorite book from home, and then share it by explaining why it is a favorite and how it fits into the home routine. Or discuss things to accomplish during the day. Truly listen, and teach children how to listen to each other by facing and watching each other as they talk. Do not expect to give everyone a chance to share thoughts with the whole group every day; instead of redirecting attention to many children during discussions, focus attention on one child's talk closely. Let that child make his important point. When you do this consistently and daily, children know that you are listening, and that you expect them to contribute thoughtfully.

Managing Journal Writing

Journals have many purposes; most often, they are places for writing personal reactions to reading, class discussions, interest topics, or everyday observations. The **response journal** is a type of journal in which students write about anything that they have read. Students of all grade levels, even kindergarten and first grade, can

Diversity in the Reading Classroom

Scaffolding the Multiple Literacies of Bilingual Latino/ Hispanic Students

Years ago, I taught with a colleague whose wife is deaf. He can hear, and is very fluent in American Sign Language. His wife's doctor thought that she had a syndrome whose symptoms are deafness and kidney failure and which is nearly always fatal. To find out more about it, the doctors needed to do a kidney biopsy. My colleague did the interpreting for his wife and medical personnel. During the biopsy, the doctor was sweating and his hands were shaking terribly. In frustration, he shouted at my friend, telling him that he needed to tell his wife to be absolutely still or her kidney could be punctured during this procedure. My colleague went white, and collapsed in a pile on the operating room floor. In spite of everything, the biopsy went well and his wife is now healthy. But he later told me of his raw fear when he came to on that operating room floor. He realized that his ability to interpret accurately could be a matter of life and death.

Likewise, Latino/Hispanic children are often called upon to serve as liaisons between their homes, communities, and schools. Their bilingualism, and the monolingualism of their families, requires them to interpret the language and teach it to others. For example, some Latino/Hispanic students must attend parent conferences to interpret for their teachers and parents. Other similar types of tasks abound, such as helping their parents pay bills, teaching younger siblings, and writing letters to relatives in their native country. Jiménez (2001, 2004) states that educators often overlook the abilities that their Latino/Hispanic students possess and use every day. These "multiple literacies" (2001, p. 741) are sophisticated, complex skills, and are essential to the families and communities of Latino/Hispanic students. Such activities can place an emotional burden on the students, because of the reversal of traditional parent–child roles. Moreover, the literacy instruction that they receive in school is often viewed as a threat to their identities, because the curriculum ignores their Spanish-language abilities and their experiences at home. In the report of a study in which he taught and interviewed immigrant Latino/Hispanic students in grades 4 through 6, Jiménez tells us: "Students indicated that literacy learning was a much more appealing activity if viewed as supportive of their Latina/o identity, if it fostered their Spanish-language and literacy development" (2004, p. 235). He recommends that educators support their bilingual Latino/Hispanic students by recognizing their abilities, as well as the burden that these abilities bring to them. Some ways to do this are:

- Call upon the background experiences of your Latino/Hispanic students during literature circles or guided reading. Use cognate vocabulary in mini-lessons.

- Talk with your bilingual students about their unique challenges and advantages.

- Support the preservation of Spanish as their native language. Use bilingual literature, word walls, and interactive writing. Teach students how to write letters to stay in touch with relatives who live in other countries.

- Allow older students to tutor English-speaking students in Spanish, translate stories from English to Spanish for use in the library, or help the school produce documents that can be used with the Spanish-speaking community.

write in daily response journals. You can prompt your students with questions or statements, or simply ask them to react to the literature, without specific prompts. If you choose to use prompts, some good examples are:

- What do you think the main character should do?
- How is this story plot similar to your life?

- What have you learned about this topic by reading this book?
- What would you like to say to the author of this book?
- How would you change this book?
- What would you like to say to the main character of this book?
- Compare this book to the best book you ever read.

Use journals to help your students view writing as a means of personal response. Reserve a 15 to 20 minute block of time for journal writing for everyone, and ask everyone to write independently. Establish a "quiet zone" rule, so this time period can be used to write privately and quietly.

You can read about journal writing in more detail in Chapter 13, where you will learn how to use several types of response journals and see samples of journal writing from children as young as first grade.

Managing Independent Reading

Give your students at least 20 to 30 minutes of independent reading time per day. This means that your students will need to have access to books that are suitable for their reading levels. To facilitate this, each student will need a receptacle, to house books and a number of small items. You can use sturdy bags, magazine storage boxes, or other lightweight containers that can hold these items:

- Enough books to sustain the reader for 20 to 30 minutes; younger children may need up to 10 paperback books
- A reading log to track titles, authors, and dates
- Writing utensils and a wipe-off board
- A bag for carrying books home

Students choose the books to go into their book bags on a regular basis; organize this according to the abilities of your students. Some teachers establish a Monday morning book-choosing time; others ask their students to select books every day or two. Students can choose them from the classroom library or from the school library. You might want to consider letting them bring some from home, too, depending upon your resources.

The portable book bags help to make this period of time manageable—everything needed is within arm's reach. Establishing a firm "no wandering" rule is easy to do, because your students will have everything they need in their book bags. They will not need to wander around finding another book to read once they've finished the first one.

Using these book bags and this independent reading time, according to Calkins (2001), you can also determine a lot about how children read. Children's ability to choose books that fit their reading abilities, their reading interests, and their persistence in sticking with books once they start them, can all be assessed simply by taking note of what is in their book bags. They should also keep a reading log, in which they record the date and the title and author of the books they read daily.

This is a good time for you to find out more about your students' reading behaviors. To do this, Cunningham, Hall, and Defee (1998) suggest establishing a routine of having a conference with a few students per day during this time. (If you have 25 students, 5 per day gets the whole class done in a week!) At the beginning of the school year, model a reading conference for your students. Make sure that they know that they will be expected to do the following:

- Tell the teacher why you chose the book.
- Retell the story.
- Tell what you learned from the author.
- Tell the teacher about your predictions and thoughts so far.
- Tell the teacher what kind of book you are thinking about sharing next week.

To have a conference with your students during the independent reading period, you can either travel around the room and sit with the students, or you can ask them to bring their book bag to you. You can ask them to select a page or two from a book in their box, and to either read aloud for you or read silently. Watch closely and make notations to record oral reading, as you learned to do with running records in Chapter 4. Make brief anecdotal notes as you hold conferences. You can look for these kinds of things:

1. What kinds of books does the student choose? Does he or she need to be nudged to try other genre?
2. What does his or her reading log say about the child's reading? Is the child moving through books at an appropriate pace?
3. Is the child able to choose books that match his or her ability? Does the child need to learn how to select books on his or her own?
4. How does the student read orally? What does the student do with miscues?
5. How does the student read silently? Is the student attending to the print and interpreting the author's message?
6. How does the child retell?
7. How does the child value reading? Do you need to help him or her gain interest by making other book choices?
8. How is his or her fluency? Does he or she need to do some repeated readings to increase speed, expression, and comfort level with oral reading?

This list is meant to show all the possibilities for a reading conference. Naturally, you will not be able to accomplish all of these assessments in a two- or three-minute conversation. To manage this list efficiently, you might want to do the same assessment for each student during that week. For example, the first week, you can decide to focus on your students' miscues and make notes about self-corrections, use of phonics clues, and use of context to decode unknown words. The second and third weeks, you might want to collect information on retelling.

Another possibility is to let the students' readings drive you. You may find, for example, that a child has particular difficulty with retellings. Thus, rather than move to a different type of assessment each week, you would stick with retellings for at least one more conference, to see if you can figure out some patterns to the child's behavior.

Managing Group Reading

Essentially, there are two ways to manage the small groups that you use with guided reading. First, Cunningham, Hall, and Defee (1991, 1998), in their Four Blocks literacy framework, advocate mixed-ability groups. Second, Fountas and Pinnell (1996), in their Guided Reading literacy framework, advocate the use of "dynamic" groups of children with similar reading abilities. Management of these groups will be different, depending on your choice. The following sections describe both.

Mixed Ability Grouping

Cunningham, Hall, and Defee (1998) recommend that you group your students heterogeneously, and provide all of them with the same text. Meet with the whole class first, and prepare them for reading by previewing the text, asking for predictions, and talking about the purpose for reading. There are a variety of interesting techniques that you can use, such as the book box or a picture walk, which you will learn more about in Chapter 11. When all of your students are ready to read the selection, assign students to read in one of four ways: (1) with partners, (2) independently, (3) with the teacher, or (4) in a small group without the teacher.

These four ways of reading allow you to meet the needs of students without putting them in homogeneous ability groups. This also allows for "multi-level" teaching (Cunningham, Hall & Defee, 1998, p. 653). Students who need less support can read the selection independently or with partners. Students who need more support can read it with other students in a small group, led either by the teacher or by a peer. Some teachers get help from parents, aides, or reading resource teachers to guide one of the small groups.

To let your students know how they are assigned, make a chart for your classroom, using card pockets and index cards. Write your students' names, one per card, on the index cards. Then arrange a chart like the one shown in Figure 9.15. You can change the chart as often as you want, or you can vary the format by giving the students a choice, letting them decide how they want to read a selection.

After you have prepared everyone to read the selection, give them a question to answer or something to look for as they read. Then, the students can find their

Schedule for Guided Reading

Today's date: <u>Thursday, November 17</u>

Read with the Teacher	Read in a Group	Read by Yourself	Read with a Partner
Angelo	McKenzie	Barry	Kyle – Joey
Marcie	Omar	Eddie	Maria – Gina
Elle	Cole	Chelsea	Bailey – Wakeena
Danny	Danielle	Yuri	Tony – Tim
		Christina	Patrick – Tommy
		Manuel	Angie – Natalie

Figure 9.15 Scheduling guided reading groups.

places and guided reading begins. Students read the selection silently, or, if in partners, softly or in whispers.

In order to successfully use partners during your guided reading times, you will need to plan carefully. For smooth management of behavior and efficient use of time, assign partners yourself, and keep these partnerships constant for two or three weeks, then change them. This is one excellent reason for knowing your students well. Your interest inventories at the beginning of the school year can help you form partnerships early on. As time passes, you will know which pairs work well and which do not. Generally, it is best to avoid putting the top ability students together with the lowest ability students, because the disparity in their abilities is too wide. Likewise, putting two of the lowest ability students in the same partnership should also be avoided, because they have not yet developed the skills to adequately coach and encourage each other. Arrange the seating in the classroom so that partners are located near each other. Additionally, when you gather children with you to sit on the floor, ask partners to sit together so that you can easily facilitate strategies that require them to talk to a partner.

Train your students to work together as pairs. There are several considerations. First, students need to know the purpose for their reading. What is the intended outcome of their partner reading? You need to make this clear to them. You might want them to prepare for choral reading with the class, so they will need to reread parts of a selection orally. Or, you might want them to help each other self-monitor by asking them to read a selection silently for the first time and check up on each other at stop points. Another reason for reading together might be to fill in an advanced organizer or a story map. Whatever the reason, make sure they know why they are reading together.

Second, students need to know how they will read together. Figure 9.16 shows some of these ways. As always, when you expect something new from your students, model the type of behavior you want them to achieve. Role-play some partner reading so that your students can see and hear the activity that you expect.

While their classmates are reading in pairs or with the teacher, some students will be reading alone. This, however, is not the same type of reading that they will do during self-selected reading time. Instead, you will guide them by giving them before-reading activities, and then ask them to read the selection by themselves. Some students prefer this mode of reading; it is important, though, that you do not portray this punitively for those who do not prefer to read alone.

When it is time to read a selection, there will be students who need to be close to you during their reading. The reasons vary. Sometimes you will want to provide additional structure for a small number of students; other times, you might want to listen closely to the responses of certain students as they read. This is also a good time to do some careful kidwatching, as students decode, solve problems, and make predictions. Again, make sure that the students who sit with you to read do not view this as a punishment, and make sure to vary the makeup of the groups, so that your grouping remains flexible.

Guided reading should take place on at least two or three days a week. With younger children, you will assign a reading selection each time they meet. As they get older, it may be necessary to take two days to read one selection. On the days when you do not use guided reading, you can use literature circles or the reading workshop format.

Ways to Read as Partners

Back and forth
The partners agree to read one page at a time, switching back and forth.

Character roles
The partners decide upon character parts to read, and divide the rest of the page. You might want to help them determine which parts to read.

Keeping track
The partners take turns "keeping track" of the print for each other. One partner points to the print, while the other reads aloud for one page; then they switch roles for the next page. This is best for younger children who are not yet fluently reading.

6″ whispers together
The partners read in choral reading fashion, whispering so that only they can hear each other.

Say something
Each partner reads silently. When they come to a stop point, the partners say something to each other about the selection so far. Prior to reading, be sure to have them mark the stop points, and give them a topic to talk about at the points.

Question the author
Each partner reads silently. When they come to a stop point, ask them to collaboratively compose a question that they would like to ask the author.

Figure 9.16 Partner reading.

Needs-Based Grouping

Fountas and Pinnell (1996) advocate putting students of like abilities together, in flexible but homogeneous groups. Their rationale is that young, developing readers need intense instruction with guided reading, using leveled texts that match their abilities. These groups meet on three to five days a week, and on other days, students participate in literature circles or reading workshop groups. Thus, they would meet with homogeneous groups only during guided reading time, and would have the opportunity to meet with other groups for other purposes. These groups should be constantly monitored, and based on ongoing assessments, children should be regrouped as necessary.

A block of about 30 to 45 minutes is needed for guided reading, and during that time, you would meet with each group, one at a time. During this time, each group reads a different selection that you have chosen to match the abilities of the students in that group. Fountas and Pinnell list thousands of leveled books in

Guided Reading: Good First Teaching for All Children (1996), *Matching Books to Readers: Using Leveled Books in Guided Reading K–3* (1999), and *Guiding Readers and Writers Grades 3–6* (2001).

When meeting with each group, briefly prepare them to read with a strategy that activates background knowledge or asks for predictions. Set a purpose for reading by asking a question or giving the students something to look for as they read. Then, have each student read the selection silently, stopping only to ask for help or to reflect on predictions. During this time, observe their reading behaviors. You can take notes on self-monitoring strategies or vocabulary needs. Depending on the selection, you can give the students a stop point and talk about the events that occurred up to that point. After starting the story and checking on everyone, you can also send them back to their seats to finish the story independently, which helps to keep the group meetings brief.

While you are meeting with one group, it is of course necessary for the rest of the class to work without your guidance. This setup creates the very common problem of how to meaningfully occupy 20 or so students while you teach only five or six of them. You need to be able to teach without interruptions so that everyone stays focused and on task. Independent activities should be, first and foremost, meaningful. You could have your students read independently, read with a partner, listen to taped readings, or work at the computer.

Managing Writing Instruction

Give students plenty of time to write. For grades three and above, students need at least 30 minutes of uninterrupted writing time, and a little less than that for the lower grades. You might want to utilize a writing workshop format, in which you use the first 5 to 10 minutes for a mini-lesson and the remainder of the time for students to write independently.

If you have chosen a theme or topic, and have introduced many books on that subject, you can involve your students in long-term writing and researching projects about the topic. You can help students research and respond to books connected to the topics that they are currently studying in science or social studies. Students can pick specific areas within the theme or topic that you have chosen; for example, if the topic is weather, the students could write about cloud formation, weather reporting, tornadoes, or any other facet of weather that interests them. To guide their selections, you might want to outline some choices for them.

While students write, hold individual conferences about their writing. Guidelines for conferencing are shown in Figure 9.17 on page 328.

To keep a record of your students' writing, you can use a state of the class chart (Atwell, 1998). This chart lists all the students in your class, the dates, and the current writing stage at which the student is working. An example is shown in Figure 9.18 on page 328.

Additionally, during the writing time of your daily schedule, you might need to plan for lessons in word study. You do not need more than about 15 minutes for word study; these lessons could include activities such as making words, phonics sorts, and a variety of other phonics activities that you can find in Chapter 6. Word study of this type is appropriate for students in second grade or younger. For older students, teach dictionary skills, word analysis skills, and spelling strategies during this time.

1. Ask students to tell you about their piece. If time permits during the conference, ask them to read it to you.
2. Always keep the content of the piece your first priority.
3. Make the conference brief—three or four minutes should suffice.
4. Make suggestions but do not rewrite or take over the piece.
5. Be sure that your comments are sincere. Tell the student what you like about the paper. Then decide on just one area that needs improvement, and ask questions or offer comments for this.
6. Questions that you can ask when correcting difficulties occur are:
   a. What is the most important thing that you are trying to say?
   b. What's your favorite part? How can you add to that?
   c. I don't understand this part. Tell me more about this part.
   d. How can you get my attention, as a reader, right away?
   e. What do you want your reader to know or feel at the end of your paper?
   f. What is one thing that you would change about your paper?
   g. Are there some extra words in your writing that you can delete?
   h. What do you think you will do by the next time we talk?
7. Always end the conference with an agreement to accomplish something in the writing.

Figure 9.17 Guidelines for holding writing conferences.

Name of Student	Project	Rehearsal	Drafting	Revising	Editing	Publishing
Michael	Letter to zookeeper	2/6	2/9			
Amber	Letter to zookeeper	2/6	2/9			
Nakita	Sequel to *The True Story of the Three Pigs*	2/6	2/9	2/11		
Santiago	Report on wolves	2/6, 2/7	2/8	2/11	2/11	
Meredith	Report on wolves	2/8				
Whitney	Report on wolves	2/8	2/9, 2/10			
Travis	Alphabet book on mammals	2/6	2/7, 2/9, 2/8			
Joe	Biography of Jon Scieszka	2/7	2/7			
Darlene	Sequel to *The True Story of the Three Pigs*	2/6	2/7	2/9		

Figure 9.18 State of the class record for writing.

Home–School Connection

Ways to Read Together

Shown below is a letter that explains partner reading. ●

Dear Family,

I will be sending home books each night for your child to read. These books should be "just right" for your child, which means that he or she can read almost all the words on the page with no difficulty.

In our classroom, we read with partners frequently. You can do the same thing at home with your child, with the books that he or she brings home. Shown below are some ways you can "share the page" with your child.

Back and forth: You and your child agree to read one page at a time, switching back and forth.

Character roles: Decide upon character parts to read, and divide the rest of the page.

Keeping track: Take turns "keeping track" of the print for each other. Begin by pointing to the print for your child, while she reads aloud for one page. Then switch roles for the next page.

Say something: Divide the book into sections. Mark each section with a bookmark or sticky note. Together, read the section. (You can read silently or orally.) When you get to the bookmark or sticky note, this is your stop point. Say something to each other about the selection so far.

Try these! I think you'll enjoy this time reading together.

Sincerely,

Your child's teacher

Partner reading can take place at home, too.

Summary: Scaffolding—The Many Ways

Scaffolded instruction facilitates the reading and writing that your students do, and provides an environment for optimal learning. When you scaffold your students' reading, you make plans for strategies to use before, during, and after their reading. Providing appropriate reading materials for them is crucial to their success; three levels of difficulty apply to a match between the text and the reader: independent, instructional, and frustrational.

Scaffolded reading instruction takes many forms; such instruction, in terms of a framework shown in Figure 9.2 on page 291, illustrates the nature of the teacher's role while supporting reading. Much support is offered in methods such as read-alouds and shared reading. As students become more capable, the teacher gradually releases responsibility and allows them to be more independent in methods such as guided reading and independent reading.

Likewise, when teaching writing, teachers support their students by modeling their writing, using mental models to explain writing processes. The teacher also supports beginning writers with shared writing methods such as language experience, interactive writing, and literacy borrowing. Teacher support is gradually reduced, as students learn and write independently with the least amount of scaffolding. While writing, students use the same processes that real authors do, so teachers guide them through five stages: rehearsal, drafting, revising, editing, and publishing. Students use these stages in a recursive manner, writing and rewriting until they are finished with the product.

Workshop approaches to reading and writing were described in this chapter; they provide alternative frameworks for teaching literacy in child-centered ways.

To manage the time, movement, and behavior of your students as they learn to read and write, this chapter showed you how to organize the day so that you have blocks of time reserved for reading and writing activities. Reserve time each day for: (1) class meeting and read-aloud, (2) journal writing, (3) independent reading , (4) guided reading , and (5) writing.

The types of scaffolded reading are shown in the Reviewing the Big Picture box, along with their corresponding standards and principles.

Technology Resources

- classroom.jc–schools.net/read/index.html   This "Road to Reading" web site, sponsored by Jefferson County Schools in Dendridge, Tennessee, has several pages, one of which is called "Guided Reading Blvd." On this page, there are many links to pages on every facet of guided reading, including charts for group management, partner reading, and more.

- www.teachnet.org/ntol/howto/childlit/manageread.htm   "How to Manage Reading Groups" is the article on this web page, which is part of the Teachers Network web site.

- forums.atozteacherstuff.com/showthread.php?threadid=1069   This site provides a forum for chatting with teachers and asking questions about issues such as management, guided reading, grouping, and matching books to readers.

- www.educationworld.com/a_curr/profdev/profdev083.shtml   Authored by Cara Bafile, this article on the Education World web site is her explanation of the strategy of shared reading and how it can be adapted for middle school readers.

- home.cc.umanitoba.ca/~fboutin/frame.html   This web site is written by Boutin and Chinien of the University of Manitoba. It is an interactive site, in which the student teacher can view web pages that contain several possible classroom scenarios. These scenarios depict problems in classroom management. You can contribute by explaining how you would solve the management dilemma, and then compare your answer to that given by an experienced classroom teacher.

- k6educators.about.com/od/classroommanagement/   This About.com web site offers several links to quality web sites on classroom management. A variety of articles provide much information and practical advice on topics such as classroom jobs, nonverbal ways to manage behavior, and student-centered learning.

The New York Times
expect the world
nytimes.com

Themes of the Times

Expand your knowledge of the concepts discussed in this chapter by reading current and historical articles from the *New York Times* by visiting the "Themes of the Times" section of the Companion Web Site.

Reviewing the Big Picture
Scaffolded Reading and Writing

Scaffolded Instruction	Description	Conditions for Optimal Use	IRA Standards	INTASC Principles	NAEYC Standards	ACEI/NCATE Standards
Independent reading	Students read alone books of their own choosing.	The least amount of scaffolding takes place when students read silently. Reading workshop and literature circles utilize extensive independent reading.	1.4, 2.1, 2.2, 3.2, 4.1, 4.2, 4.3, 4.4	3, 4, 5	1, 3, 4b	1, 2.1, 3.1, 3.2, 3.4, 4
Guided Reading	Read a book silently in small groups, using stop points to discuss predictions and conclusions. Groups are either mixed ability or on needs based	The teacher scaffolds reading instruction by giving leveled reading material. While students read, the teacher observes or interacts with the student.	1.4, 2.1, 2.2, 3.2, 4.1, 4.2, 4.3, 4.4	3, 4, 5	NA	1, 2.1, 3.1, 3.2, 3.2, 3.5, 4
Shared reading	Read a book with a group. If the group consists of young emerging readers, use the big book form of a predictable book. Have students read aloud with you at the predictable parts of the book. If the group consists of older, struggling readers, give everyone a copy of a small book and read aloud while they follow along.	Books are too difficult for students to decode alone. The teacher reads aloud while students follow along.	1.4, 2.1, 2.2, 3.2, 4.1, 4.2, 4.3, 4.4	3, 4, 5	1, 3, 4b	1, 2.1, 3.1, 3.2, 3.4, 3.5, 4
Reading aloud to students	Read books aloud instead of asking students to read it themselves.	Books are at the frustrational reading level. The teacher reads aloud to provide a common experience and to show good models of reading and writing.	1.4, 2.1, 2.2, 3.2, 4.1, 4.2, 4.3, 4.4	3, 4, 5	1, 3, 4b	1, 2.1, 3.1, 3.2, 3.4, 3.5, 4
Independent writing	Students use the writing process for formal writing projects. Informal writing is not published; a journal is one type.	Least amount of scaffold for writing instruction, although mini-lessons take place during writing workshop.	2.2, 4.1, 4.3, 4.4	3, 4, 5	1, 3, 4b	1, 2.1, 3.1, 3.2, 3.4, 3.5, 4
Shared writing	"Share the pen" with interactive writing, literary borrowing, and frames and checklists.	Provides substantial scaffold by helping with spelling, writing patterns from literature, and frames that show how writing should be organized.	2.2, 4.1, 4.3, 4.4	3, 4, 5	1, 3, 4b	1, 2.1, 3.1, 3.2, 3.4, 3.5, 4
Language experience approach	Provide an experience; ask students to dictate a piece of text about it. Transcribe their words.	Allows students to compose without the demands of writing the words themselves. Shows the connection between oral language and print.	2.2, 4.1, 4.3, 4.4	3, 4, 5	1, 3, 4b	1, 2.1, 3.1, 3.2, 3.4, 3.5, 4
Write-alouds	Model writing processes by composing while thinking aloud.	The most amount of scaffolding; this method makes processes visible and can be done in mini-lessons.	2.2, 4.1, 4.3	3, 4, 5	1, 3, 4b	1, 2.1, 3.1, 3.2, 3.4, 3.5, 4

10

Explicit Instruction of Comprehension Strategies

The old man wiped his forehead with his sleeve. "Whew," he said. "It was exhausting. But you know, even transmitting that tiny memory to you—I think it lightened me just a little."

"Do you mean—you did say I could ask questions?"

The man nodded, encouraging his question.

"Do you mean that now you don't have a memory of it—of that ride on the sled— anymore?"

"That's right. A little weight off this old body."

"But it was such fun! And now you don't have it anymore! I *took* it from you!"

But the old man laughed. "All I gave you was one ride, on one sled, in one snow, on one hill. I have a whole world of them in my memory. I could give them to you one by one a thousand times, and there would still be more."

The Giver (Lowry, 1993)

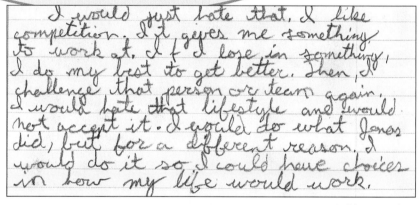

I would just hate that. I like competition. It gives me something to work at. If I lose in something, I do my best to get better. Then, I challenge that person or team again. I would hate that lifestyle and would not accept it. I would do what Jonas did, but for a different reason. I would do it so I could have choices in how my life would work.

Matt, grade 8

Just as the old man, whom Lois Lowry called "The Giver," gave his memories to Jonah in this excerpt, you can give your students the tools to find a world of memories. Show them the strategies they need to comprehend written text. Once they can do the things that good readers do as they construct meaning from the printed page, there is a whole world of memories awaiting them.

What should you teach them, and how? First, let's figure out what mature readers do when they want to understand text. In the Personal Reflection, think about how you comprehend the written word.

When you choose a novel or short story to read, what do you do . . .

- Before reading, to prepare yourself to read?
- While reading, to make sure you understand the text?
- After reading, to help yourself remember the story?

When you choose a nonfiction article, textbook, or information book to read, what do you do . . .

- Before reading, to prepare yourself to read?
- While reading, to make sure you understand the text?
- After reading, to make sure you remember the information you read?

As a mature reader, you know that there are things that a reader must do in order to comprehend text. For example, when choosing a book, you might scan the text to determine the "fit" of the book for you. Would this be a useful strategy for the students in your classroom? Absolutely! This chapter will show you how to use explicit instruction to teach several important reading strategies. When you show your students how to accomplish strategies such as previewing, predicting, self-questioning, or making inferences, you are focusing on the process of reading. Process-oriented instruction is important, because it shows your students how to accomplish the tasks involved in reading for meaning.

The kinds of behaviors you thought about in the Personal Reflection are the strategies that you use to help yourself construct meaning from print. This chapter is about those kinds of behaviors—the things that readers do to figure out the author's meaning. In Chapter 2, you learned 16 essential strategies to include in your reading curriculum. Nine of those strategies are highlighted in this chapter, because they are the ones most closely associated with constructing meaning from print. These strategies are listed in Figure 10.1, and you might recognize many of them as things that you do naturally as you read.

All of these strategies assume that the reader can process print and decode unfamiliar words independently or with little help. (You learned strategies for decoding in Chapter 7.) Teaching these strategies to your students in a direct and straightforward manner will enable them to see what you mean by doing things such as predicting, inferencing, or visualizing, among others. Constructing meaning from text is a mental process; in order for students to understand it, they need to see it. Pressley states, "the 'read, read, read' approach does not lead to as active meaning construction during reading as occurs when students are taught explicitly to use and articulate comprehension strategies when they read" (2000, p. 554). Indeed, it is important for you to teach such reading processes in an explicit and direct manner to all of your students, but it is crucial for your struggling readers

- Before reading, establish a purpose for reading and make decisions about choosing text to read, for pleasure as well as for information.
- Before reading, make logical predictions about text, based on clues on the page, as well as on knowledge of story structure or text structure of nonfiction, and knowledge of the topic chosen by the author. While reading, confirm predictions and make new ones.
- While reading, make inferences, using clues from the author as well as from background knowledge.
- While reading fiction or nonfiction, visualize text with mental pictures.
- While reading for pleasure as well as for information, use self-regulation skills to monitor comprehension and apply appropriate strategies when it breaks down.
- When reading for information, use self-questions to enable construction of meaning.
- After reading fiction, identify all the story elements in a retelling.
- After reading fiction, briefly summarize the story, using as few details as possible.
- After reading nonfiction, identify the author's main ideas in a summary.

Figure 10.1 **Nine essential strategies for constructing meaning from print.**

(Allington & Cunningham, 2002; Harvey & Goudvis, 2000). Cambourne, reporting on his work with teachers who identified themselves as constructivist, says:

> By making explicit the invisible, often taken-for-granted processes and knowledge that effective literacy behavior requires, teachers helped learners in at least two ways. First, for students who did not come from homes that provided repeated opportunities to discover these processes, teachers provided repeated demonstrations of the skills, understandings, and know-how that students might not otherwise get the opportunity to understand. Second, the teachers provided opportunities for students who had a confused understanding of how reading and writing work to clarify their confusion. (2002, p. 34)

Remember Chapter 2, which described explicit instruction as part of a model of instruction? You learned that explicit instruction includes two valuable teaching strategies: explaining and mental modeling. In this chapter, you will learn how to put both of those teaching techniques to use as you show students how to comprehend.

Now let's examine each of these reading strategies separately, and then an example of classroom teaching for each. In most of these classroom scenarios, the teacher uses explanations as well as mental modeling. So that you can become familiar with the technique of mental modeling, the words the teacher speaks while modeling are in boldface print.

Choosing Text

One of the best ways to encourage positive independence in reading is to ask children to pick their own reading selections. The power of choice in motivating children to read is one of the most consistent findings in surveys of elementary grade children (Gambrell, 1998). Mathewson (2004) offers a model of reading that includes the influences of attitude and motivation. According to Mathewson, teachers who consider the importance of their students' attitudes toward reading and their motivation to read would do these things in their classrooms:

1. Learn about their students through "conversations, interviews, observations, compositions, free book selections, and other approaches," so that they can foster positive attitudes toward reading.
2. Provide "well-stocked library shelves, magazine storage boxes, reading tables, comfortable chairs, card catalogs, and book-news bulletin boards" so that "favorable reading intentions" are supported.
3. Encourage students to read materials that satisfy them. Thus, "using free book selection as opposed to fixed assignments allows students to guide their own reading progress and encourages formation of positive attitudes toward reading."
4. Encourage students to read large amounts of satisfying text. Planning for "frequent reading sessions during the school day and encouraging students to read at home are important strategies" to forming desirable reading habits and breaking down children's oppositions to reading.
5. Give students much opportunity to read at their independent levels at a relaxed pace, rather than forcing them to "slog through difficult text" on a regular basis (2004, pp. 1,455–1,456).

All of these teaching strategies require that children select their own text to read on a regular basis. This text should be personally satisfying, relate to the students' interests, be readily available in the classroom, and be appropriately easy enough for the students to read independently at a relaxed pace. Choosing such text requires some thought on the part of the reader (Brown, Palincsar & Armbruster, 2004) and reflects the reader's purpose for reading (Rosenblatt, 1978). It is an acquired skill; it needs to be shown to inexperienced readers.

Choosing Text to Read for Enjoyment

To help your students gain independence in choosing a book to read, you can teach them how to examine the book and think about what its title, pictures, and end pages tell them. They can also make decisions about the difficulty of the vocabulary in the book. Now, read about how Mrs. Nickles, a second grade teacher, models choosing a book, because she wants her students to become more strategic about their independent reading. In order to make her modeling authentic, she decides to show them this process with a children's book that she has not yet read, *The Upside Down Boy* (Herrera, 2000). As you read, notice the mental modeling that she does in the first part of the lesson, which is shown in boldface print. She thinks out loud as she models the things she does when she selects an unfamiliar book to read. After she models, she shows the students a list of these behaviors, which serves as an explanation of the process of choosing a book. Finally, students are given the opportunity to add their own ideas to this list.

Mrs. Nickles' Lesson

Mrs. Nickles asks her second graders to sit on the floor near her. She shows them the book *The Upside Down Boy* (Herrera, 2000).

She says, "I went to the library to pick out some books yesterday. I wanted to find a few that I have never read, perhaps to add to our classroom library. You know how I love to collect books! I was looking for some good ones, and I wanted some that I would like to read just for fun. I found this one, called *The Upside Down Boy*. I've never read it before and I'm thinking about reading it. I'd like to show you how I pick out books when I'm at the library or bookstore, and share with you the things I think about."

Mrs. Nickles points her finger to her forehead, indicating that she was thinking out loud, and continues: "I'm trying to decide if I want to read this book. OK, so my first thought is about the title, *The Upside Down Boy*. That's an interesting title! I wonder why the author picked that one. Hmm, let me look for the author's name. Sometimes that helps, because I might know about the author from other books that I've read. I see the author's name, Juan Felipe Herrera, but I don't recognize the name. I don't think I've ever read a book by Mr. Herrera before. But another way to think about this is to look at the pictures on the cover. That might help. I see a boy flying in the air, above a city. He's sort of upside down. Well, that's interesting. This picture makes me wonder about this book. What could it be about—a story with a title and cover picture like that? So I need to look for more clues.

I'll look at the flaps of the book cover, because this is a good place for information about the story. The words there tell me that the story is about a boy named Juanito. His family is a migrant family from Mexico, and they decide to stop moving around from place to place. They're going to settle down so Juanito can go to school for the first time. Wow, this is interesting. I'm curious about the story now. The cover flap also says this about Juanito: 'Everything he does feels upside down.' So there's the reason for the title.

Now I'm just going to take a look at the first page. I want to be sure that the words aren't too difficult for me, so if I see any words that give me trouble, I will count them, starting with my pinky finger. Every time I see a hard word, I will put down a finger. If my thumb and pointer finger are still up when I finish the page, this book will probably be OK for me. Hmmm, let me see. . . . Well, when I read over the first page, I don't see any words that give me trouble. And this first page has already got me interested. The first sentence is always a good way for me to tell if I'll like the book. Listen to it: 'Mama, who loves words, sings out the name on the street sign—Juniper. Who-nee-purr! Who-nee-purr!' What a great beginning! The boy's mother is pronouncing the street sign in Spanish. I'm already interested in knowing about this family from Mexico. I think I'll keep this one. I want to know what happens to Juanito in his new home."

Once her mental model is complete, Mrs. Nickles pauses and says, "As you listened to me think out loud about choosing a book, you may have noticed there were several things that I did to help me decide whether I wanted to read *The Up-side Down Boy.* I'd like to make a list of those things, so that we'll have some ideas to use when we want to choose books. What were some of the things I did?"

Several students volunteer answers as Mrs. Nickles writes. Then she says, "Now, I'd like for you to close your eyes and think about going to the library. Think about what you do when you want to pick out a book to read for enjoyment. What helps you decide?"

The students give suggestions, which Mrs. Nickles writes. When they are finished, her list looks like this:

Things That Help You Choose a Book

- Title

- Author's name

- Pictures on the cover

- Pictures on the title page

- The end flaps of the book jacket

- Words on the first page (Count the hard ones! Fewer than five hard words means it's OK!)

- The table of contents

- If it's part of a series

- The subject of the book

- The type of book it is

- If your friends say it's a good one

- The reason you want the book (Is it for fun? Is it for information?)

- If the teacher has read it aloud in class

She explains, "As you can see, when you pick up a new book to read, you can decide whether you really want to spend time with it by doing a few simple things. We'll go to the library this morning, and everyone may check out a book. I'll take this chart with us to remind us of these things we can do to choose a book. If you think of any new ways to choose a book, we'll add them to the chart when we return to the classroom."

To accomplish the objective of showing students how to choose books to read for pleasure, as Mrs. Nickles does, you can plan lessons using the following guidelines:

1. Select a fiction book with which to model the strategy. This should be a book that is not already in your classroom library, and that is somewhat unfamiliar to your students. Some teachers model this using a novel for adults.
2. Tell the students your purpose for choosing the book.
3. Use the mental model to show the features of the book that you examine to help make your decision. Features should include the title, author, difficulty of vocabulary, pictures, recommendation from friends, and reviews or introductions on the book cover or flaps.
4. After modeling, ask students to help make a list of the features that you used in the model. Create a chart. Duplicate the chart in bookmark form, if you wish.
5. Take students to the library and give them the opportunity to practice using the list of features. Ask them to think of additional things to add to the chart.

Choosing Text to Read for Information

Textbooks are no longer the main source of information for your students. A whole world of information awaits them on the Internet. The volume of information that your students can access on any subject imaginable is mind-boggling—and it expands daily. However, a whole world of misinformation is also available there. Anyone with a little bit of time can produce a web site. Thus, it is essential that your students develop critical reading skills so that they can make decisions about the credibility and usefulness of web sites and other technological resources (Alvermann, Moon & Hagood, 1999; Leu, 2002). Indeed, as your students use the huge amount of resources available to them, they need an array of skills that are different from the skills needed to gain information from textbooks and other printed resources. These ever-evolving "new literacies" enable them to access, gather, categorize, critically evaluate, and share information from resources that bring the entire world to their fingertips (Leu, 2002, pp. 313–314).

This teacher shows his students how to critically select information from Internet resources

Additionally, reading hypertext is a process quite different from reading traditional printed material. Often, hyperlinks to other, related web sites are spaced throughout the web page, offering the reader a chance to jump to another page that contains more information on the same topic. While this availability of information is exciting, it can also be distracting to young readers, who "may find that without the linear format they find in traditional print, they are unable to follow the author's message and make sense of what they are reading" (Carroll, 2004). In order for students to choose web sites wisely, they need to know what the site has to offer. Careful reading of an array of formats is necessary.

Plan your lessons for showing students how to choose information on the Internet with the following procedures:

1. With the students, brainstorm ways that "surfing the net" is difficult when looking for specific information.
2. At the computer screen, model and explain as you search for information for a specific topic.
3. Be sure to emphasize the importance of using a child-friendly search engine such as Yahooligans.
4. Show the students how to narrow choices, focus on only the most pertinent information, and ignore links that do not look as if they will be of immediate help. Explain, as you move through the sites, why you have chosen to ignore some links and click on others.
5. Bookmark links or sites that may be useful later.
6. Afterwards, ask students to help make a list of the procedures you used. Create a chart.
7. From the chart, make a checklist that can be used during each search.
8. Give students a chance to practice. Ask everyone to begin a search for information they will need to complete a project, report, or assignment.

Making Predictions

K-8

Predictions are part of the "psycholinguistic guessing game" of reading, as explained by Goodman (1967), who says of his work with children, "I saw readers tentatively and selectively using graphophonic, syntactic, and semantic cues as they predicted and inferred (guessed) where the text was going" (1994, p. 1,098). At the word and sentence level, readers reduce their uncertainty about unknown words or meanings by making informed guesses about print, based on these clues on the page. When encountering larger pieces of text, such as a page or paragraph, the reader is also making these informed guesses about what comes next, based on what he or she already knows and, especially if the text is a predictable one, on what has occurred in previous pages (Anderson, 2004; Dewitz, Carr & Patberg, 1987; Duke & Pearson, 2002).

Making Predictions with Stories

You can show students how to predict while reading stories by making it a visible, tangible process. Modeling this process is important; you can do this by talking about your predictions as you read stories to your students. You can use a variety of teaching strategies that encourage predictions, such as the book box, picture book previews, or predictive story mapping. These and other such strategies are described in Chapter 11. While using these, think out loud. Identify the clues that lead you to your predictions: title, author, pictures, words, and your background experiences.

Mrs. Rodgers, a third grade teacher, uses the story *The Sweetest Fig* (Van Allsburg, 1993) to model predictions with fiction text, using clues from the pictures and the title of the book. First, she models by thinking aloud. She shows her students how her experiences, the pictures, and the title of the book help her think about possible characters and events in the story. Then, she clarifies the strategy of predicting by explaining it and outlining a set of steps that readers can follow as they read. Look for her model in the boldface print.

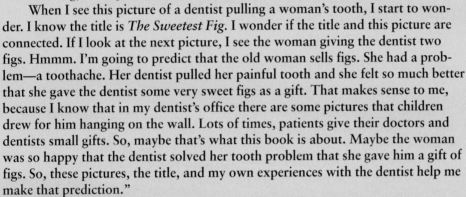

Mrs. Rodgers' Lesson

Mrs. Rodgers begins by saying, "Class, I'd like for you to hear what is going on inside my head as I make predictions about this book. [*The Sweetest Fig*, Van Allsburg, 1992.]

When I see this picture of a dentist pulling a woman's tooth, I start to wonder. I know the title is *The Sweetest Fig*. I wonder if the title and this picture are connected. If I look at the next picture, I see the woman giving the dentist two figs. Hmmm. I'm going to predict that the old woman sells figs. She had a problem—a toothache. Her dentist pulled her painful tooth and she felt so much better that she gave the dentist some very sweet figs as a gift. That makes sense to me, because I know that in my dentist's office there are some pictures that children drew for him hanging on the wall. Lots of times, patients give their doctors and dentists small gifts. So, maybe that's what this book is about. Maybe the woman was so happy that the dentist solved her tooth problem that she gave him a gift of figs. So, these pictures, the title, and my own experiences with the dentist help me make that prediction."

When she finishes modeling, Mrs. Rodgers explains, "When you read, you need to always be thinking about what comes next. When you start a book, make predictions about the whole book. And as you're reading, keep thinking about what will happen next. You can get clues about predictions from several places. Let's think about the clues I used, and write them on this chart paper. What clues helped me?"

"Pictures!" says Joey.

"That's right, Joey. I'll write that down. And what else? Keina?"

"You thought about your dentist's office," says Keina.

"Exactly. I used the pictures and my own ideas to help make a prediction. Let's put that on the list. There's one more thing. What is it?"

Keina says, "The title helped, too."

"It certainly did. I'll add that. Now, when you make predictions, think about these clues. Then, think about how stories go. You need to figure out the characters and what happens to them. To do that, ask yourself some questions like the ones on this strategy chart. Those answers will be your predictions."

Mrs. Rodgers shows them the chart, which looks like this:

Things That Help Make Predictions in Stories

- Cover of the book
- Title
- Author
- Pictures
- Things you already know

Questions to ask:
- What will the characters be like?
- Where will they be?
- When will the story take place?
- What will the problem in the story be?
- What will happen next?
- How will the story end?

Mrs. Rodgers continues, "We are always predicting. The weatherman gives us weather predictions. We make guesses when we play games. We try to figure out what might happen next in a movie or T.V. show. And, when reading, we make guesses about what comes next on the page. Good readers do this all the time. We'll read *The Sweetest Fig* together. When I stop throughout the story, we'll talk about your predictions."

The steps to follow for a lesson plan similar to Mrs. Rodgers' lesson on how to predict with fiction are:

1. Select a piece of fiction that is unfamiliar to your students and that invites thoughtful guessing and reflection. A book that has interesting twists and turns of plot, and perhaps a surprise ending, would be ideal.
2. Use the mental model to show students your thoughts as you make one prediction. Begin reading aloud, and stop at a point in the story that invites a prediction. Tell your prediction, and tell why you made it.
3. During the model, show students at least one or two of the clues that are helpful for making predictions: title, author, pictures, words on the page, and personal experiences. You do not have to use all the clues at once.
4. After modeling, have students help make a list of clues used in your model.
5. Create a chart. You can duplicate it in bookmark form, if you wish.
6. Finish reading the book. Stop at appropriate stop points to make additional predictions with the students. Use the chart as a guide for clues to use.
7. Keep the chart handy, and as students read more books, add other ideas for clues that help make predictions.

Making Predictions with Nonfiction

One of the strongest conclusions drawn from research on reading comprehension is that "students' comprehension, particularly inferential comprehension, is improved when relationships are drawn between students' background knowledge and experiences and the content included in reading selections. This may involve invoking appropriate knowledge structures before reading, [and] making and verifying predictions before and during reading" (Pearson & Fielding, 1991, p. 847). Vacca states, "For comprehension to occur, the reader must activate or build a schema that fits with information encountered in a text. When a good match occurs, a schema allows the reader to organize text information more efficiently, make inferences and fill in knowledge gaps in a text" (2002, p. 191). Readers learn how to do this by being taught explicitly and directly; such use of available clues does not happen by merely expecting students to read a lot (Duffy, 2002; Pressley, 2000).

Using graphic organizers before reading helps students make predictions that follow text structure. When you give your students a pictorial representation of the structure of the text, they have a better idea of what to expect as they read. According to Goldman and Rakestraw, "readers' abilities to use the cues present in the surface text depend on having prior knowledge of the structures of text and how to use them in the understanding process. Structural cues in the text cannot be effective if readers lack the prior knowledge needed to recognize and interpret these cues" (2000, p. 313). Thus, much practice with graphic organizers that are designed to reflect the structure of the text becomes necessary.

Chapter 5 describes five different types of text structure that are evident in most nonfiction children's books, and lists several of these books. Using a book that clearly shows the structure, introduce your students to the idea of text structure by using a graphic organizer as you make predictions. (The Toolkit for *Teachers* (Nettles, 2006) includes examples of organizers that can be used to analyze text structure.) When you make predictions, be explicit about the kinds of information the author is offering. Let your predictions follow the structure of text.

For example, Villaume and Brabham (2001) describe a lesson in which a teacher and her second grade students discussed predictions about a book on dinosaurs. In the book, two types of dinosaurs were depicted on one page. After some initial predictions were made based on the pictures, the teacher showed them a blank graphic organizer that looks like a Venn diagram. Immediately, they began to name similarities and differences in the types of dinosaurs depicted. Because of their familiarity with the graphic organizer, they were reminded of the kind of information available to them and were able to make predictions based on the structure of the text. In fact, at one point in the lesson, when students were unsure of what to add, all the teacher had to do was point to the blank organizer, which refreshed their memories of the type of information the author of the book was giving them.

Let's look at an example. Using *Weather*, an informational book by Seymour Simon (1993), Mrs. Thomas shows her fourth grade students how to make predictions. Notice that she uses clues from the print, her background knowledge about the topic, her background knowledge about the structure of text, and a graphic organizer that helps put it all together. She also clarifies the process of predicting by listing the clues that her students can use, which is part of her explanation. You'll see the mental model in boldface print.

Mrs. Thomas' Lesson

Mrs. Thomas says to the class, "I'm reading the book *Weather*, by Seymour Simon. I know that making predictions helps me understand what I'm reading in information books, so I will do that while reading *Weather*. Let me tell you what I'm thinking as I make predictions."

Mrs. Thomas points her finger to her forehead, indicating that she is thinking out loud, and continues: "I'm on the second page of print, which shows a big picture of the sun. This large picture makes me think that the sun is important to weather.

"Now I need to look over the page and get some clues from the words. I see three paragraphs. I can tell they are paragraphs because of their indentations. OK, I've learned from experience that the best way to quickly get some ideas about the page without reading the whole page is to read the first sentence of each paragraph. So, watch my fingers as I find these sentences.

"Here's the first one: 'Earth's weather is driven by the intense heat of the sun.' So the sun is important, and in fact, it says the weather is 'driven' by the sun. Well, I know the sun is not driving a car! I've heard the word 'driven' used this way, though. I've heard people say things like, 'He was driven by his desire to get good grades.' That means he wanted to get good grades, so he did a lot of things to make that happen. Here, the word 'driven' makes me think that the sun makes lots of things happen in our atmosphere. So, I predict that the author will tell about events in weather that the sun causes. And if I look at our graphic organizer for this page, it looks like a cause/effect organizer. So that's good. I'll keep going.

"Here's the first sentence of the second paragraph: 'The atmosphere lets sunlight pass through.' Hmm. Sunlight again! It's a very important topic on this page. OK, so the sunlight goes through the atmosphere. Then what? I'm guessing that the sun makes the atmosphere warm up.

"Now, for the third paragraph: 'Insolation and the greenhouse effect strike a balance and make our planet livable.' OK, this is just a little bit tricky. I'm not sure of what the word 'insolation' means. I'll have to find out about that. I can predict a little bit about 'greenhouse effect,' though. I go to the farmer's market near my house and buy plants in the greenhouse. There, the roof is made of glass, so the sun shines into the house and keeps it warm inside for the plants. Even on cold days, it's nice and warm inside the greenhouse. So, I'm predicting that 'greenhouse effect' has something to do with the sun's warmth being kept in the earth's atmosphere. That way, we stay warm. Maybe that's what Mr. Simon means by 'insolation,' too. I wonder how the sun's heat stays in, though. There's no roof up there in the sky! I'll need to read to find out. I'm going to look for a definition of this word in the text."

Mrs. Thomas continues, "OK, so those are my thoughts. I've made a prediction that the sun's rays warm us because they are somehow trapped in the earth's atmosphere. I'll write that on a graphic organizer so we can remember it and look for this information as we read. As you can see, this graphic organizer shows that the heat of the sun causes things to happen. This is the kind of information I think I'll find out as I read more of Mr. Simon's book. I'd like for you to make a prediction, too, and we'll write your ideas on this organizer. As we read, we can check to see if our predictions can be confirmed."

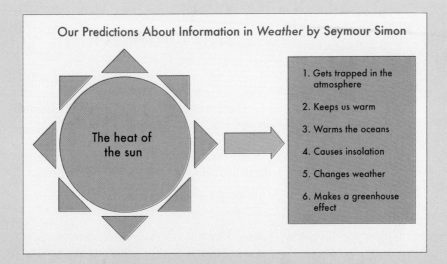

Our Predictions About Information in *Weather* by Seymour Simon

The heat of the sun

1. Gets trapped in the atmosphere

2. Keeps us warm

3. Warms the oceans

4. Causes insolation

5. Changes weather

6. Makes a greenhouse effect

"Predicting," explains Mrs. Thomas, "means making guesses about what you'll find out when you read. But you can't just make any old guess, especially if you're trying to get some information from the book. You need to use the author's clues to help you make predictions," she said. "That way, you can be surer that your predictions will make sense."

Mrs. Thomas pulls out the chart paper and says, "All right, let's make a chart that helps us remember things as we read and predict. I've listed one clue that we can use to make predictions—the title. Let's list some more. Think about the clues I used. Share ideas with your partner and then with the rest of the class. We'll list all the clues on this chart. And as we read more, we'll add to this list."

Making Predictions About Information Books: Clues for Making Predictions

- Title of the book
- Author's name
- Pictures
- Maps, charts, or photographs
- Headings and titles of sections
- First sentence of each paragraph on the page
- Kinds of words the author uses
- Vocabulary definitions
- The way the graphic organizer looks

Mrs. Thomas finishes by saying, "OK, we'll read to find out about my prediction. Then, let's make another prediction about information on the next page. You can use the chart to help you remember the clues."

Diversity in the Reading Classroom

Alleviating Language Roadblocks

Explicit instruction in reading processes is necessary for students of diverse backgrounds. For students who are learning English, it is crucial. In order to make sure that we are clearly understood by ELL students, teachers need to alleviate language roadblocks. Part of the problem that ELL students have is that their use and command of academic language lags behind their command of conversational language by about 5 to 10 years (Cummins, 1994). There are many reasons, but the nature of English is one of them. Corson (1995) explains why. About 60 percent of English words used in written text come from Greek and Latin sources, and these words have multiple syllables and low frequency. Most of conversational language comes from Anglo-Saxon lexicon, with vocabulary that is low in syllables and of high frequency. Thus, students who are learning English may grasp conversational English, while taking years to develop proficiency with written, academic language.

However, there is plenty of good news. With a projection of a 47 percent increase in the number of Spanish-speaking students in U.S. schools by 2020, it makes sense to look at the strengths that they bring to the classroom (Williams, 2001). Students who speak Spanish do have some advantages over other ELL students, because Spanish is also a language rooted in Latin. The connection between Spanish and English becomes clear in cognates, which are words that are similarly spelled in both languages. Many cognates that are academic words in English are actually everyday words in Spanish, making them relatively easy to learn. Thus, using cognates during instructional conversation and in content lessons will scaffold learning and help alleviate language roadblocks for students whose language background is Spanish.

Additional ways to alleviate language roadblocks suggested by Williams (2001) include the following:

- Create a cognate word wall and incorporate the words into all lessons.

- Avoid idioms or synonyms during instructional talk. Keep your vocabulary clear, but avoid the mistake of simply speaking louder.

- Use wait time (Rowe, 1974), which is a pause of at least three seconds after asking questions and seeking a response. The effect is a slowing down of the classroom conversation, allowing everyone time to think and reflect.

- Read aloud daily, to offer exposure to rich vocabulary in meaningful context.

- Encourage classroom conversation that is similar to family dinner-time discussion.

- Make sure you understand what students have to say. Give them opportunities to repeat, and ask questions like, "What do you mean?" or "Please tell me more." Check frequently for the students' understandings, as well.

- Respond to all comments, even if they are incorrect or seem odd.

The procedure that Mrs. Thomas uses for making predictions with nonfiction follows these guidelines:

1. Choose an unfamiliar nonfiction book to use in the lesson. Make sure that it has sufficient clues for making predictions.
2. Use the mental model to show students how to make predictions with nonfiction.

3. Explain that the clues for making predictions are a bit different when using nonfiction, because of the structure of the text. Use pictures, charts, photographs, headings and subheadings, prior experiences, first sentence of each paragraph, highlighted vocabulary, and information in the margin of the page, as well as the title, author, and information on the cover of the book.
4. Show students an appropriate graphic organizer that reflects the text structure of the book. As you make predictions, fill in the organizer.
5. Afterwards, ask students to help you list the clues that can be used to make predictions.
6. Create a chart.
7. Finish reading the book, making additional predictions at stop points. Add to the list of clues as needed.

Making Inferences

Inferring is the process of gleaning meaning from text in which the author does not reveal all of the information in an explicit manner. Readers must use the words on the page, pictures (if they are available), and their own background knowledge to decipher the author's implications. Appropriate inferences are more likely to occur if the reader is able to connect what he or she already knows with the printed text (Anderson, 2004; Anderson & Pearson, 1984; Hansen, 1981; Richards & Gipe, 1992). Making inferences while reading means that readers are not merely making a translation between print and spoken word; rather, there is a transaction between the reader and the author in order to make meaning (Kintsch, 2004). Harvey and Goudvis explain, "Writers don't spill their thoughts into the page, they leak them slowly, one idea at a time, until the reader can make an educated guess or an appropriate inference about an underlying theme in the text or a prediction about what is to come" (2000, p. 23).

Inferential thinking is difficult to accomplish, because it is equivalent to "reading between the lines," or going deeper than what is explicitly stated. It means that students are processing print beyond the level of mere words, and drawing conclusions as they read. Harvey and Goudvis (2000, p. 35) suggest the use of "anchor experiences" for teaching inferential thinking. The teacher presents an unusual object, such as an apple corer, and asks the students what it is used for. Because the object is specialized and unusual, students will most likely not know its purpose. After a few guesses, the teacher shows the students an apple, which the students link with the corer and make the guess that it peels apples. Likewise, when reading, the reader must try to figure out print that is not explicit. Readers can make better guesses when they have more information, just as the apple helps them figure out the purpose of the corer. The anchor experience helps them remember what they must do to draw a conclusion from text: look for more information.

Explaining to students how to do this with some tips is helpful, especially if you combine this procedure with mental modeling. In the following lesson example, Mr. Wood shows his third grade students how to make an inference, using the book *Double Fudge* (Blume, 2002). He first models this reading process by thinking out loud at a stop point in the story. These thoughts are displayed in boldface print. Then he offers an explanation and asks his students to help him make a chart of ideas to use, making this reading process a strategic one for his students.

Mr. Wood's Lesson

Mr. Wood and his students are reading *Double Fudge* together by sharing the page. While his students read silently from copies of the book at their desks, Mr. Wood reads aloud. Occasionally, he stops at points in the story and talks with the students about the latest episode. In Chapter 8, the students enjoy a scene in which the main character, Peter Hatcher, is with his family in the gift shop at the United States Bureau of Printing and Engraving in Washington, D.C. Peter's five-year-old brother, Fudge, has had an interest in money lately, so the Hatchers take a trip there to satisfy his curiosity. While standing in the gift shop, Peter's father bumps into someone who offers quite a surprise. Mr. Wood reads this portion aloud:

> For a minute Dad looked blank. Then he did a double-take. "No," he said. "It can't be. Are you telling me you're Cousin Howie Hatcher?"
> "None other. And you're Cousin Tubby, aren't you?"
> "Cousin *Tubby?*" Fudge said.
> I was thinking exactly the same thing but I don't always say what I'm thinking, the way Fudge does.
> "I'm known as Warren now," Dad told Cousin Howie. (Blume, 2002, p. 77)

Mr. Wood says, "Now, let's stop and think a moment about what's happened here. I need someone to tell us what has happened so far. Felicia?"

Felicia says, "Peter's dad sees a man in the gift shop that's his cousin."

"And what does his cousin call him?"

"Cousin Tubby."

"That's right. Now, if we think carefully about what the author is telling us, and look carefully at the print, we can get a clue about what Fudge means. Let me tell you what I was thinking as I read this."

To use his mental model, Mr. Wood puts his finger to his head and says, "When I read this, I was a little bit confused when I got to the line in which Peter said that he doesn't always say what he's thinking, the way Fudge does. The author seems to be leaving some information out. So, I knew that I would have to search for clues. That's when I noticed something interesting about the print. I saw that the writing is different on the word 'Tubby.' If you look at the word, you see that it looks a little bit like cursive writing. That kind of print is called 'italic.' I've seen this before, and I know that it means that the author wants me to say that word with some real expression. So, while I was reading it out loud to you, I thought about how Fudge might react to hearing his dad called 'Tubby.' He probably never heard that before. So, I made my voice sound surprised. On the name 'Tubby,' I said, '*Tubby?*' That way, you knew as you were listening that Fudge was surprised to hear this strange nickname for his dad. And I got a big clue a couple of sentences later, when his dad said, 'I'm known as Warren now.' So, the word 'now' is telling me that Peter and Fudge's dad, Warren Hatcher, used to have a nickname, but he doesn't anymore. And this was all very surprising to Peter and Fudge."

After thinking out loud, Mr. Wood explains, "So, when we use clues from the print, like the italic, plus words that the author says, like the word 'now,' we can put that information together to figure out some of the author's hidden meanings. That's called making an *inference*. The author doesn't need to tell us everything. She can just make little hints and we can guess. That makes the story more interesting. What information can we use to make good guesses? Let's list things that will help."

Mr. Wood and the students make a list, which looks like this:

Things That Help with Inferences

- Word clues
- Picture clues
- The way the print looks
- Punctuation
- Your own ideas

Put these together to guess what the author is telling you.

Keep reading to check your inference.

He continues, "We'll keep reading. I'll stop you at another point in the story and you can practice making an inference using the ideas on this chart. When you do this, remember some of the things I told you that I was thinking about."

Mr. Wood uses mental modeling and explaining to show students an inference he made in this story. You can plan a lesson similar to his by using these guidelines:

1. Choose a story that contains at least two events that require inferential thinking. This setup means that the author allows the reader to draw conclusions based on implications and hints.
2. Read aloud, stopping at a stop point in the story that requires an inference.
3. Model by thinking out loud the conclusions that you draw from the information given by the author.
4. As you model, point out the clues that lead to your inference, such as pictures, words, typographical clues in the print, or background experiences.
5. Ask students to help name these clues and make a chart.
6. Continue reading and stop at the next place in the story that requires an inference. Ask students to help decide which conclusion can be drawn from available information at this point. Refer to the chart for help as needed.

Using Visual Imagery

Reading evokes images; good authors can make the reader "see" what is being represented by the words on the page (Gambrell & Bales, 1986; Gambrell & Koskinen, 2002; Pressley, 2000). This is **visual imagery.** (Other terms for the same idea are *visualizing, mental imagery,* and *imagery.*) Making mental pictures while reading "appears to occur naturally" when both children and adults read various types of text (Sadoksi & Paivio, 1994, p. 591). When teachers instruct their students to form mental pictures, even the youngest children seem to know what to do. Asking students to make pictures in their minds to help them remember important things is helpful for two reasons: (1) It is easy to do and children seem to be able to do it quickly and readily; and (2) It is a stronger technique for remembering facts than merely asking them to think about what they've read (Gambrell & Koskinen, 2002; Sadoski & Paivio, 2004).

Visualizing makes reading personal, because every reader's mental image will be different. Visual imagery is dependent upon the reader's background experiences. Even though the author's words give the reader an idea of what the characters, setting, and events look like, readers still picture different things. Proof of that is at the movie theater. Have you ever been to a movie that was produced from a book that you had already read? How different was the movie image from the mental image that you produced? Most of the time, readers find that the movie is quite different—and many times, not as satisfying.

Visualizing Fiction

You can help readers understand that this is part of the reading process and make your visual imagery "real" by talking out loud as you describe what you see in your mind's eye. To model this process, it is best to read aloud or use shared reading, and use stop points where the text is particularly descriptive. At the first few stop points, model your own mental images for the students by simply telling them what you see and identifying the clues that lead you to that image. Use phrases like these:

> "If I were the illustrator, I would draw . . ."
>
> "The mind movie that is going on in my head right now shows . . ."
>
> "I can see this, even when I close my eyes. In my mind picture, I see . . ."

Now, take a look at an example of a lesson taught by second grade teacher Mrs. Charles, who reads *Cloudy with a Chance of Meatballs* (Barrett, 1978) with her students. First, she models by thinking aloud, and you will see her mental model in the boldface print. After that, she explains the process of visualizing.

Mrs. Charles' Lesson

Mrs. Charles begins by saying, "When we read this book, you'll be able to tell that the author, Judy Barrett, used words that tell us about this place called Chewandswallow. When we read her descriptions, we can get pictures in our heads about this place. The illustrator, Ron Barrett, drew pictures that make the book even funnier. But before I show you the pictures, let's read some of the words. I want to tell you about the 'mind movie' that I see in my mind when I read this. Then we'll look at the pictures.

"On the eighth page, the author describes how Chewandswallow is different from any other town. She tells us that the weather provides the food that the townspeople eat every day. I've got these words displayed on the projection screen so you can see them. Please read them silently now."

The students read, and then Mrs. Charles says, "Oressa, can you read those sentences aloud for us, please?"

Oressa reads the words, which tell of rain made of soup and juice; snow made of mashed potatoes and green peas; and stormy winds that blow in hamburgers.

Pointing her finger to her head to show that she is thinking aloud, Mrs. Charles says, **"Now, before I show you the pictures, let me tell you about the picture that I get in my head when I read this. Wow. This is quite a mind movie that I have! I'm thinking about what the sky must look like. If I needed to draw the picture for this page, I would draw the sky, and make raindrops coming down. But I can see these raindrops in my mind. They would have to be in colors. I'm imagining that it's raining tomato soup, so my raindrops are red. And the snow would be white mashed potatoes, but the snowflakes would be big and clumpy. Some of the snowflakes would be little green balls, like peas. And instead of white, fluffy clouds, I see bunches of hamburgers floating in the air. Some of them are even cheeseburgers! They look delicious, especially since it's lunchtime, but it's a strange sight! Now, I'm going to keep this picture in my head, because it might help me understand the story."**

After this mental model, Mrs. Charles explains by saying, "One of the best ways to help yourself understand something that you read is to picture it, or visualize it. Visualizing is when you make a mental picture of the author's words. That's what I was doing. I read the words and I could actually see, in my head, the place that the author was describing. When I got to the end of the page, I asked myself, 'What picture would I draw for this?' To visualize while you read, you can remember a few things. They are listed on this chart. Take a look."

How to Visualize Stories

Look for the author's descriptions:

- Characters: How do they look?

- Setting: What does it look like?

- Things that happen: How do the characters look when they do things?

Mrs. Charles continues, "This chart will help you remember what to do when you visualize. Now I'd like for you to practice. I'm going to read the entire story of *Cloudy with a Chance of Meatballs* to you. I think you're really going to like this book! But I'm not going to show you the pictures at first. We'll stop on some of the pages of the book and talk about the mind movies that we can make as we read the author's words."

The students listen as Mrs. Charles reads, and they share their visualizations with their partners. Afterwards, Mrs. Charles passes around a hat that contains several small slips of paper, upon each of which she has typed a quote from the story. Each student chooses one quote from the hat, reads it, and draws the picture that he or she visualizes. Finally, Mrs. Charles reads the story to them again, showing them the pictures. Her students are fascinated with Barrett's illustrations and compare them to their mental visualizations.

Teach your students about visualizing by making plans for similar lessons. The steps you will need to take are:

1. Select a book that contains strong descriptions of characters, settings, or events. It can be a picture book or a chapter book. Find passages or sentences throughout the book that are written in vivid, clear, descriptive vocabulary, and that create distinct pictures in your mind. Mark these places in the book.
2. Begin reading the book or chapter aloud, and stop at the first marked passage. Read this portion without showing the pictures.
3. Tell students the visual image that is created in your mind by thinking out loud. Identify the features of the story that you look for as you make this mental picture, such as the author's description of the character's physical appearance, descriptions of the setting, or stylistic devices. Be sure to explain how your own past experiences help create this image, too.
4. Show students a chart that outlines the things to look for when creating mental images.
5. Finish reading the book with the students.
6. After reading, give them (or let them choose) sentence strips on which you have written quotes from the story. These quotes should evoke strong imagery.
7. Ask students to illustrate the quotes, then share their illustrations with others.

Visualizing Nonfiction

Good readers form mental pictures of text, but this activity is difficult when reading about unfamiliar topics. The power in visual imagery is in the evocation of the reader's prior knowledge; thus, if a student knows little about the topic, it will be hard for that student to create mental images (Harvey & Goudvis, 2000). In that case, your students' mental images will be dependent upon the author's ability to depict the topic, with words that connect to things and experiences that are familiar (Tovani, 2000). Sometimes authors make it easy for us, such as in this sentence: "The heart of a blue whale is the size of a small car." Written by Seymour Simon in *Whales* (1989), this type of imagery comparison helps readers visualize and is more effective than writing something like, "The heart of a whale is about 14 feet long, 5 feet wide, and $4\frac{1}{2}$ feet high." But some expository text does get bogged down in facts, weights, measurements, and figures. Thus, it is important to show students how to make mental pictures of the text. A chart or bookmark with reminders, along with mental modeling, will help. A procedure for visualizing nonfiction is as follows:

1. Choose a passage from nonfiction text that lends itself to visual imagery.
2. Read the passage aloud.
3. Model by thinking aloud the mental imagery that you create when reading this passage. Tell about the clues that help you make mind pictures, such as descriptive words, specialized vocabulary, or your own experiences.
4. Make a sketch of the image as you talk.
5. Ask students to help make a list of clues that help create mental imagery.
6. Read the remainder of the selection, and stop at another point that evokes visualization.
7. Ask students to describe to each other what they see in their mind's eye, and sketch.

Metacognition and Self-Regulated Comprehension

Metacognition is "knowledge about thinking, and metacognition about reading is specifically knowledge about reading and how reading is accomplished" (Pressley, 2002, p. 304). Such knowledge about reading, when held by the student, allows the student to monitor himself or herself while reading, and control his or her own reading processes, strategies called "self-regulated comprehension" (Hacker, 2004, p. 757).

Many studies have found that immature and struggling readers are not aware that they must make sense out of what they read; they equate reading with the simple act of decoding words. They also are oblivious to their misunderstandings; when they read and make meaning-based errors, they do not realize that this type of error is detrimental to their comprehension of the text (Garner, 1994).

Good readers are able to monitor their meaning construction; they recognize when their comprehension has broken down. Durkin (1993) identifies three types of breakdowns: (1) failure to understand the meaning of a word, (2) failure to make sense of a whole piece of text, and (3) failure to recognize the preestablished purpose for reading this particular text. For each of these types of metacognitive awareness, Durkin also outlines three "fix-up strategies" (p. 297) that a good reader uses to reestablish comprehension: (1) Continue to read for additional clues about an unknown word; (2) Reread the text to clarify misconceptions; and (3) Adjust rate of reading to suit the purpose.

Hacker (2004) explains that self-regulated reading involves self-questioning, so that the reader continually checks his or her understanding to see if the ideas are supported by the text. However, self-regulation goes beyond this step, because self-questioning is limited to the reader's own interpretation of the text. Thus, teachers

Modifying Instruction for

ELL

Visualizing

GRADE LEVEL: 3–4 (ADAPTABLE FOR ALL GRADES)

- **Objective**

  Students will visualize, define, and illustrate geographical terms.

- **Preparation**
  - Find photographs of geographical terms that are in the text your students will read. (These photographs can be downloaded from many web sites. Just type the term in your favorite search engine.)
  - Prepare definitions for geographical terms. Make these definitions highly visual, using terms the students will understand and will be able to visualize.

- **Materials**
  - Geography or social studies textbook
  - Descriptions of geography terms
  - Index cards
  - Pictures of geography terms
  - Maps
  - Crayons or markers

- **Procedure**
  1. In a geography or social studies textbook, read descriptions of geographical terms.

  2. Describe these terms for the students so that they can visualize them. For example, the definition for *peninsula* is usually written as "a piece of land that has water almost all the way around it." Change this to something more visual: "I can see the peninsula. It looks like Florida. It is land that is connected to some other land at the top, and then it sticks out in the water. There is water all around the bottom part of the peninsula."

  3. Show photographs and maps to make the terms clear. For example, for "peninsula," show a photograph of a peninsula and then a map of Florida.

  4. Give students an index card. Ask each student to be responsible for one geographical term, and draw a picture of the term on an index card. Have students write the word and its equivalent in Spanish or other language.

  5. On the back side of the card, ask students to write the meaning of the term based on what they visualize. Check this against the description written in the textbook.

  Modifications for ELL are printed in color.

6. On word cards that show Spanish/English cognates, put a star or some other identification mark. Ask Spanish-speaking students to tell the class how to pronounce these words in Spanish, because not all cognates are pronounced exactly the same across languages. Point out these cognates to students, emphasizing the fact that there are many cognates in social studies, science, and other school subjects. Geographical terms have these cognates in Spanish and English:

   bay—la bahía

   city—la ciudad

   coast—la costa

   desert—el desierto

   island—la isla

   lake—el lago

   mountain—la montaña

   ocean—el océano

   peninsula—la peninsula

   river—el río

7. Reread the descriptions in the textbook aloud to the students. When terms are mentioned, ask students to hold up the corresponding picture card. Discuss these as needed.

● Adaptation

This lesson can be adapted to any subject area textbook. Any topic that is described in the text and can be reduced to pictures on cards may be used.

can encourage readers to check their understanding against other sources. Readers should compare what other authors have to say about the same topic. Additionally, they can talk with other readers for new perspectives on the topic. These strategies help the reader broaden his or her self-regulation of reading, and they prevent the reader from being tied to a single interpretation of the print.

Because of the nature of nonfiction text, self-regulation is also very important when reading for information. As you learned in Chapter 5, nonfiction is often more difficult than fiction for children to understand, because they lack background knowledge about unfamiliar topics, and because informational vocabulary is topic-specific. Moreover, young readers often read nonfiction in a passive manner, without stopping periodically to contemplate their understanding of the information being presented (Coté & Goldman, 2004; Dreher, 2002).

Thus, "readers must not only be aware of gaps and problems in their understanding, but must also bring to bear strategies to resolve the problems" (Coté & Goldman, 2004, p. 678). Comprehension monitoring alone is not sufficient. Selectively reinstating information, rereading, and hypothesis checking are the kinds of strategies that good readers do when they become aware of misunderstandings.

You will need to teach your readers how to develop these skills; they are not always developed naturally. There are many helpful strategies that facilitate self-regulation in Chapter 12. To see how to use explicit instruction to show students how to regulate their own reading, take a look at the next example lesson. In this example, Mrs. Cooper shows her second graders how to stop at a confusing part of the nonfiction book *Hungry, Hungry Sharks* (Cole, 1986a).

Mrs. Cooper's Lesson

Mrs. Cooper shows her students the book *Hungry, Hungry Sharks.* She said, "Sometimes, when I'm reading books for information, like this one, it's helpful to stop and think about what I've read so far. Sometimes I need to reread, and other times I need to make guesses and check them out. I'd like to show you how I do this, with two pages from this book that confused me a little bit. Let me read aloud these pages for you."

She reads pages 20 and 21, which describe blue sharks, often called the "wolves of the sea." These pages also explain how blue sharks, which stay together in packs, often follow ships in the ocean. Mrs. Cooper puts her finger to her forehead to indicate thinking aloud, and says:

"I've read these two pages and now I need to stop a think a minute. Things are a little confusing. What is the author trying to teach me? The pages are about blue sharks, but I see pictures of old ships on the page. To help clear up my confusion, I'll read this page again. It says that sharks are 'wolves of the sea,' and that they often swim after a ship for days. OK, so that's why there's a picture of old sailing ships on the page. These are ships from hundreds of years ago. Now, I wonder why the sharks followed those ships. I'll make a guess. I think it's because they were looking for food. Did they want to attack the sailors? I think they did. Let me read on and find out." Mrs. Cooper points to the next page.

The next page tells me that the sharks heard the noises from the ships. And, listen to this sentence: 'Then they stay to eat garbage that is thrown into the water.' Well, that makes sense. So, back in the days when sailors dumped all their garbage overboard, sharks followed their ships for days. They weren't swimming after the sailors, like I thought. Instead, they were going after the food! But I wonder if sharks still do this. Do crews still throw garbage overboard? Do sharks still follow modern-day ships? I think I need to look this up. Maybe I'll try to do a web search."

Mrs. Cooper continues by explaining, "When you read for information, sometimes the pages are a little harder to read than the stories that you're used to. You can help yourself by stopping any time things get confusing. You can also stop at every page, just to check yourself. When I get confused, I reread the confusing sentences, and then I make hypotheses about what the author is trying to tell me. If I need to, I think about places where I can get more information."

Mrs. Cooper's lesson shows her students self-regulation skills. It's important to show students that there are things a reader can do to solve misunderstandings while reading. Plan lessons for this, using the following procedure:

1. Select a passage from a book that can cause problems in comprehension. Read it aloud, and tell students that it is a confusing passage for you. Tell them that when reading becomes confusing, the reader needs to stop and apply strategies that will improve understanding.

2. Use the mental model to show students the ways to "fix up" miscomprehension: rereading, hypothesis-checking, looking for clues in pictures and words, identifying difficult vocabulary, slowing down the reading rate, and thinking about the author's purpose.

3. After modeling, ask students to help list the "fix-up" strategies to use when comprehension breaks down.

Self-Questioning While Reading Nonfiction

Smith says, "Reading is asking questions of printed text. And reading with comprehension becomes a matter of getting your questions answered" (1997, p. 99). The nature of reading involves the satisfaction of curiosity or the confirmation of hypotheses. Good readers are constantly asking questions and expecting answers as they read. When the reader generates his or her own questions while reading, that reader is processing the text meaningfully, as well as monitoring his or her own reading (Palinscar & Brown, 1984). Experimental research supports the strategy of teaching students to generate their own questions, either as a strategy on its own or as part of a combination of strategies, such as in Reciprocal Teaching (Lysynchuk, Pressley & Vye, 1990; National Reading Panel, 2000a; Palincsar & Brown, 1984; Rosenshine & Meister, 1994; Wagoner, 1983). (You can learn more about Reciprocal Teaching in Chapter 12 and Appendix B.)

Mental modeling is especially helpful for the strategy of self-questioning. So many times, students expect teachers to do all the questioning of them; they do not expect to do the asking! Students need to see that active comprehension depends upon interaction with the text, and active participation in trying to satisfy their curiosity as they read.

Read Mr. Knight's lesson. He shows his third grade students how to self-question with a page from their social studies text, *Living in Our World* (Boehm,

Good readers ask themselves questions and look for the answers as they read.

Hoone, McGowan, McKinney-Browning & Miramontes, 1997, p. 265). First, he explains the strategy, with the use of a strategy chart. Then, he models thinking out loud.

Mr. Knight's Lesson

Mr. Knight explains, "When you read textbooks or nonfiction books, sometimes lots of information is presented at once on a page or in a chapter. It helps to keep checking as you read, to see if you understand all this information. One way to do that is to ask questions! Before reading, just look at each of the features of the page and turn it into a question. Then, while you read, try to answer them. Mr. Knight says, "Now, I'd like to show you how I use this strategy, while reading a page from your social studies book." He points to his forehead to indicate that he is thinking aloud and says:

"When I look over this page, I see lots of things that I wonder about. I can get all kinds of ideas from the page, and these ideas can help me figure out what the author is trying to teach me. I see the title of this section is actually on the previous page. It's 'State Governments.' So this chapter is about state governments. That's easy. I know that we live in Pennsylvania, so my question is, 'Will the authors of this book tell me anything about my state government?' I'll be wondering about that as I read.

"Then, when I look at page 265, I see the subtitle, 'The Governor Leads the State.' That makes sense to me. I've heard of the governor before, and I know that he's the state leader. But I'm wondering about his job, compared to what I know about other leaders. I can ask the question, 'What is the governor's most important job?' When I read this page, I will be looking for an answer to that.

"I also see the pictures on the page. There is one of a girl holding her bicycle at the top of the page. That makes me wonder, 'What does this girl and her bike have to do with this? How does this picture relate to the idea that the governor leads the state?' When I read, I want to be sure to look for information about that.

"And I see vocabulary words highlighted. Obviously, if the author has decided to highlight them to make them stick out on the page, they must be pretty important! Here are the words 'public property.' That puts a question in my head, too. 'What does the governor do with public property?' I have an idea in my head about what public property is. I think it is property that belongs to everyone in the state. So, what will this author tell me about how the governor takes care of public property?"

After modeling, Mr. Knight says, "So, you see, I used all the information on the page to ask myself questions as I read. Now, when I read, I can check to see how well my questions are answered. Sometimes they are, and sometimes they aren't. That's when I would need to go read something else to find out my answers. I'd like for you to try this. Look at page 266, and with your partner, talk about the questions you can ask yourself."

Take a look at the procedures for this self-questioning lesson:

1. Choose a piece of text that contains plenty of information and physical features that could easily be transformed to questions, such as headings and subheadings, thought-provoking photographs, pictures, graphs, charts, and highlighted vocabulary.
2. Model by thinking out loud. Show students how to create questions about the text using features on the page.
3. Read the passage again, and look for answers to the self-questions.
4. Give students the opportunity to generate questions in another piece of text. This technique will take repeated practice for students to become comfortable with generating questions that go beyond trivia and literal information.

Identifying Story Elements When Retelling

As you learned in Chapter 5, narrative text, or fiction, has particular characteristics. Not all narrative texts are stories, but most stories do have similar elements: A character is in a setting, has a problem, makes attempts to solve it, and eventually resolves the problem. During the 1970s and 1980s, reading researchers became interested in pinpointing effective strategies for reading comprehension. A large body of research established a link between teaching children the elements of a story and their ability to understand and recall that story (Gambrell, Koskinen & Kapinus, 1991; Idol, 1987; Mandler & Johnson, 1977; National Reading Panel, 2000a; Morrow, 1984; Pressley, Johnson, Symons, McGoldrick & Kurita, 1989; Stein, 1978; Winograd & Bridge, 1986).

Direct instruction in story elements or story grammar, which consists of setting, characters, plot, and resolution, leads to improved recall of story information (Ruddell & Unrau, 2004a). Asking children to retell the story after reading it is a powerful way to assess their understanding of it, as shown in Chapter 4. Instructional tools, such as checklists to remind your students of the elements of story, can help them self-monitor as they read, as well as retell the story afterwards.

However, if you want students to use story grammar to help them remember what they've read, and you want them to retell stories to show you their abilities, you will need to use retelling as an instructional tool as well. Whenever you talk with your students about stories, talk about and label the story elements. Make your students aware of the structure of stories early on, so that this kind of thinking becomes part of their schemata for stories. As Trabasso and Bouchard (2002) explain:

This learning gives the reader knowledge and procedures for deeper understanding. It allows the reader to construct more coherent memory representations for what occurred in the story. Readers learn to identify the main characters of the story, where and when the story took place, what the main characters did, how the story ended, and how the main characters felt. Readers learn to construct a story map recording the setting, problem, goal, action, and outcome of the story as they unfold over time. (p. 181)

In the next example lesson, Mrs. Hanna models for her second graders the very essential skill of identifying story elements. In particular, this example shows how she models the identification of the problem in the story, which is necessary to understanding the story itself. She uses *Jamaica's Find,* by Juanita Havill (1986), because her students are already somewhat familiar with the story, which makes the demands of decoding low, allowing them to concentrate on this strategy.

Mrs. Hanna's Lesson

Mrs. Hanna gathers the students around her, and shows them the book *Jamaica's Find*. She says, "I know you're familiar with this book. We enjoyed reading it awhile back. I'd like to use it today to show you an important strategy that you can use when you read books that are unfamiliar to you. When you read, you need to know about all the important parts of the story. If you somehow miss one of these parts, you can get the story all messed up in your head. So look for these things when you are reading. They are listed on this chart."

Mrs. Hanna shows the class this chart:

Important Parts of the Story		
Beginning	Characters	Who is the story about?
	Setting	Where does it happen?
Middle	Problem	When does it happen? What does the character want? Why?
	Events	What happens because of this?
End	Resolution	How is the problem solved? How does the story end?

She then says "When you read *Jamaica's Find,* the first things you want to look for are the characters. This chart tells you that they'll be at the beginning of the book. So, right away, you start thinking about whom the story is about. Of course, the title gives you a big clue, too. You can figure out that someone named Jamaica will probably be important. Now, what else is at the beginning of the book?"

The students discuss the setting at the beginning of the book, which is the park. It later changes to Jamaica's home. Then, Mrs. Hanna says, "I'd like to show you how I find the next part of the story, the problem, because it's one of the hardest ones to find."

She points her finger to her forehead to indicate that she is thinking aloud, and says, "I know that the problem is usually introduced in the middle of the story, after the setting and characters are introduced. In this book, at the beginning, Jamaica went to the park, and found a hat and a stuffed dog. She turned the hat in to the Lost and Found counter, but she kept the dog. Now I am on page 15, which is near the middle of the book. I get the feeling that something is wrong here, when Jamaica gets home. Look at this sentence. I'll point to it for you. Jamaica's mother says, 'But Jamaica, you should have returned the dog, too.' This gives me a clue. Now I'm thinking that Jamaica's mother was not happy about keeping the dog. The words tell me that, and the picture shows me that Jamaica does not look happy about what her mother is telling her. I know if I brought home a stuffed animal from the park, my mother would not want me to keep it, either. She would say that it doesn't belong to me, and maybe even that it's too dirty to have in the house! As I read more, I can look for more clues to tell me about this problem. I'll read the words to see what the other characters say, check out the pictures to see if anyone looks unhappy, and think about what my own mother would say. That will help me understand Jamaica's problem."

Then Mrs. Hanna gives each student a copy of a story map, which has been modified and now serves as a checklist for retelling. She asks them to retell the story in writing, using the checklist as a reminder for the elements that they needed to include.

The procedure she uses is as follows:

1. Choose a book that has clear and identifiable story elements and is familiar to the students. Using a familiar book lessens the demand for decoding and allows students to concentrate on story structure.
2. Show students a chart that lists the elements and the likely location of them in the story.
3. Discuss the story elements that students can identify in this familiar story.
4. Choose the most difficult element for this story. Use the mental model to show students how you know how to identify this in the story. (Often, the problem is difficult to determine, as is the theme.) Explain the clues that you use to determine the element: pictures, words, location of events in the story, and personal experiences.
5. Give students a retelling checklist to use in retelling the story, making sure to include all elements.

Summarizing Stories

Summarizing means to recall and share the most important parts of a piece of text after reading. Only the bare essentials of the text are retold; thus, summaries are brief and not detailed, and are considered one way to respond to the story (Applebee, 1978). This version is shorter and less detailed than a retelling of the text and is an important way of enabling and providing evidence of comprehension (Baumann, 1986; Duke & Pearson, 2002; Meyer & Poon, 2004; National Reading Panel, 2000a).

The hardest part about summarizing is leaving out the details. Children often want to retell, rather than summarize, so that they can include all the events, characters, and character traits (Harvey & Goudvis, 2000). Summarizing instead requires them to tell only the bare minimum of information about the story, giving a synopsis of the author's words. This requirement is especially difficult if the student enjoyed the story, and wishes to share all of it with others. To show them how to summarize, modeling is vital. While modeling, impress upon them the necessity for brevity.

It is helpful to provide a frame that eliminates details and focuses only on the most essential elements: character, setting, the problem, and its outcome. Events and details can be left out, so that the story is synthesized to a skeleton. Glazer (1998) offers a frame that helps students capture these essential elements and write or verbalize a summary in three sentences or less. Using an adaptation that allows for a four-sentence summary, Mr. Rinehart teaches his fourth graders to summarize *Charlotte's Web* (White, 1952).

Mr. Rinehart's Lesson

Mr. Rinehart says, "Now that I've finished reading *Charlotte's Web*, I want to tell others what it is about. But I want to use as few words as possible, because people don't have time to listen to all the details, and because they can read about details when they check out the book. Now, let's review a bit. We know how to retell a story. What do we need to remember if we're going to retell? Ross?"

"We have to tell the name of the character and what his problem is," says Ross.

"Absolutely," says Mr. Rinehart. "What else?"

"The place and the time," responds Ross.

"Yes, the setting. Thanks, Ross. And what about the character's problem? What usually happens in the middle of the book? Chelsea?"

Chelsea thinks for a moment and then says, "Well, things happen in the middle of the book. Events!"

"That's true. And usually, why are these events happening?" asks Mr. Rinehart.

"These are the things the character does to try to solve his problem," says Chelsea.

"Exactly! And at the end, the problem is solved, which is called the resolution. Now, if you're going to retell a story, you want to include all of these elements of story: character, setting, problem, events, and resolution. But, in a summary, you don't have that much time. Let's try a little experiment so that you can see the importance of being brief."

Mr. Rinehart pulls out a stopwatch and said, "Think about a movie or video that you have seen lately. Think of what you would tell someone if you had to describe the movie to them. But, here's the trick: You get only 30 seconds! Close your eyes now and think of what you want to say."

Mr. Rinehart pauses as the students think of their mind movies. Then he says, "I'll time you while the first person shares, and then you can switch places and the other person in your group can share for 30 seconds. Ready? Go!"

The students excitedly share their descriptions with each other. Afterwards, Mr. Rinehart explains, "You might have noticed that you cannot tell everything about the story in a quick summary like that. All you want to do is give other people an idea of what the book is all about. That way, maybe they'll want to read it, too. Take a look at this chart."

Mr. Rinehart shows the students this chart:

Beginning Characters Setting	*Character* was *where*. The story took place *when*.
Middle Problem	*Character's* problem was_____.
End Resolution	The problem was solved when_____.

He said, "This chart shows you the most important parts of a story, and where they are usually located in a story. And on the right side, it shows you the sentence you can write to tell about that part of the story. So if you follow this chart, you can tell about a story in just four sentences! Let me show you how I do this, with *Charlotte's Web*."

Mr. Rinehart puts his finger to his forehead to indicate that he is thinking aloud, and says, "Hmmm, as I think about it, Wilbur was the main character in this story. He is the one that had all the problems in the story. Now, the setting is where and when the story took place. Well, Wilbur lived on a farm, the Zuckerman's farm. That's the 'where' part of the setting! And my first sentence directs me to say where the character was in the story. I'll write: 'Wilbur the pig lived on the Zuckerman farm.'

"The next sentence directs me to tell when the story took place. Well, I think about how it began, in the spring, and how it ended, the next spring, so I know that the 'when' part of the setting is over the course of a year. I can write this sentence next: 'The story took place from one spring to the next.'

"OK, now for the problem. Well, I've finished reading this whole book, but it's hard to remember just the most important parts. I'll take a look back at the Table of Contents to refresh my memory. Chapter 5, called 'Charlotte,' was where he met his new friend. And, scanning down the list of chapter titles, I see Chapter 7, 'Bad News.' Ah, I remember. That's when Wilbur found out that Mr. Zuckerman was planning to slaughter him for bacon and ham. And then the author, E. B. White, spent the rest of the book—all these pages—telling us about the things Charlotte did to save Wilbur's life. So the middle of the book is all about that problem and the attempts to solve it, using Charlotte's web. The sentence that I will write must tell the problem. I think I'll write: 'Wilbur's problem was that Mr. Zuckerman planned to slaughter him for bacon and ham.'

"Now, for the resolution. Well, I know that eventually Wilbur's life was saved because of the words that Charlotte wrote in her web. Everyone thought he was so special that he couldn't possibly be killed. So that should be my last sentence:
'The problem was solved when Wilbur's spider friend Charlotte wrote words in her web that saved his life.'
"Now you can read my four-sentence summary. I'll hang it up on the board."

Mr. Rinehart displays his summary:

Wilbur the pig lived on the Zuckerman farm. The story took place from one spring to the next. Wilbur's problem was that Mr. Zuckerman planned to slaughter him for bacon and ham. The problem was solved when Wilbur's friend Charlotte, a spider, wrote words in her web that saved his life.

Mr. Rinehart continues, "I'd like for you to try it. You can practice with a partner. Let's try to summarize the book *Matilda* (Dahl, 1988), which we just finished last week. We'll do that one together. Then, you can try one on your own with a favorite book."

To plan your lesson on summarizing the story, use the following outline:

1. Review the story elements.
2. To emphasize the importance of brevity, ask students to tell about a favorite movie in 30 seconds or less.
3. Show the story summary frame. Use the mental model to show students how to find each of the elements required in this frame.
4. Ask students to complete the frame using a book that everyone has shared. Compare answers.
5. Give students the chance to practice on their own, using a different book.

Identifying Main Ideas in Nonfiction Text

You may recall from Chapter 5 that children's understanding of nonfiction is enhanced when they know that reading for information means they may encounter text that can be structured in five ways: (1) descriptive, (2) sequential, (3) comparative, (4) indicative of cause/effect relationships, and (5) a presentation of problems and solutions. Identifying the author's main idea is dependent upon the student's ability to determine what is important within one of these frameworks (Armbruster, Anderson & Ostertag, 1987; Duke & Pearson, 2002; Kintsch, 2004; Meyer & Poon, 2004; National Reading Panel, 2000a). Modeling for students how to identify important information in content area texts is a matter of verbalizing the clues that you use when you try to learn what the author is teaching you. Shown next is the lesson that Mrs. Jefferies uses when teaching her third graders how she finds main ideas in a nonfiction tradebook, *From Tree to Paper* (Davis, 1995). In this lesson, she shows the students how to use a graphic organizer, picture cards, and note-taking to write a report about main ideas, as well as to verbalize the main ideas of an informational book. The use of cards and pictures allows students to rearrange their ideas if needed. Also simple pictures representing ideas can be used for making a list of notes from which students can verbalize the main ideas of the text (Harvey & Goudvis, 2000).

Mrs. Jefferies' Lesson

Mrs. Jefferies says, "This book has taught me a lot of things about how paper is made—things I never knew before. What I need to do, if I am going to write about this, is remember all the important information from the book that I can. So I'll write some facts that I remember on some small cards, and put them out on the desk in front of me. See if you can help me remember some of these facts."

As Mrs. Jefferies and her students recall some facts from the book, she writes them on cards. Then, she puts her finger to her forehead to indicate thinking aloud and says: **"When I look at all these facts, and remember what the book was about, I think of a line. The tree is here.** [She draws a tree on the left side of a large sheet of paper.] **And the paper is on the other side.** [She draws a square to represent a piece of paper on the right side of this paper.] **Why do I think of a line? Well, the title of this book gave me a clue, because—as we said earlier—it helps us know, even before reading, that the author will tell us about the process that people go through, from beginning to end, to make paper. So a line seems to be a good way to organize all this information, because it shows each step from the beginning, where the tree is shown, to the end, where the paper is made."** Her graphic is shown here.

– –	
Tree	Paper

Then Mrs. Jefferies explains, "Looking at all the facts that we wrote on these cards, we can remember the order in which our author, Ms. Davis, told us about them. She wrote a book that tells a sequence. She didn't do some of the things that other authors might do, such as compare paper to other things, or present the problems associated with making paper. Instead, this author chose to write her whole book about what happens from the beginning, when the tree is in the forest, to the end, when children are using paper. So our graphic organizer needs to tell the order in which all those events happened. If we want to write about how paper is made, just as Ms. Davis did, we need to get the order correct. Let's see if we can remember the order in which paper is made. You may refer to the book if necessary."

The students help Mrs. Jefferies put the small fact cards in sequence, and place them along the line of the graphic organizer. When they are satisfied with the sequence, they glue the cards on the graphic organizer.

Mrs. Jefferies continues, "Now that I have a plan for my report, I must write! First, I need to introduce to my reader the topic of my book. I need to begin by telling the readers what they will find out. So, watch what I'll write."

This book shows how paper is made.

She then says, "Now, I can write some sentences that describe my pictures and tell about these facts. Let's look at the first fact that we wrote on the cards."

Trees are cut down in the forest.

"We need to add a signal word, 'first.' That will tell our readers that this summary tells about a book that has several steps in it. So I'll write this sentence."

First, trees are cut down in the forest.

"We can continue writing more sentences, telling all the steps. That is how to get started with a report. To write nonfiction, make plans with an organizer and draw pictures to help you remember your ideas about each part of the report. Now, you can try this. You may finish this report about making paper, if you wish, or you may start one of your own."

The next day, Mrs. Jefferies says, "Yesterday, we learned how to write the main ideas of an information book by putting all these picture cards in order on this graphic organizer. But suppose we don't need to write a report. Suppose I give you an assignment to tell the class, in your own words, the most important ideas from this book. What could you do? Let me show you."

Mrs. Jefferies points to each of the picture cards that are on the chart. She says, "I know that the first thing to say about making paper is that trees are cut down. So, I'll just write some notes to remind me. I'll write on this book board: **cut trees.**"

After writing, Mrs. Jefferies says, "Next, I can write just a couple of words again. I'll write: **make chips.** I write this to remind me of how the people at the paper factory need to get the trees chopped into millions of little wooden chips. And now, I can keep going. What other steps can I put on my list?"

Mrs. Jefferies continues in this manner until all points are summarized. Then, she says, "Now all I need to do is tell someone the important points of this book! I can use my notes to remind me of what to say."

The steps used in this lesson are:

1. Read aloud a nonfiction book or article that has clearly defined main ideas.
2. Ask students to recall the facts in the book. Use a blank graphic organizer to help them recall facts.
3. Write the facts on cards and ask students to illustrate them.
4. Place the cards in appropriate places on the organizer. Discuss the sequence of events or the relationships between ideas. Rearrange the cards as necessary.
5. Draft a sentence for each card. Use appropriate signal words. Write these sentences on a chart or the overhead transparency.
6. After modeling one or two sentences, give students the chance to finish writing the remaining facts for the book that you used when modeling. Then, give them the chance to write a report for one of their own.
7. A day or two after writing, show students how to take notes for a verbal summary of main ideas. Looking back at the graphic organizers and pictures, write one or two words for each idea. Make a sequential list of these ideas. Students can use these to retell important ideas from the book.

Home–School Connection

What to Do When You Don't Understand

You can send the following letter to parents or caregivers, explaining the idea of self-regulation. It outlines some "fix-up" strategies that can be reinforced with home reading. ●

Dear Families,

Have you ever read poorly written, confusing instructions for putting together a toy, bicycle, or household appliance? Halfway through the page, did you find yourself scratching your head and wondering, "Huh?" What do you do when print like this makes no sense? Read it again? Slow down? Look for pictures? Give up in disgust?

Sometimes children feel the same way about things they read. But if they stop themselves when they get to a difficult place that they don't understand, that's good! That means that they realize they do not understand what they are reading. Encourage this kind of thinking. When you read with your child, stop at the end of every page or two, and ask, "Does this make sense?" If it doesn't, "fix it up"!

When your child realizes that something doesn't make sense, they can fix up their understanding. Some ways to do this include:

- They can slow down. This is especially true if they are studying or reading textbooks. Sometimes, children read everything the same way. But good readers do not read textbooks and comic books with the same speed.
- They can reread. They can go back to the part of the page that troubles them and read it again. Often, reading it again out loud helps to clarify things.
- They can locate difficult words. Encourage them to highlight or write down words that give them trouble. Talk about these words and tell them to bring these words to school for discussion.
- They can read ahead. Sometimes, if they read the next few sentences, things become clear again.

Just like you do when you realize the page doesn't make sense, your child can stop, think, and fix it up! Happy reading!

Sincerely,

Your child's teacher

Caregivers can help children monitor their comprehension as they read.

Summary: Reflecting on Children's Construction of Meaning

As schema theory tells us, good readers determine meaning based on what they encounter in print as well as what they already know from past experiences. Good teachers do not merely expect this type of understanding to take place when their students read. Using explicit instruction, you can show your students how to comprehend. This chapter described nine reading behaviors that comprise the process of constructing meaning from print: (1) choosing a book or web site, (2) making predictions, (3) making inferences, (4) visualizing, (5) self-regulating, (6) self-questioning, (7) identifying and retelling story elements, (8) summarizing stories, and (9) identifying and summarizing main ideas in nonfiction. Because these are private, mental processes, you need to transform them into visible behaviors. You can accomplish this by explaining the construction of meaning. Using concrete terms to explain each of these, you can show them how to follow steps in a strategic procedure. You can also do this with mental modeling, in which you think out loud as you go through the processes yourself. By using both of these types of instruction, you will take some of the mystery out of reading comprehension.

All of the strategies shown in this chapter, and the corresponding standards and principles, are outlined in the Reviewing the Big Picture box.

Technology Resources

- **school.discovery.com/schrockguide/eval.html** Part of "Kathy Schrock's Guide for Educators," this web page leads you to some guides and evaluation sheets for critically evaluating web sites. There is an evaluation sheet for each grade level.

- **lib.nmsu.edu/instruction/eval.html** "The Good, the Bad, and the Ugly: Why It's a Good Idea to Evaluate Web Sources" web site was written by Susan Beck, head of Reference and Research at New Mexico State University Library. She includes evaluation criteria for evaluating web sites, as well as examples and suggestions for successful Internet assignments.

- **curry.edschool.virginia.edu/go/readquest/strat/** This page from ReadingQuest. org lists more than 25 strategies to use in teaching reading comprehension, many of which are discussed in this book.

- **www.smsd.org/custom/risingstar/readingwebquest.htm** This site is a reading comprehension webquest. Following the directions and investigating the links give you some solid, research-based information on teaching comprehension.

expect the world

The New York Times
nytimes.com

Themes of the Times

Expand your knowledge of the concepts discussed in this chapter by reading current and historical articles from the *New York Times* by visiting the "Themes of the Times" section of the Companion Web Site.

Reviewing the Big Picture

Reading Strategies

Strategy	Description	Appropriate Type of Text/ Grade Level	IRA Standards	INTASC Principles	NAEYC Standards	ACEI/NCATE Standards
Choosing reading materials	Children need to be empowered as readers so that they know how to select their own reading materials. Their selections need to reflect self-awareness of their own abilities as well as their purpose for reading. Students need to critically analyze web sites for their value in providing information.	Fiction and nonfiction/K-2, 3-5, 6-8	2.2, 2.3, 4.1, 4.2, 4.3, 4.4	4, 6, 7	4b (Using read-alouds or shared reading)	2.1, 3.1, 3.4, 3.5
Making predictions	Students use information on the page and their prior knowledge to make reasonable guesses about the print. Predictions take place at the word level, when a reader is trying to figure out an unknown word; and at the text level, when a reader is trying to make sense of the page.	Fiction and nonfiction/K-2, 3-5, 6-8	1.4, 2.2, 2.3, 4.1, 4.3, 4.4	4, 6, 7	4b (Using read-alouds or shared reading)	2.1, 3.1, 3.4, 3.5
Making inferences	This is the process of understanding text in which the author does not explicitly state its meaning.	Fiction and nonfiction/K-2, 3-5, 6-8	1.4, 2.2, 2.3, 4.1, 4.3, 4.4	4, 6, 7	4b (Using read-alouds or shared reading)	2.1, 3.1, 3.3, 3.4, 3.5
Visualizing	Readers who are making sense of the print can make mental pictures of the author's words.	Fiction and nonfiction/K-2, 3-5, 6-8	1.4, 2.2, 2.3, 4.1, 4.3, 4.4	4, 6, 7	4b (Using read-alouds or shared reading)	2.1, 3.1, 3.4, 3.5
Self-regulating reading comprehension	Good readers are aware of their own understanding of text and are cognizant of ways to remedy comprehension that has broken down.	Fiction and nonfiction/K-2, 3-5, 6-8	1.4, 2.2, 2.3, 4.1, 4.3, 4.4	4, 6, 7	4b (Using read-alouds or shared reading)	2.1, 3.1, 3.3, 3.4, 3.5
Self-questioning	Good readers ask questions of the text and expect answers as they read.	Fiction and non-fiction/3-5, 6-8	1.4, 2.2, 2.3, 4.1, 4.3, 4.4	4, 6, 7	NA	2.1, 3.1, 3.3, 3.4, 3.5
Identifying story elements and retelling	Children tend to understand a story better if they have been taught to look for story elements as they read. In most stories, the elements are character, setting, plot, and resolution.	Fiction/K-2, 3-5, 6-8	1.4, 2.2, 2.3, 4.1, 4.3, 4.4	4, 6, 7	4b (Using read-alouds or shared reading)	2.1, 3.1, 3.4, 3.5
Summarizing stories	This is the ability to capture the essence of a story or a nonfiction selection in just a few words, after the reading has taken place.	Fiction/3-5, 6-8	1.4, 2.2, 2.3, 4.1, 4.3, 4.4	4, 6, 7	NA	2.1, 3.1, 3.4, 3.5
Identifying and summarizing main ideas in expository text	Readers can better construct meaning from informational texts when they know what to look for in expository writing.	Nonfiction/3-5, 6-8	1.4, 2.2, 2.3, 4.1, 4.3, 4.4	4, 6, 7	NA	2.1, 3.1, 3.4, 3.5

11

Facilitating Your Students' Prior Knowledge

She got off the suitcase and opened it up right there on the sidewalk.

Jeffrey gasped. "Books!"

Books, all right. Both sides of the suitcase crammed with them. Dozens more than anyone ever needed for homework.

Jeffrey fell to his knees. He and Amanda and the suitcase were like a rock in a stream; the school-goers just flowed to the left and right around them. He turned his head this way and that to read the titles. He lifted the books on top to see the ones beneath. There were fiction books and nonfiction books, who-did-it books and let's-be-friends books and what-is-it books and how-to books and how-not-to books and just-regular-kid books. On the bottom was a single volume from an encyclopedia. It was the letter A.

"My library," Amanda Beale said proudly.

Maniac Magee (Spinelli, 1990)

Jeffrey Magee was not like normal kids. He would catch touchdown passes with one hand, hit homeruns offa fast pitcher, or untying one of the hardest knots in the world. That's how Jeffrey Magee got the name maniac — for doing things kids can't do.

Ethan, age 11

My final year of teaching elementary school was the year I taught fourth grade near Baltimore, Maryland. I had just moved to Maryland that summer. The school, teachers, children, and curriculum were all very new to me. To my dismay, one of the goals in the social studies curriculum was that of learning Maryland history. I knew nothing of Maryland history! So each week, I stayed one step ahead of the children and read the next chapter in the history textbook that the children were required to use, educating myself a bit. Then, I assigned the appropriate chapter for the children to read and questions at the end of the chapter for them to answer.

You can imagine the success of this approach. The textbook was dreadful! Dull! My students were bored. I was bored. Their quiz grades were poor. We certainly were not achieving my goals. I knew that I would have to do something.

So I decided to spice up my approach a bit. I asked the students to read each chapter. Then, after reading, I used some drama. I pretended to be a figure in Maryland history, and made that chapter come alive. I retold the main events in the chapter to the students, using the voice of the famous person in history. The students eagerly looked forward to the completion of each chapter. After I made these presentations, I gave them their quiz. Scores soared. Whew. At last, I was making history interesting. Patting myself on the back, I was relieved that my objectives were met.

But were they? Think about what was happening with my fourth graders in the Personal Reflection.

Personal Reflection

Did I meet my objectives? What makes you think so?

If I measured success by the quiz scores, then, yes, I met the objective of making sure that my fourth graders knew Maryland history. However, if I measured success by my students' ability to read the book and understand it, I still failed. The problem is that I read the book for them, I presented the facts to them in an interesting manner, and I tested them. The students did not have to read for understanding. In fact, the more astute ones in the bunch probably figured this out fairly early on, and merely pretended to read! There was no reason for them to read; all they had to do was wait until I made a dramatic presentation, then they could listen and watch, learn the history I wanted them to learn, and completely ignore the book.

Now, suppose that I had changed some things in this lesson around. What might have happened if I had introduced history to them, using drama, *before* they read? What if I had dressed in costume? I could have brought an appropriate prop or two to class, and told them interesting stories from the viewpoint of the important people in Maryland's history. I could have introduced some interesting biographies to them, such as *Leonard Calvert and the Maryland Adventure* (Jenson, 1998); *What Are You Figuring Now? A Story about Benjamin Banneker* (Ferris, 1990); *The Story of Harriet Tubman, Conductor of the Underground Railroad* (McMullan, 1991); and historical fiction such as *Star Spangled Secret* (Kimball, 2001) and *The Flag Maker* (Bartoletti, 2004). Then, after giving them this background information and enticing them to know more, I could have asked them to read the textbook assignment. How do you think their understanding of the history book would have changed?

It would have improved a great deal, according to research. As you will recall from Chapter 1, schema theory tells us that the knowledge that the reader brings to the text is just as important as what is on the printed page (Anderson, 2004; Anderson & Pearson, 1984; Rumelhart, 1980). This theory explains how "schemata, or knowledge already stored in memory, function in the process of interpreting new information and allowing it to enter and become a part of the knowledge store. Whether we are aware of it or not, it is this interaction of new information with old knowledge that we mean when we use the term *comprehension*. To say that one has comprehended a text is to say that she has found a mental 'home' for the information in the text, or else that she has modified an existing mental home in order to accommodate that new information" (Anderson & Pearson, 1984, p. 255).

Thus, if I had helped my fourth graders build some existing schemata for events in Maryland history, their reading of the history text would have been a much more meaningful process of connecting the print with some knowledge that they had already gained prior to reading. In other words, rather than spending time after they read the chapter clarifying what they misunderstood when they attempted to read, I could have prepared them to read with sufficient background knowledge to understand the context of the chapter. They could have, based on my presentations before reading, made some predictions about what they would find out in the chapter, and verified those predictions by reading. Had I done this, I would have facilitated the children's comprehension of the text. They would have learned the history, which was my objective, but also they would have done it without ignoring the text. They would be obtaining information much more independently, and their ability to read efferently would have grown.

This chapter will show you how to facilitate children's comprehension of what they read before they begin to read it. By the chapter's end, you will see the importance of prereading preparation in your classroom by activating and assessing prior knowledge, so that your students are more likely to comprehend all kinds of text. As Spinelli says in *Maniac Magee*, the "fiction books and nonfiction books, who-did-it books and let's-be-friends books and what-is-it books and how-to books and how-not-to books and just-regular-kid books" can all be part of your students' reading repertoires. And while they may not carry all their books around in a suitcase, as Amanda did in *Maniac Magee*, you can help them enter the world available to them through books. More importantly, you can help develop their desire for it.

Two Types of Prior Knowledge

Schema theory tells us that when a reader opens the book, he or she brings to the page an understanding of the world around her, and an understanding of the nature of print (Adams & Bruce, 1982; Anderson, 2004). These understandings help readers read books, because they enable readers to connect to the topic chosen by the author, as well as to the structure of the text that they are attempting to read. Both are needed for adequate development of prior knowledge.

Knowledge of the Topic or Theme

Your students come to you with an array of experiences. The things that they know about the world around them, either through personal experiences or through vicarious experiences, will help them understand what they read (Anderson, 2004; Duke & Pearson, 2002). Knowledge about the topic of the book they are about to read can help them make mental images and make connections to the author's words (Gambrell & Koskinen, 2002). Figure 11.1 shows questions to ask yourself about the topic that is evident in the text your students will be reading.

Suppose your readers are reading *Train to Somewhere,* by Eve Bunting (1996). Their appreciation for this book is enhanced by their knowledge of the events that took place from the 1850s to the 1920s in the United States, when thousands of orphan children were sent west on trains for their "placing-out," to be adopted by families who wanted more children (usually to help with work on the farm). In fact, Bunting activates such topical prior knowledge herself by briefly explaining this historical background in an introduction to the book.

Teacher-Planning Questions to Ask about the Topic of the Text

When planning to use a piece of literature in your classroom, examine it in light of what your students already know about it. Ask yourself the following questions:

Fiction	Nonfiction
What is the theme or author's reason for writing this story?	What is the topic, concept, or piece of information presented by the author?
Have your students experienced this theme, and can they contribute to conversations about it before reading?	How much do your students know about the information presented in the text before they read?
Do your students easily infer the existence of theme, or will they need additional support to make inferences while reading?	While reading, will your students be able to connect their prior knowledge of this topic with the printed text?
After reading, will your students be able to state the theme of this piece of fiction in 1–3 words?	After reading, will your students be able to state the most important idea of this informational piece in just a few words?

Figure 11.1 Questions to ask about the topic of the text when preparing your students to read.

To assess your students' prior knowledge about the topic of a text, Holmes and Roser (1987) suggest some ways to determine how much they know before they read. I have adapted these suggestions for use with fiction as well as nonfiction; these methods are shown in Figure 11.2.

Helping students recall and use their past experiences related to the theme or topics of a story is just one important way to facilitate their understanding.

Knowledge of the Structure of Text

Your students also need schema for the way that text is organized. Knowledge of story structure and nonfiction text structure enables readers to use prereading strategies that will help them better understand the text (Duke & Pearson, 2002;

Assessing Your Students' Prior Knowledge of the Topic

Fiction	Nonfiction
Free Recall	
Tell me what you know about _____. (Insert the major theme of the story.)	Tell me what you know about _____. (Insert the main idea of the text.)
Word Association	
When you hear the words _____ and _____, what do you think of? (Insert words related to the theme of the story.)	When you hear the words _____ and _____, what do you think of? (Insert words related to the main idea or topic of the text.)
Recognition	
Show the students some words or phrases and ask them to tell which ones might be related to the book. Use words that are related to the theme of the story.	Show the students some words or phrases and ask them to tell which ones might be related to the book. Use words or phrases that are related to the main idea.
Structured Question	
Ask the students a set of prepared questions that will help you determine their specific knowledge about the topic. The questions should reflect the theme of the story.	Ask the students a set of prepared questions that will help you determine their specific knowledge about the topic. The questions should reflect the text structure.

Figure 11.2 Ways to assess your students' prior knowledge of topics for fiction and nonfiction.

Goldman & Rakestraw, 2000; Paris, Wasik & Turner, 1991). When students know the kind of text they are reading, the schema they have for that type of text helps them understand it. Research has consistently shown us that knowledge of story elements (that is, characters, setting, problem, resolution, and theme) is helpful for readers of all ages and abilities (Morrow, 1984; Gordon & Pearson, 1983; Idol, 1987; Fitzgerald & Spiegel, 1983). Likewise, knowledge of the structure of nonfiction text seems to improve comprehension and factual recall, regardless of how the text structure is taught or practiced (Duke & Pearson, 2002). Thus, the other important part of activating background knowledge is recalling the structure of the text.

Let's think about your readers again. Because they are reading historical fiction, *Train to Somewhere*, they need to realize that this is a piece of fiction based on historical fact. Thus, they know that the story will have a main character and a problem that needs to be solved. This information helps readers anticipate events and confirm predictions. But suppose that your readers are reading a nonfiction account of this event in our history, *Orphan Train Rider: One Boy's True Story* (Warren, 1996). If a reader realizes that this is a chronological description of the

Examining the Structure of Text

Fiction	Nonfiction
Does this piece of fiction have the elements of a story, in which a character typically has a problem to solve and attempts to solve it?	Which of the five most common text structure forms does the author use to present the information (description, sequence, compare/contrast, cause/effect, problem/solution)?
Will your students be able to readily identify the main character?	Are your students familiar with the text structure type(s) used by the author?
Will your students be able to determine the main character's problem?	Is there just one text structure or several? Will your students be able to readily identify the text structure(s)?
Will your students be able to determine the resolution to the problem and the story ending?	Will your students be able to determine the author's main point?
Will your students be able to complete a story map based on the elements of this story?	Will your students be able to complete a graphic organizer, based on the text structure of this selection?

Figure 11.3 Questions to ask yourself about the text and your students as you prepare them to read.

experiences that one man had as a boy on the Orphan Train, he or she can begin to understand the sequence of events that took place and their relationship to our nation's history. This understanding is dependent upon the reader's knowledge of the differences between fiction and nonfiction, and the particular structures of each of these genres.

In order to determine what is most important for your students to know before reading a selected text, you will also need to consider the structure of the text. Such examination of the text will help you determine the types of questions to ask to assess their prior knowledge, and can also help you create graphic organizers or story maps for your students to complete.

Once you have determined that the students' prior knowledge of the topic is sufficient for them to begin reading, you need to connect that information to the structure of the text. Figure 11.3 shows the kinds of questions you need to ask yourself about the nature of the text before you expect your students to read it. To see how this process works, look at a lesson in which Mrs. Hart is preparing her fifth graders to read *Number the Stars,* by Lois Lowry (1989). This work of fiction is set during the time of the German Nazi occupation of Denmark in the 1940s. Take note of how she activates prior knowledge about the topic of the book, as well as its story elements.

Mrs. Hart's Lesson

To determine students' prior knowledge of the topic, Mrs. Hart says, "I've got one of my favorite books to show you. It is called *Number the Stars*, by Lois Lowry, and it is a story about a girl who is your age. Before we begin reading it, I want to tell you a little bit about the setting of the story. It takes place in 1943 in Denmark, during World War II. Where is Denmark? Take out your social studies books, and find the atlas. With your partners, see if you can find Denmark on the world map."

Notice that Mrs. Hart used a structured question to determine students' prior knowledge about the geographical location of the story, which is important for them to know as they construct their understanding of the events in the story.

After the students have done this, Mrs. Hart asks a free recall question: "World War II began in 1939. At that time, a dictator named Adolf Hitler ruled Germany. Tell us what you know about him."

This inquiry elicits several responses, most of which indicate a vague understanding about Hitler's attempt to take over most of Europe and his persecution of millions of Jews. At this point, Mrs. Hart feels that her students have some schemata about the history that surrounds this story; however, she wants to make sure that their prior knowledge is helpful to them, so she says: "Hitler was a dictator who had the misguided belief that Germany needed to be free of Jewish people. He used his soldiers, called the Nazis, to invade several countries in Europe, systematically captured the Jews living there, sent them to concentration camps, and eventually killed them. By 1943, Nazi soldiers had invaded Denmark and occupied the city of Copenhagen. Find that city on your map. Soon, Hitler ordered that all Jewish people in Denmark must be captured and sent to death camps. But the Danish people resisted this. They planned to gather up all the Jewish people they could and send them on boats to safety in Sweden. Many Danish people hid their Jewish friends in their homes, hiding whole families in their attics and basements. This was hard to do. Most Danish people were fair-skinned, blonde, and blue-eyed. Their Jewish friends usually had dark hair and brown eyes. This difference made it easy for Nazi soldiers, who stood on every street corner, to find anyone that they thought was Jewish and send them to a concentration camp. The soldiers could search people's homes and apartments anytime they wanted to. The punishment for hiding Jews was death.

"Now, take a look at this book box. In it, I have several items or pictures that are related to the story. I'll show them to you:

- A map of Denmark
- A picture of the Nazi swastika
- A picture of a blonde-haired and blue-eyed girl
- A picture of a dark-haired and brown-eyed girl
- A picture of a store that has a "Closed—out of business" sign attached to it
- A necklace with a Star of David charm
- A photo album full of baby pictures
- A flashlight
- A picture of a Nazi soldier
- A picture of a cemetery

Mrs. Hart continues: "Remember, this is a fictional story, but it is based on true events in world history. That makes it a piece of historical fiction. So, to make sure we understand this story, we'll need to think about what all stories contain: setting, characters, problem, events, and solution. Now, think about what you know about stories. Which of these items show you the setting? Which might give you a hint about the characters in this story? Which items might indicate a problem in the story? Talk with your partners; then let's see if we can fill in a story map with our ideas."

Staying Focused

A careful review of the text to be read takes some thoughtful consideration, and the result often is not what it appears to be. If you focus on an irrelevant topic, you might foster misconceptions about it. In addition, if you do not keep your students focused on the author's intended message, it is possible that your students will become distracted from the task of comprehending the text. This danger is

Diversity in the Reading Classroom

The Period of Silence

Have you ever asked a question of a student and gotten nothing in return? Instead, perhaps you got a blank stare, or the student quickly diverted his eyes to the floor? Contrary to the old saying, silence is not always golden. Yet students who are learning English for the first time often go through this period of silence, when they rarely participate in class discussions or answer questions, even when called upon.

Such is true of many students from diverse backgrounds, for various reasons (Au, 1993). Early English language learners often remain silent because they cannot generate language as well as they can understand it. Moreover, cultural differences sometimes account for this silence. Some children of diverse backgrounds have response patterns that are different from the norm in our country. For example, in some cultures, children are not encouraged to take the lead in conversations with adults. In others, people wait slightly longer than we do to speak after the other person has stopped speaking, thus creating a lull in the flow of conversation; and in still other cultures, boys are expected to be loud while girls are expected to be quiet (North Central Regional Educational Laboratory, n.d.).

And yet it is vitally important to assess and activate the prior knowledge of *all* students before they read in instructional situations. How can you do this while still respecting the reluctance of some of your learners to speak? Some suggestions are:

- Use concrete objects and pictures to introduce new concepts or vocabulary. Ask students to pronounce these ideas in their language.

- Explain to students, in explicit lessons, the differences between the structure of traditional storytelling and the structure of written fiction.

- Encourage talk without insisting on it.

- Reexamine your own views of classroom discourse. Do you always insist that students raise their hands to speak? Many students from diverse backgrounds would be more comfortable, and more willing to talk, with a less structured conversational style.

- Explain to students that asking questions and volunteering information are acceptable in your classroom.

- Use multicultural literature that reflects the background of the students in your classroom. Allow them to share their thoughts and relevant information pertaining to the literature. For example, before reading *Chato's Kitchen* (Soto, 1995), teacher Robin Teets asked her students to tell about the Mexican foods that are listed on the inside of the front cover of the book. They spoke of ingredients and cooking instructions in such detail that Ms. Teets brought in the ingredients and they all made chili together!

particularly likely for students who struggle with reading (Williams, 2002). Likewise, activating background knowledge and making predictions will facilitate your students' understanding if you stick with those predictions, referring to them and verifying them throughout the reading of the text. Simply activating prior knowledge is not enough (Duke & Pearson, 2002).

For example, suppose your students are reading *Tacky*, by Helen Lester (1988). This delightful book is about a penguin named Tacky, who was an "odd bird." Tacky does not dress the same way that his penguin friends do, and he is not neat, orderly, and quiet, as his friends are. Instead of marching in an orderly line, he sings loud, silly songs and dances wildly. When some hunters pay a visit, and threaten to shoot Tacky and his friends, he saves the day by singing so loudly that they are bewildered, and run away. When preparing your students to read this book, you'll need to consider these things:

1. It is a piece of fiction.
2. The animals are personified, with human problems.
3. The author's purpose is to help us celebrate individuals who do not follow the crowd.

Based on the assumption that you want your students to understand the underlying theme or point of the book, you will need to activate prior knowledge in a manner that emphasizes the main character's problem. In this case, you will need to discuss with the students the problems of being different, and how these differences can become strengths. Following are some appropriate discussion questions for activating prior knowledge for this book. Notice that each of these questions stimulates discussion about the theme of *Tacky:*

1. "Suppose your mom takes you shoe shopping. She gives you a choice between two pairs of shoes to buy. One looks like the same kind of shoes that all your friends wear, but it is uncomfortable and doesn't fit right. The other pair is comfortable, but looks different from the kind your friends wear. Which would you choose? Why?"
2. "What makes a good leader?"
3. "What does it mean when someone says, 'Be yourself'?"

There is no need to spend lots of time activating prior knowledge about penguins. Even though the main character in the story is a penguin, it is a personified animal character, and his problems are human ones. Prereading discussions about penguins can be interesting, but are not really related to the author's message. Students can miss the point if the discussion takes too many turns off the path.

There are several helpful ways to facilitate your students' use of prior knowledge when they read. Because of the unique features of different types of text, it is important to use strategies that are appropriate for the type of text you are using. It is also important to recognize the difference between teaching strategies and reading strategies. A **teaching strategy** is a set of consistent teaching behaviors that the teacher uses to help students accomplish a task or objective. According to Alexander and Jetton (2000), who reviewed the literature on the nature of strategic reading, a **reading strategy** is a specialized set of procedures that readers use to facilitate their understanding of text.

The next section includes teaching and reading strategies designed for use with fiction, followed by strategies designed for use with nonfiction. The appropriate grade level is indicated for each; however, many of them can be adapted or modified for other levels.

Strategies to Use with Fiction Literature

Book Box

Actively engaging the thinking of your students is extremely important when you prepare them to read. The book box is a teaching strategy that does this well for fiction selections and is appropriate for primary grades. Book boxes are similar to prop stories (Glazer, 1989), which I introduced in Chapter 6. (Prop stories are collections of props, stored in a box, that you make available to young children in classroom play areas. They use the props in the box to reenact their favorite stories.) Similarly, the book box (Tompkins, 2003) is a collection of artifacts or pictures that relate to the story your students will read. In order to activate prior knowledge about the story elements, the book box should contain one object or picture for each element. Prior to reading, tell the students that you are going to give them some clues about the story that they are about to read, and show them, one at a time, the contents of the box. As you do this, ask them to think about how these objects or pictures can be related to the story, and how to create a story in their heads. For younger or immature readers, be sure to introduce the objects and pictures in the same sequence that they occur in the story. For mature readers, the sequence is not as important. Predictions can be written on a story map. While reading, return to the objects and talk about predictions that can be confirmed. After reading, make the box available to students as an aid in retelling the story.

To create a book box, collect objects or pictures that represent the elements of the story that your students are going to read, and place them in a container. You can decorate a box to suggest the theme of the book, or to add to speculation about one of the elements. For example, you could cover a box with wrapping paper decorated with the Star of David for the book *Number the Stars*. You can also use some other receptacle that represents the theme of the story. For example, a book box for *Hey, Al!* can be a travel bag or suitcase, as the main characters make a journey to Paradise. This approach allows the box itself to become part of the array of items that lead to thought and predictions about the book.

Make sure that each of the story elements—characters, setting, problem, events, and resolution—are represented. Only one object or picture for each element is necessary, but you might want to introduce important secondary characters as well as the main character. Represent the characters in picture books by photocopying their pictures or showing the pictures from the book to your students. Or you can represent them with dolls, stuffed animals, or magazine pictures. Important vocabulary can become part of your book

Students can generate many ideas about the book before they read it.

box. Write the words on large word cards and illustrate them or tape each card to its corresponding object.

You can vary this strategy. After they have been introduced to the book and have made predictions, your students can keep a reading log handy, and jot down their ideas for additional items to go in the book box. Another variation is to incorporate a teaching strategy called "Story Drama" described by Walker (1996). When using this strategy, read with your students until you reach an interesting or dramatic episode. At this point, give students props that can help them role-play their predictions of how the story might end. Figure 11.4 shows an example of a book box used with first graders.

While this teaching strategy, because of its use of concrete objects, might seem to be most appropriate for young children, don't overlook it when teaching intermediate grades or middle school students. Learners of all ages can benefit from the concrete representation of ideas; I have used this strategy with adult learners, who quickly formed schema for the story by talking about the objects and pictures. Moreover, these visual and concrete representations of ideas are especially helpful to English language learners of all ages.

Book Box for *The Cat in the Hat,* by Dr. Seuss (1957)

Label the box "Fun in a Box." On the outside of the box, tape a large plastic key ring hook, so that it appears that the box is held together with a hook. Inside, place these items:

- A cat plush toy, which has a laundry detergent cap placed on its head
- Two magazine photos—a boy and a girl, both looking very bored
- A picture of a mother waving goodbye
- A picture of a rainy day or of thunderclouds
- A picture of a house
- Two fuzzy creature or monster plush toys to represent "Thing One" and "Thing Two"
- A plastic fish and fish bowl
- A ball
- A dish
- A fan
- A little toy man
- A picture of a hallway
- A kite
- A small broom or dustcloth

Figure 11.4 An example of a book box.

Picture Book Introductions

Picture books lend themselves to making predictions beautifully. Young children love focusing on the pictures of a well-written picture book; indeed, this is how many children develop their interest in reading, because they want to see how the pictures match the words. Teachers can capitalize on this appeal by encouraging children to look at the pictures before they begin to read a book. Chapter 6 introduced the teaching strategy of the picture walk, which is when you and the students look at the pictures throughout the book and make predictions about the story based on the sequence of pictures. When using pictures to facilitate predictions, instead of using all the pictures in the book (or "walking" through the pages), you can be more selective about the pictures you show and elicit predictions in a quicker and more specific manner. Your interactions in this teaching strategy are more focused, more precisely directed to the point of the story. This technique helps get children ready to read a book by whetting their appetite for it. Conceptually, the strategy of introducing books with pictures is quite simple. All you really need to do is let them see the pictures before they read, and talk about their predictions. But it is so much easier said than done!

Calkins (2001) tells us about the problems with activating prior knowledge, and warns against asking children to offer too much information before they read. Likewise, some students are easily distracted by comments and discussions that wander from the topic, and this distraction might actually impede comprehension (Williams, 1993).

To see how this happens, consider this example of classroom interaction between a first grade teacher and her students. They are preparing to read *Titch*, by

This teacher uses pictures in the book to help her students form schemata and make predictions.

Pat Hutchins (1971), which is about a little boy who is the youngest of three siblings. Pete, his brother, is the oldest and biggest. Mary, his sister, is also bigger than Titch. Easy-to-read sentences and bright, clear pictures show us that Pete and Mary have all the fun. They are big kids, so they are able to ride big bikes, fly high kites, and play real musical instruments. But Titch is so small that he must contend with struggling to keep up on his tricycle, wave a tiny little pinwheel, and blow on a small wooden whistle. Read what happens in Miss Mann's classroom.

Miss Mann's Lesson

Miss Mann shows her students the cover of the book that they are going to read, *Titch*. It shows a picture of a young boy holding a pinwheel, standing next to a leafy plant and a tricycle.

Miss Mann asks, "What do you think this story will be about?"

Sam offers, "He has a pinwheel."

Maggie says, "Yeah, it's blowing around, and he's playing with it."

"I had a pinwheel. I got it at the Easter egg hunt," says Mitchell.

"Yeah, so did I!" pipes in Marcus. "Mine had sparkles on it."

"I found a bunch of Easter eggs at my Easter egg hunt," says Marissa. "But I got mad 'cause Billy got to the big one at the same time I did and he grabbed it."

"Did you get a pinwheel, too?" asks Miss Mann.

"No, but I got some candy and an Easter necklace," replies Marissa.

"Well, how about the pinwheel? How do you think it fits in this story?" asks Miss Mann.

"I don't know," says Marissa.

"I think he's gonna ride the bicycle," says Ryan. "The boy is gonna ride a bike to his friend's house."

"Yeah, I like to ride my bike. I go to my friend's house all the time on my bike," says Mitchell.

"I got a BMX bike for my birthday!" says Frankie. "It has two speeds."

"OK, it's time to read," says Miss Mann. "Let's see if we can find out what happens to the boy in this story."

As you probably already know, first graders are eager to share—so much so, in fact, that they can quickly carry a conversation to many different places! Miss Mann's students were doing what young children will do if they are not given a direction. They talked of Easter egg hunts and going to friends' houses and BMX bicycles. None of these topics are part of the book *Titch*.

When introducing books to children, it is important to focus the talk on the topic of the book. It is a challenge to do this in a manner that engages the students' thinking, piques their curiosity, and remains true to the flavor of the book. Look at the example below to see how Miss Mann could change her picture book introduction to do these things.

"I'd like to show you a book that I think you will enjoy. It's called *Titch*. Titch is a young boy who has an older brother and an older sister. Look at this picture on the first page. You can see Titch, his sister Mary, and his brother Pete. Notice how much bigger they are than Titch. The next page shows Pete and Mary on their big bikes. When we turn the page, you'll see one of the reasons why Titch has a problem. Take a look. See, he is little, so he must have a little tricycle. He's at the bottom of a big hill. What is his problem?"

"He can't get the trike up the hill," says Mitchell.

"That's right, that is part of his problem," says Miss Mann. "Titch is little, and his brother and sister are big. He tries very hard to keep up with them and do the same things that they do, and he can't always do it. Take a look at another picture. You can see, on this page, that Pete and Mary have kites that fly high above the trees and houses. When we turn the page, what do we see?"

"A pinwheel! Titch has a pinwheel!" say several of the children.

"He sure does! Why would that be a problem?"

"Because he wants to fly a kite."

"Exactly! Titch wants to do the same things that his big brother and sister do, but he's just too little. But the author, Pat Hutchins, lets him solve that problem in a very interesting way. Let's read this book and found out what she makes Titch do to solve his problem."

Miss Mann uses the pictures to focus an introduction on the theme of the book. She shows the first three pictures in the book, inviting discussion about those, and then shows two more pictures later in the book. This book introduction invites response and engages thought, but does not open the discussion to lots of disconnected possibilities. Young readers, especially struggling ones, need to focus on the topic of the book that they are about to read. You need to make sure that your picture book introductions do just that. Be selective about the pictures that you show. Make sure that you keep the prereading talk focused on the topic or theme of the book. Not all pictures need to be revealed with every book; indeed, showing too many can spoil the enjoyment or the surprise ending.

Story Impressions

A teaching strategy that connects reading to writing is called *story impressions* (McGinley & Denner, 1987). It uses carefully chosen vocabulary to give students an idea of the elements of the story. This is an "impression," or simply the idea of the story. Once they see the words and form an impression, they write their own idea of the story as they believe it will transpire while they read. McGinley and Denner report that the accuracy of the students' ideas is of little relevance to their understanding of the story, and that the acts of forming impressions and verifying predictions contribute to their comprehension. Figure 11.5 on page 386 shows the procedure and an example.

Although this teaching strategy was designed for use with older readers, it can be successfully used with children as young as first grade. To do this, a teacher might show them about 10 word cards from the story, and a Beginning-Middle-End chart, as shown in Figure 11.6 on page 387. After identifying all the words, students work together to determine "where they go" on the B-M-E map, and then tell the story that they picture in their heads, based on the placement of the words.

Procedure for Story Impressions

1. Read the story carefully. Choose some words from the story that represent each of the story elements: setting, character, plot, and resolution. McGinley and Denner (1987) recommend that you use three words per element, with about 10 to 15 words for a short story or chapter, and about 15 to 20 words for a novel.
2. Type the words in a single vertical column. Keep the words in the order in which they will be encountered in the text. Display this list with the overhead projector or MS PowerPoint slide.
3. Introduce the story to the students by saying, "These are clues that will help you think about this story. You can use them to make predictions about what you think this story will be about. Look at the words, and form a mental picture in your mind of the story. Then share your ideas."
4. Use mental modeling to show your students how you can "see" at least part of this story in your mind. Then ask students to make suggestions of what they think this story will be about. Write their story on the board or overhead transparency.
5. Ask students to read the story, and compare the author's ideas to theirs.
6. Once students are comfortable with the strategy, make "story impressions lists" for them to use individually or in small groups. (You can duplicate these lists on bookmarks so they are handy during reading.) Ask students to write their story versions alone or with a partner, and to share these before reading. Then, read to confirm and compare predictions.

Example of a Story Impression for "The Hippopotamus at Dinner" from *Fables* (Lobel, 1980)

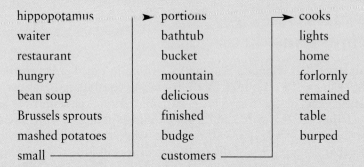

hippopotamus	➤ portions	➤ cooks
waiter	bathtub	lights
restaurant	bucket	home
hungry	mountain	forlornly
bean soup	delicious	remained
Brussels sprouts	finished	table
mashed potatoes	budge	burped
small	customers	

(Note to teacher: These words should be written in a single column.)

This is the way I think the story will happen:

Figure 11.5 Story impressions strategy.

Adaptation of Story Impressions with First Graders: "The Snow Glory" from *Henry and Mudge in Puddle Trouble* (Rylant, 1987)

Henry	flower	ate
Mudge	snow	mad
spring	glory	listen
outside	pick	
blue	throw	

(Note: Write words in a single vertical column.)

Beginning	Middle	End
Henry	blue	listen
Mudge	flower	
outside	snow	
spring	glory	
	pick	
	throw	
	ate	
	mad	

Figure 11.6 Adapting story impressions for first graders.

Strategies for Use with Nonfiction Text

Anticipation Guide

An effective way to activate prior knowledge about the author's topic is to ask students to read some statements about the topic, and decide, based only on what they know, whether they agree with them. This list of statements is called an **anticipation guide** (Readence, Bean & Baldwin, 1989), which is a teaching strategy that can serve the purpose of activating prior knowledge, as well as assessing what your students already know about the topic.

To create an anticipation guide, determine the main points made by the author of the text you want your students to read. Then, use what you know about your students to decide what they might already know about these concepts. Write no more than 10 points for the students to react to; make sure these statements are in-depth and challenge notions that the students might have about the topic. They should not be a mere check of factual knowledge; they can be statements that represent opinions or viewpoints. For example, some good anticipation guide statements for a textbook chapter on American government would be:

- U.S. citizens should vote on Election Day and help choose their government leaders.
- The president of the United States makes all the laws for this country.
- This is a free country—you can say whatever you want to say.

Type the statements and leave space for reaction before and after reading. Prior to reading, present the guide to the students, and ask them to make notations about whether they agree with them. Then ask them to read the selection, keeping these statements nearby so that they can reflect on them as they read. Afterwards, have students make additional notes about their thoughts. See Figure 11.7 for two

Anticipation Guide for *Whales* by Seymour Simon (1989)

Before Reading		Statements	After Reading	
Yes	No	1. Whales are very big mammals.	Yes	No
Yes	No	2. A whale needs to come to the surface of the water to breathe.	Yes	No
Yes	No	3. Whales are dangerous animals.	Yes	No
Yes	No	4. Whales need to be protected because they are in danger of becoming extinct.	Yes	No
Yes	No	5. Mother whales feed their babies by giving them milk.	Yes	No

Anticipation Guide for Chapter 1, "Out of Africa,"
from *Tell All the Children Our Story*, by Tonya Bolden (2001)

Before Reading		Chapter 1	After Reading 1	
Yes	No	1. King Charles II formed the Royal African Company in 1672 and sent many slaves from Africa to North America.	Yes	No
Yes	No	2. The first African American baptized in the American colonies was William Tucker, baptized in 1624.	Yes	No
Yes	No	3. The first Africans that were sent to the United States were indentured servants.	Yes	No
Yes	No	4. By the mid-1700s, there were 240,000 slaves in the 13 colonies.	Yes	No
Yes	No	5. The Church of England prohibited the enslavement of Christians.	Yes	No

Figure 11.7 Two examples of anticipation guides.

examples of anticipation guides for nonfiction text, using two very different types of text: *Whales* (Simon, 1989) and *Tell All the Children Our Story: Memories and Mementoes of Being Young and Black in America* (Bolden, 2001).

Brainstorming

One of the simplest ways to find out how much your students know about a topic is to ask them about it. When they **brainstorm,** they are recalling what they already know; thus, you will be able to assess their prior knowledge as well as make their collective knowledge visible for everyone in the group. The beauty of brainstorming is its versatility; it is a teaching strategy that enables you to facilitate comprehension. As your students become comfortable with it, it becomes a strategy that they initiate on their own before reading and writing.

Begin by using a mental model. For example: "When I get ready to gather information from a journal article, I think about what I already know. Sometimes, if I'm going to write a report, I make a list of things I know. This list helps to give me some idea of what to look for as I read the article. For example, look at this list, which I made last week when I was doing some research for a paper I'm writing."

After showing an example from your own work, introduce the text you want your students to read. Say, "Tell us what you know about _____." Then list their responses. Use this list to generate predictions or discuss important vocabulary before they read. Keep the list handy as students read the text and verify predictions. Remember that activation of prior knowledge works best when teachers explicitly compare predictions to text while reading (Duke & Pearson, 2002).

Brainstorming with cooperative groups is a useful way to generate ideas about a topic. Campbell and Harris (2001) show how to use brainstorming in cooperative groups of adults; here, this activity is adapted to work for older children. Give each small group a stack of slips of paper. Put the stack in the middle of the table, and make sure everyone has a pencil. Say, "We'll brainstorm everything we know about _____. Think about this topic and write down something that you know about it on one of the slips of paper. Put this slip in the middle of the table for everyone to see. Then get another slip and write your next thought. Keep doing this until you cannot think of anything else. You may look at the thoughts that your team members write down, because they might give you an idea for something else. When we're all finished, as a group, take a look at all of the thoughts that each of you wrote on these slips of paper. Tape these slips on a large piece of newsprint. Leave out the ones that are duplicates or repetitions. This will be your cooperative ideas chart."

Once the small groups have completed their charts, you can display them and compare them to the rest of the charts in the class. This display is a collective body of knowledge from the entire class. You could also use them for making predictions and drawing conclusions in the small groups.

Another way to gather lots of ideas is to use a strategy called *Two Minute Fast Facts.* Ask each student to write the numbers from 1 to 25 down the side of a piece of paper. Introduce the topic, and tell students to list everything they know about this topic in two minutes, and add more numbers on the list if needed. Time the students: when two minutes have passed, ask the students to draw a line under the last fact that they wrote. Now, ask the students to read the chapter, article, or book and look for these facts as they read. Also have them think about new facts that

Modifying Instruction for

ELL

Reading from a Science Textbook

GRADE LEVEL: K–1

- **Objective**

  After participating in an experiment and then reading about it in a big book, students will write sentences that describe the outcome of the experiment.

- **Preparation**

  This lesson plan is written for the big book *Matter and Energy* (Harcourt Science, 2002), which accompanies the Harcourt Science series for first grade. Any other similar concept book can be used. Many science and social studies textbook series publish companion big books to go with their units of instruction.

- **Materials**

  - Big book *Matter and Energy* (Harcourt Science, 2002)
  - Concrete items to use in an experiment on floating or sinking: beach ball, toy boat, bar of soap, rock, piece of driftwood, tub of water

- **Procedure**

  1. Activate prior knowledge by asking students to name each of the common items. If possible, ask an aide, parent, or tutor to help name the objects in the native language of the ELL students in your classroom.

  2. Show the students the tub of water and ask, "I wonder if these things will float in this tub of water. How can we find out?" Elicit responses, and guide students to the idea that they must experiment by putting the objects in the water to find out.

  3. Make a chart that looks like this:

Floats	Sinks

  4. Put the objects in the tub of water to determine if they float or sink.

  5. Write the name of the object under the appropriate heading. Use English and the language of your ELL students.

  Modifications for ELL are printed in color.

6. Now read pages 13 to 15 to the students. Show them the pages as you read, and point to the words and pictures. Use gestures as necessary.

7. Write important vocabulary on cards and add these to the word wall. Write the words on cards in both languages.

8. Ask students to write two sentences and illustrate them. Have them label their drawings in their native language.

   A _____ floats in water.

   A _____ sinks in water.

they learn as they read. After reading, give the students another two minutes to list new facts that they learned. You can adapt this strategy for younger students by asking them to write an idea about the topic on an index card, and when the two minutes are over, sharing the card with the group. Tape all the cards to the chalkboard, grouping them into appropriate categories.

This strategy is particularly useful with short pieces of text that contain much factual information, such as textbook chapters or newspaper articles. Older students enjoy seeing the list of facts grow and are often excited by racing the clock as they remember what they've learned. This "fast facts" strategy is good to use if you want to broaden your students' understanding about a rather common topic. For example, I have used this technique when teaching with the book *How Many Days to America?* by Eve Bunting (1988). I ask the students to list all the things they know about Thanksgiving before reading. Then, they read or listen to this thought-provoking book, which tells how a Caribbean family immigrates to the United States during the month of November. After reading the story, the list of thoughts about Thanksgiving always changes, with more emphasis on the value and purpose behind the holiday.

This is similar to another brainstorming strategy called *quickwrites* (Routman, 2000), in which the students are invited to brainstorm in the form of writing. Routman suggests giving students a prompt and allowing 3 to 10 minutes of uninterrupted writing. Students can write as much as they can, not concerning themselves with mechanics or form. The resulting text can serve as the beginnings of a draft, or as a list of ideas for future writing.

Concrete Experiences

If your students are not familiar with the topic that is in the book that they are preparing to read, you need to be sure to enhance their knowledge of that topic. This strategy is especially important for nonfiction, especially in subject areas in which students may have some misconceptions. It is also important when students read historical fiction or contemporary fiction that is based on factual historical events. The teaching strategy of **concrete experiences** can help.

Concrete experiences can take many forms. The key word is "concrete," because the assumption is that the students lack firsthand experiences with the subject, and need to see, hear, touch, smell, or taste the concept in order to have knowledge of it. I remember when some of my first graders were reading a story that contained the word "earth." Their association with this word was quite remote; they understood it in terms of the word "globe." When asked to explain the word, they described it as a big round ball that has water and land on it. But they did not realize that "earth" was also what they stood on literally every day, and that the soil under their feet could also be "earth." So we went outside and dug holes for a few minutes, examining the dirt and talking about the "land" part of the earth. Once returning inside, I showed them some sentences like this one:

The farmer turned over the _____ with his shovel.

Then we determined some words that could go in the blank, including the word "earth."

What are some other concrete experiences that would be helpful for your students? The answer depends upon the subject and the children. To use your time wisely, pick an experience that directly relates to the topic of the book and can be done fairly quickly. You also want to make sure that the experience will not lend itself to misconceptions.

Take a look at these ideas for using concrete experiences:

- Experiments
- Dramatic presentations
- Role playing
- Short videos or films
- Historical reenactments
- Field trips
- Manipulation of concrete objects
- Cooking
- Nature walks

Notice that many of these experiences are typically done after reading a selection. For example, many science textbooks explain a concept, and then give directions on how to conduct an experiment that utilizes that concept. In order to activate prior knowledge in a concrete manner, you should turn that upside-down. Do the experiment with the students first, and let them see the results. Then have them read to find out why it happened.

 K–8 The KWL Strategy

This popular teaching strategy, called *What I Know—What I Want to Learn—What I Learned* (**KWL**), was developed by Ogle (1986) to help students use their prior knowledge of and interest in a subject to guide them in investigating and reading more about the topic. In its simplest form, the strategy consists of a graphic organizer, that is completed through guidance by the teacher, and looks like the three-column one shown in Figure 11.8. Ogle recommended that this strategy be used with nonfiction. Its steps are:

1. Brainstorm the topic and list what you already know.
2. List additional information that you would like to learn about the topic.
3. Investigate the topic by reading and researching.
4. List what you learned.

Bryan suggests that the teacher "question the known" (1998, p. 618), thereby challenging the students to think about the gaps in their understanding of the topic and develop questions that would help them direct their inquiry to finding out more about the topic. She also modified this strategy so that students can brainstorm and list possible sources of information. Thus, she has presented the strategy as KWWL: *What I Know, What I Want to Learn, Where I Can Learn This, and What I Learned* (p. 618). This is a particularly helpful modification of the strategy when you want your students to learn about different types of expository text, such as biographies, encyclopedias, Internet resources, and so on. Schmidt

What We Know	What We Want to Know	What We Learned
• Native Americans lived in our area of Pennsylvania. • They lived here before white people lived here. • Some of our towns in Pennsylvania are named after Native Americans.	• What is the name of the tribe of Native Americans who lived here? • What happened to the Native Americans who lived here? • Where are they now?	Delawares—They moved westward and ended up in Oklahoma. Erie—They lived along the south shore of Lake Erie, but most were wiped out by the Iroquois in 1654. Susquehannocks—They lived along the Susquehanna River. They caught diseases brought by European settlers. They were attacked by Marylanders and the Iroquois. They were destroyed as a nation in 1675. Shawnees—They were constantly at war with European settlers. They moved west to Oklahoma.

Figure 11.8 Example of a KWL chart from a second grade class.

Things to Do Before Reading

Here is a letter you can send to families about pre-reading activities. ●

Dear Families,

When you select a book from the bookstore or library, what do you do? Do you check out its length? Do you read the back cover or inside flaps? Do you think about what you already know about the author or the topic of the book? Do you find yourself making guesses, or predictions, about how the book might turn out?

All of these things that mature readers do to "figure out" a book before reading it are important to understanding it, and they are part of what we call "activating background knowledge."

To prepare your child to read a book at school, I teach him or her to read the title and think about what it says about the book. If the book has pictures, we look at some of them and make guesses about the content of the book. Sometimes we already know about the author, so we think about that author's work, and make some predictions. Words from the book will also give us clues, so sometimes I take some words from the book, and ask your

Caregivers can help their children prepare to read a book.

child to make predictions about it based on what he or she knows about these words.

It is also important to know the type of book your child is reading, because that can help prepare him or her for it. In class, your child is learning to tell the difference between fiction and nonfiction.

If it is fiction, it will most likely be a story, with characters, setting, and a plot. Usually, but not always, the plot is when a character has a problem to solve. If the book is nonfiction, it will be an informational book, written by an author whose purpose was to teach something or make an important point.

You can help your child by doing some things before reading. First, determine whether the book is fiction or nonfiction, then do one or more of these things:

- Thumb through the book and look at two or three of the pictures.
- Think about the title and author.
- Read just the first page or the first paragraph.
- Talk about the possibilities that you see in this book. This is called making predictions.
- If the book is fiction, remember that most stories consist of characters with a problem to solve. Make predictions about the character and the problem he or she might have.
- If the book is nonfiction, remember that the author is trying to teach you something or make an important point. Make predictions about what you would learn from this book.

You can make a short list of these predictions if you wish, or just keep them in your head. Finally, ask your child to read the book to verify the predictions!

Sincerely,

Your child's teacher

advocates modifying the KWL strategy by adding a fourth column to the graphic organizer, called "More Questions" (1999, p. 789). Once the children have researched areas of interest and have listed their new understandings, Schmidt suggests that they write additional questions for further study.

All of these variations of the strategy encourage inquiry about a topic of interest and are best suited for activating prior knowledge about the topic. The KWL strategy and its variations are also appropriate when you wish to use multiple sources of information, such as magazine articles, trade books, encyclopedia articles, web sites, and newspapers. Keep in mind also that the strategy can be done as a large group, with the class dictating while the teacher transcribes on the chart, in small groups with a scribe for a common chart, or individually. Moreover, KWL is a teaching strategy that can become a reading strategy. Once students become accustomed to completing the KWL chart as a group, you can duplicate the chart for each student, and ask them to use it for their own personal brainstorming and fact-finding purposes. This way, it becomes a mechanism for organizing information as they read and take notes for written reports.

There is one caution about the use of KWL. It is possible that when you ask the students to brainstorm for the "What I Know" column, they will supply you with misconceptions. Many teachers are understandably hesitant to display information that is erroneous. To work around this, you can label the column, "What I Think I Know" or "My Current Knowledge about _____."

Summary:
The Value of Prior Knowledge

Mature readers prepare themselves to read. This concept is indicated in educational research, but it also holds true in our everyday reading lives. As a reader, I know that I need to preview a book before I purchase it or check it out. Reading the back cover, skimming a few pages, and checking the first paragraph to see if it holds my interest are ways that I prepare myself to read. I think about what I already know about this subject, and ponder the possibility that the book will connect with my prior knowledge. Most of the time, if I make a hasty decision and fail to preview a book, I am disappointed. I have a small stack of books in a closet that are evidence of failure to prepare myself for reading.

The same holds true for children. This chapter has shown you some strategies for helping children use what they know to bridge the unknown—a new book. Discussed in it were the importance of activating and assessing prior knowledge when reading fiction, using a variety of techniques, including focused discussions, predictions with book boxes or story impressions, and picture book introductions. Use of some of these techniques included a caution regarding the tendency of children to wander off topic, creating misconceptions. This chapter also introduced several strategies for use with nonfiction, including concrete objects, KWL, anticipation guides, and brainstorming. Using these strategies in your classroom helps your students prepare themselves for a wonderful journey with a book.

To read summaries of the strategies featured in this chapter, see the Reviewing the Big Picture box, which also includes the corresponding teaching standards and principles for each strategy.

Technology Resources

- **www.allamericareads.org/pdf/chapter/before_reading.pdf** A document sponsored by All America Reads, a web site devoted to motivating secondary school readers. This page contains some excellent "Before Reading" strategies.

- **curry.edschool.virginia.edu/go/readquest/strat/abc.html** This ReadingQuest web page is called "ABC Brainstorm." It is a variation of collecting ideas through brainstorming. The web site lists several other comprehension strategies as well.

- **www.mcps.k12.md.us/departments/isa/staff/abita/english/reading_strategies. htm#priorknow** Retrieved from a very thorough web site sponsored by Montgomery County Public Schools in Maryland, this page lists 18 reading strategies, many of which are to be implemented before reading. The strategy is defined, and then the authors explain how it takes place. When it should be used (before, during, or after reading) is included, as are technological resources needed to complete the strategy.

---

expect the world

The New York Times
nytimes.com

Themes of the Times

Expand your knowledge of the concepts discussed in this chapter by reading current and historical articles from the *New York Times* by visiting the "Themes of the Times" section of the Companion Web Site.

Reviewing the Big Picture
Strategies for Activating Prior Knowledge

Strategy	Description	Most Appropriate Type of Text/ Grade Level	IRA Standards	INTASC Principles	NAEYC Standards	ACEI/NCATE Standards
Book box	Put objects and pictures that are related to the story in a decorated box. Present the book box items one at a time, inviting predictions about story elements.	Fiction/K–2, 3–5	2.2, 2.3, 4.1, 4.2	4, 7	4b (Use with read-alouds or shared reading)	2.1, 3.1, 3.2, 3.3, 3.4
Picture book introductions	Show students selected pictures from the story. Use them to generate predictions and discussion about the story.	Fiction/K–2	2.2, 2.3, 4.1, 4.2	4, 7	4b (Use with read-alouds or shared reading)	2.1, 3.1, 3.2, 3.3, 3.4
Story impressions	Provide students with a list of words that represent each element in a story. Ask them to predict the story based on the impression they get from the list, and to write their own version of this story.	Fiction/3–5, 6–8	2.2, 2.3, 4.1, 4.2	4, 7	NA	2.1, 3.1, 3.2, 3.3, 3.4
Anticipation guide	Write statements that are related to the text. Make some of them factual and some of them false. Have students read the statements, make predictions about the text, and indicate whether the statements are true. Read to confirm.	Nonfiction/3–5, 6–8	2.2, 2.3, 4.1, 4.2	4, 7	NA	2.1, 2.8, 3.1, 3.2, 3.3, 3.4
Brainstorming	Ask students to generate lists or webs of ideas related to the topic in the text they will read.	Nonfiction/K–2, 3–5, 6–8	2.2, 2.3, 4.1, 4.2	4, 7	4b (Use with read-alouds or shared reading)	2.1, 2.8, 3.1, 3.2, 3.3, 3.4
Concrete experiences	Provide manipulative materials and experiences related to the text.	Nonfiction/K–2, 3–5	2.2, 2.3, 4.1, 4.2	4, 7	4b (Use with read-alouds or shared reading)	2.1, 2.8, 3.1, 3.2, 3.3, 3.4
KWL	Ask students to list things they already know about the topic and things that they would like to find out. After reading, have them explain what they learned.	Nonfiction/K–2, 3–5, 6–8	2.2, 2.3, 4.1, 4.2	4, 7	4b (Use with read-alouds or shared reading)	2.1, 2.8, 3.1, 3.2, 3.3, 3.4

12

Facilitating Your Students' Comprehension

"Can you tell me what it says, Nigel?" she asked.

"That's too hard," Nigel said.

"Lavender?"

"The first word is I," Lavender said.

"Can any of you read the whole sentence?" Miss Honey asked, waiting for the "yes" that she felt certain was going to come from Matilda.

"Yes," Matilda said.

"Go ahead," Miss Honey said.

Matilda read the sentence without any hesitation at all.

"That is really very good indeed," Miss Honey said, making the understatement of her life. "How much *can* you read, Matilda?"

"I think I can read most things, Miss Honey," Matilda said, "although I'm afraid I can't always understand the meanings."

Matilda (Dahl, 1988)

My favorite character in Matilda is Miss Honey. She is a kind, friendly, and caring teacher. Miss Honey is a very special person to Matilda because she taught and listened to her when her parents didn't.

Allie, grade 4

Your students have selected a book to read. They have made predictions about it and they have discussed prior experiences with the topic. They are ready to read!

What now? Start by thinking about what happens when you read the Personal Reflection.

- If your comprehension breaks down when you read, what do you do?
- What makes reading most comfortable for you?

Because reading is a covert activity, it is easy to assume that its processes are going along smoothly when children read. But reading is not always happening the way it should. Sometimes children misunderstand what they read. Sometimes they read a word as something other than what it is, producing a misunderstanding, and they do not even realize it. Sometimes they are mouthing the words very carefully and correctly, but they have no idea what the words are telling them. Children who are accomplished readers—like Roald Dahl's delightful character Matilda—stop themselves and fix the problem when these things happen. Children who are poor readers do not. Many times, poor readers do not even realize that they have misconstrued the message of the print.

Even the best young readers could be missing much of what is available to them when they read. Children who can read and retell the sequence of events perfectly often do not "read between the lines," getting at what the author is really trying to say. Many readers have trouble interpreting meanings beyond what is literal and explicit.

This chapter is about facilitating comprehension as students read and helping students figure out what to do when they misunderstand their reading. The importance of teaching comprehension cannot be understated; real reading *is* comprehending. The National Reading Panel reports that there is a solid scientific basis for concluding that seven categories of text comprehension instruction improve comprehension in nonimpaired readers. These types of instruction are: "comprehension monitoring, cooperative learning, use of graphic and semantic organizers, question answering, question generation, story structure, and summarization" (2000a, p. 15). All seven of these, plus others, are explained in this chapter.

Sometimes you will use teaching strategies that help students do things that good readers do, such as predict, infer, visualize, and summarize. These strategies focus on the processes of reading and enable students to comprehend the text as a whole. Your support will be tangible and visible, perhaps in the form of written reading guides, or questions and interactions at stop points. At other times, your students will quietly, and on their own, use reading strategies that you have taught them, such as monitoring their own comprehension as they read, generating their own questions, or making predictions and confirming them. The goal of it all is understanding of and reaction to what is read.

Teacher Questioning

Questioning is the classic teacher behavior (Gall, 1984). Why do teachers question when they teach reading? Questions serve two purposes. One is to check comprehension. The other is to facilitate it. Teachers who use questions to check comprehension typically wait until after the story has been read in its entirety. That approach focuses the lesson on the product of reading, and while it may be useful for determining how well students read, a steady diet of asking students questions after reading is not conducive to developing their comprehension, particularly if the questions ask for factual and literal recall (Anderson & Biddle, 1975). Durkin (1978–1979) pointed this out in a classic study conducted in 1978, in which she observed 36 intermediate-grade classrooms. After classroom observations of the manner in which teachers teach comprehension, she found that the teachers in her study relied too much on product-oriented questioning. They asked questions of students, expecting them to comprehend text without showing them how to gain meaning from the print. In fact, during most of their instructional time, teachers assessed their students' comprehension rather than teach comprehension strategies. After twenty years—and much research—Pressley, Wharton-McDonald, Mistretta-Hampston, and Echevarria (1998) reported similar results in a study of 10 fourth- and fifth-grade classrooms. Pressley and others observed that, while teachers were testing comprehension, they were not teaching strategies for understanding text.

If you want to facilitate comprehension and make it more likely that comprehension will occur, then questioning students while they read is appropriate. This type of questioning focuses on the process of reading and engages students' thinking about the text. As mentioned in Chapter 4, an *engagement perspective* is a way of teaching and assessing that focuses on active learning and "enable(s) all students to succeed and become motivated, strategic, and competent readers" (Wilkinson & Silliman, 2000, p. 352). While interacting with students as they read, the manner in which you ask questions, seek response, and encourage students to think about the text will have much to do with their view of reading as a meaning-construction process.

There is an art to asking questions. Research has shown the importance of teacher–student verbal interaction in the classroom; in particular, the questions teachers ask have an impact on their students' comprehension (Anderson & Biddle, 1975; Gall, 1984). According to Duke and Pearson, "students' understanding and recall can be readily shaped by the types of questions to which they become accustomed" (2002, p. 222). The strategies on the following pages can be used while students are reading, at stop points or between chapters. These behaviors also hold true for discussions held before and after reading.

Ask Text Structure–Based Questions

To focus on the process of reading, make your questions fit the text that your students have in their hands (Beck and McKeown, 1981). If students are reading a piece of fiction, ask questions that help them focus on the elements of story.

Diversity in the Reading Classroom

Needs of Asian American Children

One of the fastest growing ethnic groups in the United States is Asian Americans, whose ethnic origins include four major groups: East Asian (Chinese, Japanese, Korean); Pacific Islanders; Southeast Asian (Thai and Vietnamese); and South Asian (Indian and Pakistani). Each of these subgroups have different histories, languages, and ways of adapting (Feng, 1994). However, stereotypes and misconceptions about Asian American children prevail. The greatest misconception is the idea that Asian children are high-achieving "whiz kids" and are "problem-free" (p. 2). This stereotype is misleading and creates a problem for some children. Many times, Asian American children "do not reach the starry heights of the celebrated few, and an alarming number are pushing themselves to the emotional brink in their quest for excellence" (p. 3).

Asian American children face an enormous number of challenges in the classroom, and many of them pertain to student–teacher or student–student verbal interchanges. Cultural differences that involve language affect the way in which these students interact with others, and their actions can be misleading. Asian American children often do not volunteer to respond to questions and have been socialized to speak in a soft voice. When they respond to a question, they hesitate before speaking, and have a tendency not to use the word "no." Their nonverbal behaviors include repeated head nodding, lack of eye contact, and smiles that may indicate confusion and embarrassment more than pleasure (Huang, 1997). Teachers who are unaware of these cultural nuances can easily misconstrue all of these behaviors.

Talking with students about what they have read and questioning them as they move through the pages are all part of the discourse that takes place in the strategies described in this chapter. But with the cultural differences that abound, there is potential for failure. Listed here are several ways to support Asian American children as they participate in reading and writing activities in your classroom (Feng, 1994; Huang, 1997; Pang, Colvin, Tran & Barba, 1992; Thornburg, 1993):

- Find out the specifics of your students who are immigrants. Traumatic experiences in war or refugee camps can influence children's reactions to the classroom environment.
- Pay attention to your students' reactions to things in their environment. Do not rely on head nodding or smiles to indicate agreement.
- Carefully select children's literature about Asian Americans. Books should avoid stereotypes about Asian backgrounds and should depict settings in the United States with strong characters and plots. A few recommendations are: *Dear Juno* (Pak, 1999), *Grandfather Counts* (Cheng, 2000), *Child of the Owl* (Yep, 1977), and *Wingman* (Pinkwater, 1975).
- Learn some words in the students' native language(s) and use them in classroom lessons, on the word wall, or in language experience charts.
- Allow, but do not expect, children to share stories from their personal experiences.
- Allow students to volunteer to answer questions, rather than expecting them to answer questions in front of a group of peers.
- Have students work in pairs so that the Asian American students can interact on a one-to-one basis.

Likewise, if your students are reading informational text, ask questions that focus on the main ideas of the work. Figure 12.1 shows the types of questions you can ask that reflect story elements, and Figure 12.2 shows the questions you can ask that mirror the structure of informational text.

Characters
- Who is the main character in the story? What are the clues that tell you this?
- How would you describe the character?
- How does the author make the character(s) seem real?

Setting
- Where does the story take place? What are the clues that tell you this?
- When does the story take place? What are the clues that tell you this?
- How important is the setting to this story? Could the story happen in some other place or time? Why or why not?
- Does the setting change in this story? How important is the setting change?

Problem
- What is the problem in the story? What are the clues that tell you this?
- How do the characters react to this problem?

Events
- What events result from the characters' problem-solving actions?
- Which events caused other events?
- What's *really* going on here?
- What does the author want us to think here?

Resolution
- How is the problem solved?
- What is the character's reaction to the resolution?
- How would you describe this story resolution?
- How satisfied are you with this story ending?

Theme
- Why did the author write this story?
- What lesson is learned?

Figure 12.1 Questions that reflect story structure.

Ask Prediction-Check Questions

To check the predictions that they have made and confirm them from their reading; you can ask at appropriate stop points a simple question such as, "Which of your predictions happened?" When asking for specific predictions, be sure to make them fit the text being read. For example, when asking for a prediction for *Hey, Al* (Yorinks, 1986), you could ask, "Where do you think the bird will take Al and Eddie?"

Explore more than one possibility. After you receive one prediction, ask questions that encourage divergent thinking, such as: "What's another possibility?" "What is a different idea?" or "What else could happen?"

Descriptive text pattern

- Describe the (topic that the author describes).
- Name the characteristics of the (topic that the author describes).
- What is remarkable about the (topic that the author describes)?
- What questions are still unanswered about (topic)?

Sequential text pattern

- Tell the events that are most important.
- Describe to someone how to make a (topic of the book).
- What do you know about (topic) so far?

Cause/Effect text pattern

- What is the cause of (topic of the book)?
- What is the effect of (topic of the book)?
- Why does (topic of the book) happen?

Compare and contrast text pattern

- Tell how (first topic) is different from (second topic).
- Tell how (first topic) is similar to (second topic).
- What other (topics) are similar to (the topic the author describes)?

Problem and solution text pattern

- When (topic) happens, what do people do to try to solve the problem?
- Which solutions work best? Why?
- Which solutions are not helpful? Why?

Figure 12.2 Questions that focus on nonfiction text structure.

Pay attention to the depth and breadth of your students' predictions. There are no "right" predictions, only plausible ones that can be backed up with information and inferences from the text. A risk-free classroom atmosphere helps to facilitate predictions, because your students aren't afraid to make a logical prediction that differs from the author's actual words. Moreover, risk-taking is necessary for your students who are learning English as a second language. "Children must feel free to take risks, to try out their new language, and to err" (McCauley & McCauley, 1992, p. 528).

Even so, it is extremely important to keep your finger on the pulse of the predicting that goes on in your students' readings. Your students need to know that predictions are logical conclusions drawn from the clues that have been given in the text. In children's literature, there are generally three sources for predictions: the author's words, the pictures in the book, and the prior knowledge of the reader. Good readers do not guess wildly; instead, they make very logical guesses about what will come next on the page.

To cultivate reflective readers who predict logically, ask students to justify the conclusions that they have drawn. It is crucial for them to be able to explain why

Prediction Chart with Reasons and Confirmation

What I predict will happen	Why I am making this prediction	What actually happened
Page: _____		
Page: _____		
Page: _____		
Page: _____		

Additional examples of prediction charts are included in the *Toolkit for Teachers of Literacy* book.

Figure 12.3 Sample prediction chart.

they have made a prediction, based on the text, the pictures (if available), and their own experiences. Research indicates that "making and justifying interpretations of the text" can be expected of children as young as second grade (Pearson & Duke, 2002, p. 249). You can ask them to point to the evidence on the page, or tell how the prediction connects to something that they already know. Some teachers ask students to use sticky notes to mark pages and jot down their predictions. After reading, the students return to their notes and confirm the predictions. You can also ask prediction questions during shared reading. Using a sticky note, cover a word in the text and as you read aloud, stop at the covered word and ask students to make predictions about it. Write their guesses on the sticky note, and then reveal the first letter. Make revisions to the predictions accordingly. This type of predicting allows students to think about the cueing systems that enable them to solve problems in the text (Clay, 1991; Goodman, 1994; Halliday, 1975). Figure 12.3 shows an example of a prediction chart that can be used to scaffold this process.

Begin Discussions with Statements

Good "questions" do not necessarily end with a question mark. Sometimes requests or declarative statements work just as well. Rather than asking a question to start the discussion, make a thought-provoking statement. Then ask students to respond to the statement. For example, suppose you were working with some fifth graders who have chosen to read *Pedro's Journal* (Conrad, 1991), a book about Christopher Columbus's journey across the Atlantic Ocean in 1492. You might make this assertion: "Some people think that Christopher Columbus really did not do such wonderful things. I'd like to know what you think." This kind of opening to the discussion is similar to the kinds of things adults say as they share information about books with each other, and lends itself to much eager talk among children.

Ask Questions That Include

Use inclusive questions, rather than exclusive ones. Exclusive questions are those that exclude some students from the discussion, usually inadvertently. For example, the teacher asks, "How many of you have a pesky younger brother?" About half the students in the group raise their hands. What happens to the remainder of the group? The teacher has essentially cut some students out of the conversation. Only the children who have younger brothers can answer, and of those, only the ones with brothers who are pests are invited to join in. A better way to state that question is: "Think about a pesky little boy that you know. How is he like Peter's little brother Fudge in Judy Blume's (1972) *Tales of a Fourth Grade Nothing?*"

Other very common exclusive questions are similar to these: "Who has been on a camping trip before?" or "How many of you have visited New York City?" These questions are more inclusive when worded this way: "Think about what it might be like to go camping. Describe it for us." Or, "Think about what you know about New York City. Share that with your partner." Regardless of whether the students have actually experienced these things, they can share their thoughts based on what they know or think.

Avoid Rhetorical Questions

Rhetorical questions are another type of question often used by teachers, who are seeking a specific answer to an interpretive question. However, as Calkins asks, "In the whole scheme of things, why does it matter whether a child can repeat back the teacher's interpretation of a text?" (2001, p. 478). Rhetorical questions are wasted breath, because it takes no thought at all to simply agree with the teacher. An example is, "Don't you think that Gilly Hopkins is being a little bit rude to her new foster mother?" Instead, ask, "Why was Gilly so rude?"

Avoid "Yes or No" Questions

Questions that require only "yes" or "no" as answers are complete conversation stoppers. Imagine this exchange: The teacher asks, "Is Eddie, the dog in *Hey, Al* (Yorinks, 1986), a good dog?" The student replies, "Yes." Where does the teacher go from there? Any talk was stifled by a question that requires a one-syllable answer. Additionally, the teacher has implied that there is only one desired answer, and the only thing the students need to do is figure out what the teacher wants. A better way to ask this question is: "Think about Eddie, the dog in *Hey, Al*. What words can you use to describe him? Why?"

Give Wait Time

The typical pattern of interaction in classrooms is called **recitation,** which is a pattern of teacher question, student response, and teacher feedback. While the recitation prevails in classrooms across the country, and is part of the culture of schooling, Au (1993) tells us that this type of interaction is not necessarily appropriate for students of diverse backgrounds. Indeed, much research over the years has been critical of this pattern of interaction, indicating that it may not be conducive to thought-provoking interactions that are part of an engagement perspective to teaching reading for any of your students (Doyle, 1986).

However, one of the most intriguing conclusions to come out of teacher–student interaction research in the past thirty years is the idea of *wait time.* Rowe (1974) introduced this teaching strategy of a three-second pause that the teacher uses after asking questions and expecting response. Once the question is asked, the teacher pauses before calling on a student to respond, and then pauses again before giving feedback to that response. This type of interchange slows down the typical "recitation" and, according to Rowe, produces more thoughtful responses and more involvement from the students. This finding has been supported by several other researchers, most of whom investigated the effects of wait time usage in science lessons (White & Tisher, 1986).

Using wait time while talking to children about text can at the very least give everyone a chance to think before they talk. Look at the difference between the two examples shown in Figure 12.4. Notice that in Example #1, the teacher directs the question only to Derrick. The rest of the class has permission to tune out! Example #2 shows that the teacher gives the entire class something to think about, pauses, and then asks for an individual response. Thus, everyone is expected to think about the question. This gives the students some breathing room; they need time to reflect upon the discussion statements and questions. Au speaks of the importance of changing teacher–student interactions so that they resemble conversational talk (1993); using wait time may be one way to do this.

Example #1

Teacher: Derrick, based on these items in the book box, what do you think is the setting of the story, *Number the Stars?*

Derrick: Denmark.

Teacher: What gave you the clues?

Derrick: Because there's a map of Denmark in the box.

Teacher: Good prediction!

Example #2

Teacher: Everyone, look at the items in the book box. Based on what you see there, think about what might be the setting of the story. (Pause.) Now, someone share your thoughts with us. (Pause.) Derrick?

Derrick: I think it's in Denmark.

Teacher: (Pause.) That's a logical prediction, Derrick! Tell us where you got the clues.

Derrick: Because I see a map of Denmark in the box.

Figure 12.4 Giving everyone an opportunity to think about the question.

Encourage Student Interaction

Another way to accomplish conversational talk is to encourage students to talk to each other. Because the teacher–student interaction called recitation is such a strong component of our schooling culture, it is hard to break the pattern of dependency on the teacher (Au, 1993). One way to begin is to arrange the room so that they are all looking at each other. Sometimes children will look only at the teacher when they talk. Encourage the students to look at each other. If they find this difficult, avert your eyes as they talk. Tell them that you will be doing this, and have volunteers model student–student interaction. Additionally, sit with the group rather than stand at the front of the room, so that you are not the center of attention.

Au (1993) describes **talk story-like** interactions, based on her research with Hawaiian children. She found that these students, when allowed to use the kind of interaction that they use at home, make more logical inferences and talk about ideas from the text more frequently than when they are required to participate in the traditional recitation pattern of classroom talk. This kind of talk allows students to speak when they are ready, rather than wait to be called upon, and share personal connections and stories from home. A main feature of this type of interaction is the cooperation between students; they willingly jump in and help each other out when telling stories or offering responses.

Ask Questions That Require Thought

Ruddell reports that teachers who are influential tend to stimulate "active thinking and meaning construction," and are "highly skilled in their orchestration of question levels and concurrent use of questioning strategies as they effectively monitor student responses" (1994, p. 293). Tracey and Morrow describe their observations of exemplary primary grade teachers, and report that they saw "extensive use of questioning" in these classrooms (2002, p. 229).

Questions that require the students to infer information from clues and apply what they already know are most useful. This technique contrasts with questions that are literal, requiring answers that are reliant upon factual recall or are explicitly stated in the text.

By using *inferential questions*, you can ask students to "read between the lines." The author gives clues about the answers but does not come right out and state them. The reader must infer the answers, based on what the author implies. For example, in William Steig's *Sylvester and the Magic Pebble* (1969), Sylvester, a young donkey, finds a shiny pebble, and discovers that it has magic qualities, giving its holder whatever he wishes. While holding it, a fierce-looking lion approaches him. Panicking, Sylvester wishes he were a rock, so that he would go unnoticed by the lion. Instantly, he becomes a rock. An example of an inferential question for this book is this: "For how long was Sylvester a rock?" This is an inferential question because the author never tells us how long he was a rock, but we can determine that based on the information given to us in the words and pictures.

Another example, for the ending of the same book, is this question: "Why did Mr. Duncan put the pebble in a safe?" Again, we need to infer the answer to that question from all the information given to us in the book. The reader is transacting with the text to put together bits and pieces of information from the author to actively draw a conclusion.

Another way to ask questions is to draw out your students' prior knowledge. These questions require the reader to have some experiences with the story's concepts. Some clues for the answer may be partially implied in the book, but the reader needs to put this together with what he or she already knows. Of course, the question must be related to the text, but it extrapolates and carries the understanding of the text to another level. Readers relate this text to their own experiences and background knowledge.

An example comes from reading *The Alphabet Tree,* by Leo Lionni (1968). In this story, the word bug teaches letters to join together and form words. Eventually, they also learn to make words and sentences. At the end of the story, the letters line up together to send a very important message to the president. An example of a question that relies on the reader's knowledge is "Why is the message sent to the president an important one?" There is no information regarding this in the book; the reader must use what he or she knows about the world to make an inference and answer the question. Another such question for that book is "How is this book like one of Lionni's other books, *Swimmy* (1963)?"

Use Probing Questions

After the teacher asks a question and gets a response from a student, it is frequently helpful to continue asking additional questions that help to improve the original response. This technique is called **probing** and is associated with effective teaching (Nettles, 1987). Four types of probes to know are described here, using examples from a discussion of *Tar Beach* (Ringgold, 1991):

- *Clarifying*—The teacher asks the student to make his or her answer more clear. For example, the teacher asks, "Why did Cassie say that the George Washington Bridge was her most prized possession?" A student answers, "She

This student locates the place in the story that supports his answer to a question.

could fly over it." A clarifying probe here would be, "Tell us what you mean by that."

- *Extending*—The teacher asks the student to elaborate on the initial answer by adding more. For example, the teacher asks, "What does Cassie tell us about the union building her father is helping to build?" A student answers, "He works for a construction company." An extending probe is, "Tell us more about what the author says about her father's job."
- *Justifying*—The teacher requires the student to support his answer with information. Suppose the teacher asks, "What kind of troubles does the family have?" And the student answers, "Her dad doesn't always work." A justifying probe asks, "What clues does the author give you about that?"
- *Applying*—The teacher asks the student to relate an initial response to a different concept by predicting, inferring, comparing, and contrasting. If the teacher asks, "On the last page, the author tells us that flying is easy. Why is it easy?" The student answers, "Because all you need is somewhere to go that you can't get to in any other way." An applying probe would be, "So, what does the author mean by this?"

Give Feedback

Rosenshine and Stevens (1984) make some recommendations about giving feedback, based on findings from correlational research in studies of teachers' use of questions. When students answered questions poorly, effective teachers in several studies tended to help students arrive at the correct answer, or to revise the question. Thus, Rosenshine and Stevens suggest the following techniques:

- Stick with the student rather than redirecting the question to someone else.
- Rephrase the question so that it is clearer.
- Give hints or clues.

In their research, Rosenshine and Stevens found that when students' answers were satisfactory, effective teachers often did not give much feedback, other than a nod of the head or a short acknowledgement such as "Right" or "OK." They report that maintaining the momentum of the session was the most important consideration for the teacher, and that students tended to do well even if the teacher gave no feedback at all to correct answers. While this research involved practice sessions rather than literature discussions or guided reading lessons, we can conclude that feedback should be direct and brief, keeping students focused during classroom interactions.

Teaching Strategies That Facilitate Comprehension

Several teaching strategies have been designed to be used while your students are reading. They use questions and other types of teacher–student interactions, and serve the purpose of facilitating comprehension while reading. They can be used during guided reading sessions, literature circles, or reading workshops.

Question-Answer Relationships

Raphael (1986) offers a strategy that helps children sort out questions that are asked of them and determine the source of information that would help them with the answer. In the **Question-Answer Relationships** strategy, you can show them that there are four types of questions:

- *"Right there."* The answer to the question is found in the book, usually in the same sentence. Readers can point to the answer. This type of question is often asked in workbooks after students have read the story.
- *"Think and search."* The answer is found in the book, but in different places. Readers need to put information together from different pages in order to answer the question. Teachers often ask this type of question while students are reading, at stop points, or after reading to talk about what was learned.
- *"Author and you."* The answer is not explicitly stated in the story. The author gives hints, and the reader puts this together with what he or she already knows to get the answer. Teachers often ask this type of question after reading to generate some thought about the story.
- *"On my own."* The answer is entirely up to the reader. The author gives no clues. Many times, the reader does not have to read the story to answer this type of question, so it can be asked before reading, to brainstorm or predict.

To teach these question types, you need to model and explain them. When asking questions, be sure to talk about the sources of their answers and label them. For example, you can say something like, "I'd like to know what you think. The answer for this question will come from your head, not from the book." Put the categories on a chart so that students can refer to it as needed.

Teaching students these types of questions helps them to answer the ones that you ask, but also to generate questions of their own. As students read a piece of text, ask them to write one question of each type, to be used in a chapter review or literature discussion. A graphic organizer for managing this task is shown in Appendix B.

Directed Reading Thinking Activity

The **Directed Reading Thinking Activity (DRTA)** is a method of instruction that can be used with any stories read by your students. Its basic premise is to include prediction in the process of preparing to read, as well as in the process of reading the story (Stauffer, 1975). The teacher prepares the students by asking them to look at the pictures on the cover and first page, and to think about how the pictures lead to a prediction of the story. Additionally, the students and teacher discuss the title, which might lend itself to making predictions. Vocabulary is not taught prior to reading; Stauffer said that there was no need to preteach vocabulary, because it is controlled in basal programs (and more recently, in leveled readers). Instead, students are asked to follow these rules:

- Read to the end of the sentence.
- Use pictures to help.
- Sound it out.
- Ask for help.

Students are also asked to make predictions about the story and to continually verify them as they read. The teacher chooses stop points throughout the story, and at each, asks them to confirm their predictions. An important part of this strategy is for students to explain how their predictions are confirmed; they must provide evidence from the text. The procedure is shown in Figure 12.5.

A variation of the DRTA is the DLTA, called the **Directed Listening Thinking Activity.** Richek (1987) suggests this variation, which is a lesson in the same format, with the teacher reading the selection to the students. Reading to the students allows students to accomplish the same objectives without the demands of decoding, and allows nondecoders and English language learners to work with challenging pieces of children's literature.

Reciprocal Teaching

Developed by Palincsar and Brown (1984), the **Reciprocal Teaching** strategy shows students how to use four processes involved with constructing meaning: predicting, questioning, summarizing, and clarifying. Extensive research backs up this strategy, which indicates that there is "very strong empirical, scientific evidence that the instruction of more than one strategy in a natural context leads to the acquisition and use of reading comprehension strategies and transfer to standardized comprehension tests" (Trabasso & Bouchard, 2002). The teacher must model the technique first, using a small segment of text. Then, the teacher and students switch roles. The procedure is shown in Appendix B.

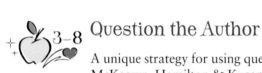

Question the Author

A unique strategy for using questions during reading is **Question the Author** (Beck, McKeown, Hamilton & Kucan, 1997). Originally designed to be used with content area textbooks, it has been broadened to be used with fiction, also. The strategy helps students overcome some of the mystery of their textbook by talking about it in terms of its author, which truly allows for students to actively transact with the text. In this strategy, the teacher explains to the students that authors are people who might or might not have made themselves clear in their writing. The purpose is to empower the reader. According to the authors, "If students understood that their task as readers was to make what they read understandable, it might promote the kind of active engagement in reading that is needed for learning to take place" (p. 15). Beck and her colleagues recommend the use of "queries," or questions that are designed to help students construct meaning while they are reading, rather than simple assessment-type questions. The procedures for planning and implementing Question the Author are shown in Figure 12.6 on page 414.

Say Something

Say Something is an interactive, verbal activity that provides scaffolding while children read (Harste, Burke & Watson, as cited in Harste, Short & Burke, 1988). While reading, students pause at stop points and share their thoughts with each

The Directed Reading Thinking Activity

Activating Background Knowledge

Have students recall important information that relates to the story. Provide background experiences if it is necessary. Use questions such as these:

- This story is about _____. What do you know about _____ ?
- In this story, _____ happens. What do you suppose will happen if _____ ?
- Imagine this problem: _____. Let's list possible solutions.

Guided Silent Reading

Preparing to Read

To introduce the story, read the title to students, show them the cover and cover page, tell them the author's name, and show them a few appropriate pictures. You can also show them a list of words that they will see in the story. Ask them to make a prediction about the outcome of this story based on all of this information. Have them write these predictions in their journals or whisper them to their partners, or write them on the board for everyone to see. Use questions such as these:

- What does this title tell you about the story?
- What prediction can you make based on what you know about the author?
- What does this list of vocabulary make you think of? How could they fit into the story?
- Look at the picture on page _____. What prediction does it bring to mind?

Guiding Silent Reading

Before teaching this lesson, you need to plan and verify appropriate stop points to ask for predictions. This number should be low; depending on the length of the story, only one or two stop points are necessary. Tell the students to read silently to the first stop point, giving them a silent signal for letting you know when they are finished. When everyone reaches this cut-off point, discuss what was read so far in relation to the predictions made. After predictions have been discussed and verified, if you wish to extend the discussion, ask a question that does not rely on factual recall. With this question, require the students to infer based on what the author is saying, as well as on what they already know. Use questions like these:

- What has happened to your predictions?
- How well do you and the author agree?
- Based on what you know now, what predictions do you want to make or change?
- Where do you think the author is leading you?
- Ask your teammate a question about this part of the story.
- If you had the opportunity to ask the author a question, what would it be?

Responding

At the end of the story, have a wrap-up discussion that ends the lesson. Discuss the author's intentions in writing this story, as well as the students' reactions to it. Use questions such as these:

- How would you describe this book to someone? Why?
- Overall, what happens to predictions in this book?
- What is the author's reason for writing the book? What lessons are learned?

Figure 12.5 Using the Directed Reading Thinking Activity (DRTA) strategy.

1. From the text that students will read, decide potential problems that may occur.
2. Segment the text into stop points that are dependent upon potential problem spots.
3. Have the students read, stopping at the first stop point. Use questions like these:
   - What is the author trying to say here?
   - What is the author's message?
   - What is the author talking about?
4. As students continue to other stop points, ask the following types of questions:
   - Does this make sense with what the author told us before?
   - How does this connect to what the author told us in the previous section?
   - Does the author tell us why? How do you know?
   - Why do you think the author tells us this now?
5. When using fiction, follow steps 1 through 4 where appropriate, adding these questions, which are unique to narrative text:
   - How does the author make things look for the character now?
   - Given what the author has already told us about this character, what do you think he's up to?
   - How does the author let you know that something has changed?
   - How has the author settled this for us?
6. Use a mental model to show students how to do this strategy, until they become comfortable with this unique way of viewing the text.

Figure 12.6 The Question the Author Strategy.

other. They can "comment on what was just read, make predictions about what will happen next, or share experiences related to the selection" (p. 337). Calkins (2001) describes a variation of this strategy in which the classroom is divided into "reading buddies" who "stop and talk" or "stop and jot." In the classroom that Calkins observed, the teacher who used the "stop and jot" strategy was reading the story aloud to her students, and whispered the page number at each new page, so that the students could mark it in their response journals. Some suggestions you can use for encouraging response include:

Say something to your partner about . . .

- this character.
- how the story makes you feel right now.
- what is *really* happening.
- what you think about the author right now.
- what you think will happen next.
- the way this story ended.
- what you could write.

Modifying Instruction for ELL

The DLTA

GRADE LEVEL: K–1

- ### Objective

  The students listen to the teacher read *Grandfather Counts* and retell the story.

- ### Preparation

  Invite the parent of a Chinese American student to your classroom to show students how to write and pronounce the numbers 1 to 8 in Chinese.

- ### Materials

  - Copy of *Grandfather Counts* (Cheng, 2000)
  - Number cards
  - Pictures or objects to glue to the number cards

- ### Procedure

  Activating Background Knowledge

  1. Show the students the book *Grandfather Counts*, and talk about the potential story based on the picture of the little girl and the old man holding up three fingers. Connect this picture to the title. Write predictions on a chart or on the chalkboard.

  2. Display large cards numbered from 1 to 8 on the wall or chalkboard.

  3. Ask students to illustrate the numbers by cutting out magazine pictures and gluing them to the number cards. You can also have them glue small manipulatives, such as bottle caps or buttons, to the cards, or draw the correct number of objects on each space.

  4. Write the English name for each number underneath its numeral.

  5. Now ask one of your Chinese American parents, a tutor, or an older sibling to help fill in the Chinese representation of the numbers 1 to 8. Ask the volunteer to write the Chinese characters for the word as well as the alphabetic equivalent, and pronounce these words for your students. The completed cards should look like this:

1 one	2 two	3 three	4 four	5 five	6 six	7 seven	8 eight
yi	er	san	si	wu	liu	qi	ba
一	二	三	四	五	六	七	八
x	xx	xxx	xxxx	xxxxx	xxxxxx	xxx xxxx	xxxx xxxx

(continued)

6. Tell students that you will read the book aloud, and that they will need to listen carefully for their predictions. Begin reading the story aloud.

7. Stop after reading the page that shows Helen running out of the house. Ask:
   - "Did your predictions happen?"
   - "Why were they putting new wallpaper in Helen's room?" (Gong Gong, her Chinese grandfather, has come to stay. He is using Helen's room.)
   - "What is the problem?" (Helen feels angry because she's lost her room to a grandfather she barely knows.)
   - "What will happen next? Why do you think so?"

8. Continue reading and stop after reading the page that shows the train going by and Gong Gong and Helen sitting on the wall. Ask:
   - "Did your predictions happen? Show us where."
   - "What is Gong Gong doing on this page? How can you tell?" (He's counting the train cars. He holds up one finger for each car that goes by.)
   - "What do you think Gong Gong and Helen will do next? Why?"

9. Continue reading and stop after reading the page that shows Helen going to her old room that night after her bath. Ask:
   - "Did your predictions happen? Show us where."
   - "Why is this page exciting? (Gong Gong has written Helen's name in English, and also her Chinese name, Hua, which means "flower." They are both learning new words in a new language.)
   - "What will happen next? Why do you think so?"

10. Finish reading the book. Ask:
    - "What happened to your predictions?"
    - "What else can Helen learn from Gong Gong?"
    - "What is the best part about this book?"

11. Reread the story, and ask students to join in when counting the numbers in Chinese.

12. Ask students to retell the story, using a Beginning, Middle, and End chart, on which they draw pictures and label their drawings, using their native language, to show the events in the story.

Modifications for ELL are printed in color.

Metacognition and Self-Regulating Strategies

Questioning can help you monitor and assess the comprehension of your students. But that is just the beginning. Read the following passage:

A stitch is a short, sharp pain in the abdomen or side. You sometimes get a stitch during exercise (usually running) if you are not used to it. It is caused by blood being sent to exercising muscles. This starves the abdominal muscles of blood and makes them go into spasm, causing pain. People cannot feel a stitch; they can only see it. Warming up allows people to prepare themselves for exercise. (adapted from Day, 1994, p. 17)

What happened to your thinking in this passage? Did you scratch your head, wondering if you missed something? I modified the paragraph by inserting a sentence, just before the last sentence, that is incongruent with the facts given in the rest of the paragraph. When you read this sentence, and realized its inconsistency, the discomfort that you felt because you realized that you really did not understand the passage, is called *metacognitive awareness*. **Metacognition** is "the knowledge and control we have of our own cognitive processes" (Baker, 2002, p. 77). In other words, metacognition is your ability to think about your own thinking as you read. As Pressley tells us, "Good readers monitor as they read, with the result that the good reader is very metacognitively aware during reading" (2002, p. 296).

Once that discomfort occurred when you were reading the paragraph, did you go back and reread, trying to make some sense of it? Did you wish there was more information, perhaps some clues for you in a later paragraph? These brain activities reflect your **self-regulation abilities** (Hacker, 2004). Many strategies can help a reader when comprehension breaks down, such as reading more carefully or rereading the hard parts of the text (Pressley, 2002).

Metacognitive awareness is usually more apparent in mature readers; however, very young children, when solving simple problems, may be able to monitor their own thinking. Poor readers, regardless of their age, typically do not have or use adequate metacognitive abilities, but even good readers do not always recognize or admit that their comprehension has broken down. Metacognitive awareness and self-regulation strategies can be taught. In fact, Pressley describes the "metacognitively sophisticated teacher," who knows "that comprehension skill does not develop very well on its own, but that the comprehension strategies used by good comprehenders can be taught, beginning with teacher explanations and modeling of the strategies followed by scaffolded student practice of comprehension strategies during reading" (2002, p. 306). Comprehension monitoring, which is another term frequently used for self-regulation, is also supported by the findings of the National Reading Panel (2000a).

Shown in the next few sections are teaching strategies that help students become aware of their own reading processes, as well as self-regulatory strategies that help them remedy comprehension problems.

Click and Clunk

One strategy to help students overcome comprehension difficulties while reading is offered by Klingner and Vaughn (1999), called **Click and Clunk.** When students understand what they are reading, this "clicks." However, a "clunk" occurs when there are words, concepts, or ideas that confuse them. The strategy is shown in Figure 12.7. You can model for students what to do when comprehension "clunks," then give students a "Click and Clunk" card.

Stop at each stop point.

It Clicks!
Think about words that were not easy.
Think about the story.
Ask yourself, "Does this make sense?"
If it makes sense, it CLICKS! Keep reading!

If it does not make sense, look on the back of the "clunk" card to find one of the fix-up strategies.

What to Do With a Clunk
Find the clunk.
Go back and read the page again. Get some clues from the sentences.
Go back and read a sentence again. Get some clues to help you understand the word.
Break the word apart and look for parts. See if the word makes sense.
Try to read part of the next page. See if it makes sense.
Slow your reading down.

Figure 12.7 The Click and Clunk strategy.

A variation of the Click and Clunk strategy that focuses on word recognition is shown in Shea's *Taking Running Records* (2000). It suggests fix-ups for single words that give students difficulty. Below, Mr. Purdomo, a second grade teacher, models the Click and Clunk strategy for his students, using this variation.

Mr. Purdomo's Lesson

Mr. Purdomo tells the students, "I'll tell you a story. When I was a fifth grader, many years ago, my teacher told me to read *The Secret Garden* (Burnett, 1911). I started to read it, and I simply couldn't get the book finished. It just didn't make sense to me. I had to write a book report and I was in real trouble. Has that ever happened to you?

"Today I will read a story to you, and describe how I make it make sense as I read it. Normally, I would read silently, but since you cannot read my mind, I need to read aloud and tell you my thoughts as I do that. I will also use this 'Click and Clunk' chart. This is a chart that helps you understand what you read as you read it.

"When the story makes sense, it clicks, so you don't have to do anything else. If the story does not make sense, it clunks, and the back of this card tells you what to do. Watch while I show you how I used this strategy."

He reads aloud the story "Down the Hill," from *Frog and Toad All Year* by Arnold Lobel (1976). At the end of each stop point, he models by thinking aloud. At the end of page 11, where he stops at the word "steer," he says: "This page does not yet make sense. I am bothered by this word. I'll check my 'clunk' list. I can go back and reread this sentence and see if I can get some clues. When I reread, I'll just put in another word that makes sense without trying to worry about sounding it out. 'I could not—drive—the sled without you, Frog.' That makes sense—sort of. But I know that this word isn't 'drive.' It begins with 's–t' and has an 'e–e' in the middle. However, that does make the sentence and the page make sense. I'll check this word out when I'm finished. Let me write it down on the back of my bookmark."

Fix-up Strategies Bookmarks

When the student realizes that comprehension has broken down, he or she must know what to do about it. Durkin (1993) suggests some simple strategies for addressing difficulties when reading. These strategies are simple, yet cannot be assumed. Students need to be taught to use them and must know when to use them. The students can:

- *Slow reading down*—This strategy is necessary if students have not adjusted their rate of reading to suit their purpose. For example, if they are reading a science textbook chapter for the purpose of studying for a test, they should read much slower than they would if they were reading a joke or riddle book.
- *Back up and reread parts of the whole passage*—This technique is necessary if students have reached a point in the passage and realize that they are not understanding it. They have missed major points and need to go back to pick them up.
- *Look in the surrounding sentences for clues*—This approach is necessary if students have misread a word and it does not make sense in the context. They need to read on and see if they can try another word. Or, they can go back and reread a sentence or two to pick up additional clues.

All of these strategies can be listed on a bookmark for referral as the students are reading. Have the students compose these bookmarks with you, so that they negotiate the words and terms to use.

Reading Line-by-Line

Adapted from a strategy for finding the main idea of text (Slavin, Stevens, Madden & Farnish, 1987), **Reading Line-by-Line** is an activity that requires students to read one line of a passage at a time. This change results in a slowing down of their reading, and allows them to think about their comprehension of the passage. Asking students to consider slowing down as they read difficult passages is a strategy for use of remedying comprehension failures; therefore, this activity can help students realize the importance of careful reading.

Reading Line-by-Line

"The Birthday Surprise" by James Marshall	Prediction: Change or stay the same?
1 It was two days before Cody's birthday. He saw a box in the hall closet.	Write your prediction here.
2 A card on the box said, "Do not open until your birthday." Cody couldn't take his eyes off the box.	Did your prediction change? If it did, write another prediction here.
3 He read the card again. But Cody just couldn't wait.	Did your prediction change? If it did, write another prediction here.
4 "No one will know," he said. Cody unwrapped the box. Another note was inside! It said, "I caught you!" Then someone laughed.	Did your prediction change? If it did, write another prediction here.
5 Cody turned around and saw his brother Ross. "Ha! Ha!" said Ross. "How do you like my joke?"	Did your prediction change? If it did, write another prediction here.

Questions to ask after reading line-by-line:

1. Did your predictions change?
2. If so, what changed your mind?
3. When did you figure out what would happen?
4. What words confused you? How did you figure them out?

Figure 12.8 Line-by-line reading for metacognition.

Use short selections of text, using either fiction or nonfiction, and choose places in the text to separate the sentences into segments. Have the students read each segment separately, stopping to make predictions about the next segment and monitor comprehension. Students are to jot down predictions after reading the line, and then at each line thereafter, to indicate whether their prediction stays the same. See the example in Figure 12.8.

Self-Reflective Questioning

Pressley explains, "Good comprehenders are capable and active readers. . . . During reading, good comprehenders respond to the text, asking questions about the content, contructing mental imgages representing the meaning in text, and paraphrasing the text" (2002, p. 297)

When listening to your students read, get into the habit of asking questions such as:

- "Does this make sense?"
- "What else would make sense here?"
- "What does this mean?"
- "What is the author saying?"

Robin Teets, a reading specialist in Virginia, works with primary grade struggling readers and trains her students to ask themselves these questions very early in the year. She begins by reading aloud a book that is familiar to them and that they can decode. Everyone has a copy and the students follow along as she reads aloud. Along the way, she intentionally makes mistakes, stops, and uses the mental model to talk about the strategies she can use to remedy the mistakes. As the students become more proficient in their own reading, she reads aloud a familiar book and intentionally makes mistakes. The students must stop her, point out the error, and offer her solutions for fixing the problem.

You can train your students to ask themselves these questions. Tape a card on their desks that looks like this:

> **When I make a guess, I need to ask myself:**
>
> **"Does this make sense?"**

Story Structure Cards or Bookmark

As you saw in Chapter 5, stories have predictable structures. This common factor is helpful for readers to know, because once they are exposed to many, many stories, and become aware that all stories have these predictable elements, they expect certain qualities about stories as they read. Ruddell and Unrau explain, "The understanding of these text patterns, in effect, enables the reader to form a plan for reading" (2004a, p. 1, 481). If readers get to points in the story and have not yet encountered these qualities, they know that they have missed something. For example, suppose your students are reading a story, such as *Hey, Al* (Yorinks, 1986). They can expect the main character to be introduced at the very beginning of a story; indeed, Al is introduced in the first paragraph of this story. Any child who has gotten to the second page of the story and still does not know the main character is missing an important piece of information. Students' metacognitive abilities help them realize that something is wrong.

To help students get into the habit of answering story structure questions every time they read a piece of fiction, teach them the clues that help them answer questions about the elements of the story. Use mental modeling to teach these clues, which are shown in Figure 12.9 on page 423. Have them use the clues as reminder's to rely on sense-making as they read.

Home–School Connection

Ways to Help Your Child Self-Regulate During Reading

Shown here is a letter about self-regulating reading that you can send to parents. ●

Dear Families,

One of my goals in teaching reading is to help your child "self-regulate" his or her reading. This means that when reading, your child is aware of how well he or she understands it. And, if not, your child knows what to do to fix the problem.

You can encourage your child to pay attention to his or her own reading. Here are some suggestions:

1. Have your child use a monitoring bookmark when reading. It gives suggestions for monitoring and figuring out difficult words. The bookmark, called "My Reading Bookmark," is shown here.
2. Give your child a sticky note when he or she reads a story. Ask your child to write down words that are difficult to figure out. Tell your child to cross them out if he or she figures them out. Discuss together any words that are left on the list when your child is finished reading. Tell him or her to bring really difficult words to school.
3. Give your child a small notebook to keep while reading. Ask your child to "write something" at selected pages while reading a story. This should be about his or her reactions to the story. Talk about what your child writes.

Students can practice self-regulation skills at home.

4. Give your child a "Story Structure Bookmark," which is shown below. As the child reads, ask him or her to look for the items on the card. If the child cannot determine these elements of the story, have him or her put a question mark by the element of story that is troubling. Discuss these.

My Reading Bookmark

1. Ask yourself, "What is happening?" If you don't know, go back a bit and read again.
2. If that doesn't work, read ahead just a little bit. See if that helps make sense.
3. When you don't know a word, find parts of the word you know.
4. Get your mouth ready and try a sound that makes sense.
5. Try your guess in the sentence.
6. Ask yourself, "Does this make sense?"

Story Structure Bookmark

- Who are the improtant characters?
- What is the setting?
- What is the problem?
- What do the characters do to solve the problem?
- How does the problem get solved?

Sincerely,

Your Child's Teacher

Clues for Determining Elements of the Story

Main character

- The name is in the title.
- The main character is introduced at the beginning of the story, either the first page or the first chapter.
- The main character's picture is on most pages.
- The main character is mentioned on every page.
- The main character is the one with a problem.
- The main character makes things happen, or things happen to him.

Setting

- Pictures show when and where the story takes place.
- Words talk about places, weather, and time.
- The setting is introduced in the beginning of the story, but it might change.

Problem

- Pictures show unhappy things going on.
- Word clues say things like, "She didn't know what to do."
- Words tell how the character feels about a problem, such as sad, worried, puzzled, angry.
- The problem usually begins in the middle of the story, or after the main character is introduced.

Events

- These are things that the character does to solve the problem.
- Many times, one event leads to another.
- The events begin to happen in the middle of the story.

Resolution

- Word clues tell that things are starting to get better for the main character.
- Words tell how the main character feels now: happy, relieved, better, peaceful.
- This happens at the end of the story, but not always the very last page.

Theme

- This is usually something that you know after reading the entire story.
- The author's words teach us lessons or important things about life.
- Sometimes the characters say or do things that help us figure out how to deal with this problem in our own lives.

Figure 12.9 Story structure clues.

Who is the main character?
What is the setting?
What is the problem?
What does the main character do to try to solve the problem?
How is the problem solved?
What is the theme?

Figure 12.10 Story structure card.

Reproduce story structure questions on an index card or bookmark, and ask the students to keep this tool handy. Before reading stories, review the questions with the children. You can also give them stop points to check themselves for each element. If they discover that they have not found the answer to these questions as they read, they should mark this place with a question mark and alter their reading. Story structure questions are shown in Figure 12.10. Following is a mental modeling lesson in which the teacher shows her students how to use a story structure card.

Miss Travis' Lesson

Miss Travis divides *Hey, Al* (Yorinks, 1986) into several stop points. She reads the story aloud to her third grade students, and at each stop point, she stops to talk about the question that was on her story structure card. She says, "I'm going to read this text aloud, and stop at certain places along the way to show you how I can help myself understand this. I'd like for you to read silently with me as I read aloud. While we read, I will also look at this card, which is called a story structure card. It contains some questions that I can ask myself as I read, to make sure that I am understanding the story."

The mental model she uses after the second page of the story follows.

"Well, Mr. Yorinks, our author, seems to be telling me here that these characters have a problem living in this apartment. Eddie is particularly unhappy. I think I've answered my next story structure card question, because he says that he wants a house. A little backyard to run around in. I can actually hear his voice, nagging and complaining. He even says that pigeons live better than they do! And look at the picture. Al has his hands thrown up in the air, and Eddie is howling. They both look unhappy, which is one of my clues for finding the problem. This makes sense, because authors usually get to the problem in the middle of the story, after the characters and setting are introduced."

Student-Generated Questions

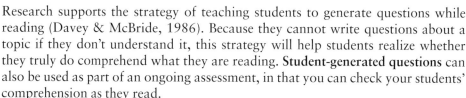

Research supports the strategy of teaching students to generate questions while reading (Davey & McBride, 1986). Because they cannot write questions about a topic if they don't understand it, this strategy will help students realize whether they truly do comprehend what they are reading. **Student-generated questions** can also be used as part of an ongoing assessment, in that you can check your students' comprehension as they read.

To do this, create stop points for a story, and at each one, have your students write a question. Students can record their questions on a bookmark, in their reading logs, or on sticky notes. They should take turns asking each other the questions as you stop throughout the story. Be sure to model for them how to ask questions that make other people think. You can use the types of questions specified in the Question-Answer Relationships strategy described earlier in this chapter.

To adapt this strategy for readers in grades 1 and 2, give each student a page for which he or she is responsible. After reading, ask each student to write one question about the events on that page to share with the group. See the example in Figure 12.11, using *Geraldine's Big Snow* (Keller, 1988).

Text Coding

Harvey and Goudvis (2000) recommend using sticky notes to mark passages in the text. Children can write "huh?" or "?" on the top half of a sticky note and place it at the point of confusion in the text. As they read, and clarify their confusion, they move the sticky note to the spot where their confusion is cleared or their question is answered. At this point, they can draw a lightbulb on the bottom half of the sticky note, indicating their understanding. If the misunderstanding is not cleared up, they leave the sticky note where it is, and write a question for discussion with the group or teacher after reading. Another way to do this is to give the students stop points, and have them mark their understanding at these points with either a checkmark or a question mark.

Title of Book: GERAIDINE'S Big Snow

Write a question about the story. Ask it to the group.

Why did Mr. Peter get books?

Figure 12.11 A first grader's self-generated question.

Students can read as buddies to verify predictions and find answers to questions.

Think-Alouds

Throughout this book, you have read about the teaching strategy of mental modeling (Duffy, Roehler & Herrmann, 1998), which involves the teacher modeling reading processes and strategies by thinking out loud. The idea is to show students what happens when good readers apply strategies such as predicting, inferring, and visualizing as they read. The same strategy can be used to help students regulate their own reading. As they read, they can stop periodically and think out loud, explaining the processes that they are using. The **think-aloud** strategy (Baumann, Jones & Seifert-Kessell, 1993; Davey, 1983) does just that. As Baumann and others explain, "Think-alouds require a reader to stop periodically, reflect on how a text is being processed and understood, and relate orally what reading strategies are being employed" (1993, p. 185).

Davey (1983) states that the strategy can be used with students of any age; however, it will work best with students who can decode on their own. To implement this strategy, see the procedure shown in Appendix B.

Summary: When You Know You've Succeeded

My son Tommy began pretend-reading when he was very young, probably about age eighteen months. Decoding came much later, in first grade. A constant source of frustration for this child (who was quite a perfectionist) was the fact that he knew, without anyone telling him, that he was not "really reading" if he was not decoding the words exactly as they are printed on the page. Once, while reading a picture book when he was six, he said, "That doesn't make sense. I'm trying to put that word in there and it doesn't make sense!" Even though he was frustrated, I was smiling. I knew he was well on his way to being a good reader.

This chapter showed you some ways to help your students along this way. When you facilitate their understandings while they read, you provide scaffolds for them that make comprehension more likely to occur, and you pave the way for independent reading. The classic teaching behavior—questioning—is one of the ways you can scaffold their reading, if you do it thoughtfully. This chapter described ways to use questions so that your students have the maximum number of opportunities to think about and reflect upon their responses, enabling meaningful interaction with the book.

As you know, your students' comprehension of what they read is your goal. One of the ways to facilitate this achievement while they read is to teach metacognitive and self-regulation skills. This chapter introduced strategies that help your students become aware of the processes they are using while reading and offered solutions for solving comprehension problems. All of these strategies are summarized in the Reviewing the Big Picture box, along with their corresponding teaching standards.

As I found out by watching Tommy read, perfection is not necessary when reading, but sense-making is. When your students realize that the words in their heads do not match the print or make sense as they move through the print, they have truly grown as readers. This is your goal.

Technology Resources

- **www.pvc.maricopa.edu/~sheets/lmw/model.htm** This web page is titled, "Learning Your Way: A Meta-Cognitive Approach to Study Strategies." The author, Richard Sheets, explains the premise behind training students in metacognitive strategies.

- **tip.psychology.org/meta.html** On this web page, the author offers a brief yet thorough explanation of metacognition.

- **www.lasw.org/questions_probing.html** Explanations of types of teacher questions are offered on this web page.

- **www.exploratorium.edu/IFI/resources/workshops/artofquestioning.html** "The Art of Questioning," by Dennis Wolf, is reproduced here as part of the Institute for Inquiry web site.

- **www.aee.vt.edu/methods/que-skil.htm** This web site lists some helpful hints for questioning, including probing questions.

expect the world
The New York Times
nytimes.com

Themes of the Times

Expand your knowledge of the concepts discussed in this chapter by reading current and historical articles from the *New York Times* by visiting the "Themes of the Times" section of the Companion Web Site.

Reviewing the Big Picture

Facilitating Comprehension During Reading

Strategy	Description	Appropriate Type of Text/Grade Level	IRA Standards	INTASC Principles	NAEYC Standards	ACEI/NCATE Standards
Teacher questioning	Several types of teacher questioning behaviors are described.	Fiction or nonfiction/ K–2, 3–5, 6–8	1.4, 2.2, 4.1	4, 6, 7	4b	2.1, 3.1, 3.2, 3.3, 3.5
Question-answer relationships	Teach students how to ask four types of questions: right there, think and search, author and you, and on my own	Fiction and nonfiction/ 3–5, 6–8	1.4, 2.2, 4.1	4, 7	NA	2.1, 3.3, 3.4, 3.5
Directed reading thinking activity and directed listening thinking activity	DRTA: break a story into stop points; ask students to make predictions and confirm them at each stop point. DLTA: adaptation of the strategy for nonreaders; the students listen to the teacher read aloud.	Fiction/ K–2, 3–5, 6–8	1.4, 2.2, 4.1	4, 7	DLTA: 4b	2.1, 3.2, 3.3, 3.4, 3.5
Reciprocal teaching	Show students how to use four processes as they read: predicting, questioning, summarizing, and clarifying. Break text into segments and let students take turns as leader, helping their peers use these processes.	Nonfiction/ 3–5, 6–8	1.4, 2.1, 2.2, 4.1	4, 5, 7	NA	2.1, 3.1, 3.2, 3.3, 3.4
Question the author	At appropriate stop points, have students think of things they would like to ask the author. Talk about the text as product of an author.	Fiction and nonfiction/ 3–5, 6–8	1.4, 2.2, 4.1	4, 7	NA	2.1, 3.1, 3.2, 3.3, 3.4
Say something	At stop points, ask students to say something appropriate about the text to a partner.	Fiction/ K–2, 3–5, 6–8	1.4, 2.2, 4.1	4, 5, 7	4b	2.1, 3.2, 3.3, 3.4

Strategy	Description	Genre/Grade				
Click and clunk	Create a chart for students to use when the text "clunks." List fix-up strategies appropriate for text grade level.	Fiction and nonfiction/ 3–5	1.4, 2.2, 4.1	4, 7	NA	2.1, 3.2, 3.3, 3.4
Fix-up strategies bookmarks	Create bookmarks that list strategies for monitoring comprehension.	Fiction and nonfiction/ 3–5, 6–8	1.4, 2.2, 4.1	4, 7	NA	2.1, 3.2, 3.3, 3.4
Reading line-by-line	Divide a selection into segments; only a sentence or two per segment. Read the passage one line at a time and make predictions about the next line.	Fiction or nonfiction/ 3–5	1.4, 2.2, 4.1	4, 7	NA	2.1, 3.2, 3.3, 3.4
Self-reflective questioning	Show students how to ask questions that monitor their comprehension as they read.	Fiction or nonfiction/ K–2, 3–5	1.4, 2.2, 4.1	4, 7	4b (use with shared reading)	2.1, 3.1, 3.2, 3.3, 3.4
Story structure card or bookmark	Create cards that outline the story elements and questions that students can ask themselves as they read, for self-monitoring.	Fiction/3–5	1.4, 2.2, 4.1	4, 7	NA	2.1, 3.2, 3.3, 3.4
Student-generated questions	At stop points, have students write questions for each other about that portion of the text.	Fiction or nonfiction/ 3–5, 6–8	1.4, 2.2, 4.1	4, 5, 7	NA	2.1, 3.1, 3.2, 3.3, 3.4, 3.5
Text coding	Show students how to use sticky notes to mark places in text that confuse them.	Fiction or nonfiction/ 3–5, 6–8	1.4, 2.2, 4.1	4, 7	NA	2.1, 3.1, 3.2, 3.3, 3.4
Think-alouds	Model reading strategies by thinking aloud; give your students the chance to do the same.	Fiction or nonfiction/ K–2, 3–5, 6–8	1.4, 2.2, 4.1	4, 6, 7	4b	2.1, 3.1, 3.2, 3.3, 3.4, 3.5

13

Reading, Writing, and Responding

Finally, with a big sigh of relief, Ramona leaned back in her chair to admire her work: three cat masks with holes for eyes and mouths, masks that could be worn by hooking rubber bands over ears. But Ramona did not stop there. With pencil and paper, she began to write out what she would say. She was so full of ideas that she printed rather than waste time in cursive writing. Next she phoned Sara and Janet, keeping her voice low and trying not to giggle so she wouldn't disturb her father any more than necessary, and explained her plan to them. Both her friends giggled and agreed to take part in the book report. Ramona spent the rest of the evening memorizing what she was going to say.

Ramona Quimby, Age 8 (Cleary, 1981)

Lauren, grade 4

Ramona was excited about the book report she and her friends were going to do. In the Personal Reflection, think about the book reports that you have done over the years.

Think about reading instruction during your school years. What kinds of things were you asked to do after reading a book? What were your reactions to these?

According to Rosenblatt (1978), there are two kinds of stances for reading. When students read to gain information, find out about a specific topic, make comparisons, look for causes or effects, discover problems and their solutions, or identify the story elements, they are reading *efferently*. Notice that efferent reading can take place with either fiction or nonfiction. This stance is quite typical of the kind of reading that children are usually asked to do in school. Rosenblatt argues that requiring children to read for information too much can discourage them from reading.

An aesthetic stance toward reading is a much more pleasurable—and natural—one. Rosenblatt says that giving students the opportunity to read for enjoyment and become emotionally involved in the text is conducive to their development into lifelong readers. Readers can also enjoy nonfiction texts aesthetically, depending upon their interests. Many children—especially reluctant readers —prefer to read informational books because of their interest in a particular topic, such as sports, animals, or crafts. Rather than asking a myriad of questions or assigning a plethora of things to do with their books, teachers need to develop an excitement and thirst for the written word.

Once again, it seems that balance is the key to appropriate instruction. Teaching your students to read efferently cannot be avoided—nor would you want to avoid efferent reading. Children need to know how to glean information from what they read, because this is one of the purposes of reading. They also need to know what to look for as they read, so that they can monitor themselves and independently check their comprehension. At the same time, if you overemphasize efferent reading, you can turn them off. Calkins (2001) warns us that too many requirements for responses take up time that our students should be spending reading another book. Moreover, story maps for every story, writing assignments that have no meaning, worksheets full of questions after every chapter can add to poor or apathetic reading attitudes. Even a steady diet of the kinds of activities that we might think are fun or cute can detract from the real purpose for reading. Making sure that they can read and get the intended message of the author in print is responding from the efferent stance. A personal and eager connection to reading, so that students relate to what they read and are anxious to share their reading with others, is responding from an aesthetic stance. The excitement of Beverly Cleary's Ramona was so contagious that her friends giggled in anticipation of being part of the book report. Spreading that kind of enthusiasm is your challenge. More than anything, when your students put down one book and are anxious to pick up another, that is the kind of response to cultivate.

This chapter is about eliciting reactions to literature—efferently as well as aesthetically. Indeed, in some teaching strategies, students will have the opportunity to take an efferent stance as well as an aesthetic stance. Both types of responses can take many forms; written, verbal, and artistic responses are all represented.

Many of the responses that I describe in this chapter are written ones. Chapter 9 described the writing process, which is the process that real writers use to produce published work. Here, the described writing is less formal, written for the purpose of responding to literature. This **informal writing** can be shared with others, but its end product does not necessarily need to be in published form. Let me explain the difference between these types of written pieces and more formal written pieces with a story.

When my son Charlie was in second grade, his teacher asked her students to write about their pets. She chose this topic so that the students would have something familiar to write about to share with others; she planned to put their finished pieces on display for Open House night. Our cat, Rudy, had died when Charlie was four years old. Unfortunately, for various reasons, he never got another cat, but Charlie asked his teacher if it was acceptable to write about the cat that passed away. It was, and he wrote. Quite eloquently, he wrote of Rudy's charms and shortcomings, and ended the paper with: "Rudy died when I was four. I miss Rudy. But if you look under the table behind the couch in our family room, you can still see his cat hairs."

Much as I would have liked for this piece of writing to be more private, hanging on that hallway wall meant that it was shared with many! The types of student writing that you'll read about in this chapter are informal and are not necessarily shared with such a wide audience. Many written responses are in a journal, shared only with the teacher, a reading buddy, or the child's family. Other informal pieces are retellings or summaries, written for the purpose of responding to literature. They can become part of the child's portfolio, collected throughout the year. This approach enables them to be used for assessments, or they can serve as drafts for published pieces that could eventually become formal writing pieces. Another type of writing described in this chapter is the writing that they do to organize their thoughts for response talks or discussions.

The next few pages describe several types of responses: retellings, summaries, text searches, response talks, response journals, and literary borrowing. Additionally, you'll find several ideas for literacy portfolios in *Toolkit for Teachers*.

Retellings

The simplest way to react to a piece of text is to retell it, without placing value or judgment on any events (Applebee, 1978). If a student can accurately retell a story or an expository piece, his or her efferent understanding of it is fairly certain (Glazer, 1998; Tierney & Readence, 2005).

As you might recall from Chapter 4, retellings offer the teacher a more complete picture of the child's comprehension than that produced when he or she answers comprehension check questions. When you ask a child to retell what he or she remembers from reading a text, you can get a much richer, more detailed account of his or her understandings. He or she must recall, and then generate the details of the story or text on his or her own, without questioning from the teacher. This activity can be a challenge for children, especially those who are accustomed to answering questions. In Chapter 10, you read about how to use explicit instruction to show your students how to find story elements to include in their retellings. Because retellings are one way to respond efferently to text, they are mentioned again here.

You can use a number of different types of retelling assessment checklists. One is included in the *Toolkit for Teachers* book, and was adapted for the purpose of using after completing a running record.

If you wish to use story or text retelling as an instructional tool, it is most helpful for your students to use it as a way to help them label story elements and remember them as they read. A retelling reminders bookmark, which can be adapted for use with any grade level, is shown in Figure 13.1. This bookmark can serve as a scaffold for helping students remember what to look for as they read, and also to remember what to include as they retell.

An excellent source for retelling scaffolds is Hoyt's *Revisit, Reflect, Retell* (1999). Hoyt makes suggestions for encouraging retellings, including team retelling, in which each student in a team is responsible for one of the story elements.

When asking students to retell nonfiction, be sure to use the text structure as a guide. Various graphic organizers can be used to help students with text structure. Many good, reproducible organizers are offered online from web sites designed for that purpose, including:

Write Design (**www.writedesignonline.com/organizers/**)
Education Place (**www.eduplace.com/graphicorganizer/**)

Figure 13.2 on page 436 shows an example of retelling problem and solution nonfiction, written by a second grader who was responding to *Ibis, A True Whale Story* (Himmelman, 1990).

Summaries

A summary is a synopsis of the author's words and is shorter yet more difficult than a retelling. Summarizing fiction as well as nonfiction is an important literacy strategy (Baumann, 1986; Duke & Pearson, 2002; Kintsch, 2004; Meyer & Poon, 2004) and is also recognized by the National Reading Panel (2000a) as one of the important comprehension strategies that children should know. When summarizing a story or a piece of nonfiction, a student assumes an efferent stance to thinking about the literature and explains to others what he or she knows about the text in abbreviated form. Moreover, a summary can include the student's aesthetic reaction to the text, if he or she offers personal connections to it.

A story summary does not include all the events or characters; a summary of nonfiction does not include all the facts. Students are directed to choose only the most pertinent details to tell in a summary; this requires them to place importance on some events or statements. After reading the entire text, students must figure out what is most important about the book to share. Some guidelines for summarizing are:

- Take out words that do not tell about the most important idea.
- Take out words that are repetitive.

Retelling reminders
Who is the main character?
Who are the other characters?
Where are they?
What time is it?
What does the character want?
What does the character do to get this?
How does the character get what he or she wants?
How does the story end?

Figure 13.1 Bookmark to use for retelling.

- Use one word to replace a list of items.
- Write a sentence that tells the most important idea.

The next few sections describe helpful strategies for teaching summarization.

Procedural Text

Kletzien and Dreher (2004) suggest the use of procedural text to help students develop their own use of informational writing. Reading how-to books can help them see the importance of brevity, clarity, and sequential ordering as they write

Problem

Ibis is stuck in a fishing net.

Solution

People reached into the water and Pulled the net off Ibis

Figure 13.2 A retelling that follows the problem/solution pattern.

for the purpose of informing. Read several examples of these books to them, making note of what makes these books helpful and clear to the reader. Then, your students can write instructions on how to do or make something that interests them. Use index cards and ask them to write each step on a separate card. This strategy allows them to rearrange the cards as they write, making sure that the proper sequence is attained. Once they are satisfied with the sequence, they can glue the cards on a large sheet of rectangular paper. Sharing these with a writing buddy can help them determine the clarity of their writing, and they can revise accordingly.

Categorizing Facts

One way to help struggling readers and writers summarize is to ask them to list facts and categorize them. Specify the number of facts they should find, so they know how much to look for in the text, and then help them organize the facts into logical categories. To do this, hand out six or eight index cards. Ask the students to write one fact on each card. Ask them to categorize the cards according to the kind of information that they have. Then, they can create a page of facts for each category. They can just glue the cards onto the page. On the last page, they should write a sentence that "wraps up" their findings. Once it is all stapled together, they have created an organized collection of facts learned. This project can be done individually or collaboratively.

The key to this strategy is the process of categorizing the facts into logical groups; model for the students thought processes while picking out facts and grouping them. While you may want to ask students to revise and expand upon their writing so that its final product is in "publishable" form, the emphasis here is on the process—the student's ability to choose facts and group them appropriately. This organization prepares them for note-taking. See Figure 13.3 for an example.

Little Books

One of the hardest parts about writing a summary is the necessity for brevity. Routman (1991) tells us about a book that students can make from a single sheet of paper and use for a variety of purposes. Use these **little books** for summarizing, because it helps students keep their words brief and simple.

In Chapter 10, you saw an example of how to explicitly teach summarizing with mental modeling. After you have modeled a summarization of a piece of literature, show students the little book and explain how this story can be duplicated in the book, using just eight pages. While the students read, stop at stop points and review the elements of story. Talk about which ones are most important to include in a little book. After reading, have students create a little book and draw pictures for each of the story elements. Instructions for making a little book are included in Appendix B.

Sketch to Stretch

One way to encourage summarizing is through the use of drawings and symbols. Harste, Short, and Burke (1988) suggest a teaching strategy called **sketch to stretch,** in which the teacher invites the students to draw their interpretations of the story or event in the story. This technique is helpful for children who struggle with writing and English language learners. After reading a story or part of a story, ask the student to draw symbols or pictures to represent the elements in the story and their reaction to it. The goal is to visually represent ideas for the summary, not to illustrate it. The completed sketch serves as a guide for sharing the summary verbally with members of the student's small group.

This idea can be used with nonfiction as well. Use a large piece of manila paper and fold it horizontally so that a large rectangle of space is available for drawings. One rectangular space is needed for each chapter or main idea. With your help, students determine which facts, dates, or ideas they need to remember, and represent them in their drawings. Symbols, letters, or numbers can be used to represent ideas. Once they complete their sketches, ask your students to use them to verbally summarize what they learned in the text. This activity can help them study important information prior to a test, or it can help them write a summary

Summarizing by Categorizing Facts with Index Cards

1. Give each student eight 3″ × 5″ index cards.
2. Have the students read a piece of nonfiction that contains at least eight facts. (You can modify this activity to make it six cards.)
3. Tell students to record a fact that they learned on each index card, and illustrate it if desired.
4. Help them organize their index cards into categories, and label the categories.
5. Now, glue each of the index cards from a single category onto a separate sheet of 11″ × 14″ paper. Head each page with its category title.
6. Write a concluding sentence on the last page.
7. Staple these together to form the book.

For example, Jamal read the section about spiders in the book *Animals Nobody Loves*, by Seymour Simon (2001). He wrote the following eight facts:

Spiders don't normally bite people.	Spiders trap bugs in their webs.
Flies and mosquitoes get stuck in their webs and spiders eat them.	The black widow is poisonous.
If you trap a spider, it might bite you.	Spiders get rid of pests.
People are afraid of spiders.	You should not bother spiders.

Jamal decided on these categories:

Spiders and People

How Spiders Eat

Poisonous Spiders

Figure 13.3 Summarizing with eight facts.

Then, he cut out the facts and pasted them into the following six-page fact book.

Facts I Learned

in <u>Animals Nobody Loves</u>
by Seymour Simon

by Jamal

Table of Contents

Spiders and People - Page 1

How Spiders Eat - Page 2

Poisonous Spiders - Page 3

Conclusion - Page 4

Spiders and People

People are afraid of spiders.	If you trap a spider, it might bite you.
Spiders don't normally bite people.	Spiders get rid of pests.

You should not bother spiders.

Page 1

How Spiders Eat

Spiders trap bugs in their webs.

Flies and mosquitoes get stuck in their webs and spiders eat them.

Page 2

Poisonous Spiders

The black widow is poisonous.

Page 3

Spiders are interesting and helpful arachnids.

The End

Page 4

Figure 13.3 (continued).

Figure 13.4 Example of a sketch for Chapter 1 of *Sam the Sea Cow*, created by Jimmy, a second grader.

of the chapter. See Figure 13.4 for an example of a sketch used to represent a summary, drawn by Jimmy, a second grader, using *Sam the Sea Cow* (Walker, 1992).

Text Searches

Finding useful and important information in texts is one of the most common purposes for reading. Yet it is one of the hardest things for children to do (Dreher, 2002). Dreher offers a model of text searching that, when taught to students, gives them a strategic plan for finding relevant information from textbooks. There are five steps to this plan:

1. *Forming goals*—The student determines an objective for searching information.
2. *Selecting categories*—The student determines which categories of information will lead to the information; the index or table of contents will be helpful.
3. *Extracting information*—The student determines which information is most relevant.
4. *Integrating the information*—The student combines and synthesizes the new information with what he or she already knows.
5. *Recycling*—The student decides whether more information is needed and recycles through all the components of the search until the goal of finding the right information is met.

These five text search steps can be modeled with textbook material or with web sites. Once the relevant information is found, students can respond to questions, write a summary, or make notes for a report. The next sections describe specific strategies for searching text.

Highlighting

Jody Grove, a second grade teacher in Pennsylvania, teaches her students how to find important information in text. She selects short pieces of nonfiction, such as magazine articles, or *Scholastic News* issues, or one or two pages from the textbook. After activating prior knowledge about the topic, she directs the students to read questions at the end of the chapter or article. They use these questions as springboards for predictions, and as guidelines for finding important information. After making predictions about what they will find out, Mrs. Grove asks the students to read the selection silently, with highlighter markers in hand. She asks them to look for confirmations to their predictions and answers to their guiding questions. When they find this information, they highlight the sentences that give them the information.

Web-Based Searches

Another type of text search uses the Internet. Finding relevant, reliable, and useful information from the Internet is one of the most important skills you can teach your students, regardless of their age (Smolin & Lawless, 2003). Leu tells us, "New forms of information and communication technology (ICT) such as the Internet are rapidly generating new literacies required to effectively exploit their potentials" (2002, p. 310). Thus, **new literacies** "include the reading and writing skills, strategies, and insights necessary" to get the most information possible out of "rapidly changing information and communication technologies that continuously emerge in our world" (2002, p. 313). New literacies require your students to critically evaluate information taken from the Internet, to be skillful in searching for important information in the complex world of ICT, to work well with others in searching for information, and to have sharp reading and writing skills. In fact, Leu explains that "new literacies build on but do not usually replace previous literacies, because "the ability to read text will become more important because it allows us to access information faster than listening, and speed counts in rich, complexly networked information environments. . . . The ability to write text will become more important because written text can be easily stored and organized to generate new knowledge" (2002, p. 315).

Perhaps the biggest difference between new literacies and traditional reading and writing abilities lies in the nature of *hypertext,* which is text that is "accessible in nonsequential, user-directed format" (Spires & Estes, 2002, p. 115). Reading hypertext means that the reader chooses from many paths throughout the text, taking him or her to locations of related materials, all of which are potentially important for the reader's use. Thus, when reading information on a web site, your readers need to be able to read multilinearly (Bolter, 1991). This task may prove to be too difficult for some readers. Shapiro (cited in Spires & Estes, 2002) states that readers need to be prompted to think about the information relationships that they encounter when reading hypertext.

Critically evaluating web-based resources is also difficult for many readers, and perhaps it is unrealistic for us to expect young readers to be able to weed out unneeded, unwanted, and erroneous information, which is a "task that has been historically relegated to editors of traditional print publishing companies" (Spires & Estes, 2002, p. 118).

One of the simplest ways to help your students find appropriate web sites and use their time wisely on the Internet is to create web pages. After you have identified sites that would be helpful to your students in a particular unit of study, create a web page that lists these sites. You can easily create web pages with Microsoft Word and post them on the Internet. Doing this allows your students' families to access the web sites that you recommend for them; you can also save the links on a disk and keep the disk in your classroom. You can find assistance at these sites:

- **teacherweb.com**
- **www.backflip.com**

Another way to scaffold students as they search for information on the Internet is with WebQuests. Originally designed by Bernie Dodge (1995), these are "inquiry-oriented units of study that propose an open-ended problem for students to solve with the resources put at their disposal in the hypertext environment" (Spires & Estes, 2002, p. 118). WebQuests work well for students of all abilities; a Quest sends students to several potential texts on the same topic—all at different readability levels. The WebQuest also organizes web-based information sources for students, and helps give them the ability to make choices about the information they can access. The sources that are available on WebQuests are predetermined by the teacher, which allows for control over web-based resources, eliminating the difficulties inherent in dealing with the Internet. A helpful web site that offers help to teachers who want to create WebQuests is **www.filamentality.com/wired/fil/**. Dodge (1995; 1998) explains the origins of WebQuest technology at **webquest.sdsu.edu/about_webquests.html**, and maintains "The WebQuest Page" at **webquest.sdsu.edu**. The Resources section of this chapter lists some sites that help explain the concepts behind this type of information search, as well as some collections of exemplary WebQuests.

Response Talks

Talking about books is something that mature readers do. To people who view reading as an important part of life sharing a good book with someone else is a natural extension of reading. The ability to make personal connections with literature is what aesthetic responding is all about (Rosenblatt, 1978). Response talks, also called book talks (Calkins, 2001) or **grand conversations** (Peterson & Eeds, 1990), help students to make these connections, to reach deeper understandings of the text, and to experience literature as a social endeavor. Read on for some suggestions on how to do this.

At the beginning of the year, establish a strong sense of community in the classroom. Children need to see each other when they talk. Teach children how to look at each other, and not at you, during these discussions. They need to trust each other and feel comfortable saying what they think in a risk-free atmosphere. The objective of response talks is not to test your students, but to encourage reflective thinking about reading with their peers.

One of the easiest and yet most important things you can do to encourage emerging authors is to show them what published authors do in **authorship talks.** Many times, children, especially the youngest ones, do not think of a book as

Modifying Instruction for ELL

Using WebQuests with
Animals Nobody Loves

● Objective

After choosing an animal from *Animals Nobody Loves* (Simon, 2001), students will participate in a WebQuest to investigate important facts about the animal.

● Preparation

- Divide students into groups of three, making sure that the student who is learning English as a second language is in a group with a familiar reading buddy.
- Each triad should be able to work at a computer that has access to the Internet.
- Create a web page of WebQuests, if you prefer. Suggested WebQuests for investigating *Animals Nobody Loves* are:

  oncampus.richmond.edu/academics/education/projects/webquests/australia/ (crocodiles)

  www.zoomschool.com/subjects/rainforest/ (rat, crocodile, piranha)

  www.mcs.k12.in.us/les/ihnen/oceans.htm (octopus, man-of-war, shark)

  oncampus.richmond.edu/academics/education/projects/webunits/adaptations/ (bear, bat)

  php.ucs.indiana.edu/~ijackson/introduction.html (all types of animals)

  leader.education.louisville.edu/student/daalla01/webquest/index.htm (spiders)

● Materials

- Copies of *Animals Nobody Loves* (Simon, 2001) for each student
- Computers with Internet access
- WebQuests listed earlier, or other WebQuests that pertain to animals; animals described in Simon's book are: shark, bat, grizzly bear, cobra, vulture, spider, hyena, devil ray, rattlesnake, gila monster, rat, cockroach, crocodile, skunk, man-of-war, fire ant, coyote, octopus, wasp, and piranha
- Word cards for each of the animals, written in Spanish (or other native language)

● Procedure

1. Show students the table of contents from *Animals Nobody Loves*. Examine it and talk about it to make predictions about what this book might teach the reader.

2. Put the names of the animals on a word wall. Make sure to put their Spanish (or other native language in your classroom) equivalents on the cards as well.

Modifications for ELL are printed in color.

(continued)

3. If there are Latino/Hispanic English language learners in your classroom, point out the Spanish cognates in this book: cobra (la cobra), hyena (la hiena), rat (la rata), cockroach (la cucaracha), crocodile (el cocodrilo), coyote (el coyote).

4. Choose an animal to read about, or ask students for suggestions for the animal that they would like to hear about. Read aloud the chapter about the chosen animal to give students an idea of the author's style, as well as to pique the students' interest in animals that are scary, unfriendly, or ugly.

5. Put students in groups. Ask each group to choose an animal to investigate.

6. Give students a WebQuest to use for investigating the animal that they chose.

7. Have each student complete a report. For students who have difficulty writing, suggest the use of a little book of facts.

something that was produced by a real person. After reading a book, talk with your students about its author. Chat with them about the choices that the author made. Many children's authors have web sites that offer information about their lives and their work. This sort of discussion leads to rich insights into authorship, which is valuable for young writers. Figure 13.5 lists some discussion starters for talking about authorship.

Use every opportunity to model responses to literature. Talk about your own reading and about how important books are to your life. For example, in morning class meetings, use some time to talk about books. You can say things like, "I'm reading a fantastic book right now and I'm really anxious to see what the main character does next." To encourage natural talk about books, tell your students to think about how they tell friends about a movie or television show. Ask them to use the same natural kind of talk in book discussions. Many times, students have had years of experience in recitations, the question-and-answer periods that are so common in classrooms. Students are often so focused on responding to the teacher's efferent questions that they are not sure of what to do when someone simply asks them for a reaction. They need to become comfortable with using a more natural kind of response to books, and talk about books rather than answer questions about them.

Ask few, if any, questions. Instead, open conversation with thought-provoking statements that are related to the book. For example, when using the book *The Giver* (Lowry, 1993), say, "I think ignorance made the people in this story very happy," rather than asking, "Why did being ignorant make these people happy?" Then, invite response.

Ask your students to say more when they do not offer enough response. One fine third grade teacher, Cathy Hayden, who teaches in Pennsylvania, uses a simple hand signal when she wants her students to say more or to complete their verbal sentences. Without saying a word, she puts her hands together as if holding a rubber band, and pulls both of them out, as if stretching the rubber band. This signal allows her to keep her interruptions and teacher talk to a minimum, and at the same time, set high expectations for classroom conversations.

Authorship Discussions

- Identify the setting, and talk about why the author may have picked that setting. Ask questions like, "If you were the author, where would you have set the story?"
- Talk about the characters. Look up the author on a web site, and find biographical information. Is there a person in the author's life who influenced the author's creation of this character? Who influences your life? Is there a potential character for your writing?
- Discuss where you think the author got the idea for this story. Is it from real life? From his or her children? From past experiences? What ideas from your life can you use in your writing?
- Talk about your favorite part of the story. Ask questions such as, "Would you want to read another book like this? Why or why not? What would you tell the author if you could?"
- Think of ways to change the point of view in well-known stories. Use Jon Scieszka's *The True Story of the Three Pigs!* (1989) as an example.
- After reading nonfiction, look up information about the author. What kind of credibility does this author have? How does he or she gather information for writing?
- What influences the nonfiction author to write about this subject?
- Reread the dedication page. Talk about how that person might have influenced the author.

Figure 13.5 Talking about authors.

Expect your students to cite evidence for their responses. Have students prepare for talks with sticky notes. Give them small bookmark-type sticky notes before reading. As they read, ask students to mark the points of the selection that interest them, confuse them, or have a personal connection for them. When it is time for the response talk, have them keep their books open when they participate. They should return to the place marked by the sticky note, read the important passage aloud, and tell their reaction to it.

When you finish reading an excellent book, what do you do? Are you glad that the book is over? Did you wish it would hurry up and end? Or were you hoping you could prolong the story as you approached its end? **Ways to linger** are described by Calkins (2001), who tells of a classroom in which the teacher actively pursues her students' ideas about how to linger over a good book. The teacher was reading a book aloud to her students. When they got to the end, she asked them to sit quietly for a moment and think about the book. Then, she broke them into groups, gave each group a copy, and asked them to "invent some way to look back to take in the whole of the book" (Calkins, 2001, p. 484). Afterward, she listed their responses, and they talked about the book for another week, using their suggestions.

"Ways to linger" captures the true essence of aesthetic reading. If your students are so involved in reading a book that they want to think of ways to make it

WebQuests give students the opportunity to interactively investigate topics on the Internet.

longer and ways to reflect upon what they've read, they have indeed personally transacted with the text. This strategy is appropriate for grades three to eight. An adaptation of the ways to linger chart is shown in Figure 13.6.

Response Journals

Response journals are convenient and efficient for recording your students' informal writing. If your students keep a journal, they always have a handy place to write responses to their reading. Use the journals before reading for predictions, during reading for notes and questions of concern, and after reading for writing favorite quotes or recording responses. Have students put the date, title of the book, and author's name for each entry. Often, the entries that students make in their response journals serve as springboards for more formal pieces that can be published for authentic purposes. For example, if a student's reaction to a book was particularly favorable, he or she can write a peer book review for use in the school library. There are many types of entries that you can use; take a look at the ones described next.

Dialogue Journal Responses

Dialogue journal responses are written by two people in the same journal. To use this type of entry, pair your students into reading buddies. After reading a fiction or nonfiction selection, tell them to write a response to the text in the journal.

1. Find a place in the book that made you feel one of these ways:
   - You loved it.
   - You hated it.
   - It made you angry.
   - It confused you.

   Reread that part. Write your reactions in your journal. Discuss it again, now that you have finished the book.
2. Think about each of the elements of the story: characters, setting, problem, events, and resolution. How do these elements add to the author's message? What makes each of them important? Write and share your ideas.
3. Think about these questions, and write the answer to one of them in your journal. Be ready to talk about your answer.
   - What is the author's whole message?
   - Why did the author write this book?
   - What is the author trying to tell me with this whole book?
   - How might this book change the way you do things or the way you think about things?
4. Compare this book to other books you know. Write your comparison. Which one do you like most? Why? Be ready to share your ideas.
5. Think about the author's ending. Why do you think the author chose this ending? Write your ideas in your journal. Be ready to talk about it.

Figure 13.6 Suggestions for ways to linger.

Then, ask them to give the journal to their buddy. Each person in the pair is to write his reaction to what was written by his buddy. This activity allows students to respond aesthetically to the text as well as to the comments of their classmates, thus emphasizing the social nature of literacy. Responses can occasionally be elicited with prompts such as these:

- What was your favorite part? Why?
- What do you think the main character should have done instead?
- What would you like to tell the author?
- What disappointed you? Why?

You can give students the choice of responding to a prompt or choosing their own related topic for writing in the journal.

Double-Entry Journals

Journals in which parts of the text are listed or copied on one side of the page and the student's reactions to those parts are listed on the opposite side of the page are called **double entry journals.** These journals allow for aesthetic responses, and make a nice connection between reading and writing. Ask students to make two columns on a page of the journal. Have students find information or events in the

Diversity in the Reading Classroom

Overcoming Cultural Differences

Lazar (2004) describes the work of a preservice teacher, Julia, who held an internship in a Philadelphia school. Julia tutored Dante, a boy who struggled with reading and writing. Her objective was to motivate Dante to write, and she decided that writing about his home town would be a relevant assignment for him. To encourage him and to provide models, Julia read poetry about city life and a story about the love of one's home town, both excellent pieces of literature that depicted diverse cultural settings. Then she suggested that he brainstorm some ideas, so that he could create a travel brochure for the city of Philadelphia. She was disappointed when he showed little interest in the project. Why did this happen?

Cultural differences between teachers and their students have a big impact on classroom teaching and learning. Clotfelter (2001) reports that while most teachers are female and white, their students are becoming more and more diverse. In 1996, there were 14% more black students and 45% more Latino/Hispanic students in U.S. public schools than there were in 1986. Moreover, many teachers would rather not teach in schools that are different from the ones they attended as children (Gay, 1993). "White privilege" (Lazar, 2004, p. 34) contributes to this chasm of understanding. Without realizing it, white teachers enjoy a long list of simple, everyday privileges that their students of color often do not, such as buying foods that fit their cultural tradition in the grocery store, finding someone who can cut their hair, or seeing people of their race positively pictured on TV or in the newspaper. Such lack of common ground can produce difficulties in the classroom (McIntosh, 1990).

Julia, the intern in Lazar's study, had chosen literature that she thought was appropriate for the assignment, and indeed it probably was. However, her student's disinterest showed her that this was not enough. She needed to help Dante make a personal connection with writing. Travel brochures were not part of his experience or schema. He saw no reason for writing such a thing; therefore, he quit writing.

After some reflection, Julia planned a lesson in which she gave Dante the opportunity to choose his writing topic, and he responded enthusiastically. He eventually wrote about his dream of becoming a basketball player. Lazar (2004) reports the need to expand this type of writing experience to reading and writing about people who overcame obstacles to realize their dreams, a theme that is important in classrooms where students do not see such role models in their everyday lives.

Au (1998) explains that educators can bridge the cultural gap in classrooms if they see the importance of connecting the things that their students learn in school with their personal experiences. Teachers need to use literature that reflects diverse cultures, link assignments to their students' experiences, and teach literacy skills for authentic purposes. Moreover, students benefit when teachers instruct in a "culturally responsive" manner (García, 2000, p. 826; Au, 1993, p. 13) and shed their beliefs that children from diverse households lack the experiences and knowledge necessary for classroom success.

book and write the page number or copy the quote in the left column. On the right column, write their reactions to it. If you want to provide more scaffolds for this, you can give them page numbers and tell them to find the interesting information on that page. This project can be done with fiction or nonfiction; it allows for aesthetic response to either type of text. See Figure 13.7 for an example of a double-entry journal response to *Roll of Thunder, Hear My Cry* (Taylor, 1976).

Interesting Events in *Roll of Thunder, Hear My Cry*	My Reactions
p. 40—Little Man, Stacey, Christopher John, and Cassie dug a hole in the road. The white kids' school bus got stuck in it and its axle broke.	I think I would've done the same thing. Cassie and her brothers were tired of getting splashed with mud from the bus all the time. And it wasn't fair that the black kids had to walk to school and the white kids got to ride a bus.

Figure 13.7 Example of a double-entry journal response.

Point of View Entries

Allow students to assume the role of one of the characters in a story, and describe in their journal what happened to them as well as their reactions to the events. This is a **point of view entry**. They should write in first-person singular, because they are pretending to be one of the characters. This is an efferent response, because students are not reacting personally or emotionally; instead, they are using their understanding of the story to retell events from a point of view different from the narrator's. See Figure 13.8 on page 450 for an example of this type of journal entry, written by a first grader who took the point of view of the alligator in *There's an Alligator Under My Bed* (Mayer, 1987).

Most of the time, this strategy is done with fiction; however, you can use it with biographies, and ask students to respond from the point of view of an important person in the life of the famous person. For example, some fifth grade students were reading *You Want Women to Vote, Lizzie Stanton?* (Fritz, 1995). Chapter 5 is an account of Elizabeth Cady Stanton's opportunity to speak to the New York State Legislature about women's rights in 1854. Although she was a grown woman, her father, Judge Cady, did not approve of her outspoken views and did not support her publicly or privately. After reading Chapter 5, one of the students, Natalie, wrote a point of view entry (Figure 13.9) by assuming the role of Lizzie's father.

Hoyt (1999) suggests that reading partners who are reading the same piece of fiction write point of view entries together. One of the partners assumes the role of questioner, while the other partner takes on the role of one of the characters in the story. The questioner asks a question, and his partner answers it from the point of view of the character. No talking can take place during this transaction; all questions and responses are written. Students switch roles after an agreed-upon number of questions have been asked.

Point of view entries can lead to more formal written pieces. Introduce the idea of changing one's perspective with a poem from Shel Silverstein, "Point of View," in *Where the Sidewalk Ends* (1974). You can show point of view with the unusual children's book *Barn* (Atwell, 1996), which begins, "I was raised in a coastal fog so thick the crows had to walk the cornfield that morning." The next page continues, "For over a hundred years I was a plain old farm barn."

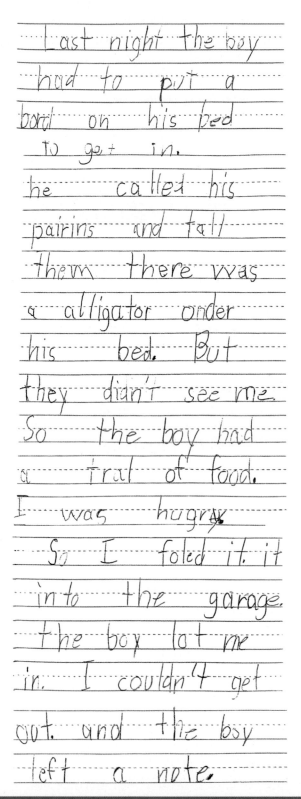

Last night the boy
had to put a
bord on his bed
to get in.
he called his
pairins and tall
them there was
a alligator onder
his bed. But
they didn't see me.
So the boy had
a tral of food.
I was hugray.
So I foled it. it
into the garage.
the boy lot me
in. I couldn't get
out. and the boy
left a note.

Figure 13.8 An example of a point of view journal entry written by a first grader.

Chapter 5—*You Want Women to Vote, Lizzie Stanton?*

Point of View: Judge Cady, Lizzie's father (Written by Natalie)

My daughter is making a big mistake. Women should not be making speeches to the legislature. The laws should not be changed. Women don't need to vote. They need to stay at home and take care of the children. My grandchildren don't see their mother very often, and now she's going to run off and make speeches. She's embarrassing her family!

Figure 13.9 A point of view journal entry used with a biography.

Finally, read to your students a book written by a group of fourth graders in Wisconsin, *A Day in the Life of Bubblegum* (Glanzer, Hitchman, Smith, Koval & Wiener, 2001). This delightful book, full of humor only fourth graders can appreciate, was published by Scholastic, under their "Kids Are Authors" program. You can learn more about publishing your students' written efforts at their web site, **teacher.scholastic.com/activities/kaa/**.

Sharing Quotations

Picking out meaningful, interesting, funny, sad, and moving quotes is a good way to respond to literature, because it is concrete; students can point to words. Once they have identified places in the text, they can move to more difficult skills such as interpreting, drawing conclusions, verbalizing their reactions, and symbolizing. **Quotation sharing** can be done in many ways. Students can write them in their journals and refer to them during discussions. They can read their favorite quotes aloud, using appropriate tone and expression, and then share the reason for choosing the quote.

A strategy offered by Harste, Short, and Burke is called, "Save the Last Word for Me" (1988, p. 332). To adapt this strategy for use with journals, ask each student to choose a quote from the text and copy it onto a page in their journal. On the back side of the page, have them write why they chose the quote. (They need to choose more than one, so they have backups if their teammates have already selected the same one they chose.) In small groups, students can then take turns sharing their quote. The first student selects the quote he or she wants to share, then reads it aloud without comment. The rest of the group discusses their reactions to that quote. When finished, the person who chose that quote tells why he chose it— "the last word." Turns are taken in this manner until everyone has a turn.

Another way to share quotes is to ask students to choose favorites from books read in the past. Each student writes a quote on an index card, and puts his or her name on the back of the card. Collect several of these over a period of days, putting them in a specially marked box or coffee can. Then, when you are ready to share, pull one quotation card at a time out of the box or can. The student who contributed the quote reads it, and everyone must guess the book from which the quote was copied. Then the student shares why he chose the quotation.

Journal writing gives students an opportunity to respond aesthetically to literature.

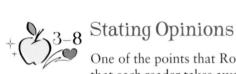 ## Stating Opinions

One of the points that Rosenblatt (1978) made with the transactional theory was that each reader takes away something different from the printed page. Everyone's reaction to a single piece of literature is different, depending on their background knowledge, their experiences, their interests, and their development. You can help your students' literacy growth by encouraging their aesthetic responses to books, even if their opinions differ from your own, or from those of their peers.

As a means of encouragement, type several statements about a book. These statements should be open-ended, in that the reader could either agree or disagree with them. For example, one statement for *Charlotte's Web* (White, 1952) could be, "It was cruel for Mr. Zuckerman, the farmer, to plan to kill Wilbur, the pig." Cut the statements into strips. Students can draw a strip from a hat, read it, and then write their reaction. They must either agree or disagree, and explain why. They should also support their answers with quotes or ideas from the text, and write down the page numbers of text that supports their answers. Then, they should bring their journals to a discussion.

Harvey and Goudvis (2000) describe a similar method of encouraging students to state opinions about factual information learned from their reading. The teacher gives the students a short piece of nonfiction to read, such as an article from a children's news magazine, a newspaper article, or a segment from a website. As they read, they find the answer to a question addressed in the article. The question should be one for which there are opposing viewpoints, such as "Should we drill for oil in Alaska?" or "Should citizens in this country be allowed to own guns?" The article should offer clear evidence for each viewpoint.

Home–School Connection

Rave Reviews

Nancy Steider, a first grade teacher in Pennsylvania, sends a copy of her students' published work home to a different family every two or three days. Attached to the back cover is an envelope that contains a sheet on which parents can make comments. The comment sheet is quite simple, and looks like this: ●

Students enjoy sharing their written responses.

Don
10/14

To be able to sit down and have my child read me a book about her classmates is very exciting. Great Job!

Sherry
10/22

Our family loved this book! The artwork is great. Thanks!!

Kim
10/23

Good job!!! This book is creative and fun to read. You're superstars!

Leah
10-28

What a wonderful idea! I've enjoyed every page of fun-looking portraits!

The teacher gives the students a note-taking sheet:

Evidence For	Evidence Against	My Opinion

Students should write evidence for and against each viewpoint in the appropriate columns, and include the page number of each statement. Students then write their own opinions in the last column.

Comparing and Rating Books

When your students finish a book, they have added it to their repertoire of literature that they know. Making connections between stories helps students understand the element of theme; comparing nonfiction books helps them read critically and make judgments about the quality of informational literature that is available to them. As readers of many books, your students are qualified to rate them. Students can rate and compare books by writing in their journals or discussing them with their groups. They finish prompt statements such as:

"This book is really different from the last book of its kind that I read, because . . ."

"This book affected me more than the last book of its kind that I read, because . . ."

"Of the two books that I read on this subject, I value this one more. The reasons are . . ."

"I read this one and another one written by this author. I like this one better because . . ."

The true reason for rating books is to share its value with others. You can make book ratings useful by asking students to look over their notes in their journals, and then write brief reviews of books on index cards. These cards can be inserted in the library pockets of the books in the school library or your classroom library. When students are searching for a library book, they can read these peer reviews to help make their decisions.

Literary Borrowing

Chapter 9 introduced the concept of literary borrowing (Lancia, 1997). This is a scaffolded writing experience in which the teacher shares a piece of literature with students, identifies stylistic devices or other unique features used by the author, and asks students to try their hand at the same type of writing. Your students can use literary borrowing as a springboard for writing published pieces, but this is also a wonderful way to respond to literature without the demands of publishing. Your students can keep records of different types of writing in special journals for this purpose. They can collect examples of different types of writing used by authors, such as stylistic devices, descriptions of settings or characters, use of nonfiction text structure patterns, and poetry. Students can copy quotations, phrases, sentences, or poems, or they can just list the author, title, and page number. Then, they can try writing their own examples. These pieces of writing that come from literary borrowing enable your students to react to text and develop as writers.

For example, one type of writing that can come from literary borrowing is the personal narrative. Begin by reading aloud to your students books that describe characters and the events in their lives. Invite your students to think about similar events in their own lives. After each read aloud session, ask students to add to a list of such events. This list will serve as a source of ideas for writing personal narratives. After your students become comfortable writing these autobiographical accounts, introduce the idea of writing fiction. Explain that authors often use true events and fictionalize them by changing people's names and exaggerating the facts. After modeling this for them, ask them to choose one event from their list to fictionalize.

Nancy Steider, a first grade teacher in Pennsylvania, shows her students how to write narratives after reading *Olivia* (Falconer, 2000). The first few pages of this book read:

> This is Olivia. She is good at lots of things. She is *very* good at wearing people out. She even wears herself out.

Using the same pattern that Falconer uses, her emerging writer students begin writing narratives very early in the year. A portion of a narrative written by Tommy, a first grader in Steider's class, is shown in Figure 13.10 on page 456. Notice that he was able to write in the third person, yet describe himself, because he followed the example of Falconer's book. Some books that can be used to introduce personal narratives to your students include: picture books such as *Olivia* (Falconer, 2000) and *Thank You, Mr. Falker* (Polacco, 1998), as well as chapter books such as *Because of Winn-Dixie* (DiCamillo, 2000) and *The Skin I'm In* (Flake, 1998).

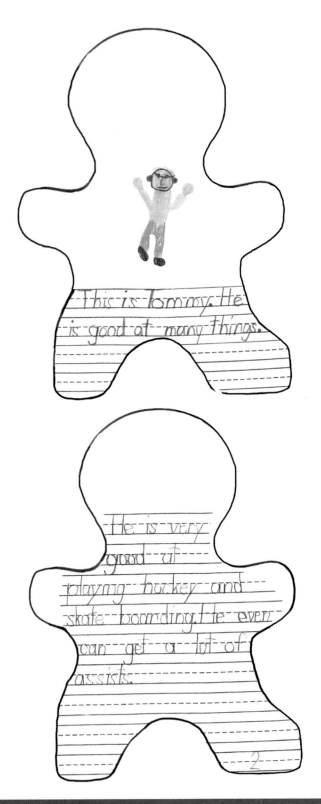

This is Tommy. He is good at many things.

He is very good at playing hockey and skate boarding. He even can get a lot of assists.

2

Figure 13.10 Portion of a personal narrative written by a first grader.

Summary: Responsible Responses

Requiring students to "publicize" their responses to reading means that you have a great responsibility. First, literature responses must be meaningful and have a purpose. Before assigning responses, ask yourself, "Why am I doing what I'm doing?" If the answer is to put pretty things on the walls or to send cute projects home, reconsider your motives. Responses need to be done for one purpose—that of completing the reading process. Second, literature responses must be treated with respect. A risk-free classroom atmosphere in which all students must listen to each other and thoughtfully consider what their classmates say about literature is essential. Third, there are two equally important ways to respond to all kinds of literature—efferently and aesthetically. Both need to be modeled and encouraged in order for your students to complete the reading process.

This chapter showed you a myriad of ways to offer opportunities to respond efferently as well as aesthetically. Several types of responses were described: retellings, summaries, text searches, response talks, response journals, and literary borrowing. I've listed all of these strategies in the Reviewing the Big Picture box, along with corresponding teaching standards and principles.

Technology Resources

Shown here are some children's book titles and related WebQuests. You can introduce the theme or topic with the book, and then give students the WebQuest to investigate.

Sam the Sea Cow (Jacobs, 1995)

- oncampus.richmond.edu/academics/education/projects/webquests/whale/ (Rescuing a baby beluga whale, fifth and sixth grades)
- oncampus.richmond.edu/academics/education/projects/webquests/oceans/ (Ocean pollution, fifth grade)
- projects.edtech.sandi.net/grant/oceanpollution/ (Ocean pollution, fourth through sixth grades)

Hoot (Hiaasen, 2002)

- homepage.mac.com/varkgirl/owlquest/ (Owls, second grade)
- www.snc.edu/educ/mse/courses/summerIT/students/benesh-zoeller/ (Landfills, fourth through eighth grades)
- oncampus.richmond.edu/academics/education/projects/webquests/fixitup/ (Creating parks, sixth through eighth grades)

The Wump World (Peet, 1970)

- oncampus.richmond.edu/academics/education/projects/webquests/paper/ (Recycling and saving the environment, third grade)
- oncampus.richmond.edu/academics/education/projects/webquests/photosynthesis/ (Photosynthesis, fourth grade)

One Day in the Tropical Rainforest (George, 1990)

- php.indiana.edu/~ljara/task.html (Rainforest environment, fourth through sixth grades)

Number the Stars (Lowry, 1988)

- oncampus.richmond.edu/academics/education/projects/samplers/stars.html (The Holocaust, sixth through eighth grades)
- http://www.spa3.k12.sc.us/WebQuests/Anne%20Frank/index.html (Anne Frank, sixth through eighth grades)

Brother Eagle, Sister Sky: A Message from Chief Seattle (Jeffers, 1991)

- oncampus.richmond.edu/academics/education/projects/samplers/nativeamericans.html (Native Americans, third through fourth grades)

So Far from the Sea (Bunting, 1998); *Grandfather's Journey* (Say, 1993)

- www.spa3.k12.sc.us/WebQuests/JAPAN%20WEBQUEST/index.html (Japan, fourth through sixth grades)
- www.education.umd.edu/Depts/EDCI/edci385/webquests3/Webquest5/webquest5.html (Japan, sixth through eighth grades)

Esperanza Rising (Ryan, 2000); *Sing Down the Moon* (O'Dell, 1970)

- coe.west.asu.edu/students/stennille/ST3/webquest.html#Introduction (Diversity, fourth through sixth grades)

The New York Times
expect the world
nytimes.com

Themes of the Times

Expand your knowledge of the concepts discussed in this chapter by reading current and historical articles from the *New York Times* by visiting the "Themes of the Times" section of the Companion Web Site.

Reviewing the Big Picture
Response Strategies

Strategy	Description	Appropriate Type of Text/ Grade Level	IRA Standards	INTASC Principles	NAEYC Standards	ACEI/NCATE Standards
Retelling checklists, bookmarks, and graphic organizers	Give your students scaffolds such as checklists, bookmarks, or graphic organizers to aid in remembering the elements or parts of the text to retell.	Fiction or nonfiction/ K–2, 3–5, 6–8	1.1, 2.2, 4.1, 4.4, 5.1	4, 7	4b (Use with read-alouds or shared reading)	2.1, 2.8
Summarizing with procedural text	Show students how to summarize by using sequential text that lists a set of steps.	Nonfiction/ K–2, 3–5	1.1, 2.2, 4.1, 4.3, 5.1	4, 7	4b, 4c (Use with read-alouds or shared reading)	2.1, 2.8, 3.1, 3.3, 3.4
Summarizing by categorizing facts	Show students how to summarize by asking them to list and categorize important facts.	Nonfiction/ K–2, 3–5	1.1, 2.2, 4.1, 4.3, 5.1	4, 7	4b, 4c (Use with read-alouds or shared reading)	2.1, 2.8, 3.1, 3.2, 3.3, 3.4
Summarizing with "little books"	Show students how to summarize, then give them books that encourage brevity.	Fiction or nonfiction/ 3–5, 6–8	1.1, 2.2, 4.1, 4.4, 5.1	4, 7	NA	2.1, 2.8, 3.1, 3.2, 3.3, 3.4
Sketch to stretch	After reading a selection, ask students to draw symbols or pictures to represent each important idea. Describe these in writing or verbally.	Fiction or nonfiction/ K–2, 3–5, 6–8	1.1, 2.2, 4.1, 4.4, 5.1	4, 7	4b, 4c (Use with read-alouds or shared reading)	2.1, 2.8, 3.1, 3.2, 3.3, 3.4
Highlighting	Teach students to find important information in text by highlighting.	Nonfiction/ K–2, 3–5	1.1, 2.2, 4.1, 4.4, 5.1	4, 7	4b, 4c (Use with read-alouds or shared reading)	2.1, 2.8, 3.1, 3.2, 3.3, 3.4

Reviewing the Big Picture (continued)

Strategy	Description	Appropriate Type of Text/ Grade Level	IRA Standards	INTASC Principles	NAEYC Standards	ACEI/NCATE Standards
Web pages	Put important web sites on a web page for student research.	Nonfiction/ K–2, 3–5, 6–8	1.1, 2.2, 4.1, 4.4, 5.1	1, 3, 4, 5, 6, 7	4b, 4c	2.1, 2.8, 3.1, 3.2, 3.3, 3.4, 3.5
WebQuests	Construct problem-solving tasks for students based on a topic of interest and using text from the Internet.	Nonfiction/ K–2, 3–5, 6–8	1.1, 2.2, 4.1, 4.4, 5.1	1, 3, 4, 5, 6, 7	4b, 4c (Use WebQuests designed for the K–2)	2.1, 2.8, 3.1, 3.2, 3.3, 3.4, 3.5
Response talks	Talk about text in natural ways by having conversations rather than recitations.	Fiction or nonfiction/ K–2, 3–5, 6–8	1.1, 2.2, 4.1, 4.4, 5.1	3, 4, 5, 6, 7	4b, 4c (Use with read-alouds or shared reading)	2.1, 2.8, 3.1, 3.2, 3.4, 3.5
Authorship talks	Talk with students about text, discussing the author and the author's purpose and sense of audience.	Fiction or nonfiction/ K–2, 3–5, 6–8	1.1, 2.2, 4.1, 4.4, 5.1	4, 5, 6, 7	4b, 4c (Use with read-alouds or shared reading)	2.1, 2.8, 3.1, 3.2, 3.4, 3.5
Ways to linger	List ways to reflect on a book reading. Don't hurry to end discussions because the book is finished. Use time to reflect. Students write their responses or discuss.	Fiction or nonfiction/ 3–5, 6–8	1.1, 2.2, 4.1, 4.4, 5.1	4, 5, 6, 7	NA	2.1, 2.8, 3.1, 3.2, 3.4, 3.5
Dialogue journal responses	Students use journals to "chat" with each other about literature responses.	Fiction or nonfiction/ 3–5	1.1, 2.2, 4.1, 4.4, 5.1	3, 4, 5, 7	NA	2.1, 2.8, 3.1, 3.2, 3.4, 3.5

Activity	Description	Genre/Grade				
Double-entry journals	Students write events from literature, then their reactions, in a journal.	Fiction/ 3–5, 6–8	1.1, 2.2, 4.1, 4.4, 5.1	4, 5, 7	NA	2.1, 2.8, 3.1, 3.2, 3.4, 3.5
Point of view entries	Students write about literature from another perspective.	Fiction/ K–2, 3–5	1.1, 2.2, 4.1, 4.4, 5.1	4, 5, 7	NA	2.1, 2.8, 3.1, 3.2, 3.4
Sharing quotations	Students find quotations from text and discuss, categorize, and write about them.	Fiction and nonfiction/ 3–5, 6–8	1.1, 2.2, 4.1, 4.4, 5.1	3, 4, 5, 7	NA	2.1, 2.8, 3.1, 3.2, 3.4
Stating opinions	Students agree or disagree with statements written about the text.	Fiction or nonfiction/ 3–5, 6–8	1.1, 2.2, 4.1, 4.4, 5.1	3, 4, 5, 7	NA	2.1, 2.8, 3.1, 3.2, 3.4, 3.5
Comparing and rating books	Students compare and rate fiction or nonfiction texts.	Fiction or nonfiction/ K–2, 3–5, 6–8	1.1, 2.2, 4.1, 4.4, 5.1	4, 7	4b, 4c (Use with read-alouds or shared reading)	2.1, 2.8, 3.1, 3.2, 3.4, 3.5
Literary borrowing	Using a piece of text as a guide, students write their own text using the same pattern, structure, or devices.	Fiction or nonfiction/ K–2, 3–5, 6–8	1.1, 2.2, 4.1, 4.4, 5.1	3, 4, 7	4b, 4c (Use with read-alouds or shared reading)	2.1, 2.8, 3.1, 3.2, 3.4, 3.5

14

Helping Students Become Fluent Readers

"'My Name,' by Sahara Jones," I began.

"Louder," she ordered.

"'My Name,' by Sahara Jones," I said again.

"Louder, and with expression!"

I swallowed. "'MY NAAAAME,' by SaHAra JONES!" I yelled. The class laughed.

"Good," said Miss Pointy. "Go on."

I can see how my daddy thought my name was a good idea at the time I was born. He must have thought that naming me after the biggest part of Africa would make me special. But special wears off. At least, it did for my daddy. He left me and my mom when I was in the third grade. We're not sure where he is.

When he left, Mom changed our last name back to Jones, which was her name before she got married. "You can change your first name, too, if you want," she told me. "We don't need nothing that man gave us."

That last line wasn't so hard to write. Why was it so hard to read? I swallowed again.

"Go on," said Miss Pointy. "You're doing great."

Sahara Special (Codell, 2003)

Jacqueline, age 12

Sahara Jones, the main character in Codell's fascinating book *Sahara Special* (2003), was clearly nervous about reading aloud for her peers, even though the text she was reading was her own writing. How do you feel about reading aloud for others? Think about that in the Personal Reflection.

When you were in elementary or middle school, how did you feel about reading aloud for other people?

How do you feel about reading aloud for others now?

What makes reading for others easy or hard for you?

A Reading Lesson— Or Is It?

Let's take a look at a second grade classroom. Mrs. Robin is conducting a reading lesson with a small group of children. These children have been grouped according to their reading ability; the book they are reading is at the second grade reading level. They all have books from the basal reading series in front of them and open to the page of the story they are about to read. After explaining to them that they will read from *Tyrone the Horrible* (Wilhelm, 1988), she asks Melanie, the first child sitting to her right, to read aloud. After Melanie reads a page, she asks Billy to read a page aloud. Following that, she asks Frankie, then Michael, then Carly, and then Anna to read. If anyone makes a mistake in pronunciation, she asks him or her to read the sentence aloud again. The children are well behaved, but we can see Michael turning pages and "reading ahead" in the story. Carly frequently looks around the room, fidgeting. Frankie mispronounces several words. When Mrs. Robin asks him to reread his sentences, Michael snickers, causing Frankie to glare at him. At last, when the story is complete, Mrs. Robin asks questions of everyone in the group. Her questions are worded in such a way that she asks the students to draw conclusions about what they have read and make comparisons about the story to their own lives. Anna and Michael are able to answer her questions fairly well, and seem somewhat interested in talking about the story. The remaining four try to avoid answering questions and are anxious to leave the group. At the end of the lesson, Mrs. Robin gives the students a workbook page assignment in which they must answer questions about the story.

Does this classroom scenario bring back memories? It's a common one, even now. Let's reexamine the scene. You probably noticed that Mrs. Robin really did not do anything before the students read the story. During their reading, she monitored the group and called on the next reader. While it is extremely important to maintain good classroom behavior, we could not say that Mrs. Robin was truly *teaching* while she was doing this. She also asked children to repeat their reading if they made mistakes. We cannot say that she taught anything here, either, because she assumed that they knew how to correct their own mistakes. After the children read, she asked some good questions, and she might have realized that most of the group did not understand or care about this story. Essentially, only two children got anything at all out of this story. Can we assume that it was because of anything their teacher did? Probably not.

Mrs. Robin was doing a fine job of controlling overt student behavior and a decent job of asking appropriate questions. However, she was making at least four assumptions:

1. The students were interested in the reading selection.
2. The students would understand its vocabulary and the authors' implications.
3. The students would be able to read orally unprepared.
4. The students would know what to do with unknown words.

Asking good questions helped her determine who understood the story and who did not. However, has Mrs. Robin done anything to ensure the students' understanding of the story or vocabulary? Has she taught in such a way that understanding of the story is her first priority? Not at all.

Notice that nowhere in the description of the classroom scenario is the word *teach*. That is because Mrs. Robin is not teaching; she is simply presiding over a group of children. What Mrs. Robin is practicing is called **round-robin reading.** This kind of practice still exists in many classrooms across this country—you might have recognized it as something you've sat through. Assuming that the purpose for reading is to understand the author's message, what is wrong with this teaching practice? Simply put, round-robin reading does not promote understanding.

For years, I have asked my undergraduate students to participate in a mock round-robin session. I ask about ten volunteers to orally read, unprepared, from an educational journal article, while the remainder of the class reads silently. Every time I ask questions about the article, few, if any, of my students are able to answer the questions. The same thing happens in elementary and middle school classrooms when children are not prepared to read aloud. Let's examine the reasons why.

The Pitfalls of Round-Robin Reading

Needless Subvocalizations

When reading silently, we sometimes **subvocalize,** which means that we mentally pronounce the words on the page. Many reading experts agree that normal, fluent silent reading does not require a mental pronunciation of every word we see. Gibson and Levin (1975) suggest that subvocalizing might help readers comprehend difficult material; however, Smith (1971) hypothesizes that subvocalizing occurs only when the text becomes more difficult. Thus, readers subvocalize because they are reading more slowly and trying to comprehend text that is difficult for them. According to Durkin (1993), it is quite possible that when readers are participating in a round robin, and they are trying to follow along with the oral reading of a poor reader, their subvocalization increases. This result is undesirable, because it leads to "needlessly slow rates—plus annoyance" (1993, p. 52). It detracts from the business at hand—understanding the text. Therefore, while reading experts say that subvocalizations may help a reader who is struggling through a piece of text, subvocalizing is not necessary for normal, everyday reading, and indeed, it slows reading rate needlessly.

Oral Reading Difficulties

Reading aloud for others is a desirable skill and is supposed to be done so that a piece of text is shared and enjoyed by all. This assertion, however, is dependent upon two assumptions: (1) The reader is prepared to read aloud for others, and (2) There is an interested audience. Round-robin reading does not ensure either of these things. Do you remember round-robin reading in your elementary school days? Perhaps you dreaded being called upon to read aloud because of your fear of making mistakes in front of your peers. This kind of anxiety is unnecessary and may even produce poor oral readers. It certainly produces poor listeners, because there is nothing worse than trying to listen to a group of readers stumble through text that is too difficult for them.

Mismanaged Student Behavior

At first glance, it would seem that keeping children together in a group and calling upon them individually to read aloud would enable the teacher to manage behavior easily. But think about the children in Mrs. Robin's group again. Michael was turning pages and "reading ahead" in the story. Carly was frequently looking around the room and fidgeting. When Mrs. Robin asked Frankie to reread, Michael snickered at his classmate, causing what is most likely to be a continuing source of discord between the boys. There were only two children who were somewhat interested in talking about the story. Thus, how well is the students' behavior actually managed?

Another behavior occurs when students make errors during round-robin reading. Usually, when the reader makes an error, someone is all too willing to correct the mistake. This interruption robs the reader of the chance to correct his or her own error, in addition to adding to anxiety related to making mistakes in front of peers. Allington reports (1980) that this seemingly helpful behavior deprives struggling students of the self-monitoring skills they need as mature readers. Moreover, students who are learning to speak English need a supportive, "low-anxiety" environment (McCauley & McCauley, 1992, p. 527). Being corrected by peers and the teacher while attempting to pronounce unknown words—in a new language—is not part of such an environment.

When I conduct the mock round-robin "experiment" in my undergraduate classes, there is always at least one student who reveals that she was not really paying attention to the article; instead, she was looking ahead in the article to determine which part of it would be "hers" to read aloud. This comes from a mature reader who attends a university, preparing to become a teacher! Many students reveal that this is what they did when they were younger; reading aloud for their peers produced such anxiety that they felt the need to practice, so they tried to figure out the sentences the teacher would ask them to read.

If this is so, then outward appearances can be quite deceiving to the teacher who thinks her group is well managed. If students are not paying attention to the message being read, the goal of reading is not being met. So, at what cost is "good" classroom behavior achieved?

Conclusions About Round-Robin Reading

We saw a fictional teacher, Mrs. Robin, attempt to teach reading. Round-robin reading, a common teaching practice, does not focus on the processes of reading, nor does it give children a chance to respond in a meaningful way to their reading. Instead, this practice assumes that children already know how to actively engage themselves and understand what they read, without ever showing them how. Certainly, Mrs. Robin can assess a few things, such as how many words a child mispronounces. However, anxiety may have contributed to poor reading in some of her students; thus, she could not get a true picture of their reading abilities. The problems inherent in the practice of round-robin reading are summarized here:

1. Students do not comprehend what they are asked to read.
2. Students might be subvocalizing too much as they try to follow another reader, resulting in annoyance and needlessly slow rates.
3. The true purpose of oral reading—that of sharing—is not realized.
4. Students are not actively engaged in the task at hand—comprehending the text.
5. Because of the anxiety it causes and its emphasis on correct word pronunciation, it conveys the wrong ideas about reading.

It is the premise of this book that the goal of all reading instruction is to enable understanding of what is read. Reading is not really reading unless you've understood—and personally reacted to—what the author wrote. Thus, merely reading words out loud on demand is not reading. So, what are the alternatives to round-robin reading? How do you foster "real" reading in the classroom? In this chapter, we'll examine some strategies for purposeful oral reading instruction. But first, let's examine why it's important.

Why Read Aloud?

The National Reading Panel (2000a) concludes that fluent oral reading is one of the five most important reading competencies to teach. What is fluency, and why is it so important? *Fluency* is the ability to read quickly, accurately, expressively, and with comprehension (National Reading Panel, 2000a; Johns & Bergland, 2002; Samuels, 2002). Fluency is important because students who can read fluently do not need to stop and devote attention to decoding single words.

Remember the automaticity theory, which you learned about in Chapter 1? This theory states that readers need to be able to automatically recognize print, so that they can pay attention to the comprehension of the author's message, rather than concentrate on pronouncing or decoding words (LaBerge & Samuels, 1974; Samuels, 2004; Samuels & Kamil, 1984). Samuels tells us that emerging readers

Diversity in the Reading Classroom

Teaching Middle School Students Who Struggle with Literacy

Reading is difficult for many African American, Latino/Hispanic, and Native American middle school students, as well as students with learning disabilities. Middle school students who struggle with reading must also contend with the common belief that they are apathetic toward it (McCray, 2001). However:

> It is becoming more apparent that many young adolescents in the United States are not simply choosing to eschew reading in favor of other nonliterate activity. Rather, as reports at the national, state, and local levels indicate, millions of youngsters at the intermediate and middle school levels read below a fourth-grade level and experience deficiencies in basic reading skills. (McCray, 2001, p. 298).

Thus, many middle school students who struggle with reading do so not because they don't want to read, but because they can't.

According to surveys conducted by McCray, Vaughn, and Neal (2001), middle school students were not apathetic about their lack of literacy and were well aware of the importance of being able to read and write well. Moreover, these students were keenly observant of their teachers' abilities in literacy instruction. Students surveyed did not want the teacher to read everything for them, as this conveyed a lack of respect and low expectations. Middle school students were cognizant that they need time to read in order to get better at reading, and that they need to read on their own, not relying on the teacher for reading assignments. At the same time, they indicated that they were frustrated by unreasonable expectations without explanations and modeling to show them how to accomplish literacy tasks that they do not know how to do.

Cambourne (2001) tells us that many students will not put forth the effort needed to read and write because they have not been convinced that the effort is worth it. When students of any age have been repeatedly exposed to print that makes no sense to them, and when they have witnessed little or no instruction in how to construct meaning from print, they stop trying.

Moreover, according to Cambourne, expectations of struggling readers have historically been low. Teaching practices such as fixed ability grouping, tracking, and constant negative feedback lead to low expectations of students, which in turn lead to students holding low expectations of themselves. Even well-meaning practices have often taken students' self-reliance away from them. Years of depending on the teacher to supply the unknown word or read the directions for them can lead to readers no longer accepting the responsibility for their own growth, and expect the teacher to make everything easier. García (2000) points out that reading instruction for bilingual students is often passive; "most of their time was spent listening or watching their teachers" (p. 825).

Middle school students from diverse backgrounds who struggle with reading and writing need to regain control over their literacy learning. Here are some suggestions for how to help them:

- Always emphasize comprehension as the goal of reading and writing.

- Set high but reasonable academic expectations.

- Avoid practices such as round-robin reading.

- Use children's and adolescent literature with compelling messages and characters that are from diverse backgrounds.

- Give positive messages that lead to self-efficacy.

- Use drama, role-playing, and poetry.

- Allow your students to do things for themselves, such as reading their own directions and correcting their own mistakes when reading aloud or writing.

develop their fluency abilities over time and through developmental stages. When readers reach the point at which they are able to recognize words quickly and simultaneously comprehend the message, their reading is fluent. This means that the reader can read with accuracy and speed, without pausing or stopping to decode. Fluency, then, allows readers to devote their efforts to comprehending the print.

Likewise, comprehension aids fluency. As readers sweep their eyes across the page, they notice clues like punctuation and specialized print such as italic. Their understanding of these clues, as well as command of the words themselves, enables them to read expressively. A reader's phrasing, tone, and pitch indicate that he or she knows how the message on the page should sound. Another word for this ability to make the print sound natural is **prosody.** While a student reads, his or her comprehension enables him or her to read with prosody, in a way that sounds conversational. Thus, fluency and comprehension are closely related, and time spent on oral reading fluency instruction is well worth the effort (National Reading Panel, 2000a).

Another reason for developing good oral reading is its close relationship to other types of reading skills. Pinell, Pikulski, Wixson, Campbell, Gough, and Beatty (1995), in a study of the oral reading behaviors of children, report that children who are the most fluent readers are also the ones who tend to be more self-motivated to read. This may be reflective of the "Matthew effect," in that readers who are good at reading tend to read more, which in turn makes them even better at reading (Stanovich, 1985).

Moreover, teachers seem to be influenced by their students' oral reading abilities. Rasinski and Padak (1998) studied the results of reading inventories conducted with over 600 children in grades 2 through 5. These students had been referred by their teachers for Title I reading services because of their poor reading abilities in the classroom. They found that on average, these children were almost at the instructional level in their comprehension and word recognition abilities. In other words, with some extra help, they could probably improve these areas. However, their reading rates were typically far below this—usually at 60 percent of the instructional level reading rate for their grade level. Thus, these readers were reading slowly and laboriously, even though their comprehension and word recognition abilities were almost on grade level. Rasinski states that the oral reading rate of children like these is a "significant factor in classroom teachers' perceptions of their students' proficiency or lack of proficiency in reading" (2000, p. 146).

Even so, Rasinski warns that though teachers seem to associate poor reading with a slow rate, they may be ignoring the connection. Often, when considering how to help their poorest readers, they assume that as long as a child is making meaning from the text, it does not matter how long it takes him or her to read a passage. But consider two situations when reading rate is very important: (1) when reading orally for peers, and (2) when reading for a test. Clearly, students who read slowly and laboriously are at a disadvantage both times.

Johns and Bergland (2002) explain fluency as a four-part entity, consisting of comprehension, expression, rate, and accuracy. In good oral reading, all of these fluency components work together seamlessly. There are specific strategies that you can use to help your students develop each of the four, enabling them to read with prosody and with understanding. The next four sections explore each of them separately.

Oral Reading and Comprehension

Some teachers have concerns with the emphasis their school district administrations place on fluency instruction. One said, "It seems like a shame to spend all that time on reading aloud. I'm worried about their comprehension." Many times, educators emphasize speed or automatic word recognition, forgetting about the reason for reading in the first place—comprehending the written word. The teacher quoted earlier is worried about this, and does not want to convey the message to students that oral reading is only about pronouncing words correctly and quickly.

In order to be truly fluent, readers need to comprehend what they read. They need to understand the relationship between printed signals and the spoken word, so that when they see marks such as commas on the page, they know to pause. Readers need to be familiar enough with print to know how punctuation influences meaning. They also need to know the vocabulary and its meanings; it is not enough to merely pronounce words correctly. Rather, they need to know subtle meanings of words, which enable them to read with the expression intended by the author.

Teaching your students how to comprehend so that it aids their fluency involves modeling. In particular, you need to model by reading and thinking aloud as you teach them strategies that help them become fluent readers.

Typographical Signals

Durkin (1993) explains the importance of teaching students about the signals that authors use to clarify their writing. These **typographical signals** not only help the reader comprehend the passage; they also influence the sound of oral reading. For example, read aloud these two sentences:

> Michael ordered ice cream and coffee.
>
> Michael ordered ice, cream, and coffee.

As you can see, the placement of commas affects the meaning of the sentence. Typographical signals indicate a change in the intonation in your voice and the pauses in your reading. The same words, combined with different signals, convey entirely different meanings.

Typographical signals can also change your prosody—your pitch, tone, and phrasing. Now read the same words with different signals. Notice how your voice and expression change as you read.

> Michael ordered ice cream—and coffee!
>
> Michael *ordered* ice cream and coffee!
>
> Michael ordered ice cream . . . and *coffee?*
>
> *Michael* ordered ice cream and coffee?

Each of these sentences tells the reader about Michael's action, but each of them convey a different meaning and reaction to the event, because of the signals given to the reader in print.

Types of Typographical Signals

Commas—Indicate a pause. The reader needs to "chunk" the text into the phrases indicated by commas.	Or maybe my teacher phoned, saying that even though I don't get the best grades in fifth grade, I am definitely the smartest kid in the class. (p. 1)
Periods—Indicate the need for a longer pause, at the end of the sentence.	Dad had to whack me on the back. Tiny pieces of chewed up carrot flew out of my mouth and hit the counter. (p. 2)
Italicized or underlined print—Indicates emphasis and usually results in loud, forceful expression. Authors also often use italic to indicate that the character is thinking these words, but not saying them aloud. The reader might need to change his voice slightly to convey this.	"How could you?" I shouted. *"How could you? Isn't one enough?"* (p. 2) *Another Fudge*, I said to myself. *They're going to have another Fudge.* (p. 3)
Question marks—Indicate a question and a need for a slight rise in intonation at the end of the sentence.	"Where are you going?" Mom asked. (p. 4)
Ellipses—Indicate a pause, often because of an interruption in the dialogue, or an unfinished sentence. The reader usually needs to make his voice trail off.	"You little . . . " I started to say, but Fudge was already yapping away to my father. (p. 5)
Exclamation points—Indicate deep emotion, such as excitement, fear, happiness, or surprise.	"Enough!" I said. (p. 6)

Figure 14.1 Typographical signals and their effect on oral reading, taken from *Superfudge* (Blume, 1980).

Your students already know these subtle differences in meaning, because they use them all the time in their speech. Your job is to show them how typographical print requires them to respond to the text appropriately. Opitz and Rasinski (1998) suggest modeling the use of these signals by reading aloud a book that has plenty of them and showing the print to the students as they listen. See Figure 14.1 for a list of such typographical signals and examples of sentences taken from *Superfudge* (Blume, 1980).

Find and Read

One of the easiest ways to develop oral reading skills is to ask your students to look for something in a selection that they have already read silently. In this strategy, you ask the students to **find and read** specific parts of the text. During guided reading, you can stop at a stop point and say, "Find the part of the story that

Find and Read

Directions: Cut this page into strips and give each student a section. After they read Chapter 1 of *The Giver* (Lowry, 1993), ask them to follow their directions and be ready to read their pieces aloud.

Find the part that tells what the voice over the loudspeakers said after the pilot of the stray airplane was noticed.
Find the part that tells about how Jonas had used the word "released" inappropriately when he was small.
Find the part that tells what happened when Asher was late for school.
Find the part that describes how the family unit shared their feelings in the evening.
Find the part that tells how Jonas feels about the upcoming month of December.
Find the part that tells what might happen to one of the new children that Father has been nurturing.

Figure 14.2 Parts for students to find and read aloud from *The Giver*.

tells. . . ." Students look for this page, and you ask someone to read it aloud. Another way to vary this activity is to write the directions on slips of paper, one per student. Each student, after reading silently, looks up his part and reads it orally. Be sure to remind students to use signals that help them figure out how to make their voices sound. Opitz and Rasinski (1998, p. 26) as well as Cunningham, Hall, and Cunningham (2000, p. 173) describe similar strategies in which students find information or conclusions in the text, and read them aloud for their peers. Figure 14.2 shows an example of directions to give students when reading *The Giver* (Lowry, 1993).

Oral Reading and Expression

Why is it important to be able to read aloud for other people? As adults, the vast majority of reading that we do is silent. The reason to read aloud is to share the page with other people. Authors write for the purpose of communicating with others; readers read in order to receive that message. Thus, when a reader reads aloud, he or she is sharing that message with an audience, which is part of the author's intention. Part of the reader's responsibility in sharing print is to convey the subtle meanings that exist within the print. The reader must make inferences from the printed page and verbalize them in pitch and tone. In order to share the meanings intended by the author, a reader must be expressive.

I remember my great disappointment several years ago, when I took time off from work to travel to another state and listen to a well-known researcher in education. While I know that he had some very compelling things to say—things that were of interest to me professionally—I simply could not pay attention. He spoke in monotone; his voice droned on through the afternoon. I had read many of his books and articles, yet his voice expression revealed none of the passion of his writing. By contrast, I went to another workshop a few months later, and listened to a different speaker. She knew how to captivate her audience with her voice. She whispered, shouted, exclaimed, and paused mysteriously. Her topic was rather mundane, and at first was only somewhat interesting to me; nevertheless, she made me laugh and cry. I still haven't forgotten the things she said.

Readers can do the same thing. If your students are comfortable with their reading, and know how to use the text to their advantage, they can make the page come alive. Decoding is automatic, and the words fall out as easily as if they were chatting in a conversation. Moreover, some literature was written to be read aloud. Its words seem to roll off the tongue, like music. Some stories are so compelling, with such interesting and quirky characters, that it is hard to resist sharing them with others. Teaching children to read orally means to teach them the reason for reading orally—sharing something worthwhile with others. This experience requires a genuine audience, preferably one that has not yet heard or read the story. It also requires that children have the opportunity to practice reading before they read aloud. This does not mean round-robin reading, or orally rereading every story read silently by the group. There are some strategies that you can use to show them how to use available clues to read with prosody and appropriate speed, described next.

Say It Right!

Once the book is finished, your students can play with its language by reading selections from it aloud, using different tones of voice and emotions (Olson & Homan, 1993). This strategy is excellent practice for reading with expression; children enjoy it because they can "ham it up" a bit. Choose some interesting quotations from the book that your students have already read in its entirety. Then select some mood or emotion words that can be used to read the quotations aloud. You can do this with the entire class, if you choose one quotation and mood word per child to read to the large group. Or, you can break the class into small groups and have them select quotations and mood words, then read to their teammates. For added variation, you can also have partners read a quotation in choral reading fashion. Below are some suggested mood word prompts.

Read this as if you were . . . :

> delighted
> wicked
> mournful
> joyful
> worried
> frightened
> depressed

Appendix B includes an example of Say It Right! Opitz and Rasinski suggest a similar strategy called Say It Like the Character (1998, p. 24). In this strategy, you ask the students to read the

This student reads aloud to share a favorite story with his classmates.

story silently first, and think about the characters' emotions. Using a mental model, you need to show the students the clues that the author gives to convey characters' moods and feelings. Sometimes these clues are words, such as "cried," "sobbed," or "gasped." Other times, these clues are typographical, such as the use of italic type or capital letters to show emphasis. After discussing the clues, model a sentence of dialogue spoken by one character, reading it aloud with appropriate emotion. Ask your students to do the same by reading aloud a sentence to their partner.

Readers' Theater

A story that has many important characters and a compelling plot can be adapted for Readers' Theater. You can have the students create their own scripts, or you can adapt the story into a script yourself. Usually, all that needs to be done is to choose a narrator to read all parts of the story that are not dialogue. Students who choose to portray the characters read character parts. Many times, you can have the students read right out of the book. Other times, you will need to change the words in the book a bit, or retype the same words into a script so that it is easier for the students to read their parts. This way, you can leave out extraneous details that might be too cumbersome for the narrator. See Figure 14.3 for a sample of a script adapted for first graders from Marc Brown's *Arthur's Computer Disaster* (1997).

Characters:

Narrator	Arthur
DW	Buster

Narrator: Arthur loaded the game.

Buster: Look out for the Squid Squad!

Arthur: I'm running out of oxygen.

Buster: Look! A treasure chest!

Arthur: That's it! That's *the thing*! I found it!

Buster: Let me open it!

Arthur: *I* found it.

Narrator: They both dove for the mouse. The keyboard crashed to the floor.

Arthur: Uh-oh.

DW: You're in big trouble.

Narrator: Just then the phone rang. Everyone jumped. It was Mom.

Figure 14.3 Readers' Theater script adapted from *Arthur's Computer Disaster* (Brown, 1997).

Some books lend themselves quite well to adaptation for Readers' Theater. You need stories that have a number of characters, so that you can assign each character to a different student. Additionally, most stories will need a narrator. Thus, you can divide your class into small groups of about four or five and give each group a different story. After reading it silently, they can determine which parts to assign to group members and begin reading aloud their parts. Appendix B includes a list of books or stories that require little or no adaptation for scripts.

Readers' Theater is a motivating way to practice oral reading expression.

Additionally, you can find many fine scripts that have already been created for you, such as Ratliff's *Introduction to Readers' Theatre: A Guide to Classroom Performance* (1999). There are also some relevant web sites listed in the Technology Resources section at the end of this chapter, and you can find several others by typing "Readers' Theater" into your favorite search engine.

Partner Reading

Partner reading is helpful in primary grades; especially first grade, when children tend to read everything orally. Silent reading does not always come naturally to very young children; they need to hear the words as they read them. Thus, when they are working with compatible reading buddies who have similar ability levels, they can read a book orally for the first time, without reading silently first. For some beginning readers, reading orally is how they process print. To do this, partners need to be reading the same kinds of books, at roughly the same ability levels. Putting a weak reader with a strong reader as partners makes no sense, because the stronger reader will do all the work, and the weaker reader gets no practice. Partners must sit side-by-side in a private place, and if one book is shared, the book must be held between them so that both partners can see it. (Reading should not take place upside-down!) Designate places in the room to which partners may go to read together. Some partner reading suggestions include:

1. Read together, in unison.
2. Read by taking turns, either page-by-page or two or three pages at a time.
3. Read by assigning character parts. Stories such as "Spring" in *Frog and Toad Are Friends* (Lobel, 1970) and "The High Board" in *George and Martha Back in Town* (Marshall, 1984) need just two characters. The first student reads until the second character speaks. All narration between the dialogue can be shared equally. Or put students in triads in which one student is the narrator while the other two read the characters' dialogue.
4. One partner reads an entire book to the other, and then the other partner reads one.
5. The readers share a book. One partner begins reading, with the understanding that when he is tired or wants to hand over the book, he can count on his partner to take over.

Modifying Instruction for

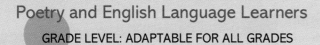

ELL

Poetry and English Language Learners

GRADE LEVEL: ADAPTABLE FOR ALL GRADES

● Objective

After listening to poetry selections, students read poetry aloud, for the purpose of sharing it with others.

● Materials

- Suggested books of poetry; see the list at **www.ablongman.com/nettles**
- Copies of selected poems on transparencies or MS PowerPoint slides

● Procedure

1. Read aloud a short poem, preferably with rhyme and humor. Show students the words on the screen, and point to words as you read aloud.

2. Read the poem a second time, and invite students to read aloud with you. Be sure to include bilingual poetry whenever possible, from books such as *My Mexico— Mexico Mio* (Johnston, 1996) or *Laughing Out Loud, I Fly: Poems in English and Spanish* (Herrera, 1998).

3. After students are comfortable with brief poems, read aloud a longer poem that has repeated lines or refrains. Students join in, reading the repeated line or refrain in chorus fashion. Write the word or refrain on a sentence strip and hold it up when it is time for the students to read it.

4. After a few days of reading poetry as a class, read aloud a poem that can be broken into parts. Give the boys one part and the girls the other part. Read aloud in chorus.

5. Once students have developed some confidence and interest in poetry, read aloud a poem that has lines each student can read aloud individually. For example, Shel Silverstein's "Whatif" poem (1981) can be divided into speaking parts, with each child assigned to a "whatif" line. Make sure that students who are learning English have ample opportunities to practice their speaking parts with a partner or with you.

6. Read aloud a poem that students can adopt and read on their own, with use of props and masks. For example, Silverstein's "Lazy Jane"(1974) can be read with one student on the floor, while the other sprinkles torn paper for "raindrops."

7. Read aloud a poem that can be used as a pattern for writing. "Good Books, Good Times!" by Hopkins (1990) is one from which students can write their own version. It is also an excellent poem for reading in parts.

Modifications for ELL are printed in color.

Keep in mind that this strategy is for beginning readers in primary grades, or for older children who are not yet proficient at reading. When your students are able to read silently alone for about 20 minutes or more, they are ready to let go of partner reading. Your goal is to develop private, silent readers who understand and respond to the text. This occurrence usually begins by the end of first grade; however, it happens either earlier or later for many children.

Poetry Parties

One of the fondest memories I have of teaching in elementary school is that of watching one of my fourth grade reluctant readers present "The Loser," by Shel Silverstein (1974, p. 25), to his peers. He drew a picture of his head, cut it out, and taped it to a trashcan turned upside-down. He sat on the trashcan, pulled his shirt over his head, and read Silverstein's delightful poem about a boy whose mother told him the familiar admonition, that he would lose his head if it was not fastened onto his neck!

Poetry, by nature, is meant to be read aloud. It is also a great medium for developing oral reading fluency, because much of it is predictable, repetitious, rhythmic, and simply fun to listen to. Allow your students to select their own poem from an anthology, or write one of their own. Give them a class period to practice reading the poem silently, then orally, making sure to practice intonation, expression, and speed. Have them practice with trusted partners who can give them encouragement. Assign a day on the calendar as a "Poetry Party" day, bring in a snack, and invite your students to share readings.

One unique way to get the students to share poetry is to adapt a strategy already used by many teachers. In many classrooms, teachers choose a student to be "Student of the Week." They devote a bulletin board to the program, and the chosen student may decorate it with photographs, pictures, or other items that they would like to share with their classmates. Cathy Hayden, a third grade teacher in Pennsylvania, initiated this type of program in her classroom, calling it "What a Kid!" Her students may bring in things to share, but they are also asked to memorize or read a favorite poem. She informs parents about their child's "What a Kid" day two weeks in advance, and invites them, if they wish, to share a snack related to the theme of the poem with the class. Here is an excerpt from the letter she sends to parents:

As you might guess, the children are excited about being highlighted in our classroom. Your child will benefit from your help selecting and practicing the poetry he or she will be sharing. Your child should write or type the poem, decorate it, and bring it to school. After displaying your child's illustrated poem on the bulletin board, the poem will be placed in a class book called *Plum Crazy About Poetry*, which is being composed by our class this year. (Hayden, personal communication, July 28, 2003)

Keep in mind that the best way to encourage this type of interest in reading poetry is to share it with your students daily. Some wonderful anthologies or poem books that lend themselves well to reading aloud include:

Life Doesn't Frighten Me (Angelou, 1993)
Joyful Noise: Poems for Two Voices (Fleischman, 1988)

Mammalabilia (Florian, 2000)
Laughing Out Loud, I Fly: Poems in English and Spanish (Herrera, 1998)
Hello, School! (Lillegard, 2001)

Choral Reading

Reading together is fun. When students read *chorally*, they work together as a team and support each other as they read short selections. There are several ways to read together:

1. *Refrains*—The whole group reads a short predictable passage or refrain while the teacher narrates the rest.
2. *Divided parts*—Each child receives a line and reads it in sequence.
3. *Group reading*—The passage is divided into two or three parts. The class is divided into the same number of groups. Each group reads its assigned part in sequence.
4. *Whole class*—The entire class reads the whole text together.

Once you have shown your students how to do each of the different types of choral reading, you can let them choose their own ways to read for a given selection.

When you use choral reading, choose short selections that can be divided into speaking parts. Opitz and Raskinski (1998) recommend that when you start teaching your students how to use choral reading, you begin with brief, familiar text that most students have memorized anyway, such as the Pledge of Allegiance. Poetry is a natural choice for all ages, especially if it is humorous, rhyming, and playful. "Alligator Pie" (Lee, 2001, p. 8) is a great choice for choral reading with young children.

Oral Reading and Rate

Rate of reading refers to how fast students can read with understanding. According to Opitz and Rasinksi, rate "reflects one part of reading fluency and can indicate how meaningfully students process text" (1998, p. 73). Good readers know how to adjust their speed to their purpose, but they can read quickly, comfortably, and with appropriate pauses and few interruptions in the flow of words.

Words per Minute

Oral reading rate is often determined in words per minute and can be easily calculated. Ask the student to read aloud a short passage that is at his or her independent level. Use the reading to determine the student's words per minute rate. The formula shown in Figure 14.4 computes the number of words that the child reads in a minute, or WPM. Once you have determined a student's WPM, you can compare it to the rates of his or her peers, giving you an indication of how fast a student is reading compared to his or her age group.

While it is generally agreed that speed of reading is important (Fountas & Pinnell, 2001; Johns & Bergland, 2002; National Reading Panel, 2000a; Opitz & Rasinski, 1998; Tyner, 2004), it is also agreed that pinpointing an optimum WPM rate for each grade level is difficult. Some recommended rates for first graders that are listed in Figure 14.4 were taken from the work of Forman and Sanders (cited in Johns & Bergland, 2002); recommended rates for all other grade levels were taken from the work of Fountas and Pinnell (2001).

Assessing WPM is simple using Figure 14.4 and can be done while you are assessing other things. When you ask a student to read a passage, the only tool that you need to determine WPM is a stopwatch. Suppose you are observing one of your second graders, Max. You want to gather some information about how well he comprehends a short passage, but you also want to know how fast he reads. You ask him to read aloud the first two pages of *Marvin Redpost: Super Fast, Out of Control!* (Sachar, 2000), which contain 162 words. On these two pages, the author does a nice job of establishing characters and a problem, which makes this selection a good one for determining comprehension. Time Max while he reads, and record the number of seconds. Then, ask Max to retell what he remembers about the reading. Make notes about his ability to name the characters and the problem. As explained in Chapter 4, use a retell checklist to determine Max's comprehension.

Now you can also compute Max's WPM and compare it to other second graders. Suppose Max reads this passage in 123 seconds. This yields a WPM of 79, which, according to Fountas and Pinnell (2001), is within the range expected of second graders. That range goes up to 100 words per minute, however. Max may need some practice with fluency rate if you are testing him at the end of his second grade year.

You can determine reading rate with more specificity, using tables of rates that are broken down into parts of the school year. Some reading researchers have established such norms, for grades one through six, for the beginning, middle, and end of the academic year (Hasbruck & Tindal, 1992; Hudson, Lane, & Pullen, 2005). However, these norms are based on **Correct Words Per Minute** (CWPM), which is different from WPM. CWPM is the number of words read *correctly* in one minute. (This rate is also called Words Correct Per Minute, or WCPM.) Thus, you ask a student to read any passage at the independent level for exactly one minute. Stop at 60 seconds and count the number of words read. Next, determine how many errors the student made in that time. (Do not count repetitions or self-corrections as errors.) Subtract the number of errors from the number of words read in a minute. This is the student's CWPM. You can find the resulting score on the norms chart to compare it to the score established by grade-level peers. The CWPM norms chart recommended by Hudson, Lane, and Pullen is in the May 2005 edition of *The Reading Teacher* (p. 711).

Keep in mind the difference in recording WPM and CWPM. When you count CWPM, you ask the student to read for exactly 60 seconds and stop. Thus, while the assessment is quick and to the point, it is purely a reading rate measure, with little or no consideration of any other aspects of the reading process. Recording WPM is less "test-like." By establishing a period of talking with and observing five students per day as they read and talk about their independent reading, you can measure reading rate while you measure other reading processes, in a naturalistic fashion. The passage that you use should be episodic, and you can allow the child to finish reading it. Thus, you can also analyze miscues, record retelling ability, or count the number of repetitions or self-corrections. Such an assessment may take a few more seconds, but it more closely mirrors a true reading situation.

Repeated Readings

Samuels (1979, 1997), in a classic report on reading fluency, advocates a simple, yet widely overlooked technique—**repeated readings.** The strategy consists of rereading "a short, meaningful passage several times until a satisfactory level of fluency is reached" (1997, p. 377). Based on the automaticity theory, which says that readers must decode text automatically in order to have enough mental energy to comprehend, repeated readings help the poorest readers in the classroom gain confidence as well as fluency.

To use this strategy, give your students short selections (50 to 200 words) from easy-to-read stories that are of interest to them. Ask the students to read them aloud, while you record their reading rate and word recognition. Then have them read it aloud for you again, while you record their rate with a stopwatch. Continue to do this until the child reaches a satisfactory reading rate, as indicated by their WPM rate. Samuels advocates emphasizing speed over accuracy in this technique, because if word accuracy is emphasized, the student becomes wary of mistakes and slows down, which impedes fluency. Thus, encourage the child to work on reading at a speed with which he can say most of the words clearly and accurately.

Figure 14.5 shows two graphs completed after five repeated readings with a fourth grader. The first one records the reading rates in seconds. The reader read the first page of Chapter 1 in *Charlotte's Web* (White, 1952), which is 155 words long. Her rates decreased from 87 seconds during her first reading to 68 seconds at her fifth reading. The second graph records WPM; she was able to improve her WPM from 107 to 137 after five repeated readings. You can use either of these graphs to show your students their improvement; remember, the goal is to decrease the number of seconds required to read the passage, and increase the number of words per minute.

The repeated readings strategy was designed for poor readers; not all of your students need it or benefit from it. Moreover, it is a strategy to be done privately, with the teacher recording. It is not appropriate for sharing in groups.

Oral Reading and Accuracy

Remember the teacher who was concerned that her school district was placing more value on reading fluency than on comprehension? Perhaps part of the problem is that her school administrators are emphasizing word pronunciation and

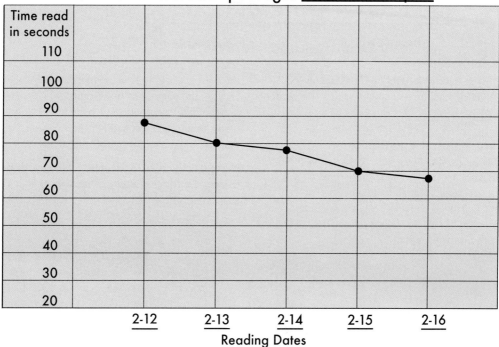

Repeated Readings Graph: Time Taken to Read
Passage: __Chapter One - Charlotte's Web - "Before Breakfast"__
Number of words in passage: __155 words - p.1__

Time read in seconds: 110, 100, 90, 80, 70, 60, 50, 40, 30, 20

Reading Dates: 2-12, 2-13, 2-14, 2-15, 2-16

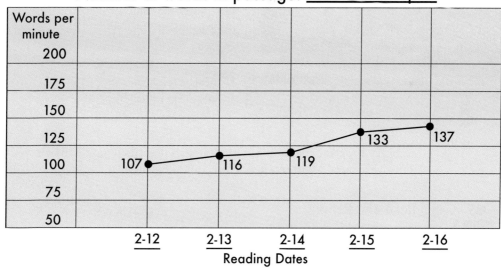

Repeated Readings Graph: Words Per Minute
Passage: __Chapter One - Charlotte's Web - "Before Breakfast"__
Number of words in passage: __155 words - p.1__

Words per minute: 200, 175, 150, 125, 100, 75, 50

107, 116, 119, 133, 137

Reading Dates: 2-12, 2-13, 2-14, 2-15, 2-16

Figure 14.5 Two graphs that show the results of repeated readings with a fourth grader.

Home–School Connection

Daily Oral Reading Homework Assignment

Shown here is a letter to send home to caregivers. It explains a fluency reading assignment, which can be done on a weekly basis. ●

Dear Families:

Enclosed is your child's homework reading book. Each night this week, please ask him or her to read page _____ aloud to you. This will be the page that I will assess on Friday. You may ask him or her to read any additional page or story in the book if you wish, but this is the page that I will record.

This student reads to her mother every evening.

The book is easier than your child's actual reading level, because the purpose of this assignment is to improve his or her oral reading fluency. It is important that your child is able to decode most or all of the words on the page, so that reading it aloud is smooth and fluid.

Please let me know if your child encounters difficulty reading the words in this book. As your child reads aloud, think about these things:

- Does your child read with expression that is appropriate for the story?
- Does your child pause at commas and dashes?
- Does your child stop at periods and question marks?
- Does your child read all the words, without omitting any?
- Does your child read smoothly, without repeating words?
- Does your child pronounce all the words correctly?
- Does your child read with appropriate speed, so that he or she is clear and interesting to listen to?

After the oral reading assessment on Friday, I will send home results.

Sincerely,

Your child's teacher

accuracy over understanding. The strategies described next will help your students improve accuracy without giving up comprehension.

Read and Relax

Johns and Bergland (2002) suggest the **read and relax** strategy, which is actually a silent reading activity. Based on the idea that students need to read lots of text that is easy enough for them to read quickly and comfortably, they recommend setting aside a daily time for students to read books of their own choosing. The student needs to choose a book that he or she can read with 99 percent word recognition accuracy and with 90 percent comprehension. After selecting the book, the child sits comfortably, alone, and reads silently. This time spent reading facilitates comfort with the text, and reinforces the idea that reading is supposed to lead to comprehension. While all the students are reading, the teacher circulates and asks students one at a time to join him or her and privately read portions of their book aloud. This strategy works best if the students know why they are doing it. You need to explain the importance of smooth, fluid, accurate reading, which can come only from reading books that give the reader no decoding difficulties at all. You also need to model this strategy, using the mental model to show students how to select such a book and then model reading from it with appropriate prosody.

Tape, Check, Chart

Another strategy suggested by Johns and Bergland (2002) allows students to assess their own accuracy when reading. **Tape, Check, Chart** is an adaptation of the re-peated readings teaching strategy, explained in the previous section. To use this strategy, give the student a selection that can be read with at least 90 percent accuracy. Make a photocopy of the selection and ask the student to read it aloud while recording it on audiotape. Afterwards, have the student listen to the tape and put a checkmark above each miscue. Then, the child makes another tape recording of reading the selection, and listens to it again, marking miscues once again, using a different color pen for the checkmarks. Finally, the student reads, records, and lis-tens to the tape a third time, and then finds his or her miscues again, using a third color. The idea is for the child to see how accuracy improves with each repeated reading. Asking a child to listen to his or her own reading is a powerful way to build autonomy and self-regulation.

Summary: Easy-Listening Reading

Radio stations that play "easy-listening" music cater to listeners who want to hear music that has rhythm and flowing melody and that blends smoothly into the background of everyday life. Such music does not necessarily make me stop and think, nor does it cause me to wrinkle my nose in distaste because it is loud, jar-ring, or halting.

   The same is true of oral reading. Good oral readers simply sound good when they read. They do not halt, hesitate, repeat, or substitute needless words. They are fluent readers. In this chapter, you learned that there are four components to flu-ency: comprehension, expression, rate, and accuracy. Strategies for all of these were presented, and are summarized in the Reviewing the Big Picture box, with the standards and principles included. These strategies can help your students learn how to share the page in the manner in which the author intended it to be shared—with people who are interested in enjoying a good story or poem, or who want to learn information from an expert.

- www.prel.org/products/re_/fluency-1.htm   Pacific Resources for Education and Learning is the sponsor of this web site, which is an article titled, "A Focus on Fluency."

- www.jimwrightonline.com/pdfdocs/prtutor/prtutor_lesson3.pdf   From "Kids as Reading Helpers: A Peer Tutor Training Manual," Jim Wright here offers suggestions on fluent partner reading and listening while reading.

- teacher.scholastic.com/professional/teachstrat/readingfluencystrategies.htm   Lisa Blau is the author of "Five Surefire Strategies for Developing Reading Fluency." This article is in Scholastic's Teacher web site.

- www.nichd.nih.gov/publications/nrp/findings.htm   This site houses the National Reading Panel report on the value of fluency instruction.

- www.cdli.ca/CITE/langrt.htm, aaronshep.com/rt/   These web sites are good sources of free scripts and other information about Readers' Theater.

---

expect the world

The New York Times
nytimes.com

Themes of the Times

Expand your knowledge of the concepts discussed in this chapter by reading current and historical articles from the *New York Times* by visiting the "Themes of the Times" section of the Companion Web Site.

Reviewing the Big Picture

Strategies in Chapter 14

Strategy	Description	Type of Text/ Grade Level	IRA Standards	INTASC Principles	NAEYC Standards	ACEI/NCATE Standards
Typographical signals	Teach students how to respond to punctuation marks and other signals. Model reading aloud while showing them the signals.	Fiction/3-5, 6-8	1.4, 2.2	4, 5, 6, 7	NA	2.1, 3.1, 3.3, 3.5
Find and read	After reading a selection silently, ask students to find parts of the story and read them aloud.	Fiction/K-2, 3-5	1.4, 2.2	3, 4, 6, 7	4b (Use with shared reading)	2.1, 3.1, 3.3, 3.4
Say it right	Copy sentences from a book and write several mood words. Ask students to read the sentence aloud, using a selected mood word.	Fiction/3-5	1.4, 2.2, 4.1, 4.3	4, 5, 6, 7	NA	2.1, 3.1, 3.3, 3.4
Readers' theater	Adapt a story into a script that contains lines for several students.	Fiction/K-2, 3-5, 6-8	1.4, 2.2, 4.1, 4.3	3, 4, 5, 6, 7	4b (Use with shared reading)	2.1, 3.1, 3.3, 3.4, 3.5
Partner reading	Put students into pairs to read together. Try a variety of ways to share the page.	Fiction/K-2, 3-5	1.4, 2.1, 2.2, 4.1, 4.3	3, 4, 5, 7	4b (Use with shared reading)	2.1, 3.1, 3.2, 3.4
Poetry parties	Have several poetry anthologies available. Ask students to pick a favorite poem to read aloud, either in partners or alone. Assign a day for a party, have snacks and drinks while reading aloud for each other.	Poetry/K-2, 3-5, 6-8	1.4, 2.2, 4.1, 4.3	3, 4, 5	4b (Use with readalouds or shared reading)	2.1, 3.1, 3.2, 3.4
Choral reading	Students read selected passages in unison, as a whole group, in small groups, or in individual parts.	Fiction/K-2, 3-5, 6-8	1.4, 2.1, 2.2, 4.1, 4.3	3, 4, 5, 7	4b (Use with read-alouds or shared reading)	2.1, 3.1, 3.2, 3.4
Words per minute	Determine how many words your students can successfully read in a given amount of time.	Fiction or non-fiction/K-2, 3-5, 6-8	1.4, 2.2, 3.1, 3.3	3, 4, 5, 7	4b (Use only with students who are able to decode)	2.1, 3.1, 3.2, 4
Repeated readings	Give a student a short selection of text at about his or her instructional level. Ask him or her to practice reading it aloud several times. Each time, chart the number of errors made. Watch the errors decrease and fluency increase.	Fiction or non-fiction/K-2, 3-5	1.4, 2.2, 3.1, 3.3	3, 4, 7	4b (Use only with students who are able to decode)	2.1, 3.1, 3.2, 4
Read & relax	Give students very easy books to choose from and read independently for several minutes.	Fiction or non-fiction/K-2, 3-5, 6-8	1.4, 4.1, 4.2, 4.3, 4.4	3, 4, 5, 7	4b (Use only with students who are able to decode)	2.1, 3.1, 3.2, 3.4
Tape, check, chart	Record students' reading. Ask them to listen to their readings to determine how many miscues occurred.	Fiction or non-fiction/K-2, 3-5	1.4, 2.2, 3.1, 3.3	3, 4, 7	4b (Use only with students who are able to decode)	2.1, 3.1, 3.2, 3.3, 3.4, 4

15

Adapting
Instruction

Before I had gone to special ed and got my new meds it would have been impossible for me to sit still and make a list of good and bad things. I didn't have time for lists. I didn't have time for anything that lasted longer than the snap of my fingers. But after I got my good meds, which were in a patch I stuck on my body every day, I started to settle down and think. And not just think about all the bad things that had already happened. I started thinking about the good things I wanted to happen. And the best part about thinking good things was that now I could make them come true instead of having everything I wanted blow up in my face.

Joey Pigza Loses Control (Gantos, 2000)

Joey thought this was ok. at first, but he soon realized his father was wrong. Finally, Carter was always mean to the baseball team and Joey could've been mean to them as well. But, in the end Joey see's that these actions may lead him down a road of trouble or even prison. Even though Joey left his father I knew he would have a good life after that.

Alex, grade 7

Every classroom has a Joey Pigza (Gantos, 2000). To teach them all, you need to understand how these individual differences influence the reading that these children do. All the quality children's books and lesson plans in the world will not work if you have not considered whom you are trying to teach. Glazer points out our responsibilities:

> Children who have been unsuccessful with literacy will probably develop poor feelings about themselves and their interactions with written text. It is our obligation as professionals to find a way for each of our children to learn. . . . All people are different. It is important to respect the differences, see them as treasures, and nurture the very best in each person. (1998, p. 37)

To get started in thinking about ways to adapt instruction, take a look at the Personal Reflection.

Personal Reflection

Think about the hardest thing you ever learned how to do:

- Why was it so hard?
- Did you enjoy learning it?
- What things did you do to accomplish this task?
- Who helped? How successful was their intervention?

Not only do you need to believe in the capabilities of your readers; you also need to convince your students to believe in themselves as readers. Reading will be unattainable to students who are not confident that their hard work will pay off. Self-efficacy is a perception that readers have of themselves—they believe they can succeed at reading tasks. This self-perception is associated with students' abilities to use reading strategies successfully and regulate their own comprehension (Schunk & Zimmerman, 1997). Thus, when your students think they are capable of comprehending the printed page, they persist at reading tasks until they understand it.

In Chapter 3, you learned of some of the strengths that English language learners bring to the classroom, as well as the challenges that they face as they learn to read, write, and speak English. You learned of some ways that you can capitalize on their strengths and help them meet those challenges. What about the rest of your learners? How can you help *all* of your readers? That is the focus of this chapter. Rather than look at groups of children by "special need" categories such as learning disabled, gifted, emotionally handicapped, ESL, or ADHD, I prefer to examine their reading behavior. Thus, this chapter presents strategies that can be used with any of your students who need additional scaffolding, either because they struggle with reading or because they struggle with the conventional classroom setting. First, let's look at some general suggestions for teaching in a manner that includes all of your students, then, more specific strategies, in three areas. I will show you strategies for children who need additional scaffolding when working with whole text as well as with the parts of text. Additionally, you will learn some ways to help your students experience the heart of reading. When reading these strategies, rather than thinking of them as "remediation techniques," think of them as opportunities to teach more, and to open more doors for children who need to experience all types of reading in a positive way.

Reaching Everyone

In the United States, the Individuals with Disabilities Education Act mandates that children with disabilities be provided with an appropriate education in public schools, alongside their peers who are not disabled. The commonly known term for this is **inclusion.** "Including 'the included,'" according to Miller, means that "placing a child in a classroom with access to a teacher is simply not enough. Instead, in order for full inclusion to occur, children must become genuine members of the class. They should be fully engaged and accepted by their peers, not just treated politely and professionally by their teacher" (2001, p. 820).

In order to "teach and reach," it is important to make sure that all of the learners in your classroom receive the instruction that you intended. This idea might seem obvious; however, many times, teachers teach without realizing that they've left someone out of the lesson. It's an easy thing to do when you are worrying about the logistics of managing a classroom. The following sections will show you ways that lessons and classroom environments can be modified to reach all of your students. Take a look at a teaching scenario, in Mr. Joseph's classroom.

Mr. Joseph's Lesson

Mr. Joseph has gathered a group of students who need to work with vocabulary. His objective is for students to read and be able to use words that begin with the "re" prefix.

Mr. Joseph begins by signaling, "May I see your eyes, please?"

He pauses while the students settle in and look at him.

"Thanks. Now I know you are all listening. Today we're going to work with some new words that you'll need to know. Let's take a look at them."

He has taped a column of words on the board:

> redial
>
> rewrite
>
> reread
>
> remake
>
> rewind

Mr. Joseph asks, "Everyone look at these words and think of something to tell us about all of these words."

Danny says, "They all begin with 'r'."

Mackenzie adds, "Yeah, they all have 'r' then 'e'."

"Yeah, and I see some words I know in there: 'write,' 'read,' and 'make'!" adds Kyle.

"That's exactly right!" says Mr. Joseph. "If you look closely, you'll see that you do know these words. The only thing new about them is that each of them begin with the prefix 're.' I'll read them aloud. You say them after me." The students echo his reading of the list; then Mr. Joseph says, "Now, we're going to look at one of these words, but first, let's all think for a minute. I want all of you to think about what you do when you call someone on the phone. Suppose you want to call a friend and invite him or her over to play. What do you have to do if you want to call someone on the phone?"

Mr. Joseph pauses while everyone thinks. Then, Mike says, "You have to know their phone number and punch it in."

"That's right, Mike. And the word that we use for that is 'dial.' The word comes from the days when all phones had dials on them. Here's an old phone right here. As you can see, if you want to call someone on this phone, you need to put your finger in the hole and turn it around. That's called a dial. Here, everyone can give it a try now."

After the students all dial the phone, Mr. Joseph says, "Now, look at this word."

He points to this word card: *redial*. Then, he tapes it to the board, inserted into this sentence: *Mike needed to <u>redial</u> the phone number because he dialed the wrong number.*

Mr. Joseph continues, "I'll read the sentence: 'Mike needed to redial the phone number because he dialed the wrong number.' He points to each word as he says it. Then, he points to the word "redial," and says, "Everyone look at this word and think about it. Tell us something about this word."

After a pause, Kyle says, "It has 're' at the beginning."

Mike adds, "Yeah, and it has a word in it. The word is—di– di– dial? Oh, the word 'dial' is in it!"

"That's what we just did on that old phone!" says Danny.

"That's the word that says, 'redial!'" says Mackenzie.

"That's correct! Now, that little combination of letters—re'—tells us something very important, and it does the same thing for all of these words. You can get a clue about it from the sentence. If Mike needed to 'redial' the phone number because he dialed the wrong number, what does 'redial' mean? Mackenzie?"

"He has to dial it again because he messed up the first time."

"That's exactly right. So, when we see that 're'on a word, it's often called a prefix. We know that these two little letters, when they are stuck on a bigger word like this, are telling us something. Most of the time, the prefix 're' is telling us that the word attached to it is supposed to be done over again.

"Now, watch what I do with this word card. I see the word 'redial' on it. I will fold back part of the card so that the prefix 're' is separated from the root word 'dial.' That way, all I see is just part of the word at a time. I want you to do that. I will point to one of these words on the board. You write it on the card and then find the prefix and fold it so that you can see the root word by itself. Then, open up the card and say the word. I'll put the directions on your table so that you can see and hear them again. Look at this now."

Mr. Joseph puts a sign that he has prepared on the table in front of the students:

> First, look at me to get your word.
>
> Second, write it on the card.
>
> Third, find the prefix and fold it.
>
> Fourth, look at the root word by itself and say that word.
>
> Last, unfold the card and say the whole word.

After the students have finished, Mr. Joseph gives each of them an "action directions" sheet. This sheet has a sentence written on it, which is a set of directions using one of the words in the list. The direction cards say:

Danny—First, write the name of your favorite hockey player. Then <u>rewrite</u> it.
Kyle—First, read this comic strip aloud. Then <u>reread</u> it.
Mackenzie—First, make a paper airplane. Then <u>remake</u> it.
Mike—First, pretend to heat up your favorite sauce. Then <u>reheat</u> it.

Mr. Joseph pauses, and then says, "Here's what you need to do. First, silently read your directions sheet and look for the underlined word. Next, figure out what the sentences tell you to do. Then, think about how you can use props or your body to show us your word. Be sure to keep your word a secret. Finally, when it is your turn, you will wait until you see our eyes. Then act out your word, and we will try to guess your underlined word. Okay, start now."

The students read their cards and "perform" for their classmates. All the words are identified and discussed.

Learning Modalities

When reading this lesson, you might have noticed that these students are using many sensory experiences to learn about the prefix "re." First, Mr. Joseph taught his lesson in **visual mode.** He put the words on a chart and displayed it on the board. Notice that he lined them up visually in a column, so that students could all easily see the "re" prefix in front of each root word. He pointed to words as he talked about them, and slid his hand under the words in the sentence as he read them. To make sure that his students understood his directions, he wrote them in clear sentences on a small poster and put it in front of students on the table for them to see up close. Finally, when he wanted his students to dramatize the word, he gave each of them a written sentence to read on his "action directions" sheet. All of these techniques ensure that his students will see the words and concepts that they are learning. Moreover, having everything written down for students to see fosters independence, because they were expected to read the words, sentences, and directions. When using visual mode, teachers make sure that their students can see the topic being taught, in many different forms. Printed words, pictures, videotapes, charts, computer graphics, and concrete objects are some of the things that students can look at to learn about a topic.

K–8

Second, Mr. Joseph gave his students an auditory experience. **Auditory mode** is when students listen in order to learn, so he made sure that everyone was paying attention before he spoke. Mr. Joseph read the list of words aloud and asked students to echo the list, so that they heard the words twice—once when he said them, and once when they said them. When they needed to follow directions, he verbalized the directions once, and then showed students the directions so that they could see them. Finally, when the students were expected to listen to each other, he directed them to wait until they could see everyone's eyes before they began.

The **kinesthetic modality** is the mode of learning in which children use their bodies or sense of touch to remember things. This modality is the hardest to implement in a classroom, especially for abstract concepts; however, it is often the modality that generates the most interest with children. Mr. Joseph used the kinesthetic modality several times in his lesson. First, he asked the children to write their own word cards, rather than merely providing them with a card already written. Second, when explaining the concept of dialing a telephone, he showed them a phone with a dial, and let them try dialing it, because he knew that most children in his class probably have touch-tone phones in their homes. Third, he asked them to fold their word cards so that they could see the prefix and the root word separately. Finally, he asked the students to dramatize a word to their classmates, using concrete objects as aids. All of these ways of using their bodies and senses of touch may add to their understanding of new words.

Some researchers describe the ways in which learners learn best as **learning modalities** or **learning styles** (Dunn, 1988; Carbo, 1988). Providing students with visual, auditory, and kinesthetic modes of learning capitalizes upon their strengths and facilitates the optimum conditions for their learning. On a broader level, Gardner (1993, 1999) introduced the idea of **multiple intelligences,** giving us categories of human capabilities, such as linguistic intelligence, musical intelligence, or interpersonal intelligence. There is some argument among reading researchers about the scientific basis for these ways of learning; however, all of these ideas remind us that children are not all alike, and they do not all learn the same way. Cunningham and Cunningham explain:

> They come with their own personalities, learning strengths, and learning weaknesses. Regardless of what you call them—multiple intelligences, learning styles, personalities—or exactly how many types exist, children have them. The best instruction in any subject seeks multiple ways to accomplish the same goals so that regardless of how a child prefers to learn or learns best, an opportunity to learn in that way is available (2002, p. 91).

The lesson with Mr. Joseph shows us his interest in making sure that his students learn vocabulary through a variety of means; he does not settle for just one method of presentation of the words. To ensure active engagement of all of his students, he makes sure that they all can see, hear, and interact with the words.

Communicative Language

To get your point across, you need to be direct. Remember that children are active learners; thus, if you want them to accomplish something, tell them what to *do* instead of telling them what *not* to do. If you see a student running in the hallway and say, "Walk in the hallway, please," you'll get much better results than if you say, "Don't run!" or "How are you supposed to be moving in the hallways?"

Notice that Mr. Joseph ended his directions with words like "Do that now," or "Okay, start now." This is a clear directive on his part; children who have difficulty focusing on a task benefit from this signal. Keep in mind that many children from diverse backgrounds better understand verbal directives that are explicit, rather than implied. Statements need to be in a direct manner, "so that requests and expectations are clear to students" (Au, 1993, p. 81).

Known to Unknown

As you might recall from Chapter 2, schema theory tells us that children bring experiences to the printed page that help them understand the author's meaning (Anderson, 2004; Anderson & Pearson, 1984; Rumelhart; 1980). This makes the start of every lesson quite simple—begin with what they know.

Mr. Joseph moved from the known to the unknown by showing his students the list of words in a column. He spaced the words carefully so that students would immediately be able to see beyond the "re" in the words, and recognize words that they already know. From here, he was able to teach the idea that the prefix "re" means to "do it again." Notice also that Mr. Joseph used consistent examples of words with the "re-" prefix. When helping students understand a concept, it is important to use examples that are clear and without variation. For this reason, Mr. Joseph did not include words such as "refuse," "revise," and "react." These words do not contain the "re-" prefix that means "to do again." Thus, moving from the known to the unknown is a little easier.

This principle applies to everything you teach, from a single letter to a whole book. For example, if you want to teach the letter "D" to your kindergarten students, begin by showing the children the name of a classmate whose name begins with that letter, such as David or Danielle. If you want your fifth grade students to understand the main idea of *Number the Stars* (Lowry, 1989), first have them brainstorm and discuss what they know about the Holocaust and German occupation of European countries prior to World War II.

Building upon the background knowledge of all your students is helpful. However, this concept appears to be especially important when teaching students who are English language learners. Jiménez tells us that "students respond in positive ways when their teachers demonstrate sensitivity to their concerns, when they demonstrate knowledge of their language and culture, and when they design instruction to build on culturally familiar activities" (2004, p. 216).

Questions That Include

Look back at Mr. Joseph's lesson, when he began to show them the rotary dial phone. He wanted to begin a discussion on what one must do in order to make a phone call. This is what he said:

> "I want all of you to think about what you do when you call someone on the phone. Suppose you want to call a friend and invite him or her over to play. What do you have to do if you want to call someone on the phone?"

But let's suppose he had done this differently. Suppose he had asked: "How many of you have ever called a friend before?" This most likely would have generated a competitive chorus of hand-raising and children shouting, "I have, I have! Oh, oh, oh! Me, me, me!" This excitement about answering the question can indicate that the children are interested in the lesson. However, if we look closer, we realize that a question like that one is essentially a subtle way of excluding students who cannot positively answer his question.

Wisely, Mr. Joseph knew that all his students had experiences with phones. Thus, he used that as a starting point, and expected everyone to think about a response to his question. After pausing and allowing this to happen, he encouraged a student to respond.

As you learned in Chapter 12, questioning needs to involve everyone. When you want to ask questions, remember to include all of the students in the group, and provide them all with the opportunity to answer questions. Many times, teachers unwittingly exclude students from entering the discussion by how they word their questions. Consider this question, asked of a group of first graders as they prepare to read *Dear Zoo* (Campbell, 1982):

"How many of you have ever been to the zoo?"

At first glance, this question might seem appropriate, because it helps to build background knowledge about and interest in the topic of the story. Most of the group excitedly raises their hands. But suppose that three or four of these students have never been to the zoo. Immediately, the implication is that they are excluded from the discussion, even if they have some vicarious knowledge about zoos. Instead, consider this question:

"What are zoos like?"

Such a question assumes that everyone, regardless of his or her firsthand experiences with the zoo, has some idea to contribute to the conversation. Moreover, this question generates more thoughtful responses right away, because you now have invited some brainstorming and discussion, based on what everyone knows about the topic of zoos. Certainly, children who have actually visited a zoo will be able to contribute information that they have gathered firsthand; but any child who has ever heard of or seen pictures of a zoo can offer insights.

Look at the "questions that exclude" in Figure 15.1. Notice that each of these questions invites a subtle roll call of children who have been lucky enough to have the experience. That is certainly not the true purpose of these questions. Reword the questions, so that they include everyone. You can see the "questions that include" in the right column of Figure 15.1.

Student Interests

To explain the importance of interests, let me tell you a bit about my first year of teaching, which was a year of many eye-opening experiences. One thing I'll never forget is the impact of the simplest efforts on my part. I got this job in October; the school year had already begun. First grade enrollment in this school was too high, so each teacher picked five students to leave her classroom and make up a new class—mine. You can imagine the anxiety all around; children who had just begun school a month before were now thrust into a new classroom, with a new teacher.

Questions That Exclude	Questions That Include
• "How many of you have a dog?" • "How many of you have ever been to the beach?" • "How many of you have helped your mom cook supper?" • "How many of you have a little brother who bothers you all the time?"	• "What are dogs like?" • "Think about the beach. Describe it for us." • "What do you need to do when you help cook?" • "Think of a little brother—either yours or someone else's. Tell us about how little brothers can be bothersome."

Figure 15.1 Questions that exclude and include.

I had about two days to prepare this empty classroom to receive my new class. I wanted to make the atmosphere bright and inviting, but had few resources to do anything elaborate. I had some posters that I had bought at flea market sales and through book clubs, and hung some of these around the room. One of the other first grade teachers realized that Amanda, a child who had been selected to join my class, was very nervous about leaving her old classroom. She brought her by the classroom on the day before my class was to begin, and Amanda noticed one of the posters on the wall. It was a picture of horses. I had put it up only because it was all I had. But Amanda loved horses. She read about them, wrote about them, and dreamed of owning one someday. When she saw this simple poster, she beamed broadly. Now this new classroom was okay.

I wish I could say that I had the foresight to survey my new students before they entered my classroom, to discover their interests and attitudes towards reading. I was lucky that Amanda accepted her new classroom based on that simple little poster alone. (Later in the year, I gave it to her when we redecorated the room.) As you learned in Chapter 4, knowing your students' interests and incorporating these interests in your lesson plans, your classroom library, and your conversations will go a long way toward motivating them to become involved with their learning. All people, no matter how old they are, pay more attention to things that interest them (Shirey & Reynolds, 1988).

Certainly, not all of your lessons can be about things such as horses, hockey, favorite TV shows, or whatever else interests your students. But there are simple ways to make these topics part of your daily instruction. For example, suppose that you want to show your students an example of using commas in a series, and you know that you have some hockey fans in your class. Here is an example sentence that you could give them: "Marcus packed his helmet, jersey, and skates in his hockey bag."

Mr. Joseph did incorporate interests in a rather subtle way, using the "action directions" sheets. He gave all the students one that was "tailor-made" for them:

Danny—First, write the name of your favorite hockey player. Then rewrite it.

Kyle—First, read this comic strip aloud. Then reread it.

Modifying Instruction for

ELL

Creating Motivational Posters with
Charlotte's Web

GRADE LEVEL: 3–5

- **Objective**

  After reading and discussing *Charlotte's Web* (White, 1952), the students will use print media in their primary language to create motivational posters.

- **Preparation**

  - Divide students into groups of three, making sure that the student learning English as a second language is paired with a familiar reading buddy.

- **Materials**

  - *Charlotte's Web* (White, 1952), Chapters 11 and 12
  - *La Telerana de Carlota* (Spanish version of *Charlotte's Web*, 2005)
  - Response journals
  - Commerically produced posters and signs of motivating quotes and pictures
  - Materials for producing posters
  - Old magazines and newspapers in English and in the primary languages of your students

- **Procedure**

  1. Read *Charlotte's Web* aloud to students, or have them read it to each other in pairs. If you have Spanish-speaking students in your class, they can use the Spanish edition of the book, *La Telerana de Carlota*.

  2. After reading Chapter 11, "The Miracle," discuss Charlotte's strategy for saving Wilbur's life; she weaves words in her web to describe the pig, which causes quite a stir among the humans at Zuckerman's farm. Talk about words that describe.

  3. After reading Chapter 12, "A Meeting," and Chapter 13, "Good Progress," discuss the steps that Charlotte and the animals take to build a new word into her web. After reading the scene where Templeton the rat goes to the dump to find magazine clippings, talk about the kinds of words that advertisers use to describe their products.

  4. Ask students to use old magazines to find and cut out words that could describe Wilbur. English language learners should use magazines and newspapers written in their primary language. Each pair of students should share their words with each other. Write all of these words on cards and hang them on the word wall, or on a large picture of a spider's web.

  Modifications for ELL are printed in color.

5. After finishing the book, talk about how many of the quotations from the book are memorable and have meanings applicable to everyday life. For example, Charlotte says to Wilbur, in Chapter 12, "People believe almost anything they see in print." Discuss quotations like these. Ask students to choose their favorites, write them in their response journals, and share them with each other. Students can also share quotations from other books, such as "Aguántate tantito y la fruta caerá en tu mano" ("Wait a little while and the fruit will fall into your hand"), from *Esperanza Rising* (Ryan, 2000, p. 2).

6. Show students commercially made posters and signs that have quotations on them. Talk about their use in classrooms and places of business. Talk about how people think about and use famous quotations in their lives. Read some famous quotations, such as "A penny saved is a penny earned," and discuss how they are used in everyday life.

7. Have students look in magazines and advertisements for phrases to use in creating flyers or posters for the classroom. Students should use their native languages and illustrate the posters. For example, Freeman and Freeman show an example of a classroom sign that reads, "Clase Releja Calidad," which means, "This Class Shows Quality" (1993, p. 554–555).

Mackenzie—First, make a paper airplane. Then remake it.

Mike—First, pretend to heat up your favorite sauce. Then reheat it.

Danny, he knows, loves hockey. Kyle reads comic strips all the time; in particular, he likes Garfield. Mackenzie is very handy with crafts. And Mr. Joseph remembered that Mike was recently talking about making barbecue sauce with his dad. All of these things made their way into this lesson!

Additionally, one of the best ways to reach all of your students is through choices. This gives them autonomy, aids in their decision-making abilities, and sets the same expectation for everyone without frustrating the ones who struggle. Many classroom practices can be offered as choices. Gifted students as well as learning-disabled and struggling readers can benefit from choices in assignments, methods of reporting, and ways of reading. O'Donnell (2005) explains the importance of giving choices to preteen and adolescent boys who dislike reading; they benefit from the feeling of ownership that book choice gives them. Figure 15.2 shows three types of choices that can be used in the language arts classroom.

Finally, keep in mind that the human brain stores information based on functionality, so new learning must have meaning to your students. Making your lessons authentic and related to things that are interesting to the children in your classroom will help to engage them.

High Expectations

Sometimes, in the interest of meeting the needs of students, teachers inadvertently lower expectations. If you assign homework, it should be assigned to and expected from everyone, even your struggling students. If you expect other children in your class to write research reports, your struggling readers should be expected to write

Choices in the Classroom

Reading Options

When reading a selection together for guided reading, you can offer your students three choices:
1. Read alone, without help from a partner or the teacher.
2. Read with a partner, without disturbing others.
3. Read with the teacher.

Retelling Options

When asking students to retell a story, you can ask them to choose one of the following:
1. Write the retelling in a few sentences, making sure to include all the parts of the story.
2. Draw the retelling; include and label all the parts of the story.
3. Tell the teacher the story verbally, using a retelling checklist to guide you as necessary.

Responding Options

After reading a selection, give your students the opportunity to respond to the book, using one of the following ways:
1. Tell your partner what you think about the book.
2. Dramatize a scene from the book.
3. Role-play one of the characters in the book.
4. Write a letter to the author.
5. Artistically portray a scene from the book.
6. Write a review of the book.
7. Write your own version of the book or a scene from the book.
8. Write a song about the book.
9. Convince your parents to read the book.
10. Copy your favorite quotes from the book and tell why.

Figure 15.2 Ways to provide classroom choices.

reports, too. Nothing is more motivating than the satisfaction of a job well done. Learners who struggle should be given the opportunity to experience this feeling, too. García (2000) reports that historically, bilingual children in urban schools have not received high-quality reading instruction; part of the problem is that of low expectations. Likewise, Jiménez explains that while "sheltered English instruction" is necessary, Latino/Hispanic students appreciate and respond to "a demand for high student performance, and the provision of a challenging curriculum" (2004, p. 216).

Classroom Library

To meet the needs of all of your students, be sure that they all have something to read. You will need books in a wide range of difficulty levels, and you will need to make them available to your students in the classroom, as well as in their homes.

One of the biggest problems that struggling readers and children in lower-income homes have is the lack of books to read at home (Allington, 2001), so be willing to lend your classroom books to them. Allington also reports that the classroom library is essential to successful literacy instruction, and that "classrooms with a larger supply of books had kids who read more frequently" and "had more kids reading books they could manage successfully" (p. 54). He recommends "at least 500 different books in every classroom with those split about evenly between narratives and informational books and about equally between books that are on or near grade-level difficulty and books that are below grade level" (p. 55).

New teachers often find this one of the hardest aspects of their new job, because they have not yet accumulated books the way their veteran teacher friends have, over the years. Additionally, new teachers often do not have the money to purchase many new books! As your collection grows, use the school library relentlessly. Ask your librarian to help you find several books on the same subject; most are happy to do so. Once you've got these books, keep a list of their titles and authors, so that you'll know which ones to borrow again next year.

Another way to keep your classroom library stocked is to assign this job to your students. Ask two students per week to be "Library Checkers," and send them to the library with a box in a wagon or cart. Ask them to return with a box full of books that they would like to include in the classroom for the week. (Of course, make arrangements with your librarian ahead of time!)

Keep in mind that your own classroom library needs to grow, because the school library may not always be able to supply your needs. Unfortunately, libraries in urban and low-income neighborhood schools typically have half the number of books that wealthier schools have (Guice, Allington, Johnston, Baker & Michelson, 1996). Thus, you may be on your own in supplying your students with books. You might need to become a book bargain hunter. Check out flea markets, garage sales, and library sales for children's books that are in good condition but cheap. New books can be purchased through school book clubs, at considerable discount for teachers. Online booksellers also offer discounts on children's books to teachers. Don't neglect to look around your own school! Storage closets often house old textbooks and basals. Some teachers tear out the best stories from the old basals and bind them in cardstock covers. You may not want to use everything you find, but even if you find a few copies of just one good story, the search is worth the effort.

When you fill your classroom with "well-stocked library shelves, magazine storage boxes, reading tables, comfortable chairs, card catalogs, and book-news bulletin boards" (Mathewson, 2004, p. 1,455), along with time allocated for lots of reading and writing, you are providing a classroom atmosphere and setting that communicates a powerful message to your students—one that tells them that literacy is important, expected, and cherished.

Independent Reading

In our zeal for encouraging readers to grow and build their reading skills, we very often push our students ahead before their time. This is typical of basal-based instruction, where the ease of having leveled or graded vocabulary-controlled selections in an anthology lulls us into thinking that as soon as a child reads one story, he or she is ready to quickly move on to a more difficult story. Such is not always the case. Too many times, we assume that children who have shown some success with a book are ready to move on to more difficult reading right away. Thus, they do not have the opportunity to be exposed repeatedly to new vocabulary in many contexts, nor are they afforded the chance to become comfortable with more sophisticated language patterns and story structures.

Children—even those who are good readers—need to read lots of books that they can easily handle, without help. They need time to read these independent level books daily. Once you have determined the independent level of a reader, give him or her ample opportunity in your classroom to read books at that level. This means that you will need to provide books outside the basal. Consider this to be an essential part of reading instruction, rather than an extra free time activity that the student can miss if something else comes up. If you have a struggling reader, do not be afraid to move him or her drastically down to a level that is comfortable for him to read fluently. A child who has struggled with reading for a long time needs to experience easy reading, at a level that requires no help at all. Sometimes teachers ask these readers to read books that are still just a bit challenging for them. This method does not provide enough scaffold, because the child needs to become fluent and confident, and can do that only with books in which the words are automatically recognized and the meaning readily understood. According to Calkins, "This is the only way that a child can feel how reading is supposed to go" (2001, p. 164). Even good readers, who know how reading is supposed to go, should experience extended periods of error-free independent reading. This practice allows them to continue reading with confidence and ease.

Kidwatching

The only way to find out how well your students are reading is to watch and listen to them as they read for you privately. As I explained in Chapter 2, Yetta Goodman (1978, 1985) advocates "kidwatching," which means observing your students closely and determining what they can do with reading. This means sitting next to them and listening. Watch their eyes and finger movements. Notice their facial expressions. Talk briefly with them about strategies to use for decoding unfamiliar words, strategies for determining meaning, or strategies for self-monitoring.

Schedule two-minute conferences daily with at least three or four of your students. This meeting should be done privately, at a table in the back of the room or some other place where students can read aloud uninterrupted. You can ask them to read selections of their choice, or give them selections that are just a little bit challenging for them. Find out what they do when they make miscues.

You can also ask students to read silently during this two-minute observation time, and make the same types of observations. The most important thing to remember is that in order to find out about your students' reading behaviors, you will need to observe them up close.

Student Autonomy

In order to foster independence when they read, your students will need to experience and muddle through their own mistakes. Sometimes, when listening to our students read, we jump in and help them correct a reading error right away, in a well-intentioned effort to help out. We need to allow students the chance to self-correct their errors; this is the only way they will develop metacognitive and self-regulatory skills. Therefore, when you listen to them read, and they make mistakes, be quiet for just a moment! Give them a chance to fix their errors. I suggest three to five seconds. Good readers will usually correct themselves right away. Struggling readers will begin to self-correct, if you teach them self-regulation strategies such as self-questioning, so that they consistently ask themselves, "Does this make sense?" Expect and train your students to do the same thing for each other, when reading aloud together in partners or in groups.

Multilevel Lessons

To include all of your students in every lesson, be on the lookout for ways that everyone can contribute to the interaction. Cunningham and Cunningham describe "multilevel activities," which are activities that "are not frustrating for those with much to learn, boring for those with little to learn, or both when aimed at those in the middle" (2002, p. 91). There are many ways to make any learning activity multilevel. One of the things that Mr. Joseph did was word his questions carefully so that everyone had a chance to offer something that they know about the words they were learning. After placing the list of words on the board, he directed the students, "Look at these words and think of something to tell us about all of these words." This type of request allows your students to respond on their own levels. Some readers may notice that the first letters of all the words that you listed begin with the same letter. Or, some readers may notice that a page of print also contains an interesting picture that leads to a prediction. This opens many possibilities for exploring what all of your students know.

Looking Closely at Reading Behaviors

The next section discusses what happens when you watch your students up close, and notice some needs for additional scaffolding. I'll begin with ways of working with whole text, then move to ways of working with the "parts" of reading (letters, sounds, and words), and finally, I will discuss ways to scaffold the "heart"— or the aesthetic side—of reading.

Scaffolding a Search for Meaning in Whole Text

Sometimes, you will observe students struggling with the "whole" of reading. While they may be able to read individual words, they may have trouble understanding the story line, the author's implications, or the main idea. Let's look at ways to help them now.

Missing the Big Idea

Recently, a friend of mine called me about a problem with her daughter, Nicole, who was in second grade. Nicole is very bright, very verbal, and loves to read. But she had a problem in school. It seemed that her teacher, who recognized Nicole's exceptional verbal abilities, had her reading materials that were far above second grade, some as high as fifth grade. Nicole was able to read the words in these books and stories and was quite proud of herself because of this. She came home with glowing reports of being the "best reader" in class, and she bubbled over with the enthusiasm about reading "higher" books. Yet when Nicole brought home some of these books, her mother became alarmed when she realized that her daughter was unable to retell what she had just read in most of them.

Nicole had lost the "big idea" of longer pieces of text. Like Nicole, some students sound good when they read aloud, but have little ability to retell the story from beginning to end. These students might even be considered "good" readers, because they are able to pronounce words well and can perform well on comprehension tests that consist of short passages with multiple-choice questions. Often, they are unaware of their own inability to comprehend, because they can read the words and get through a book without thinking much about it. This is, of course, the root of the problem. While they are decoding well, they are not thinking about the meaning of the text.

First, have these students read easier books for a while. While this may seem unnecessary because of their ability to decode well, it is essential for them to "map out" the story in their heads as they read. Therefore, story structure needs to be simple and straightforward in their fiction texts until they are able to retell all the elements of a story. Nonfiction texts need to contain only a few, clear main ideas, described in a straightforward fashion.

Second, teach these students the structure of text. Work with fiction first, because its structure is more consistent. When you read stories aloud, always introduce the book in terms of how it will consist of a character with a problem to solve, and some attempts to solve that problem. Working with nonfiction should always center around the question, "What is the author trying to teach me in this book?" Talk about these things before, during, and after shared or guided reading.

Third, sit next to the child and read together. Ask the student to read a page, then read a page yourself, and finish the book in this manner. After every page, make comments about what is happening. Questions are not necessary; instead, just react to the story. For example, in a story like *There's an Alligator Under My Bed* (Mayer, 1987), where the main character sets up an elaborate trap of food throughout his house, in an effort to catch an imaginary alligator, you could say, "Gee, I wonder if all that food will be gone when he wakes up tomorrow . . .?" or "Wow, I'd be too scared to get up in the middle of the night to do all that."

Finally, show the student how to monitor himself or herself while reading. Model how to do this by asking yourself at the end of each page, "Does this make sense?" Additionally, model retelling by pausing at stop points and asking, "What has happened so far?" and retell the events up to that point. Strategies such as story structure cards (from Chapter 12) and the retelling checklist (from Chapter 13) will be helpful.

Retelling in Fragments

Jake was a sixth grader who had a problem with reading. He read page by page. Essentially, he understood what he read in disconnected pieces. He could tell me a single event, or a description of a character, but he did not connect to a whole story, because he either lost interest or lost attention along the way.

Jake's problem is not unusual. Often, we inadvertently exacerbate this problem with response opportunities like "Tell me your favorite part of the story," or "Explain how the main character is like someone you know." Once the student answers these response questions satisfactorily, we assume that he or she understood the entire text, which, of course, is not always true. It is quite possible to name any part of the story as his "favorite part," without knowing what happened at the end, or without truly understanding the author's implications. It is also possible to relate to the character in the story without knowing the plot.

Jake and other readers like him need to experience whole text in its entirety. Again, it is important to have these students read easier material for a while. This step ensures that they will finish the text without getting disinterested or disoriented in a magnitude of plot twists or details.

Make sure that readers like this know that an understanding of the "whole" is expected after reading. Use book introductions to help students get a schema for the story or selection before reading. You can also use strategies such as Story Impressions, shown in Chapter 11, in which you show the student a list of vocabulary presented in the order found in the text. Tell the student to get an impression of the entire story that he or she will read before reading the book. Have the child make predictions about the whole story or book before reading, rather than just on pieces of the story at stop points. You might ask students to write their impression of the entire story before they read, so that they have mapped out each element in their minds. As they read, they should check to see how their ideas match the author's ideas.

See Figure 15.3 for a summary of these ways to help readers with retelling.

Lack of Self-Regulation

Corey, a third grader, was reading aloud for me. I noticed that sometimes he mispronounced a word or generated a nonsense word. Usually, the first letter or so of these miscalled words matched the words on the page, but they did not make sense. When this happened, Corey always paused, sometimes very briefly, and corrected himself. I could even see him shake his head, as if to tell himself, "Oh, no, that's not right. Try again."

By contrast, Brian, also a third grader, read the same selection. He, too, mispronounced words or created his own nonsense words that were phonetically similar. His miscues made little or no sense. The difference in the reading behaviors of these two boys is that Brian did not pause and self-correct. He continued on, finishing the text, without realizing that his word choices did not make sense. Not surprisingly, when it was all over, he was confused about the details of the story.

When a Reader Retells in Bits and Pieces

1. Give the child easier books to read for a while.
2. Give the child a schema for the entire story, before reading.
3. Use the Story Impressions strategy.

Figure 15.3 Helping the student who retells in fragments.

Brian needs to self-monitor his comprehension. Once he realizes that his understanding of the text has faltered, he can self-regulate his reading with appropriate strategies to help him regain comprehension. All of these behaviors are part of a student's metacognitive abilities, described in Chapter 12.

One of the strategies shown in Chapter 12, the Click and Clunk strategy, teaches the child to pause, and then ask, "Does this make sense?" If he determines that it does not, he applies a fix-up strategy, or a combination of them. They are: (1) reread, (2) read ahead for more clues, and (3) slow down. The key to the success of these strategies is the child's awareness of sense-making. If the child says "yes" to the question, but it really is not making sense, he or she needs more support with monitoring.

Therefore, get up close. Sit down next to the child and watch him read. When the child says a word that makes no sense, let him or her go to the end of the sentence, to give a chance to receive more clues. Then ask, "Think about what you said for this word. That doesn't make sense to me. One of the best things to do is to reread it to figure it out. Let's reread it, slowly, and think about what it says." The next time the student reads alone, help him or her look at the selection first, making predictions and getting a sense of the text. Give the student a few sticky note bookmarks to mark stop points, and a "click and clunk card" reminder to stop, think, and apply fix-ups as necessary.

The Need for a Challenge

Roberto was a fourth grader in a classroom that I observed and was a highly competent reader. He enjoyed reading; he was also interested in a variety of topics and hobbies. He read more quickly than everyone else in the classroom; he could read materials at about the seventh grade level. The problem was that Roberto was bored. His school district did not have a pull-out program for gifted children, which meant that his instruction was entirely reliant upon his classroom teacher. When his teacher asked the class to read a selection from the basal anthology, Roberto quickly read, and then had to wait for everyone else to finish reading before discussion began. He eagerly participated in discussion; in fact, he often dominated the conversation and the teacher asked him to give other students a chance to talk. He was, however, becoming impatient and moody.

A student like Roberto needs a **compacted curriculum** (Dooley, 1993), which means that the students who are gifted or who consistently read beyond grade-level expectations are permitted to progress through required reading materials such as basal selections at a pace with which they are comfortable. His reading should be independent, as he will probably be able to read the text more quickly than the rest of the class.

While reading, these students need **process modifications,** which are activities and questions that require higher levels of thought, which should be designed so that they can do them alone. Such modifications involve engaging students like Roberto in critical and creative thinking about the text. With these students, you can create reading guides that facilitate these types of thinking skills, and ask them to think about responses to the questions before, during, and after reading. Dooley suggests some questions that can be used to encourage critical thinking; adaptations of these are shown in Figure 15.4.

Flack (2000) suggests that gifted students can stay with the basal program that is already in place in the classroom, but they need to be challenged with strategies that involve supplementary books, research skills, and independent writing. Some of his suggestions include:

Critical Thinking Questions to Ask About a Children's Book

Before Reading

- What do you know about this topic? How does this knowledge help you think about the text?
- What do you know about the author? How does this information help you think about the text?
- As you read, watch for the author's influence on the text.

During Reading

- What information does the author give you that is irrelevant to the topic or story?
- Why does the author choose to write this selection from this perspective?
- What idea, belief, or theme is the author's intention? What other ideas, beliefs, or themes would work?

After Reading

- Is the resolution satisfying? Why or why not?
- Was the point of view the best one for this selection? Why or why not?
- Are the author's language and style suitable for this selection? Why or why not?
- What are the most important issues in the selection?

Figure 15.4 A reading guide that encourages critical reading.

1. Give these students the opportunity to research the topic of the theme before the rest of the class reads it. This step allows them to look up print and electronic resources on the topic to be used during the thematic unit by the class a week or so later.

2. Use biographies to enhance students' understanding of any theme or topic of study. After reading the basal selection, ask students to select a biography related to the selection topic or a biography of the author.

3. Expand vocabulary. Challenge your students to use a variety of sources to learn a new word every day, and use it appropriately.

4. Do not assume that these students know how to use reading strategies on their own. Find out how much they know about predicting, inferring, visualizing, and summarizing. Include them in mini-lessons as needed.

5. Provide fiction in which the main characters are gifted and talented. Introduce these books to students and provide access to them in the classroom library for self-selected independent reading. Some suggested titles are:

The Report Card (Clements, 2004)   *Stargirl* (Spinelli, 2000)
Pictures of Hollis Woods (Giff, 2002)   *The Skin I'm In* (Flake, 1998)
Sahara Special (Codell, 2003)   *The Giver* (Lowry, 1994)
Silent to the Bone (Konigsburg, 2000)

Scaffolding the "Parts" of Reading

Students who have difficulties with words, either because they cannot decode letters or because they cannot figure out word meanings, probably also have problems with constructing meaning of the whole text. Thus, it is important to scaffold students in their quest to put the "parts" of reading together. In the next section, we'll examine some strategies that help.

Missing the Phonetic Connection

Ellie, a second grader, read slowly and haltingly. When she came to a word she did not know, you could see her mouth getting ready to say something. The trouble was that what she was trying to say did not match what was written on the page. This usually happened when she approached a word longer than about four letters, or starting with a blend, or containing a vowel digraph in the middle. Because she did not know what to do, she usually created a nonsense word, often one that does not sound anything like the one in print. Automaticity (LaBerge & Samuels, 1974; Samuels, 2004; Samuels & Kamil, 1984) was not there yet.

When your students are not connecting the sounds of the language with the letters that represent them, they will have difficulty decoding words, just as Ellie did. Simply reminding a student like Ellie to "sound it out" does not help; in fact, it probably makes matters worse. This student knows she is supposed to get something when she sounds out a word, but she's not getting anything that makes sense, because she does not know which sounds to make!

First, a student like Ellie needs easier books to read. While it may help to have some "decodable books" available, be cautious about using them exclusively. These books use the same word patterns throughout, and are sometimes considered the "best" type of book to use with beginning or struggling readers, because they are easy to decode. The problem is that they do not use natural language patterns and often make little sense to most children, like these sentences: "Mag had a bag. Mag had a rag bag." Moreover, some research tells us (Mesmer, 2001) that there is little evidence to support their use beyond a very limited time for children who will accept them. (Many children simply don't like them.) First, Hiebert (1999) recommends that teachers provide a combination of texts in classrooms—books that are highly decodable, books that contain many highly recognizable words, and books that are highly predictable.

Second, make sure that these children have a bank of words that they know. Let them keep word collections, and add to them frequently. Give them time to write daily, and expect them to use words from the banks in their writing. Show them how word families are made, and how one word in the bank will produce many, many more, simply by changing one letter.

Third, use the Making Words strategy with this child and others who are having this same difficulty. (See Chapter 7 for details on this strategy.) This technique gives students the opportunity to see the connections between words in word families and the ease with which sounds and letters can be manipulated.

Fourth, teach these students to decode through the use of word families, or by analogy (Adams, 1990; Cunningham & Cunningham, 2002; Treiman, 1985). Make sure that they know that a combination of onsets and a rime creates several words. Thus, if a student knows the word "day," show him or her how to figure out the words "way," "play," "Sunday," and "wayside."

Fifth, encourage the use of invented spellings in journals and other types of informal writing, which "fosters phonemic awareness and sequential decoding" (Cunningham & Cunningham, 2002, p. 97). As you read students' journal entries, find out what they know about letter/sound relationships. Make plans for mini-lessons to teach the needed ones.

Finally, always maintain the expectation that meaning needs to be made when the child reads. Sit up close and watch him or her read. When the student starts to sound out a word, say things like these, if they are applicable to the text she is attempting:

"What word that begins with *d* would make sense here?"

"Think about the story. What word could go there?"

"Sometimes, but not always, the pictures help you make sense of the word. This picture might help. Now, the word starts with 'm.' What word might this be?"

The "Decoding Freeze"

Marco, a first grader, was unsure of himself as a reader. He gave up very easily, and when he came to a word he did not know, he stopped and looked at me for help. He did not attempt unknown words by himself.

Students like Marco need to learn independence as readers, which breeds confidence. The most important thing you can do for a reader like this is to keep quiet! Do not jump in and help out right away, no matter how difficult it may seem. Give the student a few seconds to try it himself. Sometimes, this leads to a conclusion; other times it does not, but most importantly, it conveys the message that he must decode on his own.

If the seconds of silence produce nothing, Brown advocates that you try a general type of prompt that encourages the student to try his or her own solutions, such as, "Something tricked you; try again" (2003, p. 728).

If the child is still not confident, what to do next depends on the child and the text, according to Brown. A child who is just beginning to learn about print needs to focus on the first letter of a word as a starting point. This "first sound" clue, combined with meaning clues and picture clues, can lead to the word. Rather than insist on letter-by-letter decoding, you can simply point to the first letter and ask, "Look at this word again. What is the first sound?" Once this answer is determined, ask, "What word that starts with that sound would make sense here?" If picture clues are helpful, point them out, but make sure that the student knows that pictures don't always help. This type of reader benefits from predictable text with clear, supportive illustrations, so make sure that he or she spends lots of time with these books.

If the reader is beginning to understand the relationships between letters and sounds and can move beyond the first letter when decoding, use prompts that allow him or her to do that. Make sure that the word is phonetically regular. Cue the reader by pointing to the first letter, and say, "Try looking at the first letter. What's the sound?" Then, if the middle of the word is still phonetically regular, slide a pencil point under the rest of the word, and say, "Keep your motor running. What sounds come next?" Another prompt could be, "Bulldoze it fast!" After a word is produced, ask, "Does that make sense?" Again, if the picture would be helpful, you can use that as a clue, but remind your readers that pictures don't always provide enough information.

This teacher allows her students to self-correct reading errors.

"Bulldozing" the word is an important concept, whose idea is to show students that blending is a smooth and quick transaction (Brown, 2003, p. 728). Because children at this stage are often clumsy and slow with blending, you want them to realize that the word is a whole entity, to be spoken in smooth syllables, rather than a collection of disjointed sounds. Children who have moved beyond simple predictable books and are now tackling the mechanics of decoding often become frustrated with this stage, because reading does not sound natural anymore. You will need to model for them the smooth blending of phonemes, and show them how to "bulldoze" the sounds quickly. These readers need simple, easy-to-read books that are decodable but with plots or main ideas that make sense.

If the children are older, or have reached the stage where fluency is increasing, use prompts that point out word patterns or chunks. If the word is a member of a word family, ask questions about its pattern, such as, "Do you see a word part or chunk that you know?" Another prompt is, "This word looks like a word that you know. Do you see it?" If necessary, point out a word that is a member of the same family; for example, "This word looks like the word 'day.' Use the word 'day' to help you figure it out." You can also tell them to cover up a part of the word so that they can see the familiar chunk. If they pronounce words that make no sense, ask, "Does that make sense in this sentence?" If necessary, prompt them to change the vowel sound from long to short, or vice versa.

Prompting readers as they struggle with print is not an exact science; however, there are some general guidelines that can help. Figure 15.5 lists these.

Vocabulary Needs

Chad, a sixth grader, was not fond of reading. He much preferred sports, math, and video games. When reading he was able to decode most words. Yet, when asked about a word, even one defined in context, he just shrugged and said, "I don't really know that word." Sometimes his lack of vocabulary knowledge affected his comprehension, because he missed words that describe character traits, the setting, or discussions of the problem in the story. His teacher found that he performed fairly well on formal vocabulary work in the classroom, doing things such as looking up definitions and writing sentences; however, this knowledge gained never transferred to his reading.

Chad was equating reading with sounding good. Because he could say most of the words printed before him, he saw no value in making sense of them. This, of course, inhibits his understanding of text, particularly as he continues to do more reading of harder and more sophisticated text.

To help students like Chad, focus on active use of text. Ask the student to read aloud for you and stop at the end of a page that contains a difficult word. Point to the word and ask, "Why is this word important to this page?" If the student does not know the word, say, "In your head, put another word there that would make sense.

When a Student "Freezes" at an Unknown Word

Marco, a first grader, gave up very easily when he came to a word he did not know. He would not even attempt unknown words by himself. Possible solutions include:

1. Make sure that the book is at the appropriate level for the child. Do not let the child continue to read texts that are frustrating.
2. Always wait 2–3 seconds for a self-correction.
3. The first prompt should be general, such as "Something tricked you. Try again," or "Look at your clues. What can you try?"
4. Beginning readers who are reading predictable text need no more than the first letter prompt and a meaning prompt, such as, "Look at the first letter. What is the first sound? Now, what word that starts with that letter would make sense here?"
5. Transitional readers who are becoming aware of vowel sounds and final consonants need a prompt to blend, such as, "Bulldoze it. Say it fast."
6. Readers who are becoming fluent need to focus on word chunks, using prompts such as, "Do you see a word part that you know?"
7. If the child cannot produce the word after two prompts, tell him or her the word and move on. Make note of areas of need.
8. If the word is not phonetically regular or simply too difficult for this child, simply supply the word and move on.
9. Pictures should be prompted only if they will help. Make sure that readers know that pictures do not always match the text.
10. After a word is attempted, always ask, "Does that make sense?"

Figure 15.5 Helping the child who is unsure of unknown words.

Then think of another word, and another one." This strengthens use of context clues and gives the student a bank of similar words to help with meaning. Because of its reliance on the use of context clues, another vocabulary strategy that will help is the Cloze Passage Definition, described in Chapter 8. Also described in Chapter 8 is a highly motivating strategy called the Keyword Method (Konopak, Williams & Jampole, 1991; National Reading Panel, 2000b; Pressley, Levin & Delaney, 1982), which helps students use mnemonics to remember new words. Students associate a new word with a familiar word, and then picture it in their minds.

Scaffolding the "Heart" of Reading

The "heart" of reading is perhaps the most important goal of all—instilling a love of reading and recognition of its value in life. Yet, for some youngsters, this is the most difficult goal to meet, because something along the way has turned them off of reading. When you recognize poor attitudes or indifference toward reading, try some of the strategies described in the next section.

A History of Reading Struggles

One young lady, Courtney, was in fifth grade. More than most children, she hated to read. Her first grade year was a rocky one; she had difficulty learning to read. Decoding was a struggle for her; she did not know (and was not taught) strategies for figuring out unknown words. This lack affected her fluency and she never quite figured out how reading is supposed to sound. She was placed in the remedial reading program by the end of first grade, but her friends were all very good readers. She hated to leave her classroom and her friends only to join a group of struggling readers, many of whom were disruptive and laden with other problems. By third grade, Courtney was still reading at the first grade level, and hated every minute of it.

Happily, a strong fourth grade teacher recognized the problem. While Courtney was good at using context clues to compensate for her lack of decoding skills, for three years, she had been expected to read texts that were simply too hard for her. As she learned new decoding skills, she did not have the time to practice them in a smooth, fluent manner. Additionally, she refused to read at home, which meant that the only reading she was doing was in the classroom, where the texts were frustrating. So, her fourth grade teacher began giving Courtney a steady diet of books that were easy to read, and much classroom time to do it. Her daily homework was reading from these books. Along with this, she continued to teach Courtney metacognitive skills, showing her how to continually self-question and figure out which decoding strategies to apply. Eventually, Courtney became a stronger reader, and began making good grades in all her subjects. Her confidence was restored. She was pulled out of the remedial program and continued to flourish. One day, knowing that she loves dogs, I recommended to her a wonderful book about a girl and her dog—*Because of Winn Dixie* (DiCamillo, 2000). I told her that I had just bought the book and she could borrow it. Courtney immediately shook her head and refused to take it. "Uh-uh! I hate to read!" she said. Even after all her growth, she still held on to an old fear.

Courtney's situation is not unusual. But there are ways to prevent Courtney's dilemma from happening. When she struggles, give her time to read books on the independent level. The importance of this step cannot be overemphasized! A struggling reader needs time—*much* time—to read books that are easy for her to read. Once she masters some decoding skills, do not move ahead until you see fluency and comfort with books at that level. Then introduce books that are a little bit harder.

Make use of series books. These books lured Courtney back to reading! While some teachers shy away from series books because they are not "good" literature, Courtney's teacher introduced several to her students, and sent home a list of suggested series books. One piqued Courtney's interest, and she asked her mother to take her to the library in search of it. Since then, she's been hooked on this series!

Certainly, not all series books are award-winning stuff, but they have qualities that make them appealing for use with children who won't read. First, they are predictable and familiar, which is comforting to struggling readers. Once readers have been introduced to the main characters in the first book, they do not need to get to know them again. Second, many series books are written about topics that are popular with children, making them viable candidates for disinterested readers, especially those in the middle school. Allington (2001) argues that many series books, while they are too predictable and flat to be considered quality literature, just may be the books that prepare many struggling readers for more sophisticated reading. Series books can be used for the students' independent reading time, both at school and at home. They can help your readers develop fluency and give them practice with decoding skills in a comfortable setting.

One summer day, Courtney reported to me that she spent the entire day reading so that she could finish her book, *Sammy Keyes and the Psycho Kitty Queen* (Van Draanen, 2004) and she couldn't wait to start the next one. Quite an accomplishment for a child who was a reluctant reader! Appendix B lists some favorite series. In most cases, the author has written numerous titles for each series, so look for several books to make up the series.

Consider what you do with books, and how students view reading. When they realize that each book they read will be followed by a test, they do not view reading as a natural thing to do. Instead, it becomes just another school subject. This is even true of gifted readers who do not struggle with the mechanics of reading. They, too, need to see reading as a pleasurable, "grown-up" activity that is not part of their academic load. Just imagine going on vacation with an armload of books to read while relaxing at the beach. Now imagine someone telling you that you had to take a test after finishing every one of them!

Therefore, when you hold a conference with your students once a week, talk to them about their reading, just as you would talk to another adult. Have conversations about reading, asking questions that show your support rather than your interrogation of their comprehension. Sometimes, the best question is not a question at all, but a statement instead. In talking to your readers privately, at least once a week, for a few minutes, you will be able to get a picture of their reading. Figure 15.6 shows some questions and statements that you can use to chat with your readers.

Boys Who Refuse to Read

A sure way to turn kids onto reading is to let them read what they like. This trick became very evident working with Brendan, a fifth grade boy who knew how to read fairly well but refused to. Brendan was a capable reader and was a smart young man who had a lot of interest in math, science, and sports. As a youngster in first and second grades, he read voraciously and was involved in many writing projects that his teachers assigned. He read a little bit at home, but much of his free time (outside of homework) was spent in hockey practices and games. He slowly

---

1. "I've been curious about this book. Tell me what you think about it."
2. "I read this book and just didn't like it at all. Can you help me change my mind?"
3. "When I got to this part in the story, I was so angry! Tell me your reaction."
4. "I really wanted the story to end differently. Here's what I would have written. . . . What about you?"
5. "This is my favorite part, and here's why. Tell me what you think."

Figure 15.6 Chatting about books naturally.

Nonfiction and series books often "hook" reluctant readers.

began to lose interest in reading. He disliked the required reading selections in the fifth grade basal. When learning social studies or science, his teachers assigned textbook reading only, which bored him. He began complaining about homework, and he refused to read at school unless he absolutely had to. Finally, an observant librarian showed him some books that she had put in a special display in the library. The titles were atypical of books he usually read at school—titles such as *Just Disgusting* (Griffiths, 2005) and *Oh, Yuck! The Encyclopedia of Everything Nasty* (Masoff, 2000). Slowly, he began to read again. These books exhibited the kind of humor that Brendan appreciated at this age, and were the kind of light-hearted fare that held his interest.

Brendan is typical of many boys approaching adolescence. He did not find that the effort it took for him to read assigned books was worth the energy. Recent research has paid much attention to the academic problems of boys, linked to their difficulties with reading. Brozo (2002) reports that boys are more likely than girls to have reading disabilities and attention-deficit disorders. Boys tend to lose interest in reading by the time they reach middle school, and their literacy scores begin to drop (O'Donnell, 2005). Many factors contribute to this problem, including an attitude that reading is a girl's activity, the lack of male role models who read, a desire to fit in with their peers who view reading and academic excellence as "nerdy," and a steady diet of basal stories or instructional texts that do not interest them.

Jon Scieszka, author of many wildly popular children's books such as *The Stinky Cheese Man and Other Fairly Stupid Tales* (1992), sponsors a program called Guys Read (available online at www.guysread.com), which offers support, information, and bibliographies for boys who do not like to read. Likewise, in *To Be a Boy, To Be a Reader*, Brozo (2002) suggests 300 titles that might interest preadolescent and adolescent boys, including fiction that contains main characters in appropriate role models.

While building a library of books boys like, don't forget the informational books. Often, nonfiction books about things that interest them—such as sports, how-to crafts, science projects, and biographies—are the keys to hooking disinterested—and nonreading boys. Reference books such as *Guinness World Records 2005: Special 50th Anniversary Edition* (2004) or *Ripley's Believe It or Not* (2004) are highly interesting to many reluctant readers, including girls, because the text is compact and accompanied by intriguing photographs. Additionally, magazines and newspapers should be in plentiful supply, because these contain short, straightforward articles that are of interest to reluctant readers.

Blair and Sanford (cited in O'Donnell, 2005), in a study of boys' reading choices in Canada, found that boys spend much more time on literacy tasks than teachers and parents think they do. However, these tasks are not the typical reading skills that we think about in school settings. For example, they look for and analyze video game cheat codes in magazines, they categorize and compare statistics of trading card characters, and they efficiently use web sites and online resources. Blair and Sanford reported five themes that interest boys most: personal interests, action, success, fun, and purpose. Thus, when the required classroom readings provide none of these, boys will create ways to make reading and writing personally meaningful. Hence, boys will do things like draw comic strips, create trading card characters, or make up competitions. O'Donnell reports that choice is the key to getting the boys hooked onto reading. Letting boys choose the text they are to read improves their attitudes and interaction with books. Figure 15.7 summarizes the ways to help boys who struggle with reading.

Impatient Readers

When my son Tommy began first grade, he fully expected to be able read by the time he came home from school on the first day. While he was able to read a few predictable books at home, he had not yet become comfortable with decoding. He was sorely disappointed when he realized that reading would take a while to learn, and that he could not yet read Rowling's *Harry Potter* books on that first day of school!

His teacher sensed his excitement about reading and wanted to capitalize on it. Immediately, she began sending home easy-to-read books that required some decoding, yet were suitable for him to read independently, so that he could gain confidence and fluency. Using a combination of picture clues and the few decoding skills that he knew, Tommy was able to begin reading within the first couple of weeks of school. However, he was impatient! He noticed that one of his friends was taking home much harder books, and he was determined that he could do the same thing. He asked his teacher to let him take home some harder books, convinced that he would read them. Wisely, she resisted, even though she was sorely tempted to capitalize on his enthusiasm. She knew that he needed to develop fluency and that he therefore needed to read books that were easy for him for a while. She used the repeated readings strategy with him, to help him become more fluent and eliminate problems with prosody. (You can find this strategy in Chapter 14.) Within a couple of months, he was confident, he read smoothly and with expression, and he began to monitor his own comprehension. Now, he was ready for harder books on his own.

When Boys Refuse to Read

Brendan, a fifth grade boy, knew how to read fairly well but refused to. He was bright and had a lot of interest in math, science, and sports. As he approached middle school, he slowly began to lose interest in reading. Soon, he refused to read unless he had to. Solutions include:

1. Provide books that boys of this age enjoy, including humor, cartoons, and nonfiction.
2. Consider "junk reading" books as "hooks" to more sophisticated reading.
3. Provide lots of magazines and newspapers for classroom reading.
4. Broaden the science and social studies curriculum to include more than just textbook reading.
5. Allow boys to make choices when reading.

Figure 15.7 Helping nonreading boys.

The lesson learned here is to make sure that your students are reading books that will help them gain confidence. These "eager beavers" are tricky; they are so enthusiastic and can be so convincing that we often are too quick to introduce them to harder books. Teach them how to choose books on their own, using the "three finger rule," Allington's variation of the popular "five finger rule." (Allington, 2001, p. 52). When they find a book, ask them to read the first page or two. They should put up a finger every time they must stop to figure out a word. Three fingers up means the book is too hard. If you want children to develop confidence and fluency, they need to find an easier book. They will need to read books at this level for at least a couple of weeks, until they can read the books without errors at all.

Likewise, explain this concept to parents. Sometimes parents are impatient, too. Sometimes they expect reading to be a skill-building exercise, where the learner simply climbs higher with harder books as soon as he shows that he can read harder words. But reading with fluency and confidence takes time and repeated exposure to these harder words. Sometimes all the child needs is more time to develop and grow with books that suit him or her. Show them how to select books that are easy enough for their children, and send home books to be read daily. The strategies for working with these students are summarized in Figure 15.8.

A Need for Multicultural Literature

Osman was a student in fourth grade. His parents, agriculture workers from Mexico, spoke no English. He was considerably older, taller, and more physically developed than the rest of the boys in the class. While he could speak English, he rarely spoke and did not participate in most class activities. As a fourth grader, he could read on the third grade level; therefore, he was in the pull-out Title I remedial reading program, where he went to class for an hour every day. The choices he had to read were from the basal, which was a carefully selected program for struggling readers in the school district. The selections were mostly of the highly decodable variety—stories about animals or middle-class white children. Osman quickly lost interest in them. He often slept during class.

Osman had multiple challenges, as children of diverse backgrounds often do. His cultural background was quite different from that of the school he attended. His reading achievement was below his grade level. And he was disinterested in reading. Yet the attempts to solve his problems, using decodable text and putting

When a Student Wants to Read But Can't

1. Insist on easy reading for a while.
2. Show the student how to choose easy books using the three-finger rule.
3. Use the repeated readings strategy.
4. Send home easy books.
5. Explain to parents the importance of easy reading and time with books.

Figure 15.8 Helping the student who cannot read at the correct grade level.

Diversity in the Reading Classroom

Children Find Themselves in Literature

One of the reasons for using children's books in the classroom is to offer our students opportunities to make personal connections with literature. Falling in love with books means identifying with the characters, relating the events to our own lives, and discovering more about ourselves in the process. Well-chosen literature helps us make schools places where children can learn about their world and their place in it. But what happens if a child never has the opportunity to make that personal connection?

In a classroom void of multicultural literature, it is quite possible that children of diverse backgrounds will not make that connection. For the transactional theory (Rosenblatt, 1938, 1978) to truly have an influence in your classroom, you need to make multicultural literature a part of your classroom library. Thus, all of your readers will see themselves in the books they read. With fiction, they will be able to identify with the characters and relate story events to their own life events. With biographies, they will be able to see the possibilities in their own lives based on the accomplishments of people just like them. And with nonfiction, they will learn of history that can—and perhaps shouldn't—repeat itself. Yet many teachers rely on textbooks for content area instruction, and reading instruction in most classrooms comes from the basal series selected by the school. Thus, classroom time spent with printed material is limited to textbooks. And textbooks, even the best ones, cannot open worlds like literature can.

Hefflin and Barksdale-Ladd tell us, "From the time they enter school, most African American children read literature that seldom offers messages about them, their past, or their future. All too often books used in primary classrooms contain too few African American characters, or they include characters who are African American in appearance only. . . . In short, today's African American children often cannot find themselves in the literature they are given to read" (2001, p. 810). The same is true of almost any other minority, including children with physical and mental challenges.

Use multicultural literature in these ways:

1. When studying a content-area theme, such as transportation, animals, the history of your state, or simple machines, find contributions to these subjects from people of a variety of ethnicities. Include these books in your resource materials for students to use when researching.

2. Have plenty of multicultural titles available in the classroom library for self-selected independent reading.

3. Wherever possible, purchase or borrow books in both Spanish and English.

4. Use multicultural titles for your read-aloud sessions. Do not limit these books to special months of the year, such as Black History month, but make them a part of your daily read-alouds.

him in a special classroom, exacerbated his difficulties. Isolating him from his classmates and forcing him to read from text that made no sense to him may have widened the gap between Osman and his peers.

Children like Osman need to see themselves in children's books. Through the transactional theory, Rosenblatt (1938, 1978) explains the importance of children's personal connections to reading. Yet it is impossible for many children of diverse backgrounds to do so, especially if they are low-achieving readers, because they must try to sort through text that borders on nonsense.

Home–School Connection

What to Do When Your Child Asks: "What's That Word?"

Shown here is a letter that contains a list of suggestions for helping children when they are "stuck" on a word while reading at home. ●

Dear Families,

Sometimes, when your child reads at home, he or she gets "stuck" on a word. Here are some ways to handle this:

1. *Try silence first!* Wait five seconds and allow your child to try figuring out what to do by himself or herself. This shows the child that you want him or her to be independent.

2. *Suggest reading on.* Tell her to keep reading and try to figure out the word from what the rest of the sentence says. Often, your child will get clues and will be able to fill in the missing word quickly.

3. *Go back and figure out the word.* After reading the rest of the sentence, if the word is still unknown, then try to go back and figure it out.

4. *Help with "sounding it out."* Break the word into manageable parts. See if there are parts of the word that your child already knows. Use that to figure out the part the child does not know. Remember, you do not have to start from the first letter of the word to sound it out. (For example, if the word is "millions," show your child this part of the word: *"ill."* Have the child say it, then put the *"m"* in front of it.)

5. *Use "risk-free" comments.* Your child needs to feel confident about making logical guesses when confronted with unknown words. Comments that help are:

   "What sound can you try now?"
   "Put that word in the sentence. Does this make sense? What would make more sense?"
   "Try that word and see if it works."
   "What do you think?"

Sincerely,

Your child's teacher

Caregivers can learn ways to prompt their children as they read.

Using multicultural literature might help. Because of Osman's low reading ability, reading good multicultural books aloud to him can help him to identify with main characters that are like him. Likewise, strategies such as DLTA (described in Chapter 12) can help lay foundations for reading processes such as making predictions, inferencing, and determining vocabulary meanings.

Many multicultural titles were introduced in Chapter 3. On page 517 are some useful web sites for finding and selecting quality multicultural literature. Included are web sites that provide bibliographies of children's books containing main characters with physical and mental challenges.

- **www.multiculturalchildrenslit.com**   This website contains links to African American, Chinese American, Japanese American, Jewish American, Korean American, Latino American, and Native American literature.
- **usinfo.state.gov/journals/itsv/0200/ijse/ijse0200.pdf**   From the Electronic Journal of the Department of State (2000), this web site lists Arab American, Asian American, Black American, Hispanic American, and Native American literature web sites.
- **scholar.lib.vt.edu/ejournals/ALAN/fall95/Ericson.html**   The role of the home in multicultural children's literature is explored in this web site.
- **www.shens.com**   Shens is actually an online bookstore, but the site displays some excellent multicultural literature, including a collection of Cinderella stories from around the world.
- **www.ucalgary.ca/~dkbrown/index.html**   This site contains a guide to children's literature on the World Wide Web, with many links to multicultural literature.
- **www-wsl.state.wy.us/natrona/latinas.html**   Latin American literature is featured on this web site.
- **www.edchange.org/multicultural/voices.html**   Multicultural poetry is featured at this web site.
- **www.geocities.com/afam_literature/index.html**   African American literature is the focus of this web site.
- **www.planetesme.com**   Esme Codell, the author of *Sahara Special*, sponsors this web site, which contains multiple links to multicultural literature.
- **www.nichcy.org/pubs/bibliog/bib5txt.htm#hear**   This site lists titles for physical challenges, deafness, blindness, Down's syndrome, ADHD, and others.
- **frankrogers.home.mindspring.com/multi.html**   Several links to sites that provide information and bibliographies for books with a wide variety of multicultural themes.

Summary:
Teaching and Reaching

Reaching all your readers is the only way to be truly successful in your classroom. Teaching makes no sense if your learners are not going to learn. Your responsibility is to make sure all of them do. The first part of this chapter described ways to modify instruction so that you can reach all learners, in all grade levels, with all kinds of text:

- Use all learning modalities.
- Use clear, communicative language.
- Teach from the known to the unknown.
- Use questions that include.
- Incorporate student interests.
- Set high expectations for everyone.
- Provide a large classroom library.
- Give everyone time to read independently in books they *can* read.
- Get up close and watch.
- Foster student autonomy.
- Make lessons multilevel.

Once you notice reading behaviors that indicate a need for intervention and extra scaffolding, plan a conscious effort to provide support in your classroom. This chapter described ways to do this, for the whole, the parts, and the heart of reading, by introducing to you 11 readers with a variety of needs. The situations and teaching strategies presented in the chapter are summarized in the Reviewing the Big Picture box, along with their corresponding teaching standards and principles.

Technology Resources

- **www.ascd.org/portal/site/ascd** The Association for Supervision and Curriculum Development (ASCD) web site contains a web page titled "Educational Topics." There are several topics available, and "Differentiating Instruction" is one of them. It describes the classroom in which all students' needs are met, answers frequently asked questions, provides testimonials from teachers, and offers several links to articles and other informative sites.

- **www.cast.org/ncac/DifferentiatedInstruction2876.cfm** The National Center on Assessing the General Curriculum is a consortium devoted to helping educators ensure success for all students through differentiated instruction. This web page includes evidence of effectiveness, descriptions, and strategies.

- **www.ldonline.org/ld_indepth/teaching_techniques/differentiation.html** This site, "Learning Disabilities On-line," offers this page on differentiated instruction.

- **www.education.pitt.edu/leaders/ABOUT_US.HTM** Literacy Educators Assessing and Developing Early Reading Success (LEADERS) is a consortium funded by the Pennsylvania Department of Education. This group produced a web page, "Differentiated Instruction," written by Bruce Fischman. Fischman provides clear explanation and many links to additional sources for help in meeting all students' needs.

---

expect the world

The New York Times
nytimes.com

Themes of the Times

Expand your knowledge of the concepts discussed in this chapter by reading current and historical articles from the *New York Times* by visiting the "Themes of the Times" section of the Companion Web Site.

Reviewing the Big Picture
Adapting Instruction for the Whole, Parts, and Heart of Reading

Observation of Student Behavior	Strategies to Meet the Student's Needs	IRA Standards	INTASC Principles	NAEYC Standards	ACEI/NCATE Standards
Nicole reads words but does not understand text	Provide easier text, teach structure of text, read together and interact, model self-monitoring strategies	1.4, 2.2, 3.2, 3.3	3, 4, 5	3, 4b (with emergent readers)	2.1, 3.1, 3.2, 3.3, 3.4, 3.5, 4
Jake retells in bits and pieces	Provide easier text, use book introductions, use story impressions	1.4, 2.2, 3.2, 3.3	3, 4, 5	3, 4b (with emergent readers)	2.1, 3.1, 3.2, 3.3, 3.4, 3.5, 4
Brian is not aware of a lack of understanding	Teach self-monitoring and self-regulating, use click and clunk strategy, observe reading behaviors closely, talk about choices made while reading, give sticky notes to mark stop points	1.4, 2.2, 3.2, 3.3	3, 4, 5	3, 4b (with emergent readers)	2.1, 3.1, 3.2, 3.3, 3.4, 3.5, 4
Roberto needs to be challenged beyond the regular curriculum	Use a compacted curriculum, use process modifications, give opportunities to research, read biographies, expand vocabulary, teach mini-lessons on reading strategies, provide fiction with gifted main characters	1.4, 2.2, 3.2, 3.3	2, 3, 4, 5	3, 4b (with young children who learned to read earlier than peers)	2.1, 3.1, 3.2, 3.3, 3.4, 3.5, 4
Ellie does not connect letters with sounds	Provide easier text, use decodable books and books with high-recognition vocabulary and predictable books, use word banks, give time to write daily, use making words, teach phonics with word families, show that meaning is always expected from text	1.4, 2.2, 3.2, 3.3	3, 4, 5	3, 4b (with emergent readers)	2.1, 3.1, 3.2, 3.3, 3.4, 3.5, 4
Marco "freezes" at an unknown word	Keep quiet as he attempts words on his own, prompt him to try his own solutions for decoding, use decoding prompts suitable for his reading development	1.4, 2.2, 3.2, 3.3	3, 4, 5	3, 4b (with emergent readers)	2.1, 3.1, 3.2, 3.3, 3.4, 3.5, 4
Chad does not know enough words	Focus on active use of text, help strengthen use of context clues, use the cloze passage definition strategy, use keyword method	1.4, 2.2, 3.2, 3.3	3, 4, 5	NA	2.1, 3.1, 3.2, 3.3, 3.4, 3.5, 4
Courtney can read but won't	Provide books at the independent level, use series books, chat about books in natural conversations during conferences	1.4, 2.2, 3.2, 3.3, 4.1, 4.3	3, 4, 5	NA	2.1, 3.1, 3.2, 3.3, 3.4, 3.5, 4, 5.3
Brendan refuses to read	Provide books that interest boys, introduce programs such as Scieszka's guysread.com, provide nonfiction books, provide magazines and newspapers, broaden subject area reading to include more than textbooks, allow choices	1.4, 2.2, 3.2, 3.3, 4.1, 4.3	3, 4, 5	NA	2.1, 3.1, 3.2, 3.3, 3.4, 3.5, 4, 5.3
Tommy wants to read harder books too quickly	Insist on easy reading for awhile, teach ways to find books on their own, use repeated readings, involve parents, send home books at suitable level	1.4, 2.2, 3.2, 3.3, 4.1, 4.3	2, 3, 4, 5	3, 4b (with emergent readers)	2.1, 3.1, 3.2, 3.3, 3.4, 3.5, 4, 5.3
Osman, a Mexican-American student, needs to see himself in children's books	Provide quality multicultural literature, do not isolate student, broaden curriculum to include more than textbooks and basals, use DLTA	1.4, 2.2, 3.2, 3.3, 4.1, 4.3	3, 4, 5	3, 4b (with emergent readers)	2.1, 3.1, 3.2, 3.3, 3.4, 3.5, 4, 5.3

Appendix A

State Department of Education Sites for Location of State Standards Pertaining to Reading and Language Arts

These web sites list the academic standards adopted by each state in the United States. Keep in mind that standards-based education is changing daily; you might be redirected when you attempt to look up a state education department web site.

Alabama: *alex.state.al.us/standardAll.php*

Alaska: *www.educ.state.ak.us/ContentStandards/English.html*

Arizona: *www.ade.state.az.us/standards/language-arts/articulated.asp*

Arkansas: *arkedu.state.ar.us/curriculum/benchmarks.html#Language*

California: *www.cde.ca.gov/re/pn/fd/documents/english-language-arts.pdf*

Colorado: *www.cde.state.co.us/cdeassess/standards/pdf/reading.pdf*

Connecticut: *www.state.ct.us/sde/dtl/curriculum/frlanga.pdf*

Delaware: *www.doe.state.de.us/Standards/English/ELA_toc.html*

District of Columbia: *www.k12.dc.us/dcps/curriculum/content/elem-stl.htm*

Florida: *www.firn.edu/doe/curric/prek12/frame2.htm*

Georgia: *www.georgiastandards.org*

Hawaii: *www.hcps.k12.hi.us/PUBLIC/contst1.nsf/2be12f699cdba2840 a2567830069239d/fbc32f9bf7fcc6bd0a2567e000146fc7/$FILE/ Language+Arts+Booklet.pdf*

Idaho: *www.sde.state.id.us/dept/docs/standards/SiteMap.htm*

Illinois: *www.isbe.net/ils/ela/standards.htm*

Indiana: *www.indianastandardsresources.org/standardSummary.asp? Subject=eng&Grade*

Iowa: *www.state.ia.us/educate/index.html*

Kansas: *www.ksde.org/outcomes/communications.html*

Kentucky: *www.education.ky.gov/KDE/Instructional+Resources/Curriculum+ Documents+and+Resources/Core+Content+for+Assessment/Core+ Content+Downloads.htm*

Louisiana: *www.doe.state.la.us/DOE/assessment/standards/ENGLISH.pdf*

Maine: *www.state.me.us/education/lres/ela.pdf*

Maryland: *mdk12.org/instruction/curriculum/reading/index.html*

Massachusetts: *www.doe.mass.edu/frameworks/ela/0601.pdf*

Michigan: *www.michigan.gov/documents/MichiganCurriculum
Framework_8172_7.pdf*

Minnesota: *education.state.mn.us/html/intro_standards_language.htm*

Mississippi: *www.mde.k12.ms.us/ACAD/ID/Curriculum/LAER/outline.html*

Missouri: *www.dese.state.mo.us/standards/comarts.html*

Montana: *www.opi.state.mt.us/index.html*

Nebraska: *www.nde.state.ne.us/ndestandards/AcadStand.html*

Nevada: *http://www.doe.nv.gov/standards/standela/english.html*

New Hampshire: *www.ed.state.nh.us/education/doe/organization/curriculum/
Assessment/EnglishLanguageArts.htm*

New Jersey: *www.state.nj.us/njded/cccs/s3_lal.htm*

New Mexico: *www.ped.state.nm.us/cilt/standards/language/index.html*

New York: *www.emsc.nysed.gov/ciai/ela/elals.html*

North Carolina: *www.dpi.state.nc.us/curriculum/languagearts/2004draft/
eladraftcurriculum.pdf*

North Dakota: *www.dpi.state.nd.us/standard/content/ELA/index.shtm*

Ohio: *www.ode.state.oh.us/academic_content_standards/pdf/ENGLISH.pdf*

Oklahoma: *http://www.sde.state.ok.us/home/defaultie.html* (Then click on PASS)

Oregon: *www.ode.state.or.us/search/results/?id=8*

Pennsylvania: *www.pde.state.pa.us/k12/lib/k12/Reading.pdf*

Rhode Island: *www.ridoe.net/standards/frameworks/english/default.htm*

South Carolina: *www.myscschools.com/offices/cso/english_la/documents/
standards2002.pdf*

South Dakota: *www.state.sd.us/deca/OCTA/contentstandards/reading/index.htm*

Tennessee: *www.state.tn.us/education/ci/cistandards2001/la/cienglangartby
standard.htm*

Texas: *www.tea.state.tx.us/rules/tac/chapter110/index.html*

Utah: *www.uen.org/core/*

Vermont: *www.state.vt.us/educ/new/html/pubs/framework.html*

Virginia: *www.pen.k12.va.us/VDOE/Instruction/English/englishCF.html*

Washington: *www.k12.wa.us/curriculumInstruct/reading/pubdocs/Reading
EALR-GLE.pdf*

West Virginia: *wvde.state.wv.us/policies/p2520.1_ne.pdf*

Wisconsin: *www.dpi.state.wi.us/standards/elaintro.html*

Wyoming: *www.laramie1.k12.wy.us/instruction/statestandards/Language%
20Arts%20Standards.pdf*

Additionally, national standards in reading are addressed at these sites:
*www.ccsso.org/projects/Interstate_New_Teacher_Assessment_and_
Support_Consortium*
www.acei.org
www.reading.org
www.ncate.org

Appendix B

Strategies for Promoting Literacy Instruction

In this appendix are several activities, strategies, and samples of materials ready to be used in the classroom. Additional materials and sample lessons are available on the Companion Web Site at *www.ablongman.com/nettles1e* as well as in the special book *Toolkit for Teachers of Literacy*.

Reading Process Mini-Assessments

Reading Process Mini-Assessments are simple assessments that you can complete in five minutes or less to collect information about how students process print, understand the author's message, and respond to the text. Following are the types of skills that can be assessed using a Mini-Assessment. A sample* of a Word Recognition Rate Mini-Assessment is provided as well.

- *Word recognition rate*—How many words does the student recognize?
- *Reader-text match*—What is the student's reading level?
- *Words per minute*—What is the student's reading rate?
- *Repetitions*—How often does the student repeat words or phrases?
- *Self-monitoring ability*—How often does the student correct himself or herself when he or she makes a miscue?
- *Use of miscues that make sense*—How many of the student's miscues make sense in the context?
- *Use of miscues that are visual*—How many of the student's miscues are graphophonologically similar to the print?
- Retelling ability—How well does the student retell the story (fiction) or the important ideas (nonfiction)?

* Complete samples of Mini-Assessments are provided in the book *Toolkit for Teachers of Literacy*.

Word Recognition Rate Mini-Assessment

Student: _____ Student's grade level: _____

Date: _____ Title of selection: _____

Level or approximate readability of selection: _____ # of words: _____

Scorable miscues	Tally or Number
Incorrect or substituted word	
Omission	
Insertion	
Teacher assistance	

# of words in text – # of inaccurate words = _____ (# of words read correctly)

Formula for word recognition rate:

$$\frac{\textit{# of words read correctly}}{\textit{# of words in the text}}$$

Word recognition rate: _____
Anecdotal notes: _____

Sample Rubric* for Analyzing Student Writing

FIRST GRADE—STORY WRITING

Name of child: _____

Title or description of paper: _____

TRAIT #1: IDEAS (FIRST GRADE—STORY WRITING)

5	3	1
The writer clearly writes a single story line. His or her ideas are all clearly related to this story.	The writer seems to have a story in mind, but strays occasionally from the story line.	The writer does not express thoughts about a single story. The writing contains many disconnected sentences that do not seem to tell a story.
Relevant title and pictures are present.	Title and/or pictures are present but need more clarity.	The title and pictures are absent, or they are present but not relevant at all.

Score for Ideas (Story Writing): _____

TRAIT #2: ORGANIZATION (FIRST GRADE—STORY WRITING)

5	3	1
The story clearly contains the most basic elements of story: character(s) with a problem that is eventually solved.	The story introduces character(s), but the problem and its resolution are not always clear.	The story line is hard to distinguish. Character(s) and problem are not clear.
The sequence of events is clearly evident, with a definitive beginning, middle, and end.	Parts of the beginning, middle, and end are apparent.	There is no clear beginning, middle, and end to the story.

Score for Organization (Story Writing): _____

TRAIT #3: VOICE (FIRST GRADE—STORY WRITING)

5	3	1
The reader knows who is narrating the story without question.	The writer sometimes shifts voice or does not make the voice clear from the beginning.	The writer seems indifferent or uninvolved. As a result, the writing is flat or lifeless.

Score for Voice (Story Writing): _____

TRAIT #4: WORD CHOICE (FIRST GRADE—STORY WRITING)

5	3	1
The writer always uses nouns and verbs appropriately and effectively.	The writer sometimes uses nouns and verbs appropriately and effectively.	The writer does not use nouns and verbs appropriately or effectively.
The writer uses many descriptive words and phrases.	The writer uses some descriptive words and phrases.	The writer does not attempt to make the writing more interesting. The story is a simple narrative. It appears as if he or she attempts to use only easy-to-spell words.

Score for Word Choice (Story Writing): _____

TRAIT #5: SENTENCE FLUENCY (FIRST GRADE—STORY WRITING)

5	3	1
The story flows well; all sentences connect with each other and are related to the story ideas.	Some sentences connect with each other. Some sentences are choppy or run-on.	Most sentences are unclear, choppy, and disconnected.
The story is pleasant to read and sounds good when read aloud.	The story is fairly easy to read and has potential for being smooth and easy to read.	The story does not seem like a story; sentences do not flow together well.

Score for Sentence Fluency (Story Writing): _____

* The complete form for this and other numerous rubrics are included in the book *Toolkit for Teachers of Literacy*.

Sample Organizers for Facilitating Text Structure

Story Frames: Character Analysis

Title: _____

_____ is an important character in this story, because

_____.

He/She wanted _____, but

_____.

So, he/she _____.

I think that _____ is _____,

because _____.

Report Frames for Expository Text: Descriptive Text That Helps to Change Schema

Title: _____

This book is about _____.

Before I read this book, this is what I knew about this topic: _____

_____.

After reading this book, I found out _____.

I found out _____ new things about _____ _____. These facts

are: _____ _____ _____ _____

_____.

Writing Projects Your Students Can Publish

Publishing the works of your students gives meaning to their writing, because the published works are designed to be read by other people, for authentic reasons. The following are publishing projects that you can conduct with your students.

- *Advertisements for books*—After reading any fiction or nonfiction book, create an advertisement for it. Display the finished ads in the library as part of Read Across America Day or National Library Week.
- *Alphabet books*—After reading any nonfiction book, use the information learned to create an alphabet book on the same topic. Each letter needs to be represented by an example of the topic. Show students examples of alphabet books such as Pallotta's *Freshwater Alphabet Book* (1996). Loan these alphabet books to the school library, or use them in your classroom.

- *Big books*—Read a fairy tale book or a popular picture book. Write your own version of the story and create a big book. Loan the big books to preschool and kindergarten teachers to use in shared reading with their classes.
- *Bilingual books*—Work together in pairs. Students who are English language learners help native English speakers write a book in two languages. The book can be a retelling of a familiar story or fairy tale, or an original piece. This project can also be done with nonfiction pieces, or with newsletters and flyers that go home to parents and caregivers.
- *Calendars*—After reading any fiction or nonfiction book, create a themed calendar with captioned pictures. Give these to parents, family, and friends as gifts.
- *Wordfull wordless books*—Examine wordless picture books. (A list of them is provided in Chapter 6.) Choose one and write the story to accompany the pictures. Publish this and read it to a buddy in kindergarten or first grade.
- *Coloring books*—After reading any fiction or nonfiction book, create a coloring book on the same topic or theme. Write captions for the book, and give it to a young friend as a gift.
- *Counting books*—After reading a nonfiction book, create a counting book on the same topic. Share the book with kindergarteners or loan it to a kindergarten teacher.
- *Dictionaries*—After reading a nonfiction book, create a dictionary of terms that are relevant to the topic. Illustrate the dictionary entries to make a picture dictionary. Loan the book to the school library.
- *Easy chapter books*—Read some transitional chapter books such as *Russell Sprouts* (Hurwitz, 1987). Write a chapter book for transitional readers to be shared with second and third graders.
- *Field guides*—After reading a nonfiction book, write an illustrated field guide on that subject. Topics such as animals, ocean life, plants, and weather work best. Loan this to the school library.
- *Letters*—Write letters of thanks, inquiry, persuasion or support. Letters can be mailed to visitors, popular authors, government officials, or the editor of the local newspaper.
- *Magazine*—After reading a nonfiction book or doing research on a topic, create a magazine on the same theme. Send the magazines home to parents or loan them to the school library.
- *Newsletters*—Write a class newsletter or school newspaper. Include reviews of recently read books.
- *Scripts*—After reading a piece of fiction, write a script for a theatrical production of the story. Or write a script for Readers' Theater. Invite friends, family, or other classes to the production.
- *Song lyrics*—Write lyrics to songs, based on book themes or topics. Share the songs with the school music teacher, parents, and friends.
- *Sticker books*—After reading a nonfiction book, collect stickers on the same topic. Paste one sticker on each page, and write a caption for it. Share these books with preschool and kindergarten children.

Literature Circles: Discussion Starter Questions that Focus on Story Elements and Encourage Aesthetic Response

In literature circles, you take a backseat as your students assume more responsibility for their reading. As they meet to discuss their readings, students respond to their reading through discussion. You will participate, but not in the traditional sense of evaluating the students. As a facilitator, you can provide a list of questions to help generate discussion.

Fiction

Questions about the character:
- Why did *(the main character)* act in this manner? What makes you think so?
- What would happen if we put *(the main character)* in another situation, such as _____?
- Are *(the main character's)* actions right? Why or why not?

Questions about the setting:
- Suppose this story took place in another place or time, such as _____. What would happen?
- Tell how the setting in this story reminds you of a place or time in real life.

Questions about the events:
- Which of these events is the funniest/saddest/scariest? Why?
- Tell what you were thinking when _____ happened.

Questions about the resolution:
- How would you have solved the problem differently?
- What lessons were learned by the characters?

Questions about nonfiction:
- What is the author trying to teach you in this selection?
- What is the author's point?
- What have you learned here that you did not know before?
- What new words have you learned? What do they mean?
- What is the most interesting fact in this book? Why?
- What surprised you?
- What did you notice about _____?

Things to do Independently During Guided Reading Time

When working with students in a small group, a big challenge is to keep the rest of the class working independently without interruptions. Following are a number of activities you can incorporate into your classroom management plan.

While working independently during Guided Reading Time, students can:

- Finish reading the selection they started while meeting with their guided reading group.
- Read independently from books in their book bags. At the beginning of each day, all students should fill their book bags with books that they can read on their own.
- Read with a partner from books in "browsing boxes" (Fountas & Pinnell, 1996, p. 58). These are boxes that you fill with books at the appropriate reading levels for each group. You can color code the box and fill it with copies of previously read books.
- Listen to taped readings. Provide tapes of selections that your students have read recently, along with copies of the book. At a listening center, students can reread the book while listening to the tape. You can make these tapes, or invite parents, the principal, or community volunteers to make tapes. Students who are reading fluently can also make tapes. Write in reading journals. At the end of the meeting with each group, give students a response question to answer in their journals.
- Work at the computer to write a story or literature response, send e-mail to penpals, or use literacy-related software.
- Read poetry. You can provide copies of favorite poems in a booklet, poetry anthologies, or word cards, so that students can put together the phrases of the poem and read.
- "Read around the room" (Fountas & Pinnell, 1996, p. 59). This is done with a pointer, which is a dowel rod, chopstick, or ruler. Students use the pointer to read charts on the wall, big books, the word wall, environmental print, language experience charts, and any other print hanging in the classroom.
- Work on Readers' Theater. Students can write scripts or practice reading scripts. (Reader's Theater is explained in Chapter 14.)
- Do word activities. Students can use magnetic letters to spell words, or word cards to make sentences.

A QAR Graphic Organizer: Write Some Questions!

The Question-Answer Relationships strategy can help your students learn to extract important details from their readings. Teaching students these types of questions also helps them generate questions of their own. You can use the graphic organizer on p. 529 to manage this activity. Make a copy of this organizer to hand out to students, or have them create their own chart. As students read a piece of text, have them write one question of each type and identify where the answer can be found.

Reciprocal Teaching

Reciprocal Teaching has been shown to be a valuable reading comprehension strategy. The procedure is:

1. Divide the text into manageable segments. Model the rest of the steps with the first segment of the text, then allow one of the students to switch roles and be the teacher for the second segment. Continue in that manner for each segment, giving each of the students in the group an opportunity to "be the teacher."

Right There	Think and Search	Author and You	On My Own
The answer can be found on a page.	Clues for the answer are in lots of places in the book.	The author gives hints about the answer. Your own ideas help answer it, too.	The answer is in your head. The author does not give you clues.
Question:	Question:	Question:	Question:
The answer is on page ____.	The clues that help find this answer are:	The author's clue is: I already know:	I already know:

2. For each segment, do the following:
   a. Predict—Ask the group to make a prediction about this portion of the text.
   b. Read —Either read this segment of the text to the group, or have them read it silently, depending upon the amount of scaffolding you need to provide.
   c. Question—Ask a question about this segment. Have the group answer the question.
   d. Summarize—Tell or write the main points of the segment.
   e. Clarify—Address confusing terms, unclear ideas, or unanswered questions.
3. This strategy can be done with the whole class, or in cooperative groups. One way to use small groups of four is to give each student a step to be responsible for: Student A asks the question, Student B predicts, Student C summarizes, and Student D clarifies. (All students read each segment.)

Think-Alouds

Similar to mental modeling, the think-aloud strategy helps students regulate their own reading by having them stop periodically and explaining the processes they are using as they read. The procedure is:

1. Select short, manageable text that contains some degree of difficulty for your students, such as some unknown vocabulary, inferences, or ambiguities.
2. Choose one of five reading strategies to teach: making predictions, visualizing, connecting to prior knowledge, self-monitoring, and fix-up strategies.
3. Read the text aloud while the students follow along.
4. Stop at points in the text to think out loud, showing students how you accomplish the reading strategy.

5. After several sessions in which you have modeled the same strategy for your students, give them the chance to try it with a partner. Give each pair a copy of carefully selected text that is on their instructional level and rather short. Narrative poetry, short stories, brief magazine articles, or just a page from a basal selection would work well.
6. Students take turns reading with their partners and stop at agreed-upon stop points. Each student takes a turn thinking aloud, while the other student listens and offers thoughts and feedback. Each student in the pair should get a chance to think aloud. Steps for thinking aloud are:
   a. Say out loud what is going on in my head while I read.
   b. Ask myself, "Does this make sense?"
   Do this several times.
7. When students read independently, give them a checklist to record their strategy use. Have them put a check in the spaces that tell their thought processes as they read.

Checklist for Reading Strategies Learned with Think-Alouds

	Not much at all	A little bit	Lots of times	All the time
Made predictions				
Made pictures in my mind				
Thought about a time this happened to me				
Found a problem in my reading				
Figured out a way to fix the problem				

How to Make a Little Book

Little books can help organize and summarize information briefly and simply. After reading, have students create a skinny book using the following instructions and draw pictures for each of the story elements.

1. Using an $8\frac{1}{2}$" x 11" piece of paper, fold up the bottom to the top horizontally. The bottom will meet the top. Crease your folds as you go.

Fold

2. Fold it in half horizontally again. It will now measure $8\frac{1}{2}$" x $2\frac{3}{4}$".

Fold

3. Fold in half verically, matching the left edges to the right edges. It will measure $4\frac{1}{4}$" x $2\frac{3}{4}$" now.

Fold

4. Open to the half sheet with the folded crease on the bottom. Cut the paper on the center crease to the center fold.

Cut

5. Open the paper. Find the diamond-shaped center. Recrease the edges, then push in the sides to the center.

Push →   ← Push

6. Push in the side edges so that the vertical creases meet in the center to form the spine of the book.

Spine →

← Push

Say It Right Strategy

The Say It Right strategy offers your students excellent practice for working on fluency. By choosing interesting quotations from a book that your students have read, and then selecting some mood words that can be used to read the quotations aloud, your students can learn to read with expression. Quotes from Louis Sachar's *Holes* (1998) and directions for reading with emotion are shown here. You can cut them apart and have the students pull one out of a hat, or assign numbers.

Quotations from *Holes*

1. If you get bitten by a yellow-spotted lizard, you might as well go into the shade of the oak trees and lie in the hammock. There is nothing anyone can do to you anymore.

2. The reader is probably asking, "Why would anyone go to Camp Green Lake?"

3. Camp Green Lake is a camp for bad boys.

4. The judge said, "You may go to jail, or you may go to Camp Green Lake."

5. If you take a bad boy and make him dig a hole everyday in the hot sun, it will turn him into a good boy.

6. It was all because of his no-good-dirty-rotten-pig-stealing-great-great-grandfather!

7. They always seemed to be in the wrong place at the wrong time.

Mood Words

a. Read this as if you were delighted.

b. Read this as if you were wicked.

c. Read this as if you were mournful.

d. Read this as if you were joyful.

e. Read this as if you were worried.

f. Read this as if you were frightened.

g. Read this as if you were depressed.

Literature Selections for Readers' Theater

Books or stories that require little or no adaptation for scripts include the following:

"Alone" by A. Lobel (Reading Rainbow Readers, 2001, p. 4)
"The Bad Kangaroo," from *Fables* (Lobel, 1980, p. 28)
"The Book" by J. Marshall (Reading Rainbow Readers, 2001, p. 48)
"Chicken Licken" (Scieszka, 1992, p. 4)
"Frogs at the Rainbow's End," from *Fables* (Lobel, 1980, p. 14)
"The Stinky Cheese Man" (Scieszka, 1992, p. 48)
"A Summer Day" by J. Rocklin (Reading Rainbow Readers, 2001, p. 54)

Examples of Wonderful Series Books

There are qualities about series books that make them appealing for use with struggling readers—they are predictable and familiar; many are written about topics that are popular with children; they may help prepare struggling readers for more sophisticated reading; they can be used for independent reading time; and they can help readers develop fluency and give them practice with decoding skills in a comfortable setting.

For Primary Readers

Amelia Bedelia (Parish, P.)
Arthur (Brown, M.)
Clifford, the Big Red Dog (Bridwell, N.)
Corduroy (Freeman, D.)
Curious George (Rey, H. A.)
Franklin (Bourgeois, P.)
Frog and Toad (Lobel, A.)
Henry and Mudge (Rylant, C.)

Little Bear (Minarik, E. H.)
Little Critter (Mayer, M.)
Lyle the Crocodile (Waber, B.)
Madeline (Bemelmans, L.)
The Magic Tree House (Osborne, M. P.)
Mister Putter and Tabby (Rylant, C.)
Moonbear (Asch, F.)
Where's Spot? (Hill, E.)

For Transitional and Intermediate Readers

The Agony of Alice (Naylor, P. R.)
Amber Brown (Danziger, P.)
American Girls series
Anastasia (Lowry, L.)
The Babysitter's Club (Martin, A.)
The Bailey School Kids (Dadey, D.)
The Blossoms (Byars, B.)
The Borrowers (Norton, M.)
The Boxcar Children (Warner, G.)
Bunnicula (Howe, J.)
Cam Jansen (Adler, D.)
Encyclopedia Brown (Sobol, D.)
The Hardy Boys (Dixon, F.)
Herculeah Jones Mysteries (Byars, B.)
The Indian in the Cupboard (Banks, L. R.)
The Jigsaw Jones Mysteries (Preller, J.)
Junie B. Jones (Park, B.)

Kids of the Polk Street School (Giff, P. R.)
Little House on the Prairie (Wilder, L. I.)
The Littles (Peterson, J.)
The Magic School Bus (Cole, J.)
Nancy Drew (Keene, C.)
Nate the Great (Sharmat, M.)
Pee Wee Scouts (Delton, J.)
Pippi Longstocking (Lindgren, A.)
Ramona (Cleary, B.)
Ricky Ricotta's Might Robot (Pilkey, D.)
Russell Sprouts (Hurwitz, J.)
Sideways Stories from Wayside School (Sachar, L.)
Skinnybones (Park, B.)
Soup (Peck, R. N.)
Sports-series (Christopher, M.)
The Stories Julian Tells (Cameron, A.)

For Middle School and Adolescent Readers

Anne of Green Gables (Montgomery, L.)
A Series of Unfortunate Events (Snicket, L.)
The "Baseball Card Adventure" series (Gutman, D.)
Dragon of the Lost Sea and sequels (Yep, L.)
Harry Potter series (Rowling, J. K.)
Hatchet and sequels (Paulsen, G.)

MacDonald Hall series (Korman, G.)
The Mennyms and sequels (Waugh, A.)
The Narnia Chronicles (Lewis, C. S.)
Redwall (Jacques, B.)
Sammy Keyes (Van Draanen, W.)

Glossary

Aesthetic Response An emotional response, by the reader, to a piece of literature.

Affective The domain of human thinking that is concerned with feelings and emotions.

Affixed Words Words that contain a prefix, a suffix, or both.

Alternative Assessments Informal assessments that go beyond formal standardized tests and reflect the actual language and literacy behaviors of students.

Anticipation Guide A list of statements about a topic that students must read and then decide, based only on what they know, whether or not they agree with them.

Attitude Surveys Instruments used to determine students' attitudes toward reading and writing.

Auditory Mode The mode of learning in which children listen in order to learn.

Author's Chair Students share their written pieces with each other by sitting in a special chair and reading their writings to the rest of the class.

Automaticity The theory that explains the development of the automatic word recognition of vocabulary for fluency.

Balanced Approach The judicious mix of content and instructional methods when teaching reading.

Basal A commercially produced set of books and materials used for teaching children to read; reading selections are usually vocabulary controlled for grade levels.

Big Book An enlarged version of a piece of children's literature that allows the entire group to see the words and read along.

Brainstorm Students generate lists or webs of ideas related to the topic in the text that they will read.

Cause/Effect Text Structure Authors use this structure when explaining events in history or natural phenomena that happen as a result of other events.

Characters The personalities that carry the action in a story.

Click and Clunk A strategy to help students overcome comprehension difficulties while reading. When students understand what they are reading, this "clicks." A "clunk" occurs when there are words, concepts, or ideas that confuse them. The teacher models what to do with "clunks."

Compacted Curriculum Students who are gifted or who consistently read beyond grade level expectations are permitted to progress through required reading materials such as basal selections at a pace with which they are comfortable.

Comparison Text Structure The author compares two things in order to make a concept clear.

Comprehensive Literacy Instruction Instruction of literacy based on the premise that understanding of the written word is the most important goal; incorporates teaching strategies that use children's literature, address specific reading strategies and skills, and encourage love of reading and writing.

Concrete Experiences The teacher provides manipulative materials and experiences that are related to the text.

Constructivism The idea that learners create new knowledge by connecting what they know to their experiences in an environment that is thought-provoking and engaging.

Content Words Words that have meaning by themselves, such as nouns, verbs, adjectives, and adverbs.

Context Clues Clues to the meaning or pronunciation of an unknown word that are derived from the text itself.

Correct Words Per Minute (CWPM) A measurement of reading fluency specifying the number of words a student reads correctly in one minute; also called *Words Correct Per Minute (WCPM)*.

Covert Responses Thoughts and ideas that are going on in students' heads as they read.

Cueing Systems The ways in which readers translate print into meaning, using syntactic, graphonological, and pragmatic cues.

Culturally Responsive Instruction Instruction in which the teacher aligns teaching methods with students' cultures and values to improve academic learning.

Decodable Text Books that contain only the few words and sentences that beginning readers can decode by putting letters together with sounds.

Decoding The ability to get the intended meaning from the printed page by using the graphic symbols.

Decoding by Analogy Using the patterns of known words to produce the pronunciation of unknown words.

Descriptive Text Structure A structure in which the author simply describes the topic.

Dialogue Journal Responses Responses to literature that are written by two people, usually reading buddies, in the same journal.

Directed Reading Thinking Activity (DRTA) A method of instruction, which can be used with any story read by students, that includes prediction in the process of preparing to read as well as in the process of reading the story.

Double Entry Journals Journals in which parts of the text are listed or copied on one side of the page, and the student's responses to those parts are listed on the opposite side of the page.

Drafting When the reader begins to put ideas down on paper.

Efferent Response A cognitive response to a piece of literature, by the reader, for the purpose of gaining information.

Elkonin Boxes A strategy in which the teacher and students "stretch out" the phonemes of a word, then use a concrete object to represent each one.

Emergent Storybook Readings Pretend reading that consists of a verbal retelling of the text, page by page.

Engagement Perspective An approach to teaching whereby learners are actively involved in their quest to make sense of the printed word.

Environmental Print The everyday print that surrounds us, such as signs.

Explanation Information concerning the desired behavior is outlined in a set of steps or procedures.

Explicit Teaching Direct instruction, by the teacher, to explain, model, demonstrate, and make the skills of literacy clear.

Extrinsic Rewards Rewards that originate outside the learner.

Facilitative Teaching The process by which the teacher enables student understanding by providing materials, tools, and teaching strategies that make it more likely that students will be successful at a given task.

Fiction Literature that is the invention of the author's mind.

Find and Read Students are asked to look for something in a selection that they have already read silently and then are asked to read it aloud.

Fluency The ability to read with proper speed, accuracy, comprehension, and expression.

Formal Assessments Assessments, such as standardized tests, that are created by commercial testing companies or state educational agencies, and compare students' performance on a variety of literacy skills to the performance of students in the same grade level across the country.

Function Words Words that serve a function in a sentence, such as to indicate a certain subject or number, a state of being, or the position of a thing.

Grapheme The written representation of sounds in words.

Graphophonological Cues Visual and sound cues, based on letters, that help the reader determine the pronunciation of a word in print.

Guided Reading A method of teaching reading to small groups of children who read from text that is chosen by the teacher and is at their instructional level.

Hink Pinks A strategy that gives students practice in combining onsets and rimes.

Inclusion The Disabilities Education Act mandates that children with disabilities be provided with an appropriate education in public schools, alongside their peers who are not disabled.

Inferring The process of gleaning meaning from text in which the author does not reveal all of the information in an explicit manner.

Inflected Word A word with an affix that does not change its meaning; instead, its plurality, tense, or degree is altered.

Informal Measures Collections of student data gathered from anecdotal notes, from observations, reading and writing strategies checklists, samples of student writing for portfolios, interest inventories, running records of oral reading, decoding checks, concept of print observations, and many others. Assessments such as these are not standardized, and are generally created by the teacher and give an in-depth look at specific objectives that the teacher has taught on an ongoing basis.

Informal Reading Inventory An assessment tool that consists of a set of graded passages that students read aloud, while the teacher records errors. Based on the number of words recognized, as well as the number of correctly answered questions, the teacher determines each student's level for instruction or independent reading.

Informal Writing Students write for the purpose of responding to literature. Student writings can be shared with others, but the end product does not necessarily need to be in published form.

Interactive Writing The teacher and students share the pen to write a brief message.

Interest Inventory An instrument used to determine the interests that students have.

Interest Words Words that are part of children's environment, play, and everyday lives.

Intrinsic Motivation Motivation that originates from a desire within the learner.

Invented Spellings Children's spellings that closely approximate the real word, using some of the letters that should be in a correct spelling, but not all of them.

Keyword Method A strategy in which students use a keyword and picture to associate with the target word in order to remember the target word.

Kidwatching An approach to assessment in which teachers watch their students carefully, making notes and conducting quick, informal assessments to determine the strengths and needs of each student.

Kinesthetic Modality The mode of learning in which children use their bodies or sense of touch to remember things.

KWL A strategy in which students list things they already know about the topic, and things that they would like to find out before reading. After reading, students explain what they learned.

Language Experience Approach A strategy that gives students the opportunity to dictate or help write a story or narrative about a common experience.

Language Experience Text The written story or narrative that was dictated by students.

Learning Modalities/Learning Styles The ways in which learners learn best, either by visual, auditory, or kinesthetic means.

Leveled Books A collection of books organized by levels of difficulty from the easy books of the emergent reader to the more difficult books of the advanced reader.

Literature Circles Students, reading the same piece of self-selected literature, join in small group discussions about their responses to that piece of literature. Each student is assigned a specific role in the group.

Little Book Small books made from a single sheet of paper.

Making Words A strategy in which students manipulate rimes and onsets to make words.

Mental Modeling The teaching behavior by which teachers make their cognitive activity explicit by verbalizing their thought processes.

Metacognition The ability of students to monitor their thinking while reading.

Metalinguistic Awareness The understanding of the ways that we talk about our language.

Miscue Anything a reader says that is different from what is printed on the page.

Miscue Analysis An assessment based on a student's oral reading. The teacher records errors, and determines trends and consistencies in the student's reading behavior by analyzing miscues.

Multiple Intelligences Gardner's (1999) categories of human capabilities: linguistic intelligence, musical intelligence, interpersonal intelligence, logical-mathematical intelligence, spatial intelligence, body-kinesthetic intelligence, intrapersonal intelligence, and naturalist intelligence, and possibly existential intelligence.

New Literacies Include the reading and writing skills, strategies, and insights necessary to gather the most pertinent information from rapidly changing communication technologies of today's world.

Nonfiction Literature that gives factual information about persons, places, and things.

Onset The first consonant phoneme of a word or syllable, or the part of the word or syllable that precedes the vowel.

Overt Responses Written, verbal, artistic, dramatic or graphic responses by readers that show evidence of their thoughts.

Partner Reading A strategy used with beginning readers in the primary grades in which students are paired with compatible reading buddies that are close in ability to read a book together.

Phoneme The smallest unit of sound in spoken language.

Phonemic Awareness The ability to manipulate sounds without any knowledge of letters.

Phonics The relationship between letters and the sounds that they represent in written language.

Phonological Awareness The ability to think about and verbalize sensitivity to the sounds of our language, including words that rhyme, counting syllables in a word, or separating the beginning of a word from its ending.

Picture Walk A strategy in which the teacher selects important pictures from the story to show to the children before they read or listen to the story.

Plot The action, conflict, and excitement the characters go through to solve a problem.

Point of View Entry Students assume the role of one of the characters in a story, and describe in their journal what happened to them as well as their reactions to the events.

Pragmatic Cues Cues that readers get from their social environment.

Predictable Books Patterned books that often use repeated phrases and rhyme.

Prefix A word part that is attached to the beginning of a word and alters its meaning.

Pretend Reading A verbal retelling of the text, page by page.

Probing The teacher asks additional questions that help to improve students' original response.

Problem/Solution Text Structure Authors use this structure when explaining a nonfiction event that is a problem and the eventual resolution of the problem.

Process Approach A method of teaching writing that mirrors the way professional authors write.

Process Modifications Activities and questions that require higher levels of thought, that are designed so that gifted students can do them independently.

Prop Stories Children act out their favorite stories using classroom props.

Prosody The ability to make the print sound natural by reading expressively using appropriate phrasing, tone, and pitch.

Publish Students share their final copies with their intended audience.

Question-Answer Relationships A strategy that helps children sort out the four types of questions that are asked of them and determine the source of information that would help them with the answer.

Question the Author This strategy helps students overcome some of the mystery of their textbook by talking about it in terms of its author, which truly allows for students to actively transact with the text.

Quotation Sharing Students pick out meaningful, interesting, funny, sad, and moving quotes as a way to respond to literature.

Readability A formula or graph that determines the approximate grade level of reading materials, based on word length and number of sentences.

Read and Relax A silent reading activity for building fluency and comprehension in which students read text that is easy enough for them to read quickly and comfortably.

Reader Responses The ways a teacher asks students to think about and show their reactions to what they have read.

Reading Strategy A specialized set of procedures that readers use to facilitate their understanding of text.

Reading Workshop A method of teaching reading with literature in which the teacher sets aside time for independent reading of quality children's books, along with opportunities for students to respond to their reading through journals and conferences with the teacher.

Reciprocal Teaching This strategy shows students how to use four processes involved with constructing meaning: predicting, questioning, summarizing, and clarifying.

Recitation The typical pattern of interaction in classrooms where the teacher questions, the students respond, and the teacher gives feedback.

Rehearsal The phase in which students prepare to write and think of topics for their writing.

Repeated Readings The strategy in which students are asked to reread a short, meaningful passage several times until a satisfactory level of fluency is reached.

Rereadings Frequent rereading of a familiar book.

Resolution The place in a story where the problem is solved.

Response Journal A type of journal in which students write about anything that they have read.

Retelling Analysis An informal assessment in which students tell what they remember from the reading. This gives the teacher insight on students' comprehension of the text, ability to sequence the details, and ability to include all the story elements or main ideas of the text.

Revision Any change in a written text whether it be large or small, form or substance, minor or major.

Rime The vowel and any consonants that follow the first consonant phoneme in a word or syllable.

Root Word The word to which one or more affixes has been added.

Round Robin Reading A classroom reading practice in which each student in the group is asked to read part of the text aloud while the others read along silently.

Running Record An assessment tool designed to assess text difficulty for the student, as well as to give the teacher information about her oral reading behaviors, which aids in making instructional decisions.

Say Something An interactive, verbal activity that provides scaffold while children read. While reading, students stop at stop points and share their thoughts with each other.

Scaffolded Instruction Any instructional tool or technique that a teacher uses to enable students' literacy efforts.

Scaffolds Instructional supports that help students accomplish a learning task.

Schema Theory The theory states that the background knowledge, or what the reader brings to the page, is just as important as what is printed on the page.

Schemata Concepts that the reader has in his/her mind, including knowledge of the way print works, knowledge

of life in general, ideas, memories of experiences, and opinions.

Self-regulation Abilities A reader's ability to apply reading strategies when comprehension breaks down, such as reading more carefully or rereading the hard parts of the text.

Semantic Cues Meaning cues that readers get from a composite of the print, pictures, and content of the whole text.

Sequential Text Structure The author uses sequence when explaining events in time or the order of events in a procedure.

Setting The place and time in which a story occurs.

Shared Book Experience A strategy teachers use to give a group of children support as they learn to read text, usually done with big books.

Shared Reading Teachers support students' reading by decoding the words for them while they listen and read along where possible.

Sight Words Words that are instantly recognized by the reader.

Sketch to Stretch Students draw their interpretations of a story or an event in the story.

Sound Charts Charts teachers hang in their classrooms that show the phonics elements that they want their students to remember.

Stance The manner in which a student approaches a piece of text, or the way in which he mentally prepares to read.

Storyboards A strategy that capitalizes on the use of pictures to make predictions, and reinforces the process of putting events in sequential order.

Student-generated Questions Questions that students create while reading that can aid comprehension.

Subvocalizations Mentally pronouncing difficult words to aid in comprehension while reading silently.

Suffix The word part that is attached to the end of a word and alters its meaning.

Syntactic Cues Structure or grammar cues that help the reader make predictions based on what makes sense in the English language.

Talk Story-Like Students are allowed to use the kind of interactions that they use at home when discussing a piece of literature.

Tape, Check, Chart A strategy that allows students to assess their own accuracy when reading orally by taping their reading and then checking for miscues.

Teaching Strategy A set of consistent teaching behaviors that the teacher uses to help students accomplish a task or objective.

Temporary Spellings Children's spellings that closely approximate the real word, using some of the letters that should be in a correct spelling, but not all of them.

Terse Verse A strategy that gives students practice in combining onsets and rimes.

Theme The author's purpose for writing a story.

Theory An explanation, based on thought and observation, about how the reading process takes place.

Think-Aloud A strategy that requires a reader to stop periodically, reflect on how a text is being processed and understood, and relate orally what reading strategies are being employed.

Transactional (Reader Response) Theory The ways in which readers transact, or become involved with the text, constantly thinking about how the author's words relate to them personally.

Typographical Signals The graphic signals authors use to clarify their writing.

Using Words You Know A strategy that useful for teaching patterns in words by helping students spell and read new words, based on known words.

Visual Imagery The ability to visualize or make mental pictures while reading various types of text.

Visual Mode The mode of learning in which children can see the topic being taught, in many different forms.

Ways to Linger The teacher lists ways for students to reflect, in written form, on the book after reading it.

Word Banks Students' personal word collections.

Wordless Picture Books Children's picture books that contain no written text.

Word Wall A large space on the wall in the classroom, on which the teacher hangs word cards.

Word Sort A strategy, in which, the teacher asks students to find words in a story or basal selection. Once students find the words and write them on cards, they must sort them according to the way they sound.

Workshop Approaches Literature-based methods of helping students, in social settings, read and write about works of fiction and nonfiction.

Writing Aloud A strategy in which the teacher shows students how to write by thinking out loud and verbalizing the mental processes involved in completing a task.

Writing Process Approach Students use the five stages of the writing process to write both formally and informally, for authentic purposes and real audiences.

Zone of Proximal Development The level at which optimal learning occurs.

References

Adams, M. J. (1990). *Beginning to read: Thinking and learning about print*. Cambridge, MA: MIT Press.

Adams, M. J. (2004). Modeling the connections between word recognition and reading. In R. Ruddell & N. Unrau (Eds.), *Theoretical models and processes of reading* (5th ed., pp. 1219–1243). Newark, DE: International Reading Association.

Adams, M., & Bruce, B. (1982). Background knowledge and reading comprehension. In J. Langer & T. Smith-Burke (Eds.), *Reader meets author: Bridging the gap* (pp. 2–25). Newark, DE: International Reading Association.

Allen, R. V., & Allen, C. (1967). *Language experiences in reading*. Chicago: Encyclopedia Britannica Press.

Alexander, P. A. & Jetton, T. L. (2000). Learning from text: A multidimensional and developmental perspective. In M. Kamil, P. Mosenthal, P. D. Pearson, & R. Barr (Eds.), *Handbook of reading research* (Vol. 3, pp. 285–310). Mahwah, NJ: Erlbaum.

Allington, R. (1980). Teacher interruption behaviors during primary grade oral reading. *Journal of Educational Psychology, 72*(3), 371–372.

Allington, R. (2001). *What really matters for struggling readers: Designing research-based programs*. New York: Longman.

Allington, R. (2002). Research on reading/learning disability interventions. In A. Farstrup & S. J. Samuels (Eds.), *What research has to say about reading instruction* (3rd ed., pp. 261–290), Newark, DE: International Reading Association.

Allington, R. (2005, June/July). The other five "pillars" of effective reading instruction. *Reading Today, 22*(6), 3.

Allington, R., & Cunningham, P. (2002). *Schools that work: Where all children read and write*. Boston: Allyn & Bacon.

Allington, R., & McGill-Franzen, A. (2004). Looking back, looking forward: A conversation about teaching reading in the 21st century. In R. Ruddell & N. Unrau. (Eds.), *Theoretical models and processes of reading* (5th ed., pp. 5–32). Newark, DE: International Reading Association.

Alvermann, D., Moon, J., & Hagood, M. (1999). *Popular culture in the classroom: Teaching and researching critical media literacy*. Newark, DE: International Reading Association.

Anderson, C. (2000). Sustained silent reading: Try it, you'll like it! *The Reading Teacher, 54*(3), 258–259.

Anderson, R. C. (2004). Role of the reader's schema in comprehension, learning, and memory. In R. Ruddell & N. Unrau. (Eds.), *Theoretical models and processes of reading* (5th ed., pp. 594–606). Newark, DE: International Reading Association.

Anderson, R. C., & Biddle, W. B. (1975). On asking people questions about what they are reading. In G. H. Bower (Ed.), *The psychology of learning and motivation* (Vol. 9, pp. 9–129). New York: Academic Press.

Anderson, R. C., & Pearson, P. D. (1984). A schema-theoretic view of basic processes in reading comprehension. In P. D. Pearson (Ed.), *Handbook of reading research* (pp. 255–291). New York: Longman.

Anderson, R., Heibert, E., Scott, J., & Wilkinson, I. (1985). *Becoming a nation of readers: The report on the Commission on Reading*. Washington, D.C.: The National Institute of Education.

Applebee, A. (1978). *The child's concept of story: Ages two to seventeen*. Chicago: University of Chicago Press.

Applegate, A., & Applegate, M. D. (2004). The Peter effect: Reading habits and attitudes of preservice teachers. *The Reading Teacher, 57*(6), 554–563.

Ariza, E. (2002a). Nonverbal communication. In H. Zainuddin, N. Yahya, C. Morales-Jones, & E. Ariza (Eds.), *Fundamentals of teaching English to speakers of other languages in K–12 mainstream classrooms* (pp. 48–55). Dubuque, Iowa: Kendall/Hunt.

Ariza, E. (2002b). A rainbow of children: A sampler of cultural characteristics. In H. Zainuddin, N. Yahya, C. Morales-Jones, & E. Ariza (Eds.), *Fundamentals of teaching English to speakers of other languages in K-12 mainstream classrooms* (pp. 457–478). Dubuque, Iowa: Kendall/Hunt.

Armbruster, B., & Osborn, J. (2002). *Reading instruction and assessment: Understanding the IRA standards*. Boston: Allyn & Bacon.

Armbruster, B., Anderson, T., & Ostertag, J. (1987). Does text structure/summarization instruction facilitate learning from expository text? *Reading Research Quarterly, 22*(3), 331–346.

Ashton-Warner, S. (1963). *Teacher*. New York: Simon & Schuster.

Atwell, N. (1987). *In the middle: Writing, reading, and learning with adolescents*. Portsmouth; NH: Boynton/Cook.

Atwell, N. (1998). *In the middle: Writing, reading, and learning with adolescents* (2nd ed.). Portsmouth, NH: Boynton/Cook.

Au, K. H. (1993). *Literacy instruction in multicultural settings*. Fort Worth, TX: Harcourt Brace Jovanovich.

Au, K. H. (1998). Social constructivism and the school literacy learning of students of diverse backgrounds. *Journal of Literacy Research, 30*(2), 297–319.

Au, K. H. (2000). A multicultural perspective on policies for improving literacy achievement: Equity and excellence. In M. Kamil, P. Mosenthal, P. D. Pearson, & R. Barr (Eds.), *Handbook of reading research, Vol. 3,* (pp. 835–851). Mahwah, NJ: Erlbaum.

Au, K. H. (2002). Multicultural factors and the effective instruction of students of diverse backgrounds. In A. Farstrup & S. J. Samuels (Eds.), *What research has to say about reading instruction* (3rd ed., pp. 392–413). Newark, DE: International Reading Association.

Au, K., Carroll, J., & Scheu, J. (1997). *Balanced literacy instruction: A teacher's resource book*. Norwood, MA: Christopher-Gordon.

Austin, G., Rogers, B., & Walbesser, H. (1972). The effectiveness of compensatory education: A review of the research. *Review of Educational Research, 42*, 171–182.

Avila, E., & Sadoski, M. (1996). Exploring new applications of the keyword method to acquire English vocabulary. *Language Learning, 46*(3), 379–395.

Baker, L. (2002). Metacognition in comprehension instruction. In C. Block (Ed.), *Comprehension instruction: Research-based best practices* (pp. 77–95). New York: Guilford.

Baker, L., & Brown, A. (1984). Metacognitive skills and reading. In P. D. Pearson, M. Kamil, R. Barr, & P. Mosenthal (Eds.), *Handbook of reading research* (Vol. 1, pp. 353–394). New York: Longman.

Bamberger, H., & Hughes, P. (1995). *Super graphs, Venns, and glyphs*. New York: Scholastic.

Baumann, J. (1986). *Teaching main idea comprehension*. Newark, DE: International Reading Association.

Baumann, J., Jones, L., & Seifert-Kessell, N. (1993). Using think-alouds to enhance children's comprehension monitoring abilities. *The Reading Teacher, 47*(3), 184–193.

Beck, I. L. (1989). Improving practice through understanding reading. In L. Resnick & L. Klopfer (Eds.), *Toward the thinking curriculum: Current cognitive research* (1989 ASCD yearbook, pp. 40–58). Alexandria, VA: Association for Supervision and Curriculum Development.

Beck, I. L., & Juel, C. (1992). The role of decoding in learning to read. In J. Samuels & A. Farstrup (Eds.), *What research has to say about reading instruction* (2nd ed., pp. 101–123). Newark, DE: International Reading Association.

Beck, I. L., & McKeown, M. G. (1981). Developing questions that promote comprehension: The story map. *Language Arts, 58*(8), 913–918.

Beck, I. L., & McKeown, M. G. (2001). Text talk: Capturing the benefits of read-aloud experiences for young children. *The Reading Teacher, 55*(1), 10–20.

Beck, I., McKeown, M., Hamilton, R., & Kucan, L. (1997). *Questioning the author: An Approach for enhancing student engagement with text*. Newark, DE: International Reading Association.

Berent, I., & Perfetti, C. (1995). A rose is a REEZ: The two-cycles model of phonology assembly in reading English. *Psychological Review, 102*(1), 146–184.

Bergman, J. (1992). SAIL: A way to success and independence for low-achieving readers. *The Reading Teacher, 45*(8), 598–602.

Bishop, R. (1997). Selecting literature for a multicultural curriculum. In V. Harris (Ed.), *Using multiethnic literature in the k-8 classroom* (pp. 1–20). Norwood, Massachusetts: Christopher-Gordon.

Bissex, G. (1980). *Gnys at wrk: A child learns to write and read*. Cambridge, MA: Harvard University Press.

Blachowicz, C. (1986). Making connections: Alternatives to the vocabulary notebook. *Journal of Reading, 29*(7), 643–649.

Boehm, R., Hoone, C., McGowan, T., McKinney-Browning, M., & Miramontes, O. (1997). Communities are built near resources. In *Living in our world* (pp.106–110). Orlando, FL: Harcourt Brace.

Bolter, J. (1991). *Writing space: The computer, hypertext, and the history of writing*. Hillsdale, NJ: Erlbaum.

Bormuth, J. R. (1968). The cloze readability procedure. *Elementary English, 45*, 429–436.

Bottomley, D., Henk, W., & Melnick, S. (1997/1998). Assessing children's views about themselves as writers using the Writer Self-Perception Scale. *The Reading Teacher, 51*(4), 286–296.

Bridge, C., Winograd, P., & Haley, D. (1983). Using predictable materials vs. preprimers to teach beginning sight words. *The Reading Teacher, 36*, 884-891.

Brown, A., Palincsar, N., & Armbruster, B. (2004). Instructing comprehension-fostering activities in interactive learning situations. In R. Ruddell & N. Unrau (Eds.), *Theoretical models and processes of reading* (5th ed., pp. 780–809). Newark, DE: International Reading Association.

Brown, K. (2003). What do I say when they get stuck on a word? Aligning teachers' prompts with students' development. *The Reading Teacher, 56*(8), 720–733.

Brozo, W. (2002). *To be a boy, to be a reader: Engaging teen and preteen boys in active literacy*. Newark, DE: International Reading Association.

Bruner, J. (1986). *Actual minds, possible worlds*. Cambridge, MA: Harvard University Press.

Bryan, J. (1998). K-W-W-L: Questioning the known. *The Reading Teacher, 51*(7), 618–620.

Bryan, J. (1999). Readers' workshop in a kindergarten classroom. *The Reading Teacher, 52*(5), 538–540.

Bunting, C. (1988, March). Cooperating teachers and the changing views of teacher candidates. *Journal of Teacher Education, 39*(2), 42–46.

Burns, P., & Roe, B. (2002). *Informal reading inventory: Preprimer to twelfth grade* (6th ed.). Boston: Houghton Mifflin.

Bus, A. (2002). Joint caregiver-child storybook reading: A route to literacy development. In S. Neuman & D. Dickinson (Eds.), *Handbook of early literacy research* (pp. 179–191). New York: Guilford.

Button, K., Johnson, M., & Furgerson, P. (1996). Interactive writing in a primary classroom. *The Reading Teacher, 49*(6), 446–454.

California Department of Education. (1998). *English-language arts content standards for California public schools, kindergarten through grade twelve*. Retrieved December 2, 2004, from http://www.cde.ca.gov/re/pn/fd/documents/english-language-arts.pdf

Calkins, L. (1994). *The art of teaching writing*. Portsmouth, NH: Heinemann.

Calkins, L. (2001). *The art of teaching reading*. New York: Longman.

Calkins, L., Montgomery, K., Santman, D., & Falk, B. (1998). *A teacher's guide to standardized reading tests*. Portsmouth, NH: Heinemann.

Cambourne, B. (2001). Why do some students fail to learn to read? Ockham's razor and the conditions of learning. *The Reading Teacher, 54*(8), 784–786.

Cambourne, B. (2002). Holistic, integrated approaches to reading and language arts instruction: The constructivist framework of an instructional theory. In A. Farstrup & S. J. Samuels (Eds.), *What research has to say about reading instruction* (3rd ed., pp. 25–47). Newark, DE: International Reading Association.

Campbell, D., & Harris, L. (2001). *Collaborative theme building: How teachers write integrated curriculum*. Needham Heights, MA: Allyn & Bacon.

Campbell, D., Cignetti, P., Melenyzer, B., Nettles, D., & Wyman, R. (2004). *How to develop a professional portfolio: A manual for teachers* (3rd ed.). Boston: Allyn & Bacon.

Carroll, M. (2004). *Cartwheels on the keyboard: Computer-based literacy instruction in an elementary classroom*. Newark, DE: International Reading Association.

Carbo, M. (1988). The evidence supporting reading styles: A response to Stahl. *Phi Delta Kappan, 70*(4), 323–327.

Center for Applied Linguistics. (1997). Policy statement of the TESOL board on African American Vernacular English. Retrieved November 29, 2004, from http://www.cal.org/ebonics/tesolebo.html

Center for the Improvement of Early Reading Instruction. (2004). Improving reading comprehension of America's children: 10 research-based principles. In R. Robinson, M. McKenna, & J. Wedman, *Issues and trends in literacy education* (3rd ed., pp. 128–132). Boston: Pearson/Allyn & Bacon.

Chall, J. (1983). *Stages of reading development*. New York: McGraw-Hill.

Chall, J. (1989). Learning to read: The great debate twenty years later. A response to "Debunking the great phonics myth." *Phi Delta Kappan, 70*(7), 521–538.

Chall, J. (1996). *Learning to read: The great debate* (Rev. ed., with a new foreword). New York: McGraw-Hill.

Chall, J., & Dale, E. (1995). *Manual for the new Dale-Chall readability formula*. Cambridge, MA: Brookline Books.

Chomsky, C. (1971). Write first, read later. *Childhood Education, 47*(6), 296–299.

Clark, L. K. (1988). Invented versus traditional spelling in first graders' writings: Effects on learning to spell and read. *Research in the Teaching of English, 22*(3), 281–309.

Clark, R. P. (1987). *Free to write: A journalist teaches young writers*. Portsmouth, NH: Heinemann.

Clay, M. (1972). *Sand: The concept about print test*. Auckland, New Zealand: Heinemann.

Clay, M. (1979). *The early detection of reading difficulties*. Auckland, New Zealand: Heinemann.

Clay, M. (1979). *Stones: The concept about print test*. Auckland, New Zealand: Heinemann.

Clay, M. (1985). *The early detection of reading difficulties* (3rd ed.). Portsmouth, NH: Heinemann.

Clay, M. (1989). Concepts about print in English and other languages. *The Reading Teacher, 42*(4), 268–276.

Clay, M. (1991). *Becoming literate: The construction of inner control*. Birkenhead, Auckland, New Zealand: Heinemann.

Clay, M. (1993). *An observation survey of early literacy achievement*. Portsmouth, NH: Heinemann.

Clay, M. (2000). *Running records for classroom teachers*. Portsmouth, NH: Heinemann.

Clotfelter, C. (2001). Are whites still "fleeing"? Racial patterns and enrollment shifts in urban public schools, 1987–1996. *Journal of Policy Analysis and Management, 20*, 199–221.

Clymer, T. (1963). The utility of phonic generalizations in the primary grades. *The Reading Teacher, 16*, 252–258.

Clymer, T. (1996). The utility of phonic generalizations in the primary grades (RT Classics). *The Reading Teacher, 50*(3), 182–187.

Cole, G. (1998). Reading lessons: The debate over literacy. New York: Hill and Wang.

Collier, V. (1987). Age and rate of acquisition of second language for academic purposes. *TESOL Quarterly, 21*, 617–641.

Compton-Lilly, C. (2003). *Reading families: The literate lives of urban children and their families*. New York: Teachers College Press.

Cooper, J. D. (2003). *Literacy: Helping children construct meaning* (5th ed.). Boston: Houghton Mifflin.

Cooter, R., Mills-House, E., Marrin, P., Mathews, B., Campbell, S., & Baker, T. (1999). Family and community involvement: The bedrock of reading success. *The Reading Teacher, 52*(8), 891–896.

Corson, D. (1995). *Using English words*. Dordrecht, The Netherlands: Kluwer.

Coté, N., & Goldman, S. (2004). Building representations of informational text: Evidence from children's think-aloud protocols. In R. Ruddell & N. Unrau (Eds.), *Theoretical models and processes of reading* (5th ed, pp. 660–681). Newark, DE: International Reading Association.

Cox, C. (1999). *Teaching language arts: A student- and response-centered approach* (3rd. ed.). Boston: Allyn & Bacon.

Cox, B., Fang, Z., & Otto, B. (2004). Preschoolers' developing ownership of the literate register. In R. Ruddell & N. Unrau (Eds.), *Theoretical models and processes of reading* (5th ed., pp. 281–312). Newark, DE: International Reading Association.

Cramer, R. L. (2001). *Creative power: The nature and nurture of children's writing*. New York: Longman.

Crawford, A. (1993). Literature, integrated language arts, and the language minority child: A focus on meaning. In A. Carrasquillo & C. Hedley (Eds.), *Whole language and the bilingual learner* (pp. 61–75). Norwood, NJ: Ablex.

Crawford, A. (2004). Strategies for teaching reading and writing to English language learners. In J. Gillet, C. Temple, & A. Crawford, *Understanding reading problems* (6th ed., pp. 398–434). Boston: Allyn & Bacon.

Cummins, J. (1994). The acquisition of English as a second language. In K. Spangenberg-Urbschat & R. Pritchard

(Eds.), *Kids come in all languages: Reading instruction for ESL students* (pp. 36–62). Newark, DE: International Reading Association.

Cunningham, P. (2005). *Phonics they use* (4th ed.). Boston: Pearson/Allyn & Bacon.

Cunningham, P., & Allington, R. (2002). *Classrooms that work: They can all read and write*. New York: Longman.

Cunningham, P., & Cunningham, J. (1992). Making words: Enhancing the invented spelling-decoding connection. *The Reading Teacher, 46*(2), 106–115.

Cunningham, P., & Cunningham, J. (2002). What we know about how to teach phonics. In A. Farstup & S. J. Samuels (Eds.), *What research has to say about reading instruction* (3rd ed., pp. 87–109). Newark, DE: International Reading Association.

Cunningham, P., Hall, D., & Cunningham, J. (2000). *Guided reading the Four Blocks way*. Greensboro, NC: Carson-Dellosa.

Cunningham, P., Hall, D., & Defee, M. (1991). Nonability grouped, multilevel instruction: A year in a first grade classroom. *The Reading Teacher, 44*(8), 566–571.

Cunningham, P., Hall, D., & Defee, M. (1998). Nonability-grouped multilevel instruction: Eight years later. *The Reading Teacher, 51*(8), 652–664.

Cunningham, P., Moore, S., Cunningham, J., & Moore, D. (2000). *Reading and writing in elementary classrooms* (4th ed.). New York: Longman.

Dahl, K. L., Scharer, P., Lawson, L., & Grogan, P. (1999). Phonics instruction and student achievement in whole language first grade classrooms. *Reading Research Quarterly, 34*(3), 312–341.

Daniels, H. (2002). *Literature circles: Voices and choice in book clubs and reading groups*. Portland, ME: Stenhouse.

Davey, B. (1983). Think-aloud: Modeling the cognitive processes of reading comprehension. *Journal of Reading, 27*(1), 44–47.

Davey, B., & McBride, S. (1986). Effects of question-generation training on reading Comprehension. *Journal of Educational Psychology, 78*, 256–262.

DeFord, D. (1980). Young children and their writing. *Theory into Practice, 19*(3), 157–162.

DeFord, D., Lyons, C., & Pinnell, G. (1991). *Bridges to literacy: Learning from Reading Recovery*. Portsmouth, NH: Heinemann.

Delpit, L. (1988). The silenced dialogue: Power and pedagogy in educating other people's children. *Harvard Educational Review, 58*(3), 280–298.

Delpit, L. (1995). *Other people's children: Cultural conflict in the classroom*. New York: New Press.

Dewitz, B., Carr, E., & Patberg, J. P. (1987). Effects of inference training on comprehension and comprehension monitoring. *Reading Research Quarterly, 22*(1), 99–122.

Dixon, C., & Nessel, D. (1983). *Language experience approach to reading and writing: Language-experience reading for second language learners*. Hayward, CA: Alemany Press.

Dixon-Krauss, L., (1996). *Vygotsky in the classroom: Mediated literacy instruction and assessment*. White Plains, NY: Longman.

Dodge, B. (1995, February). Some thoughts about webquests. Retrieved May 14, 2005, from http://webquest.sdsu.edu/about_webquests.html

Dodge, B. (1998, February). The Webquest page. Retrieved May 14, 2005, from http://webquest.sdsu.edu/.

Donovan, C., & Smolkin, L. B. (2002). Considering genre, content, and visual features in the selection of tradebooks for science instruction. *The Reading Teacher, 55*(6), 502–520.

Dooley, C. (1993). The challenge: Meeting the needs of gifted readers. *The Reading Teacher, 46*(7), 546–551.

Doyle, W. (1986). Classroom organization and management. In M. Wittrock (Ed.), *Handbook of research on teaching* (3rd ed., pp. 392–431). New York: MacMillan.

Dreher, M. J. (2002). Children searching and using informational text. In C. Block & M. Pressely (Eds.), *Comprehension instruction: Research-based best practices*, (pp. 289–304). New York: Guilford.

Dreher, M. J. (2002–2003). Motivating teachers to read. *The Reading Teacher. 56*(4), 338–340.

Drucker, M. J. (2003). What reading teachers should know about ESL learners. *The Reading Teacher, 57*(1), pp. 22–29.

Duffy, G. (2002). The case for direct explanation of strategies. In C. C. Block & M. Pressley (Eds.), *Comprehension instruction: Research-based best practices* (pp. 28–41). New York: Guilford .

Duffy, G. (2003). *Explaining reading: A resource for teaching concepts, skills, and strategies*. New York: Guilford.

Duffy, G., Roehler, L., & Herrmann, B. A. (1998). Modeling mental process helps poor readers become strategic readers. In R. Allington (Ed.), *Teaching struggling readers: Articles from the Reading Teacher* (pp. 162–167). Newark, DE: International Reading Association.

Duke, N., & Pearson, P. D. (2002). Effective practices for developing reading comprehension. In A. Farstrup & S. Samuels (Eds.), *What research has to say about reading instruction* (3rd ed., pp. 205–242). Newark, DE: International Reading Association.

Dunn, R. (1988). Teaching students through their perceptual strengths or preferences. *Journal of Reading, 31*(4), 304–309.

Durkin, D. (1966). *Children who read early*. New York: Teachers College Press.

Durkin, D. (1978–1979). What classroom observations reveal about reading comprehension instruction. *Reading Research Quarterly, 14*(4), 481–533.

Durkin, D. (1993). *Teaching them to read* (6th ed.). Boston: Allyn & Bacon.

Eccles, J. (1983). Expectancies, values, and academic behaviors. In J. T. Spence (Ed.), *Achievement and achievement motives* (pp. 75–146). San Francisco, CA: Freeman.

Eeds, M. A., & Peterson, R. (1991). Teacher as curator: Learning to talk about literature. *The Reading Teacher, 45*(2), 118–126.

Ehri, L. (1994). Development of the ability to read words: Update. In R. Ruddell, M. Ruddell, & H. Singer (Eds.), *Theoretical models and processes of reading* (4th ed., pp. 323– 358). Newark, DE: International Reading Association.

Ehri, L., & McCormick, S. (2004). Phases of word learning: Implications for instruction with delayed and disabled readers. In R. Ruddell & B. Unrau (Eds.), *Theoretical models and processes of reading* (5th ed., pp. 365–389). Newark, DE: International Reading Association.

Ehri, L., & Nunes, S. (2002). The role of phonemic awareness in learning to read. In A. Farstrup & S. J. Samuels (Eds.), *What research has to say about reading instruction* (3rd ed., pp. 110–139.). Newark, DE: International Reading Association.

Eldredge, J. L. (1999). *Phonics for teachers: Self-instruction, methods, and activities.* Upper Saddle River, NJ: Merrill.

Elmore, R., & Rothman, R. (Eds.). (1999). *Testing, teaching, and learning: A guide for states and school districts.* Washington, D.C.: National Research Council. Available online www.nap.du

Epstein, M. (2002). The emergence of conventional writing. New York: New York City Board of Education. (ERIC Document Reproduction Service No. ED464121)

Feng, J. (1994). *Asian-American children: What teachers should know.* Retrieved December 18, 2004, from University of Illinois at Urbana-Champaign College of Education Early Childhood and Parenting Collaborative Archive of ERCI/EECE Digest Web site: http://ceep.crc.uicu.edu/eecearchive/digests/1994/feng94.html

Fillmore, L. W. (2004). Loss of family languages: Should educators be concerned? In R. Robinson, M. McKenna, & J. Wedman (Eds.), *Issues and trends in literacy education* (3rd ed., pp. 73–87). Boston: Pearson Education.

Fitzgerald, J., & Spiegel, D. L. (1983). Enhancing children's reading comprehension through instruction in narrative structure. *Journal of Reading Behavior, 15,* 1–17.

Flack, J. (2000). The gifted reader in the regular classroom: Strategies for success. In J. Smutny (Ed.), *Illinois Association for Gifted Children Journal: Theme Issue* (pp. 22–29). Palatine, IL: Illinois Association for Gifted Children (ERIC Reproduction Service No. ED453625).

Flores, B., Cousin, P., & Díaz, E. (1998). Transforming deficit myths about learning, language, and culture. In M. Opitz (Ed.), *Literacy instruction for culturally and linguistically diverse students: A collection of articles and commentaries.* Newark, DE: International Reading Association. (ERIC Document Reproduction Service No. ED 438506)

Florida Department of Education. (1999). *Sunshine state standards: Grade level expectations, language arts, grades 3–5.* Retrieved December 2, 2004, from http://www.firn.edu/doe/curric/prek12/frame2.htm

Flynt, E. S., & Cooter, R. (1999). *English-Espanol reading inventory for the classroom.* Englewood Cliffs, NJ: Prentice Hall.

Fountas, I., & Pinnell, G. S. (1996). *Guided reading: Good first teaching for all children.* Portsmouth, NH: Heinemann.

Fountas, I., & Pinnell, G. S. (1999). *Matching books to readers: Using leveled books in guided reading, K–3.* Portsmouth, NH: Heinemann.

Fountas, I., & Pinnell, G. S. (2001). *Guiding readers and writers grades 3–6: Teaching comprehension, genre, and content literacy.* Portsmouth, NH: Heinemann.

Fractor, J., Woodruff, M., Martinez, M., & Teale, W. (1993). Let's not miss opportunities to promote voluntary reading: Classroom libraries in the elementary school. *The Reading Teacher, 46*(6), 476–484.

Freeman, D., & Freeman, Y. (1993). Strategies for promoting the primary languages of all students. *The Reading Teacher, 46*(7), 552–558.

Fry, E. (1977). Fry's readability graph: Clarifications, validity, and extensions to level 17. *Journal of Reading, 21*(3), 242–252.

Fry, E. (2002). Readability versus leveling. *The Reading Teacher, 56*(3), 286–291.

Fuhler, C. (2000). *Teaching reading with multicultural books kids love.* Golden, CO: Fulcrum.

Gadsden, V. (2000). Intergenerational literacy within families. In M. Kamil, P. Mosenthal, P. D. Pearson, & R. Barr (Eds.), *Handbook of reading research* (Vol. 3, pp. 871–887). Mahwah, NJ: Erlbaum.

Galda, L., & Beach, R. (2004). Response to literature as a cultural activity. In R. Ruddell & N. Unrau (Eds.), *Theoretical models and processes of reading* (5th ed., pp. 852–869). Newark, DE: International Reading Association.

Gall, M. (1984). Synthesis of research on teachers' questioning. *Educational Leadership, 42*(3), 40–47.

Gambrell, L. (1998). Creating classroom cultures that foster reading motivation. In R. Allington (Ed.), *Teaching struggling readers: Articles from the Reading Teacher* (pp. 108–121). Newark, DE: International Reading Association.

Gambrell, L., & Bales, R. J. (1986). Mental imagery and the comprehension-monitoring performance of fourth- and fifth-grade poor readers. *Reading Research Quarterly, 21*(4), 454–464.

Gambrell, L., & Koskinen, P. (2002). Imagery: A strategy for enhancing comprehension. In C. Block & M. Pressley (Eds.), *Comprehension instruction: Research-based best practices.* (pp. 305–318). New York: Guilford.

Gambrell, L., Koskinen, P., & Kapinus, B. (1991). Retelling and the reading comprehension of proficient and less-proficient readers. *Journal of Educational Research, 84*(6), 356–362.

Gambrell, L., Palmer, B., Codling, R., & Mazzoni, S. (1996). Assessing motivation to read. *The Reading Teacher, 49*(7), 518–533.

Ganske, K., Monroe, J., & Strickland, D. (2003). Questions teachers ask about struggling readers and writers. *The Reading Teacher, 57*(2), 118–128.

García, G. E. (2000). Bilingual children's reading. In M. Kamil, P. Mosenthal, P. D. Pearson, & R. Barr (Eds.), *Handbook of reading research* (Vol. 3, pp. 813–834). Mahwah, NJ: Erlbaum.

Gardner, H. (1993). *Multiple intelligences: Theory and practice.* New York: Basic.

Gardner, H. (1999). *Intelligence reframed: Multiple intelligences for the 21st century.* New York: Basic Books.

Garner, R. (1994). Metacognition and executive control. In R. Ruddell, M. Ruddell, & H. Singer (Eds.), *Theoretical models and processes of reading* (4th ed., pp. 715–732). Newark, DE: International Reading Association.

Gay, G. (1993). Building cultural bridges: A bold proposal for teacher education. *Education and Urban Society, 25*(3), 284–299.

Gibson, E., & Levin, H. (1975). *The psychology of reading.* Cambridge, MA: MIT Press.

Glazer, S. M. (1989). *Oral language and literacy development.* In D. Strickland & L. M. Morrow (Eds.), *Emerging literacy: Young children learn to read and write* (pp. 16–26). Newark, DE: International Reading Association.

Glazer, S. M. (1992). *Reading comprehension: Self-monitoring strategies to develop independent readers.* New York: Scholastic Professional.

Glazer, S. M. (1998). *Assessment is instruction: Reading, writing, spelling, and phonics for all learners.* Norwood, MA: Christopher-Gordon.

Goldenberg, C. (1991). Learning to read in New Zealand: The balance of skills and meaning. *Language Arts, 68*(7), 555–562.

Goldenberg, C. (2004). Literacy for all children in the increasingly diverse schools of the United States. In R. Ruddell & N. Unrau (Eds.), *Theoretical models and processes of reading* (5th ed., pp. 1636–1666). Newark, DE: International Reading Association.

Goldman, S. R., & Rakestraw, J. A. (2000). Structural aspects of constructing meaning from text. In M. Kamil, P. Mosenthal, P. D. Pearson, & R. Barr (Eds.), *Handbook of reading research* (Vol. 3, pp. 311-335.) Mahwah, NJ: Erlbaum.

Gombert, J. (1992). *Metalinguistic development.* Chicago: University of Chicago Press.

Goodman, K. (1967). Reading: A psycholinguistic guessing game. *Journal of the Reading Specialist, 6,* 126–135.

Goodman, K. (1973). *The psycholinguistic nature of the reading process.* Detroit, MI: Wayne State University Press.

Goodman, K. (1994). Reading, writing, and written texts: A transactional sociopsycholinguistic view. In R. Ruddell, M. Ruddell, & H. Singer (Eds.), *Theoretical models and processes of reading* (4th ed., pp. 1093–1130). Newark, DE: International Reading Association.

Goodman, Y. (1978). Kid watching: An alternative to testing. *National Elementary Principals Journal, 57*(4), 41–45.

Goodman, Y. (1985). Kidwatching: Observing children in the classroom. In A. Jagar & M. Smith-Burke (Eds.), *Observing the language learner* (pp. 9–18). Urbana, IL: National Council of Teachers of English.

Goodman, Y. (1986). *Children coming to know literacy.* In W. Teale & E. Sulzby (Eds.), *Emergent literacy: Writing and reading* (pp. 1–14). Norwood, NJ: Ablex.

Goodman, Y., & Goodman, K. (2004). To err is human: Learning about language processes by analyzing miscues. In R. Ruddell & N. Unrau (Eds.). *Theoretical models and processes of reading* (5th ed., pp. 620–639). Newark, DE: International Reading Association.

Goldman, S. R., & Rakestraw, J. A. (2000). Structural aspects of constructing meaning from text. In M. Kamil, P.B. Mosentahal, P.D. Pearson, and R. Barr (Eds.), *Handbook of reading research* (Vol. 3, pp. 311–335). Mahwah, NJ: Erlbaum.

Gordon, C. J., & Pearson, P. D. (1983). *The effects of instruction in metacomprehension and inferencing on children's comprehension abilitie*s (Tech. Rep. No. 277). Urbana, IL: University of Illinois, Center for the Study of Reading.

Goswami, U. (2000). Phonological and lexical processes. In M. Kamil, P. Mosenthal, P. D. Pearson, & R. Barr (Eds.), *Handbook of reading research* (Vol. 3, pp. 251–267). Mahwah, NJ: Erlbaum.

Graves, D. (1994). *A fresh look at writing.* Portsmouth, NH: Heinemann.

Graves, D. (2003). *Writing: Teachers and children at work (20th anniversary ed).* Portsmouth, NH: Heinemann.

Graves, M., & Graves, B. (2003). *Scaffolding reading experiences: Designs for student success* (2nd ed.). Norwood, MA: Christopher-Gordon.

Graves, M., & Watts-Taffe, S. (2002). The place of word consciousness in a research-based vocabulary program. In A. Farstrup & S. J. Samuels (Eds.), *What research has to say about reading instruction* (3rd ed., pp. 140–165). Newark, DE: International Reading Association.

Graves, M., Juel, C., & Burns, B. (2001). *Rubrics and other tools for classroom assessment for teaching reading in the 21st century.* Needham Heights, MA: Allyn & Bacon.

Graves, M., Juel, C., & Graves, B. (2001). *Teaching reading in the 21st century* (2nd ed). Needham Heights, MA: Allyn & Bacon.

Gray, M., & Troy, A. (1986). Elementary teachers of reading as models. *Reading Horizons, 31,* 179–184.

Green, J., & Meyer, L. (1990). The embeddedness of reading in classroom life: Reading as a situated process. In C. Baker & A. Luke (Eds.), *The sociology of reading* (pp. 141–160). Amsterdam, Netherlands: Benjamins.

Groff, P. (1998). Where's the phonics? Making a case for its direct and systematic instruction. *The Reading Teacher, 52*(2), 138–141.

Guice, S., Allington, R., Johnston, P., Baker, K., & Michelson, N. (1996). Access?: Books, children, and literature-based curriculum in schools. *The New Advocate, 9*(3), 197–207.

Guthrie, J., & Wigfield, A. (2000). Engagement and motivation in reading. In M. Kamil, P. Mosenthal, P. D. Pearson, & R. Barr (Eds.), *Handbook of reading research:* (Vol. 3, pp. 403–422). Mahwah, NJ: Erlbaum.

Guthrie, J., Wigfield, A., Metsala, J., & Cox, K. (2004). Motivational and cognitive predictors of text comprehension and reading amount. In R. Ruddell & N. Unrau (Eds.), *Theoretical models and processes of reading* (5th ed., pp. 929–953). Newark, DE: International Reading Association.

Hacker, D. (2004). Self-regulated comprehension during normal reading. In R. Ruddell & N. Unrau (Eds.), *Theoretical models and processes of reading* (5th ed., pp. 755–779). Newark, DE: International Reading Association.

Hade, D. (1997). Reading multiculturally. In V. Harris (Ed.), *Using multiethnic literature in the K–8 classroom* (pp. 233–256). Norwood, MA: Christopher-Gordon.

Halliday, M. A. K. (1975). *Learning how to mean: Explorations in the development of language*. London: Edward Arnold.

Halliday, M. A. K. (1978). *Language as social semiotic: The social interpretation of language and meaning*. Baltimore: University Park Press.

Hansen, J. (1981). The effects of inference training and practice on young children's reading comprehension. *Reading Research Quarterly, 16*(3), 391–417.

Harp, B. (1996). *The handbook of literacy assessment and evaluation*. Norwood, MA: Christopher-Gordon.

Harris, T., & Hodges, R. (1995). *The literacy dictionary: The vocabulary of reading and writing*. Newark, DE: International Reading Association.

Harste, J., Woodward, V., & Burke, C. (1984). *Language stories and literacy lessons*. Portsmouth, NH: Heinemann.

Harste, J., Short, K., & Burke, C. (1988). *Creating classrooms for authors: The reading-writing connection*. Portsmouth, NH: Heinemann.

Harste, J., Short, K., & Burke, C. (1995). *Creating classrooms for authors and inquirers: The reading-writing connection* (2nd ed.). Portsmouth, NH: Heinemann.

Harvey, S., & Goudvis, A. (2000). *Strategies that work: Teaching comprehension to enhance understanding*. Portland, ME: Stenhouse.

Hasbruck, J., & Tindal, G. (1992). Curriculum-based oral reading fluency norms for students in grades 2 through 5. *Teaching Exceptional Children, 24*(3), 41–44.

Hayes, D. (1988). Speaking and writing: Distinct patterns of word choice. *Journal of Memory and Language, 27*, 572–585.

Heath, S. B. (1983). *Ways with words*. Cambridge, UK: Cambridge University Press.

Heath, S. B. (1994). The children on Trackton's children: Spoken and written language in social change. In R. Ruddell, M. Ruddell, & H. Singer (Eds.), *Theoretical models and processes of reading* (4th ed., pp. 208–230). Newark, DE: International Reading Association.

Hefflin, B., & Barksdale-Ladd, M. A. (2001). African-American children's literature that helps students find themselves: Selection guidelines for grades K–3. *The Reading Teacher, 54*(8), 810–819.

Helman, L. (2004). Building on the sound system of Spanish: Insights from the alphabetic spellings of English-language learners. *The Reading Teacher, 57*(5), 452–460.

Henk, W., & Melnick, S. (1995). The reader self-perception scale (RSPS): A new tool for measuring how children feel about themselves as readers. *The Reading Teacher, 48*(6), 470–482.

Hennings, D. (2000). *Communication in action: Teaching literature-based language arts*. Boston: Houghton Mifflin.

Henry, J., & Wiley, B. J. (1999). *Answers to frequently asked questions about interactive writing: Classroom connections*. Columbus, OH: Reading Recovery Council of North America. (ERIC Document Reproduction Service No. ED 453510)

Hickman, P., Pollard-Durodola, S., & Vaughn, S. (2004). Storybook reading: Improving vocabulary and comprehension for English-language learners. *The Reading Teacher, 57*(8), 720–730.

Hiebert, E. (1999). Text matters in learning to read. *The Reading Teacher, 52*(6), 550–566.

Hiebert, E., & Martin, L. A. (2002). The texts of beginning reading instruction. In S. Neuman & D. Dickinson (Eds.), *Handbook of early literacy research* (pp. 361–376). New York: Guilford.

Hiebert, E., & Martin, L. A. (2004). The texts of beginning reading instruction. In R. Ruddell & N. Unrau (Eds.), *Theoretical models and processes of reading* (5th ed., pp. 390–411). Newark, DE: International Reading Association.

Hoffman, J., Roser, N., & Battle, J. (1993). Reading aloud in classrooms: From the modal toward a "model." *The Reading Teacher, 46*(6), 496–503.

Holdaway, D. (1979). *The foundations of literacy*. Portsmouth, NH: Heinemann.

Holmes, B., & Roser, N. (1987). Five ways to assess readers' prior knowledge. *The Reading Teacher, 40*(7), 646–649.

Horowitz, R., & Freeman, S. (1995). Robots versus spaceships: The role of discussion in kindergarteners' and second graders' preferences for science text. *The Reading Teacher, 49*(1), 30–40.

Hoyt, L. (1999). *Revisit, reflect, retell: Strategies for improving reading comprehension*. Portsmouth, NH: Heinemann.

Huang, G. (1997). Beyond culture: Communicating with Asian American children and families. Retrieved December 18, 2004, from http://www.casanet.org/library/culture/communicate-asian.htm

Hudson, R., Lane, H., & Pullen, P. (2005). Reading fluency assessment and instruction: What, why, and how? *The Reading Teacher, 58*(8), 702–714.

Huey, E. (1908). *The psychology and pedagogy of reading*. Cambridge, MA: MIT Press.

Idol, L. (1987). Group story mapping: A comprehension strategy for both skilled and unskilled readers. *Journal of Reading Disabilities, 20*(4), 196–205.

International Reading Association. (2002). *What is evidence-based reading instruction? A position statement of the International Reading Association* [Brochure]. Newark, DE: International Reading Association.

International Reading Association Professional Standards and Ethics Committee. (2004). *Standards for reading professionals* (Rev. ed.). Newark, DE: International Reading Association.

Jiménez, R. (2001). It's a difference that changes us: An alternative view of the language and literacy learning needs of Latina/o students. *The Reading Teacher, 54*(8), 736–742.

Jiménez, R. (2004). Literacy and the identity development of Latina/o students. In N. Ruddell, & N. Unrau (Eds.), *Theoretical models and processes of reading* (5th ed., pp. 210–239). Newark, DE: International Reading Association.

Johns, J., & Bergland, R. (2002). *Fluency: Questions, answers, evidence-based strategies*. Dubuque, Iowa: Kendall/Hunt.

Johnson, D. (2001). *Vocabulary in the elementary and middle school*. Boston: Allyn & Bacon.

Johnson, D., & Pearson, P. D. (1984). *Teaching reading vocabulary*. New York: Holt.

Kail, R., Chi, M., Ingram, A., & Danner, F. (1977). Constructive aspects of children's reading comprehension. *Child Development, 48*, 684–688.

Kamil, M. L., & Bernhardt, E. B. (2001). Reading instruction for English language learners. In M. Graves, C. Juel, & B. Graves (Eds.), *Teaching reading in the 21st century* (pp. 460–503). Boston: Allyn & Bacon.

Kear, D., Coffman, G., McKenna, M., & Abrosio, A. (2000). Measuring attitude toward writing: A new tool for teachers. *The Reading Teacher, 54*(1), 10–23.

Kintsch, W. (2004). The construction-integration model of text comprehension and its implications for instruction. In R. Ruddell & N. Unrau (Eds.), *Theoretical models and processes of reading* (5th ed., pp. 1270–1328). Newark, DE: International Reading Association.

Kletzien, S., & Dreher, M. (2004). *Informational text in k–3 classrooms: Helping children read and write*. Newark, DE: International Reading Association.

Klingner, J., & Vaughn, S. (1999). Promoting reading comprehension, content learning, and English acquisition through Collaborative Strategic Reading (CSR). *The Reading Teacher, 52*(7), 738–747.

Konopak, B., Williams, N., & Jampole, E. (1991). Use of mnemonic imagery for content learning. *Journal of Reading, Writing, and Learning Disabilities International, 7*(4), 309–319.

Krashen, S. (1993). *The power of reading*. Englewood, CO: Libraries, Unlimited.

Krashen, S. (1996). *Every person a reader: An alternative to the California Task Force Report on Reading*. Culver City, CA: Language Education Associates.

LaBerge, D., & Samuels, S. (1974). Toward a theory of automatic information processing in reading. *Cognitive Psychology, 6*, 293–323.

Lancia, P. (1997). Literary borrowing: The effects of literature on children's writing. *The Reading Teacher, 50*(6), 470–475.

Lazar, A. (2004). *Learning to be literacy teachers in urban schools: Stories of growth and change*. Newark, DE: International Reading Association.

Lenters, K. (2004/2005). No half-measures: Reading instruction for young second-language learners. *The Reading Teacher, 58*(4), 328–336.

Leslie, L., & Caldwell, J. (1990). *Qualitative reading inventory*. New York: HarperCollins.

Leslie, L., & Caldwell, J. (2000). *Qualitative reading inventory – 3* (3rd ed.). Boston: Allyn & Bacon.

Leu, D. (2002). The new literacies: Research in reading instruction with the Internet. In A. Farstrup & S. J. Samuels (Eds.), *What research has to say about reading instruction* (3rd ed., pp. 310–336). Newark, DE: International Reading Association.

Leu, D., Castek, J., Henry, L., Coiro, J., & McMullan, M. (2004). The lessons that children teach us: Integrating children's literature and the new literacies of the Internet. *The Reading Teacher, 57*(5), 496–503.

Levin, J., Levin, M., Glasman, L., & Nordwall, M. (1992). Mnemonic vocabulary instruction: Additional effectiveness evidence. *Contemporary Educational Psychology, 17*(2), 156–174.

Lortie, S. (1975). *Schoolteacher*. Chicago: University of Chicago Press.

Luria, A. (1980). *Higher cortical functions in man*. New York: Consultants Bureau.

Lyons, C. (1999). Letter learning in the early literacy classroom. In I. Fountas & G. Pinnell (Eds.), *Voices on word matters: Learning about phonics and spelling in the literacy classroom*. (pp. 57–66). Portsmouth, NH: Heinemann.

Lysynchuk, L., Pressley, M., & Vye, N. (1990). Reciprocal teaching improves standardized reading comprehension performance in poor comprehenders. *The Elementary School Journal, 90*(5), 469–484.

Mandler, J., & Johnson, N. (1977). Remembrance of things passed: Story structure and recall. *Cognitive Psychology, 9*(1), 111–151.

Many, J. (2004). The effect of reader stance on students' personal understanding of literature. In R. Ruddell & N. Unrau (Eds.), *Theoretical models and processes of reading*, (5th ed., pp. 914–928). Newark, DE: International Reading Association.

Martinez, M., & Roser, N. (1985). Read it again: The value of repeated readings during storytime. *The Reading Teacher, 38*(8), 782–786.

Martinez, M., Roser, N., & Strecker, S. (1998/1999). "I never thought I could be a star": A Readers' Theatre ticket to fluency. *The Reading Teacher, 52*(4), 326–334.

Martinez-Roldán, C. M., & López-Robertson, J. M. (1999/2000). Initiating literature circles in a first-grade bilingual classroom. *The Reading Teacher, 53*(4), 270–281.

Marshall, J. (2000). Research on response to literature. In M. Kamil, P. Mosenthal, P. D. Pearson, & R. Barr, *Handbook of reading research* (Vol. 3, pp. 381–402). Mahwah, NJ: Erlbaum.

Mathewson, G. (2004). Model of attitude influence upon reading and learning to read. In R. Ruddell & N. Unrau

(Eds.), *Theoretical models and processes of reading*, (5th ed., pp. 1431–1461). Newark, DE: International Reading Association.

McCauley, J. K., & McCauley, D. S. (1992). Using choral reading to promote language learning for ESL students. *The Reading Teacher*, *45*(7), 526–533.

McCormick, S. (1987). *Remedial and clinical reading instruction*. Columbus, OH: Merrill.

McCracken, R. A., & McCracken, M. J. (1972). Modeling is the key to sustained silent reading. *The Reading Teacher*, *31*, 406–408.

McCray, A. D. (2001). Middle school students with reading disabilities. *The Reading Teacher, 55*(3), 298–300.

McCray, A., Vaughn, S., & Neal, L. (2001). Not all students learn to read by third grade: Middle school students speak out about their reading disabilities. *Journal of Special Education, 35*(1), 17–30.

McGinley, W., & Denner, P. (1987). Story impressions: A prereading/writing activity. *Journal of Reading, 31*(3), 248–253.

McIntosh, P. (1990, Winter). White privilege: Unpacking the invisible knapsack. *Peace and Freedom*, 10–12.

McKenna, M., & Kear, D. (1990). Measuring attitude toward reading: A new tool for teachers. *The Reading Teacher*, *43*(9), 626–639.

Mesmer, H. A. (2001). Decodable text: A review of what we know. *Reading Research and Instruction, 40*(2), 121–142.

Meeting spotlights ELL issues. (2004, June/July). *Reading Today*, 34.

Meyer, B. J. F., & Freedle, R. O. (1984). Effects of discourse type on recall. *American Educational Research Journal, 21*(1), 121–143.

Meyer, B. J. F., & Poon, L. W. (2004). Effects of structure strategy training and signaling on recall of text. In R. Ruddell & N. Unrau (Eds.), *Theoretical models and processes of reading* (5th ed., pp. 810–851). Newark, DE: International Reading Association.

Miller, H. M. (2001). Including "the included." *The Reading Teacher, 54*(8), 820–821.

Miller, H. M. (2004). Teaching and learning about cultural diversity: A dose of empathy. In R. Robinson, M. McKenna, & J. Wedman, (Eds.), *Issues and trends in literacy education* (pp. 92–95), Boston: Allyn & Bacon.

Morrison, T., Jacobs, J., & Swinyard, W. (1999). Do teachers who reading personally use recommended practices in their classrooms? *Reading Research and Instruction, 38*(2), 81–100.

Morrow, L. M. (1984). Reading stories to young children: Effects of story structure and Traditional questioning strategies on comprehension. *Journal of Reading Behavior, 16*, 273–288.

Morrow, L. M. (1991). Promoting voluntary reading. In J. Jensen, D. Lapp, J. Flood, & J. Squire (Eds.), *Handbook of research on teaching the English language arts* (pp. 681–690). New York: Macmillan.

Morrow, L. M. (1992). The impact of a literature-based program on literacy achievement, use of literature, and attitudes of children from minority backgrounds. *Reading Research Quarterly, 27*(3), 250–275.

Moss, P. (2004). Teaching expository text structures through information trade book retellings. *The Reading Teacher, 57*(8), 710–718.

Moustafa, M. (1997). *Beyond traditional phonics*. Portsmouth, NH: Heinemann.

Nagy, W., & Scott, J. (2004). Vocabulary processes. In R. Ruddell & N. Unrau (Eds.), *Theoretical models and processes of reading* (5th ed., pp. 574–593). Newark, DE: International Reading Association.

National Commission on Teaching and America's Future. (1996). *What matters most: Teaching for America's future.* New York: National Commission on Teaching and America's Future. Retrieved November 20, 2004 from http://www.myaea.org/uploadFiles/teachingforamerica's future.pdf

National Reading Panel. (2000a). *Teaching children to read: An evidence-based assessment of the scientific research literature on reading and its implications for reading instruction.* (NIH Publication No. 00-4769). Washington, D.C.: National Institute of Child Health and Human Development.

National Reading Panel. (2000b). *Teaching children to read: An evidence-based assessment of the scientific research literature on reading and its implications for reading instruction: Reports of the Subgroups.* (NIH Publication No. 00-4754). Washington, D.C.: National Institute of Child Health and Human Development. Retrieved July 12, 2005 from http://www.nichd.nih.gov/publications/nrp/report.htm

Nettles, D. H. (1987). *A study of the variation in probing behaviors of teachers across two subject areas and two levels of student ability.* Unpublished doctoral dissertation, University of South Florida, Tampa, FL.

Neuman, S., & Celan, D. (2001). Access to print in low-income and middle-income communities: An ecological study of four neighborhoods. *Reading Research Quarterly, 36*(1), 8–26.

Neuman, S., & Roskos, K. (1989). The influence of literacy-enriched play settings on preschoolers' conceptions of print. Retrieved January 14, 2005 from http://www.eric.ed.gov/ERICWebPortal/Home.portal?_nfpb=true&eric_viewStyle=list&ERICExtSearch_SearchValue_0=concepts+of+print&ERICExtSearch_SearchType_0=eric_metadata&eric_pageSize=10&eric_displayNtriever=false&eric_displayStartCount=21&_pageLabel=RecordDetails&objectId=0900000b80048e08. (ERIC Document Reproduction Service No. ED 316848).

No Child Left Behind Act of 2001, Pub. L. No. 107-110. (2001). Retrieved November 21, 2004 from http://frwebgate.access.gpo.gov/cgibin/getdoc.cgi?dbname=107_cong_bills&docid=f:h1enr.txt.pdf

North Central Regional Educational Laboratory. (n.d.). Critical issue: Addressing literacy needs in culturally and linguistically diverse classrooms. Retrieved December 18, 2004 from http://www.ncrel.org/sdrs/areas/issues/content/cntareas/reading/li400.htm

O'Donnell, L. (2005, February/March). Are Canadian boys redefining literacy? *Reading Today, 22*(4), 19.

Ogle, D. (1986). K-W-L: A teaching model that develops active reading of expository text. *The Reading Teacher, 39*(6), 564–570.

Ohlhausen, M., & Jepsen, M. (1992). Lessons from Goldilocks: "Somebody's been choosing my books but I can make my own choices now!" *The New Advocate, 5*(1), 31–46.

Olness, R. (2005). *Using literature to enhance writing instruction.* Newark, DE: International Reading Association.

Olson, M., & Homan, S. (1993). *Teacher to teacher: Strategies for the elementary classroom.* Newark, DE: International Reading Association.

Opitz, M. (1992). The Cooperative Reading Activity: An alternative to ability grouping. *The Reading Teacher, 45*(9), 736–738.

Optiz, M. (1995). *Getting the most from predictable books.* New York: Scholastic Professional Books.

Opitz, M., & Rasinski, T. (1998). *Goodbye, round robin: Twenty-five effective oral reading strategies.* Portsmouth, NH: Heinemann.

Oster, L. (2001). Using the think-aloud for reading instruction. *The Reading Teacher, 55*(1), 64–69.

Palincsar, A., & Brown, A. (1984). Reciprocal teaching of comprehension-fostering and comprehension-monitoring activities. *Cognition and Instruction, 1,* 117–175.

Palmer, R. G., & Stewart, R. (2003). Nonfiction tradebook use in primary grades. *The Reading Teacher, 57*(1), 38–47.

Pang, V., Colvin, C., Tran, M., & Barba, R. (1992). Beyond chopsticks and dragons: Selecting Asian-American literature for children. *The Reading Teacher, 46*(3), 216–224.

Paratore, J. (2002). Home and school together: Helping beginning readers succeed. In A. Farstrup, & S. J. Samuels (Eds.), *What research has to say about reading instruction* (3rd ed., pp. 48–68). Newark, DE: International Reading Association.

Paris, S., Lipson, M., & Wixson, K. (1994). Becoming a strategic reader. In R. Ruddell, M. R. Ruddell, & H. Singer (Eds.), *Theoretical models and processes of reading,* (4th ed., pp. 788–810). Newark, DE: International Reading Association.

Paris, S., Wasik, B., & Turner, J. (1991). The development of strategic readers. In R. Barr, M. Kamil, P. Mosenthal, & P. D. Pearson (Eds.), *Handbook of reading research* (Vol. 2, pp. 609–640). White Plains, NY: Longman.

Pearson, P. D., & Duke, N. K. (2002). Comprehension instruction in the primary grades. In C. Block, (Ed.), *Comprehension instruction: Research-based best practices* (pp. 247–258). New York: Guilford .

Pearson, P. D., & Fielding, L. (1991). Comprehension instruction. In R. Barr, M. Kamil, P. Mosenthal, & P. D. Pearson (Eds.), *Handbook of reading research* (Vol. 2, pp. 815–860). White Plains, NY: Longman.

Pearson, P. D., & Johnson, D. (1978). *Teaching reading comprehension.* Orlando, FL: Holt, Rinehart, & Winston.

Pearson, P. D., Roehler, L., Dole, J., & Duffy, G. (1992). Developing expertise in reading comprehension. In S. J. Samuels & A. Farstrup (Eds.), *What research has to say about reading instruction* (2nd ed., pp. 145–199). Newark, DE: International Reading Association.

Pennsylvania Department of Education. (1999). *Academic standards for reading, writing, speaking and listening.* Retrieved August 14, 2004 from http://www.pde.state.pa.us/k12/lib/k12/Reading.pdf

Pennycook, A. (1985). Actions speak louder than words: Paralanguage, communication, and education. *TESOL Quarterly, 19*(2), 259–282.

Peregoy, S., & Boyle, O. (2004). English learners reading English: What we know, what we need to know. In R. Robinson, M. McKenna, & J. Wedman (Eds.), *Issues and trends in literacy education* (3rd ed., pp. 103–123). Boston: Allyn & Bacon.

Perfetti, C. (1985). *Reading ability.* New York: Oxford University Press.

Peterson, R., & Eeds, M. (1990). *Grand conversations: Literature groups in action.* New York: Scholastic.

Piaget, J. (1926). *The language and thought of the child* (M. Worden, Trans.). New York: Harcourt Brace & World.

Piaget, J. (1969). *The psychology of intelligence.* Totowa, NJ: Littlefield, Adams.

Pinnell, G., Pikulski, J., Wixson, K., Campbell, J., Gough, P., & Beatty, A. (1995). *Listening to children read aloud.* Washington, DC: U.S. Department of Education, National Center for Education Statistics.

Polette, K. (2005). *Read and write it out loud!* Boston: Pearson Education.

Pressley, M. (2000). What should comprehension instruction be the instruction of? In M. Kamil, P. Mosenthal, P. D. Pearson, & R. Barr (Eds.), *Handbook of reading research* (Vol. 3, pp. 545–562). Mahwah, NJ: Erlbaum.

Pressley, M. (2002). Metacognition and self-regulated comprehension. In A. Farsrup & S. J. Samuels (Eds.), *What research has to say about reading instruction* (3rd ed., pp. 291–309). Newark, DE: International Reading Association.

Pressley, M., Johnson, C., Symons, S., McGoldrick, J., & Kurita, J. (1989). Strategies that improve children's memory and comprehension of text. *Elementary School Journal, 90*(1), 3–32.

Pressley, M., Levin, J., & Delaney, H. D. (1982). The mnemonic keyword method. *Review of Educational Research, 52*(1), 61–91.

Pressley, M., Rankin, J., & Yokoi, L. (2000). A survey of instructional practices of primary teachers nominated as effective in promoting literacy. In R. Robinson, M. McKenna, & J. Wedman (Eds.), *Issues and trends in literacy education* (2nd ed., pp.10–35). Needham Heights, MA: Allyn & Bacon.

Pressley, M., Wharton-McDonald, R., Mistretta-Hampston, J. M., & Echevarria, M. (1998). The nature of literacy instruction in ten grade 4/5 classrooms in upstate New York. *Scientific Studies of Reading, 2,* 159–194.

Pritchard, S. (1989). Using picture books to teach geography in the primary grades. *Journal of Geography, 88*(4), 126–136.

Pulaski, M. A. (1971). *Understanding Piaget: An introduction to children's cognitive development.* New York: Harper & Row.

Purcell-Gates, V. (1996). Stories, coupons, and the *TV Guide:* Relationships between home literacy experiences and emergent literacy knowledge. *Reading Research Quarterly, 31*(4), 406–428.

Raphael, T. (1986). Teaching question answer relationships, revisited. *The Reading Teacher, 39*(6), 516–523.

Rasinski, T. (2000). Speed does matter in reading. *The Reading Teacher, 54*(2), 146–151.

Rasinski, T., & Padak, N. (1998). How elementary students referred for compensatory reading instruction perform on school-based measures of word recognition, fluency, and comprehension. *Reading Psychology: An International Quarterly, 19*(2), 185–216.

Rasinski, T., & Padak, N. (2001). *From phonics to fluency: Effective teaching of decoding and reading fluency in the elementary school.* New York: Addison-Wesley Longman.

Ratliff, G. L. (1999). *Introduction to readers theatre: A guide to classroom performance.* Colorado Springs, CO: Meriwether.

Read, C. (1971). Preschool children's knowledge of English phonology. *Harvard Educational Review, 41*(1), 1–34.

Readence, J., Bean, T., & Baldwin, R. (1989). *Content area reading: An integrated approach.* Dubuque, IA: Kendall/Hunt.

Reitsma, P. (1983). Printed word learning in beginning readers. *Journal of Experimental Child Psychology, 36*(2), 321–339.

Richards, J. C., & Gipe, J. (1992). Activating background knowledge: Strategies for beginning and poor readers. *The Reading Teacher, 45*(6), 474–476.

Richek, M. A. (1987). DRTA: Five variations that facilitate independence in reading narratives. *Journal of Reading, 30*(7), 632–636.

Richgels, D. (2002). Informational texts in kindergarten. *The Reading Teacher, 55*(6), 586–595.

Riekehof, L. L. (1987). *The joy of signing* (2nd ed.). Springfield, MO: Gospel.

Robb, L. (1994). *Whole language, whole learners.* New York: Morrow.

Robinson, R., McKenna, M., & Wedman, J. (2000). *Issues and trends in literacy education.* Boston: Allyn & Bacon.

Rosenblatt., L. (1938). *Literature as exploration.* New York: Appleton Century.

Rosenblatt, L. (1978). *The reader, the text, and the poem: The transactional theory of the literary work.* Carbondale: Southern Illinois University Press.

Rosenblatt, L. (2004). The transactional theory of reading and writing. In R. Ruddell, & N. Unrau. (Eds.), *Theoretical models and processes of reading* (5th ed., pp. 1363–1398). Newark, DE: International Reading Association.

Rosenshine, B., & Meister, C. (1994). Reciprocal teaching: A review of the research. *Review of Educational Research, 64*(4), 479–530.

Rosenshine, B., & Stevens, R. (1984). Classroom instruction in reading. In P. D. Pearson (Ed.), *Handbook of reading research* (pp. 745–798). New York: Longman.

Ross, E. (1986). Classroom experiments with oral reading. *The Reading Teacher, 40*(30), 270–275.

Routman, R. (1991). *Invitations: Changing as teachers and learners K–12.* Portsmouth, NH: Heinemann.

Routman, R. (2000). *Conversations: Strategies for teaching, learning, evaluating.* Portsmouth, NH: Heinemann.

Rowe, M. B. (1974). Relation of wait-time and rewards to the development of language, logic, and fate control. Part II—Rewards. *Journal of Research in Science Teaching, 11*(4), 291–308.

Ruddell, R. (1994). The development of children's comprehension and motivation during storybook discussion. In R. Ruddell, M. Ruddell, & H. Singer (Eds.). *Theoretical models and processes of reading* (4th ed., pp. 281–296.). Newark, DE: International Reading Association.

Ruddell, R. (2006). *Teaching children to read and write: Becoming an effective literacy teacher* (4th ed.). Boston: Allyn & Bacon.

Ruddell, R., & Unrau, N. (2004a). Reading as a meaning-construction process: The reader, the text, and the teacher. In R. Ruddell & N. Unrau (Eds.). *Theoretical models and processes of reading* (5th ed., pp. 1462–1521.) Newark, DE: International Reading Association.

Ruddell, R., & Unrau, N. (Eds.). (2004b). *Theoretical models and processes of reading* (5th ed.). Newark, DE: International Reading Association.

Rumelhart, D. (1977). Toward an interactive model of reading. In S. Dornic (Ed.), *Attention and performance* (Vol. 6, pp. 573–603). Hillsdale, NJ: Erlbaum.

Rumelhart, D. (1980). Schemata: The building blocks of cognition. In R. Shapiro, B. Bruce, & W. Brewer (Eds.), *Theoretical issues in reading comprehension* (pp. 33–58). Hillsdale, NJ: Erlbaum.

Sadoski, M., & Paivio, A. (1994). A dual coding view of imagery and verbal processes in reading comprehension. In R. Ruddell, M. Ruddell, & H. Singer (Eds.), *Theoretical models and processes of reading* (4th ed., pp. 582–601.) Newark, DE: International Reading Association.

Sadoski, M., & Paivio, A. (2004). A dual coding theoretical model of reading. In R. Ruddell, & N. Unrau (Eds.). *Theoretical models and processes of reading* (5th ed., pp. 1329–1362.) Newark, DE: International Reading Association.

Samuels, S. J. (1979). The method of repeated readings. *The Reading Teacher, 32*(4), 403–408.

Samuels, S. J. (1997). The method of repeated readings (RT Classic). *The Reading Teacher, 50*(5), 376–381.

Samuels, S. J. (2002). Reading fluency: Its development and assessment. In A Farstrup & S. J. Samuels (Eds.), *What* research has to say about reading instruction* (3rd ed., pp. 166–183). Newark: DE: International Reading Association.

Samuels, S. J. (2004). Toward a theory of automatic information processing in reading, revisited. In R. Ruddell, & N. Unrau (Eds.), *Theoretical models and processes of reading* (5th ed., pp. 1127–1148). Newark, DE: International Reading Association.

Samuels, S. J., & Kamil, M. (1984). Models of the reading process. In P. D. Pearson (Ed.), *Handbook of reading research*, New York: Longman.

Sanacore, J. (2004). Genuine caring and literacy learning for African American children. *The Reading Teacher, 57*(8), 744–753.

Sciezka, J. (2005). Guys read. Retrieved February 28, 2005, from http://www.guysread.com/

Schickedanz, J. (1989). The place of specific skills in preschool and kindergarten. In D. Strickland & L. M. Morrow (Eds.), *Emerging literacy: Young children learn to read and write* (pp. 96–106). Newark, DE: International Reading Association.

Schmidt, P. (1999). KWLQ: Inquiry and literacy learning in science. *The Reading Teacher, 52*(7), 789–792.

Schmitt, M. (1990). A questionnaire to measure children's awareness of strategic reading processes. *Reading Teacher, 43*(7), 454–461.

Schunk, D. H., & Zimmerman, B. J. (1997). Developing self-efficacious readers and writers: The role of social and self-regulatory processes. In J. T. Guthrie & A. Wigfield (Eds.), *Reading engagement: Motivating readers through integrated instruction* (pp. 34–50). Newark, DE: International Reading Association.

Searls, E. F. (1985). Do you, like these teachers, value reading? *Reading Horizons, 25*(4), 233–238.

Shanahan, T. (2002). What reading research says: The promises and limitations of applying research to reading education. In A. Farstrup & S. J. Samuels (Eds.), *What research has to say about reading instruction* (3rd ed., pp. 8–24). Newark, DE: International Reading Association.

Shanker, J., & Ekwall, E. (2000). *Ekwall/Shanker reading inventory*. Boston: Allyn & Bacon.

Shea, M. (2000). *Taking running records*. New York: Scholastic Professional.

Shearer, A., & Homan, S. (1994). *Linking reading assessment to instruction: An application worktext for elementary classroom teachers*. New York: St. Martin's.

Shepard, A. (1993). *Shared stories on stage*. New York: Wilson.

Shepard, L. (2004) *The role of assessment in a learning culture.* In R. Ruddell & N. Unrau (Eds.), *Theoretical models and processes of reading* (5th ed.), pp. 1614–1635), Newark, DE: International Reading Association.

Shirey, L. L., & Reynolds, R. E. (1988). Effect of interest on attention and learning. *Journal of Educational Psychology, 80*(2), 159–166.

Short, K., & Klassen, C. (1993). Literature circles: Hearing children's voices. In B. E. Culinan (Ed.), *Children's voices: Talk in the classroom* (pp. 66–85). Newark, DE: International Reading Association.

Singer, H. (1994). The substrata-factor theory of reading. In R. Ruddell, M. Ruddell, & H. Singer, *Theoretical models and processes of reading* (4th ed., pp. 895–927.) Newark, DE: International Reading Association.

Sipe, L. (2001). Invention, convention, and intervention: Invented spelling and the teacher's role. *The Reading Teacher, 55*(3), 264–273.

Slavin, R. (1995). *Cooperative learning* (2nd ed.). Boston: Allyn & Bacon.

Slavin, R., Stevens, R., Madden, N., & Farnish, A. M. (1987). *Cooperative integrated reading and composition: Reading Comprehension, RC—101 to 134*. Baltimore, MD: Johns Hopkins University.

Slavin, R., Madden, N., Dolan, L., Wasik, B., Ross, S., & Smith, L. (1994). Whenever and wherever we choose: The replication of Success for All. *Phi Delta Kappan, 75*(8), 639–647.

Smith, F. (1971). *Understanding reading*. New York: Holt.

Smith, F. (1997). *Reading without nonsense* (3rd ed.). New York: Teachers College Press.

Smith, C. (2000). *Creating lifelong readers: A practical guide for parents and tutors*. Bloomington, IN: ERIC Clearinghouse of Reading, English, and Communication. (ERIC Document Reproduction Service No. 437612).

Smolin, L., & Lawless, K. (2003). Becoming literate in the technological age: New responsibilities and tools for teachers. *The Reading Teacher, 56*(6), 570–577.

Solley, B. (Ed.). (2000). *Writers' workshop: Reflections of elementary and middle school teachers*. Boston: Allyn & Bacon.

Spandel, V. (2001). *Creating writers through six-trait writing assessment and instruction*. New York: Addison-Wesley Longman.

Spiegel, D. L. (1992). Blending whole language and systematic direct instruction. *The Reading Teacher, 46*(1), 38–44.

Spindler, G. (1982). *Doing the ethnography of schooling*. New York: Holt, Rinehart, & Winston.

Spires, H., & Estes, T. (2002). Reading in web-based learning environments. In C. Block & M. Pressley (Eds.), *Comprehension instruction: Research-based best practices* (pp. 115–125). New York: Guilford.

Spohn, J. (2001, February 21). Potluck and pleasure reading. *Pittsburgh Post-Gazette*, S-8.

Squire, J. (1994). Research in reader response, naturally interdisciplinary. In R. Ruddell, M. Ruddell, & H. Singer (Eds.), *Theoretical models and processes of reading* (4th ed., pp. 637–652). Newark, DE: International Reading Association.

Stahl, S. (1992). Saying the "p" word: Nine guidelines for exemplary phonics instruction. *The Reading Teacher, 45*(8), 618–625.

Stahl, S., Duffy-Hester, A., & Stahl, K. (2000). Everything you wanted to know about phonics (but were afraid to ask). In R. Robinson, M. McKenna, & J. Wedman (Eds.), *Issues and trends in literacy education* (2nd ed., pp. 47–72). Needham Heights, MA: Allyn & Bacon.

Stanovich, K. (1985). Matthew effects in reading: Some consequences of individual differences in the acquisition of literacy. *Reading Research Quarterly, 21*(4), 177–186.

Stauffer, R. G. (1970). *The language experience approach to the teaching of reading*. New York: Harper & Row.

Stauffer, R. G. (1975). *Directing the reading-thinking process.* New York: Harper & Row.

Stein, N. (1978). *How children understand stories: A developmental analysis.* (Technical report no. 69). Urbana-Champaign: University of Illinois, Center for the Study of Reading.

Stenner, A. (1996). *Measuring reading comprehension with the Lexile Framework.* Durham, NC: Metametrics.

Stewart, M. T. (2004). Early literacy instruction in the climate of No Child Left Behind. *The Reading Teacher, 57*(8), pp. 732–743.

Stieglitz, E. (2001). *The Steiglitz informal reading inventory: Assessing reading behaviors from emergent to advanced levels* (3rd ed.). Boston: Allyn & Bacon.

Stratton, B., Grindler, M., & Postell, C. (1992). Discovering oneself. *Middle School Journal, 24*(1), 42–43.

Strickland, D. (2002a). Early intervention for African American children considered to be at risk. In S. Neuman, & D. Dickinson (Eds.), *Handbook of early literacy research* (pp. 322–332). New York: Guilford.

Strickland, D. (2002b). The importance of effective early intervention. In A. Farstrup & S. J. Samuels (Eds.), *What research has to say about reading instruction* (3rd ed., 69–86). Newark, DE: International Reading Association.

Strickland, D., & Morrow, L. M. (Eds.). (1989). *Emerging literacy: Young children learn to read and write.* Newark, DE: International Reading Association.

Strickland, D., & Taylor, D. (1989). Family storybook reading: Implications for children, families, and curriculum. In D. Strickland & L. M. Morrow (Eds.), *Emerging literacy: Young children learn to read and write* (pp. 27–34). Newark, DE: International Reading Association.

Sulzby, E. (1985). Children's emergent reading of favorite books: A developmental study. *Reading Research Quarterly, 20*(4), 458–481.

Sulzby, E. (1992). Research directions: Transitions from emergent to conventional writing. *Language Arts, 69*(4), 290–297.

Sulzby, E., Teale, W., & Kamberelis, G. (1989). Emergent writing in the classroom: Home and school connections. In D. Strickland & L. M. Morrow (Eds.), *Emerging literacy: Young children learn to read and write* (pp. 63–79). Newark, DE: International Reading Association.

Teachers of English to Speakers of Other Languages. (1997). Policy statement of the TESOL board on African American vernacular English. Retrieved November 29, 2004 from http://www.cal.org/ebonics/tesolebo.html

Teale, W. (1986). Home background and young children's literacy development. In W. H. Teale & E. Sulzby (Eds.), *Emergent literacy: Writing and reading* (pp. 173–206). Norwood, NJ: Ablex.

Teale, W., & Sulzby, E. (Eds.). (1986). *Emergent literacy: Writing and reading.* Norwood, NJ: Ablex.

Teale, W., & Sulzby, E. (1989). *Emergent literacy: New perspectives.* In D. Strickland & Lesley Morrow (Eds.), *Emerging literacy: Young children learn to read and write* (pp. 1–15). Newark, DE: International Reading Association.

Temple, C., Nathan, R., & Burris, N. (1982). *The beginnings of early writing.* Boston: Allyn & Bacon.

Temple, C., Ogle, D., Crawford, A., & Freppon, P. (2005). *All children read: Teaching for literacy in today's classrooms.* Boston: Allyn & Bacon.

Thornburg, D. (1993). Intergenerational literacy learning with bilingual families: A context for the analysis of social mediation of thought. *Journal of Reading Behavior, 25*(3), 321–352.

Tierney, R., & Cunningham, J. (1984). Research on teaching reading comprehension. In P. D Pearson, (Ed.), *The handbook of reading research.* New York: Longman.

Tierney, R., & Readence, J. (2000). *Reading strategies and practices: A compendium* (5th ed.). Boston: Allyn & Bacon.

Tierney, R., & Readence, J. (2005). *Reading strategies and practices: A compendium* (6th ed.). Boston: Allyn & Bacon.

Tompkins, G. (2006). *Literacy for the 21st century* (4th ed.). Upper Saddle River, NJ: Merrill Prentice Hall.

Tovani, C. (2000). *I read it, but I don't get it: Comprehension strategies for adolescent readers.* Portland, ME: Stenhouse.

Trabasso, T., & Bouchard, E. (2002). Teaching readers how to comprehend text strategically. In C. Block & M. Pressley (Eds.), *Comprehension instruction: Research-based best practices* (pp. 176–200). New York: Guilford.

Tracey, D., & Morrow, L. M. (2002). Preparing young learners for successful reading comprehension. In C. Block & M. Pressley (Eds.), *Comprehension instruction: Research-based best practices* (pp. 219–233). New York: Guilford.

Trachtenburg, P. (1990). Using children's literature to enhance phonics instruction. *The Reading Teacher, 43*(9), 648–654.

Trieman, R. (1985). Onsets and rimes as units of spoken syllables: Evidence from children. *Journal of Experimental Child Psychology, 39*(1), 161–181.

Trelease, J. (1993). *Read all about it! Great read-aloud stories, poems, and newspaper pieces for preteens and teens.* New York: Penguin.

Trelease, J. (2001). *The read-aloud handbook* (5th ed.). New York: Penguin.

Tyner, B. (2004). *Small-group reading instruction: A differentiated teaching model for beginning and struggling readers.* Newark, DE: International Reading Association.

United States Department of Education. (n.d.). *Helping your child series.* Retrieved September 4, 2004 from http://www.ed.gov/parents/academic/help/hyc.html

United States Department of Education. (2002). *Cómo ayudar a su hijo a ser un buen lector.* Retrieved September 4, 2004 from http://www.ed.gov/espanol/parents/academic/lector/index.html

Vacca, R. T. (2002). *Making a difference in adolescents' school lives: Visible and invisible aspects of content area reading.* In A. Farstrup & S. J. Samuels (Eds.), *What research has to say about reading instruction* (3rd ed., pp. 184–204.) Newark, DE: International Reading Association.

Valdés, G. (1996). *Con respito: Bridging the differences between culturally diverse families and schools.* New York: Teachers College Press.

Villaume, S. K., & Brabham, E. G. (2001). Guided reading: Who is in the driver's seat? *The Reading Teacher, 55*(3), 260–263.

Vygotsky, L. (1978). *Mind in society: The development of higher psychological processes.* Cambridge, MA: Harvard University Press.

Vygotsky, L. (1986). *Thought and language.* Cambridge, MA: MIT Press.

Wagoner, S. (1983). Comprehension monitoring: What it is and what we know about it. *Reading Research Quarterly, 18*(3), 328–346.

Walker, B. (1996). *Diagnostic teaching of reading: Techniques for instruction and assessment.* Englewood Cliffs, NJ: Prentice Hall.

Walker, L. (1997). *Readers theatre strategies in the middle and junior high classroom.* Colorado Springs, CO: Meriwether.

Watson, G. (1996). *Teacher smart!* West Nyack, NY: The Center for Applied Research in Education.

Weaver, C. (2000). The basalization of America: A cause for concern. In R. Robinson, M. McKenna, & J. Wedman, *Issues and trends in literacy education* (2nd ed.). Needham Heights, MA: Allyn & Bacon.

White, T. G., Sowell, J., & Yanagihara, A. (1989). Teaching elementary students to use word-part clues. *The Reading Teacher, 42*(4), 302–308.

White, R., & Tisher, R. (1986). Research on natural sciences. In M. Wittrock (Ed.), *Handbook of research on teaching* (3rd ed., pp. 874–905.). New York: MacMillan.

Wilhelm, J. (2001). *Improving comprehension with think-aloud strategies: Modeling what good readers do.* New York: Scholastic Professional.

Wilkinson, L., & Silliman, E. (2000). Classroom language and literacy learning. In M. Kamil, P. Mosenthal, P. D. Pearson, & R. Barr, *Handbook of reading research* (Vol. 3, pp. 337–360). Mahwah, NJ: Erlbaum.

Williams, J. A. (2001). Classroom conversations: Opportunities to learn for ESL students in mainstream classrooms. *The Reading Teacher, 54*(8), 750–757.

Williams, J. P. (1993). Comprehension of students with and without learning disabilities: Identification of narrative themes and idiosyncratic text representations. *Journal of Educational Psychology, 85*(4), 631–641.

Williams, J. P. (2002). Using the theme scheme to improve story comprehension. In C. Block & M. Pressley (Eds.), *Comprehension instruction: Research based best practices* (pp. 126–139). New York: Guilford.

Willis, A. (2000). Critical issue: Addressing literacy needs in culturally and linguistically diverse classrooms. *North Central Regional Educational Laboratory.* Retrieved December 18, 2004, from http://www.ncrel.org/sdrs/areas/issues/content/cntareas/reading/li400.htm

Winograd, P., & Bridge, C. (1986). The comprehension of important information in written prose. In J. B. Baumann (Ed.), *Teaching main idea comprehension* (pp. 18–48). Newark, DE: International Reading Association.

Wood, D., Bruner, J., & Ross, G. (1976). The role of tutoring in problem-solving. *Journal of Child Psychology and Psychiatry, 17*(2), 89–100.

Yaden, D., Rowe, D., & MacGillivray, L. (2000). Emergent literacy: A matter (polyphony) of perspectives. In M. Kamil, P. Mosenthal, P. D. Pearson, & R. Barr (Eds.), *Handbook of reading research* (Vol. 3, pp. 425–454). Mahwah, NJ: Erlbaum.

Yopp, H. (1995). A test for assessing phonemic awareness in young children. *The Reading Teacher, 49*(1), 20–29.

Yopp, H., & Yopp, R. (2000). Supporting phonemic awareness development in the classroom. *The Reading Teacher, 54*(2), 130–143.

Yopp, R., & Yopp, H. (2001). *Literature-based reading activities* (3rd ed.). Boston: Allyn & Bacon.

Zigler, E., & Muenchow, S. (1992). *Head Start: The inside story of America's most successful educational experiment.* New York: Basic.

Children's Book References

Adler, D. (1990). *A picture book of Helen Keller*. New York: Trumpet.

Adler, D. (2000). *Cam Jansen and the birthday mystery*. New York: Puffin.

Agee, J. (2002). *Palindromania!* New York: Farrar, Straus and Giroux.

Aliki. (1986). *How a book is made*. New York: Harper & Row.

Allard, H. (1985). *Miss Nelson is missing!* Boston: Houghton Mifflin.

Alvarez, J. (2002). *Before we were free*. New York: Alfred Knopf/Random House.

Ancona, G. (1994). *The piñata maker/El piñatero*. San Diego, CA: Harcourt Brace.

Angelou, M. (1993). *Life doesn't frighten me*. New York: Stewart, Tabori & Chang.

Appleby, E. (1984). *The three billy goats gruff*. New York: Scholastic.

Asch, F. (1999). *Moonbear's Shadow*. New York: Aladdin.

Atwell, D. (1996). *Barn*. Boston: Houghton Mifflin.

Babbit, N. (1975). *Tuck everlasting*. New York: Farrar, Straus and Giroux.

Banks, L. R. (1980). *The Indian in the cupboard*. New York: Avon.

Barrett, J. (1978). *Cloudy with a chance of meatballs*. New York: Aladdin.

Barroux, S. (2004). *Mr. Katapat's incredible adventures*. New York: Viking/Penguin Group.

Bartoletti, S. C. (2004). *The flag maker*. Boston: Houghton Mifflin.

Barton, B. (1991). *The three bears*. New York: HarperCollins.

Bateman, T. (2001). *A plump and perky turkey*. New York: Winslow.

Bemelmans, L. (1958). *Madeline*. New York: Viking.

Berenstain, M. (1991). *Nose, toes, antlers, tail*. Racine, WI: Western.

Berger, M., & Berger, G. (2001). *What makes an ocean wave?* New York: Scholastic.

Bierhorst, J. (2001). *Is my friend at home? Pueblo fireside tales*. New York: Farrar, Straus and Giroux.

Bird, S. (2004). *Sue Bird: Be yourself*. Kirkland, WA: Positively for Kids.

Blair, M. (1996). *The red string*. Los Angeles: J. Paul Getty Museum Publications.

Blake, Q. (1996). *Clown*. New York: Holt.

Blume, J. (1976). *Tales of a fourth grade nothing*. New York: Yearling.

Blume, J. (1980). *Superfudge*. New York: Dutton.

Blume, J. (2002). *Double Fudge*. New York: Dutton.

Boedoe, G. (2004). *Arrowville*. New York: Laura Geringer/HarperCollins.

Bolden, T. (2001). *Tell all the children our story: Memories and mementos of being young and black in America*. New York: Abrams.

Bottner, B. (1986). *The world's greatest expert on absolutely everything is crying*. New York: Dell.

Bourgeois, P. (1994). *Franklin is messy*. New York: Scholastic.

Bourgeois, P. (2001). *Oma's quilt*. Toronto, Ontario: Kids Can.

Brett, J. (1995). *Armadillo rodeo*. New York: Scholastic.

Bridges, R. (1999). *Through my eyes*. New York: Scholastic.

Bridwell, N. (1991). *Clifford, we love you!* New York: Scholastic.

Brown, M. (1980). *Pickle things*. New York: Trumpet.

Brown, M. (1983). *Arthur's Thanksgiving*. Boston: Little, Brown.

Brown, M. (1991). *Arthur meets the president*. Boston: Little, Brown.

Brown, M. (1995). *D.W. the picky eater*. Boston: Little, Brown.

Brown, M. (1996). *Arthur's reading race*. New York: Random House.

Brown, M. (1997). *Arthur's computer disaster*. New York: Random House.

Brown, M. (1999). *Arthur in a pickle*. New York: Random House.

Browne, A. (1988). *I like books*. New York: Scholastic.

Bunting, E. (1988). *How many days to America?* New York: Trumpet.

Bunting, E. (1995a). *Cheyenne again*. New York: Clarion.

Bunting, E. (1995b). *Dandelions*. San Diego, CA: Voyager/Harcourt.

Bunting, E. (1996). *Train to somewhere*. Boston: Clarion.

Bunting, E. (1997). *I am the mummy Heb-Nefert*. San Diego, CA: Voyager/Harcourt.

Bunting, E. (1998). *So far from the sea*. New York: Clarion.

Bunting, E. (2001). *Gleam and glow*. San Diego, CA: Harcourt.

Bunting, E. (2003). *Whales passing*. New York: Blue Sky.

Bunting, E., & Bloom, S. (2002). *Girls A to Z*. Honesdale, PA: Boyds Mills.

Burnett, F. H. (1911). *The secret garden*. New York: Dell.

Burningham, J. (1970). *Mr. Gumpy's outing*. New York: Henry Holt.

Busby, P. (2003). *First to fly*. New York: Random House.

Butler, D. (1988). *My brown bear Barney*. New York: Greenwillow.

Byars, B. (1996). *Dead letter: A Herculeah Jones mystery*. New York: Puffin.

Cameron, A. (1981). *The stories Julian tells*. New York: Dell Yearling.

Campbell, R. (1982). *Dear Zoo*. New York: Simon & Schuster.

Canizares, S. (1998). *Storms*. New York: Scholastic.

Canizares, S., & Moreton, D. (1998). *Sun*. New York: Scholastic.

Canizares, S., & Reid, M. (1998). *Coral reef*. New York: Scholastic.

Carle, E. (1969). *The very hungry caterpillar*. New York: Philomel.

Carle, E. (1984). *The very busy spider*. New York: Scholastic.

Carle, E. (1987). *Have you seen my cat?* New York: Scholastic.

Carle, E. (2002). *Slowly, slowly, said the sloth*. New York: Philomel.

Carlstrom, N. W. (1986). *Jesse Bear, what will you wear?* New York: Scholastic.

Casey, P. (2001). *One day at Wood Green Animal Shelter*. Cambridge, MA: Candlewick.

Charles, N. N. (1994). *What am I? Looking through shapes at apples and grapes*. New York: Blue Sky.

Chavarria-Chairez, B. (2000). *Magda's tortillas/Las tortillas de Magda*. Houston, TX: Piñata.

Cheng, A. (2000). *Grandfather counts*. New York: Lee & Low.

Choi, N. S. (1991). *Year of impossible goodbyes*. New York: Dell.

Choi, Y. (2001). *The name jar*. New York: Alfred A. Knopf.

Christopher, M. (1972). *Face-off*. Boston: Little, Brown.

Cleary, B. (1981). *Ramona Quimby, age 8*. New York: Scholastic.

Clements, A. (1996). *Frindle*. New York: Simon & Schuster.

Clements, A. (2004). *The report card*. New York: Scholastic.

Cline-Ransome, L. (2001). *Quilt alphabet*. New York: Holiday House.

Codell, E. R. (2003). *Sahara special*. New York: Scholastic.

Cohlene, T. (2003). *Little firefly: An Algonquian legend*. New York: Troll.

Cole, J. (1986a). *Hungry, hungry sharks*. New York: Random House.

Cole, J. (1986b). *This is the place for me*. New York: Scholastic.

Cole, J. (1990). *The magic school bus lost in the solar system*. New York: Scholastic.

Collard, S. (2002). *Beaks!* Watertown, MA: Charlesbridge.

Colligan, L. (1988). *Help! I have to write a paper*. New York: Scholastic.

Conrad, P. (1991). *Pedro's journal*. New York: Scholastic.

Cox, P. (2000). *Sam sheep can't sleep*. New York: Scholastic.

Coxe, M. (1996). *Cat traps*. New York: Random House.

Cummings, P. (1994). *Clean your room, Harvey Moon!* New York: Aladdin.

Dadey, D., & Jones, M. T. (2000). *Mrs. Jeepers' monster class trip*. New York: Scholastic.

Dahl, R. (1988). *Matilda*. New York: Puffin Books.

Danziger, P. (1999). *I, Amber Brown*. New York: Scholastic.

Davis, W. (1995). *From tree to paper*. New York: Scholastic.

Day, T. (1994). *The Random House book of 1001 questions and answers about the human body*. New York: Random House.

Delton, J. (1988). *Cookies and crutches: A Pee Wee Scout mystery*. New York: Yearling.

Diaz, J. (1993). *The rebellious alphabet*. New York: Holt.

DiCamillo, K. (2000). *Because of Winn-Dixie*. Cambridge, MA: Candlewick.

Dixon, F. (1994). *The mystery of Cabin Island: A Hardy boys mystery* (Reissued ed.). New York: Grosset & Dunlap.

Dixon, F. (2005). *Extreme danger: Hardy boys undercover brothers*. New York: Aladdin.

Dodd, E. (2000). *Dog's a-b-c*. New York: Dutton.

Donner, K. (1999). *Buffalo dreams*. Portland, OR: Westwinds.

Dorris, M. (1992). *Morning girl*. New York: Hyperion.

Dorris, M. (1996). *Sees behind trees*. New York: Hyperion.

DuQuette, K. (2002). *They call me Wooly: What animal names can tell us*. New York: Putnam's Sons.

Eastman, P. D. (1961). *Go, dog, go*. New York: Random House.

Ehlert, L. (1992). *Moon rope/Un lazo a la luna*. San Diego, CA: Harcourt Brace.

Ellis, D. (2002). *Parvana's journey*. Toronto, Ontario: Groundwood.

Falconer, I. (2000). *Olivia*. New York: Atheneum.

Ferris, J. (1990). *What are you figuring now? A story about Benjamin Banneker*. Minneapolis, MN: Carolrhoda.

Finchler, J. (2002). *You're a good sport, Miss Malarkey*. New York: Walker.

Flack, M. (1997). *Angus and the ducks* (Reprint ed.). New York: Farrar, Straus and Giroux.

Flake, S. (1998). *The skin I'm in*. New York: Hyperion.

Fleischman, P. (1988). *Joyful noise: Poems for two voices*. New York: Trumpet.

Fleischman, P. (2003). *Sidewalk circus*. Cambridge, MA: Candlewick.

Fleming, D. (2002). *Alphabet under construction*. New York: Holt.

Fleming, C. (2003). *Boxes for Katje*. New York: Farrar, Straus and Giroux.

Florian, D. (2000). *Mammalabilia*. San Diego, CA: Harcourt.

Fox, M. (1989). *Feathers and fools*. Orlando, FL: Harcourt Brace.

Fox, M. (1994). *Tough Boris*. Orlando, FL: Harcourt Brace.

Fradin, D., & Fradin, J. B. (2003). *Fight on! Mary Church Terrell's battle for integration*. Boston: Clarion/Houghton Mifflin.

Freeman, D. (1955). *Mop top*. New York: Puffin.

Freeman, D. (1968). *Corduroy*. New York: Viking.

Freschet, B. (1977). *Little Black Bear goes for a walk*. New York: Scribner.

Fritz, J. (1982). *Homesick: My own story*. New York: Paperstar/Penguin Putnam Books for Young Readers.

Fritz, J. (1987). *Shh! We're writing the Constitution*. New York: Scholastic.

Fritz, J. (1995). *You want women to vote, Lizzie Stanton?* New York: Putnam's Sons.

Fry, Y. Y. (2001). *Kids like me in China*. St. Paul, MN: Yeong & Yeong.

Galdone, P. (1981). *The three billy goats gruff*. Boston: Houghton Mifflin.

Galdone, P. (1984). *The teeny-tiny woman*. New York: Clarion.

Galdone, P. (1986). *Over in the meadow*. New York: Simon & Schuster.

Gantos, J. (2000). *Joey Pigza loses control*. New York: Farrar, Straus and Giroux.

Garza, C. L. (1996). *In my family/En mi familia*. San Francisco: Children's.

Gave, M. (1993). *Monkey see, monkey do*. New York: Scholastic Cartwheel.

George, J. C. (1959). *My side of the mountain*. New York: Trumpet.

George, J. C. (1990). *One day in the tropical rain forest*. New York: HarperCollins.

George, L. B. (1995). *In the woods: Who's been here?* New York: Trumpet.

Giff, P. R. (1985a). *Kids of the Polk Street School: In the dinosaur's paw*. New York: Dell.

Giff, P. R. (1985b). *Watch out, Ronald Morgan!* New York: Puffin.

Giff, P. R. (2002). *Pictures of Hollis Woods*. New York: Dell Yearling.

Giff, P. R. (2004). *A house of tailors*. New York: Wendy Lamb.

Gilman, P. (1988). *The wonderful pigs of Jillian Jiggs*. Toronto, Ontario: Scholastic.

Glanzer, E., Hitchman, A., Koval, R., Smith, L., & Wiener, E. (2001). *One day in the life of bubble gum*. New York: Scholastic.

Goffin, J. (2000). *Oh!* New York: Abrams.

Gonzalez, T. (2004). *Catch and connect*. Kirkland, WA: Positively for Kids.

Gourley, C. (1999). *Welcome to Samantha's world—1904: Growing up in America's new century (American Girls Collection)*. Middleton, WI: Pleasant.

Griffiths, A. (2005). *Just disgusting*. New York: Scholastic.

Guarino, D. (1989). *Is your mama a llama?* New York: Scholastic.

Guinness World Records. (2004). *Guinness World Records 2005: Special 50th anniversary edition*. London: Guinness World Records.

Gutman, D. (2003). *Mickey and me: A baseball card adventure*. New York: HarperCollins.

Haddix, M. (2002). *Among the betrayed*. New York: Simon & Schuster.

Hadingham, E., & Hadingham, J. (1990). *Garbage! Where it comes from, where it goes*. New York: Simon & Schuster.

Haduch, B. (2001). *Food rules! The stuff you munch, its crunch, its punch, and why you sometimes lose your lunch*. New York: Puffin.

Hall, Z. (1998). *The surprise garden*. New York: HarperCollins.

Hall, Z. (2000). *The surprise garden*. (Big book ed.). New York: Scholastic.

Harcourt Science. (2002). *Matter and energy*. Orlando, FL: Harcourt.

Hart, A. (2003). *Fires of jubilee*. New York: Aladdin.

Havill, J. (1986). *Jamaica's find*. Boston: Houghton Mifflin.

Havill, J. (1993). *Jamaica and Brianna*. Boston: Houghton Mifflin.

Heide, F. P., & Pierce, R. H. (1998). *Tio Armando*. New York: HarperCollins.

Henkes, K. (1987). *Sheila Rae, the brave*. New York: Greenwillow.

Hennessey, B. G. (1990). *Jake baked the cake*. New York: Viking.

Herman, G. (1996). *There is a town*. New York: Random House.

Herrera, J. F. (1998). *Laughing out loud, I fly: Poems in English and Spanish*. New York: HarperCollins.

Herrera, J. F. (2000). *Upside down boy/El niño de cabeza*. San Francisco: Children's.

Hiaasen, C. (2002). *Hoot*. New York: Alfred Knopf/Random House.

Hill, E. (1980). *Where's Spot?* New York: Putnam.

Himmelman, J. (1990). *Ibis: A true whale story*. New York: Scholastic.

Hoffman, M. (2002). *The color of home*. New York: Penguin Putnam.

Holliday, L. (1999). *Why do they hate me? Young lives caught in war and conflict*. New York: Pocket.

Hopkins, L. B. (1990). *Good books, good times!* New York: Trumpet.

Hopkinson, D. (2003). *Shutting out the sky: Life in the tenements of New York, 1880–1924*. New York: Scholastic.

Horenstein, H. (1997). *Baseball in the barrios*. Orlando, FL: Harcourt.

Howe, J., & Howe, D. (1979). *Bunnicula: A rabbit tale of mystery*. New York: Atheneum.

Hurwitz, J. (1983). *Rip roaring Russell*. New York: HarperCollins.

Hurwitz, J. (1987). *Russell sprouts*. New York: HarperCollins.

Hutchins, P. (1968). *Rosie's walk*. New York: Aladdin.

Hutchins, P. (1971). *Titch*. New York: Aladdin.

Ibbotson, E. (2004). *The star of Kazan*. New York: Dutton.

Jacobs, F. (1992). *Sam the sea cow*. New York: Walker.

Jacques, B. (1986). *Redwall*. New York: Penguin Putnam.

Jeffers, S. (1991). *Brother Eagle, Sister Sky*. New York: Dial.

Jensen, A. (1998). *Leonard Calvert and the Maryland adventure*. Centreville, MD: Cornell Maritime.

Jimenez, F. (2000). *La mariposa*. Boston: Houghton Mifflin.

Johnson, A. (1992). *The leaving morning*. New York: Orchard Books.

Johnson, C. (1955). *Harold and the purple crayon*. New York: Harper & Row.

Johnston, T. (1996). *My Mexico—Mexico mio*. New York: Penguin.

Katz, K. (1999). *The colors of us*. New York: Holt.

Keats, E. J. (1964). *Whistle for Willie*. New York: Viking.

Keats, E. J. (1999). *Clementine's cactus*. New York: Viking.

Keller, H. (1988). *Geraldine's big snow*. New York: Scholastic.

Kellogg, S. (1987). *Chicken little*. New York: Morrow.

Keene, C. (1996). *The sign of the twisted candles: A Nancy Drew mystery*. (Reissued ed.). New York: Grosset & Dunlap.

Kimball, K. M. (2001). *Star spangled secret*. New York: Aladdin.

Kirk, D. (2000). *Miss Spider's ABC*. New York: Scholastic.

Konigsburg, E. L. (1996). *The view from Saturday*. New York: Scholastic.

Konigsburg, E. L. (2000). *Silent to the bone*. New York: Simon & Schuster.

Korman, G. (1999). *Something fishy at MacDonald Hall*. New York: Scholastic.

Kraus, R. (1971). *Leo the late bloomer*. New York: Windmill.
Krull, K. (2000). *Lives of extraordinary women: Rulers, rebels (and what the neighbors thought)*. San Diego, CA: Harcourt.
Kubler, A. (1999). *Man's work!* London: Child's Play.
Laskey, K. (2003). *A voice of her own: The story of Phillis Wheatley, slave poet*. Cambridge, MA: Candlewick.
Lauber, P. (1999). *What you never knew about fingers, forks, and chopsticks*. New York: Simon & Schuster.
Lawrence, J. (2002). *This little chick*. Cambridge, MA: Candlewick.
Lear, E. (1973). *Whizz!* London: Macmillan.
Lee, D. (2001). *Alligator pie*. Toronto, Ontario: Key Porter Kids.
Lehman, B. (2004). *The red book*. Boston: Houghton Mifflin.
LeSieg, T. (1972). *In a people house*. New York: Random House.
LeSieg, T. (1980). *Maybe you should fly a jet! Maybe you should be a vet!* New York: Random House.
Lester, H. (1988). *Tacky the penguin*. New York: Trumpet.
Lewis, C. S. (1950). *The chronicles of Narnia*. New York: HarperCollins.
Lewison, W. C. (1992). *Buzzz said the bee*. New York: Scholastic Cartwheel.
Lillegard, D. (2001). *Hello, school!* New York: Alfred Knopf.
Lindgren, A. (1997). *Adventures of Pippi Longstocking*. New York: Viking.
Lionni, L. (1963). *Swimmy*. New York: Pantheon.
Lionni, L. (1968). *The alphabet tree*. New York: Trumpet.
Lobel, A. (1970). *Frog and toad are friends*. New York: Harper-Collins.
Lobel, A. (1971). *Frog and toad together*. New York: Harper-Collins.
Lobel, A. (1976). *Frog and toad all year*. New York: Harper-Collins.
Lobel, A. (1980). *Fables*. New York: Harper & Row.
Lowry, L. (1979). *Anastasia Krupnik*. Boston: Houghton Mifflin.
Lowry, L. (1989). *Number the stars*. New York: Bantam Doubleday Dell.
Lowry, L. (1993). *The giver*. New York: Bantam Doubleday Dell.
Lowry, L. (2000). *Gathering blue*. New York: Laurel Leaf.
Maccarone, G. (1996). *Recess mess*. New York: Scholastic.
Maizlish, L. (1996). *The ring*. New York: Greenwillow.
Marshall, J. (1984). *George and Martha back in town*. Boston: Houghton Mifflin.
Marshall, J. (1985). *The cut-ups*. New York: Viking.
Martin, A. (1986). *Kristy's great idea: Babysitter's club*. New York: Scholastic.
Martin, B. (1983). *Brown bear, brown bear, what do you see?* New York: Holt.
Martin, B. (1991). *Polar bear, polar bear, what do you hear?* New York: Holt.
Martin, B., & Sampson, M. (2001). *Little granny quarterback*. Honesdale, PA: Boyds Mill.
Martin, R. (1992). *The rough-face girl*. New York: Scholastic.
Massoff, J. (2000). *Oh, yuck! The encyclopedia of everything nasty*. New York: Workman.

Maxner, J. (1990). *Nicholas cricket*. New York: HarperCollins.
Mayer, M. (1987). *There's an alligator under my bed*. New York: Dial.
Mayer, M. (1993). *Just like Dad*. New York: Golden.
McCloskey, R. (1941). *Make way for ducklings*. New York: Viking.
McMillan, B. (1990). *One sun*. New York: Holiday House.
McMillan, B. (1991). *Play day: A book of terse verse*. New York: Holiday House.
McMullan, K. (1991). *The story of Harriet Tubman, conductor of the Underground Railroad*. New York: Parachute.
Metropolitan Museum of Art. (2002). *Museum ABC*. New York: Little, Brown.
Miller, D. (2002). *Are trees alive?* New York: Walker.
Mills, L. (2005). *Hans Christian Andersen's* Thumbelina. New York: Little, Brown.
Minarik, E. (1996). *A kiss for Little Bear*. HarperCollins.
Miranda, A. (1994). *Does a mouse have a house?* New York: Simon & Schuster.
Montgomery, L. (1998). *Anne of Green Gables*. (Re-issued ed.). New York: Random House.
Mora, P. (1992). *A birthday basket for Tia*. New York: Simon & Schuster.
Mora, P. (1994a). *Listen to the desert/Oye al desierto*. New York: Clarion.
Mora, P. (1994b). *Pablo's tree*. New York: Simon & Schuster.
Mosel, A. (1968). *Tikki Tikki Tembo*. New York: Holt.
Munsch, R. (1980). *The paper bag princess*. Toronto: Annick.
Napier, M. (2002). *Z is for zamboni*. Chelsea, MI: Sleeping Bear.
Naylor, P. R. (1986). *The agony of Alice*. New York: Aladdin.
Nelson, P. (2002). *Left for dead: A young man's search for justice for the USS* Indianapolis. New York: Delacorte/Random House.
Norton, M. (1952). *The borrowers*. San Diego, CA: Harcourt.
Numeroff, L. J. (1985). *If you give a mouse a cookie*. New York: HarperCollins.
Numeroff, L. J. (2002). *If you take a mouse to school*. New York: HarperCollins.
O'Connell, J. (2000). *Ten timid ghosts*. New York: Scholastic Cartwheel.
O'Dell, S. (1970). *Sing down the moon*. New York: Random House.
O'Malley, K. (1999). *Leo cockroach, toy tester*. New York: Walker.
O'Neill, A. (2002). *Recess queen*. New York: Scholastic.
Oppenheim, J. (1989). *"Not now!" said the cow*. New York: Bantam Doubleday Dell.
Oppenheim, J. (1993). *"Uh-oh!" said the crow*. New York: Bantam Doubleday Dell.
Oppenheim, J. (1994). *"Not now!" said the cow*. (Big book ed.). New York: Trumpet.
Osborne, M. P. (1999). *Magic tree house: Tonight on the* Titanic. New York: Scholastic.
Otto, C. (2002). *Spiders*. New York: Scholastic.
Oughton, J. (1992). *How the stars fell into the sky*. Boston: Houghton Mifflin.
Packard, M. (1993). *My messy room*. New York: Scholastic.
Pak, S. (1999). *Dear Juno*. New York: Viking.

Pallotta, J. (1996). *The freshwater alphabet book*. New York: Trumpet.

Papov, N. (1988). *Why?* New York: North South Books.

Parish, P. (1981). *Amelia Bedelia and the baby*. New York: Avon.

Park, B. (1997). *Skinnybones (Revised ed.)*. New York: Random House.

Park, B. (2001). *Junie B., first grader (at last!)*. New York: Random House.

Park, L. (2002). *When my name was Keoko*. Boston: Clarion/Houghton Mifflin.

Paterson, K. (2002). *The same stuff as stars*. Boston: Clarion/Houghton Mifflin.

Paulsen, G. (1987). *Hatchet*. New York: Simon & Schuster.

Pavlova, A. (2001). *I dreamed I was a ballerina*. New York: Atheneum.

Peck, R. N. (1974). *Soup*. New York: Dell Yearling.

Peet, B. (1970). *The wump world*. Boston: Houghton Mifflin.

Pérez, A. I. (2002). *My diary from here to there/Mi diario de aqui hasta alla*. San Francisco: Children's.

Peters, L. W. (1988). *The sun, the wind, and the rain*. New York: Holt.

Peterson, J. (1967). *The Littles*. New York: Scholastic.

Pilkey, D. (2001). *Ricky Ricotta's giant robot vs. the voodoo vultures from Venus*. New York: Scholastic.

Pinkwater, D. (2001). *Fat camp commandos*. New York: Scholastic.

Pinkwater, M. (1975). *Wingman*. New York: Dell.

Pinto, S. (2003). *The alphabet room*. New York: Bloomsbury.

Polacco, P. (1994). *Pink and Say*. New York: Philomel.

Polacco, P. (1998). *Thank you, Mr. Falker*. New York: Philomel.

Polacco, P. (2000). *The butterfly*. New York: Philomel.

Potter, B. (1987). *The tale of Peter Rabbit* (Reissued ed.). New York: Scholastic.

Preller, J. (2000). *A Jigsaw Jones mystery: The case of the ghost-writer*. New York: Scholastic.

Raczka, B. (2002). *No one saw: Ordinary things through the eyes of an artist*. Brookfield, CT: Millbrook.

Reading Rainbow Readers (2001). *Friendship stories you can share*. New York: Seastar.

Recorvits, H. (2003). *My name is Yoon*. New York: Frances Foster Books/Farrar, Straus and Giroux.

Rey, H. A. (1941). *Curious George*. New York: Scholastic.

Rey, H. A. (1952). *Curious George rides a bike*. Boston: Houghton Mifflin.

Riley, L. (1997). *Mouse mess*. New York: Scholastic.

Riley, L. (1999). *Mouse mess*. (Big book ed.). New York: Scholastic.

Ringgold, F. (1991). *Tar beach*. New York: Scholastic.

Ringgold, F. (1999). *If a bus could talk: The story of Rosa Parks*. New York: Simon & Schuster.

Ripley Entertainment. (2004). *Ripley's believe it or not*. Orlando, FL: Ripley Entertainment.

Rohmer, H. (1989). *Uncle Nacho's hat*. San Francisco: Children's.

Rosen, M. (1989). *We're going on a bear hunt*. New York: Simon & Schuster.

Rosenberry, V. (2004). *Vera rides a bike*. New York: Holt.

Rowling, J. K. (1997). *Harry Potter and the sorcerer's stone*. New York: Scholastic.

Rupp, R. (2003). *Weather!* North Adams, MA: Storey.

Ryan, P. N. (2000). *Esperanza rising*. New York: Scholastic.

Rylant, C. (1987). *Henry and Mudge in puddle trouble*. New York: Simon & Schuster.

Rylant, C. (1994). *Mr. Putter and Tabby pour the tea*. San Diego, CA: Harcourt.

Sachar, L. (1978). *Sideways stories from Wayside School*. New York: Avon.

Sachar, L. (1998). *Holes*. New York: Farrar, Straux and Giroux.

Salisbury, K. (1997a). *My nose is a hose*. New York: McClanahan.

Salisbury, K. (1997b). *There's a bug in my mug*. New York: McClanahan.

Sateren, S. (2002). *Going to school in colonial America*. Mankato, MN: Capstone.

Say, A. (1993). *Grandfather's journey*. Boston: Houghton Mifflin.

Schulman, J. (Ed.), (1993). *The Random House book of easy-to-read stories*. New York: Random House.

Schwartz, A. (1984). *In a dark, dark room and other scary stories*. New York: HarperCollins.

Scieszka, J. (1989). *The true story of the three little pigs!* New York: Viking Penguin.

Scieszka, J. (1992). *The stinky cheese man and other fairly stupid tales*. New York: Viking Penguin.

Segal, L. (1977). *Tell me a Trudy*. New York: Farrar, Straus and Giroux.

Sendak, M. (1963). *Where the wild things are*. New York: Scholastic.

Seuss, Dr. (1940). *Horton hatches the egg*. New York: Random House.

Seuss, Dr. (1957). *The cat in the hat*. New York: Random House.

Seuss, Dr. (1958). *Yertle the turtle and other stories*. New York: Random House.

Seuss, Dr. (1960). *Green eggs and ham*. New York: Random House.

Seuss, Dr. (1963). *Hop on pop*. New York: Random House.

Seuss, Dr. (1965). *Fox in socks*. New York: Random House.

Seuss, Dr. (1974a). *Great day for up*. New York: Random House.

Seuss, Dr. (1974b). *There's a wocket in my pocket*. New York: Random House.

Seuss, Dr. (1978). *I can read with my eyes shut!* New York: Random House.

Shannon, D. (2002). *David gets in trouble*. New York: Blue Sky.

Sharmat, M. W. (1972). *Nate the Great*. New York: Coward-McCann.

Shaw, N. (1986). *Sheep in a jeep*. Boston: Houghton Mifflin.

Shecter, B. (1977). *Hester the jester*. New York: Harper & Row.

Silverstein, S. (1964). *A giraffe and a half*. New York: HarperCollins.

Silverstein, S. (1964). *The giving tree*. New York: Harper & Row.

Silverstein, S. (1974). *Where the sidewalk ends*. New York: HarperCollins.

Simon, S. (1989). *Whales*. New York: HarperTrophy.

Simon, S. (1993). *Weather*. New York: Morrow.

Simon, S. (2001). *Animals nobody loves*. New York: Scholastic.

Sis, P. (2000). *Dinosaur!* New York: Greenwillow.

Slate, J. (1996). *Miss Bindergarten gets ready for kindergarten*. New York: Dutton.

Slepian J., & Seidler, A. (1967). *The hungry thing*. New York: Scholastic.

Slobodkina, E. (1947). *Caps for sale*. New York: HarperCollins.

Smith, D. (2002). *If the world were a village: A book about the world's people*. Toronto, Ontario: Kids Can.

Snicket, L. (Handler, D.) (2001). *The ersatz elevator: A series of unfortunate events*. New York: HarperCollins.

Sobol, D. (1985). *Encyclopedia Brown, boy detective*. New York: Bantam.

Soto, G. (1992). *The skirt*. New York: Bantam Doubleday Dell.

Soto, G. (1993). *Too many tamales*. New York: Putnam.

Soto, G. (1995). *Chato's kitchen*. New York: Putnam & Grosset/PaperStar.

Soto, G. (1996). *The old man and his door*. New York: Putnam & Grosset.

Spinelli, J. (1990). *Maniac Magee*. Boston: Little, Brown.

Spinelli, J. (2000). *Stargirl*. New York: Knopf.

Steig, W. (1969). *Sylvester and the magic pebble*. New York: Simon & Schuster.

Stevens, J. (1995). *Tops and bottoms*. New York: Scholastic.

Stevens, J. & Crummel, S. (1999). *Cook-a-doodle-doo!* Orlando, FL: Harcourt Brace.

Stevens, J. R. (1995). *Carlos and the squash plant/Carlos y la planta de calabaza*. Flagstaff, AZ: Rising Moon/Northland.

Taback, S. (1997). *There was an old lady who swallowed a fly*. New York: Viking.

Taback, S. (1999). *Joseph had a little overcoat*. New York: Scholastic.

Tan, A. (2001). *Sagwa, the Chinese Siamese cat*. New York: Simon & Schuster.

Tavares, M. (2000). *Zachary's ball*. Cambridge, MA: Candlewick.

Taylor, M. (1968). *Henry explores the jungle*. New York: Simon & Schuster.

Taylor, M. (1976). *Roll of thunder, hear my cry*. New York: Viking Penguin.

Treffinger, C. (1947). *Li Lun: Lad of courage*. New York: Walker.

Tudor, T. (2001). *A is for Annabelle*. New York: Simon & Schuster.

Uchida, Y. (1981). *A jar of dreams*. New York: Aladdin.

Uegaki, C. (2003). *Suki's kimono*. Toronto, Ontario: Kids Can.

Van Allsburg, C. (1993). *The sweetest fig*. Boston: Houghton Mifflin.

Van Draanen, W. (2004). *Sammy Keyes and the psycho Kitty Queen*. New York: Alfred Knopf.

Vaughan, M. (1995). *Tingo tango mango tree*. Morristown, NJ: Silver Burdett.

Vieira, L. (1994). *The ever-living tree: The life and times of a coast redwood*. New York: Trumpet.

Vinje, M. (1996). *The new bike*. Grand Haven, MI: School Zone.

Waber, B. (1965). *Lyle, Lyle, crocodile*. New York: Houghton Mifflin.

Waber, B. (1972). *Ira sleeps over*. Boston: Houghton Mifflin.

Walsh, E. S. (1981). *Theodore all grown up*. San Diego, CA: Voyager Books/Harcourt Brace.

Warner, G. C. (1942). *The box car children*. Toronto, Ontario: Whitman.

Warren, A. (1996). *Orphan train rider: One boy's true story*. Boston: Houghton Mifflin.

Waters, K. (2001). *Giving thanks: The 1621 harvest feast*. New York: Scholastic.

Waugh, S. (1996). *The Mennyms*. New York: HarperTrophy.

Wheeler, J. (2001). *September 11, 2001: The day that changed America*. Edna, MN: ABDO.

White, E. B. (1952). *Charlotte's web*. New York: HarperCollins.

White, E. B. (2005). *La telarana de Carlota (Charlotte's Web)*. New York: Rayo/HarperCollins.

Wilder, L. I. (1935). *Little house on the prairie*. New York: HarperCollins.

Wilhelm, H. (1988). *Tyrone the horrible*. New York: Scholastic.

Wilhelm, H. (2002). *I love my shadow*. New York: Scholastic.

Williams, L. (1986). *The little old lady who was not afraid of anything*. New York: HarperCollins.

Williams, R. L. (1994a). *All through the day with cat and dog*. Cypress, CA: Creative Teaching.

Williams, R. L. (1994b). *Cat and dog*. Cypress, CA: Creative Teaching.

Williams, R. L. (1994c). *Where do monsters live?* Cypress, CA: Creative Teaching.

Williams, S. (1989). *I went walking*. San Diego, CA: Voyager Books/Harcourt Brace.

Wiseman, B. (1959). *Morris the moose*. New York: HarperCollins.

Wolkstein, D. (1993). *Horse and toad. A folktale from Haiti* (Big book ed.). New York: Scholastic.

Wood, A. (1989). *Little Penguin's tale*. San Diego, CA: Harcourt.

Wood, A. (1992). *Silly Sally*. San Diego, CA: Harcourt.

Wood, D. (2002). *A quiet place*. New York: Simon & Schuster.

Wulffson, D. (2000). *Toys! Amazing stories behind some great inventions*. New York: Holt.

Yep, L. (1977). *Child of the owl*. New York: Harper & Row.

Yep, L. (1982). *Dragon of the lost sea*. New York: HarperCollins.

Yorinks, A. (1986). *Hey, Al*. New York: Sunburst.

Young, E. (1989). *Lon po-po*. New York: Scholastic.

Young, E. (1992). *Seven blind mice*. New York: Scholastic.

Ziefert, H. (1984). *Sleepy dog*. New York: Random House.

Ziefert, H. (2003). *You can't see your bones with binoculars: A guide to your 206 bones*. Maplewood, NJ: Blue Apple.

Index

Boundaries
    of books, 177
    of sentences, 184–185
    of words, 182–183
Brainstorming, 389, 391, 397
"Bulldozing," 508

Caregivers
    mental modeling shared with, 63
    reading process explained to, 32
    web sites for, 88
Categorizing of facts, 436–437,
        438f–439f, 459
Cause/effect text structure,
        157–159, 165
Center for the Improvement of
        Early Reading Instruction,
        47
Character evidence map, 141, 141f
Characters, 138–141, 165
Chinese language, 73
Choral reading, 86f, 478, 485
Clarifying, 409–410
Class meeting, 318–320
Classroom
    cueing systems used in, 14
    diversity in, 46
    for English language learners
        cultural experiences, 78–79
        encouragement of primary
            language, 75, 77–78
        humor, 75
        laughter, 75
        lessons as language learning
            experiences, 82
        reading aloud, 79, 82, 86f
        risk-free atmosphere, 74–75
        rules, 75
        scaffolds, 83
        time to learn, 84
    language forms in, 71
    learning climate in, 178
    library in, 290f, 498–499
    play areas in, 176–177, 211
    theory influences on, 9–10
    writing center in, 206
Classroom decoding checks,
        117–118, 119f, 134
Classroom learning, 6
Classroom library, 290f, 498–499
Clay's Concepts About Print test,
        112
Click and Clunk, 417–419, 429,
        504
Cloze passages, 263, 263f–264f,
        279
Cognate languages, 70

Cognates
    description of, 83f, 84
    in guided reading, for English
        language learners,
        292–293
Cognitive academic language
        proficiency, 71, 90
Cognitive modeling, 51
Communication
    cultural differences in, 72–73
    culturally responsive, 85
    nonverbal, 73
Communicative language, 492–493
Compacted curriculum, 504
Comparison text structure, 157, 165
Comprehending, 18, 21
Comprehension
    assessments of
        description of, 118
        matching readers to text,
            122–127
        miscue analysis, 119, 121–122,
            134
        retelling analysis, 122, 134
        running records, 118–119,
            122–123, 134
    breakdowns in, 353
    definition of, 373
    fluency and, 18, 20–21, 469–472
    inferential, 343
    oral reading and, 470–472
    prior knowledge as basis for, 22,
        24–25
    self-regulated, 353, 355
    teaching strategies to facilitate
        Click and Clunk, 417–419,
            429, 504
        description of, 410
        directed listening thinking
            activity, 412, 415–416,
            428
        directed reading thinking activ-
            ity, 411–412, 413f, 428
        question the author, 412, 414f,
            428
        question-answer relationships,
            411
        reading line-by-line, 419–420,
            420f, 429
        reciprocal teaching, 412, 428
        say something, 412, 414, 428
        self-reflective questioning,
            420–421, 429
        story structure cards, 421,
            423f, 424, 429
        student-generated questions,
            425, 429

text coding, 425, 429
    think-alouds, 426
Comprehensive instruction
    "balance" used in, 39
    decision-making model of, 40f
    description of, 38
    model of, 39, 40f
    summarization used in, 45
Concepts of print
    addressing of, 185
    assessments of
        alphabet recognition checklist,
            114, 114f–115f, 134
        checklist, 112, 113f, 134
        Clay's Concepts About Print
            test, 112
        Graves, Juel, and Burns
            emergency literacy
            assessment, 112
        overview of, 133
    definition of, 110
Concrete experiences, 251,
        391–392, 397
Conflict, 144–145
Consonant continuants, 220
Consonant phonemes, 219, 221f,
        223f
Constructivism, 24–25
Content words
    definition of, 258
    meaning strategies for
        cloze passages, 263,
            263f–264f, 279
        context clues, 260–261, 261f
        keyword method, 266–267
        mnemonics, 266–267, 279
        predict-o-gram, 262, 262f, 279
        semantic feature analysis, 265,
            266f–267f, 279
        word and sentence prediction
            charts, 263–264, 265f,
            279
        word parts, 269–271, 279
    teaching of, 258–259
Context
    function words understood by,
        250–251, 258, 278
    words in, 259
Context clues, 260, 261f, 509
Continuant sounds, 191
Conversational talk, 408
Conversations, 98
Cooperative Children's Book
        Center, 91
Cooperative groups, 389
Correct words per minute,
        479–480

"teaching the heart" strategies for, 89, 89f
"teaching the whole" strategies for, 86f, 87
technology resources for, 91
terms associated with, 69f
verbal speech understood by, 71
visualizing lesson plan for, 354–355
web sites for, 88
WebQuests for, 443–444
Environmental print, 181–182, 183f
Evidence-based instruction, 8
Exclusive questions, 406, 495f
Expectations, 497–498
Explanations
  characteristics of, 49–50
  description of, 48, 65
  example of, 50
  need for, 50
  overview of, 65
  rationale for, 48
  value of, 51
  when to use, 50
  written, 48
Explicit phonics instruction, 222, 224, 242
Explicit teaching
  Center for the Improvement of Early Reading Instruction description of, 47
  description of, 47–48, 65
  explanations. See Explanations
  mental modeling. See Mental modeling
  overview of, 65
  strategies for, 48
  teacher behaviors, 47
Extending, 410
Extrinsic rewards, 43
Eye contact, 73

Facilitative instruction, 64
Facilitative teaching, 54–55, 58f, 65
Feedback, 410
Fiction
  historical, 142
  nonfiction vs., 150, 163
  predictions making with, 340–342
  stories. See Stories
  structure of, 377f
  summary of, 163
  teaching strategies for
    book box, 381–382, 397
    picture book introductions, 383–385, 397

story impressions, 385, 386f–387f, 397
technology resources for, 164
visualizing of, 350–352
Figurative language, for English language learners, 61–62
Find and read strategy, 471–472, 485
Five-a-Day Folder system, 99
Fix-up strategies bookmarks, 419, 429
Fluency
  accuracy and, 482–483
  automaticity and, 18, 20–21, 467
  comprehension and, 469–472
  definition of, 18, 467
  description of, 17, 30
  elements of, 469
  expression and, 472–478
  indicator of, 18, 20–21
  native language, 75, 77
  rate and, 478–481
  reading assignments for, 482
  repeated readings for, 480, 481f
  vocabulary and, 20–21
Focus, 378–380
Frames and reminders checklists, 307–308, 309f
Fry readability formula, 124, 125f, 131, 135, 286
Function words
  definition of, 250
  example of, 250
  teaching strategies for
    context, 250–251, 258, 278
    interactive writing, 253, 255, 278
    language experience approach, 251–253, 254f, 278
    predictable books, 251, 253
    repetition, 251
    word banks, 256, 256f, 278
    word walls, 256–258, 278

Generalizations, 229–232, 231f, 243
"Ghost talk," 192, 213
Gifted students, 504
Giggling, 73
Glyphs, 103f–104f
Grammar cues, 12
Grand conversations, 442
Graphemes, 225
Graphophonological cues, 13
Graves, Juel, and Burns emergency literacy assessment, 112
Group reading, 319f–320f, 324–327
Guided reading, 291, 294, 295f, 331

Highlighting, 441, 459
High-stakes tests, 96
Hink pinks, 234, 243
Historical fiction, 142
Humor, 75
Hypertext, 339, 441

Ideas
  awakening of, 3
  main, 364–366, 368–369
Impatient readers, 513–514
Inclusion, 489
Inclusive questions, 406, 493–494, 495f
Independent reading, 7, 41, 288–291, 319f, 322–323, 331, 499–500
Independent writing, 301–305, 331
Inductive learning, 229f
Inductive word solving, 227–229, 243
Inferences
  description of, 44f, 53
  making of, 347–349, 368–369
Inferencing, 53–54
Inferential questions, 408
Inferential thinking, 347
Inferring, 347
Informal assessments, 57, 97
Informal reading inventory, 127, 127f, 135
Informal writing, 433
Informational texts. See also Nonfiction
  cause/effect structure of, 157–159, 165
  comparison structure of, 157, 165
  descriptive structure of, 152, 165
  problem/solution structure of, 159–160, 162–163
  sequential structure of, 152–153, 155–157, 165
Instruction
  "balance" in, 39, 57, 59–64
  content balanced with, 57, 59–62
  culturally responsive, 7, 74, 151
  facilitative, 64
  literacy. See Literacy instruction
  planning of, 39
  quality of, 178
  reading, 4, 15, 225
  scaffolded, 39
  strategies for, 8
  student's role in, 45–46
Instructional decisions, 60
Interactive writing, 86f, 207–209, 208f, 213, 253, 255, 278, 306–307

Reading (continued)
    for boys, 511–513
    choral, 86f, 478, 485
    comprehending and, 18, 21
    daily independent, 7, 41
    decoding and, 18, 20–21
    efferent, 432
    emergent storybook, 172
    for enjoyment, 336–339
    environment for, 283
    extrinsic rewards for, 43
    fluency in, 17–21
    functions used in, 18
    group, 319f–320f, 324–327
    guided, 291, 294, 295f, 331
    "heart" of, 509–516
    independent, 7, 41, 288–291,
        319f, 322–323, 331,
        499–500
    inference making during,
        347–349
    instructional supports for,
        287–300
    intrinsic motivation for, 43
    oral. *See* Oral reading
    paired, 86f
    partner, 89f, 326f, 475, 477, 485
    practice in, 56
    predictions used by students
        during, 13
    pretend, 172–173, 211
    readiness for, 168
    recreational, 106
    refusal, 511–513
    round-robin, 465–467
    scaffolds for, 284f, 286–300
    schema theory of, 24–25, 26f,
        30, 34–35, 43
    self-regulated, 353, 355–357, 422
    shared. *See* Shared reading
    silent, 289–290
    as social endeavor, 41, 56
    speed of, 478–480
    struggles in, 510–511
    summarization after, 45
    support for, 283–284
    teaching of
        balanced approach to, 217
        National Reading Panel recom-
            mendations for, 218
        "teaching the heart" approach,
            42–43, 60
        "teaching the parts" approach,
            42
        "teaching the whole" ap-
            proach, 41
    text selection for, 336–340
    vocabulary knowledge and,
        15–16

    volume of, 46
    word knowledge and, 246
    writing and, 41, 129, 282
Reading aloud
    description of, 298–300, 299f,
        331
    for English language learners, 79,
        82, 86f
    pretend reading secondary to, 172
    reasons for, 467, 469–470
"Reading backpacks," 77
Reading behaviors
    assessment of, 101f
    scaffolding a search for meaning
        in whole text, 501–505
    scaffolding the "heart" of read-
        ing, 509–506
    scaffolding the "parts" of read-
        ing, 506–508
Reading comprehension, 60
Reading instruction
    influences on, 4
    phonics-based, 225
    research on, 15
Reading line-by-line, 419–420,
    420f, 429
Reading process
    components of, 45–46
    description of, 32
    explaining to caregivers, 32
    mental modeling for uncovering
        of, 51–52
    technology resources about,
        34–35, 64–65
Reading strategies
    definition of, 380
    description of, 42
    essential, 43–46, 44f
Reading workshop, 314–315, 315f
Reciprocal teaching, 412, 428
Recitation, 407, 444
Recreational reading, 106
Rehearsal phase of writing,
    302–303
Repeated readings, 480, 481f, 485
Repetition
    function word teaching strategies
        using, 251
    language experience approach,
        251
Rereading of books, 172, 211
Resolution of story, 146–147, 165
Response journals
    definition of, 446
    description of, 321
    dialogue journal responses,
        446–447, 460
    double-entry journals, 447–448,
        449f, 461

    point of view entries, 449, 451,
        461
    quotation sharing, 451–452, 461
    rating and comparing of books,
        454, 461
    stating opinions in, 452, 454,
        461
Response talks, 442, 444–446, 460
Retelling
    bookmarks for, 435f
    comprehension assessments
        using, 122, 134
    description of, 433–434
    for English language learners,
        120f–121f
    in fragments, 502–503, 503f
    problem/solution pattern, 436f
    story elements identified while,
        359–361, 368–369
    summary of, 459
Revising phase of writing, 304–305
Rhetorical questions, 406
Rhyming activities, 187,
    187f–189f, 212
Rhyming books, 188f
Rimes
    activities with, 191, 192f
    definition of, 117, 232
    list of, 234f
Root word, 268–269
Round-robin reading, 465–467
Running records, 118–119,
    122–123, 134

Say It Right! strategy, 473–474,
    485
Say something strategy, 412, 414,
    428
Scaffold(s)
    activities used as, 284f
    daily plan for, 319f–320f
    description of, 39, 283
    for English language learners, 83
    examples of, 64
    explanations as, 48
    facilitative teaching as, 55
    management of, 317–328
    for reading, 284f, 286–300
    for web searches, 442, 460
    for writing, 284f, 300–310
Scaffolded instruction, 39, 283
Scaffolding
    for bilingual students, 321f
    definition of, 284
    of literary instruction, 285, 285f
    summary of, 329–330
Schema theory, 24–25, 26f, 30,
    34–35, 43, 60, 68, 373, 493
Schemata, 25, 373

Photo Credits